LETTERS

OF

THE LADY BRILLIANA HARLEY,

WIFE OF SIR ROBERT HARLEY,

OF BRAMPTON BRYAN, KNIGHT OF THE BATH.

WITH INTRODUCTION AND NOTES

BY

THOMAS TAYLOR LEWIS, A.M.

VICAR OF BRIDSTOW, HEREFORDSHIRE.

LONDON:
PRINTED FOR THE CAMDEN SOCIETY.

MDCCCLIII.

This scarce antiquarian book is included in our special *Legacy Reprint Series*. In the interest of creating a more extensive selection of rare historical book reprints, we have chosen to reproduce this title even though it may possibly have occasional imperfections such as missing and blurred pages, missing text, poor pictures, markings, dark backgrounds and other reproduction issues beyond our control. Because this work is culturally important, we have made it available as a part of our commitment to protecting, preserving and promoting the world's literature.

COUNCIL

OF

THE CAMDEN SOCIETY

FOR THE YEAR 1853-4.

President,
THE RIGHT HON. LORD BRAYBROOKE, F.S.A.

WILLIAM HENRY BLAAUW, ESQ. M.A. F.S.A.
JOHN BRUCE, ESQ. Treas. S.A. *Director.*
JOHN PAYNE COLLIER, ESQ. V.P.S.A. *Treasurer.*
WILLIAM DURRANT COOPER, ESQ. F.S.A.
BOLTON CORNEY, ESQ. M.R.S.L.
PETER CUNNINGHAM, ESQ. F.S.A.
SIR HENRY ELLIS, K.H., F.R.S., Dir.S.A.
EDWARD FOSS, ESQ. F.S.A.
THE REV. JOSEPH HUNTER, F.S.A.
THE REV. LAMBERT B. LARKING, M.A.
SIR FREDERICK MADDEN, K.H. F.R.S.
FREDERIC OUVRY, ESQ. F.S.A.
THE RT. HON. LORD VISCOUNT STRANGFORD, F.R.S. F.S.A.
WILLIAM J. THOMS, ESQ. F.S.A., *Secretary.*
SIR CHARLES GEORGE YOUNG, Garter, F.S.A.

LONDON:
J. B. NICHOLS AND SONS, PRINTERS,
PARLIAMENT-STREET.

COUNCIL

OF

THE CAMDEN SOCIETY

FOR THE YEAR 1853-4.

President,
THE RIGHT HON. LORD BRAYBROOKE, F.S.A.

WILLIAM HENRY BLAAUW, ESQ. M.A. F.S.A.
JOHN BRUCE, ESQ. Treas. S.A. *Director.*
JOHN PAYNE COLLIER, ESQ. V.P.S.A. *Treasurer.*
WILLIAM DURRANT COOPER, ESQ. F.S.A.
BOLTON CORNEY, ESQ. M.R.S.L.
PETER CUNNINGHAM, ESQ. F.S.A.
SIR HENRY ELLIS, K.H., F.R.S., Dir.S.A.
EDWARD FOSS, ESQ. F.S.A.
THE REV. JOSEPH HUNTER, F.S.A.
THE REV. LAMBERT B. LARKING, M.A.
SIR FREDERICK MADDEN, K.H. F.R.S.
FREDERIC OUVRY, ESQ. F.S.A.
THE RT. HON. LORD VISCOUNT STRANGFORD, F.R.S. F.S.A.
WILLIAM J. THOMS, ESQ. F.S.A., *Secretary.*
SIR CHARLES GEORGE YOUNG, Garter, F.S.A.

INTRODUCTION.

Referring to Collins' "Historical Collections of the noble families of Cavendish, Holles, Vere, Harley and Ogle," (Lond. 1752) for the earlier notices of the distinguished family of Harley, it may be well, for the illustration of these letters, to state that Sir Robert Harley, the husband of the Lady Brilliana, was the son of Thomas Harley, of Brampton Bryan Castle, by Margaret daughter of Sir Andrew Corbet, of Morton Corbet in the county of Salop, and born at Wigmore Castle, and baptised there 1st March, 1579.[a] His father, born about 1548, was sheriff 36° Elizabeth, and again in the last year of that reign and in the first of James, in which year he had the grant from the King of the honour of Wigmore Castle. He was in frequent state employments,[b] in the council of William Lord Compton, President of the Marches of Wales, and "very considerable for his affluence both of fortune and ability, and distinguished himself by the sagacity of his counsels to the King, against the measures then in pursuit, as tending to involve his Majesty or his son in a war with his people." Quitting public employment, he retired to his estate, where he lived in the exercise of a noble hospitality, and died at an advanced age, and was buried at Brampton Bryan 19th March, 1631.[c]

The mother of Sir Robert having died when he was young, his early education was entrusted to his uncle Richard Harley, an accomplished scholar. He afterwards entered Oriel college,[d] under the tutorage of the Rev. Cadwallader Owen,[e] reputed a great disputant, and commonly known as "Sic Doceo;" at which place he must have been held in high esteem, for on the motion of the Provost, 1641,[f] his arms were placed in a window of the new hall, built about this time, where they still are to be seen. Having taken the degree of Bachelor of Arts, he removed to the Inner Temple,[g] where he associated with men of the first rank and influence in that society, and remained there until the coronation of

[a] Wigmore Register.
[b] Collins, p. 197.
[c] Brampton Bryan Register.
[d] The Auditor's Notes.
[e] Wood's Fasti by Bliss, i. 455.
[f] Letter in Appendix.
[g] Collins, p. 198.

King James,[b] at which he was made one of the Knights of the Bath. In 16th July, 1604, he was made Forester of Boringwood or Bringwood Chase, in the county of Hereford, with the office of the Pokership (the nature of which office is now involved in obscurity), and custody of the forest or chase of Prestwood, and in the 7th of King James he obtained a grant to himself, his heirs, and assigns for ever, for a weekly market and annual fair at Wigmore.

[b] 15th July, 1603.

Authorities given in Collins.

Marrying early, in the life-time of his father,[a] he resided for some time at Stanage Lodge, in the parish of Brampton; and whilst interesting himself in rural pursuits, in the improvement of breeds of cattle, sheep, and horses, and other branches of agriculture, devoted much of his time to everything connected with the business and welfare, religious and secular, of the county of Hereford, of which he was a magistrate and deputy lieutenant. He represented the borough of Radnor in the parliament 1º and 12º James,[b] and was elected one of the knights for Herefordshire in 21º James, and in 15º, 16º of Charles, which last beginning 3rd Nov. 1640, continued sitting until 1653; a parliament which, notwithstanding the dissolution of the monarchy and the summoning of no less than four parliaments by the usurping power, was re-assembled in 1659, when a Bill was passed for its dissolution,[c] and for calling another parliament, which met 25th April, 1660, and restored the monarchy.

[a] Notice of Rectors of Brampton Bryan in Harl. MSS. Brit. Museum.

[b] Willis's Notitia Parliamentaria.

[c] 16 March, 1659-60.

Sir Robert was a man of wit, learning, and piety, but of an austere and decided character. As a patriot, he was zealous and active for the redress of the many grievances under which the people of England had too just grounds of complaint; and in his religion he was deeply imbued with the views of the Puritans, of which party he was one of the most decided and influential members.

The Journals of the House of Commons, especially during the Long Parliament, evince how incessantly and zealously he was occupied in committees of that house, and in conferences with the Lords,

viii   INTRODUCTION.

^a Journals of House of Com. 13 Nov. 1640.
^b 3 Dec. 1640.
^c 17 Dec. 1640.
^d 23 Dec. 1640.
^e 3 Dec. 1641. 20 Dec. 1641. 24 Feb. 1641.
^f 20 May, 1642.
^g 3 Feb. 1643-4.
^h 19 Sept. 1642. 6 Dec. 1643.
ⁱ 23 Sept. 1643.
^k 27 Oct. 1643.
^l 9 Oct. 1643. 10 Feb. 1643-4.
^m 30 Sept. 1643.
ⁿ 30 Aug. 1641.
^o 11 Feb. 1641-2.

on almost all the most important questions of the times. To him, in committees with others, were referred the petitions of Leighton,^a Prynne,^b Bastwick,^c and other sufferers under the Star Chamber; also, the consideration of the jurisdiction of the High Commission Courts of Canterbury and York,—of the Star Chamber, and also of the court of the Council of the Marches of Wales;^d the acts and abuses of which courts had given such great cause of discontent. He was active in the proceedings against the Lord Strafford,—in the Scotch and Irish affairs,^e—in carrying out also the scheme of adventures for Ireland,^f—of the joint committee of the Commons with the Lords, to receive from the Scotch Commissioners what they had to communicate to both or either house of parliament.^g He was busily engaged in the organizing of the militia,—in providing means for carrying on the civil wars;^h lending money and plate himself, and encouraging others to do the same, towards the support of the Parliamentary cause; in which he was of the committee for the garrisonⁱ of Gloucester and the security of the western counties.^k Sir Robert was on the committee for the Great Seal;^l and also on an ordinance of Parliament for upholding the trade and settling the government of the Company and Fellowship of Merchants trading to the East Indies, &c. and also to the Levant seas. He was chairman of the committees for Elections, for the Universities, for Emmanuel College, also of one of the subdivisions of the Grand Committee for Religion. To Sir Robert was entrusted the preparation of the order to prohibit the wearing of the surplice in cathedral, collegiate, and parish churches,^m and for the better observing of the Lord's Day. He was of the committee to take into consideration the removing of the Communion tables in the Universities and the Inns of Court,ⁿ the Book of Sports, and all other matters of innovation,—of the committee for superstitious pictures,—of a committee,^o consisting of Strode, Cromwell, Hampden, and himself, to prepare letters to be sent to the Uni-

versities concerning the complaint of pressing subscriptions upon young graduates, on taking their degrees; and also of the committee on an Act to enable Members of Parliament to discharge their consciences in the proceedings of Parliament.[a] It would be tedious to refer to the very frequent connection of his name in the Journals of the House of Commons with all these matters, or with the proceedings against the Archbishop, Bishops, and other ecclesiastical persons:—The suppression of the surplice, the removal of innovations, the destruction of altars and crosses, superstitious images and inscriptions, were all highly congenial with his convictions, and not less so the rigid observance of the Sabbath, and private and public fasts. We are not surprised to find him of the committee with Pym, Strode, Nath. Fienes, Hampden and others, "to prepare a declaration of the unanimous consent and resolution of the House, for the defence of the religion established, of the King's person, and the liberty of the subject, be it by oath or any other way;"[b] and among the first of the House of Commons to take the Protestation; again, with Selden,[c] Nath. Fienes, Hampden, Sir Benjamin Rudyard and others, "to prepare and present unto the House a form of declaration, which may express the intentions of the House, for the vindicating the doctrine of the Church from the aspersions laid upon it, and concerning government, discipline, and public liturgy, and concerning consultation to be had with divines thereon, and to consider of the establishing and maintaining of a preaching ministry throughout the kingdom, and the ways and means how to do it, and renewing the Protestation of the 3 May 1641, in the Sacred Vow and Covenant of 6 June 1643; and afterwards naturally engaged busily in framing and taking the Solemn League and Covenant.[d] On the death and in place of Pym, Sir Robert was elected into the committee of the assembly of divines,[e] and zealously devoted himself to its proceedings; he reported the "amendments to the Ordinance for esta-

[a] Journals of H. of Com, 3 July, 1641.
[b] 3 May, 1641.
[c] 4 April, 1642.
[d] 25 Sept. 1643.
[e] 15 Dec. 1643.

x   INTRODUCTION.

^a 12 Dec. 1644. blishing the Directory for Public Worship,"ª and took an active part in almost all other deliberations of that intolerant and unconstitutional body.

He had wisdom to discern the tendency and ambitious ends of the army, and boldness to act upon his conviction. Happily he was averse to the extreme measures against the King, and was with his son Edward amongst the members made prisoners, (6 Dec. 1648,) for voting "that the King's answer to the propositions of both Houses was a ground to proceed upon in the settlement of the kingdom's peace." He had been made by Charles I. Master and Warden of

^b Pat. 2 Car. I. quoted by Collins.

^c Journ. Ho. of Com. 6 March, 1642-3. 3 May, 1643. 5 May, 1643.

the Mint;ᵇ subsequently displaced by the King; restored, however, by an ordinance of Parliament, 6 May, 1643,ᶜ and continued to hold the office under the proviso of "*the self-denying ordinance,*" passed 3 April, 1645. After the death of the King, upon a report of the Council of State, that the Master of the Mint refused to stamp and coin with any other stamp than formerly, the House ordered a trial of the pix to be made at his expense, and he was put out of the office, and Dr. Gourdon the physician succeeded to it, with

^d Whitelocke's Memorials, p. 588, ed. 1682.

a salary, according to Whitelocke,ᵈ of £4000 a-year; which is said also to have been the salary in Sir Robert's time.

^e MS. Notice of Rectors of Brampton Bryan, in Harl. Coll. B. Mus.

Sir Robert sustained great losses in the civil wars;ᵉ his castles destroyed, parks and farms plundered of about 500 deer, of 800 excellent sheep, 30 goodly cows, and other cattle in proportion, with a stud of 30 breeding mares and young colts; and suffering much from the detention of his rents, and himself an object of suspicion, he retired into the country, and repaired in some degree the waste of his estate; but in his later years he was much afflicted with the gout and stone, all which troubles he bore with patience and resignation to the Divine will.

It is recorded in his funeral sermon, that about three days before his death, when he arose and went to prayer, as he constantly used to do, though not able to enlarge in prayer, because of weakness, he prayed for the ruin of Anti-Christ, and for the churches of God beyond the sea, naming Savoy, Switzerland and Germany. The persecution of the Protestants of Piedmont had recently elicited the sympathy of Cromwell himself; who, receiving the sad news on the day on which the French treaty was to have been sealed,[a] refused to sign it until the King and Cardinal undertook to assist him in getting right done to them. He had nobly sent 2,000*l*. from his own purse, and appointed a day of solemn humiliation and a general collection, on which immense sums were contributed, for their relief. On this occasion Milton wrote his sonnet:

> "Avenge, O Lord, thy slaughtered saints, whose bones
> Lie scattered on the Alpine mountains cold," &c. &c.

and Mr. Morland (afterwards Sir Samuel Morland) was sent ambassador to remonstrate with the Duke of Savoy, and on his return published "The History of the Evangelical Churches of the Valleys of Piedmont, 1658."

Sir Robert had ever been the friend and patron of learning and religion, both of which he sincerely loved; and many able ministers were settled in his neighbourhood through his influence, and found a shelter from trouble and persecution under his roof. To him were many works dedicated; among others there is "a Treatise on Simeon's Song; or Instructions advertising how to live holily and dye happily:" (Lond. 1659), composed for his use, when weakness and old age confined him to his chamber, by Timothy Woodroffe.[b] Woodroffe had been tutor to Hobbs of Malmesbury, and had suffered himself much in the beginning of the civil wars, from both parties; through Sir Robert's kindness he had been preferred to the rectory of Kingsland, in his own gift, and through his influence made one of the parliamentary preachers in the cathedral of Hereford.

Sir Robert died at Brampton Bryan 6th Nov. 1656, and was there buried 10th Dec.[c] on which occasion the church at Brampton,

[a] 3 June 1655. Cromwell's Letters, &c. by Carlyle, 1846. Neal's Hist. of the Puritans, vol. iv. p. 140, Toulmin's Edition.

[b] Wood's Athenæ, vol. iii. p. 1113.

[c] B.Bryan, Reg.

events, both domestic and foreign, of the momentous years in which she lived.

The letters are printed in the order of their dates, some few undated are so placed by authority of internal evidence. Upon a more careful examination of the contents, No. 106 appears to be misdated in the year (not an uncommon mistake, when, as in these letters, the old style is used, and the new year commenced 25th March), and misplaced, and the undated letter No. 134, misplaced.

All the letters except the first, dated Ragley, the seat of her father in Warwickshire, are from Bromton or Brompton, now Brampton Bryan Castle. They are written in a bold and legible hand, with few contractions, and scarcely an erasure; but the use of capitals, and the spelling, not only of the names of persons and places, but of everyday words, are varied and irregular. A few of the letters are written by an amanuensis, in seasons of sickness, but signed by herself as usual, or with her initials. They were generally sent by an express messenger or the carrier, occasionally by a friend, or the tradesmen, but most rarely by the post of Hereford, Leominster, Shrewsbury, or Ludlow, then recently established, and not much to be depended upon: the insecurity of letters at this time gave rise to a variety of secret correspondence, one of which, very simple, is exemplified by Letters 188, 189, &c.

The earlier letters (1625—1633) are addressed to her husband; and the remainder (1638—1643), with the exception of a Letter to Sir Robert and two letters written to her friend Mrs. Wallcote of Wallcote, during her troubles at Brampton, to her son Edward, commencing in Oct. 1638, his residence in Oxford.

The letters are written with the greatest fondness of maternal affection, and abound with excellent remarks and advice on his studies, health and conduct in the University, with frequent allusions to affairs home and foreign. A deeply religious tone pervades the whole of them; it is scarcely possible to find a single letter without the evidences of practical piety. It is unnecessary to notice any particular passages. It is clear, that her mind was imbued with the doctrines and discipline of Calvin, which were at this time working powerfully in many of the most learned, pious and patriotic people, lay and clerical, of this country. Numerous allusions attest the accuracy of her information, and the interest she took in public affairs, and in the proceedings of the Parliament. She deeply sympathized in the feelings of her husband in his varied employments, and entered fully into his interests and pursuits. They agreed in regarding Episcopacy as Anti-Christ, and nothing short of "down with it, down with it, even to the ground," would satisfy their zeal.

The ministrations of Brampton Bryan under two successive rectors, accorded with their views, and afforded them ample opportunities of religious exercises, in the observance of public and private fasts; how strictly they were there observed, appears by the memorandum now in the register of that parish, a copy of which will be found in the Notes.

The rectors here alluded to, were Thomas Pierson and Stanley Gower. The Rev: Thos. Peacock, Fellow of Brazennose college, had preceded Pierson, but appears from Froysell's sermon, already mentioned, never to have resided at Brampton. Sir Robert had no doubt been acquainted with him in Oxford, and not improbably derived benefit from his advice and instruction, as he was "highly esteemed for his great learning, great sanctity of life, and counsel," and was known as the convertor of Robert Bolton, a well-known puritan divine; by whom "an account of the last visitation, conflict, and death of Mr. Peacock was published, 1646."[a] Pierson had been brought up in Emmanuel college,[b] where he resided for several years, and was the friend of the learned Calvinist William Perkins, whose works he had been engaged in editing, and also in the publication of Brightman's work on the Apocalypse, and was known as a profound scholar and theologian. Instituted in 1612, he continued to reside at Brampton

[a] Wood's Athenæ, vol. ii. p. 514.
[b] MS. Notice of Rectors of Brampton Bryan, in Brit. Museum.

xvi   INTRODUCTION.

1602—1617.

until his death, 1633. In the early years of Pierson's residence, his ministrations had not been acceptable to Thomas Harley, the father of Sir Robert, who made frequent complaints of him to Bennett, Bishop of Hereford, who used to declare, with truth, "that he received letters from the father against Mr. Pierson, and from his son in his behalf." John Harley, the grandfather of Sir Robert, never adopted the reformed doctrines, and was a zealous Romanist, and was said to have given some protection at Brampton Castle to Parsons and Champion, the Jesuits. It may be inferred, therefore, that these differences arose out of the religious views now probably first put forth at Brampton; for it is said, "that a solemn day of prayer was observed at Stanage Lodge,[a] where Sir Robert and his most pious and virtuous lady (sister of Sir Richard Newport), Mr. Pierson and his godly family, and some few neighbours, presented supplications to the Lord, to turn the heart of Mr. Harley to express kindness to his son, and friendship towards Mr. Pierson; to which it pleased the Lord to give a most gracious answer of peace; for, within a very short time, Mr. Harley, by a trusty servant, sent to Sir Robert,—' Tell my son, I will take care of the concerns of the estate, and pay his debts; and tell him, I will be friends with Mr. Pierson, and then you will be a welcome messenger;' and, accordingly, he began and continued all expressions of high esteem and real friendship for him, and gave a copyhold estate to him and his wife for their joint lives, and in his enfeebled old age received his continual ministrations," and "to his dying day, no man, except in nearest relation to him, was more in his esteem, more dear unto him, or in whom he put more confidence, than Mr. Pierson."

[a] MS. Notes on the Rectors of Brampton Bryan, in the Brit. Museum.

In Brampton, Pierson set up the strict observance of the Ember weeks and public and private fasts, frequently alluded to in these letters, "the resort to which of many godly persons from remote places was as the flight of doves to the windows of holy light;"[b] and,

[b] MS. Notes of Rectors, &c.

under authority from the Bishop of Hereford, a monthly lecture, in the adjoining parish of Leintwardine, in the manner of "the prophecyings" which had given so great offence to Queen Elizabeth, occasioning her displeasure with Archbishop Grindall, and calling forth his noble letter to her majesty;[a] after which model many other lectures were established in the neighbourhood. He was also one of the London feoffees for buying in impropriations,[b] and to maintain a constant preaching ministry where it was wanting; a design which was much applauded by the religious party in England, but which soon giving offence to the High Church party, was interrupted by the Star Chamber, when the tithes which had been purchased were seized for the King's use. He received young men into his house, to prepare for the Universities and holy orders; and in all these ways exercised a very great influence, not only in his own parish, but far and wide in that district, which is represented as having been in great religious darkness. A minister of this time, Mr. Gwalter Stephens, of Bishop's Castle, "who had lighted his candle at famous Mr. Pierson's,[b] of Brampton Bryan," used to say, that "when he preached, in his younger days, for a great space, there was never a preacher between him and the sea one way, and none near him the other, but one in Shrewsbury." Pierson objected not to the Liturgy or the gesture of kneeling in the receiving of the Lord's Supper, but scrupled the use of the surplice, and the cross in baptism; yet is said to have been liberal enough, to allow the use of both to his own curate. A Mr. Brice, of Henley upon Thames, was nominated on Pierson's death, but his old parishioners expressing their sense of the great loss they should sustain by his removal from them, he was allowed to relinquish it, and returned to his old charge, when Stanley Gower became rector, and a great blessing to the place, following the steps of Mr. Pierson.

Gower was a man of piety and learning, and had been brought up

[a] Grindall's Remains, Park. Soc. p 376.

[b] MS. Rectors of Brampton Bryan, Brit. Mus.

by Dr. Hoye, probably at Dublin, as he had been chaplain to Archbishop Usher for some time. His last ministration recorded in the register of Brampton is dated 1 May, 1642. He had been nominated and approved as one of the Assembly of Divines,[a] and removed at once to London, and became a constant attendant and active member in that assembly, being employed in the compilation of the Assembly's Confession of Faith and the larger and smaller Catechisms. He was one of the committee appointed by ordinance of Parliament for the examination and approval of such clergymen as petitioned for sequestered livings,[b] and himself in possession of one near Ludgate. He was also a select preacher before the House of Commons at St. Margaret's, and one of the presbyters and members of the Assembly to examine and ordain by imposition of hands all those whom they should judge qualified to be admitted to the sacred ministry.[c] No doubt he agreed with Sir Robert Harley in all such matters, and disapproving, like his patron, of the wicked designs upon the King, he was one of the ministers who assembled at Zion College,[d] and published " a serious and faithful representation of their judgment, in a letter to the General and his Council;" and also, "A Vindication of the London Ministers from the unjust aspersions cast upon their former actings for the Parliament, as if they had promoted the bringing the King to capital punishment."

But to return to the Lady Brilliana. Moving but little from home, her time was much given to her children and domestic matters—and, in the absence of Sir Robert, to the management of his estate, on which several judicious remarks will be found in these letters. The affairs of the country, in these sad times, afforded too great cause of anxiety to allow her to be a quiet observer of what was passing. It was but to be expected, on the breaking out of the Civil Wars, in a county which was generally devoted to the King's cause, that Brampton Bryan, the seat of one so influential on the other side, would soon

---

[a] Journals of the House of Commons, 23 April, 1642. MS. Notes on the Rectors of B. Bryan.

[b] Neal's History of the Puritans, by Toulmin, vol. iii. p. 89.

[c] Neal, vol. iii. p. 140.

[d] Neal, vol. iii. p. 491. 18 Jan. 1648-9.

attract a more than agreeable notice. Whilst Sir Robert was engaged in Parliament, she became an object of suspicion to her loyal neighbours, and after repeated minor provocations and threatenings, the plundering of his park of deer and game, and the withholding of his rents, the castle was surrounded by the soldiers of the royalists or "malignants," under Sir William Vavasour and Colonel Lingen.[a] Shut up now in Brampton Castle with her children, and neighbours "who resorted thither to keep themselves from the plunder and villanous usage then the practice of the Cavaliers,"[b] with the advice of Dr. Nathaniel Wright, a physician of Hereford, frequently in attendance upon her, and who now, with his wife, took up his quarters there, and devoted himself and his money to the cause, and that of a veteran, sent to her by Colonel Massey from Gloucester, and her own servants, she defended it with a prudence and valour worthy of her distinguished family. The siege commenced 25 July, 1643, "on a day on which she and her young children were engaged in prayer and humiliation for the mercy of God to avert the dreadful judgment then justly feared," and continued for six weeks; when the besiegers, alarmed by the operations in and about the Forest of Dean, were hurried off to the neighbourhood of Gloucester. "The first stroke of the Cavaliers in the siege was upon a poor aged blind man, who was without any provocation killed in the street."[c] During the siege, "the cook was shot by a poisoned bullet, and a running stream that furnished the village was poisoned." The church, parsonage house, and dwelling houses, together with the mill about a quarter of a mile off, with the buildings belonging to the castle, were all destroyed: and early in the following year, Sir Michael Woodhouse, governor of Ludlow (having been successful in his brutal attack on Hopton Castle,[d] which in its distress had received assistance from Brampton Castle,) came before it again, when, after a gallant defence made by the servants, under Dr. Wright's

[a] Letter ccIII.

[b] MS. Notice of Rectors.

[c] MS. Notice of Rectors.

[d] See the Journal of the Siege of Hopton Castle, by S. More, Esq. in Blakeway's Hist. of Sheriffs of Shropsh., p. 216—220.

direction, it surrendered at mercy only, and the inmates, including three of Sir Robert's younger children, were taken prisoners, after a siege of three weeks. There were taken 67 men, 100 arms, two barrels of powder, and a whole year's provisions.[a]

17 April, 1644.
[a] *Mercurius Belgicus.*

Lady Brilliana was of a delicate constitution; and, enfeebled by repeated attacks of illness and continued anxieties during her troubles, and the long absence of her husband and son, whom she fondly loved, she took a cold, alluded to in her last letter, and after a few days' illness died, soon after the raising of the first siege, in Oct. 1643, leaving three sons and four daughters, all baptised at Brampton, as follows:—Edward, 24 Oct. 1624; Robert, 16 April, 1626; Thomas, 13 Jan. 1627-8; Brilliana, 26 April, 1629; Dorothie, 12 Sept. 1630; Margaret, 25 Dec. 1631; and Elizabeth, 26 Oct. 1634.[b]

[b] *Brampton Register.*

Edward Harley, born at Brampton, 21 Oct. 1624, and baptised as above, three days afterwards, was as his mother, in his infancy, of a delicate constitution. Having passed some period at school, first in Shrewsbury and then at Gloucester, he was sent to Magdalen hall, at that time under the principal Dr. Wilkinson, and the tutorage of Edward Perkins, described by Calamy[c] "as a great man, a very ready and well studyed divine, especially in school divinity, a great tutor, and particularly famous for his giving Mr. John Corbet (the historian of Gloucester, and a good divine) his education and the direction of his studies." Magdalen hall at this time was in Oxford what Emmanuel College was at Cambridge, a famous puritanical school, and several remarkable men had been there educated, on which account, no doubt, it was selected by Sir Robert for his son. Dr. Ingram, in his Memorials of Oxford, states, "as a house of learning, it could have been inferior to none in the university in eminence at that period, since in the year 1624, under the elder Wilkinson, it reckoned 300 students on the books, forty of whom

1605—1643.
[c] *Baxter's Life by Calamy.*

were Masters of Arts." He resided there for two academical years, until July 1640, but, on account of the unhealthy state of the place, his residence was broken in the following October term, when he joined his father in London, where he was at the opening of the Long Parliament, 3 Nov: of that year. He was present too, at the trial of Lord Strafford, in April of the following year, and at that time gave himself much to the proceedings of the Parliament. His mother was eagerly bent upon his entering public employment, and though only eighteen years of age, she exercised her interest among her friends to secure his return as burgess for the city of Hereford, on the death of Mr. Weaver; in which, however, she failed. Remaining in London, he had a lodging in Lincoln's Inn, and was probably a member of that society; but in 1642 he became a captain of a troop of horse in the parliamentary army, which he joined under the command of Sir William Waller, and in a few weeks had himself the command of a regiment of foot. In one of Sir William Waller's skirmishes about this time,[a] probably at Lansdown, his horse was shot, "and on another occasion a musket-ball,[b] levelled at his heart, was bent flat against his armour, (not reckoned of such proof,) without harm." He distinguished himself particularly in the conflict at Red Marley, near Ledbury, where "at the head of his troop, he gallantly and in good order gave the charge, beat the enemy from their ambuscadoes, put their horse to flight, and in an instant of time got into the van of their foot, cutting some down, and taking others prisoners, so that few escaped."[c] He there received a severe wound in the arm, which obliged him to seek surgical assistance in London; but he was again in the field early in the following year, and in the conflict between Prince Rupert and Colonel Massie,[d] near Ledbury, in which it is said "Massie was in great peril, as the Prince sought a personal encounter with him, and shot his horse." Edward Harley was here again hurt, and he is said to have

Letters cvi., cx., cxxxiv.

Letters cxcix., cc.

Letter ccii.
[a] 11 July, 1643.
[b] Sir Edward's retrospect of his life in App.

27 July, 1644.

[c] Corbet's Hist. Rel. of Mil. Gov. of Glouc. 1645, p. 111.

[d] 22 April, 1645. Webb's Historical Introduction to the Bibliotheca Gloucestrensis, p. ciii.

carried a bullet in his body to his death. He was ordered with his men to Plymouth in Nov: 1643,[a] made Governor of Monmouth 1644, and of Canon Frome, a garrison near Hereford, in 1645, and quartered with the Major-General at Marston, near Oxford, in May 1646.

On the disabling of Humphrey Coningsby, member for the county of Hereford, he was chosen member.[b] He was at this time warmly affected to the Presbyterian cause, which his father had so zealously espoused; but notwithstanding his devotion to that party, and the spirit with which his family was regarded by the Royalists, when the faction in the army began to form the scheme of a military government, he was among the first to perceive the intrigues of Cromwell and Fairfax, and afterwards openly to oppose them in the House of Commons, for which, with Denzell Holles and others, he was impeached by the army of high treason, " for that by their power the ordinance for disbanding the army did pass." He was now disabled by an order of the House[c] which was afterwards revoked,[d] and joining with his father in December following,[e] as before noticed, in favour of the King, they were by the army made prisoners. Henceforth he was an object of suspicion to Cromwell, and in 1650, on grounds of disaffection to the government, was summoned by letter from Major Winthrop at Leominster,[f] to appear at Hereford before the Commissioners of the Militia. This summons was followed by a visit from soldiers, who searched and read his papers, and carried him and Mr. Clogie, the minister of Wigmore, to Hereford; both his brother Robert then M.P. for Radnor, and his brother Thomas, being at this time prisoners at Bristol. Refusing a bond urged upon him at Hereford for his appearance in London, he gave a promise to be there at his father's house from 18 Aug: to 1st of Sept: following, which, under authority of a pass from Wroth Rogers,[g] of the city of Hereford, he was enabled to keep. What proceedings were then taken do not appear, but he was not permitted a residence in Herefordshire for ten years.

[a] J. C. H. 13 Nov. 1643. Whitelocke.

[b] 11 Sept. 1646. Cobbett's Parliamentary History, vol. ii. p. 609.

Ibid.

[c] 29 Jan. 1647–8.
[d] 8 June, 1648.
[e] 7 Dec. 1648.

[f] Letter in Appendix, pp. 233–256.

[g] Appendix, p. 235.

In a memorandum which will be found in the Appendix,[a] he records, "that he was preserved from the cruelty of that power which put to death holy Mr. Love." Love was a Presbyterian minister;[b] the martyr of the cause; he was charged with treason, tried, and condemned, as implicated in the plot with the Scots, for bringing in Charles II., and was executed on Tower Hill.[c] When on the scaffold, attended by Manton, Calamy and other Presbyterian ministers, he exulted in the cause for which he was about to suffer; declaring in a calm and manly manner his dislike of the Commonwealth, and his detestation of the Engagement, saying, "I am for a regulated mixed monarchy, which I judge to be one of the best governments in the world. I opposed the late King and his forces, because I am against screwing up monarchy into tyranny, as much as against those who would pull it down into anarchy. I was never for putting the King to death, whose person I did promise in my covenant to preserve, and I judge it an ill way to cure the body politic, by cutting off the political head."

In the Parliament of 1656 he was again chosen for the county of Hereford, and being again secluded with other members, he was one who signed and published the Remonstrance,[d] "that they would not be frightened or flattered to betray their country, and give up their religion, lives, and estates, to be at the will, to serve the Protector's lawless intentions;" setting forth his depredations, and the power he had assumed; protesting "that the assembly at Westminster was not the representative body of England, and that all such members as shall take on them to approve the forcible exclusion of other chosen members, or shall sit and vote, or act by the name of the Parliament of England, while to their knowledge many of the chosen members are so by force shut out, ought to be reputed betrayers of the liberties of England and adherents to the capital enemy of the Commonwealth." It was the lot of himself and family still to lie under suspicion in the

[a] P. 247.
[b] Marsden's History of the Later Puritans, p. 347. Neal's History of the Puritans. Wood's Athenæ, vol. iii. p. 278.
[c] 22 Aug. 1661.
[d] Whitelocke's Memorials, p. 643, ed. Lond. 1682.

time of Richard Cromwell, when his brother Robert was arrested at Kynsham Court, in Herefordshire, not without grounds of disaffection to the Government.

At the Restoration, Edward Harley was a zealous asserter of the royal cause, and met the King at Dover, and was shortly afterwards made Governor of Dunkirke, of which garrison he took immediate possession. During the short time he held that charge, he much improved and strengthened it; and it is a fact which Marshal Schomberg owned to Sir Edward, when he came over with the Prince of Orange in 1688, " that the French had often during his time attempted to take it by surprise."[a] Lord Lansdown, in his Vindication of General Monk, gives this account of Harley:[b]— " General Monk foresaw early what might happen to be the fate of Dunkirk, and took his precaution in the very beginning to preserve it, by placing Sir Edward Harley in the command, a man of public spirit, firm to the interests of his country, and not to be biassed, tempted, or deluded to be assistant in any thing contrary to it; which appeared clearly afterwards, for the first step taken, as soon as the treaty was projected, was to remove that gallant man, and place another General there." Nor was he deceived in the estimate of Sir Edward, for he strenuously opposed the sale of it to the French, and persevered so far with the House of Commons, to pass a resolution to prepare an Act, that it should never be alienated, but be part of the King's hereditary dominions. Neither threats or promises could prevail with him to be a party to its surrender. It being known that he would refuse to deliver it up to the French, he was removed, but received a most honourable discharge of the trust from the King.[*] " When he took leave of the King before the

[a] The Auditor's notes.
[b] Quoted by Collins.

---

[*] Collins gives the commission for his appointment (14 July, 1660), and the order for his giving up the town to Lord Retorfort or Rutherford (22 May, 1661), Lord R's discharge (28 May, 1661), and also King Charles's release (3 Dec. 1663).

Lord General,[a] the Duke of Albemarle, he told him that the guns, stores, and ammunition he left them were worth more than the French were to give for the place (500,000*l.*), and that he had left him one thing more, that his Majesty might not think of, and that was 10,000*l.* in an iron chest, which he had saved, against a siege or any other exigency that might happen." By a fragment of a letter given in the Appendix,[b] it will be seen that the Earl of Montague was told by the King "that he would not have parted with Dunkirk if he could have been permitted to retain Colonel Harley in that post, which he would have preserved for his Majesty; but, said the King, I am continually disturbed, because he is represented to be a notorious Presbyterian." The King was clearly not insensible to the worth of the man who had declined a viscountcy, lest his zeal and his services for the restoration of the ancient Government should be reproached as proceeding from ambition and not conscience; and his being made a Knight of the Bath was done without his knowledge: when employed at Dunkirk, the King inserted his name in the list, with his own hand.

[a] Collins, p.204.

[b] Appendix, p. 245.

Sir Edward Harley was a member in all the Parliaments of Charles the Second, after the Restoration, either for the town of Radnor or the county of Hereford; and, as he complied not with the corrupt measures of the Court, so he never entered into the plans of others, who, under pretence of serving the public, pursued their own interest or revenge. He vigorously opposed all the acts for persecuting the Dissenters, and the act which made the holy sacrament of the Lord's Supper a civil test; and, when King James II. came to the throne, and set up a dispensing power, under cloak of which, he intended to bring in Popery, he endeavoured, without success, to prevail with Croft, bishop of Hereford, and with the Dissenters of that county, with whom he had justly a great influence, not to read the King's declaration, nor make any address upon it: and neither he nor any of his family ever took any oath to that King.

Though he was a favourer of such as dissented from the Church of England for conscience sake, and sometimes went to hear Mr. Baxter and others in London,[a] which brought him under suspicion of being still a favourer of the Presbyterian cause, yet he constantly attended church; and having, as his son Edward says, "by the grace of God, and a constant reading of the scriptures, attained a very Christian temper, he never engaged in the narrow principles with which several parties in the Church had embroiled themselves and the country:" a confirmation of which will be seen in his letter to Lord Clarendon, in the Appendix.[b] Sir Edward was a good and religious man, untainted by the evils of that most licentious age, and during the reign of King James "he weekly spent the greater part of one day, either alone or with some of his family, in imploring the mercy of God, that the storm which seemed then to be falling on the nation might be averted."

At the commencement of the Revolution he exerted himself with his sons on behalf of the Prince of Orange, and was at once made Governor of Worcester by the gentry there assembled; which city, by his great prudence, was kept in absolute quiet, whilst most others felt the shock of that great change. He was unanimously elected in the first Parliament of King William for the county of Hereford, and, consistently with the high principles which had ever actuated him, avoided all place and recompence, but devoted himself to the obtaining of such laws as might be of real service to his country; and by his means the act for abolishing the arbitrary court of the Marches of Wales was passed. To the second Parliament his return was factiously opposed, under the cry of his being an enemy to the Church; but, the successful candidate dying within a few months, he was again unanimously elected, and continued, in that and the succeeding Parliaments, constantly to oppose the extravagant ways that were taken for running the nation in debt, by raising funds

[a] Auditor Harley's Notes.

[b] P. 240-241.

under great discounts, whereby a dependence was created on the minister, and vast estates obtained .. He was much regarded in the House of Commons for his sound reasoning, and frequently closed the debates. He was well acquainted with the character of men, yet in public avoided saying anything that might the least prejudice the reputation of any person. His conversation was very entertaining; having read much of history and retained what he read, and having himself been engaged in many of the most stirring events of his own times. The Auditor records:—"Our father, Sir Edward Harley, may be truly said to have had all the accomplishments of a gentleman. His features were very exact, and (he) had great quickness in his eyes, which commanded respect. His temper was naturally very passionate, though mixed with the greatest tenderness and humanity. His passion he kept under a strict restraint, and had a manner totally subdued; but his generosity and tender compassion to all objects of charity continued to his last." He was not less generous than brave. Sir Henry Lingen having been engaged in the siege of Brampton castle, his estate was laid under sequestration, and the profits thereof ordered to be applied to make satisfaction to Sir Edward. After an inventory of all his goods and personal estate was taken, Sir Edward waited upon the Lady Lingen, and having asked whether that was a perfect inventory, he presented it to her, with all his right to the same. His cousin Smyth having cut off the entail of his estate, left it to Sir Edward; but this he gave up at once to the next of kin. As a testimony of his unfeigned love for religion, and its public maintenance, he not only rebuilt the church at Brampton Bryan in his father's life-time, but augmented the livings of Brampton Bryan, Leintwardine, Wigmore, Lyngen, Kington and Stow:" and on the death of his mother-in-law, becoming interested in the lease of the impropriate tithes of Folden in Norfolk, the property of Caius College, he proposed surrendering the same, on condition of its perpetual annexation to the vicarage;

Auditor Harley's Notes—

xxviii INTRODUCTION.

which was effected, thereby augmenting the value of it to 100*l.* a-year: and when the College offered him the nomination to the living, then void, he only so far availed himself of it, as to request the person to be nominated should be first approved by his father's friend, Dr. Tuckney, the Master of St. John's College, and at that time Professor of Divinity in Cambridge. His letters to the Master and Fellows, and also to Dr. Tuckney, will be found in the Appendix, together with a memorandum of the Master and Fellows relative to the business.

<small>Appendix, page 237.</small>

The Appendix contains a letter of Sir William Gregory, which, bidding Sir Edward to the funeral of John, Lord Scudamore, records the friendship which existed between these two worthies of Herefordshire, who had taken opposite parts in the Civil Wars. Truly, they were among the excellent of the earth. They loved and feared God, and left substantial proof of their devotion to His cause, in the restoration to the Church of tithes, of which she had been despoiled.

<small>Appendix XI. p. 245.</small>

For the two or three last years of his life he wisely retired from public, and, as his father and grandfather before him, died in peace at Brampton Bryan, 8 Dec. 1700. So exemplary was his virtue, and love to his country, that he was called by discerning persons, "ultimus Anglorum."

<small>Auditor's notes.</small>

Sir Edward was twice married: firstly, 26 June, 1654, to Mary, daughter of Sir William Button, of Parkgate, in co. Devon, by whom he had issue:—

<small>Collins.</small>

Brilliana, wife of William Popham, of Tewkesbury:
Martha, wife of Samuel Hutchins, of London, merchant:
And two Maries, who died young.

<small>Letter in Appendix, p. 218.</small>

Secondly, to Abigail, daughter of Nathaniel Stephens, of Essington, in co. of Gloucester, (by whom his children were allied to Sir Francis Walsingham, Sir Philip Sydney, and the Earl of Essex,) and by her had four sons and one daughter: viz.—

Robert, the Earl of Oxford:
Edward, the Auditor of the Imprest:
Nathaniel, a merchant, who died at Aleppo:
Brian, who died young:
And Abigail, who died unmarried 1726.

Lady Frances Vernon Harcourt's collections contain many letters of Sir Edward, but none written to his Mother, or during her life-time. They were, no doubt, all preserved and treasured up by one who loved him so fondly, and must have perished, with many valuables, in the ruin of the castle, when a considerable library of MSS. and printed books was destroyed. Portraits remain of Thomas Harley, Esq., Sir Robert Harley by Oliver, and Sir Edward by Cooper, all engraved by Vertue, and published in Collins's Historical Collection; and there is a portrait of the Lady Brilliana Harley still in the possession of her descendant, Lord Rodney, and now at his seat at Berrington, in the county of Hereford.

In addition to the originals, the Editor has had the use of a complete transcript of them, made by the Lady Frances Vernon Harcourt, and illustrated by her own notes; and it would be unjust to his friend and neighbour, the Rev. John Webb, of Tretire, whose accurate knowledge of the history of the times to which these letters refer is well known, if he did not here gratefully acknowledge the ready and valuable advice he has at all times received from him in the preparation of this Introduction and the notes which accompany the Letters.

Bridstow Vicarage, near Ross,
 2 Dec. 1853.

THE CHARACTER OF SIR ROBERT HARLEY, TAKEN FROM A SERMON PREACHED AT HIS FUNERAL, ENTITLED, "THE BELOVED DISCIPLE," BY THOMAS FROYSELL, MINISTER OF CLUN, IN SHROPSHIRE. LOND. 1658.

We have marched all this day in sable posture: I pray we may all walk in white one day with Jesus Christ. This present scene of sorrow becomes us. As the aire receives severall impressions from the superiour bodies, she looks lightsome when the heavens shine, and sad again, when they look black again upon her; so, when the celestiall providence shall change her countenance upon us, 'tis our duty to change our aspects.

Our losse is very great. We have lost a chiefe man, one that was a common and publick good. The sun of this country is set. Sir Robert Harley gave a great light to these parts. We are wont to say of fair weather, "'tis pitty it should doe any hurt," because we are loth it should ever leave us. I am sure, I may say, 'tis pitty that good men should dye and leave us—that brave Sir Robert Harley should ever be missed among us; he was as choyce a piece as our age hath known; a man that was the rariety of men; a man whom his descent had elevated above the rate of ordinary men; and a man whose veins free grace had filled with nobler blood; a man of whom I may say, in the words of my text, "Thou art greatly beloved." (Page 1—3.)

(Page 97 to the end.) And this leads me now into the discourse of this great man and great saint, whose funeralls we at this time celebrate. He was a great man by birth; he was a great saint by grace; and therefore greatly beloved. I shall not speak the greatnesse and antiquity of his honourable family, although these shining adjuncts set him out in brightnesse and splendour to the eye of the world; yet, because they make not a man greatly beloved in the eye of God, I shall rather speak of those titles of honour that are not written in dust—those things that did greaten his greatnesse.

I know he had his humanities, for we are all but men till we are glorified saints, and then our infirmities as well as sorrows shall be done away; as all tears shall be wiped from our eyes, so all stains shall be washed from our natures.

My language is not a match for his excellent vertues. His spirituall lineaments and beauties are above my pencill. I want art to draw his picture. And though little grace seems much (nay, more than it is,) in a great person, yet I think I may safely say that his gracious greatnesse did transcend his outward greatnesse. If other saints are candles, he was a torch. If others are starres, he was a starre of greater magnitude. He made his outward greatnesse but a servant to the exercise of his graces. He was a copy for all great men to transcribe in all descending ages. He was a man of desires: a saint in great letters: famous (I think) throughout the land, one where or other, for his graces. To my knowledge eminent ministers did most eminently prize him. Sir Robert Harley was a sweet name upon their lips. When they spake of him, they would speak with honour and delight in him.

(1). I have heard himself say, that God (in His great mercy) had kept him unstained from grosse sins: a great priviledge and favour of Heaven! More than many a worthy saint can say, that his life (like a fair sheet of paper) should be preserved pure and white from foul blots, and then written upon with golden letters of grace. I must tell you, this is a lovely manuscript.

(2). He was the first that brought the Gospell into these parts. This country lay under a vaile of darknesse till he began to shine. He set his first choyce upon that transcendent holy man, Mr. Peacock, in Oxford, but God took him to Heaven, which prevented his coming to Brampton. Then Providence led him to the knowledge of that now blessed servant of God, Mr. Peirson, whose exemplary graces and ministery shed a rich influence abroad the country.

And as God removed godly ministers by death, he continued still a succession of them to you. Not onely Brampton Brian, but ye also of Wigmore, and ye of Leyntwardine, owe your very souls to Sir Robert Harley, who maintained your ministers upon his own cost, that they might feed you with the Gospell of Jesus Christ.

(3). He was the pillar of religion among us. How would he countenance godlinesse? His greatnesse professing Christ brought profession into credit, and cast a lustre on it Profession began to grow and spread itselfe under his shade

(4). His planting of godly ministers, and then backing them with his authority, made religion famous in this little corner of the world. Oh! what comfortable times had we (through Gods mercy) before the wars! How did our publick meetings shine with his exemplary presence in the midst of them!

(5). He would feed heartily upon the ordinances. He came with hunger to them, and did afterward digest them into reall nutriment. How would his heart melt under the word, and dissolve into liquid tears! I have seen him thaw and distill as the weeping trees under the winter sun-beams.

(6). He did deal much in prayer. He would embark no undertaking till he had sought God. He would frait his vessell, hoyse up the mast, and spread the sailes: (he would not neglect the meanes) yet he would, by prayer, beg the winds, and wait the gales of Providence to set his ship a-going.

(7). His house was an house of prayer: 'twas the center where the saints met to seek God.

(8). He was noble in his liberality to the saints in their wants: their necessity was his opportunity.

(9). He was spirited with a keen hatred of sin and prophanenesse. He would not, I may say, he could not brook it, in any under his roof. He would often say, he cared not for the service of one that feared not God.

(10). He was a friend to Gods friends. They that did love God had his love. Gods people were his darlings: they had the cream of his affections. If any poor Christian were crush'd by malice or wrong, whither would they fly, but to Sir Robert Harley?

(11). Againe, if at any time he had been angry, he would quickly desire to be reconciled; saying, "We must take heed least the devill come between."

(12). He loved his children most tenderly; I think no man in the world carried more of a fathers dearnesse in him than he did, yet he would never bear with any evill in any of his children; he would often say to them, I desire nothing of you but your love, and that you keep from sin.

(13). The soule of his religion was sincerity; he knew no end but to serve God and to be saved. I shall, in this place, bring in a notable speech of his about a year and a halfe since: when a most eminent minister of the land came to visit him, and ask't him what comfortable evidences he had of his salvation? he answered, "he had nothing to rely upon but Jesus Christ, and he knew no religion but sincerity."

(14). He was a great honourer of Godly ministers; he carried them in his bosome; of all men in the world they sat next his heart, he did hug them in his dearest embraces; I must tell you he was their sanctuary in evill times. How oft hath he interposed between them and dangers! when sinfull greatnesse did frown upon them, this great man would show himselfe upon the stage for them. When Mr. Pierson was questioned before the Bishop, Sir Robert Harley was not afraid to appear constantly in his defence; I could tell you that he felt the frowns and displeasures of a near relation rather than he would desert that servant of Jesus Christ. When Dr. Stoughton and Mr. Workman were in trouble, Sir Robert Harley accompanied them to the High Commission, which made the Archbishop dart frowns upon him.

(15). He was also a magistrate; and herein (I must tell you) he was animated with a most nimble soul of zeal against sin. He was full of spirits against all dishonours done to God; he was a terrour to evill works; he knew no respect of persons in a businesse, wherein God was wronged. Among other things, how would he vindicate the Sabbath from contempt! Prophannesse durst not appear upon the face of it. By this means the congregations were frequented on the Lords dayes, and many thousand soules, prevented from their sinfull sports, sate under the droppings of the word.

(16). He paid a dear devotion of love to the Lords day (that pearle of the week). When the licentious sinfulnesse of times cryed it down, how often have I heard him plead it up! with excellency of arguments! and in his own practice he rose alwayes earlier upon the Lords day (and dayes of humiliation), even to the times of his extreme weaknesse. He rejoyced still when the Sabbath came, and was usually more chearfull that day than others, even in his sicknesse. He wept much when his servants suffered him to sleep on the Lords day later than he used, although he had not rested all that night.

(17). He was one that did swim deep in the tide of fasting and humiliation. I have seldom seen an heart broken upon such a day as his was wont to be. He was one that did stand in the gap, that did sigh and cry for the abominations done in the land, and for it God set a mark upon his forehead. Though his castle was ruined, yet God set a mark upon him, when the naked sword, that messenger of death, walkt the land, and lookt keen upon you; and God set His seal of safety upon his dear Lady. That noble Lady and Phœnix of Women dyed in peace; though surrounded with drums and noyse of war, yet she took her leave in peace. The sword had no force against her, as long as God preserved her, He preserved the place where she was. And the Man cloath'd with linnen set a mark also upon the forehead of his children; for when they with the castle were surrendered up, God made their enemies to treat them gently; he had his jewells sent safely to him by the hand of Providence.

(18). He was (I know not how oft) chosen by his country to the High Senate and Court of Parliament, and there (that I may speak within my knowledge) he was a bright and glorious star in that shining constellation; as some stars are more excellent than others, so was he there. He was a man of fixed principles; religion and solid reformation was all the white he shot at. He appeared all along for a setled ministery, and the liberall maintenance thereof. He procured the ordinance for settling the ministers at Hereford; his compasse, without trepidation or variation, stood constantly right to that pole, the good of his country and gospell, which he kept ever in his eye. And though his losse were vast in those destroying times, yet he laboured not for recompence of his private losses, nor receiv'd any in the world.

He was very zealous against Superstition and Heresie, and for Church Government. When one of the Parliament said to him, "Sir Robert Harley, why are you thus earnest for Presbytery? you see it is so opposed that it is in vain to seek to settle it." He replyed, "Let us so much rather be earnest for it, though we gain it by inches; what we obtain now with much difficulty and opposition shall be of use one day, when there shall not be heard so much as the sound of a hammer."

(19). He could (when he was put to it) live by faith. In the wars, when the stream of his estate (which should have maintain'd and watred him and his family) was diverted wholly from them, he would say often, " Dear children, it may be, God will bring us to want bread; some say it is base to live from hand to mouth, but I am of another mind; I finde it the best way of living, and (which was an high expression) who can be afraid of God's providence? welcome what the Lord sends, if it go well with the Church, it is no matter."

(20). His soul was paved with humble submission to God in hardest dispensations. When after the wars he returned into the country and came to see with what face Brampton look't, he rode toward his castle gate, and seeing the ruins, put off his hat, and said, " God hath brought great desolation upon this place since I saw it; I desire to say ' the Lord hath given and the Lord hath taken, and blessed be the name of the Lord;' in His good time He will raise it up again; when His house is built, God (I trust) will build mine;" and observe, that he took care to build this house a place of worship, and let his own lie buried still in its woefull ruines.

You have had the fair and sumptuous prospect of his life, which stood aloft like a beauteous city upon an hill.

Let us now follow him to his sicknesse, which (you know) confined him some years to his chamber; and here I see the seaven stars, or seaven celestiall signs, appear in the night of his sicknesse.

First. The greatest trouble of his sicknesse to him was, that it disabled him from enjoying the publick ordinances; he dearly loved the solemn assemblies; one day in Gods court was better to him than a thousand. The want of the publick ordinances was the sicknesse of his sicknesse.

Secondly. His divine employment. Most of his time (both day and night), whilst he was detained in his chamber, was spent in hearing some good book, or the Scriptures, read to him; he used very often to hear the 17 chapter of St. John and the 8 to the Romans read to him; and those two golden texts in the 8 to the Romans, " all things work together for good to them that love God," and " He that spared not His own Son, but delivered Him up for us all, how shall He not with Him also freely give us all things?" he would repeat often, saying, " he knew no such cordialls."

Thirdly. His victory over Sathan. It pleased God, about two years since, to permit Satan to buffet him severall times. Once he lay all night and slept not, and he was heard to say often, " Lord, rebuke the tempter!

Lord, give victory! Lord, be gracious!" With these expressions he spent five or six hours; in the morning he spake very chearfully, and said he would be laid to sleep; and having taken quiet rest, he awaked, and said that all the sins of his life had been laid before him that night, and those things (he said) that he had long forgotten, he then remembered. He said, the tempter had been very busie, "But, blessed be God, I did not sleep untill I had made my peace with God, through Jesus Christ." Then he chearfully said, a little while after, "God may let Satan buffet us for a time, but he shall never prevaile." After this his chearfulnesse continued without interruption.

Fourthly. His willingnesse to die. He was wont to say, many wish to live over their lives againe, that they might mend what had been amisse. "I would not be to live over my life again, least I should make it worse; I would not for all the world be young again, because I would not be so far from Heaven." And he would say to his children, when he had them about him, "I have taught you how to live, and I hope I shall teach you how to die."

Fifthly. His patience under his sharp sufferings. His disease was stone and palsie, and they that know these must look for tortures; yet in his sharpest pains and torments he would mollifie them with this consideration, —that is best which God doth. He would often say, the will of the Lord be done, above all and in all, for that is best of all; and he would support himselfe under his sharp pains with this meditation,—Heaven will make amends for all; and sometimes, when asked how he did, he would answer, " poor, but going to Heaven, as fast as I can." His lips (like an honeycombe) would drop such sweet expressions as these, "if the Lord see it best for me, that the stone in the bladder should be the way to bring me to Heaven, His will be done: it is better to die of the stone in the bladder, than of the stone in the heart." Thus (if you observe) he fed his patience under the divine hand, with divine arguments. That place of Scripture, 1 Cor. 10, 13, " there hath no temptation taken you, but such as is common to man; but God is faithful, who will not suffer you to be tempted above that you are able," he did often mention with joy; saying, it was the first place whereby God gave him comfort; and some few days before his death, when he was in much pain, he said, " blessed be God, who brings this place with comfort to me, whereby I had received first joy;" and so repeated those words, "there is no temptation," &c.; adding further, "blessed be God, blessed be what comes in the name of the Lord; Lord, be gracious." Thus you see his admirable patience.

Sixthly. His love to the Glory of God, and the Church of God. To joy under great afflictions is a hard matter; water quencheth fire, yet his joy in that which concern'd God his affliction could not extinguish. He was wont to pray constantly since the ruines and desolations of Brampton, that God would restore the Gospel hither: and two days before his death he rejoiced exceedingly, when he was told that this place of publick worship was finished. About three days before his death, when he arose and went to prayer (as he constantly used to do), though not able to enlarge in prayer, because of weaknesse, he prayed for the ruine of Antichrist, for the Churches of God beyond sea, naming Savoy, Switzerland, Germany. Upon the fifth of November, though very weak, and under great pains, yet he blessed God, for the great mercy of that day to the Church, and the nation, and to himself, who was of the Parliament when the Powder Plot was intended, and for the many mercies God had vouchsafed him to see since that time in the Church and in his own family; for his lady, the mother of his children, who (he said) was gone to Heaven before him, and for his childrens children; and for his hearing, which being lost, God restored him perfectly. Thus, the day before he dyed, he kept a day of thanksgiving to God, for all His former mercies. Oh, what spiritual and angelical elevation of heart was this! His soul was musical, like the swan; he sang before his death: which leads me to another branch.

Seventhly. His faith and assurance. A godly minister speaking to him concerning his dissolution; he said, "What matter is it if my poor cottage be falling here below! I am sure of a fair house upon the top of yonder hill." A day or two before his death, the 5 of Job being read to him in course, he said, "He that hath been with me in six troubles will not leave me in the seventh." And, lastly, having (like good old Jacob) given his blessing to all his children that were then at home, and to his grandchildren; desiring the Lord to blesse and sanctifie them particularly; I say, having done this about an hour before his death, though under extream pain, he said, "Blessed be God for this quiet peace." Thus his peace with

God shined like a candle in his heart, till his lamp of life went out with these last words, " I die, Lord be gracious!" In the flame of these words his soule (like the angell of God that appeared to Manoah) ascended, and went up to Heaven Thus this glorious saint went up to glory.

In the best times there were few or none better; in these declining times he hath left almost none like him among us. I pray God to double the spirit of deceased Elijah upon his surviving Elisha. The Lord repair the ruines of this castle, and build up this great family for the glory of His name in these parts.

Before I leave, I cannot but tell you, how God hath taken three brave men of late from us. The first upon whom the lot fell was Mr. Richard More of Linley, the next was Mr. Humphrey Walcot of Walcot, and now it hath fallen upon renowned Sir Robert Harley. I mention them here together, because these three were the triangles of our country; and whilst they lived were special friends, and of one heart for God in the concernments of His Gospell. And now I have done: onely to put you in mind a little of yourselves. You see, you are dying creatures: oh, then! consider your later end! the consideration of our last end should be the exercise of our first thoughts: to consider our end, would be the end of our sins, and the resurrection of our repentance; ashes keep fire alive; so this consideration, that we are dust and ashes, will keep our graces alive.

FINIS.

NOTES TO INTRODUCTION.

Page v. *Harley, family of.*—The family of Harley is of very ancient descent; it is still a question whether it be Roman, Saxon, or Norman, but certainly it was settled in Shropshire before the Norman Conquest, at which time Sir John de Harley was Lord of Harley Castle. In the obit or leger book of Pershore abbey there is a commemoration of one of the Harleys who defeated the Danes at Goodluck Hill, near that place, about the year 1013. Sir John de Harley, of Harley Castle, married Alice, daughter of Sir Titus de Leighton (by Letitia his wife, daughter of Hugh le Brune), and left issue Sir William de Harley, who accompanied Godfrey de Bulloigne to the Holy Land, 1098, and in honour of which he was made a Knight of St. Sepulchre. He married Katharine, daughter of Sir Jasper Croft, a knight of that order. He was buried in the abbey at Pershore, where there is a monument to him, of which it is to be observed, "that the shield on his effigies is plain, without any arms, according to the custom of most ancient times."—Collins. In the seventh descent from Sir William (24 Edw. I.) the King granted to Malcolm de Harley, his chaplain and beloved clerk, the marriage of his ward, Margaret, daughter and co-heir of Bryan de Brampton, for his nephew, Robert de Harleigh. The descent of the Bryans is traced from and beyond Maud, daughter of Sir William de Breos, Lord of Brecon, and widow of Roger Mortimer, Lord of Wigmore. The issue of this marriage was Robert, Bryan, Walter, and Joan. Robert and Bryan married two sisters, Joan and Eleanor, daughters of Sir Roger Corbet, of Morton, knight, and dividing the inheritance, the only daughter of Robert carried the Castle of Harley and other Shropshire property into the family of Grendon. Joan married Gilbert de Lacy, Lord of Castle Frome, co. Hereford. Brampton, Bucton, Byton, and other lands in Wiggesmoreland, fell to the lot of the second son, Bryan, who distinguished himself in the French wars, and was there knighted, and was recommended by the Black Prince to his father to be one of the Knights of the Garter, but died before the election. By his marriage he left *a son Bryan*, and a daughter Eleanor, married to Sir John Bromwich, of Bromwich Castle. This Bryan (2) was governor of Montgomery and Dolveren Castles, which he successfully defended against Owen Glendower; in memory of which his crest was changed from a buck's head proper to a lion rampant gules, issuing out of a tower triple-towered proper. He married Isolda, daughter of Sir Ralph Lyngen, of Stoke Edith, in the county of Hereford, knight, and left two sons, Richard and Jeffery: the former died unmarried, but Jeffery, by his first marriage with Johan ap Harry, had a daughter, Margaret, who married Hugh Wolley, and by his

Margin notes:
Abridged from Collins's Peerage of England, vol. iv. p. 231, Lond. Ed. 1768; and MS. Pedigree in Lady F. V. Harley's collections.
Sir William de Harley.
Malcolm de Harley.
Bryan de Brampton—Robert de Harleigh—William de Breos—Roger Mortimer—Robert.
Bryan (1).
Bryan (2).
Richard, ob. s. p.—Jeffery.

NOTES TO INTRODUCTION.

second marriage with Joce or Juliana, daughter of Sir John Burleigh or Burley, two sons, John and Bryan, and a daughter, Joan. Bryan (2) was killed in Brampton Bryan, on Palm Sunday, by Radnorshire felons; and John, engaged in the cause of the House of York, was knighted on the field at Gaston, near Tewkesbury: he married Joan, daughter of Sir Richard Hackluit, of Yetton, by whom he left Richard, and Alice, married first to Richard Monington, and secondly to William Tomkins, of Monington. Richard Harley married Catharine, daughter of Sir Thomas Vaughan, of Tretower Castle, in the county of Brecknock (whose descent is traced from the ancient British princes of Hereford, Brecknock, and Radnor, previous to the Norman Conquest, and from the noble families of Clares and Mortimers, as also from all the Princes of Wales), and had issue John, William, and Thomas, and a daughter, Catharine, married to Robert Hopwood.

This John Harley signalized himself as a Commander at Flodden Field (1513), and married, 11 Henry VIII. (1519-20), Anne, daughter of Sir Edward Croft, of Croft Castle, knight, by whom he had issue: John, Thomas, Rector of Brampton Bryan, William, Edward, and Margaret married to Thomas Adams, also Joyce and Elizabeth, who died unmarried; and by his second marriage, with Anne, daughter of Sir Ed. Rouse, of co. Worcester, a daughter Alice, who married Simon Macklew.

On the 30 March, 1541, John Harley covenanted for the marriage of his son John, then a minor, with Maud, daughter of Richard Warncomb, of Hereford, esquire, and afterwards co-heiress (with her sister Alice who had married, first, William Wigmore of Shobdon, and secondly, Sir James Croft,* of Croft Castle, by whom she had three sons, Edward, John, and George; and three daughters, Eleanor, married to Sir John Scudamore, of Holm Lacy, Gentleman Usher to Queen Elizabeth; Margaret, married to William Rudhall of Rudhall, esquire, and Jane, who died unmarried,) of James Warncomb, who died possessed of the manor of Lugdwardine, and divers other manors and lands in the co. of Hereford. She had for her share the manors of Aylton, Pickaley, and lands at Bodenham, Webton, Gothermet, Leyntall Starkes, Elton, and several houses in Leominster and Hereford. Of this marriage came John, slain in the French wars, Thomas, William, and Richard; and three daughters, Catharine, married first to John Cresset, of Upton Cresset, and secondly to John Cornwall the Baron of Burford; Elizabeth, married to Giles Nanfan, of Birch (now Birts) Morton, co. Worcester; and Jane, married to Roger Minors, of Treago, in the county of Hereford.

This Thomas was the father of Sir Robert.

The following circumstance gave occasion to Sir Robert being born at Wigmore Castle:

"Thomas Harley, when married, resided with his father at Brampton Bryan, who, being a zealous Romanist, prevailed with his son to attend a secret mass in the castle, of which his good wife having intimation, came to the chapel door and ask't to have her husband away, with threats, if it were denied, to acquaint Queen Elizabeth. Thereupon the doors were opened and he let go to his wife, who prevailed upon him to remove to Wigmore Castle, where Robert was soon afterwards born."

Sir Robert had expressed a wish (1621) to go and see the army in the Netherlands; which his father refused in the following letter:—

Marginal notes:
John—Bryan. Sir John.
Richard.
John, b. 1491, ob. 1542.
John—Thomas— William—Edward.
* Notice of Sir James Croft in Retrospective Review and Historical Magazine, vol. I. p. 491. Lond. 1827.
John, sl.—Thomas —William—Richard—Catharine. Elizabeth. Jane.
MS. in his grandfather's study, copied by the Auditor, 1722.
Sir Robert.

THOS. HARLEY TO SIR ROB. HARLEY.

"Good Son—As c'cerning y^r lett^r to my dau'tr of y^r desyr too goe into ye Lowe Countries too see ye noble army there, iff I wold grāte you leave, wherwith my daut^r acqu'ted me, my answer was, that you s'old never haue my c'sent, and if there were a necessytye of goinge, I wold be ye man. Alsoe I receaved from my dau'ter vpon Thursday ye letter tendinge to that purpose, wch I dyd reade that day, and the nyght following did consider therof, not too sende a bare letter, but my servant Ihon Hopkins, whom I sent to Mr Pierson that I myght acq'nte hym wth y^r letter, and to knowe whether he wold have any thinge to you, who verye frealye offered to be the messenger hymselfe, w^h I doe take most kindlye att his hands, whom I have instructed to deale with you very ffreely. Human'est errare, but no wysdom to p'severe; therefore, good sonne, lette me p'vayle soe ffarre w^h you, that no further sppeches maye growe hereof, lest there thence maye cō a ryppynge upe of them and other occacions, but rather a ————; wherin I know Mr Pierson, who loveth and honoreth you in his heart, will advise you. Therefore for once agayne intreatinge you will come to vs wth speed, w^h wylbe noe small c'forting to us all, and especially to my dau'ter. The God blese you.

"Y^r lovinge and naturall Ffather,
"T. HARLEY.

"Brōpt. Castel, 23 June, 1621."

In Sir Robert's time, Harley was occasionally spelt Harlow, Harlowe, and Harloe.
Lord Conway writes Harlow, Appendix, p. 214.
Major Winthrop writes Harlowe, Appendix, p. 233.
Whitelocke, in Memorials, writes Harlow, Harloe, and Harley.

Page vi. *Provost of Oriel.*—"John Tolson, Procter 15 April, 1607; D.D. 21 March, 1621; was Provost (1621-44); and pro-Vice-Chancellor 1642. In his time the new Chapel and Hall were built, between 1637-1642, himself contributing 1,150*l.*"—Ingram's Memorials of Oxford.

Page vii. *He represented in Parliament.*—Among Sir Robert's papers is the following in his own hand-writing:—

"COPPIES OF GENERALE LETTRES VPON NEWS OF A PARLAM^t.

"Sr T. C.

"Honorable knight and my worthy friend,—I heare that wee shall shortlie hav a parliament, wch it may bee is no newes to you. To answere yor many noble respects to mee, I desire to impart it to you, beeing newes to mee, beseeching you to bee pleased to reserve your voyces for the knights of the parlament for this county, till we all meet to deliberate of the fittest persons for that attendance, that ye choyce may not be made by affection but discretion. So in hast."

"S^r Jo. Sc.

"S^r,—I understand wee shall shortly have a parlament, the immediate consequence of wch truth amongst vs will bee the choyce of knights of the shire. I beseech you, sir,

NOTES TO INTRODUCTION.

therefore acquaint yo' grandfather with it, beseeching him from mee, that he will reserve his voyces till we all meete to consult of ye fittest men for that service, that affection possesse not the place of discretion in o' election. So in haste p'esenting you wth my newes, wch it may be is none to you, I commend you to o' good God, and rest."

"Sr R. Hop:

"S^r,—I understand for newes y^t wee shall shortly have a parlament, wch I desire to impart to you, as to my frend and loving kinsman, wth all intreating you to reserve yo' voyces for the election of the knights of this shire till we shall meete to deliberate and resolve of the fittest for that service, wherin I desire that neither faction nor affection, but discretion and true understanding, may poynt us out the men. So in hast."

"M^r Ja. Fo:

"S^r,—I have newes that ye parlament will shortly be summoned, and I pray that my love may so fare prevayle wth you to entreate you to reserve yo' voyces for electing ye knights of this shire till wee all meet to advise of such as shall be thought fitest for that service. So, etc."

Page ix. *The suppression of the surplice, &c. &c.*—"The House of Commons made an order, and Sir Robert Harlow had the execution of it, to take away all scandalous pictures, crosses, and figures within churches and without. And the zealous knight took down the cross in Cheapside, Charing Cross, and other the like monuments impartially."—Whitelocke, 5 July, 1641, p. 45.

This is certainly incorrect as to time, for in the Jour. H. Commons we find (1 March, 1641-2,) it "*Ordered*, That the Com^e on Cheapside Cross shall be revived." Again, "Cheapside Cross and other crosses were voted down."—Whitelocke, 3 May, 1643.

Evelyn says, 2 May, 1643, "I went from Wotton to London, where I saw the furious and zealous people demolish that stately cross in Cheapside."

In the Supplement to the Gent. Mag. 1764, a plate and notice is given of the demolishing of Cheapside Cross. "2 May, 1643, the crosse in Cheapside was pulled down: a troope of hors and two companies of foote wayted to garde, and, at the fall of the top crosse, dromes beat, trumpets blew, and multitudes of capes were thrown in the ayre, and a greate shoute of people with joy. The 2 May, the Almanake sayeth, was the Invention of the Crosse, and 6 day at night was the leaden popes burnt in the place where it stood, with ringing of bells and a great acclamation; and no hurt done in all these actions."

Lilly, in his Observations on the Life of Charles I. (quoted by Percy in his Reliques of Ancient Poetry, in illustration of the ballad "On the Downfall of Charing Cross") says, "Charing Cross, we know, was pulled down 1647, June, July, and August. Part of the stones were converted to pave before Whitehall. I have seen knife-hafts made of some of the stones, which, being well polished, looked like marble."

Jour. H. Com. 24 Ap. 1643. "Sir Robert Harley, Mr. White, Mr. Corbett, and others, a Committee to receive information from time to time of any monuments of superstitious idolatry in the abbey church of Westminster, or the windows thereof, or in any church or chapel in and about London. And they have power to demolish the same, where any such superstitious or idolatrous monuments are informed to be. And the churchwardens and other officers are hereby required to be aiding and assisting in the execution of this order."

Ibid. 5 Feb. 1643-4. "*Ordered*, That it be referred to the Com" for superstitious pictures, where Sir Rob. Harley has the chair, to take into their custody the copes and surplices and other chapel stuff at Whitehall, and to view the superstitious pictures about Whitehall, and to report what they are. They are likewise to search and view all the plate in Sir H. Mildmay's custody, and search and view such other things in Whitehall as they shall think fit. *Ordered*, That the product of goods, copes, and surplices seized at Whitehall, and also the plate in Sir H. Mildmay's custody belonging to his Majesty, be employed and disposed of to the Lady Essex, for payment of arrears to Sir W. Essex, her husband, who died at Oxford, and the remainder to Col. Ven, for payment of arrears due to the garrison of Windsor."

Ibid. 17 April, 1644. "*Resolved*, That the chest or silver vessel in St. Paul's shall be sold for the best advantage, and employed towards providing necessaries for the artillery by the Com" at Grocers' Hall."

23 April, 1644. "*Ordered*, That the materials informed of by Sir Rob. Harley be forthwith sold by Sir Rob. Harley, viz. the mitre and crosier-staff found in St. Paul's Church, London, and the brass and iron in Hen. VII. Chapel, Westminster, and the proceeds thereof, the necessary charges deducted, be employed according to the direction of the House."

Ibid. 25 April, 1644. "That Sir Rob. Harley do report on Saturday the ordinance for defacing copes, &c. &c."

"The ordinance for taking away altars, levelling chancel-floors recently raised, tapers, candlesticks, basins, crucifixes, crosses, images, and pictures of the Holy Trinity or Virgin Mary, and all other images and pictures of saints and superstitious inscriptions *excepted*, images, pictures, coats of arms in glass, stone, or otherwise, in any church, chapel, or a churchyard, set up or engraven for a monument of any king, prince, nobleman, or other dead person, who had not commonly been reported or taken for a saint."—Neal's Hist. of the Puritans, by Toulmin, vol. iii. p. 644.

Page x. *Master of the Mint, &c.*—Journ. H. Com. 6 March, 1642-3. "*Ordered*, that Sir Rob. Harley shall have power to give a privy mark for the pixe money in the Mint, and that he bring in an ordinance for the restoring of himself to his place in the Mint." See other notices in Journ. H. Com. 3 and 5 May, 1643.

Self-denying Ordinance.—The self-denying ordinance concludes thus: "Provided always, and it is hereby declared that those members of either house who had offices by grant from his Majesty before the parliament, and were by his Majesty displaced sitting this parliament, and have since by authority of both houses been restored, shall not by this ordinance be discharged from the said offices or profits thereof, but shall enjoy the same, any thing in this ordinance to the contrary thereof notwithstanding."—Parl. Hist. vol. iii. p. 355.

The Mastership at the Mint, worth 4,000*l.* a-year in Sir Robert's time: in the time of £4,000 a-year. Sir Isaac Newton it was considered to be worth from 1,200*l.* to 1,400*l.* a year.

NOTES TO INTRODUCTION.

Page xi. *Piedmont collection, &c.*—The collection for the persecuted Protestants in Piedmont, &c. is said to have amounted to 37,097*l.* 7*s.* 3*d.*; about 30,000*l.* was remitted in 1655 and the following year; the confusion following the Protector's death prevented the clearing of the whole amount till the Convention Parliament at the Restoration, when the remainder, 7,000*l.*, was ordered to be paid."—Neal's Hist. of the Puritans, by Toulmin, vol. iv. p. 141.

Page xii. *Thos. Froysell.*—Journ. H. Com. 17 March, 1642-3. "An ordinance for sequestering the rents and profits of the parish-church of St. Margaret's, New Fish Street, London, into the hands of certain sequestrators, to the use of Thos. Froysell, M.A., a godly, learned, and orthodox divine, who is hereby required and appointed to take care for the discharge of the cure of the said place in all the duties thereof, until both houses of parliament shall take further order, was read, and by vote upon the question assented to, &c."

Ibid. 25 March, 1643. "It was ordered, upon the petition of the common councilmen and others of ye parish of St. Dunstan's in the West, that Mr. Thos. Froizell shall preach the lecture every Thursday forenoon."

"Mr. Froysell of Clun, an ancient divine of extraordinary worth, for judgement, moderation, godliness, blameless life, and excellent preaching, who with many others, in poverty and sickness, and great suffering, continued to preserve the peace of his conscience."—Calamy's Abridgment of the Life and Times of Baxter, p. 355.

Recent generations of the Harleys since the time of Henry VII.—In the curious old mansion of Birt's Morton in county Worcester, formerly the seat of Giles Nanfan, who married Elizabeth, the sister of Thomas Harley, and first cousin of Sir John Scudamore and William Rudhall, as stated above, there is, along the cornice of a fine old panelled room, the arms and names of the following gentlemen, among whom, no doubt, an extensive cousinship was recognized:

> William Rudhall, of Rudhall, Esq.
> Jhon Blount, of Eye, Esq.
> Y^e Lord Copley.
> Sr Henry Polle, Knight.
> Sr John Scudamore, Knight.
> Sr Thos. Throgmorton, Knight.
> Sr James Croft, Knight.
> Thomas Cornwall, Esq.
> Baskerville of Erdesley, Esq.
> Thomas Harley, Esq.
> Walter Vaughan of Hergest, Esq.
> Roger Minors, Esq.
> Jhon Bridges, Esq.
> Bromwich of Bromsberro, Esq.
> John Hyett, Gent.

NOTES TO INTRODUCTION. xlvii

Hackluyt of Yetton.—Richard Hackluyt, the author of English Voyages, Navigation, and Discoveries. Lond. 1598-99, 1600, 3 vols. folio, and other geographical works, according to Wood, was of the family of Hackluyt of Yetton.—Wood's Athenæ, vol. ii. p. 186.

Page xiv. *Post of Hereford, Leominster, Shrewsbury, or Ludlow, then recently established, &c.*—See an interesting notice of the early history of the Post-office in the Gentleman's Magazine, Aug. 1853, p. 153.

In a table appended to the Description and Use of two Arithmetical Instruments, &c. by S. Morland (Sir Samuel), Lond. 1673, is a notice " concerning letters which may be sent from London."

Page xvi. *A solemn day of prayer, &c.*—Numerous allusions to fasts occur in these letters in Ember weeks, private days, &c. Sir Robert keeps a solemn day of prayer at Stanage Lodge, also a day preparatory to his entering on his parliamentary duties. The Ember days and monthly parliamentary fasts, the last Wednesday in the month, and special days, were strictly observed at Brampton. Instead of the last Wednesday the King, 5 Oct. 1643, ordered the second Friday in each month, to be so observed. The last Wednesday in December, 1644, falling on Christmas Day, and doubt having arisen with the divines whether that day should be observed as a fast—on the 19th Dec. it was ordered by the House of Commons so to be kept. The Royalists made a clamour against this as a great impiety and profaneness. The parliament—now to a man Presbyterian—taking the views of the Kirk, approved of it. Mr. Edmund Calamy, in his sermon before the House of Lords, on that day, says, " This day is commonly called Christmas Day, a day that has hitherto been much abused to superstition and profaneness. It is not easy to say whether the superstition has been greater or the profaneness. I have known some that have preferred Christmas Day before the Lord's Day—some that would be sure to receive the Sacrament on Christmas Day, though they did not receive it all the year after—some thought, though they did not play at cards all the year, yet they must play at Christmas; thereby, it seems, to keep in memory the birth of Christ. This and much more had been the profaneness of this feast—and truly I think the superstition and profaneness of the day is so rooted into it—that there is no way to reform it, but by dealing with it as Hezekiah did with the Brazen serpent. This year, God, by His providence, has buried this *feast* in a *fast*, and I hope it will never rise again. You have sent out, right honorable, a strict order for keeping this day, and you are here to-day to observe your own order, and I hope you will do it strictly. The necessities of the times are great—never more need of prayer and fasting—the Lord give us grace to be humbled in this day of humiliation for all our own and England's sins, and especially for the old superstition and profaneness of this feast."—Neal's Hist. of the Puritans, by Toulmin, vol. iii. p. 156.

In the letter from Lord Westmorland to Edward Harley in the Appendix, p. 215, there is, in a Latin Epigram, an allusion to this keeping of Christmas Day as a fast—fixing the year of that undated letter to be 1644.

On the monthly fast days, the business of the House of Commons was usually voting thanks to the preachers for the great pains taken in their sermons, requesting the preachers to print the same, and nominating two other preachers for the next fast day. After the calling of the Assembly of Divines, they were usually, if not always, selected from that body.

Soon after the death of the King, the ordinance for keeping the monthly fast was repealed and occasional ones substituted; for which this reason is assigned: "That such times of extraordinary duties of worship are apt to degenerate into mere formality and customary observances."

In the Register of Brampton Bryan is the following:—

"*Memorandum*, That whereas Dame Brilliana Harley is lycensed by Thomas Pierson, Rector of this parish of Brampton Bryan, to eate flesh on fast days, in reason of her greate weakness, wch licence was made the first day of the month, and for that her greate weakness does yet continue, the continuence of the seyd licence   according to the statute of Elizabeth, till it shall please God to render her ....

"THOMAS × PIERSON.
"March 14, 1632."   the mark of

A similar notice occurs in the Register of Sellack, in the county of Hereford:—

"1632, ye 16th Nov. Mem. That upon the day and year above written, a license was granted by Richard Prichard, Vicar of Sellack, unto John Viscount Scudamore, his Lady, and their sonne, in respect of manifest sickness and infirmityes, to eat flesh upon dayes prohibited, during the time of their sickness and infirmityes. Registered in the sight of Walter Holland, one of the churchwardens, 22 Nov, 1632."

Page xvii. *Pierson objected not to the Liturgy, but scrupled the use of the surplice, &c.*—
"Mr. Pierson's scruples, expressed in his own hand, as follow:—

"GROUNDS OF REASONS AGAINST THE CEREMONIES.

"1. I desire to see good warrant for a proper ministering garment under the Gospell.
"2. How a proper massing garment can be decent for Christ's members of the Gospel, or his service.
"3. Good warrant for ye use of significant ceremonies in God's service such as ours be.
"4. Whether these, being idolatries in Rome, should not be rejected as *idolathytes* out of God's service."—MS. Acct. of Rectors of Brampton Bryan in Harl. MSS. Brit. Mus.

Page xviii. *Stanley Gower.*—Jour. H. C. (1 Nov. 1643) directs that Stanley Gower do preach on the next Lord's Day at St. Margaret's, Westminster—being Gunpowder Treason-day.

Page xix. *Plunder and villanous usage then the practice of the Cavaliers, &c.*—
"Divers of Worcestershire, under Mr. Dingley, declared for the Parliament, and complained of the insolencies and injuries by the garrison of Worcester." Whitelocke gives a specimen of this, but of a later date, 25 Nov. 1645: A copy of a warrant from Col. Bard, the Governor of Worcester, to the constables for contributions was sent up, wherein

were these expressions: "Know that unless you bring unto me, at a day and houre, in Worcester, the monthly contribution for six months, you are to expect an unsanctifyed troop of horse among you, from whence if you hide yourselves they shall fire your houses without mercy, hang up your bodies wherever they find them, and scare your ghosts," &c.—P. 188.

Dr. Nathaniel Wright.—Nathaniel Wright, M.A. of Cambridge, took the degree of Doctor of Physic at Bourges, in France, and was incorporated at Oxford, 30 May, 1638. Wood says he was afterwards "Physician to O. Cromwell, when he was sick in Scotland."—Wood's Fasti, vol. i. p. 503.

The siege commenced on the 25 Sept. 1643.—This happening on a Tuesday, the day before the monthly fast, was kept as a special day of prayer and supplication at Brampton.

Page xx. *Lady Brilliana's children.*—The issue of Sir Robert and Lady Brilliana Harley:—

1. Edward, afterwards noticed, page xxviii.
2. Robert, knighted, married 8 Feb. 1670, Edith, daughter of ———— Pembrugge, esquire, widow of Major Hinton, but left no issue; buried at Brampton Bryan, 18 Nov. 1673.
3. Thomas, of Kinsham Court, by Abigail, daughter of Sir Richard Saltinstall, knight, had four sons, who died issueless.
4. Brilliana, wife of James Stanley, second son of Sir Robert Stanley, knight, who was second son of the Earl of Derby.
5. Dorothy, wife of William Mitchell, of co. Norfolk.
6. and 7. Margaret and Elizabeth, who died unmarried.—Collins, vol. iv. 252.

Dr. Wilkinson.—John Wilkinson was Principal of Magdalene Hall from 1605 to 1644, when he fled from Oxford—to which he was restored 1646—and became President of Magdalene College in 1648; he took his D.D. in 1613. The Hall flourished under his government, and that of his nephew Henry Wilkinson, to the Restoration; and was the chief school of Puritanism in Oxford. Wood speaks disparagingly of him, and says, "he published nothing."—Fasti, vol. i. p. 354; and again "contrasts the liberal conduct of John Oliver, President of Magdalene College, who had been displaced 1648, but restored 1660, with that of Drs. Wilkinson and Goodwyn, who had been thrust into his office by the Parliament and Oliver, for their saintship, and zeal to the blessed cause, and gave not a farthing, but raked and scraped up all that they could get thence, as the rest of the saints did in the university."—Wood's Athenæ, vol. iv. p. 300.

"SIR ROBERT HARLEY TO ED. H.

"Ned Harley,—I thank you for y^r letters, and desier so to carry ye buisness with you y^t you may alwaies thanke mee for mine, and now y^t ye Lord hath in His good providence disposed you in ye university, and with so worthy a tutor as is Mr Perkins, and under ye vigilent government of ye Principall Do^r Wilkinson, whose holy example lett every day make impression in you of ye good in wch he moves. You must consider y^t y^r end is to gett

NOTES TO INTRODUCTION.

inlargement of knowledg in ye understandinge chiefly of God in Christ, wch is life eternall, then of morrall science, wch will not only enriche y^r mind but sett of yor conversation amongst men, as shaddows do some pictures, to ye workeman's greater com'endation. Fyrst then take ye wise man's counsell to remember y^r Creator in ye dayes of y^r youth, to love Hym y^t made you when you were not, and redeemed you with ye preciouse blood of His deare Sonne when you were lost, wch you must finde to be from a vaine conversation, and love will teach you ye feare of ye Lord, and y^{ts} ye beginninge of wisdome, wch not only makes one man differ from another, as reason doth man from a beast, but giveth life to hym y^t hath it; and it will give you an elevation above ye base wayes wherein many young men wallow; and I feare ye universities do too much abound with such pigges, from wch ye preservative must be daily prayer for God's blessinge on y^r owne and ye endevours of y^r loving and graciouse tutor, whose care and counsells if you answer with diligence and obedience you will allsoe my expectation, with no little comforte; so, with my constant prayers for ye blessings of our heavenly Father upon you, I send you ye blessing of y^r loving father,
                       Ro. HARLEY.

"Brampton Castle, 19° 9bris, 1638."

Page xxi. *Edward Harley, Captain of a troop of horse, &c.*—Jour. H. Com. 13 Nov. 1643. "*Ordered*, That the men raised under the command of Col. Harley shall be forthwith sent to Plymouth by sea, part raised by imprest. The Committee of the West to take care for the raising of these men."

21 Aug. 1648. "Letter from Salop, that Sir Henry Lyngen, with a party of horse, took 60 of Col. Harley's men; and, about two days after, a party of Col. Harley and Col. Horton's men met with Sir Hen. Lyngen's men about Radnor, regained all the men, horse, and prisoners, took Sir Hen. Lyngen and Col. Croft and many others of the King's commanders prisoners, slew divers of the party, and routed the rest."—Whitelocke, p. 325.

In the Auditor's notes there is an allusion to the barbarous treatment Colonel Edward Harley received from Sir Herbert Croft and other deputy lieutenants, in sending part of a troop of horse to seize a pair of pistols given him by Lord Vere as a memorial, these being the pistols with which he charged at the battle of Newport.

Page xxii. *Mr. Clogie.*—Alexander Clogie was buried in the chancel of Wigmore church, where there is a slab in the floor under the communion table with this inscription :—

"Here lyeth, in hope of a glorious resurrection unto life eternall, the body of that holy, reverend, and learned divine, Mr. Alexander Clogie, who departed this life 24 Oct. 1698, aged 84. Minister of Wigmore 51 years."

He was the author of a Sermon, "Vox Corvi; or, The Voice of a Raven that thrice spoke these Words distinctly: 'Look into Colossians the 3rd, 15th.' The Text itself looked into and opened in a Sermon preached at Wigmore, in the County of Hereford; to which is added, 'Serious Addresses to the People of this Kingdom,' shewing the use we ought to make of this Voice from Heaven. Lond. 1694."

NOTES TO INTRODUCTION.

There is a MS. Life of Bishop Bedell in the Harl. MSS. in the Brit. Mus. supposed by Archdeacon Hone to be the MS. which Bishop Burnet made use of in the compilation of his Life of Bedell, which was published in 1685; for this reason, the writer appears to identify himself with A.C. minister of Cavan, and Burnet's authority (see Preface, page *b*) was Mr. Clogy, minister of Cavan, "a worthy and learned divine," and as having lived in the bishop's house, and shared his troubles up to the time of his death, 1642. In a letter of the Bishop of Meath, dated Dec. 14, 1685, found amongst Mr. Boyle's Correspondence, "a Life of Bedell is mentioned lately published by one Clogy, who is somewhere beneficed in England, if he be alive, and as having married the bishop's daughter." May not this Mr. Clogy,—A. C. (Minister of Cavan) be Alexander Clogie, Minister of Wigmore from 1647 to 1698? Stanley Gower, the Rector of Brampton Bryan, had been chaplain to Archbishop Usher, and to him Mr. Clogy or his family might have been known; and it is not at all improbable that, seeking an asylum in England, as he did, he might have found a friend in Mr. Gower, which may have led to his being fixed at Wigmore. There appears to be an inaccuracy in the Bishop of Meath's letter not noticed by Archdeacon Hone, for it is there said that Clogy had married the bishop's daughter; but in the Life of the Bishop it is said, " of his four children, two died in infancy, the other two, being sons, grew up to man's estate, and survived their parents."—Archdeacon Hone's Lives—Bishop Bedell, vol. ii. pp. 211, 248—257.

Mr. Clogie's marriage with Susannah Nelmes at Ludlow, 11 Dec. 1665, is noted in the Register of Wigmore. Among his children was a daughter named Brilliana, after the Lady Brilliana Harley.

Page xxiv. *Dr. Herbert Croft, Bishop of Hereford.*—See an interesting account of him in Wood's Athenæ, vol. iv. p. 309—318. In 1688, he published a short discourse concerning the reading his Majesty's late Declaration in churches. This pamphlet coming into the hands of a certain courtier, he communicated it to the King, who, upon perusal, commanded so much as concerned the reading of the Declaration (which was for the indulging of consciences,) to be printed, but suppressed all that he said against taking off the Test and penal law.

Page xxvi. *Sir Edward Harley, Governor of Worcester.*—When Governor of Worcester, "A party having brought into the city the plunder of horses and other things, Sir Edward ordered all that could be seized to be restored, except a blasphemous image of the Holy Trinity, which (having been first shewn to the Bishop,) he ordered to be broken in pieces in the open street."—Auditor's Notes.

Page xxvii. *John Lord Viscount Scudamore.*—See a view of the ancient and present state of the churches of Dore, Home-Lacy, and Hempsted, endowed by him; with remains of that ancient family, by Matth. Gibson, M.A. Rector of Dore.—Lond. 1727.

Page xxviii. *Dr. Tuckney.*—Anthony Tuckney was originally of Emmanuel College, of which he became a fellow, and thence removed to the vicarage of Boston, from which place he was selected as one of the Assembly of Divines: he is said to have assisted in composing the Westminster Confession and Catechism, and, in particular, to have drawn up the exposition of the Commandments in the larger catechism, but to have voted against subscribing to swearing to the confession, &c. set out by authority—a conduct the more deserving of notice and commendation as the instances of a consistent adherence to the principles of religious liberty were so few and rare in that age. In 1645 he became Master of his College; and in 1653 Master of St. John's, Cambridge, in which year he was named one of "the Tryers;" and on the death of Dr. Arrowsmith became Regius Professor of Divinity. He was one of the Presbyterian Divines in attendance at the Savoy conference, where he received a Royal letter from Secretary Nicholas, giving him a supersedeas from his public employments, with the promise of 100*l.* a-year for life out of his successor's income, which was punctually paid. Calamy says, "he left behind him the character of an eminently pious and learned man, a true friend, an indefatigable student, a candid disputant, and an earnest promoter of truth and godliness." His modesty was as distinguished as his learning, and he is said to have shewn more courage in maintaining the rights and privileges of the university in those lawless times than any of the heads at Cambridge. He presided over St. John's with great prudence and ability, and that college had never flourished more than under his rule. In the elections, when the president, according to the language and spirit of the times, would call upon him to have regard to the godly, his answer was, " no one should have a greater regard to the truly godly than himself, but he was determined to choose none but scholars; adding, very truly, " they may deceive me in their godliness, but they cannot in their scholarship." He published in his lifetime some small pieces, as "Death disarmed, or the Grave swallowed up in Victory, 1654;" "Balm of Gilead for the Wounds of England, applyed in a Sermon, 1654;" "A good day well improved, in 5 Sermons, 1656." After his death, were published Forty Sermons of his, preached on several occasions; also his " Prælectiones Theologicæ," containing all his theological lectures and exercises while he continued in his public employments in the university: and in 1753, Dr. Samuel Salter, Prebendary of Norwich, published a correspondence between Dr. Tuckney and Dr. Benjamin Whichcote, on moral and interesting subjects.—Neal's Hist. of the Puritans, vol. iii. p. 115, vol. iv. p. 556; Dyer's Hist. of Cambridge; and Baxter's Life, by Calamy.

LETTERS

OF

THE LADY BRILLIANA HARLEY.

1625—1643.

I.

To my deare husband Sr Robart Harley, Kinght of the Bathe.

S^r—Docter Barker has put my sister into a cours of ientell fisck, which I hope by God's bllsing will doo her much good. My sister giues you thankes for seending him to her. I pray you remember that I recken the days you are away; and I hope you are nowe well at Heariford, wheare it may be, this letter will put you in minde of me, and let you knowe, all your frinds heare are well; and all the nwes I can seend you is, that my Lo. Brooke is nowe at Beacthams Court. My hope is to see you heare this day senet, or to-morrowe senet, and I pray God giue vs a happy meeting, and presarfe you safe; which will be the great comfort of

Your most true affectionat wife,   BRILLIANA HARLEY.

Ragly: the 30 of Sep. 1625.

II.

To my deare housband Sr Robart Harley, Knight, in Blackfriers,
at my Lo. Lewsons howes.

Deare S^r—I thanke you for your letter which you sent me from Tuddington: which gaue me satisfaction of your being well, so fare on your journey: which ascurance of your health is the beest nwes

I can heare, except that of your comeing home. I ernestly desire to heare howe you came to Loundon; and doo thinke your men stay longe: but I hope they will bringe me good nwes of you, and then I shall be well pleased. Ned, I thanke God, is very well, and you will beleeve me, if I say he looses non of his grandfather loue, whoo is better than you leeft him. And no more to you at this time; but I beceache the Allmighty presarue you, and giue you happy meeting with

Your most faithfull affectionat wife, BRILLIANA HARLEY.

Brompton, the 10*th of Phe.* 1625.

III.

To my deare housband Sr Robart Harley, Knight.

S^r—I thanke you for sending me word, I may hope to see you at Easter, which time will be much longed for by me. I hope the parlament has spent as much time as will satisfy them in dooing nothing: so that nowe some good frute of theare meeting will be brought to ripnes, which is the effect of our prayers. This day I deleverd the £100 to my father: which he has payed to Mr. Davis: that mony that was wanting of it, was made vp with the £50 pounde Mr. Lacy payed for wood. The payling of the nwe parke is made an end of. Yesterday your company only was at Heariford, to shewe what they had lerned, whear Sr. Jhon Skidemore and Mr. Vahan weare judges; and so they meane to be of the reest of the companis, and they haue apointed teen of your company to learne the vse of theiare armes and so to teache the reest. This last night I not being very well, made me seend this day for the midwife, which I thinke I should haue defered to longe. I asure myself I haue your prayers, becaus you haue so great a part of mine: and I blls God that you injoy your health, which I beeg of you to take care of. I thanke God, Ned is well, and I beeg your bllsing for him: and I pray God preserue you well and giue you a happy and speedy meeting with

Your most faithful affectionat wife, BRILLIANA HARLEY.

I pray you present my humbell duty to my father, and my lady. My cosen Thomkins remembers her loue to you.

Brompton, the 17 *of Mar.* 1625.

IV.
To my deare husband Sʳ Robert Harley.

Deare Sʳ—Your two leters, on from Hearifort and the other from Gloster, weare uery wellcome to me: and if you knwe howe gladly I reseaue your leters, I beleeue you would neeuer let any opertunity pase. I hope your cloche did you saruis betwne Gloster and my brother Brays, for with vs it was a very rainy day, but this day has bine very dry and warme, and so I hope it was with you; and to-morowe I hope you will be well at your journis end, wheare I wisch my self to bide you wellcome home. You see howe my thoughts goo with you: and as you haue many of mine, so let me haue some of yours. Beleeue me, I thinke I neuer miste you more then nowe I doo, or ells I haue forgoot what is past. I thanke God, Ned and Robin are well; and Ned askes every day wheare you are, and he says you will come to-morowe. My father is well, but goos not abrode, becaus of his fiseke. I haue sent you vp a litell hamper, in which is the box with the ryteings and boouckes you bide me send vp, with the other things, sowed up in a clothe, in the botome of the hamper. I haue sent you a partriche pye, which has the two pea chikeins in it, and a litell runlet of meathe, that which I toold you I made for my father. I thinke within this muthe, it will be very good drinke. I sende it vp nowe becaus I thinke carage when it is ready to drincke dous it hurt; thearefore, and please you to let it rest and then taste it; if it be good, I pray you let my father haue it, because he spake to me for such meathe. I will nowe bide you god night, for it is past a leauen a cloke. I pray God presarue you and giue you good sugsess in all your biusnes, and a speady and happy meeting.

Your most faithfull affectinat wife,   BRILLIANA HARLEY.

I must beeg your bllsing for Ned and Rob. and present you with Neds humbell duty.

Bromton, the 5 of October, 1627.

V.

To my deare husband Sr Robert Harley, Knight.

My deare S^r—I ame glad of this opertuenity to present you with the remembranc of my deare loue. I hope you came well to Bristo; and I much longe to heare from you, but more a thousand times to see you, which I presume you will not beleeue, becaus you cannot poscibilly measure my loue. I thanke God your father is well, and so are your three soons. Ned presents his humbell duty to you, and I beeg your bllsing for them all; and I pray God giue you a happy and speady meeting with

Your most affectinat wife,   BRILL. HARLEY.

If I thought it would hasten your comeing home, I would intreat you to doo soo.

I pray you remember me to Mr. Pirson. I thanke God all at his howes are well.

Bromton, the 7th, 1628.

VI.

To my deare husband Sr Robert Harley, Knight.

My deare S^r—I thanke you for your letter, which I reseaued this weake by the carrier, and I thanke God for my father's health. I trust in our good God, in his owne good time, he will giue a happy end to your biusness. I haue rwritten a letter to my father, which I send you heare inclosed. If you thinke it will not displeas him, and it may any thinge at all seet forward your biusnes, I pray you deleuer it to him. If you do deleuer it to my father, I pray you scale it first. Allas! my deare S^r, I knowe you doo not to the on halfe of my desires, desire to see me, that loues you more then any earthly thinge. I should be glad if you would but rwite me

word, when I should hope to see you. Need has bine euer sence Sunday trubled with the rume in his fase very much. * * * * * *
The swelling of his face made him very dull; but nowe, I thanke God, he is better, and begins to be merry. He inquires for Jhon Walls comeing downe: for he thinkes he will bringe him a letter. I must desire you to send me downe a littell Bibell for him. He would not let me be in peace, tell I promised him to send for on. He begings nowe to delight in reading: and that is the booke I would haue him place his delight in. Tom has still a greate coold; but he is not, I thanke God, sike with it. Brill and Robin, I thanke God, are well; and Brill has two teethe. Ned presents his humble duty to you, and I beeg your bllsing for them all: and I beceach the Allmighty to prosper you in all you doo, and to giue you a happy meeting with

Your most faithfull affectinat wife, BRILLIANA HARLEY.

I pray you, S^r, send downe no silke grogram. I hope you haue reseuefed the siluer candell-stike.

Your father, I thanke God, is much better than he was. I pray you, S^r, present my beest loue to my sister Wacke.

Desem 4, 1629.

VII.

To my deare husband Sr Robert Harley, Knight, at his howes in Alldermanbery.

My dearest S^r—Your men came to Bromton on thursday last. I thanke God that you haue your halth. I hope the Lord will giue vs bothe faith to waite vpon him; and I trust that in his mercy he will give a good end to your biusnes. It pleases God that I continue ill with my coold, but it is, as they say, a nwe disceas: it trubelles me much, more becaus of my being with childe; but I hope the Lord will deale in mercy with me; and, deare S^r, let me haue your prayers, for I haue need of them. Docter Barker is nowe with me. I thanke God the children are all well, and Need and Robine are very glad of theire boose, and Ned is much discontended that you come not downe. I beeg your bllssing for them all, beeeaching the Allmighty to presarue you, and to giue you a joyefull and happy meeting with your

Most faithfull affectinat wife,   BRIL. HARLEY.

I pray present my humbell duty to my father. This day theare came a man from Ragley to feetche my cosen Hunkes to her mother, whoo is very sike.

Bromton, the 8 of May, 1630.

VIII.

For my deare husband Sr Robert Harley, Knight.

My deare S^r—I pray you reseaue my thankes for your letter by my cosen Pris, and by the carrier; they weare both very wellcome to me, which I thinke you beleeue, for in part you know howe deare you are to me. I ame very glad that my brother Raphe is come to Loundoun; I hope he is nowe well. I pray you to giue him counsell what to doo. I desire from my hoole hart that he may grow in the feare of God, and then he will be happy. Pinner shall send some woole to Lemster. I haue heare inclosed sent you the aquittance of the pursevant, by which you may knowe his name. I doo blles my good God, that you haue had so a good an end about the presentation of Bromton. I thinke you haue doun a very good worke, in recommending Mary Wood to my Lady Veere, to home I hope shee will doo acceptabele sarvis. I am toold of a gentell-woman by Docter Barker. She was bread with my old Lady Manering. She, they say, is religious and discreet, and very hamsome in dooing of any thinge; her name is Buckle, a Sharpsheare woman: if you like of it, I would thinke of haueing of her; for I haue no body aboute me, of any judgment, to doo any thinge. My heate continueing, I sent to Docter Barker to come and see me let bloud; he came on thursday night, and yesterday morning I sent fore a curgen at Bischops Castell, that let Mrs. Wallcot blud, and he pricke my arme twis, but it would not blled; and I would not try the third time. I hope the Lord will derect me what to doo: and for gooing abrode I will endeuor to doo it as soune as it shall pleas

God to inabell me. It is a word of comfort which you rwit me, that you hope shortly to send for your horsess. I beceache the Lord to giue you a good and happy end to all your biusness. I thanke God all the chillderen are well, and so is Ned Smith. Ned and his brother present theaire humbell dutis to you; and I begg your bllesing for them all, and your loue and prayers for my self. I beceach the Lord to giue you a speady and happy meeting with

  Your most affectinat wife for ever,   BRILLIANA HARLEY.

Mr. Littell, I thanke God, is well, and abell to goo a littell abrode.

I thanke you for my very fine wascott: by this carrier is sent vp the clocke and dublet and houses you sent for.

May the 18, 1633.

IX.
To my deare sonne Mr Edward Harley.

Good Need—I hope thease lines will finde you well at Oxford. I longe to reseaue the ashurance of your comeing well to your iournyes end. We haue had faire weather sence you went, and I hope it was so with you, which made it more pleaseing to me. You are now in a place of more varietyes then when you weare at home; thearefore take heede it take not vp your thoughtes so much as to neglect that constant saruis you owe to your God. When I liued abroode, I tasted something of thos willes: thearefore I may the more experimentally giue you warneing. Remember me to your tutor, in home I hope you will finde dayly more and more cause to love and respect. I thanke God my coolde is something better then when you left me. I pray God blles you, and giue you of those saueing grasess which will make you happy heare and for ever heareafter.

  Your most affectinat mother,   BRILLIANA HARLEY.

Oct. 25, 1638.

X.

To my deare sonne Mr Edward Harley.

Good Need—I was dublly glad to reseaue your letter, bothe for the asshureanc of your comeing weell to Oxford, and that I reseued it by your fathers hand, whoo, I thanke God, came well home yesterday, aboute foore a cloke. I am glad you like Oxford; it is true it is to be liked, and happy are we, when we like both places and condistions that we must be in. If we could be so wise, we should finde much more swetness in our lifes then we do: for sartainely theare is some good in all condistions (but that of sinn), if we had the arte to distract the sweet and leaue the rest. Nowe I ernestly desire you may haue that wisdome, that from all the flowers of learneing you may drawe the hunny and leaufe the rest. I am glad you finde any that are good, wheare you are. I belleue that theare are but feawe nobellmens sonne in Oxford; for now, for the most part, they send theaire sonnes into France, when they are very yonge, theaire to be breed. Send me word wheather my brother Bray doo send to you, and wheather Sr Robert Tracy did come to see you, for he toold your father he would; and let me knowe howe sheawes you any kindenes, when you haue a fitte opertuenity. Comend my saruis to Mrs. Willkeson and tell her I thanke her, for her fauor to you. I may well say, you are my well-beloved chilld; thearefore I cane not but tell you I mise you. I thanke God I am somethinge better with my coold then I was; your brother Robine has had no fite sence the Munday before you went away; the rest of your sisters and brother, I thanke God, are well. Remember me to your tutor. If you would haue any thinge, let me knowe it. Bee not forgetfull to rwit to me; and the Lord in mercy blles you, both with grase in your soule and the good things of this life.

Your most affectinat mother till death, BRILLIANA HARLEY.

Be carefull to keepe the Sabath.

Nov. 2, 1638.

XI.

To my deare sonne Mr. Edward Harley, in Magdeline Halle
in Oxford.

Good Ned—I beceach the Lord to blles you with those choys bllesings of his Spirit, which none but his deare ellect are partakers of; that so you may taste that sweetness in Gods saruis which indeed is in it: but the men of this world can not perseaue it. Thinke it not strange, if I tell you, I think it longe sence I hard from you; but my hope is that you are well, and my prayers are that you may be so. As you say you haue founde your tutor kinde and carefull of you, so I hope he will be still. If you wante any thinge, let me knowe it. On Saterday last I hard from your aunte Pelham: shee and all hers are well. I beleeue you haue all the inteligence of the Quene mothers arriuall and entertainement, thearefore I will omite it. Your father, I thanke God, is well; and for meself, I haue not yet shaked off my coold. Your brother Roberd by Gods mercy to him has bine yet free from his fitts, and goos to scoule carefully; and I hope he is now so wise to see his stubborneness was not the way to gaine any thinge but reproufe. I purpos, if pleas God, to send the next weeke to see you. Your father prays God to blles you. Remember me to your tutor, and I beceach the Lord to keepe you from all euil. I haue sent you some juce of licorich, which you may keepe to make vse of, if you should haue a coold. So I rest,

Your most affectinat mother,   BRILLIANA HARLEY.

Bromton, Nove. 13, 1638.

XII.
To my deare sonne Mr. Edward Harley.

Good Ned—This day I rescued a letter from you, in which you rwite me, that you had rwit to me the weake before; which letter I haue not reseued, so that I thought it longe sence I hard from you. It is my ioye that you are well, and I beceach the Lord to continue your health, and aboue all to giue you that grase in your soule which may make you haue a healthfull soule, sounde without erors, actiue in all that is good, industrious in all the ways in which good is to be gained. I am glad you finde a wante of that ministry you did inioye: labor to keepe a fresch desire affter the sincere milke of the word, and then in good time you shall inioye that bllesing againe. The Lord has promised to giue his Spirit to his chilldeŕen, which shall leade them in the truth. Begge that bllesed Spirit, and then errors will but make the truth more bright, as the foile dous a dioment. My deare Ned, as you haue bine carefull to chuse your company, be so still, for piche will not easely be tuched without leaufeing some spot. I had not hard of Duke Roberts and my Lord Crauens being taken. I hope the nwes of the Sweeds is not true; but in all theas things we must remember the warneing, which our Sauiour has giuen us, when he had toold his decipels that theare must be wars and rumers of wars; (but he saith, let not your harts be trubled; in my aprehention, as if Christ had saide) greate trubells and wars must be, both to purg his chruch of ipocrits, and that his enimies at the last may be vtterly distroyed, but you my saruants be not carefull for your selfs, you are my jewells, and the days of trubbell are the days when I take care of jewells: and, my deare Ned, tho I fermely beleeue theare will be great trubells, yet I looke with ioy beyond those days of trubell, considering the glory that the Lord will bring his chruch to ; and happy are they that shall liue to see it, which I hope you will doo. I hard that theare was a cardenalls cape brought to the Custome Howes, valued at a high rate, but none would owne it; and, to requete your inteligence, I let you knowe what I heare. The Scoch buisness is not yet ended. Theare is lately come to the court a frech duke with two or three other gentellmen or nobell men, being fleed from the French king's army, for some vnfiting words they vsed of the French kinge. The Quene mother was so transported with joy, as they say, at the sight of the quene, that shee was in a trance. This day I hard it confermed from Lounddoun that the Palsgrave in besceachgeing a towne in WestPhalia was raised and most of his army defeated, and his brother taken prisner; but this is our comfort, that the rod of the wicked shall not allways rest on Gods peopell. I haue sent Hall purposly to see you; for, sence I can not speake with you, nor see you so offten as I desire, I am willing to make make theas paper mesengers my depuety. I hope I shall heare from you by this mesenger; I thanke God your father is well, and your brother Robert has had no fitte sence you went. He goos to scoule and eates his meate well; and I hope the Lord will spare him. You must rwit to him; you know he is apte to aprehend vnkindness. When you rwite by the carrier, rwite nothing but what any may see, for many times the letters miscarry. My deare Ned, you may see how willing I am to discourse with you, that have spoune out my letter to this lentghe. I thanke God my coold is goon. I beceach the Lord to blles you, as I desire my owne soule should be bllesed:

Your most affectinat mother,   BRILLIANA HARLEY.

I haue sent you a cake, which I hope you will eate in mory of Bromton.

Bromton, Nove. 17, 1638.

XIII.

To my deare sonne Mr. Edward Harley, in Magdeline Hall, in Oxford.

Good Need—I reseued a letter from you this weake, by the carrier; it was very wellcome to me, for sence I can not see you, I am glad to haue the contentment of a paper conuersing with you, for still you are most deare to me, and I hope euer will be. When I rwit to Gorge that I had not hard from you (as I thought a longe time) I had then reseued no letter sence I did that sent by Looker, but now I haue reseued all you haue rwit to me, but that by my broth— Brays man. As I much reioyce to be asshured of your health, as much as I inioye my owne, so much more dous it reioyce me that the Lord dous so in mercy incline your hart to seeke him, and that you finde sweetnes in his ways. The Lord, whoo only has the harts of men in his hands, keep your hart cloose to his feare; that you may remember your Creator now, in the days of your youth; that in youth and old agge you may haue that joye which surpases the joy of the world, that so in your old agg you may say, Lord, remember thy sarvant whoo has allways desired to sarue thee. I did always thinke Mr. Longly would not stay long with my Lord of Middelsexcess; I whisth my Lord my brother had him. I haue not time to rwite you the nwes I heare from a shure hand; thearefore I haue sent you my brothers letter, that you my knowe the truth and particulars of it. Keepe my letter safe, and send it me againe. Another letter I send you with it, that you may knowe what I heare, and I hope, you will vse the knoweledg of things in this kinde wisely. The Scoth biusnes I hope is well composed. I would willingly haue sent you the booke, but as yet I could not geet on; but I hard it read, a booke printed by aughterity from the kinge, in which he has forbide ther booke of Common Prayer, which they weare offended at, and grated them a publick fast, which they heeld the 10 of this month, as I take it; and now they haue a publicke assembely and a parlament in May or March, I haue forgot which. I take this to be good nwes. Your father, I thanke God, is well. Your brother Robert has no fitte sence you went, and yet he has bine crost, when he desarued it; but he left of some of his cloths, and tooke a greate coold, and yesterday was exceeding ill, feauerisch, his throate sore. I had not bine so fare has his chamber sence you went, but yesterday went to see him; when I was glad I did, for vpon my giueing him somethinge, he was much better. They that weare with him did not perseauefe his illness: I thanke God, to day he is vp, and I hope it will be no ague, tho I feare it. All the rest are well, and I thanke God I am reasnabell well. The Lord in mercy blles you, and take this assurance, that I am

Your most affectinat mother till death, BRILLIANA HARLEY.

Remember my saruis to your worthy tutor. I did rescaue a letter from him by Looker, and I thanke him for it.

I haue no time to rwite to Gorge.

In hast.

Nou. 24, 1638.

XIV.
To my deare sonne Mr. Edward Harley.

Good Ned—I haue now reseued your letter by my brother Brays man. I giue God thankes that you are recouered from that indispotion you fellt, and thanke you that you did send me word of it; for I desire to knowe howe it is with you in all condistions. If you are ill, my knoweing of it stire me vp more ernestly to pray for you. I beleeue that indispotion you feelt was caused by some violent exersise: if you vse to swinge, let it not be violently; for exersise should be rather to refresch then tyer nature. You did well to take some bolsome; it is a most sufferen thinge, and I purpos, if pleas God, to rwite you the vertues of it. Deare Ned, if I could as easely conuae meself to you as my letters, I would not be so longe absent from you; but, sence I must waite for that comfort, I joy in this, that I asshure meself, your prayers and mine meete dayly at the throne of grase. I must nowe tell you, your letter, by the carrier this weake, was wellcome to me; and your father has reseued his from you, and one from your tutor. I take it for a greate bllesing, that your worthy tutor giues so good a testimony of you, and that you esteme him so highely. I blles the Lord, that has giuen you fauor in his eyes, to seet his good will vpon you. It is found experimentally true that conquerores must be as carefull to keepe what they haue gained as they were to obtained it. It is alike true, we must be, as carefull and stuedious to keepe good opinions and affections towords vs as we weare to gaine them; and I hope you will be a good practicinor of that leesson. Deare Ned, if you would haue any thinge, send me word; or if I thought a coold pye, or such a thinge, would be of any plesure to you, I would send it you. But your father says you care not for it, and Mrs. Pirson tells me, when her sonne was at Oxford, and shee sent him such thinges, he prayed her that shee would not. I thanke you for the Man in the Moune. I had hard of the booke, but not seene it; by as much as I have looke vpon, I find it is some kine to Donqueshot. I would willingly haue the French booke you rwite me word of; but if it can be had, I desire it in French, for I had rather reade any thinge in that tounge then in Inglisch. I know not sartainely wheather I haue it, tell I see it. Take it vpon likeing; if I haue it not, I will not return it backe. Your father was yesterday at Loudlow, wheare the caus was hard betwne Sr Gillberd Cornewell and his sisters, and it went against Sr Gilberd Cornewell, to his shame. I thanke God, your father is well, and so is your brother Roberd, and all the rest. Smaleman has beueried his wife; and Mrs. Steuenson remaines very ill. Deare Ned, the Lord in heauen blles you, and giue you that principell of gras, which may neuer dye in you, but that you may growe in gras, and so haue the fauor of your God, which is better then life, and the fauor of good men, which small number is worth all the millions of men besides. So, asshureing you that I will still reioyce to sheawe meself

Your most affectinat mother tel death, BRILLIANA HARLEY.

I rwit to the last weake; send me word wheather you had my letter; I would not haue it loost.

In hast.

Noue. 30, 1638.

XV.

To my deare sonne, Mr. Edward Harley.

Good Ned—This night Hall brought me your letter; but he is so perplexed aboute the horses that he seems not to be Hall. He was apointed by your father and meself to come downe by Oxford, and to haue rested theare the Seboth; but the spoileing of the horses did so distract him, that he can not say any thinge of Oxford or Loundoun. I rwite you worde by the carrier that your father did purpos to send to you this weake: my cosen Prisc sending for his horsess, your father takes that opertunity to send to your tutor. I take it for a great mercy of God, that you haue your health; the Lord in mercy continue it to you, and be you carefull of your selfe: the meanes to presarufe health, is a good diet and exersise: and, as I hope you are not wanteing in your care for your health, so I hope you are much more carefull for your soule, that that better part of yours may growe in the wayes of knowledg. And in some proportion it is, with the soule as with the body; theare must be a good dyet; we must feede vpon the worde of God, which when we haue doun we must not let it lye idell, but we must be diligent in excersiseing of what we knowe, and the more we practes the more we shall knowe. Deare Ned, let nothinge hinder you from performeing constant priuet duties of prayeing and redeing. Experimentally, I may say that priuet prayer is one of the beest meanes to keepe the hart cloos with God. O it is a sweet thinge to open our harts to our God, as to a frinde. If it had not bine for that I had recours to my God sheure I should haue fainted before this. I heare no nwes at this time from Loundoun, only Mr. Wallker is still in prison; all my frinds theare are well, and I thanke God all your frindes are well heare. Your father is cheerefully well, and your brother Robert has had no fitte sence you went. Your brother Tomas cried very much the other day, becaus he thought howe he was vsed to fight with you at Sheareswesbury. The Ember weake nowe drawes on a pase. I wisch you and your tutor weare heare then; howesoeuer I hope, you will in desires be with vs: and so our prayers, I hope, shall meete in heauen, before the Lord. I thanke God, I am much better then when I rwite last to you. I beceach the Lord to blles you, and that you may be still the beloued childe of

Your most affectinat mother, BRILLIANA HARLEY.

I haue sent a token to Mrs. Wilkinson: it is a box. Doo not you vndoo the boxe; but deleuer it to her, eather yourself, or send it by Gorge Griffits. It is two cruets of chinna, with silluer and gilt couers, and bars and feete. Doo not let the boxe be opened before she has it.

I haue giuen my cosen Prisis man a great charge of the box. If it come safe, I will giue him a reward.

Send me word how he bringes the box.

In hast affter sauper.

Desem. 11, 1638.

XVI.

To her son Edward.

Good Ned—I haue a nwe wellcome for euery letter you send, and a nwe thankes to you for it. I blles God that you are well; the Lord in mercy continue your health, for shure I am, if you be well, I counte it vpon my owne score, and thinke meself so. My deare Ned, be still wacthfull ouer your self, that custome in seeing and heareing of vice doo not abate your distaste of it. I blles my God, for thos good desires you haue, and the comfort you finde in the sarfeing your God. Be confident, he is the beest Master, and will giue the beest waiges, and they weare the beest liuery, the garment of holynes, a clotheing which neuer shall weare out, but is renwed euery day. I remember you in my prayers, as I doo my owne soule, for you are as deare to me as my life. I hope in a speciall maner, we shall remember you at the fast; and, deare Ned, thinke vpon that day, howe your father is vsed to spend it, that so you may haue like affections to ioyne with vs. Let your desire be offtner presented before your God that day; and the Lord, whoo only heares prayers, heare vs all.

Deare Ned, be carefull to vse exersise; and for that paine in your backe, it may be caused by some indispocion of the kidnes. I would haue you drinke in the morning beare boyled with licorisch; it is a most excelent thinge for the kidnes. For the booke, if you can not have it in French, send it me in Inglisch: and I will, if pleas God, send you mony for it. Deare Ned, it is very well doun, that you submite to your fathers desire in your clothes; and that is a happy temper, both to be contented with plaine clothes, and in the wearing of better clothes, not to thinke one selfe the better for them, nor to be trubelled if you be in plane clothes, and see others of your rancke in better. Seneque had not goot that victory ouer himselfe; for in his cuntry howes he liued priuetly, yet he complaines that when he came to the courte, he founde a tickeling desire to like them at court. I am so vnwilling that you should goo to any place without your worthy tutor, that I send this mesenger expresly to your tutor, with a letter to intreate him, you may haue the happines of his company, wheather souer you goo; and your father by no means would haue you goo any wheather, without him. If you should goo to my brothers, I heare theare is a dangerous passage; I desire you may not goo that way, but aboute. The Lord in much mercy blles you, and presarue you from all euell, especially that of sinn: and so I rest

Your most affectinat mother, BRILLIANA HARLEY.

Your father dous not knowe I send. Thearefore take no notis of it, to him, nor to any.

Desem. 14, 1638.

Nobody in the howes knowes I send to you.

XVII.

To her son Edward.

My good Ned—I was very glad to receaufe by Marten, the asshurance of your being well, at Barington. Your letter was wellcome, for Marten could tell me nothinge of you, but that you weare well, and that was wellcome to me. Sence I could not haue you with me, I was glad you weare with my brother, wheare I doute not, but that you weare made much of. I can not but be glad to haue you make some aquantance with my frindes. I doute not, but that you are of my beleefe, that my Lady Bray is of a very kinde and sweet dispotion. I beleeue you found my brother very kinde, tho not very full of exprestions; but if theare weare caus to try a frinde, I beleeue he would truely aproufe himself one: but that is the euill in melencoly; it actes most, inwardly; full of thoughts they are, but not actiue in exprestions. Many times they are so longe in studeing, what is fite for them to doo, that the oportuenity is past. My deare Ned, nothing heare belowe on the earth is more deare to me, than your being well. It is that, I pray for, and reioyce when I am ashured of it; but, my deare Ned, aboue all, the well being of your soule is most deare to me, next to my owne. I reioyce, that you keepe that aquantance with your self, as to take notice of the pasages in your hart; keepe that waeth still, and the more you knowe of your self, the lees you will trust in yourself, and then you will desire to be seet in that Rocke, which is higher then yourselfe, and so you will be safe. I hope theare will no such things be imposed vpon your howes, as is in some others; and I hope, if it should be, you will keep to the truth in euery thinge; and, in my opinion, he whoo stands for the truth in a smale thinge (as we thinke, for none of Gods truths in his saruis is smale), is of a more coragious spirit, then on that will only sheaw themselfes in greate matters. I hope this letter will meete you returned safe to the vniuercity, which I should be glad to be ashured of. My deare Ned, rwite to me as soune as you cane; for I longe to heare from you, and the Lord in mercy let me heare well from you. Your father is nowe at Heriford; he went theather on wensday to the musters; he returnes not tell to-morrow. I thanke God, he has his health well. Your brother Robert has had no fitte this fortnight; he is not much changed. Your brother Tomas and cosen Smith are very well, and I beleeue, they begine nowe to looke to theaire recknings; they thinke theas days haue bine short. Your sisters are, I thanke God, well; and so is all your frindes in theas parts; only my cosin Pris brought a greate coold with him, and has it still. The Lord in mercy blles you, and giue you a hart to vnderstand thos things which belonge to your peace, both in this life and your euerlasting peace; and the Lord in mercy presarue your health, and prosper your indeuors in the ways of knowledg; and still beleeue, that I take comfort in expresing meself

  Your most affectinat mother,   BRILLIANA HARLEY.
Janr. 4, 1638.

Remember my saruis to your worthy tutor. Mr. Gowor telles me, he rwit to you, and so did I, by the carrier of Lemster, when your father rwit to your tutor; for your father rwit by both the carriers, feareing the one of them might faile the deliuery of his letter.

XVIII.
To her son Edward.

My good Ned—I thinke it longe sence I hard from you, but my hope is that you are well. My thoughtes are as much vpon you now, as when you weare with me, and thearfore I must conclude, that absence abates no loue, but that which is but a shawdow of loue. I send this mesenger (whoo makes me beleeue he goos with a good will) purposly to see you, and I hope, he will bringe me the ashurance of your being well returned to Oxford. The carrier sent me word you weare not returned on Tusday last. Your father came well home from Heariford, on Saterday last; he was a littell ill at Heriford, but I thanke God, he is very well nowe. Your brother Robert has some times a fite; all the rest are well, and I beleeue they will tell theaire owne mindes to you themselfes. I hard of no other thinge they did at Heariford; but, by order from the Lords, they haue made two prouesmarchalls, to home they giue £20 pound a peace, euery yeare, to ride well armed, and each of them a man, and to let noe roges or idell persons wonder aboute the country; and the depuetie liftenantes haue entertained two shoulders to discipline all the bandès: on is taken out in your fathers company, to be his sargent; his name is Weare; he has bine in all theas wars in Jermany, and sarued vnder your ouncell Sr Tomas Conway; the others name I knowe not; and this I rwite you word of, that you may not be ignorant of what is doune in your owne cuntry. Your cosen Scriuen, they say, is to be a curenall, if any troups goo vpon any saruis. He is called Curenall Scriuen. For forane nwes, I beleeue, you haue hard that Briscake is taken; and nowe the Curantes are lisened againe, you will wekely see theare relations. Now, my deare Ned, howe much doo I longe to see you, and the Lord in mercy still giue me that comfort, that I may acounte you my beloued child, and the Lord in mercy fille you with his gras, that so you may be louely in His sight; and if you are beloued by the Lord, it is happines enoufgh. None are partakers of his loue but his childeren; and he so loued them, that he gaue his sonne to dye for them. O that we could but see the depthe of that loue of God in Chirst to vs: then shure, loue would constraine vs to serue the Lord, with all our harts most willingly. And this loue of the Lord is not commen to all. Others may partake of his mercy, as Ahab, who the Lord spared vpon his humeliation; and they may partake of his power, as the Kinge in Samaria did, when the Lord made plenty to flowe in the citty, affter so greate a famine. And all his creaturs partake of his liberallity in feeding them, and his most wise gouerning of the things heare belowe; but none tastes of his loue but his chosen ones; and if we be loued of the Lord, what need we care what the men of the world thinke of vs? We in that respect, should be like a good wife, whoo cares not, howe ill fauored all men ells thinke her, if her husband loue her. And, my deare Ned, as this loue of the Lord is his peculier gifte, only to his deare onse, let it be your cheefe care to geet ashurance of that loue of God in Christ; and, sence he has loued you, sheawe your loue to him, by hateing that which he hates, which is sinn; and it was sin that crucified our Lord, that so loued us that he gaue himself for vs. My deare Ned, the eye, which I put vpon my owne soule, I put you in minde of. Be constant in holy dutys; let publicke and priuet goo to geather. Let not the on shoulder out the other. I beleeue, before this, you haue reed some part of Mr. Caluin; send me word how you like him. I haue sent you a littell purs with some smale mony in it, all the pence I had, that you may haue a penny to giue a power body, and a pare of gloufs; not that I thinke you haue not better in Oxford, but that you may some times remember her, that seldome as you out of my thoughts: the Lord blles you.

  Your most affectinat mother,   BRILLIANA HARLEY.
Janu: 14, 1638.

  I haue sent your tutor a smale token. I can not but desire to sheawe thankes to him, who sheawes so much loue to you. I heare in closed send you the bookebinedrs letter from Woster, that you may see bookes are not so cheep theare as in Oxford.

XIX.
To her son Edward.

Deare Ned—I pray God blles you, first with thos rich grasess of his Spirit, and then with the good things of this life. I haue thought it longe sence I hard from you; and I can not be very mery, tell it pleases God, to giue me that comfort; my hope is that you are well, tho I haue bine in a greate deale of feare of it. I haue thought thens three weakes a longe time; but I hope the Lord will in mercy refresch me, with good asshurance of your being well. I may well say, that my life is bounde with yours, and I hope I shall neuer haue caus to recall or repent of my loue, with which I loue you. I rwite to you by the carrier, and to Gorge Griffets. I rwit the last weake: but I heare from none of you. I thanke God, your father is well. Yesterday he came from my Lady Cornewells, wheare he was, about the shute which shee and her daughters haue with Sr Gillberd Cornewell. Theare, he meet with Mr. Penell and his sonne, whoo is of Oxford. Your father sayes, he is a very pretty jentellman; he toold your father he would goo to see you; if he doo, vse him kindely. His mother was Sr Edwarde Griuell's daughter, and so shee was my cosen, and you haue caus to esteme your, my kindered, which I beleeue you doo. Mr Scidamore, that dwells hard by Heariford, whoo maried my Lord Scidamores sister, toold your father the other day at Heriford, that he would see you at Oxford; he has bine a brood in France and Italy: if he doo come to you, be carefull to vse him with all respect. But in the etertaineing of any such, be not put out of your self; speeke freely, and all ways remember, that they are but men; and for being gentellmen, it puts no distance betwne you; for you haue part in nobellness of bearth: tho some have place before you, yet you may be in theare company. And this I say to you, not to make you proude or consaited of your self, but that you should knowe yourself, and so not to be put out of your self, when you are in better company then ordineray: for I haue seene many, when they come in to good company, loose themselfes. Shurely they haue to highe esteme of man; for they can goo booldly to God, and loose themselfes before men. Remember, thearefore, when you are with them, that you are but with thos whoo are such as yourself; tho some, wiser and more honnerabell. Your brothers and sisters, with Ned Smith, are well. Mrs. Pirson is still ill. I pray God spare her, if it be his will. I had a letter from my Lord, the last night; I thanke God he is well. I heare that Duke Robard is brought to a castell with in 20 miles of Vienna, wheare he is keep clos prisinor; a senternall standing at his chamber doore with a drawne sword. My Lord Crauen is in the same place, but they come not to on another. My Lord Crauens ramson is 50 thousand pounds. My paper will giue me leaufe to say no more, but to conclud as I begane; the Lord blles you.

   Your most affectinat mother,   BRILLIANA HARLEY.
Janu: 19, 1638.

Remember my saruis to your worthy tutor. I had but a littell time to rwite in; yet I have scribelled ouer a longe letter.

XX.

For my deare sonne Mr Edward Harley.

Good Ned—I reseued your letter by the carrier, and by the mesenger on frieday last. Your father was very vnwilling you should goo to any place without your worthy tutors company; and I douted the carriers comeing so soune as to preuent your tutors gooing to some other place, and that made me hasten a letter to you. I desire to be thankefull that the fier in Oxford fell not out in your howes. I like it well that your tutor has made you hamsome cloths, and I desire you should goo hamsomely. Dear Ned, I am exceeding glad that you did seet Wensday a part; I hope the Lord did hear vs all; and nowe our duty is, when we haue so prayed, and so promised, to be more wacthfull and obedient to our God, that we doo not turne againe to foolly, and like brokens bowes that start a side, for so we shall loose our paines, and the sweet frute of our prayers, and bringe more sorrow vpon our soules. Deare Ned, I thanke you for ioyneing with me in desireing, I might be abell to goo to the congregation and the beauty of holynes. It is true, my sweet Ned, I may truely say, on thing haue I desired, and that I will seeke affter, that I might inioye thos sweet preueleges in Gods howes; but sence you went I haue not had that happines. The sharpnes of the weather is such as I can not beare it so longe togeather. I must waite vnder the gratious hand of my God. Your father and I, haue sent Marten, hopeing he will finde you at my brother Brayes. I desire to heare howe you doo, and I hope, I shall heare well from you, and I beceach the Lord in mercy, to continue that comfort to me. And nowe, my dear Ned, in company and in inioyeing the recreations of this life, looke to your hart, that you may resarufe a higher meashure of joye and delight for the saruis of your God; and to doo so, labor to finde out the vanity in all the things heare belowe: the vanity is this, they last not; and theare is a wearines in them, if they be still inioyed. The Lord bless you.

Your most affectinat mother,   BRILLIANA HARLEY.
(No date.)

Your brother Robert has had three or foore fits within this weake, to my great greefe; all the rest, I thanke God, are well.

On the Envelope:—

Mune knwe he should be quite out of countenance if he brought no letter, thearefore, to make vp the matter, he tells me that Mr Tomes came home the last night, and sends me word that he left you well. I hope Mune does not make it, but that it is true that you are well, which is all ways a joy to me.

XXI.

To my deare sonne Mr Edward Harley.

Good Ned—The last night the gardener brought me your letter, which was a greate refrescheing to me, for I had not bine well satisfied, neuer sence Martaine was with you, for he toold me, you said you weare sleeppy that morneing he came away, and that you spake very littell to him; and not heareing, as I thought, so longe from you, made me afraide; but nowe, I thanke God for his mercy to me, that I haue hard with comfort from you. The Lord in mercy continue your health, and, aboue, the Lord in his rich mercy giue you such life in Christ, that you may haue a stronge and liuely soule, allways actife in the ways of gras. My deare Ned, be carefull of yourself, and forget not. Doo exersise; for health can no more be had without it, then without a good diet. I much reioyce, and giue the Lord thankes, that Mr Pirkins was an instrement to bringe two in my deare brothers famerly out of darkenes into light, and from the power of sin, vnder the sweet regement of our Lord Christ Jesus. I am confident, your worthy tutor reioyces in it, that he did so shine as to bringe glory to his Lord and Master; and as the worke is begonne, and we reioyce in it, so I desire from my soule, that the Lord would perfect it. I begone with this, becaus I most reioyce in it; and nowe I must tell you, I am glad my brothers howes, is so well gouered, and that his daughter and sonne are of so good dispocions. I pray God, add gras to it, and then it will be a sweet harmmony. I am not sorry that euery one tells you, you are like my lord. I haue not bine very well theas three days, and so enforsed me to keepe my beed, as I haue doune many times, when you weare with me. I hope, I shall be able to rise to day. My letter should haue bine longer, had not I bine in beed. I heare my Lord Conway is goone suddainely into Ireland, and that he has a troup of hoors, but more of that, a nother time. Your father, I hope, is well. He purposed to be with Mr Vahans at Mockes, and to be at home this night. The Lord blles you, and beleeue that I am neuer weary in expresing meself to be,

Your most affectinat mother,   BRILLIANA HARLEY.

Janu: 26, 1638.

Deare Ned,—My agge is no secret; tho my brother Bray is something mistaken in it. When I was maried to your father, your father would haue bine asked in the chruch, but my lord would be no means consent; what his reson was, I know not. Then they haue a custome, that, when they fetch out the liscens, the agg of the woman, must be knowne; so that, if I would haue hide my agg, then it must be knowne, and then I was betwne two or three and twenty. I was not full three and twenty, but in the liscens they rwit me three and twenty, and you knowe how longe I haue bine maried, for you know how old you are, and you weare borne when I had bine maried a yeare and 3 months.

My brother Bray has bine a maried man ever since I can remember, and I neuer had much aquentance with him, but I knwe he was my brother, and so I could not be a stranger to him, and he is a very good man.

XXII.

To my deare sonne Mr Edward Harley.

Good Ned—This day I reseued your letter by the carrier; it was wellcome to me; and I blles God that you are well, beeeaching the Lord in mercy to keepe his feare in your harte, that so you may walke in the ways that leads to life, and avoide all the bye paths that tend to death. I was confident that my lady Cope would vse you courtesely, and I beleeue she keepes her state, as all nobellmens daugtres doo; tho I doo not. Your ouncell Bray sent home Spot the llast weake, and then he writ to your father, howe glad he was of you, and he expresses a large good opinion of you, which I hope you will ansure with respect to him and his. I am sorry his sonne has no better aquantance, or rather I am sorry that he relescheth thos that are of no worth in respect of goodness. My deare Ned, pray ernestley to God, to put such a principell of gras into your hart, from which you may loue thos that are worthy of loue, and then no ill company will be pleaseing to you. I heare as you doo of the displaceing of my lord Anckeram and my lord Morton, that was captaine of the gard, and the leftenant of the Tower; but I did not heare of Mr. Treashurer remoueall. I beleeue you haue hard, that my lord of Arendell eateing of oyesters, the oyesters were bluddy, and afterwards thought he sawe a man runeing at him with a drawne sword; but none ells coued see what he thought he sawe. I am sorry my lord is goone into Ireland. Doctor Deodate was sent for to Mr Roberd Moores wife, whoo is lattely come out of the lowecuntres; shee had a greate feauer. Doctor Deodate being so neere, came to see your father and meself; he did not forget to aske for you, with a greate deale of loue, and expreses a greate deale of desire affter your good; he is very well and merrier than ever I sawe him; his man toold Pheebe, that his mistris was with chillde; if it be so, shure that is the ground of his meerth. Your anchent frinde Mrs Traford is very bigg with child, and doctor Deodate dous somethinge feare her. He tells me he was allmost in loue with her, when shee sarued me, but now he can not fancy her. Mrs Pirson has quited her ague; but good Mr Simons has goot one; he has had three fitts. I beleeue your cosen Smith is not sorry for it; he growes a fine boy, and is more ciuell then he was. Your brother Robert has had no fite this fortnight. I thanke God, he is not alltogeather so stuborne as he was. The gardner would make me beleeue that you are much growne; he likes all well at Oxford, but the capes and littell fiers. It semes it has put him in loue with trauelling, for he would faine be sent againe. I asked him, if Mr Pirkins did not say I was too fond a mother. He ansured me, he said you did very well. Mr Gower toold him, he had learnt no eloquence. Your father came home well on Saterday. Tell my cosen Vahan, that your father sayes they weare all very well at his fathers, wheare he had greate entertainement. I sent this day to see Mrs Wallcott; they sent me word, that theare sonne should goo shortly to Oxford; he is at home to be fitted for it. Mr Cradock is seetled at Clanuer, wheare they say Mr Wallcott means to liue. I thinke it strange that Mr Cradocke should incorage on to preche, by which he puts his frinde vpon such a disaduantage. Mr Cradock is a worthy man, but some times he dous not judg cleerely of things, and when we meet with such men, we must looke through the clowde of theare infirmetyes vpon the suneshine of theare vertues. My paper did deceauefe me, for I thought I had had another side.

Docter Barker was with me lately, and remembered you with much kindenes; he toold me, he would rwit to you, and it semes he is as good as his word; he is a good man. You longe sence riwite for Sr Wallter Rawelys History to your father. I did not forget it, and haue sent it you by this carrier, with a book of nwes. I would haue sent you the relation of the takeing of Brisake, which is of great importance, but your father leaft it at the bischops. I haue sent you another littell booke; you sawe me haue it, when you weare with me. I haue reade it, and it pleases me better then any thinge I haue reade a longe time, and any thing that is good, which I inioye, especiall in the beest thinges, I desire you should haue part with me. Deare Ned, reade it, at your leashure, and well waye it, and then let mee knowe how you like it; for my part I am much in loue with it. Sence the ring I gaue you is broken, and that you esteme a peace of it, becaus I gaue it you, I will, if pleas God, by the next safe bearer send you another, that will not so easely breake: and tell your father keepes his promies, in giueing you a wacth, I will let you haue mine; but I will not venture it by the carrier, and I cannot heare of any that goos to Oxford. My cosen Pelham rwites with a great deale of loue of you, and aproufeing of your carage. The Lord presarue you, that you may still be aproufed of. Vse him kindeley, for I am perswaded, he is of a good nature, and has some morall good in him. My deare Ned, the Lord blles you.

Your most affectinat mother, BRILLIANA HARLEY.

Pheb: this first, 1638.

You father was not well pleased you did not rwite by the gardner, becaus he was an expres mesenger. Remember my saruis to your worthy tutor. This day Hall brought me " the Holy Court," from Worster. Remember my saruis to Mrs Willkenson.

XXIII.

For my deare sonne Mr Edward Harley, in Magdeline Hall, Oxford.

Good Ned—Sence you keep the brittell ringe tell it brake, I haue sent you on of a more dureing substance, and that you may knowe I haue worne it, I haue left the riben vpon it, which did healp to make it fite for my finger; and keepe this, tell I giue you a better. I beceach the Lord to bless you, with thos choys blessings, with which I desire my owne soule should be bllessed with. My deare Ned, be wacthfull that you grow not slake in keepeing the saboth, and in the performeing of priuet dutyes. O it is a sweet thinge to haue priuet conferance with our God, to hom we may make knowne all our wants, all our foolyes, and discouer all our weakeness, in acurance that he will supply our wants, and will not abrade vs with our infermetys. I thanke God your father is well, and so is your brothers and sisters with your cosen Smith. This opertuenity came vnlooked for, so that the time of the night rather puts me in minde of sleepeing then rwiteing. I can but tell you, I long to see you, and I hope, the Lord will giue me a comfortabell inioyeing of that mercy.

Your most affectinat mother,   BRILLIANA HARLEY.

Pheb: 2. 1638.

I hope, we shall haue a priuet day the next weake, when I trust, we shall remember you.

Remember my saruis to your worthy tutor.

XXIV.

For my deare son, Mr. Edward Harley.

Good Ned—It is my greate comfort, that you inioye your health, which I was assured of this day by your letter. It is my greater ioy that you thirst affter the sweet waters of Gods word in a powerfull menestry. I hope the Lord will grant you, your desire in that kinde. Deare Ned, labor to keepe vp the life of yur soule and be ernest with God, to blles the small means you haue, that by his bllesing, a littell may doo you much good, and that his spirit may heate the cooldness of it. I much reioyce that our hatrs did so neere meet, that you in one weake and we in another sought the Lord. As I rwit to you, I thanke God, we keept wensday last, and I blles God, I ioyned with them, and so did your sister Brill and brothers. If euer we had caus to pray, it is nowe. Shure the Lord is about a glorious wotke.; He is refineing his Chruch; and happy will thos days be, when shee comes out like goold : and if euer wicked men had caus to feare, it is nowe ; for sartainely the Lord will call them to acounte. Theaire day is at hande. Let vs be found morners, that so we may be marked. I thanke God, I am now out of my chamber againe. Your father is well and so is your brother Robert. I haue not knowne him so well neuer sence he had theas fitts. The rest are well. Mrs Pirson is so well, that shee goos abroode. Mrs Steuenson is still vnder the chrugens hands, and I feare will be. Mr Simons has his ague still ; this is all Bromton inteligenc. For that from abrode, I refer you to this inclosed princted booke. I purpos, if pleas God, to remember you with some of Bromton dyet, against Lent. I wisch you may not eate to much fisch. I know you like it ; but I thinke it is not so good for you. I hope you haue something ouer your beeds head. Remember my saruis to Mrs Willkensone. I rwit you a letter by Mr Asson ; send me word wheather you reseued it. The Lord blles you and caus you to walke vprightly before him, that so you may be his delight.

Your most affectinat mother,   BRILLIANA HARLEY.

Pheb: 8. 1638.

Mrs Trayford is brought to beed of a daughter this day ; shee sent a man a purpos to me, to desire me to be the godmother and that it might be of my name.

Remember my saruis to your worthy tutor, whom I thanke for his loue and care of you, whoo are deare to me.

I beleeue you haue seene the proclemation, which inioynes all barons, knights, and gentellmen, of Linconscheere and the other northern parts, not to be absent from theaire howes, but theair to remaine for the gard of theare cuntrey; which I feare will hinder my sister Pelhams comeing to me.

Deare Ned, rwite againe to my cosen Tomkins and to Mr Simons.

XXV.

To my deare sonne Mr. Edward Harley.

My good Ned—The Lord in mercy blles you, and giue you interest in his sonne Christ, and such a measure of holyness, that you may liue heare like his child. It is my comfort, that you inioye your health, and I beceach the Lord, to continue that mercy to you. I perswade meself you are carefull to improufe your time; this is your time of haruest, and that time being ouer-slipt, it cannot be recalled. I am glad to heare you are cheerefull. Inioy that bllesing, when God giues it you, for cheerefullness of spirit giues more freedome in the performeance of any duety. I hope, as you doo, that the nwes of so many being masacred is not true; the great God of heawen and earth looke in mercy vpon his poore peopell. It is reported, from all parts, the french haue a very great army. I can not thinke yet, that the french would take this time to come into Ingland, when we stand vpon our garde and such preperations for wars. And the report is, that theare goos 30000 fooute and 10000 hoors with the king to Yorke; so that a forieng enimye could not come in a time more disaduantages to him. But if we fight with Scotland, and are ingaged in that ware, then a foren enimy may take his time of aduantage. The caus is the Lords; and He will worke, for his owne glory. Deare Ned, you may remember I haue offten spoke to you aboute theas times; and my deare Ned, would I weare with you one day, to open my minde more largly than I can by rwriteing. They call to super, thearefore I must hasten my letter, but first I must tell you, I haue sent you by the carrier a boxe, derected to you, in which is a turky pye and 6 pyes, such as my lord, your grandfather did loue. I hope to remember you againe in lent. Send me word, wheather you reseaue them, and wheather they be good. Mr. Simons is very ill and very weake. I wisch his wife be not a widowe againe. For Mr. Walcotes sake, I will perswade them to send theare sonne to your tutor: but Mr. Cradock is the only man that preuails with them. I thanke God, your Father is well, and so is your brothers and sisters, with Ned Smith: so in hast, I rest,

Your most affectinat mother, BRILLIANA HARLEY.

Pheb: 15, 1638.

I haue sent your tutor a box of dryed plumes, the box is derected to you; tell him it is a Lenten token. Remember my saruis to him.

XXVI.

For my deare sonne Mr. Edward Harley.

Good Ned—I beceach the Lord to blles you, with thos choyes bllesings, which are only the porcion of his ellect; in which the men of this life, haue no part. They are hide from theaire eyes. Only in the day of trubell and death, then they knowe theare is a happines belongeing to Gods chillderen, which they would then partake of, and howlle, for the wante of that comfort. This day I reseued your letter, and that you are well is so much comfort to me, that when I am ascured of it, it sweetens other trubells, which I goo vnder. Deare Ned, doo not let your dyet be, this Lent, all togeather fisch. I am well pleased, if the pyes fitted your tast, and your frinds. Diuers reports theare be, and it is lightly, the papis will furnisch themselfs, as well as they can. Theare is a booke, which is rwitten by a papis that is conuerted; it discouers much; I would, if I could, haue gained it and haue sent you the booke. I forgot the last time, I rwit to you, to let you knowe the arming, which was seence vpon the seae, were Hollenders; they fought with the Dunckerckes, and had the victory; but what loos the Dunckerckes had, is not yet sartainely knowne. I beleeue you haue hard this, before this letter comes to your hand. For nwes at home, we heare that the lord cheefe justice Finch is sworne a preuy conseller; yonge Mr. Somerseet Fox is sworne on of the presences chamber, and vpon that score he must waite vpon the kinge to Yorke. They say, my lord of Wosters sonne shall be generall of the hors. This day a mesenger, which I sent to my sister Pelham, returned from thence. I thanke God, they are all well theare. My sister rwit me word, that the counsell had sent into Linconscheere 68 shoulders, which weare to be dispersed, and imployed to exersises ther traine bands. My brother Pelham being one of the kings saruants, was sent to by my lord chamberlen, to commade him to waite vpon the kinge at Yorke. We see that honnors are not all ways eassy posestions. I haue sent you a booke of nwes, and on of the weackely corentes. I woould willingly haue your minde keep awake in the knowledg of things abroode. I thanke God, your father is well, and prays God to blles you: your brothers are well. Mr Simons is vpon recouory. My cosen Prise continues ill; what it will proufe, I knowe not. And now I am telling you of thos, whoo are sike, I well tell you of one, that has left this life, and now rest from all sikeness and trubell, Mrs Traford; this day, I hard shee was dead. She dyed aboute 7 dayes affter she was brought to beed. Docter Deodate, when he was with me, told me he feared shee would not liue long affter she was brought to beed. I would haue you rwite a letter to my lady Conway. I have heare inclosed sent you a coppy of the letter I would haue you rwite to her. I beleeue she will take it very kindely. Burgh has bine very sike, which foreslowes your peace of plate. I cane not well tell the waight of it; for I was not by, when your father rwit for it. I haue rwit to Burgh to hasten it. I hope it will be such as it should be. Tell Mr Pirkins rwit to your father that you did wante it, your father said he thought you had no neede of it. It is time nowe to conclude this letter, but it must be in ascuereing you, that I reioyce to aproufe meself,

  Your affectinat mother,   BRILLLIANA HARLEY.

Mar: this first, 1638.

Remember my saruis to your worthy tutor. I thinke the carryer goo by Acton, wheare my lady Conway dwells, when they goo to Loundon.

XXVII.

For Sr Robert Harley, Kinght of the Bath.

My deare S^r,—This is only to let you knowe, we are all well, which I had rather tell you, then send the bare message by another. I blless God, that you are well; and hope the Lord, will giue you a safe returne home to morrow, wheare you are longed for. Nowe the Lord in mercy presarue you from all that is euile; desireing still to be beloued by you, as

Your most affectinat wife,   BRILLIANA HARLEY.

Mar: 12, 1638.

Endorsed in Sir Robert's handwriting, " fro' my wife."

XXVIII.

To my deare sonne Mr. Edward Harley, Oxford.

My good Ned—The last weake being not well, I could not inioye this contentment of rwiteing to you. You may remember, that when you weare at home, I was offten enforsed to keepe my becd; it pleases God, it is so with me still, and when I haue thos indispotions, it makes me ill for some time affterwards. It is the hand of my gratious God; and tho it be sharp, yet when I looke at the will of God in it, it is sweetned to me: for to me, theare is nothing can sweeten any condistion to vs, iu this life, but as we looke at God in it, and see ourselfs his saruants in that condistion in which we are. Thearefore when I consider my owne afflictions, they are not so bitter, when I looke at the will of my God in it. He is pleased it should be so, and then, should not I be pleased it should be so? And I hope, the Lord will giue me a hart still to waite vpon my God; and I hope the Lord will looke gratiously vpon me.

And my dearest, beleeue this from mee, that theare is no sweetnes in any thinge in this life to be compared to the sweetnes in the saruis of our God, and this I thanke God, I cane say, not only to agree with thos that say so, but experimentally; I haue had health and frinds and company in variety, and theare was a time, that what could I have saide I wanted; yet in all that theare was a trubell, and that which gaue me peace, was sarueing of my God, and not the saruis of the world. And I haue had a time of siknes, and weakenes, and the loose of frinds, and as I may say, the glideing away of all thos things I tooke most comfort in, in this life. If I should now say (which I may booldly) that, in this condistion, O howe sweet did I finde the loue of my God, and the endeuor, to walke in his ways; it may be, some may say, then it must needs be so, becaus all other comforts failed me; but my deare Ned I must lay both my condistions togeather; my time of freedome from afflictions, and my time of afflictions; and in the one, I found a sweetnes in the saruis of God, aboue the sweetnes of the things in this life, and in trubele a sweetnes in the saruis of God, which tooke away the bitternes of the affliction; and this I tell you, that you may beleeue howe good the Lord is, and beleeue it, as a tryed truth, the saruis of the Lord, is more sweet, more peaceabell, more delightful, then the enioyeing of all the vadeing pleashurs of the world. My deare Ned, I thanke you for your letter by the carrier this wake. Howe soeuer trubells may befall me, yet if it be well with you, I reioyce. I thanke God, that you injoy your health. The Lord in mercy continue it to you. My deare Ned, I longe to see you; but I feare it will not be a great whille. I know not well when the Acte is, and I thinke I must not looke to see you tell the Act be past. Whensoeuer it is, I beceach the Lord, giue vs a happy seeing on of another. I am sorry my lady Corbet takes no more care of her chilederen. Sr Andwe Corbet left two thousand pounds a year. Shee has a way that I should not take, by my good will with my chillderen, without it weare to correct some great fallt in them; but my deare Ned, as longe as it pleases God, I haue it, I shall willingly giue what is in my power, for the beest adwantage of you, and your brothers and sisters, as ocation offers itself. Vse your cosen Corbet kindely. I heare his broother goos alonge with the kinge to Yorke, which he dous, becaus he estemes it to be the gallentry of a yonge man. I sent you the last weake a list of thos shoulders, which they say must goo with the kinge. I heare that the Loundoners haue refused to send any of theare trained band, answering, theare weare so many strangers in Loundon, that they feared to let any of theare strentg goo from them. I hard that the kinge caused all the strangers to be numbered in Loundon, and the number of them was two hundred thousand. On wenday last your father had some of his shoulders at Brometon, whean they dyned, and spent the day in trayneing. I wished you with me, but I did not see them, for then I was not abell to goo out of my chamber: but now I thanke God, I am, and haue some thoughts, if pleas God, to goo to chruch the next Lords day. Good Mr. Gower has an ague. Mr. Simons begins to mend. My cosen Prise is something better. You forget to rwit to Mr. Gower; he has had 4 fitts. Mr. Simons tooke your letter very kindely. I must needs say, I neuer had any maide that profest more respect to you, than Mary Barton, and I beleeue it is in truth; for shee is her fathers daughter and can not desembell. I finde her as good a saruant as euer I had; if I coould but put a littell water in her wine, and make her temper her hastiness! yet I cannot say that euer shee gaue me any ill word, but theare is still the spirit of enuy raingeing amongest some of the saruants, but the humers of my saruants swaye not my affection, and, I hope, shall neuer blinde my judgment: my deare Ned the Lord blles you.

Your most affectinat mother, BRILLIANA HARLEY.

in hast, Mar: 22, 1638.

Your brothers and sisters and cosen Smith I thanke God are well.
Tell Gorg Griffets I had not time to rwit to him, which I did desire to haue doun. I haue sent him the mony for Mr Neelham, the

drawer, and I would haue him hasten the sending of the peace of cloth, which he had to drawe. I hope Gorge will bide his countryman wellcome. I had him into my chamber to see him, becaus he went to Oxford. I like it very well, that you goo with your tutor to my brother Brays. I beceach the Lord to goo alonge with you, in all your ways.

Heare inclosed is a booke of nwes. Your father I thanke God is well. He goos and pleas God on Tuesday to the bischops upon a commistion aboute some land that is in question betwne the bischop and another gentellman.

XXIX.

To my deare sonne Mr. Edward Harley.

Dear Ned—Your letter this weak was wellcome to me. It is my joy that you are well, and I blles my God for that mercy to you. I am sorry your eyes haue bine soore, and glad I am that you founde benifite by what Mrs Willkinson gaue you; but feareing your eyes should affter this rume be inclined to a rumeticke humor, I haue sent you a glas of eye watter, which is not only good to cure sore eyes but to presarufe the eyes sight. Drope a litter of the water into your eys, in the morneing and at night; but I hope this watter will come to your hands when your eyes are well. Tho I am not afraide of your eyes, yet I can not but pitty your them; for by experience, I know it to be a great paine; for once I had sore eyes, and when by experience we feele how tender the eye is, we may call to minde, how sencibille God is of all the ronges which are doun his chillderen, when he is pleased to say, that they which touche his chillderen, touch the appell of his eye: thearefore wo be to thos that are so boold; and happy are those that are in that acounte with the Lord.

Your father, I thanke God, came well home from the bichops, the last night, affter I had suped, and this day he was at Wigmore, wheare part of his cumpeny was exersised. On munday last, theare came a letter from the lord leftenants, with commande from the kinge to prees 200 men for soulders, and that they should be at theare randevous the first of Aprill; theare randevous is Assbe, as I take it, neare Yorke; neare Yorke the towne is, if that be not the name. If you weare with me, I could tell you more of my minde; all the ministers are sent to, for mony. Good Mr Steuenson has pleaded a true excuse, his poouerty, haueing 7 chillderen and the sikeness of his wife. Howe it will take, I knowe not, but shure it is true; his wife is still ill, vnder the chrugens hands, but doctor Deodat is not yet come. My deare Ned, I long to see you, and I trust the Lord will giue me that comfort. I thanke God the Lord voutsafed me, that priuelly on the last Lords day, that I was partaker of the comfort in his publike ordinance. Mr Gower did not preach, but on Mr Blineman did, whoo preached very well; he says, he knowes you, and he commends Mr Pirkins very much, which I am very glad to heare so large a commendation as he giues; he is nowe without a place, being lately put out of one. He teaches the scoule tell Mr Simons be abell. I thanke God, I tooke no hurt in gooing to chruch; a littell coold I haue, but I hope it will weare away. I ride one day a broode. I wisched you with me. I beleeue you will be glad to heare, that Mr Gower has mised two fitts. My cosen Pris remains still ill, and I can not but thinke that his drinkeing of so warme beare has donne him hurt.

Your brother Robert had one fite, a weake sence, but sense that he has bine very well, but alas! he cares not to gaine any jentile corage, comes littell to me, but when I exacte it from him; but your brother Thomas is of another minde; your sisters are well. I heare that the kinge begane his journy the 28 of this month. The lord mayor of Loundone has a commistion sealed him by the kinge, to exicute martiall lawe, if theare should be any insorection, when the king is goon. My deare Ned, the Lord in mercy blles you, so in hast I rest,

  Your most affectinat mother,   BRILLIANA HARLEY.
Bromton Mar: 29, 1639.

Remember my saruis to your worthy tutor and to Mrs Willkinson, whoo I thanke for her care of your eyes. I am sorry good Mr Pirkins has any thinge to trubell him. But my deare Ned, trubells are multiplyed vpon euery one: many are in douts, and know not what to doo in doutfull cases. Your father prays God to blles you. This night Burgh rwit he had rescued the tancherd, and would make on acording to Mr Pirkins derechon, and send it to Bromton, to be sent to you.

I forgot to rwite you worde that I was very glad you joyned with us in the Ember weake. Mrs Wallcote sent me word she would come to see me the next weake, and then it may be I shall know her minde about her sonne, but my desire is to haue my nephewe Pelham with your tutor.

The greatest * * * I can send you is that an egg was laid by heen of Mr Yats that smels like muske. I haue the egg.

XXX.

To my deare sonne Mr Edward Harley,
at Maudlin Hall in Oxford, these.

Deare Ned—I haue but littell warneing to rwite. Your father hastens the mesinger away; yet in haste, I desire to say somethinge to you, by which you may knowe howe we doo, and howe much I longe affter your good, which I desire next the good of my owne soule. My dayly prayers are for you, and my thoughts are offten with you. Your father has not bine very well theis three days, he has sent for doctor Deodate; but doo not be affraide, for I hope it is but some coold, and I am not affraide of him, tho I am sorry for him, and be you so, and pray for him. He dous not keepe his chamber: his illnes keep him at home, that he was not at Hariford, with depuety leftenants. Your cosen Croft is a lefftnenat, and is come downe for the prest men: he was with me: he came post, and tooke 2 post horsess vp in this towne. All the lusty men are afraide and hide themself. Theare are other letters come from the lord president, to command the depuety lefftenants to haue part of the trained band in rediness, against they are sent for: and the number of them in all countes are acording to that list I sent you. My lord of Arondall is .generallisomoe, and my lord of Exexe is lefftenant generall, my lord Nweport a courenell, and Sr Jacob Aschely another corenell. This bearor will tell you, that my cosen Pris is dead; he dyed yesterday; he has made your father and my cosen Smith his excexotors, which is the ocation of this bearors gooing vp to Loundon. Besides the hast of this bearor, my cosen Foxe and her mother, with other strangers; thearefore I must conclud, but it is with my ernest prayers to the Lord to blles you.

  Your most affectinat mother, BRILLIANA HARLEY.
3 *Aprill*, 1639.

  I haue sent you by this bearor a littell box, in which is my wactch, loue it better than you would another wacth; becaus it was yoor good grandfathers. You must not over winde it and it will goo very well.

  In very greate haste.

XXXI.

For my deare sonne Mr Edward Harley,
in Magdeline Halle, Oxford.

  Deare Ned—Theare is no earthly thinge that is of more comefort to me than your being well, thearefore you may easely beleeue your letters are sweet comforts to me, and so was your letter this weake. I blles my God that you haue your health, and the Lord in mercy continue that comfort to you and me. My deare Ned, I should be exceeding glad, if your tutor would be willing to let you come home at Whitesuntide: if he will but say the word, I beleeue all partyes would agree; but then I thinke you would desire to goo to the Act, and that would be to much for you; for I desire if pleas the Lord, to haue you at home the longe vacation as they call it. My deare Ned, let me knowe your minde, wheather you are willing, and wheather your tutor be so too, but so that he will be pleased to spend some time with vs at Bromtone. As they doo at Oxford, so they doo in all places, take liberty to inuaye against Puretans. We heare the Scothes haue taken the posestion of the kings howes in Eddenboro. Shure this somer is likely to produce greate matters. The Lord sheawe mercy vpon his poor saruants. I hard the queene as soune as the knige left Loundon to goo towards Yorke, went to her beed with much sorrow.

I rwite to you on wensday last by the gardner, but it was in such hast that I beleue you could hardly reede it. I rwit you word your cosen Prise had made your father and my cosen Smith his excexotors, and thus he has disposed of his estate; they say his land is worth 300 a yare; he owes 2 thousand and 5 hundered pound and some say 3 hunderd pound more. He has giuen to his two sisters chillderen, 12 hundred pounds, and to his brother, 30 pounds a yare anwety; this will he made when he was last at Loundon, and brought it your father, maneing that if any thinge did a rise aboue his deets and leggessess, it should come to his excexetors.

Remember my saruis to worthy Mr Perkins, and let him knowe, the mony shall be sent with all expedition: the sikenes of his scoller is as I aprehinde it, a happy sikenes; for for the most part we are all rather to senceles, then to aprehencif of the condition of the state of our soules. I thanke God, your father is indiferent well, he dous not keepe his chamber. Doctor Deodate is not yet come, but I beleeue, he will come this night. My deare Ned, I thanke you for hopeing with me, that I should haue my desire in gooing to chruch, which I thanke God, I did two saboths, and I hope the Lord will giue me that mercy this next saboth. I thanke God, your brother Robert has his health well, and so has the rest; some of the sarwants haue agues, but not very violently. Good Mr Simons has his ague euery day and many fairt his life. I haue toold you if you remember of a paper that some statemen make use of, when they would not haue knowne what they riwit of. Rwite me worde wheather you vnderstand what I meane. I pray God blles you and fill you with gras, that saucfeing gras which will neuer leaufe you. I haue not yet reseaufed your letter by Mr. Hackleut, but I hope I shall; so I rest

    Your most affectinat mother,   BRILLIANA HARLEY.

April 5, 1639.

I thanke you for the booke you sent, but yet I nor your father heau not reed any of it.

Heare incloesed is the key of your box, with a token from your sisters. I should be exceeding glad to see my brother Bray and my sister.

XXXII.

For Mr. Edward Harley, in Magdeline Halle, at Oxford.

Dear Ned—Axcedentally I haue this opertunity to send this letter to the carryer, and haueing forgot some nwes, which it may be you will be glad to heare, I rwit this letter to you; tho this and that which I rwite to you yesterday come by one mesenger.

We heare that the kinge of Spaine begins to deale with the monestries in Spaine, as Harry the 8 did in Ingland. My deare Ned, let me vpon this put you in minde that this year 1639, is the yeare in which maney are of the opinion that Antichrist must begine to falle. The Lord say Amen to it: if this be not the year, yet shure it shall be, in is due time. What nwes I heare conserning Jermany you may see by this inclosed, which I reseued this morneing. I thanke God, your father is reasnabell well. Doctor Deodate is not yet come, nor the mesenger returned. Antony Childe went for him on tuesday last.

The cane for you is come downe to Loudlowe. The boxe was sent for this morning, but yet it is not come: if I can haue my owne minde, it shall be sent to you, if pleas God, the next weake, with the mony that is due for your quarter, and that which is due to Mr Pirkins as your tutor.

The Lord in mercy blles you, and keepe you in his feare and fauor, and giue you fanor with his childeren.

Your most affectinat mother,   BRILLIANA HARLEY.
Apr. 6, 1639.

Remember my saruis to your tutor, and tell him I thanke him for his letter.

XXXIII.

To her son Edward.

My deare Ned — I should be glad if I weare in this mesengers place, to see you. Nowe at last I haue rescued your letter, by my cosen Hacklet; it does much reioyce me that you are well, and when I am not well, your being well refresches me, and I blles my God for his mercy to me, that you haue had your health sence you went from me; and I beceach the Lord to blles you, and to fill your soul with thos sweet grases of his spirrit, by which you may both knowe and taste the goodness of the Lord: the Lord is good, and good to his, and his saruis is perfect freedome; and happy are they that are of his famely, whoo serue him dayly, and not as a retainer. My deare Ned, be still waethfull ouer your hart, that nothing steale away your affections from your God, whoo alone has loued us and whoo alone is to be beloued.

My deare Ned, I thanke you for desireing me to be let blood, shuer if I weare auers to it, yet you might perswade me, but doctor Deodats stay was so short, and I then in a condistion not to take phisek, so that I could not bee let blood, which I did desire and doo still; but I dare not venture vpon Woodowes. I haue not bine well theas 4 days, being extremely trubelled with a beateing at my hart. I thanke God, this day I haue bine something better then I was sence thrusday; I hope the Lord will be mercyfull to me in all condistions. I thanke God, your father is well and cheerefull. Your brother Robert had a littell indispotion, inclineing to a fite the last night, but nowe he is well; your sister Brill is returned from

Lainetarden, wheare shee was to supply my place in being godmother to Mrs. Yates daughter. She was brought to beed on saterday last. I thanke you for the bookes you sent me: the 2 speeches against the Scothes, I red them both; they both sheawe of what spirit they are; Mr Euers was with me yesterday, and your father gaue him the one home with him. Yon cosen Croft and the other conducter fell out at Loudlowe, and Mr Merek went away with the comistion, but now they are goon. Your father is very willing you should come home the weeke before Whitesentide; it is the Ember weake, but then your tutor must be pleased to come with you. Let me knowe wheather you haue any desire to it. Your father has sent you by this bearer (for yet I knowe not whoo shall goo to you) the mony for your quarter, which Mr Pirkins rwite for, and the mony due to him, and the cane for you; it has bine longe a comeing, and now it is not so good as I would haue it. I haue sent you a purs, which I did promise you, and somethinge in it, only becaus it should not come emty: it has bine all Bleethes worke sence she came to me. Your father purposess to goo to morrow to the bischops about the commistion. My lady Conway rwite me word that shee had reseued a letter from you, which shee takes very kindely. The Lord in mercy blles you, and keepe you from all euell. Strangers are in the parler, and theare I must end this discours, to discours with them, but I am well pleased when I cane expres meself

Your most affectinat mother, BRILLIANA HARLEY.
Apr: 16, 1639.

Remember my saruis to your worthy tutor. I hope Piner shall bring this letter to you.

XXXIV.

To my deare sonne Mr. Edward Harley,
at Magdelin Hall, Oxford.

My deare Ned—I haue two letters to thanke you for, on by the carrier and on by the gardner; the gardner came not to Bromton tell wensday last; he says he was sike by the way, but I beleeue this has loost his creedet for gooing any more journys. My deare Ned, it is my joy that you are well, and I beceach the Lord in mercy to continue this bllesing of health to you, but aboue all, I desire you may haue that true health in your soule of a sounde minde, that so in theas days of wafereing and douteing you may hoold the truth. I was not well pleased that I did not keepe my woord in sending to you this weake. I hope the next weake your father will send, and thearefore I only rwite theas feawe lines by the carrier to let you knowe I haue sent you a pigon pye; and much good may it doo you when you eate it. Your father returned from the bischops this night. I thanke God he is well: he prays God to bless you, and so dous

   Your affectinat mother,   BRILLIANA HARLEY.
Apr: 19, 1639.

Remember my saruis to your worthy tutor.

XXXV.

To my deare sonne Mr Edward Harley.

My deare Ned—By the date of this inclosed, you will knowe that I had thought to haue sent to you the last weake; but other biusness preuented Piners comeing to you. I thanke God your father came well home from the bischops on fryeday, and I thanke God he is well. Theare are letters come from the lord presedent, to command all the depetue leftenants not to goo out of the county, and I beleeue it will be the like in Oxfordsheere, and then I must not looke to see my brother Bray. We heare that the Hariford shoulders haue killed on of the conductors, but which of them I doo not yet knowe; they say he was beueried on tusday last at Whitechruch beyond Shrewsbury. The Oxford soulders could not be wors than Harifordsheares weare. Euery on crys out vpon them for theare vilinees which they did. I take it for a mercy that your father had not a hand in it, sence they weare so ill furnished. I hard this day that my lord of Excexes was meet neare Bareke by the treshewe of Scotland, whoo toold him that the Scots had put in many men into Bareke. My lord of Execkes had 150 hundered men with him when he meet him, and vpon his words sent for 3000 more, but when he came to Bareke he found no such thinge, and then he sent the kinge word he should take heed of the tresurerer, vpon which the kinge comemanded him to his chamber; but they say he is broken away. It is confermed by euery on that the Scots haue gained all Scotland without sheeding any blood. I hard that 500 men came out of Irland, and they are put into Carlile. Your father goos to morrow, if pleas God, to Heariford to the sessions, and thinkes not to returne tell saterday. My deare Ned, I did thinke that your tutor would be vnwilling you should come home tell affter the Act; I beleeue he dons it for your benifit, and I must and doo seeke that, beyond all content to meself; but I cannot ynderstand by your letter wheather he be content you should come home as soune as the Act is past, for that I desire you should doo, and I thinke you may well do.

I beleeue my cosen Smith and his wife, and Burgh and his wife, brake theare promis with you, and did not come to you this Ester. Colborne will informe you of all your frinds heare.

I hope your worthy tutor is returned before this. I much reioyce to heare he is so carefull of you. I beceach the Lord more and more to incline his hart to sheawe a loueing care of you, and I hope you will indeuier to ansure his loue, with loue, and his care with all respect.

I am sorry you haue loost so good company as my cosen Vahan.

My deare Ned, be carefull of your health and neglect not exercise.

The Lord in mercy blles you and presarue you from all eueill.

I thanke you for the prophesy you sent me.

Remember my sarnis to your tutor. So I rest

  Your most affectinat mother, BRILLIANA HARLEY.

Apr: 22, 1639.

XXXVI.

For my deare sonne Mr Edward Harley,
in Magdeline Hall, in Oxford.

My deare Ned—I was glad to rescufe your letter, for heatherto you haue bine the great comfort of my life, which I blles my God for; but, my deare Ned, are you willing to hide your being ill from me, whoo only desires to partake with you in all that befalls you? My deare Ned, when you are ill, my prayers are more for you, and the Lord, I hope, will heare me in his Sonne, in home He alone is well pleased. My deare Ned, I hope this is but an ague, which are very much every weare; be carefull of your self, keepe a spare dyet; and, my deare Ned, O that I weare with you; but this is my comfort, my God is with you, and He cane ease you, and vphoold you, and presarue you, and I trust He will doo so. Your father is now at Heareford, and will not returne tell to morrow; but I can not well stay so long from sending to you, thearefore I haue made hast to dispacth this barer to you, and hope he will bringe me wellcome newes of your health, but, if otherways, I hope both you and I shall willingly submit to beare the hand of our God. I thanke you for the kings booke you sent me. Deare Ned, be neuer vnwilling that I should know bow it is with you; for none has a more tender aprehention of it then meself. I thanke God, your brothers and sisters are well, and I am reasnabell well, but that I haue bine much trubled with a swelling in my fase and mouth. The Lord in mercy blles you, and restore your health to you againe, and santyfy this sikenes to you, that so, both health and siknes may be aduantage to you, whoo are most deare to

Your most affectinat mother,   BRILLIANA HARLEY.

Apr: 26. 1639.

I haue sent some bessor stone, which you may take at a night when you goo to beed; and the Lord blles all means to you.

I haue sent you 2 graines of orampotabely, which I would haue you take in 2 spounefulls of cordus watter, when you finde yourself not well.

XXXVII.

To my deare sonne Mr Edward Harley, in Magdeline Hall, in Oxford.

Deare Ned—On saterday last I reseued your letter by Mr. Braughtons man; it was wellcome to me. I hope this day Jones will be with you. My prayers are for your health, and I hope the Lord will be mercyfull to me in you, and as I may so say, to spare my Joseph to me. My deare Ned, nothinge can more pleas me then to haue a simpathy with you, thearefore not to knowe how it is with you would be a torter to me; and when you are not well, sorrow is a thousand times more pleasing to me then to be merry.

My deare Ned, if it pleases the Lord that you are still not well, looke vp to your God; consider why He corrects; it is to better vs, that we may see the euill of our ways, and finde how bitter sinn is, that has brought such bitter thinges vpon us, and has, as we may say, altered Gods dealeing with vs; for the Lord delights to sheawe mercy; and we haue changed His cours, so that we infors the Lord to correct vs for our good; and deare Ned, this comfort we finde in afflictions, that then we tast howe good the Lord is, He then heares our prayers, and giues vs ease, and casts vs not of, howe weake, howe fainte, howe poore or misrabell so euer we are. To the glorry of my God be it spoken, such haue I founde Him to the poorest of all His seruants. My deare Ned, be carefull of yourself for my sake, and I hope your tutor will take care of you, or ells he deceaufs me. I long to heare of you, and I pray God I may heare well of you; but, deare Ned, rwite me the truth, still howe you doo, or ells I can neuer be in any aschurance.

Your father came well home on saterday last. I thanke God, he is very well. I am not sartaine wheather he will rwit to you or no. Your brothers and sisters are well. Mrs. Gower is brought to beed of a daugher, and I am intreted to be the godmother. Mr. Simons is now well. I hard that my lord of Esexkess went from Barek into Scoteland with 500 men, and found none theare that resisted him, or did any thing, and so he returned in peace. To morrow your father, if pleas God, goos to Hariford about prikening the soulders that must be sent out of the trained bands, which makes many of theare wifes to cry.

Mrs Pits sent me word by a saruent of hers that she sawe you at Oxford. I knowe her not, but out of her loue to your ant Wacke shee fauored you with a viset, and sent her man purposely from Rudall to let me knowe you weare well. She married my lady Chokes brother. Mr. Scidmore that I rwit you word of, would see you, was at your chamber to see you the thursday before Easter, but you and your tutor weare not theare. The Lord in mercy blles you, and presarue you in safety, and giue me comfortable seeing of you; so in hast I rest

Your most affectinat mother, BRILLIANA HARLEY.

Apr: 29, 1639.

Remember my saruis to your worthy tutor; to him I would haue rwit, but I heare he is not at Oxford.

XXXVIII.

Ffor my deare sonne Mr. Edward Harley, at Magdalen Hall,
in Oxford, deliver these.

Deare Ned—The last night I receaued your l^{tre} by Jones, wch giues me comfortable assurance of yor being well; for which I desire to blesse the Lord; and (deare Ned) as some sharpenes giues a better relish to sweet meats, soe some sence of sickenes makes us tast ye benefit of health. I belieue it was yor comfort, when you were sicke, that you expected health from yor God; and in yor health, that you haue that blessing from Him, with a desire to spinne forth yor health in ye seruice of yor God, wch is perfect freedome; & since you haue soo great priuiledge as to partake of God's mercies in all conditions, labour to see ye great and infinite loue of God in Christ, in whom all thinges are made a blessing to us; but without whom, all conditions and all thinges are a curse. Be carefull of yor health for my sake. I belieue ye sneezing powder did you noe good, and let it teach you y^t wisdome not to take medecines out of a strange hand. Your ffather returned well from Hereford ye last night, where ye deputie lieuetenants met about making choise of some of ye trayned band to be ready against ye king send for them. I hear from London that Mr. Simons (a worthy minister) and three or fower more are gone into ye low contreyes to shift for themselues. Dr Storton is very sicke. I am exceeding glad to heare that there is some hope of Mr Whatlyes recouerie. I thanke you for ye copie of ye oath you sent me. I doubt whether my lord Say & my lord Brooke be set at libertie, but I wish it be true. This morning I receaued yor l^{tre} by ye carrier, & ye last weake yor l'er sent by Mr Braughton's man: they are wellcome to me, & you deserue thankes for them. Some indisposition enforces me to keepe my bed, wch is ye cause I make vse of another's penne.* I thanke God I am not worser than when I was wont to keepe my bed. Remember my seruice to yor worthy tutor, & tell him I am engadged in ye way of thankes to him for his care of you. I desire him, yf he doe not like ye piece of plate, that he would returne it to Burghe againe, wth directions of what fashion he wold haue it, & the weight of it 28 ounces, as yor ffather wrote to Burghe this should haue been, & write to Burghe that he send it downe to you to Oxford, & not to Brompton. I will, an't please God, send you a draught of yor ffathers armes to put upon it.

I wold haue writ to Mr Perkins but that I am so bad. I pray God blesse you.

Send me word how yor watch goes.

Your most affectinat mother, BRILLIANA HARLEY.

---

* The concluding words, "your most affectinat mother, Brilliana Harley," are alone in the handwriting of the Lady Brilliana.

XXXIX.

For my deare sonne Mr. Edward Harley.

Deare Ned—I willingly take my opertunity both to giue you knowledg howe your father and meself doo, and to inquire affter you, and thearefore I cannot let this bearer goo without a letter, tho I haue but littell time to rwit in, it being affter supper. My deare Ned, when I receued your letter by Jones and by Coolborne I was indisposed, that I could not be out of my beed; but now, I thanke God, I haue more liberty, in which I haue this contentment, that I can tell my minde to you with my owne penn. I acknowledg it Gods great mercy to me that you are well; and I thanke youe for both your letter by Jones and Coolborne; and tho Jones found you well, yet I did not repent my sending to see you. I was afraide you would haue had an ague; but God sheawed both you and me what He could haue brough upon you, and His name be bllesed that He so soone withdrwe His hand. I hope I shall see you affter the Act, which I longe for, and I pray God giue me a joyefull seeing of you. I would by all means, and so would your father, haue the peace of plate changed for a bigger on of 30 ounces; the armes shall be sent you. I like the stufe for your cloths well; but the cullor of thos for euery day I doo not like so well; but the silke chamlet I like very well, both cullor and stuf. Let your stokens be allways of the same culler of your cloths, and I hope you now weare Spanisch leather shouwes. If your tutor dous not intend to bye you silke stokens to weare with your silke shute send me word, and I will, if pleas God, bestow a peare on you. You did well to keepe the beasorstone and orampotabily with you. I thinke I forgot to rwite word that when the orampotabily is taken it must be stired tell it be disolued. Your cosen Fraces thinkes it will doo miracells. I thanke God, your father is well, and on thursday next he goos, if pleas God, to Hariford. For meself, I haue not bine very well; but this day, I thanke God, I haue bine some thinge better. I haue bine a longe time in the scoule of affliction, wheare I desire not to be wary of the correction of my heauenly father, but to learne obedience vnder it.

Heare inclosed I haue sent you some foren nwes, being still desireous to haue your minde keep awake in the consideration of the affairs abroode. I thanke you for the kings booke.

My deare Ned, I comfort meself with the perswation that your cheefe care is to walke before your God in all well pleasinge, and not to deuide His saruis, and so to make a religion to your self, that is, to take so much of Gods saruis as you pleas, and to leaufe the rest, as most men doo; but tho they may passify theare conciences for a time, yet in the end theare comforts will faille theim; which I hope yours will neuer.

I pray God blles you, and presarue you from all euill; so in hast I rest,

  Your most affectinat mother,   BRILLIANA HARLEY.

I reseued the note by Jones, and thanke you for it.

May 7. 1639.

XL.

For my deare sonne Mr. Edward Harley.

Deare Ned—This mornig, with no smale contentment, I reseued your letter by the carrier; it is my joy that you are well, and I beceach the Lord to continue your health to you; and, my deare Ned, be carefull to doo exersis. I did beleue that you did forget to send the letter which you rwite me word of, but now I haue reseued it, and thanke you for it. It is strang to me how fasting and prayer can agree with treacherous weapons, as kinifes and such like; thearefore, for my part, I will vnbeleeue the one of them, eather that they doo not fast and pray, or that they doo not make prouition of such wepons. Theare was a report that the kinge was goone to Loundoun, which came to his eare, at which he was much displensed. I hard that marquise Hamlenton was gone with 7000 men to land them in Scotland. Captaine Brandsheave is gouerner of Barek. My deare Ned, theas things are of the Lord, and as none thought of such a biusnes as this is, so we are as ignorant whate the issue will be: the Lord giue vs harts of depentances vpon him.

Haueing bine ofttin not well, and confined to so sollatary a place as my beed, I made choys of an entertainement for meself, which might be eassy and of some benifit to meself; in which I made choys to reade the life of Luther, rwite by Mr. Calluen. I did the more willingly reade it, becaus he is generally branded with ambistion, which caused him to doo what he did, and that the papis doo so generally obrade us that we cannot tell wheare our religion was before Luther; and some haue taxt him of an imteperat life. Theas resons made me desire to reade his life, to see vpon what growned theas opinions weare biult; and finding such satisfaction to meself, how fallsly theas weare raised, I put it into Inglisch, and heare in closed haue sent it you; it is not all his life, for I put no more into Inglisch then was not in the booke of Marters.

Theas things of note I finde in it, firstly, what Luther acknowledgs, he was instructed in the truth by an old man, whoo led him to the doctrine of justification by faith in Christ: and Erasmas, when his opinion was asked of Luther, said he was in the right. It is true the truth was much obscured with error; and then it pleased the Lord to rais up Luther as a trumpet to proclame His truth, and as a standered barare to hoold out the ensinge of His truth; which did but make thos to apeare of the Lords side, whoo weare so before. And it is aparent to me, that no ambistious ends moued Luther; for in all the cours of his life he neuer sheawed ambistion: tho he loued lerneing, yet, as fare as I can obsarue, he neuer affected to be estemed more lerned than he was. So that in Luther we see our owne fasess; they that stand for the old truee way they bring vp nwe doctriner, and it is ambistion, vnder the vaile of religion. Another obseruation I finde in Luther, that all his fasting and striknes, in the way of Popery, neuer gaue him peace of concience; for he had greate feares tell he had throughly learned the doctrine of justification by Christ alone; and so it will be with vs all; no peace shall we haue in our owne righteousness. And one thinge more I must tell you, that I am not of theaire minde whoo thinke, if he had bine of a milder temper it had bine better; and so Erasmas says; but I thinke no other spirit could haue sarued his turne. He was to cry aloude, like a trumpet; he was to haue a Jonas spirit. Thus, my deare Ned, you may see how willingly I impart any thinge to you, in which I finde any good. I may truely say, I neuer inioy any thinge that is good but presently my thoughts reflect vpon you; but if any thinge that is euill befall me, I would willing beare it all me self, and so willingly would I beare the ill you should haue, and reioyce that you should inioy what is good. Your father is now at Hariford; I hope he will be at home to morrow. Your brothers are well, and so as your sistwers and cosen Smith. Mr. Simons is recouered, and teaches the scoule againe. Mr. Gowers ague hangs a littell vpon him. My deare Ned, I knowe you doo not loue medicines, yet I would faine haue you drinke, this May, some scuruigras pounded and strained with beare, if theare be any to be had in Oxford; it is a most excelent thinge to purge the blood.

My deare Ned, the Lord in heauen blles you, and giue me a comfortabell seeing of you. So I rest, in hast,

Your most affectinat mother, BRILLIANA HARLEY.

Remember my saruis to your worthy tutor. Tell Gorg his mother is looked for at Bromton to night. His brother is goone to Teuxbery; I beleeue you knowe his biusness.

May 10, 1639.

I haue made a pye to send you; it is a kide pye. I beleeue you haue not that meate ordinaryly at Oxford; on halfe of the pye is seasned with on kinde of seasening, and the other with another. I thinke to send it by this carrier.

XLI.

To my deare sonne Mr. Edward Harley, in Magdeline Hall, in Oxford.
For your deare self. [Sealed with black wax.]

Deare Ned—Your father haueing some biusnes to send to Loundon giues me an opertuenity to rwite to you, which I willingly doo, tho I rwit to you by the carrier last frieday. When your father went to Heariford, he was not sartaine of his gooing to Bambery; and if he did he meant to send on to let you knowe so much, that you might meet him on saterday at Bambery, wheare I hope by Gods mercy you will see your father; and I pray God you may both haue a comfortable meeting; and tho I cannot haue part in it, yet absent, my desres are with you, and I hope in good time the Lord will giue me the comfort of seeing you.

This morning I reseued your letter by Hollingworth. My deare Ned, I blles the Lord that in mercy he has so sluted you with a tutor, vpon hom your harts desire is so much seet; you might haue had a good man, and not such a shutetabellness in him to your hart. I can not blame you to feare the looseing of him; for when we fined any of like affections to vs we ought to prise them, for they are not to be had euery day. As soune as I hard that Mr Whately was sike, my thoughts weare that if Mr Wheately did dye, Bambery men would desire to haue Mr Pirkins. My poore prayers haue bine euer sense I hard it, and shall be, that the Lord would giued your tutor in the right way, most for his glory; and I hope the Lord will seettell him in the place wheare he now is, for he must as well looke how he leaufs his standing as vpon what ground he would accept of that place which is offred him: it is true his call to Bambery is right and just, but wheather it be as right he should leaufe that standeing in which he is, I knowe not. I feare me that that has bine the spoyleing of the vniuersitys and corrupting of the jentry theare breed, because that as soune as any man is come to any ripeness of judgment and holynes he is taken away, and so they still gleane the garden of the ripe grapes and leaufe sower ons behinde. My deare Ned, my God be bllesed, who has giuen you a hart to looke vp to Him, and a desire to depend on His most holy Prouidence; and the Lord in mercy establisch your hart in waiteing one Him, and then you will neuer be ashamed. It is true that you no souner peeped into the world but you had a taste of the various and changeabellness of the condistions here belowe; for no souner weare you at Glloster but you weare remoued, and from Shearwesbury; but, as you well obsarue, for which I hope both you and I shall endeuer to be thankfull, God still prouied for you; and so I trust He will doo still. My hope is, that you will still inioy your worthy tutor, which will be much contentment to me. I hope your father will be a means to seettell his thoughts. I haue heare sent you a coppy of a sermon preeched in Scotland; you must take care whoo sees it; you neuer read such a peace. I thanke God, I am reasnabell well, and your brothers and sisters, with your cosen Smith, are very well; but to my much trubell I feare your brother Robine learnes but littell.

I purpos to send this weake into Linconschere, for I haue not heard from my sister a longe time. My deare Ned, the Lord in mercy blles you, and fill you with his grase, and giue you a feeleing of his vnspeakebell loue in Christ Jesus, that so you may be tyed by the bonds of loue to all obedience to your God; and so I rest

Your most affectionat mother, BRILLIANA HARLEY.

Your fathers ante Corbet is dead, for which he is very sorry.

Bromton, May 20. 1639.

Your father meet accedentally with on at Hariford by home he rwite to you to meete him.

Your father will bringe his armes with him, if please God, to be set on the plate.

XLII.

For my deare sonne Mr. Edward Harley.

Deare Ned—I pray God blles you, and inriche you with those saucing grasess of His spirit which to inioye is happines, and mesery to be to without them.

Yestrday Lonckford returned from Loundoun, and he aschures me he sawe you well on monday last, but two lines from you would haue giuen me more contentment than all his eloquence has doun. I hope you will haue a comfortabell seeing of your father, which I hope I shall reioyce in the aschurance of, at the safe returne of your father, and I hope it will not be longe before God giue me the comfort of seeing you.

I beleeue you heare that the Scots would none of the proclamation. My lord of Ratesford sonne and one other nobell man is goone to the Couenanters. It is reported thatt the Scots haue sent the kinge the crowne and septer, with most humbell exprestions.

Howe all your frindes doo in theas parts you will heare, I hope, by your fathers man; so recommending you to the protection of the Lord, beceaching Him to keepe you in His feare, which is the begineing of all wisdome; and be aschured I am well pleased when I can expres meself

   Your most affectinat mother, BRILLIANA HARLEY.
May 23, 1639.

I hope Mr Pirkins resolution continues for his stay in Oxford: send me word how it is.

XLIII.

To her son Edward, endorsed, "for your dere self."

Deare Ned—Most gladely I reseued your letter from Woster, by my cosen Adams. I acounte it as a greate mercy of God that you had so cleere a skiee ouer you, which might make you the better tolerate the ill ways vnder your horsess fooute. I knowe not a greater joy in this world than the aschurance of your being well, thearefore I desire to blles my God, that you past part of your journey so well, and I hope I shall eare longe reseaufe the aschurance of your comeing well to Oxford.

I beleeue you remember wheather your father whent when you parted from him; from whence he brought this inteligence, that the Scots weare intrenched 12 miles of Barek, and that it is a dificulle thinge to knowe what they doo; for if any inglishe man goo to them, thay are vsed kindely, but they returne as wise as they came, for none discouers theaire counsills to them. That they sourrouneded some of my lord of Holluands company, they say is true, by which they did but verify what they had said, that they mente not to take adwntgess to doo ronge, only to defend themselfs. Theare are some Scots taken which weare comeing into Scoteland, who had bine commanders in Jermany: they are put into seuerall prisons; the particulars I beleeue you will heare from other pens, thearefore I omite it. They say, that the Frenche haue had two great ouerthrowes; for which I am sorry. Your father is in some doute wheather he shall goo to Loundone the next weake or noo; if nesescity so constraine him, I can not but be sorry, and I if it be so, I wisch I had you with me that time your father is away. Doo not take notis of this to your father. I hope if he doo goo to Loundoun, it will be by Oxford. Deare Ned, theare is so much discours of wars, that it may well put vs in minde of our spirituall warefare; in both theare is nothing more requisite then to stand vpon the wacth; to be surpirsed is both a shame and greate disaduantage to a soulder, thearefore, deare Ned, stand as it weare senternell, and be shure you be not founde sleepeing; wacth against your enimy, and the Lord of heauen, that neuer comes so neare sleepe as to slomber, keepe you in all saffety. Let me heare from you as offten as you haue opertunity. Your father, I thanke God, is well, and so is your brothers and sisters. I thanke God, your sister Margett as mised her ague theas two days. Mr. Broughton dined heare to day; he proclames a quarell against you and your tutor; but I tell him you are both gillteless. My deare Ned, the Lord blles you, and giue me the comfort of seeing you againe.

    Your most affectinat mother,   BRILLIANA HARLEY.

In hast.

June 21, 1639.

Doo with the testament I gaue you as you pleas, and if Asch send one to me for you, it shall be sent you. Remember my saruis to your tutor.

Your brother has sent you your bookes by this carrier.

XLIV.

To her son Edward.—Endorsed, "For your dear self."

Deare Ned—I rwite to you this day, before this, but this night at supper reseaufeing so good nwes of peace, I could not willingly stay tell the next weake before I did impart it to you. This night Tomas Miller came from Loundon, wheare vnexpectedely he founde my lord nwely come to Loundoun from Ireland; his letter to me I send you heare inclosed, and what he rwites to your father, I will relate you as pountually as my memory will giue me leaufe. It is thus, the Scots armey was intrenched within 4 or 6 miles of the kings: they sent comissinars to the kinge, to let the kinge knowe theare griuences, for whous safety they had the lord jeneralls hand; when they weare in his tente treateing with him, the kinge came in vnexpected; the commiscinars offred to kise his hand, which the kinge refused, but aftterwards they did. They haue agreed vpon such conditions which is much to the kings honnor; they are to haue a jenerall assembely and a parlament, and bischops; but the bischops must be subect to the assembely and parlament. The armemy in Scotland is vnintrenched; and thus we see a way by which God is pleased to lentghen our peace; for which I pray God, make us thankefull: and for my part I shall be glad if this proufe true: howesower, beleeue this, that I am,

Your most affectinat mother, BRILLIANA HARLEY.

(No date.)

I haue sent my brother Bray a chees; I would haue you carefull to send it him, but not by any expres mesenger. Send my letter to me againe.

XLV.

For my deare sonne Mr Edward Harley,
in Magdeline Hall, Oxford

Deare Ned—Your letter by Hullsy, Mr Braughtons man, I reseeued yesterday. I reioyce that you are well, and I hope your eyes are so, becaus you say nothing to the contrary; and I hope your minde and tonghe weare in good tune when you ansured in the hall; and if you should not doo as well as you desire, yet let it not discorage you. I wisch I had hard you; and, my deare Ned, I long to see you, for when you weare with me you weare halfe that littell time you stayed, vpon gooing euery day, that it did a littell vnsweeten my contentment; but I hope I shall see you now againe with comfort, which I begg of the Lord.

My cosen Pelham rwite me word that I made him a seasnabell offer of a buck, for which he thanked me. He did not say he desired on, but for feare least I should be in an eror, I tooke the thankes for my offer, for a willingnes to accept of a buck, which I haue sent him by this bearer, and if it come sweet I shall be pleased; and if it be not the fellowes fallt, I beleeue it will come very sweet: it is a very large deere, and very fat for this time of the yeare, considering your fathers park dous not at any time yeald a very fate deare, but as good a tasted deare as any is: if you see this venson you will say it is a good dare. The place where it was shot I made salt be put, that so that place may not taute the rest. My deare Ned, I would haue you give the mesenger my letter to my cosin Pelham, and direct him to carry the venson to him.

I thanke God your father is well, and so is your brothers and sisters.

I haue not hard of any allterations in publicke affaires sence I rwite last to you. I beleeue you will gees whoo was your sister Dorritys secretary. My deare Ned, the Lord blles you and fill you with thos graseses which may make you shine in the eyes of His chillderen; in hast, I rest

Your most affectinat mother,   BRILLIANA HARLEY.

Bromton: July 4, 1639.

Remember my knife.

Remember my saruis to goode and worthy Mr Pirkins. Let me knowe wheather he be as kinde to you as he was vsed to be.

I would haue you rwit me word by this barrer when your tutor will, and pleas God, let you come home.

XLVI.

For my deare sonne Mr Edward Harley,
in Magdeline Hall, Oxford.

Deare Ned—I rwite to you yesterday, and I beleeue to many others I should haue aleaged that, as an excuse for not rwiteing at this time, yet I cannot give meself leaufe to do so to you, but willingly I vse a kinde of violence to my other ocations, in takeing time to rwite to you, sence I cannot haue the contentment in speaking to you. I reseued your letter by the carrier this morning, so that Moene is now in request againe.

I blles God that you are well, and my deare Ned, be carefull of yourself; be carefull of the health of your body for my sake; and aboue all, be carefull of the health of your soule for your owne and my sake; and as to the body, thos things doo most hart which are of a deadly quallity as poyson, so nothing harts the soule like that deadly poyson of sinn; thearefor, my dearest, be wacthfull against thos great and suttile and vigilent enimys of your presious soule. I beleeue you knowe that one of the best parts of a soulder is to stand vpon his garde, and his greatest shame (next to runeing away) not to be found so; so is it in our spirituall warefare; if Sathen surprise vs, he takes vs at his will, and if we turne our bakes and rune away, O! he will persue tell we be taken. My deare Ned, I beleeue you are confident that you are most deare to me, thearefore thinke it not strange, if I am stuedious and carefull that your peace should be keept with your God, whous fauor is better then life. I longe to see you, and I hope I shall doo it shortly. I hope before this, you haue reseued your hate and stokens, but Burigh is something ngligent. Your father is, I thanke God, well; he is ride abroode. In hast, I giue you this ascurance that I am

    Your most affectinat mother,   BRILLIANA HARLEY.
Bromton, July 5, 1639.

Remember my loue to your worthy tutor. I should haue rwit to Gorg, but I haue not time. Your father has diuers times sence you went asked for strawbery butter, and in memory of you this day I made Hacklet make some. I wisch you a disch of it.

XLVII.

To her son Edward.—Endorsed, " For your deare self."

My deare Ned — On tusday last by Tomas Miller I reseued your letter, which was not a littell wellcome to me. I blles God that you are well, most ernestly desireing you may both inioy the fauor of your God, which is better then life, and the fauor of his endeared onsie, which should be more precious to vs than the good will of all the world besides. For the affaires of the Acte, I wisch you hard Miller make the relation: it seemes he meanes not to be a papis, for becaus he vnderstood nothing, he likes it not, and desires rather to be sent to Oxford at any other time then the Act. How biussy soeuer the time was to you, yet it was a vacation to him, for he knwe not what to doo with himself. I beleeue this was his greefe, that he sawe euery one so biussy and he vnderstoode not why.

I much desire to heare from you, now the Act is past, how you did in all that comeboustion: I hard by Miller, but nowe I desire to knowe how you are when it is past. Your father has bine ever sence tusday at Hariford, at the sescions, wheer a strange thinge befell him, for Stiche of Wallford put vp a bille of indictement against him for spoileing the kings highe ways, by the water that he drawes ouer his growndes. You may remember, I thinke, that your father made him pay for his hors that carriede a loade on the saboth: acording to the law he paide, and now against lawe, he seekes to reueng himself: tho it be longe sence, I dout not but your father will cleere himself and forgiue him. Your father had this day senight a falle off his hors which did much hurt him, but I thanke God, he is now much better; this day he is gone to my lord presedent, whoe has apointed all the depuety leftenants to come to him on tusday next; but they desire a further time, and haue desired your father to procure it; and that is his biusnes to my lord.

My deare Ned, I long to see you, and without your tutor seet doune the day when your father should send horses for you, your father will say the time is not yet this 3 weekes that he and your tutor agreed vpon, but I was not then bye. I hope to see you shortly, and I trust it will be with much comfort. I thanke God, your brothers and sisters are well. This day I rescued many corantes, but I haue reed but one, and that I haue heare inclosed sent you. I hard from Loundon this day, but I doo not heare that the kinge is come theather. All thinges goo one yet well.

I am glad the venson came sweet; if it did not, Miller deceufes me. The questons at the Acte, which weare much longed for, I hard read the last night, tell which time Mr Gower was keep bigg of longeing, becaus I would not open your fathers letter tell he came home.

It is pitty that such yonge men should marry. You knowe home I meane. I doo not say it is pitty that all yonge men should, for some haue need of a nurs or a giude, call them what you pleas. This incke is so bade, that I haue thought I haue had much patience to rwit so large a letter, and you must haue some to reade it.

My deare Ned, the Lord in mercy blles you, and keepe you safe vnder the shawedow of His most holy Prouidence; so I rest,

Your most affectinat mother,   BRILLIANA HARLEY.
Bromton, July 13, 1639.

Deare Ned, remember my loue to good and worthy Mr Pirkins.

XLVIII.

To her son Edward.—Endorsed, "For your deare self."

My deare Ned—Your letter this weake by the carrier I reseued yesterday, and you may beleeue it was wellcome to me, that reioyces in your being well. I am glad you past all the biusnes of the Act so well, and now I beleeue Oxford is in a calme againe. My deare Ned, I llonge to see you, and thearefore your father has sent horsses for you, which I hope will be with you at the time your tutor desires they should, or ells I mistake your letter. I hope your tutor will come with you; you say he will, but by his letter to me I doute it, for he speakes of some thinge that he will send by you. Upon your word your father has sent a hors for him, and if he come he shall be very wellcome; if he weare only your tutor he should be welcome, but being so good a man, and loueing you and vseing you so kindely as you assure me he dous, I cannot but loue and respect him; and that I cannot doo every one.

My deare Ned, I reioyce with you, and blles my God with you, that you are with one that shuts with your dispocion, for I thinke to liue with a sower nature is a greater paine then to be feed allways with sower and bitter meate, and to have the smoke in ons eyes; for my part, I loue no swernes, and I hope you are of my minde in that; yet it has bine my lot to meete with some of that dispotion.

On munday Mr. Braughton was with me; but his discours was

as short as your letter; yet I thanke you for it; tho it weare short, yet it found a very wellcome.

On tusday your father went to Loudlow, from whence he brought home with him Sr Ihon Kirle, Mr. Vahan, and Mr. Scidmore; it fell out to be at such a time when I was inforsed to keepe my beed, which I did from tusday tell this day, and now I thank God, I am vp againe. Your father purposess to goo on munday to Mrs Bramley, and to come home on tusday, and the weake affter is the assises. My lord schef barron goos no more this sirquite. Your tutor rwit to me to speake to your father, that £10 might be sent to him for your vse, which your father has doune. Remember my loue to your worthy tutor, and tell him I thanke him for his letter, and I doo not rwite to him, becaus I hope to see him at Bromton.

My deare Ned, the Lord in mercy blles you, and giude you in your journy and giue me a comfortabell seeing of you.

Your most affectinat mother,   BRILLIANA HARLEY.

Bromton, July 20, 1639.

I hope to tell you my minde about your brothers. I pray God the nwes you rwit me to true. My lord is at the bathe with my lord of Northumland.

XLIX.

For my deare sonne Mr Edward Harley.

Deare Ned—My cosen Adams returne from Woster was very wellcome to me, becaus he aschured me of your comeing well so fare on your journy, and I trust the same gratious Prouidence brought you to your journis end. Your letter was very wellcome to me, for, my deare Ned, I cannot but say that I inioy meself with more comfort when you are with me, and next seeing you, to heare from you is most pleasing to me. Heare has bine strangers euer since you went, and on Mr Acton came apurpos to see you. He was of the same howes you are of, but left it that yeare you came theather. I like him as well as any yonge jentellman I haue seene a greate while.

I thanke God your father is well, and this day gone ahunting, and your brothers with him, it being procured with much dificullty from Mr Simons.

My deare Ned, the Lord blles you and giue you that heauenly wisdome to remember your Creator in the days of your youth, that you may sarufe your God with an vpright hart, and the Lord in mercy teach you to profet in all the ways of wisdome, and leade you in the way in which you should walke. My deare Ned, omite not priuet dutyes, and stire vp your self to exercise yourself in holy conference, begg of God to giue you a delight in speaking and thinkeing of thos thinges which are your eternall treasure. I many times thinke Godly conference is as much neglected by Gods chillderen, as any duty. I am confident you will noways neglect the opertunity of profeting in the ways of lerning, and I pray God prosper your endeuors. My deare Ned, my thoughts weare filled with other obiects that morning you went away, which made me forget to giue you directions about the stufe I spake to you of; but I gaue Ions a pettren of what kinde of stufe I would haue; but I did not tell him any thinge ells; and I beleue he had not wite to conseafe my meaneing, that you should chus the culler.

Remember my loue to your worthy tutor, and still beleeue that I much reioyce when I can expres meself to be

      Your most affectinat mother,   BRILLIANA HARLEY.

My cosen Dauis presents her saruis to you.

Octo: 18. 1639.

I would have you send this inclosed letter as soune as you can to Sr Gilles Bray, but by a safe hand.

I haue sent you a baskett of Stoken apells; theare are 4 or 5 of another kinde. I hope you will not dispice them, comeing from a frinde, tho they are not to be compared to Oxford appells.

In the basket with the appells is "the Returne of Prayer." I could not find the place I spake of to your tutor, when he was with me; but since, I found it, and haue sent the booke to you, that he may see it, and judg a littell of it; for my part, I am not of that openion, that God will not grant the prayer of others, for the want of our joyeing with the rest, or that God dous stand vpon such a number; but I am not perrentory, but upon good reson I hope I shall yeald: but this I thinke and beleeue, that none joyne in prayer with others but thos that simpathise on with another; for it is not the consenting to, but the ernest desireing of the same.

L.

To her son Edward.—Endorsed, "For your deare selfe."

Deare Ned — Your letter which I receued this day by Lemster carrier was very wellcome to me. I blles God that you inioy your health, and that your eye is now well, which I beleeue has put you to some paine. I thanke Mrs. Willkinson for her care of it, in which shee supplied my place. My deare Ned, I thanke God that the Lord has added the acomplischment of this yeare to the rest you haue lived; and I beceach the Lord whoo has our times in His hand and is the preseruer of man, that He would add many years to your life, that you may be full of dayes and full of gras, that you may liue heare to the glory of your God; to which end you weare made, and that affter this life you may inhearet eternity. I am glad you remembred your birth day; I did, and I blless God that I haue had the comfort in seeing this yeare more added to you. I thanke you for the relation of the seae fight; to requite you, I haue sent you the currances of this weake. Many are of an opinion, the fleet was for Ingland. Bllesed be our God, whoo has wacthed ouer vs when we thought not of such an enimy.

If the gooldsmith dous my wacth well for that prise I shall not think it to much.

Your father is I hope well; he went yesterday to the bischops about the gift of Bucknill; for Mr Griffits is dead, and Mr Morgan has put in a cauit for the kinge, so that Mr Barthy the younger was refused to be admitted by the bischop, but your father did hope to preuale with him. I feare your father will not be at home this night. You may knowe I wisch you with me. I rescued a box from Loundon with your seale, but no letter with it. I purpos and pleas God to send it by Mr Braughton, whoo I heare goos to Oxford on Monday next, becaus it should come by a more shure hand, with a token to Mrs Wilkinson. I thanke God your brothers and sisters are well, and the Lord in mercy blles you and make you still a comfort to

Your most affectinat mother,   BRILLIANA HARLEY.

Bromton, Octo. 24, 1639.

This weake the bischop haue giuen part of a comen to on of his secretaries; his secretary went to sarue on that oposed him with a proses, the mans seruant stroke him downe with a pickeuell, and so they beat out his brains in a cruell maner.

I sent you the last weake a basket of appells. Remember my loue to your worthy tutor.

LI.

For my deare sonne Mr Edward Harley.

My deare Ned—I knwe not of this mesengers gooing to Loundon tell saterday last, sence which time I hawe bine enforced to keep my beed; this day being the first since saterday thatt I haue bine out of my beed to site up out of it, and thearefore, my deare Ned, I can only let you knwe in theas lines howe it is with me; and that still I haue a hart that dous most truly loue and tender you; and I beceach the Lord to presarue you from all euill, especially that only venome of our soules, sinn. My deare Ned, be carefull of your self, and let me heare from you as offten as you can. Your father, I thanke God, is well; he came home on fryeday last, but I fear Mr. Barthy will not haue Bucknill, for a cauite is put in for the kinge.

The greife of it has allmost killed my good cosen Dauis; on saboth day last her husband thought she had bine dead. I hard from your ante Pelham the last weake; they are all well. The Lord blles you.

  Your most affectinat mother,   BRILLIANA HARLEY.

Oct. 30, 1639. *Bromton.*

I should be glad to heare whether Bleethly be fallty or no.

LII.

For my deare sonne Mr Edward Harley.

Deare Ned—Sr Richard Newport is pleased to doo me the honnor to conuaie this letter to you, and I hope you will haue the aduantag of waiteing vpon him; and I can not but acounte it an aduantage to be in the presence of such a man.

I pray God blles you, and giue you a hart to be in loue with thos ways of wisdome, which will make you for euer happy.

Your brothers and sisters are well.

So in hast I rest

  Your most affectinat mother,   BRILLIANA HARLEY.

Oct. 31, 1639. *Bromton Castell.*

LIII.

For my deare sonne Mr Edward Harley, in Magdeline Hall, in Oxford.—Endorsed, " For your deare self."

Deare Ned—It is my ioy that you are well, and I blles my God that you haue had your health, which I was aschured of this day by your letter, which is wellcome to me. That the appells came well to your hand I am well pleased, and I hope you haue made vse of them for your descert in your chamber.

What I have hard of the fight with the greate dons, I haue sent you heare inclosed; and if the venter of the Corrantes be in prison, then take your leaufe of them in theas, which I now send you.

My deare Ned, keep my wacth tell you haue a shure hand, and if it like you, I beleeue it will not dislike me, for seldome your fancy differs from what I like; and thearefore besides my owne content I mis you, for when I cannot see what is doun, I rested content when you toold me of the things, I desired to be satisfyed in.

Mr. Braughtone was with me this day and tells me of his intention to goo to Oxford, but he was in hast, so that I could not rwit by him, nor send you the mony to pay for my wacth, which I did desire to doo, but by the next I purpos to send it.

I hope your father is well; he went yesterday to Sr Richard Nweports, whoo intends to goo to Loundon this weake or the next, and in his returne from Loundon he purposes, as he rwit to your father, to see you in Oxford.

I haue not hard of anny yet to supply Mr Simons place in teacheing scoule. I am halfe of an opinion to put your brothers out to scoule. They continue still stife in theare opinions; and in my aprehention vpon samale ground. My feare is least we should falle into the same error as Calluin did, whoo was so ernest in oposeing the popisch hollydays that he intrenched vpon the holy Saboth, so I feare we shall be so ernest in beateing downe theare to much villifyeing of the Common Prayer Booke, that we shall say more for it than euer we intended.

My deare Ned, keepe allways a wacth over your preceous soule; tye yourself to a dayly self exemnation; thinke ouer the company you haue bine in, and what your discours was, and how you found yourself affected, how in the discourses of religion; obsarne what knowledg you weare abell to expres, and with what affection to it, and wheare you finde yourself to come short, labor to repaire that want; if it be in knowledg of any point, reade somethinge that may informe you in what you finde you know not; if the falt be in affections, that you find a wearines in that discours of religion, goo to God, begg of Him nwe affections to loue those things which by nature we can not loue. Affter discours, call to minde wheather you haue bine to appt to take exceptions, or wheather any haue prouocked you, and examin your self how you tooke it. My deare Ned, you are to me next my oune hart; and this is the rule I take with meself, and I thinke it is the best way to be aquanted with our owne harts, for we know not what is in vs, tell ocations and temptation drawes out that matter which layes quiet; and in a due obsaruation, we shall finde at last, in what we are proud, in what fearefull, and what will vexe and eate our harts with care and grefe. I can speake it of meself; theare are many things which I see wise men and women trubell themselfs with, that I blless my gratious God for they neuer tuched my hart; but I will not cleere meself, for theare are some things that of meself I can not beare them: so that if I should haue only obsarued meself in some thinges, should thinke I weare of so setteled a mind I would not be moued; but I knowe theare are blastes that trubell any calme, which is not settled vpon that Rock, which is higher than our selfes. My deare Ned, I will not excus my lentgh of lines, tho it may be you may thinke it to long a letter; but rather thinke vpon the affection with which I rwite it, whoo am

  Your most affectinat mother,   BRILLIANA HARLEY.

Nour: the first, 1639. *Bromton Castell.*

I haue sent you by this carrier a loyne of veale backed, if the cooke haue doun his part it is well.

Remember my loue to your worthy tutor.

Your father, I thanke God, came well home to night late.

LIV.

For my deare sonne Mr. Edward Harley,
in Magdeline Hall, Oxford.

Deare Ned—It is not many days since I rwit to you, yet I can not let this opertunity pas without inquireing how you doo, and that is biusness sufficient for a letter from me to you. Mr Braughton, I beleeue, has bine with you. I should haue bine glad to have rwit by him, but his stay was short.

He was resouleued to make peace betwne your tutor and Mʳ Taylor; tho thos that know not Mʳ Braughton say he is a man that loues quarelling, but I finde him to be no such man. Your father, I thank God, is well; he came home on saterday last, so that he did not resoulfe of sending vp any to Loundon tell this morning.

My deare Ned, I longe to heare from you, and I can not but let you know your letters are most wellcome to me. My deare Ned, I dout not but that you are deligent in the way in which you are to store yourself with knowledg, for this is your haruest in which you must gather the fruts which beare; affter you may bring out to your owne and others profete. It is a sorrowfull repentance to repent for the loos of that which we can not recall; which many men doo in sorroweing over theare loost time. But aboue all, my deare Ned, keepe your hart cloos with your God; O let it be your resolution and practice in your life, rather to dye than sinn against your gratious and holy God. We haue so gratious a God, that nothing can put a distance betwne Him and our soules, but sinn; wacth thearefore against that enimy.

Heare inclosed I haue sent you 33 shilings to pay for the dooing of my wacth. I beleeue you will send it me by the next shure hand. I thanke God this day I haue bine out of my chamber at diner, and am indeferent well. Your brothers and sisters are well. I should be very glad to heare of a scoule master.

Be carefull of your self, and the Lord blles you, that you may be still a comfort to

    Your most affectinat mother,   BRILLIANA HARLEY.

Noue: 4, 1639. *Bromton Castell.*

Remember my loue to your worthy tutor.

LV.

For my deare sonne Mr. Edward Harley.

Deare Ned—On tusday last I reseued your letter by Mr Taylor, and this day yours by the carrier; both weare wellcome to me. Mr Taylor brought your letter to me himself, and toold me you did him the honnor to be at his marrege. He protests he neuer rwite to Oxford in his life, of any thing that might reflect in any ill kinde vpon Mr Pirkins, for he protest he much loues him, and for his wife, he says, he has asked her aboute it, and she says shee neuer hard of Bleethly. I beleeue it did trubell him that you refused to leade his wife to chruch, but I gees you know vpon what ground you denyed such a curtesy to Mrs Willkinson. My deare Ned, I blles my God that that illnes which you found, heald you no longer; I beleeue it was some coold you had taken. Be careful, my deare Ned, of your health, for my sake, and let me still knowe howe it is with you. Mr Taylor toold me he would bringe his wife to me, and that shee would giue me full assurance, that thies reports come not from him nor her, and thearefore he desires them to looke to it who are the aughters of it.

Your father did intend to rwit to your tutor about your comeing home at Christ-tide, and I hope and pleas God he will send for you.

I heare that the prince ellector had good hopes the princes of Jermany would chuse him for theare jenerall, for which employment he was gooing into Jermany, and in his way in France he was taken. Being disguised, haueing a greate train with him; the French king retains him, and he has a great gard seet ouer him. This the French king dous, becaus he would place a jenerall ouer thos troups in Sacxson Waymers place.

The biusnes in Scotland is as bad, if not wors than euer it was; theare is a Duch imbasodor, Mounsire Arttson, come ouer to excuse the fighting of the Duch ships vpon the Inglisch cost.

I thanke God your father is well; it may be he will rwite you himself.

I beceech the Lord to blles you and fill you with His gras, which is only the true riches.

Your most affectinat mother,   BRILLIANA HARLEY.
Bromton Castell, Noue. 8, 1639.

Remember my loue to your worthy tutor.

LVI.

For my deare sonne Mr Edward Harley,
in Magdelin Hall, Oxford.

Deare Ned—I did hope I should haue had this weake a fitte opertunity to rwite to you by a speciall mesenger, but some ocations put by your fathers intention to send to Loundon and so to Oxford.

This day I reseued your letter by the carrier, and on fryeday last I reseued your letter by Hall, which, tho it weare short, yet it a longe wellcome. I thanke God that you haue health, and the Lord in mercy continue it to you and make you growe in all grase, and especially in thos which may make you like to your Sauiour, that you may loue righteousness and hate sinne. My deare Ned, that it has pleased the Lord to imbitter my life with many sorrowes (yet I must say it has bine in mercy and not acording to my desert) has bine caused by my owne sinnes, which has bine the wormwood of my life; and I must say, sweet are my afflictions, if they haue and doo make me finde the bitternes of sinn. My deare Ned, I hope before longe to haue the comfort of seeing you, which I beg of the Lord. I hard from London, from my Lord, that theare is a nwe committy made for the Scote biusnes, but they treate vpon foren afaires. My lord of Holland and my lord admaral are left out with secretary Cooke. My brother goot your father of from beeing sheerife, for which I thanke God.

I thanke God your father is well, but I haue not bine well this therte days, being as I use to be, thearefore I cannot rwit so much as I thought to haue doune; tho I rest

   Your most affectinat mother,   BRILLIANA HARLEY.
Bromton Castell, Noue. 22, 1639.

Remember me to your worthy tutor, to home I would haue rwit, but that I am not very well.

LVII.

   For my deare sonne Mr. Edward Harley.

Deare Ned—This bearor stayeing on day longer then I thought he should, which giues me time to rwite theas feawe lines with my owne hand. I haue not bine out of my beed sence saterday, and you may remember howe ill I am when I first doo rise. I beleeue you will pray to the Lord for me; and I hope the Lord will giue me patience to waite in faith for His goodnes to me; for I trust the Lord will deale gratiously with me: and, my deare Ned, I had rather haue the hope of being the Lordes and sarue Him, tho in such a weake and afflicted condistion, then to inioye health and pleashurs and obey my owne harts lusts.

O! sweet is the saruis of our God, that giues sweetness in the midest of bitterness. My deare Ned, it is an ease to me to tell you how I doo; it is a thinge I cannot doo to euery one: but, my deare Ned, as I haue had comfort in you, so I hope the Lord will still giue me comfort in you. I much desire to heare of a good scoulemaster, thearefore, my deare Ned, put your tutor in minde to doo his best for one. Yow know how Mr Simons was before he was maryed, and so may he be, if he be one that is not maried. Mr Simons packes vp his goods apase and sends them away. Mr Cradock is goon from Clanuer, he was sited and would not apeare.

I mistooke in rwiteing you word, it was my lord admarall that was left out of the committy, it is my lord of Arnendell. The Lord blles you and giue us a happy seeing on another.

   Your most affectinat mother,   BRILLIANA HARLEY.
Noue. 25, 1639. *Bromton Castell.*

LVIII.

For my deare sonne Mr Edward Harley,
in Magdeline Hall, Oxford

Deare Ned—With much contentment I haue reseued this weakes letter from you. I acknowledg the Lords mercy to me in the continuance of your health, which is a joy to me in the midest of many ocations of sorrow; and I beceach the Lord I may still haue that refreschment to see it goo well with you, and to see it best with your better part, so that you may euery day more and more aproufe yourself, not only a branch but a member of Christ.

I much reioyce in the hope of seeing you, but I trust I shall haue more joy in seeing you. I am glad your worthy tutor will come with you, by which I see, he is not an obstinate man. A pare of rideing stokens I haue prouided for you, which I purpos, if pleas God, to send you by the horses that shall be sent for you; and knoweing your tutors minde for a hors and saddell, I will endeuor to haue him fitted, that tho the ways may be fooule yet his seate may be eassy. I rwit you word that my lord admarall was spoken to, but that would not doo, but it was my lord depuety of Irland that preuailed to geet your father off from being sherefe. Thinges goo wors in Scotland then euer they did, and it is said theare will be wars; for my part I did allways doute that that buisnes would not so end as many others thought; neaither am I now of theare mindes, that that kingdome will eassely be subdued. The Lord in mercy inabell all His childeren to fixe theare eyes on Him, that so, trusting in the Lord, we may neuer be dismayed. It is thought that such a number of Scote minesters will not be suffred to goo out of Scotland.

The prince elector is put in prison in France; into the same prison wheare princ Casemere is, and Jhon de Wart. It is thought the prince elector will not be seet at liberty; it was fitte he should goo vnknowne; he did disguise himself, but went with such a traine that he could not but be inquired affter. Thus we see, my deare

Ned, all condistions are liabell to misery; and the greater the person is, the greater is the misery; so that honnor dous but enhanse pouerty, or shame or imprisonment: yet man is so forgetfull of his God, that all, and most of all great men, liue in prosperity as if they weare lords of what they had, forgetting that they are but tennants at will.

Your father has promised Mr. Simons £110 for his howes, which is as much as he gaue for it, and now he has had it two years, so that now he is no louser.

Mr. Blineman is goone from Walcot.

I thanke God your father is well, and I am now abell to be out of beed. I haue not bine so well for aboue this weake as I use to be, and with it I haue been trubled with much heauiness at my hart. I thanke God your brothers and sisters and your cosen Smith are well. Deare Ned, if theare be any good lookeing glasses in Oxford, shuse me one aboute the biggnes of that I use to drees me in, if you remember it. I put it to your choys, becaus I thinke you will chuse one, that will make a true ansure to onse face.

All my frute disches are brocken; thearefore, good Ned, if theare be any shuch blwe and white disches as I vse to haue for frute, bye me some; they are not purslane, nor they are not of the ordinary mettell of blwe and white disches. I beleeue you remember what I vse to haue; if you chuse them against the horses come for you, I will take order with the men about the bringeing of them home, and will send mony to pay for them. I see your sister has a nwe hude; it semes shee lost hers and durst not tell, and so, as I gees, rwit to you for one, which I will pay you for. I haue sent you my wacth, and I beleeue it may be mended. I doo willingly giue you the rige of goold that was aboute the agget.

I am hartely sorry for the death of Mr Knightly. I heare my lady Wesmorland is brought to beed of a daughter. My lady Veere was with her, and I thinke shee is so still.

I did thinke your father would haue sent mony by Miller; it

seemes it was forget, but he indends to doo it by the men that goo for you.

Remember my loue to your tutor, to home I wisch the frueition of all happines.

I hope to see him, and thearefore I doo not rwit to him.

My deare Ned, the Lord blles you and giude you in all your thoughts words and actions, that you may still looke vpon them as seeing the ways of an vpright hart. So I rest

Your affectinat mother,   BRILLIANA HARLEY.

Noue: 29, 1639. Bromton Castell.

My Lord rwit word this weake that he thought he should not goo this yeare to Louddington.

I would haue 6 frute disches.

LIX.

For my deare sonne Mr. Edward Harley,
in Magdeline Hall, Oxford.

Deare Ned—Tomas Miller came late this nighte, which giues me but a littell time to rwit to you. I blles God that you are well, and I hope by His gratious prouidence I shall see you shortly, which I long to doo. I beceach the Lord to blles you in your journey, and to bring you in safety to the place wheare you are desired.

Dear Ned, be carefull not to ride late, nor to venture through the waters, if they be out, and I beceach the Lord to guide you. Your father will rwit to you, as he tells me, and will send your tutor 20*l.* pound for you, I am hartely sorry for * * * * oughton, I pray God deliuer him, in that intangled trubell. I am very glad that your tutor has lighted vpon on that he judges may be fitt for the scoule. I knowe his father; if he be alike, he is a very worthy man. Mr Simons makes hast away; they growe deeper and deeper in theare opinions, so that he now thinkes it is not fite to ioyne with us in the publicke fast, and so they intend to be goon on the munday before the fast. I heare that Mr Cardock is returned to Clanuer, but not to preach. I hope you may bring Mr Balham along with you. Your brother Robert has had 2 spisess of his fitts with in this weak. I pray God be merciful to him. Remember my saruis to your worthy tutor. So in haste I rest

  Your affectinat mother,   BRILLIANA HARLEY.

Decem: 6, 1639. *Bromton Castell.*

I haue sent you a paire of rideing stokenens. Deare Ned, bringe Euesebius with you.

I am glad you would not let the agget be filled; that would spoyle it. Good Ned, bring my wacth with you to me.

LX.

For my deare sonne Mr. Edward Harley,
at Magdalen Hall, in Oxford.

Deare Ned—It hath pleased God that I haue beene ill euer since you went; but yet I reioyce in Gods mercy to me, that you enioy your health, wch your letters haue assured me of. I thanke you for them, for they haue beene sweet refreshments to me. Your letter this weeke by the carrier I receiued last night, and I blesse God that I receiue such childlike expressions of loue from you. I hope I receiue the fruit of your praiers, for the Lord hath beene pleased to shew His strength in my weakenesse, to enable me to undergoe such a fit of weakenesse, wch hath made stronger bodies then mine to stoope. This day seuen night it pleased God I did miscarrie, wch I did desire to haue preuented; but the Lord wch brought His owne worke to passe, and I desired to submit to it. Your father out of his tender care ouer me sent for doctor Dayodet, who gaue me some directions, and is now gone. I thanke God I am prity well, and I hope that as the Lord hath strenghened me to beare my weakenesse in my bed, so I trust He will enable me to rise out of my bed. I was so desirous that you should know how I was, that I entreated your father to let you know in what condition I was. My deare Ned, since I canot see you, let me heare from you as often as you can. I thanke God your father is well, and so are your brothers and sisters. Mr. Baalam carries himself very well, who I haue enquired after as much as my illnesse will giue me leaue. Remember me to your tutor, who I desire to remember me in his prayers. I pray God blesse you with those eternall riches of the sauing graces of His spirit. So I rest

 Your affectionate mother,   * BRILL. HARLEY.

Brompton, January 31, 1639.

My Lady Whitney wrote my father word that she had made choice of one for Whitney.

Here enclosed I haue sent you two letters, by wch you may know Mr. Hibbons tooke a vomit contrary to all counsell, and thereupon died.

Keepe my lords letter to your seal.

LXI.

To her son Edward.

My deare Ned—Tho I rwit to you the last night, yet I cannot let the bearer goo without letting you know how I doo; when you are with me I am best pleased to tell you how I am, and so I am now you are gone.

I thanke God I am pretty well, but haue not yet gone out of my beed. I am confident you pray for me. I waite vpon my gratious God. My great comfort is to heare you are well. The Lord blles you with all bllesinges of gras and thos of this life.

 Your most affectinat mother,   BRILLIANA HARLEY.

Phe: the first.

   * The signature alone is in the handwriting of Lady Brilliana.

I want one to rwit for me,

Remember me to your worthy tutor, whoo I desire to remember me in his prayers.

Your father promised me he would rwit to you.

Directed, in the hand-writing of another,—" To my deare sonne Mr Edward Harley, at his chamber in Magdalen Hall in Oxen. these p^esent."

LXII.

For my deare sonne Mr. Edward Harley,
in Magdalene Hall, Oxford.

My dear Ned—Yesterday I reseued your letter by my cosen Dauis, and this day yours by the carrier, both weare very wellcome to me, and I desire to acknowledg Gods mercy to me, that you inioy your health, which I pray God you long doo, with a hart desirous to spend all your strentgh and health to the glory of your God.

My deare Ned, I thanke you for your ernest desire for my health. I am, I think, better for your prayers. I did not send for doctor to take phisick, for I thanke God I was not sike, but I knwe I had need of cordialls, and thos I toucke of doctor Deodate and not of Doctor Rwit. I thanke God I am now abell to site up a littell. This day I sate vp out of my beed allmost an ower. I should be glad to haue you with me, since I can let your thoughts run with me. I did not thinke I had bine with child when you weare with me. The Lord blles you, and make you still a comfort to

Your most affectinat mother,   Brilliana Harley.

Pheb. 8. 1639. Bromton.

Your father, brothers and sisters are well.

Remember my saruis to y^r worthy tutor, whoo I hope remembers me in his prayers, for I doo him in mine.

LXIII.

For my deare sonne Mr Edward Harley,
in Magdalen Hall, Oxford.

Deare Ned—The last night, by Tho: Millard, I receiued your letter, wch was a sweet refreshment to me. I know your deare loue to me wch makes you desire to heare how I doe: therfore I cannot let this messenger goe without a letter. I thanke God I am indifferent wel, though now constrained to keepe my bed for the same cause as I used to doe heretofore, but now I am a litle worse then I used then to be. I assure myselfe you forget me not in your praiers, which is the best thing that we can doe, one for another. Deare Ned, I long to see you, instead of which I hope the Lord will giue me that comfort of still hearing well of you. The Lord blesse you, and I beseech Him to giue you that holy wisdome, to guide you in all the actions of your life. Your father, I thanke God, is well, and so are your brothers and sisters and your cousen Smith. On saterday I heard from your aunt Pelham; shee and all hers are well: my brother Sir William Pelham hath refused to be knight of the shire. The French pages of newes I did not intend to haue sent you. So I rest,

Your most affectionate mother,   B: H:*

Brompton, Feb. 10, 1639.

Remember my loue to your tutor, and tell him I desire his prayers.

LXIV.

For my deare sonne Mr Edward Harley.

My deare Ned—Miller came home a littell before super; he is wellcome, becaus he bringes me the assurance of your being well,

---

* This letter is in the handwriting of another, and signed simply with the initials, evidently by herself.

which I acknowledg as a greate mercy to me, and is a sweet cordiell to me, in my being ill, for my deare Ned, your being well is much of my being so. I pray God blless you, and make you to grow strong in the feare of the Lord.

I thanke you for your care of my wacth; it is doune very well; I will send you mony, and pleas God, very shortly. My deare Ned, I thanke you for sending me your seale, when you hard it might doo me good. I will take care of it, and I hope to returne it you shortley. I beleeue your loue is such to me, that it makes you glad still to be a comfort to me and your father. Heare inclosed I haue sent you the nwes come in my lords letter to your father.

Your most affectinat mother,   Brill. Harley.

Sr Francis Deuerex elledest sonne and 4 more jentellmen and on kight weare drouned in a bote the last night pasing the water near Worster.

I hope you remember the Ember day.

(No date.)

LXV.

*For my deare sonne Mr. Edward Harley,
in Magdiline Hall, Oxford.*

Deare Ned—This morning I reseued your letter, I thanke you for it, and I much reioyce that you are well. Miller toold me that you did cut your wood for exercise, which I am glad of, but your father would not haue you cut but sawe your wood. I tell him, I thinke you doo saw it. Your father tooke some coold, which made him ill sence Miller went, but now I thanke God, he is well agayne and abroode. For meself, my dear Ned, I am still weake, and, I thinke, allmost as weake as affter lyeing in of any of my chillderen, but your sister Dorrity; yester l was vp a littell. I haue sent you a gammon of backen by this carrier, and a Lenten tocken of dried sweetmeats for your tutor, but it is directed to you; if I had bine well I had sent you a larger prouition for Lent. I hard that theare weare 500 men sent to Barwicke. I pray God direct them what to doo. The Lord blless you and presarue you in His feare. Deare Ned, be carefull of your self, and beleeue that I am,

Your most affectinat mother, BRILLIANA HARLEY.

Phe: 20, 1639.

Remember me to worthy Mr Pirkins.

I haue sent the water for Elsabethe Stanton, she may take 2 or 3 spounefulls at a time, shee should take it as soune as shee finds any inclination to a fite; the best way to take it is with 2 or 3 spounfulls of parseley water.

The dried appells are for you.

Sam Pinner waits on your brothers, and I think Blechly goos away; your father dous not like her.

LXVI.

To my deare sonne Mr Edward Harley,
in Magdilen Hall, Oxford.

My deare Ned—Tho your letter by Holingworth and another by Jhon Wall weare long comeing to my hand, and so my thanke may be of an old date, yet rescue it, for them and for your letter this weake by the carrier. I acknowledg it is Gods great mercy to me that you are well, by which I haue much contentment to scheer me in my want of other content, in my owne health. I hope you will find out some way not to keep a strickt Lent, for I am confident it is not good for you. My deare Ned, be carefull of your health; vse exersis and a good diet; goo to beed betimes and rise erlye; yet I desire not that you should put your self in such a frame that you cannot doo otherways, when theare is oction to change your cours; but aboue all, my deare Ned, looke to that precious part of you, your soul; be not you wanting to presarue its health, keep it in a spirituall heate by prayer, and let the loue of your God be the motife of all your obedience. I cannot but prise that care you haue exprest of me, and your ernest desires for my health. Docter Rwit when he went from me did ernestly desire me to haue some about me that would put me in minde to eate; for he toold me, he obsarued I neglected meself. I thanke you for rwiting to your brother to put Hacklet in minde of it, which shee has sence offner remembred then shee did before. I thanke God I am something better then I haue bine; this day and yesterday I sate vp 2 owers a day.

I beleeue you pray for me, and doo still, my deare Ned. Your father is, I thanke God, well, and tells me he will rwit to you; they say, he and Sr Wäter Pye shall be knights for this sheare. Mr. Edwards is inducted into Buckill and theare abides. Mr. Simons is now heare, he is very resolut in his way. Mr. Blineman is goon into NweIngland, and Tabithe is goon. Mr. Balls booke is come forthe about thos opinions, but I haue not yet reed it. You rwit me word you had sent me the book put out by a Jesuet, but I haue not yet reseued it, nor thos thigs Gorg rwit me word he had sent. I purpos, if pleas God, to send shortly to you, if I am well. Mr. Ballam dous well. Your brother Robin had a littell spis of a fite the last weak. I haue sent you by this carrier a turkey pye, but I dout that it is not a very good one, it is so littell. My paper puts me in mind to conclud theas lines.

  Your affectinat mother,   BRILL. HARLEY.
Bromton, Phe. 28, 1639.

Send me word wheather you reseued the band I sent you.
Remember my loue to your worthy tutor.

LXVII.

For my deare sonne Mr. Edward Harley,
in Magdilen Hall, Oxford.

My Deare Ned—It is my comfort that I inioy so constant aschurance of your health; in which mercy I hope the Lord will be still gratious to me, and I trust the Lord will croune that mercy in filling you with gras.

I thanke you for your letter by Looker, tho it may be your sister will not thanke you for her token, becaus the expettacon was disapounted, at which I could not but lafe.

Your father, I thanke God, is well, and likly, as they say, to be knight of this scheer; I do not yet heare that the rwit is come into this cuntry, tho it be in diuers others: I thanke God thees 2 days I haue risen betwne a 11 an 12 a cloke, and sate vp tell 6; and I hope I shall doo so this day, I meene, site vp so long, for I rose to day about a 11.

I haue sent you by this carry another turky pye, with 2 turkys in it; I hope the cooke has backed it well. I did thinke the glas of water would not be well stoped up. I take it as a speciall providence of God, that I haue so froward a made aboute me as Mary is, sence I loue peace and quietnes so well; she has bene extremely froward since I haue bine ill; I did not think that any would haue bine so colericke.

I pray God, if euer you have a wife, she may be of a meeke and quiet spirit. My deare Ned, the Lord bless you, and so I rest,

Your most affectinat mother,   BRILLIANA HARLEY.

Mar: 6, 1639, from my chare by the fre.

Remember my loue to your worthy tutor.

I haue now resceued the booke you sent me, and thanke you for it.

LXVIII.

For my deare sonne Mr Edward Harley,
at Magdalen Hall, Oxford.

Deare Ned—Yesterday I receiued your letter by the carrier; I much reioyce in Gods mercy to me in continuing your health. I purpose (and please God) to make you some meath, which may be good for the stone, and send it to you, that you may drinke it in a morning. I hope you are carefull not to eat too much fish this lent. I take it for a great expression of my sister Braies loue to me, in the fauour she shewes to you. I am very glad that my neece is to be married into this countrey, where I hope I shall see her. I heare that Mr Francis Newport and Sr Richard Lee are burgesses of Shrewsbury. My cousen Andrew Corbet and Sr John Corbet and Mr Peierpoint contend, who shall be knights for Shropshire. Ludlow haue made choise of Mr Goodwin to be burgesse, hauing refused my lord president his letters for Sr Robert Nepper, his son in law. Mr Harbert is chosen for Mountgomeryshire; he hath a coure of horse giuen him and a thousand pound paid him to furnish him. Your father went yesterday to Hereford: this day being the day for the choise of the knights, if they chuse your father I must be contented, though for my owne particular I haue no cause to be glad. I am in bed, which is the reason I make use of anothers pen.[*] I thanke God I am not much worse then I used to be when I am enforced to keepe my bed. I promis my selfe part of your praiers. Your brothers and your cousin Smith and your sisters are all well. I pray God blesse you and make you to grow strong in the graces of His spirit, that you may be able to withstand the temptations of the world and of satan. Remember me to your worthy tutor, and tell George Griffithes that I haue received the petticoates wch Mr Nelham did drawe, and the silke and wyre, for which Mr Nelham shall haue money, when I receiue the piece of greene cloth from him. I haue read part of the booke you sent me, and I must needs say, he that wrote it sauours of the spirits from below.

I purpose (and please God) to send you word who are chosen for this countrey. And so I rest,

Your most affectionate mother,   BRILLIANA HARLEY.

Brompton Castle, March 14, 1639.

[*] The signature alone of this letter is in the handwriting of the Lady Brilliana: by the next letter it appears, it was written by her son Thomas. Letter LXIII. is evidently in the same hand.

LXIX.

For my deare sonne Mr. Edward Harley,
in Magdilen Hall, Oxford.

Deare Ned,—A boute sixe a cloke your father returned well from Hariford, wheare this morning aboute 8 a cloke, he and Sr Walter Pye weare chosen with a vanimos consent, to be knights for this cuntry; the Lord fill them with wisdome for that worke.

I thanke God your father is very well. This morning I rwit to you by the heelp of your brother Tomas, but theas lines I send you, becaus I beleeue you will desire to heare whoo is chosen. The Lord blles you.

Your most affectinat mother,   BRILLIANA HARLEY.
Mar: 14, 1639. *Bromton.*

LXX.

For my deare sonne Mr. Edward Harley,
in Magdelin Hall, Oxford.

Deare Ned — This morning I reseued your letter, and I thanke you for it; for sence I cannot see you, I gladly entertaine your letters. I much reioyce that in all places they are so carefull to chues worthy men for so greate a buisnes, as the parlament.

I rwit you word the last weake, that your father and Sr Waltr Pye weare chosen for HerifordScheere, and that your father would not haue you goo out of Oxford, becaus he purposes to goo to Loundon shortly. I thinke he will goo the weake before Ester. On tusday next, if pleas God, your father will keep a day; I beleeue you vnderstand what day I meane. Mr. Moore and Sr Robert Howard are chosen for Bischops Castell. This weake I hard from my sister Pelham; I thanke God shee is well. But I am sorry that they haue made choys of a tutor for theare sonne in Magdeline coledg; it is on Mr. Rogers. As sonne as his ouncell has prouided him a chamber he is to come to Oxford. Your father did not goo this weake to the assises, becaus of his many buisnescess; this day he is gone to Loudlow. I thanke God he is indeferent well. Your brothers and sisters are well. Remember me to your worthy tutor; and I pray God blles you, and make you still a comfort to

Your most affectinat mother, BRILLIANA HARLEY.

Mar: 20, 1639. Bromton Castel.

Tell Gorg Griffits that his father and mother are well. I hard from them the last night.

I thanke God I begin to rise agane out of my beed.

LXXI.

To my deare sonne Mr Edward Harley.

Deare Ned—I can not let Mr. Balam goo without a letter, being glad of all opertunitys to let you know I thinke of you.

Your father, I thanke God, is well; but his many buisness and the weather has caused your father to put of his journey for a day or tow; but, and pleas God, he purposes to be at Oxford frieday or saterday next. Your father would haue you, as soune as you can, to rwit to Mr. Smith at Loundon, to let him know that the last weake your father sent vp his trunck, but no letter with it. Heare are many strangers, so that I can but cacthe a littell time to rwit to you; but I haue not keep them much company, only seene them twise. I pray God blles you, and so I rest

Your most affectinat mother, BRILLIANA HARLEY.

Mar. 31, 1640.

I haue sent you some violet cackes.

LXXII.

For my deare sonne Mr Edward Harley,
in Magdeline Hall, Oxford.

Dear Ned—This night I reseued your letter by Jhon Coolborne. I am glad you went vp to Loundon with your father, and I hope this letter will meet you safely returned to Oxford. I acount it a great mercy that your father came so well to Loundon, the weather being so fowele, and that you indured so weet a day so well. I beceach the Lord to inabell you to indure all stormes of this life, being shelltered vnder the sole protection of your gratious God. My deare Ned, I shall longe to heare from you againe; my thoughts are with you. I did thinke theas preparations weare for Scotland. I beceach the Lord to turne all the counsells of men to the aduantag of His chruch. I am now in beed, and so haue bine theas 5 days. Your brothers and sisters are well. My cosen Cornewell is goon to her mother, whoo is very sike. My deare Ned, the Lord blles you, and if it be His will, giue me a comfortabell seeing of you; which I long for.

Your most affectinat mother,   BRILLIANA HARLEY.
Bromton Castell, Apr: 11, 1640.

LXXIII.

For my deare sonne Mr Edward Harley,
in Magdeline Hall, Oxford.

My Deare Ned—Sence I can not see you, I am glad of theas opertunitys by which I may let you know my thoughts are offten with you; your father being from me, I haue not much company to take pleashure in, but this is a Chirstians comfort, that God is all ways with them. I should be glad to heare from you a relation how the king went to parlament, and at what ease you hard his speche; for I did feare theare would be a great crowde, which made me desire your father not to be theare. I heare your father had a fitt of the pastion of the hart, the day before yow went from Loundon. I beceach the Lord presaruef him from them. Heare is great presing. Mr Harberd is goon with his trop of hors; on of his soulders killed a man in Shearsbury, but they say he was prouocked to it. They are gallant and merry. The trained band is thought must goo, or ells proud men to goo in theiare places. I can not yet heare for sartaine wheare theair randeuous is.

I haue sent you by Loocker some violet cakes. Deare Ned, be carefull of your self, especially be wachfull ouer your hart.

Edward Piners chillderens beed was seet on fier, and it was Gods mercy they had not bine smothered. Piner in puting of it out, haueing none to healp him but Pheebe, whoo is with his wife, tooke coold, for he was in his shirt, and the smoke allmost tooke away his breath, that he is very ill, and I feare has a feauor; it was on firer on wensday night; they rang the bell, which feared all my howes. I pray God to blles you.

   Your most affectinat mother,   BRILLIANA HARLEY.

Apri: 25, 164 . Bromton Castell.

LXXIV.

For my deare sonne Mr. Edward Harley,
in Magdalen Hall, Oxford.

Deare Ned—This morning I receiued your letter, which was very welcome to me and since it pleases God that you inioy your health, I do with more ease beare my owne weakenes. I haue not yet this weeke receiued any letter from your father, and it would much trouble me, but that your father wrote me word that he intended to send the cooke downe this weeke. I thanke you for the kings prair, and I pray God to heare all the praiers that are now put up for a happy issue of this parliament. I haue heard of many bold speeches that haue passed there; and that passage betweene the archbishop and my lord Say is diuersly reported; but I beleue that which I receaued from you. The presse of souldiers is now passt; so that the poore fellowes may now appeare, who had hid themeselues for feare. I purpose and please God, to send to you sometime the next weeke with the money your tutor sent for. I haue not beene out of my bed since wednesday, but I thank God I am but as I use to be. I long to see you, I will not say how much, lest your tutor call it fondnesse, and not loue. I thanke God your brothers and sisters with your cousin Smith are well; but your brother Robert had yesterday morning a seice of a fit, which makes me desire he should enter into a course of physicke. Edward Pinner hath beene very sicke. I sent for docter Wright to him, who hath beene here the most part of this weeke, and hath giuen him physicke which hath done him (by the blessing of God) upon that meanes, much good. This morning he was let blood, and bled uery vile blood; and I now hope he will recouer apace, but yet he keepes his bed. I pray God blesse you, and giue me a comfortable seeing of you, which is much desired by

   Your most affectionate mother, BRILLIANA HARLEY.*

May 1, 1640.

I beleue your cousen ——— is not yet come to Oxford.

M⁸ Walkut was not long since with me. She much reioyced that she had got so excellent a tutor for her son and nephew, and how she had contriued it, that he should haue a seruitor in the house, and so should not need a man to wait upon him. He now feares an ague, and his going to Oxford is put off till he be well.

---

* The signature alone is in the handwriting of the Lady Brilliana:—the letter in that of her son Thomas.

LXXV.

For my deare sonne Mr. Edward Harley,
in Magdeline Hall, Oxford.

My deare Ned—I am not willing you should be longe without that which you stand in neede of, which makes me send this bearor to you, with £10 and 50 sh: for your tutors quartrege; and haueing this oction to send to you, I send him a littell further to see your father, whom I long to see. Affter I had rwit to you by the carrier, I reseued a letter from your father by the cooke, and on from you; they weare both wellcome to me. I thanke you that you make me partake of what you heare; for your father has not time to rwit many particulars. The state of the parlament which I receued from your father I send you heare inclosed, and that which I had from you. Returne mine againe. I beleeue you haue the lord keepers speach, and the speakers, and thearefore I doo not send them to you. I pray God giue a happy sugsess to this parlement; if not we may feare wors effects then has bine yet. You and meself haue great resen to be ernest with our God for your father.

I beleeue this weake will sheaw what they will doo, as all our expectations are vpon the parlament, so I desire all our prayers may be for it.

My deare Ned, I much long to see you and I hope I shall shortly. I haue not recoured so much strentgh as to goo out of my chamber, and at this time I am in beed. Your brothers and sisters are well, and Edward Piner mends a pace. I thinke doctor Rwite a very good doctor. I like the cooke very well.

My deare Ned, the Lord blles you and make you grow in the strentgh of gras, and that you may dayly grow in the loue of Jesus Christ, that that loue may be all in all in you; that so loueing your God aboue all, you may vse the thinges heare below as if you vsed them not. I thanke you for your care of my candellstike, which I rescued safe. I heare inclosed send you 20th. out of which, pay for the lookeing glas, and the rest you may dispose of, as pleas yourself.

I thinke Hall will bring the glas very well. So in hast I rest

    Your most affectinat mother,   BRILLIANA HARLEY.

Deare Ned, remember me very kindly to your worthy tutor. The 20th I thought to haue sent in my letter is with the £10; take it out, and giue the £10 to your tutor.

May 4, 1640.

LXXVI.

To her son Edward.—Endorsed, "For your deare selfe."

My deare Ned—I thanke you for your letter this weake by the carrier; beleeue it, your lines are sweetly wellcome to me; it is my joy that you are well; the Lord in mercy presarufe you in health both of body and mind.

I much desire to see you, and thearefore I haue rwit to your father, to desire him to giue you leafe to come home at Whitsontide.

I thanke you for imparting to me what you know of the parlament, and I will requite you with what I knowe. Theas which I send you I had from my cosen Goowdine; you may keepe them, for I had them rwit out for you. Edward Piner begins to goo abroad. Your brothers and sisters are well. I am not yet out of my beed. Remember me to your tutor.

    Your most affectinat mother,   BRILLIANA HARLEY.

May 8, 1640.

LXXVII.

To her son Edward.—Endorsed, "For your deare selfe."

My deare Ned—I rwit to you but a short letter by the carrier, intending to rwit this day againe to you, but I am not yet sartaine whoo shall carry my letter. I doo so much desire to see you, that I haue rwit ernestly to your father to giue you leaufe to come home at Whitsontide. My deare Ned, I hope it will still be so that you shall be my great comfort. The Lord in mercy make you to grow in the sweet graces of His spirit, and then you will be louely in the eyes of all Gods chillderen.

I am glad you had a day of fast, which is a spirituall feast. I heare that the parlament had granted to them a day of fast, but I cannot tell when it was.

I haue heareinclosed sent you your letter which you sent me, and I thanke you for it, and haue sent you some papers that weare sent me. I had two letters from your father this weake. I thanke God he was well, but he rwit not one word of the parlament; nor Sanky, when he rwits, he says nothing of your father, nor of the parlament. I pray God guie the two howes a happy vnion togeather; for the effects of this parlement will not be indiffrent, neather good nor euell, but eather very good or ells the contrary. The depuety leftenants haue bine at Hariford sence wensday, aboute sending the soulders. Captaine Button is to be captaine of them; he is, as they say, a proper jentellman. Roger Beeb was wilde for his brother being prest, but I could not preuaile with the wise counstablle of Bromton, and was constraind to send Samuell to the deputy leftenants; they thought it much that I could not command that of him, which if I had sent to any jentellman in the cuntry, they would haue doun more, as they said. I heare the soulders are very onruly.

I thanke God your brothers and sisters are well, and Edward Piner is abrood againe.

Good doctor Barker is, as they say, sike to death. Blechly has theas 2 days bin in griuious distres, and is in griuious agony of contience and dispare; shee says shee shall be damned. Desire Mr Pirkins to pray for her, and, deare Ned, pray for her; shee was with me, for her desire was ernest to see me and to speake with me. My deare Ned, long to see me, as I doo, to see you; and the Lord in mercy giue me comfortabell seeing you, which is much desired by

  Your most affectinat mother,   BRILLIANA HARLEY.

Deare Ned, remember me to your worthy tutor.

If you doo not come home at Witsentide, I would haue you send me one of your shirts to take meashure by, and I will, if pleas God, send them you. I like the cooke very well.

May 9, 1640. *Bromton Castell.*

LXXVIII.

For my deare sonne Mr. Edward Harley, in Magdeline Hall, Oxford.

My deare Ned—I thanke you for your letter by J——rth. It was wellcome to me, and I hope it will not be long before I see you, which comfort I begg of the Lord. On Sunday morning I receued a letter from your father, by which I found the nwes of the disolueing of the parlament to be true. Theare are many rumurs in the cuntry. The prest soulders in Presteene haue fought; and they say, if it had not bine for the trained band they had killed the captaine that is come downe for them, refuseing to goo with him, becaus he is a papis. Mr Haruy and his wife are now heare, comeing to take theaire leafe to goo into Warekschere. My deare Ned, the Lord blles you, and giue your father and you a happy meeting with

Your most affectinat mother,   BRILLIANA HARLEY.

May 13, 1640. *Bromton Castell.*

I am glade Mr Robert Pye sonn is with your tutor.

Remember me to your worthy tutor, and tell him if he come to Bromton, Mr Gower expects to haue him to preach for him.

LXXIX.

For my deare sonne Mr. Edward Harley.

My deare Ned—I hope theas lines will finde you well at Oxford. I long to heare from you, and I hope I shall, before it be longe.

My deare Ned, be carefull of your self, and especially be wacthfull ouer your precious soule, still to embrace all things that may further thos grasess in you, which may make you like those that liue holy heare, and shall be gloryfyed heareaffter.

I thanke God your father is well, and so is your brothers and sisters; for meself I am as you left me, but that I haue not you, with me.

I heare from Loundon that the Conuocation howes bracke up the 29 of May, and they haue suspended the bis: of Gloster, becaus he would not consent to theare cannons; and they haue sencured doctor Beale for his sermon. The soulders which weare at Heariford are sent to theare seuerall abodes, and theare to abide for a month. I pray God blles you, and make you still a comfort to

    Your most affectinat mother,   BRILLIANA HARLEY.
(No date.)

Remember me to your worthy tutor.
Your father gaue me this packet to send you.

LXXX.

For my deare sonne Mr. Edward Harley.

Deare Ned—On saterday night somethinge late Colborn came home; his late comeing put me in some doutefull thoughts, but I thanke God I reseued by him the aschurance of your comeing well to Oxford. I thanke you for your seale you sent me, I will keepe it safe for you. This day I reseued your letter by the carrier, I thanke you for it, and it dous much reioyce me that you are well, which I beceach the Lord to continue. I am glad my nephewe Pelham is come so well to Oxford; and, my deare Ned, be still kinde to him; tho it may be, his ouncell may make him something strang, but let your loue (if it be so) ouer come it. I beleeue he thinkes all well doun that is nwe to him and that he sees jentellmen to do with a good gras, which he thinkes they doo when they bowe to the allter; but I pray God teach him another leson; but he must be warely dealt with.

I am sorry to heare my sister has bine ill. I doo purpos, if pleas God, to send to her shortly. Your father has not bine well; he sent for doctor Rwit, but tooke nothing. On wensday last, aboute 12 a cloke at night, he was very ill, but, I thanke God, by morning, he was well, and whent into the faire as he was vsed to doo. The faire was reasnabell quiet, only some Shropsheere soulders weare vnruley; but at night they weare all quiet. The deputy leftenants had letters, that they should sertyfy the counsell how the soulders weare, and who did refuse cote and conduck money. This weake I haue hard no nwes. I thinke Mr. Gower will be with you some time the next weake, and then I hope to rwit to you. Your brothers and sisters are well. I thanke God I am as you left me. I pray God blles you, and giue me a comfortabell seeing of you, which is ernestly desired by

Your most affectinat mother,   BRILLIANA HARLEY.

Remember my loue to your worthy tutor; and let Gorge know I like the las well.

My cosen Dauis remembers her saruis to you.

Jun: 12, 1640. Bromton Castell.

LXXXI.

To her son Edward.—Endorsed, "For your deare selfe."

Deare Ned—I am glad to take the oportunity to rwite to you, when your father is at dinner; for last night my cosen Vahen and his sister with her husband and Mr. Lawes, with others of theairs, came to Bromton, and I beleeue after diner I shall haue theair company. They are come to make a full agreement with your father. Doct^r Deodate gaue your father some phisick, and is confident your fathers illness only proseeds from the splene, and is no inclination to a palcy. Woodowes did as Prichards vse to do, and deceaued your father, so that he would not take this which the doctor would haue had him take, while he was with him. I thanke God your father is as well as he usess to be. The doctor let him bloud vnder the tounge, which agreed very well with him. Dr Deodate went away on tuesday last. I thanke you, my deare Ned, for wishing I should take something of him; but my illness comes at sartaine times, and without I should send for him just at that time, I can not haue him then to giue me any thing; for he would haue me take something and be let blood two or three days before I am ill, as I use to be. If pleas God, when you are with me, I will send for docter Rwite and take something. It pleases my gratious God, so to dispose of it, that this illness which I haue, makes me very weake, for as soune as I am pretty well I am ill againe. Doctor Deodate telles me he kowes many so, and he doos much pitty me; but my comfort is, that my God will not cast off for ever.

The soulders from Heariford were at Lemster last thursday on theaire marche to theaire rendeuoues; the captaine not paying them all theare pay, they would haue returned into the towne againe, but all the towne rose, and thos that weare come out of chruch, and with thos arms they had, beate them back, but theare being a greate heape of stones out of toune, the soulders made vse of them as long as they lasted, in which time the townesmin did but littell good, till that powder was spent, and then the townesmen weare to hard; many weare hurt on both sides; the captaine would haue come into the towne, but was keep out.

Your letter this weake by the carrier was wellcome. I hope, if Mr Gower be at Oxford at the fast, that you may heare him preach that day; and I hope, we shall haue him shortly at Bromton. If Dagon begin to fall, it will downe. I thanke you for the paper you sent me; I haue not yet red it, and the booke I haue not yet seene; your father has it, and I haue not seene him much to day.

Deare Ned, take care of your self for my sake, and doo not goo to be ouer heate in the crowed at the Act. The Lord in mercy blles you and presarfe you.

Your affectinat mother,   BRILLIANA HARLEY.

July 3, 1640. *Bromton Castell.*

I haue so scribeled that I thinke you will hardly reade it.

By this carrier I haue sent you a cape. I hope it will come well to your hand.

LXXXII.

For my deare sonne Mr. Edward Harley,
in Magdiline Hall, Oxford.

Deare Ned—I believe you doo as willing reseafe my letters as I rwit them, which makes me willingly to take all oportunitys to give you aschurance I am nowaye vnmindful of you. Your father has fully agreed with my cosen Vahan and her sister, whoo went from heance this morning, and about that biuesnes he now sends to Loundon; so that this bearer is to rest at Oxford, on the fast. We heare a confidente report that the kinge is agreed with the Scoths, and I hope it is true. Your father, I thanke God, is well. I have resued the booke you sent me, and thanke you for it. I beleeue I shall like it well, for the subiet is very needfull to be knowne, and the aughter of it, is of judgment, thearefore I beleeue he has doun it well. The wellknoweing how fure our pastions are good and how fure euill, and the right way to goworne them is dificule; and in my obseruation I see but feawe, that are stutidious to gouerne theaire pastions, and it is our pastions that trubells our selfs and others.

Deare Ned, I longe to see you, and I hope I shall with comfort. Mr. Salawewell is with your father. The Lord in mercy fitt you and us for the day of fast, and I hope Mr. Gower will preach at Oxford. Mr. Heath will be at Bromton on the fast. I looke that Mr. Pirkins should rwite to me when he will let you come home.

I pray God blles you and fill you with gras, which is the best riches.

   Your most affectinat mother,   BRILLIANA HARLEY.
July 4, 1640. *Bromton Castell.*

Remember my loue to your worthy tutor. The messenger is not yet returned out of Linconscheer.

LXXXIII.

For my deare sonne Mr. Edward Harley,
in Magdeline Hall, Oxford.

Deare Ned—Mr. Gower came not home till saterday about 5 a colke. I, haueing no letters by the carrier, was something trubled, tell I reseued yours by Mr. Gower. I hope I shall now see you shortly, which I longe to do, and I pray God I may with much comfort.

I pray God blles you and bring you safe to
   Your most affectinat mother,   BRILLIANA HARLEY.
July 27, 1640. *Bromton Castell.*

Remember me to your worthy tutor. I hope we shall see him at Bromton.

I reseued a letter the last weeke from my lord by Mr Harbert. I thanke God he is very well. Mr Harberd came but for 3 days, and is returned.

LXXXIV.

For my deare sonne Mr. Edward Harley.

My deare Ned—Your letters by the carrier I haue reseued, and I thanke you for them, and the kings speach and the versess. I hope the parlament will (by Gods mercy) haue as happy proseedings and endeing as it has a hopefull begining. I hope by the next you will send me the speakers speache. I much reioyce that your father and your self enioy your health, and I beceach the Lord you may longe doo so: but, my deare Ned, I would haue you rwite me word more at large, what my cosen Smith thinkes of that which trubells you, and wheather he thinkes a plaster will be sufficient for you. Deare Ned, beleeue it, my thoughts are much with you: be carefull to improuf your time. I know Loundoun is a bewitching place. I desire to knowe wheare your fathers lodging is, and wheather you lye at his lodging. I thanke God I am indeferent well, and your brothers and sisters are very well. Send me word wheather my cosen Hrry Pelham be of the parlament, and wheather my lord is to come or no to Loundoun.

I beceach the Lord to blles you, and presarfe you in all safety.

Your most affectinat mother,   BRILLIANA HARLEY.

The versess pleas me well, and to requite you, I haue sent you some.

Nou: 14, 1640. *Bromton Castell.*

Remember me to my cosen Smith and his wife. I haue sent to your man, to doo some biuseness for me. Good Ned, put him in minde to doo it.

Deare Ned, send me word what good men are of the parlament.

LXXXV.

For my deare sonne Mr. Edward Harley.

My deare Ned—I beceach the Lord to blles you, and to fill you with His gras, and that heauenly wisdome by which you may truely see, that the ways of the men of the world are but foolly.

I did much feare you would not haue endured your iourney so well, but my God was mercifull to you and me in enabelling of you. Deare Ned, let me know whoo your father makes choys of to giue you some thinge, and I beceach the Lord to blles the means to you; and I dout not but that my cosen Smith will be carefull of you. Deare Ned, send me word wheare your father his lodging is.

I perswade meself, the enimes of Gods chruch will lay theair plots deep, but our God is aboue them, and to Him doo we looke, that neuer yet deserted His in the time of trubell. Nay, this is our comfort, that the time of trubell is a speciall time, in which the Lord has commanded His chillderen to seeke vnto Him; and the Lord dous not bide vs to seeke Him in vaine. I pray God presarfe the parlament and giude them in the good way, that they may counsell for the good of his chruch. I am glad you went to see my lady and my sister Wacke. I purpos, if pleas God, to keepe a day the next weake. I thinke it will be thursday; so I rest,

  Your most affectinat mother, BRILLIANA HARLEY.

(No date.)

Deare Ned, rwit me word, how you found Ned Pelham. I thanke God I am indeferent well, but I haue not bine very well sence you went.

Your brothers and sisters are well.

I heare my lord of Northamton is to be lord presedent of Wailles; send me word wheather you heare so.

The chesnut gellding was grauelled and theare is a great hoole in his foote, but Martine thinke he will doo well.

LXXXVI.

For my deare sonne Mr. Edward Harley,
at Magdeline Hall, Oxford.

My deare Ned—Not being sartaine wheare you are, I haue sent one letter to Loundon, and this I send to Oxford, least you should not be at Loundoun. I pray God blles you, wheresoeuer you are. This night, I hard from my brother Pelham; he is well, but some of his chillderen haue not bine well. In hast, I rest,

  Your most affectinat mother, BRILLIANA HARLEY.

Noue. 21, 1640. Bromton Castell.

LXXXVII.

For my deare sonne Mr. Edward Harley.

My deare Ned—I much reioce in the aschurence of your health with your father. I beceach the Lord continue your health and giue you thos choys grasess of His spirit, which He only bestowes vpon His chillderen. O deare Ned, it is most wellcome nwes that the parlament goos on thus happily. The Lord be with them still, and enabell your father for that greate worke. I was not sartaine wheather you would be goone to Oxford or no; becaus your father said nothing of it, which made me send this letter to Loundon. I thanke God your brothers and sisters are well. I beceach the Lord to blles you, as I desire my owne soule should be bllesed, and beleeue that I am,

Your most affectinat mother,   BRILLIANA HARLEY.

Noue: 21, 1640. *Bromton Castell.*

LXXXVIII.

To my deare sonne Mr. Edward Harley.

My deare Ned—I thanke you for your letter from Mr. Sallwells. I much reioyce that you so well endured so fare of the iourney, and I hope my God safe prouidence has brought you to London: my hart is much with you, and I desire to haue it much with my God, for you. It is my comfort that you desire to submite your self to the dispos of our gratious God; His way is best; and the Lord in mercy giue you allways the eye of faith to see it is so.

Deare Ned, be carefull of your self, and let me know how it is with you. Mr. Gower came home last night late and weet; and I feare your father and you had a weet day of it. I heare that parlament is ajourned for 10 days, but I defer my beleefe. I haue not bine yet out of my beed, but I thanke God I am indeferent well;

your brothers and sisters are well. I beceach the Lord to blles you and keepe you safe, under His holy protection; so I rest

   Your most affectinat mother,   BRILLIANA HARLEY.

Noue: 30, 1640. *Bromton Castell.*

Your truncke is sent to Oxford.

LXXXIX.

For my deare sonne Mr Edward Harley,
in Magdilen Hall, Oxford.—Endorsed, " For your deare selfe."

My deare Ned—This day I reseued your letter, which is much comfort to me. I longe much to see you, and I mise you as much; be carefull, of your self, and doo not neglect to vse the meanes, which is derected you. The last night I hard from your father by Morgan, who had bine at Loundon; I meane the apoticary; he left your father well, but full of buisness. He sawe Mr Prine and Mr Bourton come into Loundoun; they weare meet with 2000 hoors and 150 schochess, and the men wore rosemary that meet them. I haue heare sent you the 7 articells against my lord Straford; your father sent them me. The parlament goos on happily; I pray God continue it. Mrs Yats continues ill, but doctor Rwit hopes shee mendes; he is with her still. I haue sent your father a snipe pye and a teale pye, and a coller of brane, or elles I had sent you somethinge this weake. Remember me to my nephew Pelham and to your tutor. I pray God fitte vs all, for the day of fast. Your brothers and sisters are well, and I thanke God I am out of my beed againe. I pray God blles you and leade you in the path of life; and beleefe that I am,

   Your most affectinat mother,   BRILLIANA HARLEY.

Desem: 1640. *Bromton Castell.*

I haue not yet seene the glasses, they are not come from the carriers, but I thanke you for them, and I will and pleas God, send you mony for them.

Mr. James is not yet come downe; I hope he will come by you.

XC.

For my deare sonne Mr Edward Harley.

Deare Ned—I thanke you for your letter this weake by the carrier; it is my greet ioy to heare from you, and I pray God I may still heare well of you. I should be exceeding glad if your father could procure Wigmore to be a burges towne, and that you might be of the parlement. I resceued a letter from your father this night by Mr Morgan, but none by the carrier. I thanke God he is very well, but full of biusnes. He rwit me word that secretary Winedibancke was fled. I heare it is likely to goo ill with the erle of Straford. My lady Veere rwit me a letter this weake; she was then gooing to my lady of Westmorland, whouo is bigg with child. My lord her husband has had the small-pox, but I heare not a word of my sister Wacke. Mrs. Wallcote was with me this weake; she tells me shee thinkes to send for her sonne thees holydays, but shee neuer asked me wheather I would haue any thing to Oxford. Shee told me Dr. Toby Mathue was with Mr. Plooden, wheare theare was great resort of papis, which makes some feare they haue some plots; but I trust the Lord of Hosts will wacth ouer vs.

My cosen Cornewell is heare; but I thinke when the Ember fast is past, shee will be goone. If you goo to my brother Brayes theas holy days, I shall not be sorry, but I know not, wheather your father will be content. Deare Ned, let me know wheather you goo or no. My cosen Blany his wife is brought to beed of a sonne: your brother Robert was godfather. Your brother growes talle. Mrs. Yates is vpon recovery. Doctor Rwit dealt very kindely with them, and tooke much pains, and tooke but half his feese. I was sorry Mr. Griffits brought me no letter, but he aschured me you weare well. I thanke God I am reasnabell well, and your brothers and sisters are very well, and I pray God continue your health and fill your hart with gras, which will be much comfort to,

Your most affectinat mother,   BRILLIANA HARLEY.

Desem: 11, 1640. *Bromton Castle.*

I thanke you for the glases you sent me. They came all very safe; and I hope to send you the 11th for them; they are fine glasess.

Deare Ned, remember me to my nephew Pellham, and my saruis to your worthy tutor; and I hope you are carefull of your owne health.

XCI.

For my deare sonne Mr. Edward Harley.

Deare Ned---On wednesday night last I receiued your letter from Mr James, and yesterday yours by the carrier, for both I thanke you; and do you beleue that your letters are uery welcome to me, and I hope that that will alwayes make you willing to write.

Your father wrote me word that he did thinke to send for you, which I am very glad of, and that makes me send this letter to London, where I hope it will meet you. I wrote you nothing of what I haue heard of the parliament: bec: I hope you will heare it more fully at London. Deare Ned, tell your father that I desire him, if Mr Gower can be spared from comming to London, that I desire he may. Richard Sankie wrote to him to come up about the beginning of January. Mr Gower read Sankies letter to me, but I will not haue Sankie know this. I know not how this congregation will be well prouided for in his absence. I thanke God he is very well, but I see him but seldome: he kept wednesday last very worthely. Mr Tomms was at Brompton and helpt us in my family. I haue kept my bed since yesterday; I hope the Lord will bring mee well out of it. I thanke God your brothers and sisters are well. I pray God blesse you and preserue you in safety, both of soule and body.

Your most affectionate mother,   BRILLIANA HARLEY.[*]

Brompton, December 19, 1640.

[*] This letter, excepting the signature of Lady Brilliana, is in the handwriting of another; probably that of her son Thomas.

I take it for a great blessing of God that you are so well. I pray God continue your health, and be carefull of yourselfe for my sake.

XCII.

For my deare sonne Mr. Edward Harley.

Deare Ned—On thursday night Miller came home, and brought me the wellcome aschurance of your being well, with your father: and I should be glad you weare of the parlament. I much reioyce that the parlament goos one so well. I trust the Lord will finisch this good worke begonne. I am sorry my lord keeper would goo away. I belefe others wisch themselfes with him.

I hard from my brother Pelham aboute a fortnight sence; the ocation of his sending was this; I hard that the minester of Brockellbe was deade, and the place was worth 50l. a yeare; I haueing a great desire to haue a good man theare, made offer to Mr. Volye. My brother liked the report I gaue of him, and sent to haue him come and speake with him; but sent me word it was worth but 30 pounds a yeare; neather would he haue him come with a hope that he would mend it; but if he sawe he weare painefull, it was likely he would consider him. Mr. Voly was loth to goo to so small a thinge, vpon so poore hopes, and he has so much wheare he is: it did much trubell me, that my brother semed to be so straight in so great a matter; he rwit me word he had many shuters for it; I thinke they are not worth the haueing.

My deare Ned, take care of your self: doo not goo by water this winter. I heare theare is a howes shut vp by my cosen Smith, which I am sorry for. If Rafe had not goone vp of his owne buisnes, I had sent vp Rise. I could wisch your father would make you another shute of cloths, for one shute is to littell.

I thanke God I am indeferent well, and all your brothers and sisters are well.

I pray God blles you and keepe you in His feare and leade you in the pathe of life, so I rest,

Your most affectinat mother, BRILLIANA HARLEY.

Janu: 2, 1640. *Bromton Castell.*

My cosen Cornewell is yet with me.

If you haue so much time, let Rafe tell you how the boys shut out Mr. Ballam out of scoule. I was very glad that your brothers weare not with them.

XCIII.

For my deare sonne Mr. Edward Harley.

My deare Ned—I hope this letter will finde you with your father: now I thinke it longe sence I hard from you; for this weake as yet I haue not hard. Send me word wheather my brother be in Loundoun, and how he does. Now your father and you are from me, my contentment is in the happy proseedings of the parlament, which makes a mend for your fathers longe absence. I longe to see him, and I hope in due time I shall inioy that comfort of seeing you both. I beleefe by this, you are somethinge aquanted with Londoun, and, deare Ned, send me word how you like it.

Yesterday wee keepe a priuet day; Mr. Gower, Mr. Yaits, Mr. Steuenson, Mr. Voile, and Mr. More, were at it. Mr. More's wife is very ill, as she was vsed to be, a shakeing all over her. I thanke God your brothers and sisters are well, and I am indeferent well; but it has bine extreme coold weather. I pray God blles you, and make you to see and finde that there is more sweetness in the seruis of God then in all the pleashurs of the world; and be aschured that I gladly will sheaw meself

Your most affectinat mother, BRILLIANA HARLEY.

Janu: 8, 1640. *Bromton Castell.*

Mr. Prise of Pilleth dyed on wensday last.

XCIV.

For my deare sonne Mr Edward Harley.

My deare Ned—I thanke you for your letter this weake; I reseued it not tell this morning, and then it was wellcome. I thought at the first I had no letter from you, becaus yours had no shuperscription; but I was well pleased to be so disceaued. It is a great comfort to me to hear the parlament goos on so happily, and that the kinge has consented that the insendereis should be judged. Mr Braughton is now at Bromton, and I beleefe, if Mr. Tomkins be not burges for Webly, he will on munday: Mr. Gower purposes to goo to Heereford, to consult aboute the scandolous ministers, and thos places which haue none. I am glad theare is likly to be so good a corespondency betwne us and the Duch. I am glad to heare my lord is well, but I haue not hard from him yet. Theare is a very fine discours rwiten in Italien, but translated in to Latine; it is dedicated to Oxsensterne, he that was tresure to the king of Sweden; if the book desarfe the comendation I could wisch you did reade it, but I can not send you the titell of the booke. I thanke God your brothers and sisters are very well. I pray God blles you, and keepe your hart aboue all the thinges in this life; so I rest,

  Your most affectinat mother, BRILLIANA HARLEY.

Janu: 9, 1640 *Bromton Castell.*

XCV.

For my deare sonne Mr. Edward Harley.

My deare Ned—This morning I reseeued your letter by Raphe, and I hope theas lines will finde you with your father, wheare I had rather haue you be then at Oxford. I am very glad that the parlament has defered priuet biusnes for a time, to settell the publike; in which I beseach the Lord direct them and giue them a vnanimous consent in thos things which may be for the glory of God and the peace of His Church; that all theas thinges, whithout which God may be sarfed without burdening the conscienc of any of Gods childeren, may be cast out, as thos things which haue to longe trubeled the peace of the chruch. I much reioyce that your father and you are well. I beseach the Lord continue your health. My cosen Smith rwite me word that you weare perfectly well, which is much comfort to me. I heare not a word of my sister Wacke. I am sorry my lord is gone into the North.

I thanke God, I am now out of my beed; your brothers and sisters are well.

I pray God blles you and keepe you in His feare, and giue you a comfortabell seeing of,

  Your most affectinat mother, BRILLIANA HARLEY.

Janu: 22, 1640. *Bromton Castell.*

My cosen Dauis remembers saruis to you.

XCVI.

For my deare sonne Mr Edward Harley.

Deare Ned—I can not let such a sufficent mesenger goo without a letter to you. Mr. Gower had finisched but this day late. I beleefe your father will correct somethinge in it, or am deccafed. I sent Rice to carry this the more carefully, and I thinke your father may make some vse of him; for I feare on man is too littell for him. I pray God blles you.

  Your most affectinat mother, BRILLIANA HARLEY.

Janu: 23, 1640. *Bromton Costell.*

Your sister Marget is not very well, but the rest are well. I feare her made vsed somethinge to her head.

XCVII.

For my deare sonne M'r Edward Harley.

Deare Ned—I am glad of all ocations to inquire affter your health, which I hope you inioye. Munday, as I hard from you and others, was to be the day of debate about bischops. We at Bromton keep the day to shue to our God for His derection of the parlament. I beleefe that herarchy must downe, and I hope now.

My cosen Keirle sent the petion he had at Hereford to Mr. Gower to geet hands; he rwit Mr. Gower word he sent it to my younge cosen Vahan; he singned it and goot threescore and 10 hands to it, but his father did not singe it. I longe to heare from you. I beceach the Lord to blles you, and that I may see you with much comfort; so I rest

Your most affectinat mother,   BRILLIANA HARLEY.

Janu: 28, 1640. Bromton Castell.

Your brothers and sisters are well; but your sister Brill has a very greate coold.

Deare Ned, let your man deliuer this letter to my cosen Pelham, as soune as you can; I haue rwit to him about a mariage for one of my neecess.

XCVIII.

For my deare sonne M'r Edward Harley.

My deare Ned—I thank you for your letter by the Wellchman and by the carrier. I thinke the Wellchman went vp on a sleepless arent, for he toold me he went vp about a petion against the minister wheare he liued, but the man that carried the petion was not come to Loundon, nor he knwe not wheare he was; as he went vp he said that he carried the petion, and that he would goo to your father about it.

I did much feare, when I hard first of the kings speach, that it would haue caused some allteration in the parlament, but I now hope it will not. I thought the Jesuet had bine acuesed of treson. I hope the kinge will yeald to the request of the parlament in that particular. Mr. Gower was not willing to goo vp the next weake, because he thinkes theare is some rubs in the way; but I thinke he will begine his iourney on munday-comsenet. Mr. Yaits, when I toold him of Mr. Gowerses gooing, was of himself very ernest vpon the journey, but now he is content to stay tell your father sends word, wheather he should come or no; and I thinke he dous better.

I had seene the kings speech before you sent me it, but it was various from yours. I thanke you for it. Deare Ned, I thanke you for puting me in minde to send your father some biskets. I haue sent him a box with some and another box in which is some Sheawsbery caskes for your father, and 5 biskets for your self, with a paper of lemoncakes, such as I haue sent to your father: I was angry that they had ouer backed the biskets, and I would not haue sent them, but that I was loth to stay tell another weake; send me word wheather your father like them. I am glad that Gorge has seene his error and that your are frinds againe. I only rwit to your father that I had hard that Gorge was weary of saruis, and that his father toold me, he would studdy deuinety, and I desired him, if you did finde him not fite for you, that he would giue his consent that you might change him. I thank God your brothers and sisters are well. Your brother Robine, in my eye, is too tall for his scoule. He aplyes, I hope, his minde to his booke something better then he did; he is resarued, says littell, but Tome is as biussy as can be, about the parlament, and hoolds inteligence with all that will giue him true notice of things. I hope your father will not let you goo from him. I pray God blles you, and make you see betimes the vanitye of this life and the excellency of the fauor of God. I longe to see you, and rest,

Your most affectinat mother, BRILLIANA HARLEY.

Pheb: 5, 1640. *Bromton Castell.*

In the lesser box are 5 biskets for you and a paper of lemon cakes.

XCIX.

For my deare sonne Mr. Edward Harley.

Deare Ned—Mr Gower says he means to begine his iourney on munday next, but his offten changeing of his minde makes me send theas lines by the carrier, in which I thanke you for your letter by this weake. I hope the Lord will so cleere the judgments of all the parlament, so that they may see the errors of thos that terme themselfs the fathers of the chruch. Deare Ned, put your father in minde of inquireing affter Mr Gwine. I haue keept my beed theas 6 days, and I haue taken a great coold; I tooke it in gooing once or twice into the parler, this coold weather. I hope the Lord will be mercyfull to me, that I may liue to see you and your father. I thanke God your brothers and sisters are well. I hope your father will not let you goo to Oxford yet a while, for the infextion of such a diseasce is not goone in 4 weakes at the least, but I thinke it will stay longer in the beeds. I pray God blles you, as I desire my owne soule should be bllesed.

Your most affectinat mother,   BRILLIANA HARLEY.

Pheb: 12, 1640.   *Bromton Castell.*

C.

For my deare sonne Mr. Edward Harley.

Deare Ned—I hope Mr Gower will finde you with your father, wheare I am glad to haue you be, and I hope your father will not let you goe from him. I hope your father will hasten Mr Gower downe againe. I heare my cosen Vahan would not put his hand to the petion, nor did not geet any hands. Deare Ned, send me word wheather thos that haue put in the petions against bis: haue taken the hands of all such as doo not vnderstand what they haue put theaire hands to. I am toold that it is the way in all cuntrys, and that Mr Macworths gaue such derections. To me it dous not sound reasnabell; for, in my opinion, such hands should be taken as vnderstand it, and will stand to what thay haue doun.

I heare my Lord Straford is aquesused of most abominabel maters, but I haue not hard any particulars. I had a letter from my cosen Harry Pelham, in which he dous much commend you. I beleefe you finde him to sauer more of religion than his brother Hurberd. I am glad my brother is not goon to the army, and that my cosen Farfex has the honner of knightwood added to him. My lady Veere rwit me word, that shee was glad that you weare with your father, for shee thought it would be an aduantage to you.

I hope the Lord will still gooalonge with the parlament, and tho wicked men wacth for theaire failleing, that they shallbe disaponted.

I blles God that you finde yourself well; I beceach the Lord to continue your health, and aboue all, that you may inioy a sound judgment, an vpright hart, large affectionons to your God, which is the true health of the minde. Deare Ned, be carefull of yourself, and the more for my sake.

Rwit me word what imployment your father puts Gorge Griffits brother to, which Mr Griffits toold me he sent vp the last weake to your father. I haue heare inclosed sent you 11th for the glases you sent me downe; they are very good and came very well to me.

I thanke God my coold is much better then it was, and I hope gooing away.

I am now out of my beed; this is the first day. I pray God blles you.

    Your most affectinat mother,   BRILLIANA HARLEY.

Pheb: 15, 1640.   *Bromton Castell.*

CI.

For my deare sonne Mr. Edward Harley.

Deare Ned—I should be glad I could as easely see you as rwit to you. I thanke you for your letter this weake. I reioyce that your father is well, and that is my comfort in his absence. I could wisch I could vndergoo some of the paines for him, but I would haue him act the vnderstanding part. I haue allways beleefed that the Lord would purge His chruch from all theas thinges and persons, that haue bine such a hinderance to the free pasage of His glorious ghospell; and I trust, now is the time. The death of the kinge of Spaine, I thinke, will make some alterations in thos parts. I much reioyce the parlament goos one so well. I pray God they may doo so still. Your brother Tomas red me the speach, which I can not vnderstand no further then to know I doo not vnderstand the nonesence of it. Your brother is very glad of his letter, but he is very soleme at the speach, as if he did not thinke that had bine spoken. Mr Gower is, I beleeue, with you. I did hope my cosen Daniel would haue come doune this weake, that so I might haue hard more fully from you. I haue sent your father some other cakes to put in his pocket. Rwit me word, how he likes them. I am sorry the biskets weare made wors in the carage; before they went of, all theaire falte was that they weare ouer backed. It pleases me well that you are with your father. Deare Ned, I beceach the Lord to blles you, and make you growe stronge in gras, which is ernestly desired by,

    Your most affectinat mother,   BRILLIANA HARLEY.

Pheb: 19, 1640. *Bromton Castell.*

CII.

For my deare sonne Mr. Edward Harley.

My deare Ned—If you knwe how much I mise your company, you will conclude your letters are very wellcome to me. I thanke you for yours by the carrier and by the post.

I much reioyce that you and your father are so well. Deare Ned, still take care of your self, and put your father in minde to doo so.

I am sorry Irland is in so bade a case, and that the puting off of the land into a posture of defence, is so forslowed.

Mr Broughton, I beleeue, will tell you how they speake of the parlament, in the cuntry. I pray God open theare eyes, that they may see things a right. I should be sorry your father should put a stranger in trust with his estate, when he is not in the cuntry. I pray God direct him. I haue scase time to rwit any thing to you in this letter; Mr Moors man being in such hast. I pray God blles you.

Your most affectinat mother, BRILLIANA HARLEY.

Pheb: 26, 1640. *Brompton Castel.*

CIII.

To her son Edward.

Deare Ned—I haue reseued your letter by my cosen Dauis; it was wellcome tho it was short. My cosen Dauis telles me, your father is very well and that you are so, which is a great comfort to me; and I hope that the Lord will giue your father dubell strentgh, to vndergoo the waight of thos imployments which lye vpon him. And I hope you will not repent your being at Loundoun with your father, which I gees will be more aduantage to you, then if you had bine at Oxford.

My cosen Dauis is not cleere yet in his biusnes; for Mr Edwards will not out; he slites what they say; and says Mr Dauis goos about like a premouter. He says, he would be sent for vp to Loundoun, that he may informe the parlament with what vntruths my cosen Dauis has toold them. I never hard of a man that was not out of his sences, that was so careles to doo like a resnabell man, as Mr Edwards is; he seames to let himself loose to be led by his pastions. I hope my cosen Dauis makes a ronge judgment; for he thinkes my lord Straford will not haue his sentence, and that some other thinges will fall out. My cosen Dauis charges dous not pleas him, becaus it is no more.

Your letter by Jhon Wall was very wellcome to me, and I thanke you for it. I hope the Lord will disapoint all the plots of thos that haue evill will at the prosperity of Gods chruch. Your letter has giuen me much content, for I feared that some would take ocation by the Scots declaration to vrge against them; but I hope the Lord will pasefy all distempers. I am glad to heare my brother is well, and I perswade meselfe he loues you. I hope my brother is not for lord Straford. I hard my lord Straford layed some of his actions to his charge; but I hope, if he did, my brother has cleered himself.

I am glad my cosen St. Jhons is to be maried. I beleeue it is for her aduantage; tho in my opinion, when one has chillderen, it is better to be a widowe.

Mr Ballam is very sicke; I thinke it is an ague, but he eates, and so make his fits violent; he will take nothinge of Wodowes, nor Morgan, but is resouled to send to morrow for doctor Rwit, but he feares he will stay longer with him then 3*l.* will hoold out; that he is willing to giue, but he can spare no more, as he says: this 2 dayes he has bine debating of, as they tell me; but now in his fitte, he re-soulfes to send for him, and dous not recken the charges. I hope he will doo well; he is so prouedent. Your brother Tome had a sharpe fitte on saboth day night, but I thanke God his last fite was but short; he is very cheerefull and hungry, but I suffer him to eate no meate, and I giue him glisters, which I thanke God has doun him much good.

I hope in good time your father will finde a chamber in the Tempell for you. Deare Ned, put your father in minde, to inquire of Mr Gwine.

I thanke you for your letter by the carrier; your letters gives me more satisfaction then any other. I did much feare, by what I was abell to gees, that the Scots declaration would giue the contrary party ocation to sheaw themselfes; but I blles the Lord, that He has ouer-ruled the harts of men, and I hope they goo now on well, to doo that greate worke they haue in hand. I thanke you for the paper the Scots put into the Lords. I haue taken a coppy, and heare-inclosed returned yours. I confes, I longe to heare the sugsess of the conferance. Many rumors are in the cuntry. If you haue bine to heare the Scots minesters, send me word how you like them. I am glad your father has not taken coold, this coold weather; for wheare your fathers lodging is, is the cooldest place I thinke about Loundoun. I reioyce that your father is well, tho I was sorry I had no letter from him; but when he is so biussy I would not haue him rwit.

I thanke God your brother Tomas scaped his ague yesterday, and he is indeferent well. Mr Ballam is ill, and so is Same Pinner. Deare Ned, send me word when you thinke that Mr Gower can come doune.

I haue rwit to Sanky about Hacklet; for I perseaufe shee may be brought to loue him. I haue keep my beed this weake, and as yet I haue not bine a whoole day vp. I pray God blles you, and giue you gras and comfort, the portion of His chilldren; so I rest,

  Your most affectinat mother, BRILLIANA HARLEY.

Mar: 12, 1640. *Bromton Castell.*

CIV.

For my deare sonne Mr Edward Harley.

Deare Ned—Your letter was this morning a sweet cordiall to me, affter a great deale of sorrow I had for your brother Tom. It is Gods great mercy to me that your father and you are well; and I beceache the Lord to continue that mercy to you both, and then I shall be, so much the better.

I am sorry theare is that difference betwne bothe howes, and I feare theare will be more; but I trust the Lord will ouer-rule mens harts. I am glad that the Bischops begine to falle, and I hope it will be with them as it was with Haman; when he began to falle, he feell indeede.

I am glad my lady Veere has caus to reioyce in my cosen St. Jhons second mariage.

Your brother Toms ague is much increesed, and he is very weake; his fitte on wensday heald him 22 oures; he is now in his fitte, and he has it very sharply; his noos has blled much at seuerall times, and they say is a singe, it is a feauor. I haue sent for doctor Rwit or doctor Bauer. Mr Ballam sent on munday for doctor Rwit, but then he was in Glostersheere. I had safed him that labor, but your brother was then reasnabell well. He lay in Mr Ballams chamber, and Blechely, whoo lookes to him and had waethed with him, on monday night, shee left him a sleepe and prtly allmost out of his fitte, and would let them make no fier in his chamber, but when she was goon, the maid that shee left with him, made so much fier that it allmost burnt the clothes of the beed, and put him into a violent heate; now I haue him lye in the chamber by me, which pleases him very well. He weepe the other day in priuet, and toold on that he takes for his frrend, that his brother Robin was angry with him aboute the parlament nwes, and he feared he had made you angry with him; thearefore, deare Ned, rwite to him. Your brother Robin cares not to know how it goos in the parlament. I meane to know it, which I blamed him on day for, and then he rwit to you. Your brother Tom is the likest you, and loues you dearely.

I pray God blles you and giue you a comfortabell meeting with
Your most affectinat mother,   BRILLIANA HARLEY.

Blechly giues him much content, and shee takes great pains with him.

Deare Ned, let this incolesed letter be deliuered to my brother. I rwit to him, becaus I hard he was expected in the North.

Mar: 19, 1640. *Bromton Castell.*

CV.

For my deare sonne Mr. Edward Harley.

Deare Ned—Sence I cannot haue the greater part of my comfort in seeing of you, I am glad to my parte in this, that is next it.

I much desire to heare the sugsess of this weakes debates in parlament; I pray God it may be a happy one.

Your brother Tom this morning is pritty well, but he had a very loonge fitt, from 2 a clooke wesday night tell 2 a clooke this thursday night; he is very weake, but doctor Rwit puts me in good hope of him: the doctor came yesterday to me. This morning he has giuen him a purge, and I hope the Lord will blles it to him: his noos bleeds every fitt. I see him twes or thrise a day. Blechly takes a greate deale of paines with him, wacthes every fite-night with him, rises euery night to him, giues him all his glisters. I did not thinke, shee had bine halfe so carefull. I beleeue you pray for him; some times in his fitts he speakes a littell idell; but he did not, I thanke God, in this fitt; but, poore hart! he is very weake. But the doctor puts me in good hope of him. Your brother Robin dous exceedingly neglect himself, which is a great greefe to me; he is still with the saruants, and grows tall and very leane, so that Doctor Rwit did not knowe him. I pray God blles you.

Your most affectinat mother,   BRILLIANA HARLEY.
Mar: 20, 1640. Bromton Castell.

I haue sent your father by this carrier a turkey pye. Deare Ned, send me word wheather your father like it.

CVI.

For my deare sonne Mr. Edward Harley.

Deare Ned—That I haue no letter from you this weake puts me to a stand, and I should be very much trubeled, but that your father rwites me word you are well, which mercy, I hope, the Lord will still continue to you. I neuer more longed to heare how things goo then I did this weake. Many rumors we heare, but I biuld vpon nothing tell I heare it from you or your father.

I much desire to heare how the parlament tooke the ansure of the justices of this country, that sent word they knwe not by what aughtority the parlament did require the taking of the protestation. Sr William Croft is much against the parlament, and vtters his minde freely: he was much displeased that they would petition the Parlament: he toold Mr Gower he was a moufer of sedistion; and my cosen Tomkins was very hoot with him: they say the parlament dous theare owne biusness, and not the cuntryes. I shall long to heare from you. I thanke God, your cosen Smith has loost his ague, for I could not deserne he had any fite. On munday before Ester, Mr Kirll and some other gentellmen intend to seet forward with the petition, which I hope will be well taken.

I pray God blles you, and keepe you in His feare.

Your most affectinat mother,   BRILLIANA HARLEY.
Mar: 25, 1641.

CVII.

For my deare sonne Mr Edward Harley.

My deare Ned—I know not wheather Mr Laneford will keepe his resolution, to be at Loundoun as soune as the carrier, and thearefore I desire to let you knowe how your brothers doo, which I perswad meself you longe affter. I thanke God your brother Tom is pritty well but weake; your brother Robine was ill all day yesterday. Doctor Rwit made haste backe, becaws he did not like your brother when he went away. This day he tooke a vomit, which rought very well with him, and I hope he will be much better for it; and I trust the Lord will be mercyfull to them and me, in restoreing them both to health; and I beceach the Lord to continue yours, and to blles you with all bllesinges, as I desire my oune soule should be bllesed. So I rest,

    Your most affectinat mother,   BRILLIANA HARLEY.

Mar: 27, 1641. Bromton Castell.

Your sisters, I thanke God, are well. This day Sr Williham Croft is at Wigmore aboute the subsedies.

CVIII.

For my deare sonne Mr. Edward Harley.

Deare Ned—I hope you are well, and I am glad to heare you are so; but yet I know not what to thinke, that I had no letter from you, neather by the carrier nor by the post. I long to heare from you, and I beleiue you think I doo. I pray God blles you and keepe you from all euill, especially that of sinn. I thanke God your cosen Smith is well againe. So I rest,

    Your most affectinat mother,   BRILLIANA HARLEY.

Mar: 28, 1641. Brompton Castell.

I beleeue you hear that Mr Weafer, on of the burges of Hereford, is dead.

CIX.

For my deare sonne Mr. Edward Harley.

Deare Ned—The last night I receued your letter by the carrier which you rwite the last weake. I confes I was much joyed to see your hand, but I cannot but yet be sorry that I haue no letter from you this weake, nor from your father. I pray God I may heare well of you: it is my comfort, that in theas days of trubell you make the Lord your defence, and looke vp to Him, whoo goouers all the affairs of the world, and I am confident will bring this, His owne worke to a glorious end. I send this letter by the post of Loudlow, whoo is nwely seet vp; if you will rwite by him weakely, I will send, if pleas God, for the letters; for it will be eassyer then to send to Shreawesbury. I have bine ill, as I vse to be sence wensday. I pray God blles you and giue you wisdome both to walke before God and man.

Your most affectinat mother,   BRILLIANA HARLEY.

Apr: the first, 1641. *Brompton Castell.*

CX.

For my deare sonne Mr. Edward Harley.

My deare Ned— Your wellcome letter by Mr. Moore I receued the last night. I had longe longed for a letter from you; the last weake I had only a letter from you, but it was on that had bine rwite the weake before. We must all say, if the Lord dous not apeare in His allmighty power to ouer-rule the actions of men, we may feare woofull dayes. If such dayes should befalle vs, the woo would light on thoos that haue not walked with God, and Gods childeren should only tast of the sorrow of them. I am sorry for judg Mallet, I wisch he may be so wise as to see his error; but the soyle of pich will hardly be rubed of.

I haue sent Mr. Dauis of Wigmore, the derections you rwite me from your father, to Heariford; he went this morning. I pray God prosper him in it, and if it be His holy will, that you may haue that imployment. I beleeue my lord Scidmore stands for Mr. Witeny, and I beleeue Sr William Croft will looke after it; he is quite turned abownte. I purpos and pleas God, to send the keepers man to Loundoun on tusday, and then I hope to rwit you word what Mr. Dauis has doun at Heariford. You may beleeue I will rwite and doo all that I can, to further that which I do desire, and I am perswaded doctor Wright would doo all that weare in his power. I thanke God your brothers and sisters are well, and I pray God blles you with His choyest bllesings; and beleeue that you are most deare to,

    Your most affectinat mother,   BRILLIANA HARLEY.

Brompton Castell. Apr: 9, 1641.

CXI.

For my deare sonne Mr. Edward Harley.

My deare Ned—Tho longe yet at last, I receued your letter sent by Mrs. Vahans man; it was very well-come, tho it bare an old date.

Mr. Scidmore the last night sent me your fathers letter, which he brought downe, and rwite me word you weare well, which was more wellcome to me then all his strange lines.

Now I know your father desires for your sisters comeing vp, I purpos, and pleas God, she shall begine her journy, without your father contradict it, on munday or tusday come senight, becaus I desire she should goo before the weather be so hoot. I am very glad your coold is gone. I beceach the Lord in His rich mercy to blles you, and keepe you from all euille and make you grow in wisdome, so that you may still giude all your actions with descretion: so I rest,

  Your most affectinat mother,   BRILLIANA HARLEY.

I send this by the post of Hariford, becaus I know not wheather the post of Loudlow euer deleuered my letter or no. Deare Ned, be carefull of yourselfe.

Apr: 14, 1641. Brompton Castell.

CXII.

For my deare sonne Mr Edward Harley.

My deare Ned—Tho your letter by the merser weare short, yet it had a longe wellcome. I much desire to heare how my lord Straford comes of; for I beleeue many thinges depend vpon it. Once againe I thanke you for his charge, and Mr Fines his speach, which I like very well. I need not tell you I had no letter from you by the carrier, but your father rwit me word you weare heareing my lord Strayfords charg, which was excuse susphicient; and that you weare well, was pleasing to me, tho I should haue bine glad of a letter. Your brother Tom, I thanke God, has loost his ague, but he dous not yet come abroode. Your brother Robine has is ague, but his fittes are short and much eassier then they weare. Mr Ballam is very ill; his is a feauor, if it be no thinge elles. The other day he resouled to make his will, and then to meddell no more with the world; but yesterday and to day he hopes better of himself. I am very sorry for him. Doctor Rwit, I thinke, will be with him on munday next, and then I purpos, if pleas God, to take something meself. Aske your father, wheather I shall send to Oxford for your beed and Gorgess and the sheets; I can hardly spare the beeds; for it may be, some will perswade that it is better sell them theare then bringe them home; but I am not of that minde. Your sisters are well, and I should be very glad to haue Brill goo to my lady Veeres. I hope Mr Gower will come downe shortly. I am much pleased that you are now with your father, and I hope it will be much aduantage to you; and I beceach the Lord to blles all the wayes of knowledg to you; for you now see the truth of Gods word, that tho men spread like a bay tree, yet they endure but for a time.

Deare Ned, be carefull of your self; and I beceach the Lord to blles you: so I rest,

Your most affectinat mother,   BRILLIANA HARLEY.

Apr: 19, 1641.   *Bromton Castell.*

CXIII.

For my deare sonne Mr Edward Harley.

My deare Ned—It cannot but be much comfort to me to receaue the aschurance of your health, sence Loundoun is now so sikely a place, and thearefore I thanke you for your letter this weke by the carrier. It is an excelent thinge to carry a littell peece of meer in your mouth, to keepe you from any infection. Tell your father of it, it may be he will vse it; and I beceach the Lord to presarfe you, and giue me a comfortabell seeing of your father and you. In the cuntry they had broken the parlament and beheaded my lord Straford, which would not well hange togeather. I pray God remoufe all rubs that lye in the way, so that the worke can not goo forward. Our eyes must be to the Lord, whoo only can doo greete things.

Mr. Gower has not yet made an end of the relation of my lord Strafords charge; he is as much taken with the relation, as I thinke he was with heareing it.

Your brother Tom has loost his ague and is resnabell well. Your brother Robine keepes his old way in every . . . , in his dyet, and consealeing his being ill. Docter Wright left him well, but he is growne wors; but docter Wright calling of me as he came from a patient in Wostersheere, findeing him in that distemper, gaue him something, so that I hope the worst is past. This is the first day I haue take any time out of my beed. I will, if pleas God, haue some half shirts made for you. I longe to see you, and now I shall hope to doo so within thees 2 months. Your sisters are well. My cosen Dauis takes it exceeding kindely from you, and tells me he will rwit you word what he has doun. I pray God blles you as I would haue my owne soule blessed: so I rest,

Your most affectinat mother,   BRILLIANA HARLEY.

I am glad your * * * has changed the Tempell to Linconsine, becaus theare is a better preacher.

Apr. 30, 1641. Bromton Castell.

CXIV.

For my deare sonne Mr. Edward Harley.

Deare Ned—I reseued your letter which you sent with your fathers by Heareford; it was doubly wellcome to me, in that it was yours, and that it brought me the wellcome hope of the two howesess agreeing about my lord Straford. I thanke God your brothers are pritty well. Your brother Tom has lost his ague, and your brother Robine I hope will doo his shortly. I thanke God I am reasnabell well, and I long to see you, and reioyce to express meselfe,

Your most affectinat mother,   BRILLIANA HARLEY.

You did not rwit me word that you weare well, but I hope you are. Loue is watchfull. This man is in hast.

May 4, 1641. Bromton Castell.

CXV.

For my deare sonne Mr. Edward Harley.

Deare Ned—Sence my thoughtes are so much with you, I may easely writ offten to you. I take much content that I may hope to see your father and you within 2 months. I pray God giue me a comfortabell inioyeing of that my desire. Deare Ned, be carefull of your health, and aboue all, of keeping your hart cloos with your God. I did much reioyce that theare was hopes of a good agreement betwene the 2 howess, and I hope to heare more fully of it by Looker, who was looked for hard the last night; but he is not yet come. Your brother Tom, I thanke God, is so well that he comes into my chamber, and is mightyly a hungery, but your brother Robine has his ague still; his fittes are much less. He was very ill, and I preuailed with him to take a vomit, which, he says now, if he had not taken he thinkes he had bine in his graue: but he was very vnwilling to take any more phiseke, so he did not: and I feare he is a littell corbuticall; for his teethe are loose; and I feare he had a littell touch of his old deases the other day, but he had no fitt: he is alltogeather against phiseke; he thinks an ague must be worne away by gooing abroode; but theas are not such agues. Mr. Ballam mends a pacce, and so dous Sam Piner: your sisters are, I thanke God, very well, and your cosen Smith, whous only sorrow is, that I haue goot one to teach scoole for Mr. Ballam.

Mr. Gower toold me of the death of my good brother Bray. I am exceeding sorry for the loos of him; I hope my sister Wacke and my brother are well, and my lady Conway and my brothers chillderen.

I pray God blles you and keepe you in His feare: so I rest,

  Your most affectinat mother,   BRILLIANA HARLEY.

May 7, 1641. *Bromton Castell.*
I thanke God, I finde meself much better for my phisek and being

let blood. I haue bine to see your brother Robine, but I durst not goo to-day, becaus I haue taken a great coold.

CXVI.

For my deare sonne Mr. Edward Harley.

Deare Ned—I haue defered the mesenger so longe that I haue hardly time to write. I did hope Looker would haue bine in time, and now I hope he will bringe me the aschurance of your health, and your fathers, when he comes, which I longe for. Your brother Tom is well, but your brother Roberd had his ague to-day. We heare of great matters that has bine doun at Loundoun this weake, but I beleeue nothinge tell I heare it from a shure hand. I pray God blles you, and beleeue me to be,

Your most affectinat mother, BRILLIANA HARLEY.

May 8, 1641.

Endorsed,—Conwey
Carrage
Cairage
Caraige.

CXVII.

For my deare sonne Mr. Edward Harley.

Deare Ned—I haue resen to giue you thankes for your letters, for as I haue many ocations of sorrowes, so I thanke God your letters are greate refreschings to me. I am very sorry to heare that the sikenes is so much increesed. I beceech the Lord stay that judgment that it may not goo through the land; and the Lord in mercy presarue you from all infections. And deare Ned, be not so boold in gooing into plases where the sikenes is. I haue some hope that the parlament will ajourne, that your father and you may come doune within this fortnight or 3 weakes at the farthrest, which I should be glad to be assured of. I am glad my lord Saye is master of the wards. In the cuntry they haue in report hanged the archbischope. I am glad that Mr. Gwine has giuen a better imprestion of himself. I could wisch with all my hart, that my cosen Harry Pelham weare aquinted with him. My brother Pelham is a good father, but yet my dear sisters chillderen want theare mother.

I feare my brother is not ouer willing to part from his money. My nephewe Edward is now returned to Oxford from Brockellsbe. Deare Ned, I could wisch your chamber weare in Linconsine and not in the laine ouer against it; those lains weare the vnsweatests places in Loundoun, and allways the siknes is in thos placess. I could wisch you had rather bine in the Tempell or Graseine. Grasein mythinkes is a fine place. I would haue you tell your father what I thinke of your chamber and the howes. I would haue write to him about it meself, but that I thought it might trubell him to reade so longe a letter. I longe to heare how you are prouided for a man, and whoo shall mainetaine Gorge at Oxford; for I heare he has not write to his father aboute it this mornig. Merredifes hows that Mr. Simons liued in fell on firer, but thankes be to God, theare was not much hurt doun, only the walls of the kichen burnt and pulled doune; the loos is thought to be about 3*l*. Mr. Ballam is fallen sike againe; he is no ouer wise man. I thanke God your brothers and sisters are well. The protestation was taken on sabath day last at Bromton, Wigmore and Lainterdine, with much willingnes. I desire to know wheather you tooke it. I pray God blles you, and giue you a comfortabell meeting with

Your most affectinat mother,   BRILLIANA HARLEY.

May 21, 1641.   **Bromton Castell.**

I haue sent you a peace of angelica rooat: you may carry it in your pocket and bite some times of it.

CXVIII.

For my deare sonne Mr. Edward Harley.

Deare Ned—The shurenes of the carrier, tho he is slow, makes me writ by him, tho I purpos and pleas God to write by the mersser, whoo goos towards Loundoun on munday. I am glad that justice is excicuted on my lord Straford, whoo I thinke dyed like a Senneca, but not like one that had tasted the mistery of godlyness. My deare Ned, let theas exampels make you experimentally wise in Gods word, which has set forth the prosperity of the wicked to be but for a time; he flowreschess but for a time in his life, nor in his death has peace; but the godly has that continuall feast, the peace of a good contience, and his end is peace, and his memory shall not rot. I thanke God that I hard you weare well, for I haue bine in feare of it all this weake. I thanke God your brothers and sisters are well. I haue keepe my beed sence munday. Deare Ned, be carefull of your self, and I pray God blles you. So I rest,

Your most affectinat mother, BRILLIANA HARLEY.

May 21, 1641. *Bromton Castell.*

CXIX.

For my deare sonne Mr. Edward Harley,
in Wesmester, neare the Parlament Howes.

Deare Ned—I thanke you for your letter by the Wellcheman; beleeue it, your letters cannot come to offten to me. I blles God that you are well, and I hope the Lord will keepe you so, and in good time giue me, whoo longes for it, a happy seeing of you. I knwe not of Mr Yaits his gooing to Loundoun tell this day. I hope buisnes in the parlament will goo one smouthly, and I hope your father will come downe and you in June. I was allways of the minde, that Gorge would not stay with you but to sarfe his owne turne. I pray God send you a religious and a good natured saruant. Deare Ned, take my counsell, I beleeue you will not finde it beest to take Gorges his brother; it is a most teadious thinge to be sarued by a chillde, without you had other saruants that might healp out his defects; they want witt and discretion, and haue theair pastions unbrideled, wich all togeeather makes them teadious saruants;

and I consider when you are at the ends of court, and nobody about you but a child, if you should not be well, you would finde it a trubell; and so you would being well; when you imploye him in any saruis you would tast his childeischness in all he did. I speake from experience. I haue had chillderen sarue me; and I finde very yonge men and women no good saruants; and then at the end of a yeare or 2, you will haue him doo as Gorge dous; but if you weare sure he would not, yet I would not haue you take such a youth; you would finde no content in it. If Samuell weare of a good nature, I could wisch you would like him; but he has a sower nature. Pleas yourself in your choyce, and I shall be pleased; but take my word; boys are trubellsome saruants.

I thanke God your brothers are well, and so is your sisters. I am very glad to heare my lord is well, and that my lady Veere is willing to haue Brill; it is my greefe that my condition in health is such, that I can not be of more aduantage to you all than I am. I thanke you for the sparigous you sent me. I pray God blles you, and keepe you in His feare; and, deare Ned, beleeue me to be,

Your most affectinat mother, BRILLIANA HARLEY.

Mr. Ballam has made shift to geet his ague againe. Roger Beeb like a wise man is goon to be maried. I haue not bine out of my beed sence munday. I pray God bringe me well out of it.

May 22, 1641. *Bromton Castell.*

CXX.

For my deare sonne Mr Edward Harley.

Deare Ned,—I thanke you for your letter by Jelly and by the carrier; it is my greate comfort that you are well, and I hope the Lord will continue that mercy to you. I much reioyce that the Lord has sheawed Himself so mightyly for His peopell, in heareing theare prayers; that it is come so fare as that the bischops and all theiare traine is voted against. I trust in God they will be in-acted against, which I longe to heare; and I pray God take all thos thinges away which haue so longe offended. I longe much to see your father and you. I did hope to haue seene you the later end of this month; but now I heare, it will be not tell the begineing of July.

I thanke God your brothers are well, and so are your sisters. Mr. Ballam is abroad, and has begoun to keepe scoule; but as you thought when you weare in the cuntry that he was not wis, so I finde him. Sr William Croft has promised me to come to Bromton at the faire, when I beleeue I shall want your father and you.

On tusday night I had a greate fitt of the stone, but now, I thanke God, I am better. Deare Ned, be carefull of your self, and I beceach the Lord in mercy to blles you, and giue you a happy meeting, with

Your most affectinat mother, BRILLIANA HARLEY.

I am sorry that your father was displeased for not haueing his mony souner: but I did what I could, and so will doo still.

June 5, 1641. *Bromton Castell.*

CXXI.

To her son Edward.

Deare Ned—Had I not this weake reseued a letter from *** by which I heare you and your father were well, I should haue bine very much trubelled; for this weake I haue reseued no letter from your father, nor from you. I know you are careful to rwite to me, becaus you know what a comfort it is to me; thearefore I beleeue your letter has miscarried.

I very much desire to heare how the affaires goo; for I thinke theaire was neuer a more doutfull crisise; but it is the Lord who hoolds the bridell vpon all men, so that they cannot doo what they desire, but in aduancing at theare owne endes, they still bringe to pas the Lords work.

Deare Ned send me word wheather your father * * * * * * * * *

the man for a steward or no. I am grieued with all my hart that the tenants doo not pay theaire rents, that I might send it to your father, whous ocations I hard rather a hundred times weare supplyed then my owne. I should be very glad, if your father would be pleased to bye a coach and haue horrses. I thinke it would not cost him much: and insteed of other horsess, if he keepe coach horsess, which would be of as much vse as other horsess, I thinke I shall be abell to take the ayre in it; and I beleeue it would be much aduantage to my health. And good Ned, tell your father so, and let me pray you to put him in minde of it. The maire and one or two horsess are sike, and so will not be fite to be sould as yet. Your cousin Smith has some remembrance of his ague againe, but I hope it will not last longe.

I pray God blles you and presarue you in health, and giue you a happy and comfortabell meeting with

  Your most affectinate mother, BRILLIANA HARLEY.
1641. *Brompton Castell.*

The letter you rwit to me last weake I had this weake.

CXXII.

For my deare sonne Mr. Edward Harley.

Deare Ned—I cannot let doctor Deodat goo, without leting you know my thoughts are much with you, and I hope I shall see you shortly. I receued your letter by Mr. Griffits: it brought me wellcome nwes, in that it asshured me of your health, which I pray God continue to you. I thanke God your brothers and sisters are well. I am still in beed, but I hope I shall be abell to rise with in thease feawe days. I am sorry doctor Deodat has left the cuntry.

Deare Ned, be carefull of your self for my sake. I pray God bells you and giue you a comfortabell meeting with

  Your most affectinat mother, BRILLIANA HARLEY.
June 14, 1641. *Bromton Castell.*

CXXIII.

For my deare sonne Mr Edward Harley.

Deare Ned—I thanke you for puting me in minde of takeing the ayre; I beleeue it would doo me good, but as yet I haue not made triall of it; but I hope to doo, and if your father weare with me I should doo it with more cheerefullness. I thanke God I am now abell to site out of my beed, and finde meself indeferent well. Every weake begeets nwe desires in mee, for now I very much desire to heare what is become of the biusness of the bischops, which I hope shall downe; but I feare it will finde mighty opotion; but the Lord can make hard things eassy. We must all acknowledg Gods greate mercy in the discouering of so great a plot against His poore peopell. I pray God we may still make God our refuge; that so He may wacthe ouer vs, and then we shall be safe. Deare Ned, rwit me word how the pasage was of Mr Harberds Pris his carage in the parlament, becaus theare is such various reports of it. I beleeue you father takes greate pains. I beceach the Lord strentghen him and direct him in all his ways, and give me a happy and comfortable meeting with your father and you.

Mr Ballam I thinke is a very silly man; he has discouered himself what he is, in his sikness.

I feare your brothers loose theare time very much. Your brother Robrert is very much growne, and I feare spends littell time in gaineing of knowledg, which trubells me much. I hope your father will thinke of some cours for them.

I much wonder at Gorge Griffits, whoo has had so many tyes to you, that he so neglects what you would haue done. I hope your father will not let you goo to Linconsine as longe as he is in Loundoun. Mr. Edwards, you will heare by my cosin Dauis, has by fors keept Bucknell, and cars not for the order of the parlament, which I thinke will be of very ill exampell, if it be not reproufed in him. I will and pleas God, send you some handchorchers as soune as I can.

I pray God blles you, and giue you thos choys bllesings which He only bestowes vpon His beloued ons in Christ: so I rest,

Your most affectinat mother, BRILLIANA HARLEY.

Jne: 19, 1641. *Bromton Castell.*

I pray you tell your father that the cooke I tooke, I was enforsed to put away, he was so naught.

CXXIV.

For my deare sonne Mr. Edward Harley.

Deare Ned—Mr Doughty his stay something affter my cosin Dauis, giues me leaue to begine this weake with a letter to you. I pray God blles you and presarue you from all things that may hurt you eather within or without.

I hard this morning that your father had taken my cosin Wigmors estate into his hand, and vndertaken to pay all his deets. I hope it is not true: send me word wheather you heare any such thing. I would haue write to your father, but I thinke many letters would trubell him: be carefull of yourself for my sake.

Your most affectinat mother, BRILLIANA HARLEY.

June: 21, 1641. *Bromton Castell.*

Just nowe Mr Ballam tell me he is not abell to teach scoule. I pray you tell your father so.

CXXV.

For my deare sonne Mr. Edward Harley.

Deare Ned—Your letters must needs be dubly wellcome, sence they come from you, and make a supply for your fathers not writing. I acknowledg Gods greate mercy, that your father and you are well, which mercy I hope the Lord will continue to you. I am glad corenell Goreing did so well cleere himself. We heare of many more plots; one that Loundon should haue bine seet on firer, and many plots against the parlament; that theare weare porters apointed to take notice of euery parlament mans lodging. I pray you write me word wheather it weare so or no. I desire to trust in the Lord, and that dous stay my hart, or eles I should be much trubeled. I hope the Lord will direct the parlament in such a way as that they may seetell theare affairs, so as that they haue a time to goo into the cuntry, wheare I longe to see your father and you.

I haue written to your father to desire him that your brothers and cosin Smith may goo to Mr Voils tell the scoule be better prouided, or that Mr Ballam returne from Oxford: they loos theair time extremely. I make them translat some thinge out of Latin into Inglisch, but it is but a litell which they doo. Mr Griffits was with me this day; he tells me he will alow Gorge at Oxford 20l. a year; his elledest sonne is to be maried shortly to Mr Knights daughter. I haue writen to your father aboute your brother. Put him in minde to sende me an ansure, for I shall longe for one. I hard a post came downe to Loudlow on tusday, but I had neuer a letter. I thinke it now longe sence I had on from your father. I thanke you for the patterne of worke you sent me. I like it very well, and so well, that if pleas God, I purpose to woorke a shute of chars of it, and I hope you shall inioy them.

I thanke God your brothers and sisters are well, and I am indiferent well.

I pray God blles you and keepe you in His feare, and presarue you in all safety.

    Your most affectinat mother,   BRILLIANA HARLEY.
June: 25, 1641. *Bromton Castell.*

I haue sent you halfe a dusen of handcherchers, tell I send you more.

I thanke you for sending me word that your fathers bisket was goon. I hope to send him more the next weake. I am sorry the meath is not good.

CXXVI.

For my deare sonne Mr. Edward Harley.

Deare Ned—This weake I receued a letter from your father by a man of Kinton. I hope you weare well, tho you did not wirite; and this weake I haue receued no letter by the carrier. Just as I write this, the carrier sent me your letter from Loudlow, which giues me great content; for, deare Ned, you are a great comfort to me, and I hope the Lord will blles you for it. I much reioyce that your father is so well; and I trust the Lord will still inabell him to vndergoo thos waighty affairs which lye vpon him. I feare, as you doo, that it will be Augst before your father will haue time to come downe. I hope you ride some time into Hide parke to take the ayre; and for my sake be carefull of yourself. I thanke you for giuing me some hope of the bischops bill paseing this weake. I pray God effect that mighty worke. My cosen Wigmore was with me yesterday. He tells me your father was very well, but full of buisnes, and that he was 3 times to see him at his loudging, but found him not at home. He tells me you are very much growne, which I am very glad to heare. When he toold me he neuer spake with your father at his loudging, I thought what I had hard was not true. I thanke God I haue found meself much better of late then I haue bine this yeare and halfe, but not so well as I was before that time; and I thinke if your father and you weare with me, I should, I thinke, be better. Mr Ballam is goon to Oxford, and I know not what to doo by your brothers. I thanke God, they and your sisters are very well.

I haue sent your father by this carrier a box, in which is 6 pise, Mrs Osbersons pise. I hope he will like them, but I feare theare is too much spice in them. In that box, and another littell box, I haue sent your father some biskets; theare are 23—6 of them are for your self; the meath was mistaken; it was that which was of the combs; thearefore if your father doo not like it, he may have other sent vp, which is better.

I haue not hard a great while from my sister Wacke and my brother Conway. I desire to heare what your father has doun with Mr. Gwine. I pray God blles you and keepe your hart cloos to Him, so that you may experimentally know the ways of God to be the beest and pleasants way. So I rest,

  Your most affectionat mother, BRILLIANA HARLEY.

I desire to knowe how your littell man pleasess you.
July 2, 1641. *Bromton Castell.*

CXXVII.

For my deare sonne Mr Edward Harley, at Sr Robert Harley, loudging at Mr Gay his howes, Woolstaple, in Wesmester.

Deare Ned—Let theas lines tell you I am glad of all opertunitys by which you may be ashured my thoughts are with you. I hope it will not be longe before I haue the comfort of seeing your father and you, tho when I consider the biusness the parlament is in hand with, I then feare it will be longe. I pray God blless you, and giue you such a true knowledg of the thinges heare below, that you may know them to be but transetory. Your brothers and sisters are well, and I pray God keepe you so.

  Your most affectinat mother, BRILLIANA HARLEY.

July 3, 1641. *Brompton Castell.*

Piner forgot to seet doune Edward Dallys rent in the rent rolle, thearfore he has now sent it: for the rest of the tenants of Kingsland, he says he can make no rent role. Giue this note to your father.

CXXVIII.

For my deare sonne Mr. Edward Harley.

Deare Ned—I thanke for your letter: it was loaded with good newes; so that I may well say it did much cheere me. Your letters are great comforts to me; and tho I want my owne health, yet that your father and you are well makes vp much of mine.

I desire to giue our gratious God the glory of thos great things that has bine doun in the parlament; that the king has past the 3 bills, in which the high commission goos downe; and that they haue proseeded so fare against the bischops. The Lord our God, who can doo great things, I hope will perfect that greate worke. I thanke you for the acts of parlament, and for doctor Dowing booke. I did hope you would haue sent me word this weake when your father had meent to haue come downe, which I longe to heare, and more to see. Your brothers and cosen Smith went on munday last to Wallcot, and so on wensday to Clanuer, wheare they haue a very good chamber, and I hope they will do uery well theare. I thanke God I am reasnabell well, and I roos souner this time out of beed then I vse to doo. Doctor Wright came to see me, and it feell out to be when I keepe my beed. He perswad me to rise, and gaue me some cordiall; but that night I was something ill, but the next day I was well; and I thanke God this day I have bine out of the gate, but no further; and sence it pleased God I was so well affter riseing, and that it feell out accedentally that doctor Wright came to me, I haue entreated him to be with me the next time I am ill; hopeing by Gods mercy to gaine some more liberty out of my beed, which I thinke the keeping of it dous me much hurt. I promis meself your prayers. I am glad you haue toold Mr. Gwine, and I thinke it strange that his father has such an estat and will asshure so littell of it in his eldest sonne. I pray God blles you, as I desire my owne soule should be bllesed.

Your most affectinat mother,   BRILLIANA HARLEY.

July 16, 1641.   *Bromton Castell.*

CXXIX.

For my deare sonne Mr Edward Harley.

Deare Ned—I thanke you for your letter, which I receued the last weake by one of your fathers soulders, and for this weakes letter by the carrier; it is my great comfort that your father and you are well. I hope the same comfortabell hand of Prouidence will still keepe you in all safety; and deare Ned, be carefull of yourself that you doo not ouer heate your selfe, nor to goo into any infected places, and the Lord in mercy presarue you. I did hope to haue seene you and your father shortly, but now I heare theare is littell hope of the agurning of the parlament. I could wisch and desire, if it be so, that your father would aske leaue to come into the cuntry for a littell time. I thinke it would doo you and your father much good. I much reioyce that theare is hope of pasing the bill against bischops; the Lord say Amen to it; we doo not desarue to see such a mercy; but our God, I hope, will worke for His owne name sake. I hope the quene will stay her journy. I forgot to rwit you word that Mr Husbands is maried, and a most abundant loueing cuppell they say they are; and old Mrs Hubbins is goone to liue with her daughter. Mr Gower is goen into Schescheere to his sister Mrs Bursell, whoo has beuried her husband. I thinke Mr Gwine no wis man, that would not haue bine glad, with all his heart, to haue giuen any condistions to haue maried his sonne into such a famely and to such a wife.

Mr Ballam is returned from Oxford, but says he feares he shall not haue his health to teach scoule, thearefore he would only stay tell your father be prouided of a good one. Your brothers are very well at Clanuer, and I think they will learne better theare than at home; but as your father pleases, so I shall be content. Your sisters are very well: I thanke God I haue this weake goon a littell a broode, and I purpos, if pleas God I am any thinge well, and the weather dry, to goo to chruch on saboth day next. I pray God in mercy, if it be His holy will, make me partaker of thos sweet preueleges of His publick ordinancess. I pray God blles you and keepe your hart aboue all the thinges of this life, and I pray God giue you comfortabell meeting with

    Your most affectinat mother,   BRILLIANA HARLEY.
July 23, 1641. *Bromton Castell.*

I beleeue you heare that Mr Griffitt is a maryed man. I thanke you for the kings manifest.

CXXX.

For my deare sonne Mr. Edward Harley, at Sr Robert Harley his Loudging in Wesmester.

Deare Ned—I heare Mr Moore is come downe. I long to heare from him, how your father and you doo. I pray God I may heare well of you, and that I may see your father and you with comfort. If the howes will site still, yet I hope your father will come down for a littell time. I thanke God I was yesterday at chruch, in the morning, but the affternoune was so weet I durst not goo, and I thanke God I finde myselfe reasnabell well to day. Your brothers are well at Clanuer, and your sisters are well. I pray God blles you, as I desire my owne soule should be bllesed. So I rest,

    Your most affectinat mother,   BRILLIANA HARLEY.
July 26, 1641. *Bromton Castell.*

When you see my brother, tell him I present my saruis to him.

CXXXI.

For my deare sonne Mr. Edward Harley.

Deare Ned—I thanke you for your double letter, which was very wellcome to mee. It is Gods great mercy, for which I desire to be thankfull, that your father and you enioye your health. I am sorry that there is no hope of an aorgment of the parlament, for then I feare your father will not come into the cuntrey, where I longe to see you and him. Mr More cam to see mee vpon tusday last. Hee tells me that your father and you are very well: it gaue mee much content to spake with so good a frind, that could tell me how your father and you are. Hee telle mee the queene has stayd hir iorney. I pray God prosper the affaires in the parlament, and the Lord giu a good isue to the bill of the bishops. I was very glad to reciue a letter from my brother. I thinke to send for your brothers home vpon tusday next, and Mr Ballam shall teach them tell your father can get a good on. I haue kept my bed sence thursday last. I pray God bring mee well out of it. I thanke God your brothers and sisters are well. I pray God blese you and giue mee a hapy seeing of you. So I rest,

Your most affectionnat mother, BRILLIANA HARLEY.*
July 31, 1641. *Bromton Castell.*

CXXXII.

For my deare sonne Mr. Edward Harley, in Westmester.

Deare Ned—This weake I haue receued three letters from you, which made the weacke more cheerfull. Sanchky came to Bromton on tusday morning, and this day the boy Rise brought me your letter. I take it as a great mercy that you haue your health, which I hope the Lord will continue to you, that though I wante mine, yet I may haue the comfort that you inioy yours. I am sorry theare is any differance betwne the tow howesess. I beceach the God of peace to presarfe peace betwne them. I am very sorry that the sikness and small pox dous so increes, and I hope you will be willing to come into the cuntry, sence your stay in Loundoun may be of such danger to you. I can not blame you to be vnwilling to leaue so deare a father; yet remember, you come to a mother that loues you. I beceach the Lord to presarfe you from all infextions, and to

* The date and signature of this letter are alone in Lady Brilliana's handwriting.

bring you with much safety into the cuntry; and the Lord I trust will be your keeper in all placess. Deare Ned, if you come downe, be very carefull that you doo not ride to hard; for it is very dangerous to doo so this hote weather, for feare you should ouer heate your blood. The diet was so bade, as Mrs. Wallcote told me, at Clanuer, for your brothers, that I sent for them home on thursday last. I feare it has doun your brother Tome some hurt. He dous not looke well, and his stomake is goon. They did eate nothing but salt meate. Mrs. Wallcot has taken home her sonnes. I am in greate trubell to geet on to teach them; but as yet I can heare of none. Mr. Ballam has not his health, and is resoulued to goo to Oxford.

This time that I keepe my beed I was so ill, that I was constrained to send for doctor Wright; it was an inclination to the stone. I thanke God, I am now indifferent well, and abell to goo out of my chamber. My deare Ned, the Lord in mercy blles you and giue you a happy and comfortabell meeting with,

 Your most affectinat mother, BRILLIANA HARLEY.

Augt: 7, 1641. Bromton Castell.

CXXXIII.

For my deare sonne Mr. Edward Harley.

Deare Ned—I knwe not of this bearers gooing to Loundoun tell it was very late, thearefore, in short, let thease tell you, I longe to see you and your father. I beceach the Lord to keepe you in all safety, and giue you a happy meeting with

 Your most affectinat mother, BRILLIANA HARLEY.

Augs: 9, 1641. Bromton Castell.

CXXXIV.

To her son Edward.

My deare Ned—You cannot tell with what joye I rwite theas lines, in that hope to see you, though it should be but for a littell time. I hope, vnder Gods holy protection, you will have a safe journey downe, and that you will be at Brompton on wensday or thursday. Deare Ned, to see you will much reuiue me in the midst of many sad thoughts. It has very much trubelled me to see the affections of this cuntry so against your father that is worth thousands of them; and he has desarued so well of them: but you are in the right. It is for Gods caus, and then it is an honnor to suffer; * * * * * to trubell me. * * * * * since I conseaue true patience has loue joyned with it, to the persons that doo one rong, yet I thinke as the case stands thus, I shall not be very glad to see any of them. Doctor Wright came to see me on saturday last. They hate him as much as any; and if Petter doo but goo into Heareford, they call him fresch roundhead. They haue hated doctor Wright ever sence he stood for you; and I haue bine told by some that has bine by, that if any spooke against your father, he would tell them he could not indure it; that now they durst not speake before him. He toold me that Mr. Dewe did defend your father very much, and that he loued him for that, though he did not before. I had not seen him in a great while before. He is resolued to giue nothing, but he dous not knowe how it will goo with him.

I hope the horsess will come well to you. Your nag I haue giuen order should be leed, and the younge geldinge.; but, deare Ned, I pray you doo not ride vpon gray-shephard, for he has throwne Samuele twis very desperately. I hope you will be carefull of yourself, and not ride too hard in the heate of the day. I haue not toold any body that you are comeing downe. I pray God blles you, and giue you a most comfortabell meeting with,

  Your most affectionate mother,   BRILLIANA HARLEY.

I pray you aske Anthony * * * * * what Mr. Hauor proclaimed in Shobden chruch. I haue scribbled this letter. I was at the dutys of this day at the fast, so that it is late. When Dr. Wright went away he prayed me to remember his saruis to you. I haue given

Colborne 5l. I pray you let somebody bye a littell barrel of anchouies, becaus you loue them, and a bottell of salad oyle.
(No date.)

CXXXV.

For my deare sonne Mr. Edward Harley.

My deare Ned—I rwite to you yesterday, and doo it as willingly this day. The last night Bagly came home; you will beleeue I had longed for your fathers letters before they came. I now desire to heare of your safe comeing to Loundoun. I hope my lord was not goone before you came, and I hope you will make acquaintance with Sr Jhon Conyars, whoo loue, first for my sake, and then for his owne.

My deare Ned, the Lord of heauen blles you and presarue you from all euill.

Your cozen Cornewell dous not remember her loue to you. Put your father in mind to be carefull of himself: so I rest,

Your most affectinat mother,   BRILLIANA HARLEY.

Your 2 boxes are not sent vp this weake; becaus I sent your father a desell of Meath, and they could not carry them; but the next weake, and pleas God, I will send them.
Pheb: 5, 1641.

CXXXVI.

For my deare sonne Mr. Edward Harley.

My deare Ned—I did the last night, with much contentment, receaue your letter by Jhon Coolborn. I take it for a greate bllesing that you came so well to Loundoun, and that you meet with so good newes theare, as that the bischops are voted in both howes to lous theaire vots theare. I hope the Lord will perfect His owne glorious worke. You know how your fathers biusnes is neglected; and, alas! it is not speaking will sarue turne, wheare theare is not abilltise to doo other ways; thearefore I could wisch, that your father had one of more vnderstanding to intrust, to looke to, if his rents are not payed, and I thinke it will be so. I could desire, if your father thought well of it, that Mr Tomas Moore weare instrusted with it; he knowes your fathers estate, and is an honnest man, and not giuen to greate expences, and thearefore I thinke he would goo the most fruegually way. I knowe it would be some charges to haue him and his wife in the howes; but I thinke it would quite the chargess. I should be loth to haue a stranger, nowe your father is away. Deare Ned, tell your father what I haue rwiten to you, and I pray God derect him in his resolutions; and what he resoulues of, I shall be contened with; so do not forget to tell your father. I did not rwite him word of it, becaus I would not make my letter so longe to him, and I am not very well at this time; being ill, as I vse to be. I haue, by this carrier, sent vp your rwiteing boox, and your boox of bookes. I pray God blles you, and beleeue you are most deare to,

  Your most affectinat mother,   BRILLIANA HARLEY.

I thanke God my coold is goone.

Pheb: 11, 1641.   *Bromton Castele.*

CXXXVII.

For my deare sonne Mr. Edward Harley.

Deare Ned—The last night, as I went to super I receued your letter, sent by the Shwsbury post, and you may beleeue mee, it made mee eat my super with a better stomake then any sause could haue done. I doe much recoige in the kings answer to the petcion of both houses, and that my brother was one of the sixe and threetie lords that voted against the bishopes. I haue sent vp too your father, in youre boxe of books, 2 paire of riding stockings, and I haue sent by this carry, a boxe of pies for my brother and 2 chees fore him. I pray you, if hee bee not gone, doe you take car to haue them sent to my lords from me; and I haue sent your father 2 boxes of biskates. I pray God bles you: be carfull of yourselfe, and let mee heare from you as often as you can, for it is a greate comfrot to,

    Your most affectionat mother,   BRILLIANA HARLEY.*

Brompton Castel, Pheb: 11, 1641.

I am not well, as I writ to you last night, therefore I haue made vse of anothers pen.

CXXXVIII.

For my deare sonne Mr. Edward Harley.

My deare Ned—I send theas by the post of Hariford, becaus I desire your fathers ansure aboute the seeting of his grounds at Kingsland, becaus the yeare is so fare past, thearefore, I pray you, put your father in minde to rwite aboute it, for if his land be not seet, it will be greate loos to him.

I mise you very much; and deare Ned, sometimes thinke of me, tho you cannot mise me. Your brother Robine seemes to be extremely discontented. I wisch your father would rwite to him, to take his minde of it. Your frind, my cosen Cornewell, is no changeling. I thanke God, my coold is goone, and I am now abell to goo out of my chamber againe; but this was the first day. I much desire to heare what is become of our Harifordsheare petetion for bischops; but I more longe to heare the kings ansure to the petetion to take away the bis: vots in parlament.

In Hariford, they haue turned the tabell in the cathedroll, and taken away the cops and bassons and all such things. I hope they begine to see that the Lord is about to purg His church of all such

---

* The signature of this letter is alone in the handwriting of the Lady Brilliana.

inuencions of men. Deare Ned, be carefull of your self, and I beceach the Lord of heauen to blles you, and keepe you, as I desire my owne hart should be keepe.

Your most affectinat mother, BRILLIANA HARLEY.

Pheb: 17, 1641. *Brompton Castell.*

CXXXIX.

For my deare sonne Mr. Edward Harley.

My deare Ned—You desarue many thankes for your letters to me this weeke, which was exceeding wellcome to me, both for the good newes they contained, and becaus they came from you, whoo I mise; for I may booldly say, I haue not bine very merry sence you went. To me, theas mercys of God are such, as may make our harts stand amased at the goodnes of our God, and they are strong bands to tye vs in obedience to our God; for howe can we sinn against so gracious, so mercifull a God, whoo is thus pleased to put forth His wisdome and power, for the healp of His poore chillderen.

I am exceeding glad that Sr Jhon Conyars is leftenant of the tower. I hope you are acquainted with him, and I hope you haue deleuered my letter to my brother. They are now aboute a petecion to the parlament, which I hope will be ready to send vp the next weake. My deare Ned, the Lord of heauen blles you and presarue you from all euill. Put your father in minde to be carefull of himself; and I desire to know wheather he likes the meath, and wheather my brother had the pyes I sent him. We heare of letters that weare intersepted from my lord Digbe. I desire to know wheather theare was any such thing or no. My deare Ned, still beleeue I am beest pleased, when I can expres meself to be,

Your most affectinat mother, BRILLIANA HARLEY.

Pheb: 19, 1641. *Brompton Castell.*

CXL.

For my deare sonne Mr. Edward Harley.

My deare Ned—I can not lette the carrier goo without rwiteing to you, tho I rwite yesterday by the post of Heariford; for could I heare from you and send to you every day, I should be glad.

By the carrier I haue sent a box in which is a cake and 2 schees with the box; they are directed to you. I pray you scrape out the derection to you, and rwite vpon them for my lady Conyars, and let me put you in trust, to send the cake and schees to her from me, without your father contradict; for I pray you tell your father of it. I purpos to rwit to my Lady Conyars by my cosen Dauis, whoo says he will goo on munday. Mun cries out to be goon, because of his carage. I pray God blles you; so I rest,

    Your most affectinat mother,   BRILLIANA HARLEY.

Mar: 6, 1641.

CXLI.

For my deare sonne Mr. Edward Harley.

My deare Ned—I allways longe to heare from you, but this weakes inteligence in the cuntry made me more ernest to heare, and theare-fore, I with much joy receued your letter last night by the carryer: that your father and selfe inioye your health is much comfort to me; and, deare Ned, be carefull of yourself for my sake.

Many feares did aris in the cuntry, because the kinge gaue such a refusall to the requeste of both howes, but I hope the Lord will be gratious to this poore land; it was a most remarqabell thinge that shpe was cast away, in which thos fopperis weare. I wisch they may have eyes to see Gods hand.

I haue no desire at all, that a stranger should come to looke to your fathers biusness. Now your father is away, you know that I have no body I can speake to; and if Piner goo away, whoo I dare trust with any thinge, and whoo I know loues your father and me, I should much want him; thearefore I desire not to haue any other, that must so wholy put Piner away. I should haue bine glad to haue had Mr Moore, the time your father was away. I am very glad you like your cosen Conway so well. Your cosen Smith is ill, which has something trubeled me; it is not an ordinary ague he has; he is now in his fitt. I thinke doctor Wright will be with him this day.

I rwite by the post, becaus there is a man that would lay out a 1000*l.* on something for liues, and he desire a speady ansure.

I was ill affter I rwite last to you, as I vse to be, so that I can not yet make the pyes for your father. I pray God blles you, as I desire the soule should be blles of

    Your most affectinat mother,   BRILLIANA HARLEY.
Mar: 12, 1641.

CXLII.

For my deare sonne Mr. Edward Harley.

My deare Ned—I did thinke to haue made Hall stay tell munday, that so I might haue had so much time more to haue rwite to you in; but Piner sends vp 20*l.* to venture in the Irisch wars, and thearefor they desire he might goo with the carryer. I hope things goo one well in the parlament, and that the discontent with the Loundoners is not so much as it is said to be in the cuntry. I am exceeding glad that the affaires goo so well in Ireland. They are about a petecion, but they can not so well agree aboute it, and thearefore I know not when it will be ready.

I will, if pleas God, make the pys your father sends for. I wisch your father would bye a cooch and haue cooch horsess; I should hope to be abell to take the ayre sometimes. To-morrow theare is a sacrement, and I hope to be at it, thearefore I can say no mor at this time, becaus it is late.

Deare Ned, be carefull of yourself, and I beceach the Lord to blles you and to fill you with gras, and give me a comfortabell seeing of you.

Your most affectinat mother, BRILLIANA HARLEY.

(No date.)

Deare Ned, send me word wheather your father venturs any thinge in Irland, and wheather you thinke that it will be sure and profitabell aduenture into Irland, and wheather it may be doun without much truebell.

CXLIII.

For my deare sonne Mr. Edward Harley.

Deare Ned—I thanke you for your letter by Hall. I did much long to receaue the declaration to the kinge. I thanke you for it; I am sorry the kinge is pleased yet, not to conseaue anny better thoughts of this parlament. The Lord be mercifull to this poore land, and to this cuntry wheare I ame; for I thinke theare is not such another. I heare the justices haue sent vp theare ansure, why they would not take the protestation. Sr William Crof gouerns all of them. Mr Braughton tells me you had taken coold and weare not very well with it. I shall longe to heare how you doo. Deare Ned, be carefull of yourselfe, and I pray God blles you and presarue you in health. I am very well content your father should take another, that his estate might be well looked to, but I desire Piner may stay to receaue the mony, and to lay it out. I thanke God, your cosen Smith is much better. I will, if pleas God, prouid your linnes as soune as I can. I haue by this carrier sent your father 12 pyes and a schees. Mr Braghton brought me no letter from you, which made me sorry; but more sorry that you weare not well. I hope shortly you will have the peticion for this county, but Sr William Croft disswaded it, as a thing vulawfull to petecion. So I rest,

Your most affectinat mother, BRILLIANA HARLEY.

Mar: 19, 1641.

CXLIV.

To her sonne Edward.*

* * * * * * * * * * *
by your * * * * * by the keeper. I see thinges stand in a doutful maner, and our healp must be from our God, and I trust the Lord will presarue His poor childeren. I haue not bine well theas 2 days, or elles I could rwite much more to you. Mr Smith told what I rwit to you by Mr Braughton. I do not * * * * * * your sister Brill * * * * * * * * * journey * * * * . I hope Mr Moore will goo munday come sen-night, and Mr Yaets is resolued and pleas God to goo then; and becaus of the fast of the next weake, I am desirous she shoude stay till that be past. I pray God blles you, as I desire the soul should be bllesed of

Your most affectinat mother,   BRILLIANA HARLEY.
April 22, 1642.

I haue made 2 shirts for you till I make more. I purpos to send them this weake.

CXLV.

For my deare sonne Mr. Edward Harley, at Mr. Cooles howes, in Chanell Row.

My deare Ned—I cannot let Mr Moore goo without a letter to you, tho I rwite to you yesterday by the post of Ludlow. I am perswaded thinges are now come to theaire ripenes, and if God be not very mercyfull to vs, we shall be in a distressed condistion; but the Lord has promised to heare His chillderen in the day of trubell, and to deliuer them, which I am perswaded He will doo nowe.

I longe euery day to heare from you; I beceach the Lord to presarue you; and deare Ned, be carefull of yourselfe. I haue receued a box with maeth and 2 bandeleres; but the box was open, befor it

---

* This letter is much injured by damp.

came to me. I purpos, and pleas God, that your sister Brill shall begine her journey to Loundoun on munday comsenight, and Piner and Hackelet shall goo with her. Mr Yeats, I beleeue, will goo with her; your cosen Smith has not bine well, tho his ague was goone, so that I was faine to send for doctor Wright for him. He came when the keeper brought your letter, which was on friday, so he meet your letter, for which he returnes many thankes, and would not now rwite to you, becaus he desires when he dous, to rwit aboute Potters biusness, which he will, when he has spoken with a lawer. He desires you would doo him the fauor to bye him 2 muskets and rests and bandeliers, and 15 or 16 pound of poweder in a barell, and he desires you would send them by Lemster carrier, and so derected them to Brompton, and he will giue order to haue them sent to Heariford, and will send you what they cost.

I am not yet very well, and yesterday I was something ill. I pray God blles you and presarue you in all safety; so I rest,

Your most affectinat mother,   BRILLIANA HARLEY.

Apri: 23, 1642: Brompton Castell.

Doctor Wright telles me that Mr Weafer is still sike, and for his part he would haue doun his vtmost, that you might haue had that place.

CXLVI.

For my deare sonne Mr. Edward Harley.

My deare Ned—You cannot conceaue how wellcome your letters are to me; yet beleeue I giue you thankes for them. I receued one by the post and another by the carrier this weake. I see the distance is still keepe betwne the kinge and parlament. The Lord in mercy make them one, and in His good time incline the kinge to be fully assured in the faithfull counsell of the parlament. Our God has doun greate thinges, and I hope He will still glorify Himselfe in exerciseing of His mercy to vs His poore saruants. And, my deare Ned, it is my greate comfort that you haue made your God your confidence; and this is most sure, He will neuer faile you. I purpos, and pleeas God, your sister Brill shall begine her journey to Loundoun on munday next, and I hope shee will be abell to reache Wickam by wensday night; wheare I hope shee shall meete you at the Catterne wheele; shee much longes for this journey. Piner and Hackelet and Prichard goo vp with her, and Mr Yeats and his wife. This night Mr Old tells me that Mr Nweport is maried; for my Lady Nweport sent to Shrewsbury to haue the bells rounge for it. I wishee, and please God, I had the like ocation of reioyceing. Your cosen Smith is now well. Doctor Wright stayed with him 3 or 4 dayes, and gaue him somethinge, which has doun him much good.

I was ill when docter Wright was with your cosen Smith, and so I haue bine sence he went; but I haue taken nothing of him sence you went.

Deare Ned, be careful of yourselfe, and I beceach the Lord in much mercy to blles you whith all His bllessings, and I wisch you much ioye in your nwe lodging in Lincons Ine. I beleeue your father misses you, and I am sure I doo. I pray you send me word how you like your commons; so I rest,

Your most affectinat mother,   BRILLIANA HARLEY.

Apr: 29, 1642, *Brompton Castell.*

Mr Gower is very well pleased that he is chosen on of the ministers.

CXLVII.

For my deare sonne Mr. Edward Harley.

My deare Ned—But that I loue to say something to you my selfe, I might thinke this letter might be spared, sence your sister is the bearer of it, whoo can tell you how how all dous at Brompton; but, becaus shee cannot giue me the content by her discours with you, as if I did so, I am glad to take this way of discours; for I exceedingly long to see you, and I hope God will, in His good time, giue me that comfort. I haue sent you 2 shirts by your sister and haue sent for cloth to make you 4 more, which shall be sent you, as soune as I can, if pleas God.

I hope theas will meete you at Wickam, wheare I know and at Loundon, you will be very carefull of your sister; shee is yonge, thearefore, deare Ned, obsarue her carage, and let not your counsell be wanting to her, and I hope shee will have so much wisdome to take it. I am toold that Sr William Croft shall be burges if Mr Weafer dye, whoo they say is very sike. I cannot but let you know what hapned the other day, which may shame all the rest that haue spoken ill of your dear father. I was toold, that on Mr Fox spake ill of your father, which he hard of, and came to me to excuse himself, with many protestations, that he neuer did so, and how ready he would be to doo your father saruis: he is Mr Foxes sone, that is at Creete; your sister Brill can tell you all the story of it. Let your father know of it. I pray God blles you with all the grases of His spirit. So I rest,

Your most affectinat mother,   BRILLIANA HARLEY.
Apr: 30, 1642.   *Brompton Castell.*

On the back of the letter are the following arithmetical processes.

```
    b    Ll    b                        216
  216 — 9 — 767                          31
           9                            ———
         ———                             216
     216)6903                            648
      —— 42                             ———
      31¹ ———                           6696
           207                           207
           ———                          ———
           216                          6903
```

CXLVIII.

To her sonne Edward.

My deare Ned—I beleeue some buisines hindered your rwiting this weake or ells I should haue promised myself a letter from you; for you know how much I loue to have a letter from you. I should wisch you would begine a letter on monday and take the whoole weake to rwite it in, that so I might know from you how thinges goo, and how your sister Brill pleases my lady Veare. I feare theare will be blowes struck. I pray God prepare vs for thos times.

Deare Ned, tell your father that the plumer of Woster is now casting the leads; the timber was very rotten; he seems to be an honest man. I wisched you with me to day, to see him cast it. I thanke God your brothers and sisters are well. I pray God blles you, and giue you a comfortabell meeting with

Your most affectinat mother,   BRILLIANA HARLEY.

I hope you doo not forget to spend some time to learne French. I pray you send me word wheather you doo. I hope you haue reseaued the letter I sent by Mr Moore.

(No date.)

CXLIX.

For my deare sonne Mr. Edward Harley.

My deare Ned—Your letter by the post and by the carrier are both very wellcome to me; for besides the knowledge you giue me of the publicke affaires, the assurance of your health is very deare to me. We all are ingaged deepely to pray ernestly to our God, that He will giue both wisdome and corage to the parlament, and I hope the Lord will so giude them that the mouths of thos that would speake euill of them shall be stoped. I thanke you for desireing me not to beleeue rumors. I doo not; becaus I assure meself I shall heare the truth of thinges from your penn. It is the Lords greate worke, that is now a frameing, and I am confident, it will be finished with much beauty, so that the very enimyes shall be enforsed to acknowledg it has bine the Lord that has rought for His caus and chillderen; against home they will finde that theare is no deuination nor inchantment.

We hard that the Kenttiche peticion was brought by 3000 men, and that 3000 Loundoners meete them vpon Blacke Heath and theare fought, and many weare killed. And now we heare that Sr Francis Wortly drwe his sword and asked whoo was for the king, and so 18 foolowed him. I thinke this later may be true; but for the fight vpon Black Heath, I know it is not true.

I am glad our Heariford peticion is come to Loundoun, and I hope deliuered before this: your sister, I hope, meet you at Wickcam on wensday last. Deare Ned, send me word how my lady Veere vsess her, and how shee carriers herself.

I pray God blles you with a large measure of gras and with all the comforts of this life.

  Your most affectinat mother, BRILLIANA HARLEY.
May 6, 1642.

CL.

For my deare sonne Mr. Edward Harley.

My deare Ned—Tho my letter can bring you no other inteligence then of the deere affection of a mother that loues you dearely, yet I will beleeue it shall haue a wellcome. By this time, I thinke your sister has lefte wondering at Loundoun. I long to heare how she dous: deare Ned, put her in minde to be carefull of herselfe.

Mr Gower is very well pleased that he is chosen. I pray God derect them all, that theare may be a full reformation. I purpos, and pleas God, to send you 4 more shirts as soune as I can. I haue taken on to waite vpon your cosen Smith and your brothers. It is on that came out of Schescheere; he borded at Mrs Pirsens; his name is Raphe; he dous it for his diet without wages, and yet he dous it very well; he is a very honnest man; I beleeue you remember him. I pray you tell your father of it; they did much wante one to looke to them. Your sister Doll has not bine very well, and shee lookes very lamentabell. Deare Ned, I longe to see you, and I pray God giue me a comfortabell inioying of that comfort.

I pray God blles you, as I desire the soule should bee bllesed of
  Your most affectinat mother, BRILLIANA HARLEY.

They haue so mocked at our Hearifordsheere petion, that I long to heare what they say to it at Loundoun.

May 7, 1642. Brompton Castell.

CLI.

For my deare sonne Mr. Edward Harley.

My deare Ned—Mr Voile is in hast, so that I haue only time to let you know you are much in my thoughts; and as I think of you, so I much longe to see you. I pray God derect the parlament, and the Lord of heauen blles you: so I rest,
  Your most affectinat mother, BRILLIANA HARLEY.

May 7, 1642.

CLII.

For my deare sonne Mr. Edward Harley.

My deare Ned—I doo so much desire to see you, that I take offten rwiteing to you, in the place of it, tell I can see you. Piner says littell, which makes me thinke that your father said some thing to him. I pray you send me word wheather your father will take another or no: and, deare Ned, aske Mr. Smith whoo toold him what he toold Mr. Braughton. I desire much to knowe whoo it was. I hope something will be doun to docter Rogers.

I haue sent you, by the carrier, 8 botteles of cider in a box derected to you, and a runlet of sider to your father. I pray you send me on of your scokes, to make you nwe onse by. Your shirts you shall haue shortly, if pleas God. I desire to heare how Sr Jhon Conyars comes off for Onells escape.

I pray God blles you and keepe you in His feare, and giue you comfortabell seeing of

  Your most affectinat mother,   BRILLIANA HARLEY.

(No date.)

CLIII.

For my deare sonne Mr. Edward Harley.

My deare Ned—I am glad your sister Brill has the joy of seeing you, tho I can not: but I hope God will againe giue me that comfort. Your sister Brill did looke much paler; I thinke, by resen of her ernest desire to goo vp to Loundoun. I much desire to knowe how my lady Veere likes her. I thanke you for your letter by Piner; it was wellcome; but I had no letter from you by the carrier or post: but your father rwiteing to me by the post, and letting me knowe you weare to see the soulders on tuesday last, I tooke it, that that hindered you.

Deare Ned, I sent you a letter to your father from Mr Gower; I hope you receued it; and I hope it will be thought fitt that the publischers of such ventings of such matter as the enclosed sermon was, will be thought fite to be sencured; and I thinke if Mr Schirbere be reproufed, it would be very well. I pray God blles you, and giue you a comfortabell meeting with

  Your most affectinat mother,   BRILLIANA HARLEY.

Deare Ned, send me word how Sr Jhon Conyars ansured Oneles gooing out of the Tower.

May 13, 1642. Brompton Castell.

CLIV.

For my deare sonne Mr. Edward Harley.

My deare Ned,—A short letter will saruc to let you know how Harifordsheare stands, when Mr. Braughton is the bearer of it: thearefore I will say nothing of what is doun abroode, only tell you of your frindes at Brompton, wheare I longe to see you.

This day I hard out of Linconscheere: I thank God they are all well: but I see my brother Pelham is not of my minde. I thinke now, my deare sister was taken away that shee might not see that which would haue grefed her harte.

Sr William Pelham rwites me word he has giuen vp his liftenatcy and his gooing to Yorke, to the king; being his saruant, as he rwites me word, and so bound by his oth.

Deare Ned, send me word wheather your sister lookes as pale as shee did. I haue not bine well theas 3 dayes, but it is as I vse to be. Your sister Dorrity has bine exceeding ill: shee fell ill about 10 days sence. I was very unwilling to send for any docter, tell shee grwe very ill, and so ill, that I much feared her; and I sent for docter Wright, whoo went away this morning. I hope now shee will recoruer, tho I still feare her: shee lookes most lamentabell, and is growne weake; but I hope God will be mercifull to her.

I hope to send you your shirts shortly. I pray God blles you and presarue you in all safety: and deare Ned, let me heare the truth of thinges, tho it be bade. We heare that the kinge will sommon all that will be for him, to come to him.

I pray God compos thinges to His glory and His chruches advantage.

  Your most affectinat mother,   BRILLIANA HARLEY.

I haue receued docter Wrights armes you sent downe.

May 17, 1642. *Brompton Castell.*

CLV.

For my deare sonne Mr. Edward Harley, theas Loundoun.

My deare Ned—The ocation of this letter is to let you knowe that Mr. Weafer is dead. Doctor Wright has exprest a very greate deale of frindeshipe to you in this biusnes, more then this short time will let me tell you. This mornig doctor Wright came to me presently affter 7 a cloke; he thinkes that if your father can make Mr. Seaborne ferme to him, and gaine Mr. Ellton to preueale with yonge Mr. Weafer, that you will haue it. I will, in the meane time, rwite to Mr. Ellton, and doctor Wright will carry the letter to him. But this is the question, that you must be a burges of theare towne, which I bide Mr. Davis tell them you would: but it seemes he did not so cleerely; for that was one reson that made doctor Wright come to me, to let me knowe, that if you weare not burges, you could not be one. Doctor Wright is so ernest that you should haue this, that he perswaded me to send to your father, that nothing might be left vndone. If your father be displeased that I send so to him, you must healp to make my excuse. If please God, I should be very glad you might be in this imployment. The Lord prosper our indeuors and blles you. In great hast,

Your most affectinat mother, BRILLIANA HARLEY.

Samuell promises me to be with you on saterday . . I pray you rwit doctor Wright thankes, and pray your father to doo so. I did not tell now thinke he had borne so much good will to Brompton, as I see he dous.

May 19, 1642.

Deare Ned, put your father in minde, if he thinkes best to doo so, to rwite to Sr William Croft for his healpe.

CLVI.

For my deare sonne Mr. Edward Harley.

My deare Ned—I thanke you for your letter this weake by the carrier, and for your promis of one by the post; but I receued none by him. I beleeue you weare hindred from rwiteing. Samuell, I hope, came to you on saterday. I was vnwilling to leaue any thinge vndone that might further your being chosen for the parlament; in which, if it be the Lords will, I should be very glad you might acte your first saruis for the commonwellth. To tell you now what has bine doun; I must first let you know that doctor Wright is very eruest in it; as soun as Mr Weafer was dead, he sent his man to let me know so; and when I rwite him word that I desired he should try his frindes for you, he did so. When Mr Dauis came to towne, as Mr Davis toold me, he found no incoragement; but I had directed him to goo to doctor Wright, and he put him in such a way, that he had good hopes of it. Doctor Wrights frinde, as Mr Dauis toold me, was very desirous to haue you, and saide you must be made free of theare towne, to which he would giue all his assistance.

As I rwit yesterday to you, doctor Wright staid diner and tooke a letter from me to my cosen Ellton, which he saide he would delever himself. It was his counsell to me to rwite to him; for his daughter has married Mr Weafers sonne, and yonge Weaffer has power ouer many voces. Doctor Wright perswaded me to rwite to my cosen Vahan, whoo has interest in some of the alldermen. I haue doun so; and if the mesenger returne to night, I will rwite you word, what hope theare is. Mr Dauis spake of himself to Sr William Croft; he toold Sr William Croft that he, heareing in Heariford of the death of Mr Weaffer, he desired his masters sonne might haue that place, and desired him that he would be pleased to giue his assistance to it. It was doctor Wright counesele to Mr. Dauis. Sr William Croft ansured, hee would not medel in it; he would leaue all men to themselfes; and such an ansure your sweet hart made Mr Dauis. Antony Child, whoo I sent to my cosen Vahan, brought me this inclosed leter; by which you will see Mr Vahan is not come home. Childe tells me, they say at Heariford that Sr William Croft or Mr Allderne shall be. Deare Ned, let you and me commite this to the wise directions of our God, and be well contented with the issue He shall pleas to giue. I pray God blles you.

Your most affectinat mother,   BRILLIANA HARLEY.
May 20, 1642: *Brompton, at night.*

CLVII.

For my deare sonne Mr. Edward Harley, thease Loundoun.

My deare Ned—I hope you are well, though I had no letter from you by the post, and I shall longe tell I receaue the assurance of yours and your fathers being well. This day doctor Wright rwite me word, he made no question but that you would haue voices enowe in Heariford; yesterday he spent in gaineing as many as he could; this day he went to Leadbury with my letter to my cosen Ellton. Doctor Wright rwite me word, that some of the alldermen toold him that it would be very well, if you did come downe, to be 2 or 3 dayes in Heariford; but that is as your father shall thinke fite; but if pleas God, that you be made free of theare towne, and to be so you must haue Mr Seaborns assistance; if he be constant to your father, it will I hope, doo well. I was very sorry that I had not an ansure from Mr Ellton before I rwite this letter. Doctor Wright rwit me word, he hears none spoken of to haue it besides you, but Mr Prise of Wistanstone (Mr Prises father, that is of the parlament), and Mr Hoskins; but they stir not yet. I pray God blles you, and the Lord in mercy giue you suich a large porcion of wisdome, that you may be very abell to doo your cuntry saruis. I thanke God I am reasnabell well, and your brothers and sisters are well; only Doll is not well, and has bine very ill this night. Deare Ned, put your sister in minde to be carefull of her self.

Your most affectinat mother, BRILLIANA HARLEY.
May 21, 1642: Brompton Castell.

CLVIII.

To her son Edward.

My deare Ned—I must tell you once againe, that I haue had no letter from you this weake, but Sankey rwites me word that you are well, and that makes me glad. I should haue bine very glad to haue receaued derections from your father, wheather I should doo any more in getting voices for you about Heariford. I haue spoken to many who haue promised me, and young Mr Weafer, if hee doo not stand for it himself.

If Mr. Ellton is nowe in London, I pray you tell your father, that if it pleas him, he may speake to him. If you did rwite any letter by the post, he has played the naughty fellow, and then I pray you rwite no more by him. I pray God blles you, and giue you a most comfortabell meeting with

Your most affectinat mother, BRILLIANA HARLEY.
*May 27, 1642: Brompt*m *Castell.*

CLIX.

For my deare sonne Mr. Edward Harley.

My deare Ned—I did very much longe to heare from you, and I thanke God this night I receaued your letter by Samuell. I will doo no more in the biusness for Heariford, tell I see what my lord Scidmore sonn will doo.

You are much behoolding to doctor Wright, for he has stood very hard for you, tho some threaten him much for it, that they shall loose theare frindshp. If you have not this, I hope you shall haue another.

I pray God blles you: so in great hast, for it is very late, I rest,
Your most affectinat mother, BRILLIANA HARLEY.

May 28, 1642: *Brompton Castell.*

CLX.

For my deare sonne Mr. Edward Harley.

My deare Ned—I am very sorry I haue had no letter from you this weake. Deare Ned, rwite to me, tho it be but 2 or 3 words. I sent to Heariford to let them know that I hard that my lord Scidmors sonne would stande for the burgesshp, and then I did not further desire it for you; but gaue them many thankes for theare good will to you, and desired if my lords sonne did not stand, that then they would giue you theare vosies, which they then promised they would, and tooke my thankes very well. I pray God blles you and giue me a joyfull seeing of you: so I rest,
Your most affectinat mother, BRILLIANA HARLEY.

June 3, 1642.

CLXI.

For my deare sonne Mr. Edward Harley.

My deare Ned—Now I thanke you for your letter by Mr Braughton, whoo brought it this day somethinge late, so that I am shortned in time to rwite to you.

I thinke we must all acknowledeg Gods greate mercy that the plot for the takeing of Hull was discouered. I pray God derect the parlement what they ought to doo, for they haue enimyes enough to looke with on euill eye at what theare actions.

At Loudlow they seet vp a May pole, and a thinge like a head vpon it, and so they did at Croft, and gathered a greate many about it, and shot at it in deristion of roundheads. At Loudlow they abused Mr Bauges sonne very much, and are so insolent that they durst not leaue theare howes to come to the fast. I acknowledg I doo not thinke meself safe wheare I am. I loos the comfort of your fathers company, and am in but littell safety, but that my trust is in God; and what is doun in your fathers estate pleasess him not, so that I wisch meselfe, with all my hart, at Loundoun, and then your father might be a wittnes of what is spent; but if your father thinke it beest for me to be in the cuntry, I am every well pleased with what he shall thinke beest. I haue sent you by this carryer, in a box, 3 shirts; theare is another, but it was not quite made; on of them is not wasched; I will, and pleas God, send you another the next weake, and some handchersher. I rwite yesterday to you by the post of Loudlow, how my thankes was taken at Heariford.

I pray God blles you and keepe you from sinn, and from all other euills, and giue you a joyfull meeting with

Your most affectinat mother,   BRILLIANA HARLEY.

Your sister Doll is not well, shee has a great weakenes vpon her; yet I thanke God this day shee is somethinge better than shee was.

June 4, 1642: *Brompton Castell.*

CLXII.

To her son Edward Harley.

My deare Ned—You haue now made amens for not rwiteing the last weake, becaus you haue rwite by the post and promis me another letter by Hacklett, whoo I hope will be with me this night. I longe to see her that shee may let me know how you doo, which I should be glad to be an eye witness of meselfe; for beleue me I longe to see you, and I wisch you were with me to morrow on the faire day. I hope they will be quiet, tho I somethinge feare it. I am sorry you finde that paine in your head. I beseach the Lord to free you from it, and to blles the phisecke to you, which you haue taken. I shall extremely longe to heare how you are affter it; and pray, deare Ned, send me word particularly how you doo, or elles I shall not haue much contentment. I pray God that it be true, that the lords will return to parlament, which I thinke will much work upon others. Your brothers and sisters are well, only your sister Dorroty. I hope you take care of your sister Brill, and pray let me pray you to send me word, how my lady Veare likes her.

Mr Braughton is now come that he may keepe the faire quiet, and Mr Floyd has mustered vp his fors; and then you must remember he is a buissy man. My cosen Cornewall is goone. I pray God blles you, as I desire my owne soule should be bllessed: and rest

Your most affectinat mother, BRILLIANA HARLEY.

June 10, 1642.

CLXIII.

For my deare sonne Mr. Edward Harley.

My deare Ned—I thanke you for your letter by Hackelet; I much reioyce to heare you are well, and longe to see you. Your fathers horses could not be sould at the faire, thearefore I thinke and pleas God, to send them vp on munday or tusday, when I hope to rwite to you more at large, for now I haue defered rwiteing tell it be late, that I might let you know howe the faire went. I thanke God heatherto it has past quietly, but I was somethinge afraide, becaus they are growne so insolent.

I hope this night will be as quiet as the day has bine. I pray God blles your phiseke to you; and, deare Ned, let me know how you doo in euery particular. I hope to send you your other shirt by Martaine, when he bringes vp the horses.

I pray God blles you and keepe you in all safety; so I rest

Your most affectinat mother, BRILLIANA HARLEY.

I haue sent your father a box of Shrewsbury cakes.

Just as I am rwiteing theare is a quarell begoun.

June 11, 1642.

CLXIV.

For my deare sonne Mr. Edward Harley.

My deare Ned—I thanke you for your letter by the carryer. I hope your phisek has doun you good, and I pray God it may. We must all ioyne our sorrows togeather that the kinge yet hoolds of. I dout not but that the Lord will perfect His great worke, He has begoun.

I purpos, and pleas God, to send Martane with the horsses your father sent for, on munday next. I doute not but that your father will giue to his vtmost for the raiseing theas hoors, and in my opinion it weare better to borrow mony, if your father will giue any, then to giue his plate; for we doo not know what straits we may be put to, and thearefore I thinke it is better to borrow whillst on may, and keepe the plate for a time of neede, without your father had so much plate, that he could paret with some, and keepe some to sarue himselfe another time. This I doo not say, that I am vnwilling to part with the plate or any thing ells in this case; if your father cannot borrow mony, I thinke I might finde out some in the cuntry to lend him some. Deare Ned, tell your father this, for I haue not rwite to him aboute it. I haue not bine very well this day, but it is as I vse to be, and I thanke God so much better, as I keepe not my chamber. Your sister Dorroty is much better then shee was, and I hope shee will doo well, though I was much afraide of her.

I pray God blles you and giue you a comfortabell meeting with

Your most affectinat mother, BRILLIANA HARLEY.

June 17, 1642. *Brompton Castell.*

CLXV.

To her son Edward.

My deare Ned—If you beleaue how glad I am to haue this paper discours with you, you will read it as willingly as I rwite it. Since your father thinkes Hearefordsheare as safe as any other country, I will thinke so too; but when I considered how long I had bine from him, and how this country was affected, my desire to see your father, and my care to be in a place of safety, made me ernestly desire to come vp to Loundoun; but since it is not your father's will, I will lay aside that desire. But, deare Ned, as you haue promised me, so let me desire you to let me know how thinges goo. This night I hard that my lord Savile was dead. I desire to know wheather it be so or no; and wheather my lord Paget be goon to York. I heare that on Mr Mason carride a letter from the justices of this country to the king at York, to let him know that they would sarue him with theare lives and estats. I thought it had bine with the petition they made for the bischops, but they say, it was with a letter. When d^r Wright was with Mr James, he toold me you had rwite to him aboute Petters bill, and that it was well if some lords weare spoken to: he desires me to make some means to speake to my lord Brooke, which I promised him I would; thearefore, good Ned, eather speake yourselfe to my lord Brooke, or get somebody to speak to him, that when the bill comes into the lords he may further it. This day Mr. Dauis came from Heareford, wheare he went to preach, by the intreaty of some in the town, and this befell him: when he had ended his prayer before the sermon, which he was short in, becaus he was loth to tire them, 2 men went out of the chruch and cryed "pray God blles the kinge; this man dous not pray for the kinge;" vpon which, before he read his text, he toold them that m^{isters} had that liberty, to pray before or after the sermon for the chruch and state; for all that, they went to the bells and range, and a great many went into the chruch-yard and cryed "roundheads," and some said, "let us cast stones at him!"

and he could not looke out of doors nor Mr Lane but they cryed "roundhead." In the afternoon they would not let him preach; so he went to the cathedral. Thos that had any goodness weare much trubelled and weepe much.

Mr Yats dous much lament doctor Wrights being theare, and says, if he can preuaile with him, he will persuade him to goo to Shreawsbery; which I should be very glad of, becaus he has gained him enemys in standing to geet voices for you. You may see by this how wicked they are growne. I think it beest to let doctor Rogers alone till it pleas God to giue a fairer correspondency between the kinge and parlament, and then I wisch he may be soundly punished.

I thanke God I have bine very well, and so well, that I am abell to goo abroode, when I am not well as I used to be.

I haue sent you a shirt and hafe a dusen handcherchers and some powder for your hair.

I haue rwitten so misrabell that I feare you will hardly reade it, but I hope, this will be leagabell to you, that I desire the Lord to blles you, as I desire my own soul should be bllesed: so I rest,

    Your most affectinat mother,   BRILLIANA HARLEY.

I hope I shall see you this summer; I long for it. I thanke God your brothers and sisters are well. Deare Ned, send me word wheather my cosen Dauis has lost Bucknell or no; he says he has not, and Mr Edwards says he has.

June 20, 1642. *Brompton.*

CLXVI.

For my deare sonne Mr. Edward Harley.

My deare Ned—Your two letters this weake weare exceeding wellcome to me. I thanke God, that you finde yourselfe better affter your pihiseke. Deare Ned, for my sake take care of your ———.

I am very glad to heare that your sister has so much fauor from my lady Veere. I had no letter from your sister this weake. I hope the horsess are come well to your father: and by this carrier I purpos, and pleas God, to send the 2 pistolls you rwite me word your father would haue, and the gillt plate which he has sent for. I am exceeding glad to heare that my lord of Sallsbery and my lord of Clare is come to the parlement. It is a greate comfort to me to see you fixe your thoughts in theas times vpon your God. Your brother Tom has bine extreme ill, and it pleased God, that docter Wright was with Mrs Litellton, and so came to see me as he went home, which I thought fell out happily for your brother. Yesterday I was exceeding fraid of him, but this day, I thanke God, he is better, so that I hope docter Wright may leaue him to-morrow. He fell sike on tusday last; so that, deare Ned, I finde that on trubele fooloows another.

Mr William Littellton being at Loudlow last weake, as he came out of the chruch, a man came to him and looked him in the fase and cryed "roundhead;" he gaue the fellow a good box of the eare and steep to on that had a chugell and tooke it from him and beat him soundly. They say, they are now more quiet in Loudlow. I pray you put your father in mind to consider of that I rwite to him about Mr Yates, and send me word what he says, for I desire they may be punished.

I pray God blles you and giue you a comfortabell meeting with
    Your most affectinat mother,   BRILLIANA HARLEY.

Jne: 24, 1642. *Brompton Castell.*

Deare Ned, send me word wheather my lady Veere giues any thinge in this prouicione for raizing of hors for the good of this poore kingdome.

CLXVII.

For my deare sonne Mr. Edward Harley.

Deare Ned—I loue to rwite to you, and thearefore, my deare Ned, be somethinge glad to receaue my letter.

Sr William Croft came to see me: he neuer asked how your father did; spoke slighty, and stayed but a littele.

I heare that he has commanded the beackon nwe furnisched, and nwe piche put into it. I haue sent to inquire affter it; if it be so, I will send your father word. When Sr William Croft came to me, he came from my lord Harbert. . . . I pray God blles you, and the Lord in mercy send you a comfortabell meeting with

Your most affectinat mother,   BRILLIANA HARLEY.

Jun: 25, 1642.

CLXVIII.

To her son Edward.

My deare Ned—This morning I rwite to you by Mr Greene, but I cannot so offten haue an opertunity as I haue a desire to let you know my thoughts are much with you, and my prayers are for you.

I sent to Mr. Dauis, to enquire about the beackon, but he could not heare that any piche was put into it; only piche was in the howes, wheare the beackon was. I neuer hard of a man so changed as they say Sr William Croft is. He gaue me a slight visit.

I haue sent vp the pistolls your father sent for, by the carrier, which bringes up the littell truncke in which is your shirt and handcherchers, and a bundell derected to your sister. I thanke God your brother Tom is much better, and your sister Dorrity is exceedingly mended. I pray God blles you, and giue you a happy meeting with

Your most affectinat mother,   BRILLIANA HARLEY.

June 25, 1642. Brompton Castele.

I pray you tell your father that the dublet he sent for is in the truncke.

CLXIX.

For my deare sonne Mr. Edward Harley.

My deare Ned—I am not willinge to make an excuse for not rwiteing to you becaus I did so offten the last weake; but I am glad to doo it now. I hope we shall haue better nwes of the affaires than yet we haue, and I am confident the Lord will finisch this His greate worke. And the Lord in mercy hasten it, that the mouths of wicked men may be put to silence. Heariford is growne now wors than Loudlowe. You may gees wheaire they haue theaire incoragement. I haue sent your father another sermon of d^r Rogers. In my opinion, it weare a most just work to punische him: but your father knows beest what is to be doun: but sure it is pitifull that a man should goo on so.

I wisch with all my hart that the howes of lords would send for him, and that would make them startell in this cuntry; and I thinke the lords will be very sencibele of what he says, for he lays lyes enowe to theaire charge. Good Ned, put your father in minde of it. I doo longe almost to haue him punisched. I feare your father dous much neglect himself. Deare Ned, put him in minde of eateing in the morning. I pray God blles you, and giue you a comfortabell meeting with

Your most affectinat mother,   BRILLIANA HARLEY.

June 27, 1642. *Brompton Castell.*

CLXX.

For my deare sonne Mr. Edward Harley.

My deare Ned—I hard very late this night that Mr Moore would goo to Loundoun, and I cannot let him pas without a letter; for, my deare Ned, beleeue me, I long to see, and how glad should I be, if you weare heare at the fast. Docter Wright was send for to Mr James, whoo was very ill, and he, seeing Mr Moore with him, toold me he was to goo to Loundoun: but it was late, and if I doo not send very early, he will be goon; so that I can say no more but that I am,

Your most affectinat mother, BRILLIANA HARLEY.

Jun: 27, 1642.

CLXXI.

For my deare sonne Mr. Edward Harley.

My deare Ned—Had not I hard that you weare well, I should haue allmost haue feared it, becaus I had no letter from you this weake. I did hope eather Martaine or the vnder keeper would haue bine in the cuntry this weake; but, this being saterday, I haue no hope they will come.

I feare your father in theas great binsness will neglect himself; thearefore, deare Ned, put him in minde to eate something in a morning.

I long to see you, and yet, when I thinke you are a comfort to your father, I cannot wisch you from him; yet I desire you weare with me for a littell while; now euery day begeets a nwe longeing in me to heare from you, and to heare how thinges goo.

I pray God blles you and fill you with the grasess of His spirit, and the Lord in mercy presarue you in health, and giue you a comfortabell meeting with

Your most affectinat mother, BRILLIANA HARLEY.

July 2, 1642. *Brompton Castell.*

I beleeue the mending of the howes will cost a greate deale, for the plumers haue 5 sh. a day, and 5 sh. a hundered for casting the leade, besides the carpenters and masons, but I thinke your father will not repent of it when it is doun.

CLXXII.

For my deare sonne Mr. Edward Harley.

My deare Ned—The resen why I send this bearer to your father is, to let him knowe that the kinge has sent a commistion to 12 of the justices to settell the milica. I haue rwite your father theare names. I did not heare it tell late this night. I herd it presently affter diner, but it was but a flyeing report; but now I heare it from one that was at Rudall, when my cozen Rudall was sent for; tell your father that the other as I thinke is Mr Wigmore of Shobdon. I pray God derect your father and the parlament what to doo, and I thinke, if any cuntry had need of some to haue bine sent doun into it, it is this. Your father they are growne to hate. I pray God forgiue them. My deare Ned, I am not afraide, but sure I am, we are a dispised company.

I pray God blles you; in hast I rest,

  Your most affectinat mother,   BRILLIANA HARLEY.

July 5, 1642. *Brompton Castell.*

I thanke God your brothers and sisters are well.

CLXXIII.

For my deare sonne Mr. Edward Harley.

My deare Ned—I receued your letter by Mr. Hill yesterday, and I thanke God that I heare you are well; the Lord in mercy continue that comfort to me.

They goo on with the milica in this cuntry; the sherafe has sent out warents that they apeare on the 15 of this month at Herifrd. Your fathers company, I heare, they meane to make offer to you, and if you will not haue it, they will giue it to another. They trihumfe brafely, as they say, and threaten poore Brompton; but we are in the hand of our God, whoo I hope will keepe vs safe. I pray God blles you, as I desire the soule should be bllesed, of

   Your most affectinat mother,   BRILLIANA HARLEY.
July 8, 1642.

CLXXIV.

   For my deare sonne Mr. Edward Harley.

My deare Ned—I haue bine so longe in puteing vp the plate to send your father, that I haue no time to rwite any more than that I longe to see you. I am confident you are not troubled to see the plate goo this way; for I trust in our gratious God, you will haue the frute of it.

 I pray God blles you.
   Your most affectinat mother,   BRILLIANA HARLEY.

I pray you send me word wheather my lord Clare be come to Loundoun.

I doo long allmost to be from Brompton.

In the hamper with the plate, I haue sent your father a cake; it whas sent me this morning.

July 9, 1642.   *Brompton Castell.*

CLXXV.

   For my deare sonne Mr. Edward Harley.

My deare Ned—Beleeue it, your letter by Raphe and Mr. Longly and the post this weake weare very wellcome to me. It is true, as you aprehend it, that I haue great caus to blles God for His great mercy in giuing me, now at this time, a fare more full measure of health then I haue had, ever sence I was ill; for now, I thank God,

I can goo abrood at thos times that I was inforsed to keepe my beed, and this last weake was abell, at that time, to keepe a priuet fast, and the Lord that has doun this for me, the vnworthyest of all His seruants, I trust and am fully assured, will doo much more for His chruch. I haue often toold you, I thought you would see trubellsome times; but, my deare Ned, keepe your hart aboue the world, and then you will not be trubelled at the changes in it; and haveing your God for your porcion, which I am confident you haue, and it is my comfort that I can beleeue so, you are happy; for I can experimentally say, that the Lord will sheawe most mercy, when we stand in most need of it; and I am confident, the Lord will not faile His poore saruents at this time. I wisch you with me, but, deare Ned, I am glad you are at Loundoun, becaus that is a safer place.

I sent Samuell to Heariford on tusday, to obsarue what was doun. Yesterday the soulders weare called. He is not yet come home, which makes me thinke it very much, for he was seene this day at Lemster, at 4 a cloke. I did hope to haue sent the relation of all to you in this letter by the post.

Mr. Dauis of Coxall did not goo to Heariford, and Mr. Dauis of Wigmore went, but did nothinge: he says but a feawe of your fathers company did apeare. They speake bigg words, but I hope the Lord will keepe theare harts lowe.

I haue receued the box with 20 bandeleres, but the boxes with the muskets and rests the carrier has left to come in a waggon to Woster; he promises I shall haue them shortly. I pray you tell your father the reson, why I did not send the trunck of plate by Lemster carryer was, becaus the last I sent to Lemster, they said it was plate; but Bagly, that went with it, not knowing what it was, only I toold him theare was a cake in it, and so he toold the carryers wife. I hope your father receued it. I haue derected this truncke to Mr. Smith, in the Old Bayly, and I haue desired Will Griffets to deleuer it to the carrier and to take vpon him that he sends it. I pray you bide Sankey be carefull to speake to Mr. Smiths man to goo to the carryer of Loudlow to looke for the truncke; it is sowed vp in canues. I haue sent your father a note of what plate is in the truncke.

I pray God blles you and giue you a comfortabell meeting with
    Your most affectinat mother,   BRILLIANA HARLEY.

I pray you tell your father the bay gellding he sent to haue taken vp, is so, and he is in very good case.

Remember me to your sister. I haue sent her bibell in the truncke with the plate. I wisch some parlament men might be sent into this cuntry to settell the milica, and that my lord of Essekes would make Mr. Shirborne hoold his peace.

Gloues and pattern for me. M. Instrum^{ts}.
July 15, 1642.

CLXXVI.

To her son Edward.

My deare Ned—By the enclosed paper to your father, you will knowe how poore Hearifordsheare is affected; but, deare Ned, I hope you and myself will remember for whous caus your father and we are hated. It is for the caus of our God, and I hope we shall be so fare from being ashamed of it or trubelled, that we beare the reproche of it, that we shall binde it as a crowne upon us; and I am confident the Lord will rescue His chillderen from reproche.

I sent Samuell to Heariford to obsarue theaire ways. He had come home last night, but that he had a fall from his hors and put out his shoulder.

He tells me that they all at Heariford cried out against your father, and not one said any thinge for him, but one man, Mr. Phillips of Ledbury said, when he hard them speak so against your father, "well," said he, "tho Sir Robert Harley be lowe heare, yet he is aboue, wheare he is." My deare Ned, I can not thinke I am safe at Brompton, and by no means I would haue you come downe. I should be very glad if your father could geet some religious and discreet gentleman to come for a time to Brompton, that he might see sometimes what they doo in the cuntry. I trust the Lord will direct your father what way is beest, and I doute not that we shall pray, on for another.

I could wisch that my cosen Adams weare out of the howes, for I am perswaded he will give the other side what assistance he can. If you thinke good, tell your father so: your father dous not know what counsells they haue in Hearifordsheare, and what way they goo.

The captaine of the voluntiers is one Barell, he was a tradesman, and once maire of Heariford.

It is so late I will but wisch you a good night, and I pray God blles you, and in His good time giue you a comfortabell meeting with

   Your most affectinat mother,   BRILLIANA HARLEY.
July 17, 1642. *Brompton Castell.*

CLXXVII.

For my deare sonne Mr. Edward Harley.

My deare Ned—I longe to see you, but would not haue you come downe, for I cannot thinke this cuntry very safe; by the papers I haue sent to your father, you will knowe the temper of it. I hope your father will giue me full derections how I may beest haue my howes gareded, if need be; if he will giue the derections, I hope, I shall foolow it.

My deare Ned, I thanke God I am not afraide. It is the Lords caus that we haue stood for, and I trust, though our iniquitys testify aganst vs, yet the Lord will worke for His owne name sake, and that He will now sheawe the men of the world that it is hard fighting against heauen. And for our comforts, I thinke neuer any laide plots to route out all Gods chillderen at once, but that the

Lord did sheawe Himselfe mighty in saveing His saruants and confounding His enimyes, as He did Pharowe, when he thought to haue destroyed all Israell, and so Haman. Nowe, the intention is, to route out all that feare God, and surely the Lord will arise to healpe vs: and in your God let your confidence be, and I am assured it is so. One meet Samuell and not knoweing wheare he dwelt, Samuell toold him he was a Darbesheare man, and that he came lately from thence, and so he did in discours; the papis toold him, that theare was but a feawe puretaines in this cuntry, and 40 men would cut them all off.

Had I not had this ocation to send to your father, yet I had sent this boy vp to Loundoun; he is such a rogeisch boy that I dare not keepe him in my howes, and as littell do I dare to let him goo in this cuntry, least he ioyne with the company of vollentirs, or some other such crwe. I haue giuen him no more money then will sarue to beare his charges vpe; and becaus I would haue him make hast and be sure to goo to Loundoun, I haue toold him, that you will giue him something for his paines, if he come to you in good time and doo not loyter; and heare inclosed I haue sent you halfe a crowne. Giue him what you thinke fitte, and I desire he may not come downe any more, but that he may be perswaded to goo to seae, or some other imployment. He thinkes he shall come downe againe. Good Ned, do not tell Martaine that I send him vp with such an intention. I haue derected theas letters to you, and I send him to you, becaus I would not haue the cuntry take notis, that I send to your father so offten; but when such ocations come, I must needs send to him, for I can rely vpon nobodys counsell but his. I pray God blles you and presarue you in safety, and the Lord in mercy giue you a comfortabell meeting with

    Your most affectinat mother,   BRILLIANA HARLEY.

July 19, 1642. *Brompton Castell.*

My cosen Dauis tells me that none can make shot but thos whous trade it is, so I haue made the plumer rwite to Woster for 50 waight of shot. I sent to Woster, becaus I would not haue it knowne. If your father thinke that is not enoufg, I will send for more. I pray you tell your father that my cosen Robert Croft is in the cuntry. My cosen Tomkins is as violent as euer, and many thinke that her very words, is in the Heariford resolutions. I beleeue it was Mr Masons pening. He is gone to Yorke, for when he carried the letter from the gentellmen in this cuntry, he was made the kings chapline.

CLXXVIII.

For my deare sonne Mr. Edward Harley.

My deare Ned—I did hope that Richard Sanky would haue come downe this night, which made me defer my rwiteng tell now that it is time to goo to beed. Mr Ellton came aboute 4 a cloke: he tells me that the commiscioners desires to haue mony for three months pay for a hors. Sr Richard Hopton comes not at them, nor Sr Jhon Kirle; Mr Wigmore stands much vpon his points, he will scase looke vpon any one; and your cosen Tomkins made the most slightest ansure that on could make, when shee was toold, that I would goo out of the cuntry. I pray God blles you, and giue you comfortabell meeting with

Your most affectinat mother,   BRILLIANA HARLEY.
July 23, 1642.

Remember me to your sister; it is so late I could not rwite to her.

CLXXIX.

To her son Edward.

My deare Ned—I must needs thanke you for your two letters this weake; for, beleeue me, in this trubellsome time and your fathers absence and yours, your letters are of much comfort to me. My deare Ned, at first when I sawe how outrageously this cuntry carried themselfes aganst your father, my anger was so vp, and my sorrow, that I had hardly patience to stay; but now, I haue well considered, if I goo away I shall leaue all that your father has to the pray of our enimys, which they would be glad of; so that, and pleas God, I purpos to stay as long as it is poscibell, if I liue; and this is my resolution, without your father contradict it.

I cannot make a better use of my life, next to saruing my God, than doo what good I can for you. Wigmore faire is to be on munday next. You may gees at the resons why I would not speake to Mr Wigmore or his asociats to be at the faire; and thairefore I sent for Mr Ellton, whoo promised to come this night. I stayed supper till past ten a clocke, but he came not. I did hope to haue sent you word by him what they did at Heariford * * * * * horsess at Roos * * * * bought 30. Sr William Croft and Mr Wigmore, as they say, will goo with him to the kinge.

I pray you tell your father that they sent to the kinge on thursday, and till they haue an ansure they are not resolued what to doo. It is very late, theairefore I can say no more; but I pray God blles you with all His bllesinges, and I hope you will alwaies be the joye of your

Most affectinat mother,   BRILLIANA HARLEY.

July 2, 1642. *Brompton Castell.*

I thanke God all your brothers and sisters are well. I haue rescued this night the hamper with the powder and macth, but I haue not yet the muskets, but will and pleas God, enquire after them.

CLXXX.

For my much honnored frinde Mrs. Wallcote, at Wallcote.

Most worthy frinde—I had rather intreate a kindencs from you then from any I knowe; assureing meselfe you will doo the same to me, in home you have as much interest in, as in any.

I haue had of late in the mending of the leeds of my howes bine inforsed to lay out an extriordary some of money; and Edward Dally with others, oweing me rent, I can not as yet geet it; if you can lend me 40*l.* for halfe or a quarter of a yeare, I shall take it as a greate kindenes, and I will pay the interest of it with all my hart, and giue you any securety my sonne and I can giue you, which I hope will be enough for a greater some. So recommending you unto the protection of God, I rest,

  Your most affectinat frinde,   BRILLIANA HARLEY.

Augs. 18, 1642.

I desire to haue my saruis presented to Mr Wallcote and your sonne.

CLXXXI.*

For my much honnored frinde Mrs. Wallcote, at Wallcote.

My much honnored and deare frinde,—I acknowledg this as a greate fauor, and I shall be ready to expres my thankes with all the

---

* This Letter is accompanied by Mr. Walcot's acquittance, endorsed thus in Sir Edward Harley's handwriting:—

M^m. That I heard not of ye 20 ll within specified but of late: and though I was not by cours of law obliged to ye payment, yet, reckoning myself by ye law of conscience (wch is true honor) bound to pay it, if due, I bless ye Lord who hath enabled mee to pay it.

                       E. H.

Also in Mary Walcot's handwriting, on a separate paper:—

Whereas I am informed that there is some question between the hon^{ble} Sr Edward Harley and John Walcot Esq. concerning twenty pounds lent by Humphrey Walcot Esq. in the time of the late warres to the Honble the Lady Brilliana Harley, I can testifie that seuerall times since the decease of the said Humphrey, I have heard my mother in law Ann Walcot, his relict, mention the said twenty pounds, as certainly lent and never repaid.

 Witness my hand this 31st of Decem. 1667.   MARY WALCOT.

      Acq't'ce fro Mr Walcot:—

Received this twenty-first day of March 1682 of Sr Edward Harley of Bramton Castle in the county of Hereford k^t of the hon^{ble} order of the Bath by mee John Walcott of Walcott in the county of Salop Esq. the sum of twenty pounds of lawfull English money in full of all moneys debts reckonings and accompts whatsoever due vnto my late ffather Humphrey Walcott, Esq. dec^d or vnto my late mother Ann Walcot (the relict of the sa^d

testimony of true respets, and I acknowledge, that for the vertues you haue, I much loue and honnor you. I haue receued the 20*l.* you are pleased to lend me, and I haue made a bill of the resaite of it, and my sonne and meselfe haue put our hands to the resaite of it, and I will and pleas God pay you very shortly.

I desire to haue my saruis presented to Mr Wallcote and your sonne; and desire you to beleeue that I am most vnfainedly

  Your most affectinat frinde,   BRILLIANA HARLEY.
Augt: 22, 1642. *Brompton Castell.*

CLXXXII.*

To her son Edward.

My deare Ned—My hart has bine in no rest sence you went. I confes I was neuer so full of sorrow. I feare the prouicion of corne and malt will not hoold out, if this continue; and they say they will burne my barnns; and my feare is that they will place soulders so

---

Humphrey Walcott) dec^d or unto mee the said John Walcott from s^d Robert Harley late of Bramton Castle aforesaid in the said county of Hereford kn^t of the Bath dec^d or from dame Brilliana Harley dec^d or from the said Sr Edward Harley by bond bill promise agreement or otherwise from the beginning of the world untill the day of the date of these p'sents and the said John Walcott doe for me my heirs executors adm^{ors} and assigns and every of them acquitt release and for euer discharge the said Sr Edward Harley his heirs ex^{tors} and adm^{rs} and every of them by these p'sents of and from the said sume of twenty pounds and every part and parcell thereof and of and from all bonds bills reckonings and accompts for or touching the said sume of twenty pounds or any part thereof or for or touching any cause matter or thing whatsoever due or payable as aforesaid In witness whereof the said John Walcott haue hereunto put my hand and seale the said twenty-first day of March in the five-and-thirtieth year of the reign of o^r sovereign Lord King Charles the Second over England &c. a°q' D'ni 1682.

                  J. WALCOT.   (S).

Signed and sealed and delivered
 in the presence of
NEH. KETTILBY.
J. FUMDWEN.
THOMAS PROSSER.

* The original is written on cloth.

neare me that theare will be no gooing out. My comfort is that you are not with me, least they should take you; but I doo most dearly mis you. I wisch, if it pleased God, that I weare with your father. I would haue rwite to him, but I durst not rwite vpon papaper. Deare Ned, rwite to me, though you rwite vpon a peace of clothe, as this is. I pray God blles you, as I dsier my owne soule should be bllesed. Thears a 1000 dragonears came into Harford 5 owers affther my lord Harferd.

   Your   mother,   BRILL: HAR.

Desem: 13, 1642.

CLXXXIII.

To her son Edward.

My deare Ned—I thanke you for your letter by Proser; he is a trusty mesenger. I must now tell you how gratious our God has bine to vs: on the soboth day affter I receued the letter from the markis, we sett that day apart to sceeke to our God, and then on munday we prepared for a seege; but our good God called them another way; and the markis sent me word he remembered him to me, and that I need not feare him, for he was gooing away, but bide me feare him that came affter him.

Mr Connisbe is the gouernor of Heariford, and he sent to me a letter by Mr Wigmore. I did not let him come into my howes, but I went into the garden to him. Your father will sheawe you the letter; they are in a mighty violence against me; they reueng all that was doune vpon me, so that I shall feare any more parlament forsess comeing into this cuntry: and deare Ned, when it is in your power sheaw kindenes to them, for they must be overcome so. Bardlam has played the very traitor to me, and Richard Bytheway neuer comes at me: Mr Phillips takes much care and pains. Deare Ned, rwite him thankes tho it be but in a littell scripe of paper. My deare Ned, I pray you aduis with your father wheather he thinkes it best that I should put away most of the men that are in my howes, and wheather it be best for me to goo from Brompton, or by Gods healp to stand it out. I will be willing to doo what he would have me doo. I neuer was in such sorrows, as I haue bine sence you left me; but I hope the Lord will deleuer me; but they are most cruely beent against me. I thanke you for your counsell, not to take theair words; the Lord in mercy presarue you, and if it be His holy will, giue me the comfort of seeing you, in home is much of the comfort of

Your affectinat mother, BRILLIANA HARLEY.

Desem: 25, 1642.

CLXXXIV.

To her son Edward.

My deare Ned—Your wellcome letter I receued on munday last, but Hopkis was taken at Rickards Castell, but sent me your fathers letter and yours. But I heare he had 6 other letters, and they weare carryed to Mr Coningsby. He is still at Heariford. How he will be used I knowe not; for poor Griffits was cruelly used, but he is now seet at liberty. But the poore drumer is still in the dungon, and Griffits says he fears he will dye. I cannot send to releas him.

My deare Ned, I know it will greeue you to know how I am used. It is with all the malice that can be. Mr Wigmore will not let the fowler bringe me any foule, nor will not suffer any of my saruants pas. They haue forbid my rents to be payed. They draue away the yong horsess at Wigmore, and none of my saruants dare goo scarce as fare as the towne. And deare Ned, if God weare not mercyfull to me, I should be in a very miserabell condistion. I am threatened euery day to be beseet with soulders. My hope is, the Lord will not deliuer me nor mine into theair hands; for surely they would use all cruellty towards me, for I am toold that they desire not to leaue your father neather roote nor branch. You and I must forgiue them. Deare Ned, desire the prayers of the godly for us at

Brompton. I desire to * * * * * * * * as it is poscibell that I may keepe the possestion of your fathers howes for him.

I know not wheather this will come to your hand or no, but this I know, that I longe to heare from you, and I pray God blles you, as I desire the soule should be bllesed, of your

    Most affectinat mother,   BRILLIANA HARLEY.
Jany. 28, 1642.

CLXXXV.

For my deare sonne Mr. Edward Harley.

My deare Ned—I am confident you longe to heare from me, and I hope this will come to your hand, though it may be it will be long first. We are still threatned and iiniured as much as my enimyes can poscibell. Theare is non that beares part with me but Mr Jams, whoo has shouwed himselfe very honnest; none will looke towards Brompton, but such as truely fears God; but our God still takes care of vs, and has exceedingly sheawed His power in presaruing vs. Nine days past my lord Harberd was at Heariford, whear he stayed a weake; theare was heald a counsell of ware, what was the beest way to take Brompton; it was concluded to blow it vp, and which counsell pleased them all. The sherife of Radnorsheare, with the trained bands of that county and some of Hearifordsheare soulders, weare to come against me. My lord Harberd had apointed a day to come to Prestine, that so his presence might perswade them to goo out of theare county. He had commanded them to bring pay for vitals for 10 days. The soulders came to Prestine, but it pleased God to call my lord Harbrd another way, for thos in the forest of Deane, grwe so strong, that they weare afraid of them.

Now they say, they will starue me out of my howes; they haue taken away all your fathers rents, and they say they will driue away the cattell, and then I shall haue nothing to liue vpon; for all theare ame is to enfors me to let thos men I haue goo, that then they might seas vpon my howes and cute our throughts by a feawe rooges, and then say, they knewe not whoo did it; for so they say, they knewe not whoo draene away the 6 coolts, but Mr Connigsby keepes them, though I haue rwite to him for them. They haue vsed all means to leaue me haue no man in my howes, and tell me, that then I shall be safe; but I haue no caus to trust them. I thanke God we are all well. I long to see my cosen Hackellt. I pray God blles you.

Your most affectinat mother, BRILLIANA HARLEY.

Feb. 14, 1642.

CLXXXVI.

For my deare sonne Mr. Edward Harley.

My deare Ned—Your littell vollome of paper sent by Bonde had a long wellcome. I am very glad that your sister is recouered. If Mr Moores man Makelin has told you nothing, I pray you aske him, what Mr Moore bide him tell you. Docter Wright and his wife presents theare saruis to you, and Mr Phillpis has bine, and is very carefull. Mr Hill has vndertaken to bring the water into the mote. I ventured but 20^{sh} but he has had many oposits, but Mr Gower was for him. I hope it will be doun. I pray God blles you with all blessings.

Your most affectinat mother, BRILLIANA HARLEY.

I thanke God your brother and sisters are well.

Feb. 23, 1642.

CLXXXVII.

For my deare sonne Mr. Edward Harley.

My deare Ned—I rwite to you the other day by Mr Taylor, and I am as glad to doo it now, and I hope this will come safe to your hand.

I am in the same condistion as I was; still amongst my enimys, who now threeten me not with forsess, becaus the soulders are goon before Gloster; theaire randevous is S^r Ro. Cookes howes. My deare

Ned, desire your father to send me word what he thinkes I had beest doo; for if I should put away the men in my howes, I should be eury day plundered, and as basely vsed as it is poscibell, and I can receaue no rents.

Sam Piner toold who went with you, and so Leeg and Poell are indited.

Mr Yaets and Mr Lowe and Edward Pin. goo towards Loundoun the next weake. Edward Pin. biusnes is to speake with your father aboute the legacy he should pay Mr Poells daughter; he has sould land to her husband, and he would haue him take the mony of your father. I would not haue had him goo vp to Loundoun, becaus I thinke it is not a time for your father to take vp mony to pay that legacy, that the land is still in question; but your brother tells me Piners intentiene is to geet more lives on Buckton for that mony. If your father pleas to consider it, I thinke it is not so much for his profit to let on man haue so many liueings in his hand; for then they put poore tenants into them, and let the howses goo downe, and your father has but on tenant, for his tenant haueing 2 or 3. I pray you speake to your father about it. Good Mr Bayley is come to me. They rage more then euer. I pray God keepe vs from them; and, deare Ned, pray for vs and desire all good Christians to doo so. The Lord in mercy blles you, and giue me, a comfortabell seeing of you, who hoold you as deare as my owne soule.

Your most affectinat mother,   BRILLIANA HARLEY.

I longe to see your sister Brills sonn.

I think it seuen yeare tell he come.

I sent you all your linnens the last saterday.

Mr William Griffits tooke them with him, and promised to send them to his brother Gorge.

I purpos to send your man vp to you, when Piner goos, for I beleeue you will hardly haue on that is better and loues you more.

Feb. 25, 1642.

1642-3.]   LADY BRILLIANA HARLEY.   191

CLXXXVIII.*

For Mr. Edward Harley.

Deare Ned,
[*I desire you*] imagin to [*would pray*] all strength and [*your father*] go all to geather; why did I rong my judgment so as to [*to send me*] let vs the [*word what*] world. As for to loue wheare I did know [*he would haue*] all be it [*doo: if I put*] it is strang [*away the*] theare was no hoold to be taken for what my wisches [*men I shall*] thirst if [*be plundered*] once of it my hart can bost straight by her [*and if I*] is [*haue no*] forsaken [*rents, I know*] off haue I wished that when theare had bine some [*not what*] all mineche [*cours to*] for to haue seene when loue with her had bine [*take*] in season [*If I leaue*] but I [*Brompton*] perseaue theare is no art, can finde the [*all will be*] of that [**ruened**] hart that loues by chance and not by reson. [Mr *Coningsby*] if and [*swore he*] violent [*would be*] Cato Johannes, the Grecian emperour, vp with came [*in Brompton*] with a [*within five*] wast Army of hors and foote, and demand [*days*] cold and [*I heare*] with diemns [*he has*] to resign vnto him all places of strentg, togeather [*a commistion*] with all the [*to displace*] forse he had, and then he seet forward to [*all ministers*] he too [*and put*] them [*in others*] all places without resistance as you haue hard [*so it be*] to the greef [*doun with*] of many I cannot heare what is to be doun, and

* This Letter is read by a key of cut paper, the openings of which correspond with the words within the brackets.

[*the bischops*] that is [*consent*] all I can [*I would*] heare at this time, as I lived on an [*not haue y°*] penny [*beleeue*] yeare as frinds togeather, but now thee [*all that will*] is gon [*be toold*] I know [*you about*] not wheather could I but gees; I doo protest [*the bringing*] I speak [*of the water*] it not to flatter of all the women in the [*Mr Hill has*] world [*undertaken*] I newer [*it, and I*] would come at her tho grecionce came in [*hope will*] all has [*effect it*].

You must pin that end of the paper, that has the cors made in incke, vpon the littell cros on the end of this letter; when you would write to me, make vse of it, and giue the other to your sister Brill. I beceach the Lord to blles you, and deare Ned, be carefull of your-selfe. I did not send your man, whoo has a greate desire to be with you, becaus I did not know wheather you would haue him; if you would, send me worde, for I thinke you will hardly geet a better in theas days. I shall long to heare from you.

Your most affectinat mother,   BRILLIANA HARLEY.

I haue sent you your linen. Doctor Wright and M^ntris Wright presents theare saruis to you.

Mar: the first, 1642.

CLXXXIX.

To her son Edward.

My deare,

[*This day I*] went a [*heare that*] great way [*Sr Wm Cro*] so that they all pudd and watters weare when first [*has sent forth*] I sawe and [*a warent to*] hard from the yong men giue, and Rich they are of the

[*that somens,*] same year [24 *to come*] they are [*into Her:*] and sisters chillderen are not, and are of opinion as thos [*on munday*] that are [*next, to wittnes*] of a more constants mind and testament the next in degres [*to dismanors*] can come [*and crimes*] are brother [*laide to the*] the more kindred the greater affinity the more a man is [◦ *charge of*] honoured is [*your father*] they must as well become kindsmen or frindes [*yourselfe*] to theair [*Mr James*] frindes as [*Mr Dauis*] it self is satisfied and redeemed with a sartane number of [*Mr Gower*] beasts [*Mr Lowe*] which contenteth the whoole famely, and is profitabel [*Mr Yaets*] to the for [*Mr Beale*] common [*by Dickien*] good for wheare liberty is theare is priuet of [*the vnder*] are not l [*shereffe,*] and entertainements in no weare more beautifull [*so that it*] then theare [*seemes the*] to beare [*under-sherefe*] any man his howes, and not giue him meate or [*is the*] and drinke [*accusor of*] when all is spent the last host will be to the next [*you all. The*] howes and [*butler saw*] for united [*the warent*] and are receued with like curtesy and respect hospetallity [*in the baylefes*] of theare [*hand, and*] make you no diferance wheather it be of or from or a [*he rent it.*] greate and [*Meredife the*] or not [*ranger, and*] if any thing the manor is to grante it demand or if so [*Tom Child*] you and he [*and Daile*] as thinges aske the as thinges that pleas but thos that well [*of Lainterdin*] doo not [*and Hopkis*] thinkee [*of Dounen*] they you and not bond or beholden for them they enter [*are some*] theare gees [*of the* 24.] which they wasch in warme haueing long winter [*The rest of*] and when [*the names*] they full [*I know not*]. to eate euery man stoul and to himself.

Then full [*Hellische plots*] to theare [*they haue,*] biusness and make good cheere to seet and stond [*but I hope*] the a day is [*the Lord will*] not disgras [*disapoint*] to many and commonly it hapneth but selldome with offten [*them. I am*] with mirth [*still threatned,*] of all and make and chuse meate when neuer more [*I heare you*] vpon to [*are to haue*] plaine [*a company*] dealeing or more stirred vp or the neathe carefty or sutell end [*of hors. I pray*] dous not [*you send me*] discours or say nothing and the euery mens minde bring [*wordwheather*] or is to [*it be so*] or the next [*or no.*] shall with or regard

I hope Edward Piner is come to Loundoun, and that you haue receaued my letter by him, and then you will not maruell at this nonesence, which I haue writen to you to make you merry. Beceach the Lord in much mercy to blles you, and that I may haue againe the comfort of seeing you, whoo are very deare to me. Your brother is much better than he was, and does much reioyce that you wisched him with you. Tell your father what I haue writen; he may eassyly gees at the reson why I did not wright to him. I thanke God, we are all well, and I long to see your sisters sonne come downe. Deare Ned, tell your sister I pray God to blles her; and present my saruis to my brother; so I rest

Your most affectinat mother, BRILLIANA HARLEY.

Mar: 3, 1642.

CXC.

For my deare sonne Mr. Edward Harley.

My deare Ned—By what I haue writ to your father you will see what they meane to doo with me and mine. You will see my ansure, and I hope the Lord will derect me what to doo when the time comes, and I trust He that has deleuerd me will deleuer me.

The Lord in mercy presarue you and keep you, and in His good time giue vs a comfortabell meeting; and, deare Ned, pray for Brompton, and

Your most affectinat mother, BRILLIANA HARLEY.

Mar: 4, 1642.

Mr. Phillips carries himself very well, and all in my howes are of good corage.

CXCI.

For my deare sonne Mr. Edward Harley.

My deare Ned—I should haue bine very glad to haue receued a letter from you by Mr. Taylor; and deare Ned, finde some way or other to rwite to me that I may know how the world goos, and how it is with your father and yourselfe; for it is a death to be amoungst my enimys, and not to heare from thos I loue so dearely.

Heare I haue sent you a coppy of the sommons was sent me; I wisch with all my hart that euery on would take notice what way they take: that if I doo not giue them my howes, and what they would haue, I shall be proseeded against as a trator. It may be euery onse case to be made traytors; for I beleeue eury on will be as vnwilling to part with theare howes as I am. I desire your father would seariously thinke what I had beest doo; wheather stay at Brompton, or remoue to some other place. I heare theare are 600 soulders apointed to come against me. I know not wheather this sessation of armes will stay them. I cannot tell what to think, that I heare nothing of your sister Brills sonne, nor that you did not write me word, that he was come to you. I heare captaine Jeferes is drowned. I am very much behoolding to docter Wright, for he will not goo from Brompton tell he sees me out of my trubell.

Mr. Phillips carrys himselfe very well, and Mr. H   as he was vsed to doo. Good Mr Baughly is faine to come to Brompton.

Mr Legg is still at Brompton, and Mathes and the Wellchmen and Staney and 2 of Knights brothers, who were faine to fly out of theare owne cuntry. My deare Ned, I will promise meselfe a letter from you by this bearer, whoo has carried himselfe very well to me; thearefore I pray you giue him thankes for it. I pray God blles you, and in His good time giue vs a joyfull meeting, which I beleeue you thinke is longed for, by

   Your most affectinat mother, BRILLIANA HARLEY.

I heare they have put vp proclamations in this cuntry, that theare shall be no sessation of armes.

Docter Wright and Mrs Wright remember saruis to you.

Mar: 8, 1642.

CXCII.

For Mr. Edward Harley.

My deare Ned,

[*When*   *the*] in trihumph [*judges came*] to Woster [*not to Hearifrd*] then in haste in the more courtly to what purpose lately trained otherwise [*so that theare*] the viccount [*was nothing*]   enriching themselfes vnited vnder erle Simons and Richards to the hassard of [*doun against me*] or any [*at the bench,*] when I sent [*they sent for*] come protesting which now in feareing fell fomented by the supposed [*the*   *trained*] vp in pride [*bands, and haue*] not cared to speake as they from him and her, so they goo one [*taken*   *away*] meate colthes [*thearie armes;*] sowords [*some say to*] gaine as much as can be thought and haue ended the a greete to [*giue the armes*] vp and [*to my lord*]   Crauen so when all is doun it comes all togeather [*Harbreds soulders*] and the [*that wante.*] mony? [*They say*] so when all was sould the mony came short and that was so [*that they gaue*] gloues of [*half a crowne*] a peace to comfort them for all loses so they went away [*to every soulder*] howes [*to looke for*] the more [*enimyes*] wheare to the joy of ons hart to the greefe of frends [*every day. They*] went out [*haue taken*] fisch good store which may last a greate while [*Mores lad,*] not bine [*and he is in*] a good howes [*prison at*] wheare is a greate many that loues tobacco came to [*Heariford,*] to liue a time [*becaus he*] neuer thought it had bine so hard a matter hogg and dich [*was with*] Poell to [*me. If I had*] hard of the [*mony to*] come to morrow I had then sent it so now they must [*buy corne*] at another place [*and meale*] somewheare elles, or it will not doo well; but it is strange [*and malt*] I should not [*I should hope*] to render it [*to hoold*] as long as any but brauely and beaten and reduced to obedience [*out, but then*] write [*I haue 3*] yeares heance will be acknowledged to the ioy of all and greefe of [*sheeres against*] which for [*me . . .*]

When you have laught at the nonsense, pleas your self with this, that is reson; I thanke God we are well, though all would not haue it so. I longe to heare from you. Desire your father from me to be carefull of himselfe, and I pray God blles you, and giue you a comfortabell meeting with

Your affectinat mother, BRILLIANA HARLEY.

Mar: 11, 1642.

CXCIII.

For my deare sonne Mr. Edward Harley.

My deare Ned—I was very glad to receaue a letter from you by Proser and by Samleman, but I did hope you would haue bine more at large, for I doo exceedingly long to heare what you doo, and what is beest for me to doo. I heare some say, you haue an imployment, but I will beleeue nothing tell I heare it from your selfe or father. The report in this cuntry is, that my lord Capell comes very shortly to be gowernor of Shrewsbury, and the qu: is to come to Loudlow. I thanke God we are all at Brompton, and desire to knowe when you meane, and pleas God, to moue this way.

I pray God blles you and giue you a comfortabell meeting with

  Your most affectinat mother, BRILLIANA HARLEY.

Doctor Wright and Mrs Wright, whoo yet make me so much behoolding to them as that they are with me, remember theaire saruis to you.

Mar: 25, 1643.

CXCIV.

For my deare sonne Mr. Edward Harley.

My deare Ned—Your wellcome letter by the carrier I haue receued; and deare Ned, let this tell you, God has mightyly bine seene in Hearifordsheere. Mr Conningsby and Sr William Croft and Sr Wallter Pye are at Gloster. I will with all speede send Mr Hill to you. The Lord in mercy blles you.

Remember my deare loue to your father, and my bllesing to your sister. I pray God giue you a happy meeting with her that longes to see you.

  Your most affectinat mother, BRILLIANA HARLEY.

May 6, 1643.

I thanke God we are all well. To my greefe I must tell you that honnest Petter is taken. 6 seet vpon him; 3 shot at him as he was opening a gate not fare from Mortimers Cros. He fought with them valliantly and aquited himself with corage: he hurt 2 of them, and if theare had not bine 6 to on, he had escaped: he is wounded in the head and sholder, but not mortally; he is in prison at Loudlowe. I doun all that is poscibell to get him out, but it cannot be; but I hope the Lord will deleuer him. I haue found him very faithful to me, and he desired to haue come to you.

CXCV.

For my deare sonne Mr. Edward Harley.

My deare Ned—Sence God has put into your harte that you haue taken this imployment vpon you, the Lord in much mercy blles you, and make you to doo wisely and valiently: and now, my deare Ned, you may be confident my very soule goos alonge with you; and becaus I cannot be with you myselfe, I haue sent you on, to be of your troope, and haue furnisched him with a hors. You know he came at the first to Brompton, when our trubells begane, and has faithfully stayed with me, and carried himselfe honestly and with very good corage. He had a desire to come to you, and I as good a desire he should come, and I hope you will find him such a one as I say he is, if not more: the hors coost me 8*l.* I hope it will come safe to your hande, with his rider. I read your letter very well, which came by Looker; but if you would let the paper you write vpon be of the same breath of the cute paper, it would be much better. From this place make vse of the cute paper.

+ [*I pray you*] take into [*consider that*] it has [*Mr. Hill is*] all ways ready and will be still, which I know will reioyce [*much given*] and in [*to keepe*] the beest and richest and wisest so that some weare much [*company and*] to eate [*so to drinke,*] and sleepe [*and I feare*] this day Captaine Croft and his wife weare to see me and so [*will put his*] but all [*minde much to*] no purpos I long to see you more than you can thinke. [*plundering.*] but doo [*Consider well*] and that [*of it.*] Pray God blles you, and giue you comfortabell meeting with

    Your most affectinat mother,   BRILLIANA HARLEY.
May 9, 1643.

Mr Moore is come to stay at Brompton, which I am very glad of. Your brother Robine goos abonte as if he weare discontented, but I know not for what. Mr Phillips carrys himselfe very honestly and carefully, and is impatient to have you come to Brompton, wheare I should be glad to see you. Petter is still in prison at Loudlow. 5 men seet vpon him; he fought very valiently with them all; they had carrabins and pole axes. I am very sorry for him, and I haue doun all I can to geet him out. I will trye once againe what my lord Capell will doo; he was hurt in three places. Deare Ned, take it well that Mr Legg is so willing to come, and I hope you will vse him kindely.

CXCVI.

To her son Edward.

My deare Ned—I receaued your letter by the carrier of Lemster, and beleeue me, it was extremely wellcome to me, and therefore, let me preuaile with you to rwite to me as offten as you can. I am sorry you say nothing of Mr Leggs coming to you: if you doo not like him, he will willingly returne to Brompton. For Mr Mountaine (I beleeue you understand that name in France; I mean he that you thought of, for a place in your trope) I find, he was altogether given to shifting, and I dout his faithfulness. Any thing shall be digested for mony with him. I beleue it is true; thearefore deare Ned, take heede of your choys.

I hope you will let me know as soune as you can when you begine your journey; and the Lord in much mercy blles and prosper you, and giue me in His good time a joyfull seeing of you, which I long to doo; . . . as much longes for you. The water is brought quite into the greene court, and I thinke you will like the worke well. I like it so well, that I would not haue it undoun for a great . . . Petter is still in prison theare;

. . . . fident that I cannot well . . . which the ocation that all the Wellchmen are goone from me. Good Mr Moore is with me and is much comfort to me, and so is Doctor Wright and his wife, whoo promises not to leaue mee till my trubells are past.

I am confident you pray for us at Brompton, and I pray you doo so, and the Lord in mercy blles you, as I desire the soule should be bllesed, of

Your most affectinat mother,   BRILLIANA HARLEY.

Deare Ned, remember me to your sister Brill. I was very glad to receue a letter from my brother. . . .

Poore Petter wisched himselfe many times with you before he was taken. He is used better nowe then he was at Loudlow.

May 28, 1643.

CXCVII.

To her son Edward.

My deare Ned—I did hope I should haue had a letter from you this weake, by the carrier, but I mised of that comfort; but I was so much beholding to Mr Moore that he rwite me word you weare well.

I pray God send you well into the cuntry. Take heede of your choys of that man, I haue rwrite you of hearetofore.

We are pretty quiet, but still in the . . . condistion. We are still threatened. Some soulders are billeted in Pursla. I pray God send the faire well past ouer. The worke aboute the court is almost ended, and I thinke you will like it well. I rwite to my nephewe Pelham, whoo is cornet to my lord Capell, but he has not goot Petters releas. He write me an ansure with some hope of his releas. I am very sorry for him; he has bine used pittifully.

I could say much more, but I know not wheather this will come to your hand. I pray God blles you, and giue you a comfortabell meeting with

  Your most affectinat mother,   BRILLIANA HARLEY.

June 3, 1643.

I pray you remember me to your sister Brill. Doctor Wright and his wife remember theaire saruis to you.

CXCVIII.

To her son Edward.

O! my deare Ned—that I could but see you! I liue in hope that the Lord will giue me that comfort, which I confes, I am not worthy of. I heare from a good hand that you are ready to come out of Loundoun. The Lord in much mercy goo with you and make you to doo worthyly; and deare Ned, beleeue my hart and soule is with you.

I hard from Gloster on thursday last, by on I sent a purpos. Sr William Waller went on tuesday towards the west. Lef.curenell Massy is commanded to be gouerner of Gloster by my lord jenerall. I haue and am exceedingly behoolding to corenell Massy, as much as I was ever to on, I did not know; and I pray you tell your father so, and pray him to giue him thankes. I sent to him to desire him to send me an abell soulder, that might reguelate the men I haue, and he has sent me on that was a sargent, an honnest man, and I thinke an abell soulder; he was in the Jerman wars. He came to me on thursday last, but your brother has the name of the command. I writ to you the last weake, that the Wellchmen weare goone from me; this bearer will tell you the reson. Honnest Petter is come out of prison. He was greeuiously vsed in Loudlow. Turkes could have vsed him no wors; a lefftenant corenell Marrow would come every day and kicke him vp and downe, and they laied him in a dungon vpon foule straw. Mr Goodwine sheawed him kindnes. In Shreawesbury he was vsed well for a prisoner; but he is very glad he is come home againe, and so am I. The Lord in mercy blles you, and giue you a comfortabell meeting with

  Your most affectinat mother, BRILLIANA HARLEY.

Mr Phillips is very carefull, and longes to see you.

June 11, 1643.

I shall be full of douts tell the fare be past. Some soulders are come to Knighton; my old frinds that weare theare before.

CXCIX.

For my deare sonne Mr. Edward Harley.

My deare Ned—I hard from Loundoun that you with Sr Arter Hasellrike left Loundoun on Friday was senight, and that your intentions weare to hast to Sr William Waller. I haue some hope that theas lines may meet with you, which if they doo, my deare Ned, let them assure you my hart is with you; and I hope my God will blles you. This bearer can tell you the state of Heariford-schere. You know you are the comfort of my life, thearefore thinke it not strange, if my thoughts are so much with you.

The Lord in much mercy blles and presarue you, and giue you a comfortabell meeting with

  Your most affectinat mother, BRILLIANA HARLEY.

June 19, 1643.

I thanke God we are all well at Brompton.

CC.

For my deare sonne Captaine Harley.

My deare Ned—I receued your letter dated the 17 of this month, which was dearely wellcome to me, becaus it brought me word that you weare safely come to Sr William Waller, wheare the Lord of heauen and earth blles you and presarue you. My hart is with you, and I know you beleeue it; for my life is bound vp with yours. My deare Ned, sence you desire your brother to come to you, I cannot be vnwilling he should goo to you, to home I pray God make him a comfort.

If Mr Hill be with you, and you would be free of him, you may if pleas you, tell him I desire he should come to me, and so you may send him to me: if your brother will speake freely, he can tell you of his carage. My deare Ned, if you wante any thinge that I can healp you to, I pray you send to me; and be sure I will wante myselfe, before you shall. Your brother will tell you how this cuntry is, and I pray you take care of your brother, and I beceach the Lord to blles you and him, and in His good time to giue me a joyifull meeting with you.

Your most affectinat mother,   BRILLIANA HARLEY.

Your father was, I thanke God, very well on tusday last. I had not a letter from him, but Mr Moore wrote me word so. I am very sorry that my brother has doun what he has. I haue bide your brother tell you what I haue hard.

CCI.

To her son Edward.

My deare Ned—On saterday I receued your letter by Raphe. Your being well is mine, and thearefore you may beleeue I reioyce in it. That you left me with sorrow, when you went last from Brompton, I beleeue; for I thinke, with comfort I thinke of it, that you are not only a child, but on with child-like affections to me, and I knowe you haue so much vnderstanding that you did well way the condistion I was in; but I beleeue it, your leaueing of me was more sorrow then my condistion could be; but I hope the Lord will in mercy giue you to me again, for you are both a Joseph and a Beniamin to me, and deare Ned, longe to see me; and I hope when you haue spent some littell time in the army you will come to Brompton. Sence you desired your brother to come to you, I could not deny it, though I was loth to leaue him. I hope he is come, before this, safe to you; and I pray God blles you both togeather, and that I may agene haue you returne in safety with your deare father. In this cuntry they begine to rais nwe tropes, and they haue seast the country at 1200*l.* a-month. My lo. Harbert and colonel Vaueser whoo is to be gouerner of Heariford, is gone vp into Moungomeryscheere to rais soulders. All of them are returned into Hearifordsheere; Sr Wallter Pye, Mr Brabson, Mr Smaleman, Mr Wigmore, Mr Ligen, and Mr Stiles and Gardnas, whoo has quartered soulders in Kingsland, and they say, that besides the 1200*l.* a month, theare must be free quarter for soulders. They counsell, but the Lord in mercy defeate theaire counsells. I must looke for nwe one-seets, but I hope I shall looke to my rocke of defence, the Lord my God, from home is deleuerance. Out of Chescheere, I heare from a sure hand, that on the 19 of this month Sr William Brerton sent out a party of hors into Sharpschere, but when they weare plundering at Hanmere, the lo. Capells tropes supprised them; they hasted to theaire horsess and fleed, but theare was taken prisnors of them the leftenan colonell and captain leftenant Sanky, and 13 more taken prisners, and about 12 slaine, and many more wounded. They vsed the prisnors very barborously. All Lancascheere is cleered, only Latham howes. My lord of Darby has left that county, which they take ill. My deare Ned, I know you loue to heare how I doo. I thanke God, beyond my expectation or that of some in my howes, my prouistions has heald out; and I haue borrowed yet not much mony, though my tenants will not pay me, and Coolborn deales very ill with me, and will pay me no mony; and Mr Connisbys steward sent to him to know wheather he would receaue the 6 coolts, and he neuer toold me of it, but sent them word he durst not. This Mr Eaton rwite me word of yesterday.

Your brother can tell you I sent for a sargent to colonnell Massey, and he sent me one, and I hope he will doo very well. As you desired to haue some honnest man sent you, I did as much desire to send you some. Those that I thought would haue gone gladly, findes out excusess, but theas 3 desired to goo, to venture theair liues with you, or elles they would not goo from me. Doctor Write asked his man the question, but the poore gardner and Stangy desired it of themselfes, and they seet forward with good corage. I will endeuor to see wheather any will contribute to buy a hors; but thos that haue harts haue not means, and they that haue means haue not harts. I doo not send you Jack Griffets, becaus I thought you might like Phillip Loouke, whoo is a pretty inienious fellow, but if you would haue Griffets, I pray you let me know by Raphe, and I will, if pleas God, send him to you. By Raphe and the rest I haue sent yon your bookes. Deare Ned, I could say much more to you, but I haue run out my paper. The Lord of Heauen blles you and presarue you, and make you to doo worthely and to outliue all theas trubells.

 Your most affectinat mother,   BRILLIANA HARLEY.
June 30, 1643.

I am confident you will hate all plundering and vnmercifullness. I pray you aske your brother what I bide him tell you concerning Mr Hill.

CCII.

To her son Edward.

My deare Ned—My cosen Dauis has desired much to see you, and thearefore I am so much behoolding to him that he dous me the kindnes to be the bearer of these lines, by which I am glad to let you know I haue reseaued your letter by Raphe. You may beleeue, it was welcome, for I had long desired it. I acknowledge the greate mercy of my God that He presarued you in so sharp a fight, when your hors was killed. The Lord my God presarue you still, and I trust that He will still continue His mercy to . . . . that I may againe see you with comfort.

I am sorry you haue lost so many hors out of your trope; but I hope they will be made up againe. I knowe not what they will doo heareafter, but, as yet, I can get but very little towards the byeing of a hors; what it is, I haue sent you inclosed. If you want any thing I can possibilly healp you to, let me knowe it, and I will . . .

I hard this day that your father and sister weare well this day senight. What is to be knowne of theas parts this bearer will tell you. Out of Schesheare I heare that Haughton Castell is still besieged by Sir William Breerton, and it is thought cannot hoold out. Two tropes of hors went out of Chester to rais the siege of Haughton Castell, but they weare beaten backe.

My deare Ned, the Lord in mercy presarue you in all fights, and giue me . . . . and which is . . desired by

Your most affectinat mother,   BRILLIANA HARLEY.
July 11, 1643.

CCIII.

To her son Edward.

My deare Ned—I cannot but venture theas lines, but wheather you are at Loundoun or no, I know not. Now, my deare Ned, the gentillmen of this cuntry haue affected theair desires in bringing an army against me. What spoyls has bine doun, this barer will tell you. Sir William Vavasor has left Mr Lingen with the soulders. The Lord in mercy presarue me, that I fall not unto theair hands. My deare Ned, I beleeue you wisch yourself with me; and I longe to heare of you, whoo are my great comfort in this life. The Lord in mercy blles you and giue me the comfort of seeing you and your brother.

Your most affectinat mother,   BRILLIANA HARLEY.
August 25, 1643.

Mr Phillips has taken a greate deale of paines and is full of corage, and so is all in my howes, with honnest Mr Petter and good Docter Wright and Mr Moore, whoo is much comfort to me. The Lord direct me what to doo; and, deare Ned, pray for me that the Lord in mercy may presarue me from my cruell and blood thirsty enemys.

CCIV.

For my deare sonne Mr. Edward Harley.

My deare Ned—I receaued your most wellcome letter by Mr Greens man, but I had none by Fischer, which did trubell me. I hope before this, you are assured of the Lords mercy to vs in deleuering vs from our enimys.

My deare Ned, a thousand times I wisch you with me, and then I should hope, by Gods assistance, to keepe what is left your father with comefort. It is true, my affection makes me long to see you, and my reson tells me it would be good for you for to employ yourselfe for the good of your cuntry, and that which I hope shall be yours. My deare Ned, if the Lord should be so mercifull, it would be such a comfort, that it would reuive my sad hart and refresch my dryed vp spirits.

The Lord in mercy derect you and presarue you, and giue you a comfortabell meeteing with

Your most affectinat mother,   BRILLIANA HARLEY.

My deare Ned, let me know your minde wheather I had beest stay or remoue.

Remember me to your brother.

Sep. 24, 1643.   *Brompton Castell.*

CCV.

For my deare sonne Colonell Harley.

My deare Ned—Your short but wellcome letter I receaued by Prosser, and as it has pleased God to intrust you with a greater charge, as to change your trope into a regiment, so the Lord in mercy blles you with a dubell measure of abillitys, and the Lord of Hosts be your protector and make you victorious. My deare Ned, how much I longe to see you I cannot expres, and if it be possibell, in parte meete my desires in desireing, in some measure as I doo, to see me; and if pleased the Lord, I wisch you weare at Brompton. I am now againe threatned; there are some souldiers come to Lemster and 3 troopes of hors to Heariford with Sr William Vauasor, and they say they meane to viset Brompton againe; but I hope the Lord will deleuer me. My trust is only in my God, whoo neuer yet failled me.

I pray you aske Mr Kinge what I prayed him to tell you con serning Wigmore.

I haue taken a very greate coold, which has made me very ill thees 2 or 3 days, but I hope the Lord will be mercifull to me, in giuing me my health, for it is an ill time to be sike in.

My deare Ned, I pray God blles you and giue me the comfort of seeing you, for you are the comfort of

  Your most affectinat mother, BRILLIANA HARLEY.
Octo: 9, 1643.

APPENDIX.

No. I.

LETTERS FROM SIR ROBERT HARLEY, LORD CONWAY, LADY VERE, THE EARL AND COUNTESS OF WESTMORLAND, EDWARD HARLEY, AND MARY HARLEY.

To Mr. EDWARD HARLEY, at Magdalen Hall in Oxford.

Ned Harley—Comend my service to M^r provost and Mr Rouse, and lett them know that I do receeve it as an honor to mee y^{er} intentions to set up my armes in the colledge. I will go (God willinge) send it to them.

There is another seruice which I have impartid to your worthy tutor, which if you like not, new counsailes shal be taken, for I would willingly shew myself, as time shall trie, and truth shall prove, and occasion shall rest contented, your obedient father. But, if otherwise or so, the horses shal be with you on Wednesday, the 11th of the next month, that you may be heere the 14th ; and, if you have taken the schoolinge so farr as that you have learned any rhetoricke, file your tong, and bestowe it all on your tutor to p'suade hym to come along with you. In which attempt if you faile, I may say you have spent your time and I my money to small purpose, if your tutor hath not taught you to overcome hym at his owne weapon. Howsoever, *fac periculum*, use your skill, and if you prevayle, send me word by the next, and I will send a horse for the good tutor allso. The Lord in mercy sett and settle His holy feare in your heart, then which nothinge can more inlarge the joye of,

Your most lov'ge father,   RO. HARLEY.

Bro'pto: Castle, 18mo 9^{bris}, 1639.

For Mr. EDWARD HARLEY,
at Magdː Hall, in Oxon.

Ned Harley—By my last I acquainted you of my purpose to send horses for you and your worthy tutor, if your logicke or rethoricke can prevayle with hym to honoure you heere with his presence, and my resolution hereby (God will'ge) to send them that they may arrive with you on the 11th of the next month. But if the tutors affaires stand calculated for an other meridian in the verticole point of this yeare, then let this berer, in his returne from London, bring mee a cleere understonding of it, and beseeche your good tutor to be the good genius for a schoolmaster heere. Remember, you haue set saile for heaven : let Ch: be your north starr, His holy word your card, and keepe your canvase pregnant with His feare, and upon my life, you will make a happy voyage. In which hope I joye and rest,

Your most affectionate father,   Ro. HARLEY.

Bro'pto' Cast: 25ᵗ 9*bris*, 1639.

For my sonne Mr. EDWARD HARLEY,
at Brōptō Castle.

Ned Harley—I canot advertise you any thinge of your chamber, but I intend to provide one for you as soone as I can. Whilst you are at Bropton lett no day pass *sine linea*. Walke as an example in love before your brothers and sisters, that they may honoure you next mee and your good mother. See the worship of God kept up in the familye, greeve not your heavenly Father by s——ge agˢᵗ Hym. So you wilbe the joye of your earthly,   Ro. HARLEY.

Comend my love to your brothers and sisters, and to your cossin Smyth.

Little Brittan, 18ᵐᵒ 8*bris*, 1641.

For NED HARLEY.

Ned Harley—I thanke you for your lettre, which you will understande I hope to be an incouragët to write to mee. I am sorry for the sad accident at Leyntwardine. It is fitt that Pyner should th^{nc} how to provide an other tenant for the mille, and let hym coferr with Thos. Davyes of Wigmire abote the death of the man.

Divide my blessing betweene yourself and your brothers and sisters, and, if you challenge a double parte, strive to walke worthy of your title to it, which you can never do, unless you feare all s———e, which the Lord in mercye settle in your heart, that you may be the joye of your father,

Ro. HARLEY.

Com^d me to your cossin Smyth.

London, 30^e 8bris, 1641.

LADY VERE to EDWARD HARLEY.

Good Nephew—I am very sory to hear by yor sistars leter of the weakn^s in your arme. I am glad you ar in London, whear you may have the meanes wich I pray God to bles to you, and m'k vs to se the mercy in preserveiug yor life with this mark of honor. I did writ latly to you about my sad busnis, it is lick to be very burdensom to me, for I shall not know what to do, if that plas faill me. My hope is in God, who will never fail them that ar His. I know you will not be wanting in any thing wherein you may be helpfull in the busines, wich I beleue you vnderstand so well as to know what is to be done in it, and I know your fathers love and care of me. I hear not it that my nephew Tracy be come, and tell then I hear nothing can be don. God geve me a good end of it, and menes to expres the senserity of my affections, wich shall never faill in loveing and esteming you, and in aproving myself,

Yor most faithfull true loving avnt,   MARY VERE.

LORD CONWAY to COLONELL HARLOW.

Nephew—I heare that you are returned to London, hauing heard that your hurte in your arme did grow worse, when it was conceived it was in an estate of melioration. I doubt that you comme to London that you may haue a good chirurgion. I send therefore this to enquire of your health, of which I am very desirous, not onely bycause of your neereness to me, which inciteth euery one to wish wele without other reason, but bycause that I thinke your health will not be ill bestowd on you: and it is very mutch wished to you by,

Your most affectionat vnkle to serue you,

CONWAY AND KILULLA.

Sion, Sep. 28. (1643?)

The EARL of WESTMORLAND to COL. HARLEY.

Cosen—Ther needs noe apollogising wher the inconsiderablenes of your mushrom frends and seruants heer ought and must giue way to those sublimer occations wherein you with many more heroes or worthyes are wrap. I wish I were but a hewer of wood or a water tanker in this great work begun of reformation, wherein ye divel and wicked men cause yet soe many rubbs. But the vpper orbes are wise, and know what sphear is sutable to every p'portion of light. I am fixed in resolution, I assure you; noe roaming, wandring plannet; and therefore it may be, to weak sight may appeer a twinkler, though I was born high and a gentleman, though not altogether Welch; therefore must needs say, I contemn y^t monster parety, soe much now seeks to domineer. I am sorry the treaty ends without beginning. The summer will be the hotter if God (who alone can) p'uent not.

My wife is yet soe weak she sitts not vp, and therefore I thanke you for and from her, and wish you all happiness whither you goe. Resting euer,

Your poor yet truely affectionat kinsman to serve you,

WESTMORLAND.

My love and seruice to y^r good father. Doe not tel him that I am going afoot this morning to Malling Lecture, least he conclude me a Puritan.

Februar: 22.

The COUNTESS OF WESTMORLAND to COL. HARLEY.

Deare Cousin—I here this afternone that Hulle is beseged, and my Lord Fairfax and my brother in danger. Pray if you doe here any thing send me word, for I am very much troubled, and whether Beverley be taken by my Lord Nacastell: what news you hav, pray comunicat, and lay a farther obliggation one,

Your affectionat cousin,   M. WESTMORLAND.

Directed—" To my very much esteemed cousine, Coneranell Harlow."

The EARL of WESTMORLAND to COL. EDWARD HARLEY.

Cosen—Pray acquaint your father with what I was entertained with, all this day—heer coming one of the officers of Douer Castle with Sir Nicholas Miller to church, they dined with me and assure, that ther is a great plott discouered at Douer, which was to have seised on the castle upon Wensday last for the K—— without P——. The gentleman tells me he saw the kinges com'ission for it, which, vpon search, they found in a fether bed: it was directed to Captain Collins and others: some of them taken, and the maior there in hould. This Collins com'aunded the blockhouse iust vnder the castle in the dukes time, and had been easd of that charge sithence. I fear this will not sound well in times of treaty. But stil our God workes marvailously for vs: to whō be praise.

If your intents hould westward, let me know for Robins sake.

Soe rests at your com'and,   WESTMORLAND.

Mer: 10—23. (1644.)

Directed—" For my cosin, Collonell Harley,
            at Westminster."

The EARL of WESTMORLAND to COL. EDWARD HARLEY.

Cos. Col. Ned—I take this opportunety again to thank you for that favour you did vs heer, which must not be forgotten. It seems the world is pregnant with mischiefs, soe that treaty and treachery are coupled, and plotts generative begetting plotts. I was tould of the Douer busines that morning I came out of toun, but knew nothing to w^t now; for I haue spoken with one who sawe the com'ission itself, which was directed to one Increse Collins, quondam captain of the blockhous ther vnder the D. of R and L. his gra. The partees apprehended, as ye Maior of Dover &c., were brought to Maidston and ther examined yesterday, from whence I heer they will send them vp. I strain to lode intelligence, that we may be refreshed with some by return from the Mint. My wife came from church very ill on Christmas day, but, God be praised! is better now (a good condition for all the sex). Freedom bids me salute you with what I conceived vpon the coniunction of the two great planetts (which you may impart to Spencer, that great astronomer,) Christmas and Fast:—

>Quondam festa dies nunc jeiunantibus apta es,
>Ut queis non prosunt gaudia, mœsta iuvent.
>
>A holy day I was: and am soe still.
>For holy fasting saues wher riotts kill.

Soe rests,

"Tuus dum sum,"

WESTMORLAND.

St. Jhos day (1644?).

Directed—" To my loving cosen, Collonell Edward Harley, at Westminster."

Col. HARLEY to his brother Thomas.

Deare Brother—I have now exchanged the sweet country aire and sports for the dirt, fogs, and trouble of the city. The employment there, is to chase the poore hare, or crafty fox; heere, to pursue one another. The forest whence I came, hath not beasts more savage as we meete every day. The lustfull goat, fawning dog, greedy wolf range freely, and what is worst, every one abounds with these wild inhabitants, and want sagacity to pursue and courage to destroy them. If every private person would be an honest hunter, we should not complaine of so many Nimrods. If you have recovered, and can spare your *watry hunter*, I shall be very glad to receave him from you. The assurance of your health will be very wellcome to,

       Your most affectionate brother,

                  EDW. HARLEY.

Westminster, 6 Martii, 1650-1.
For his deare Brother,
 Mr. Thomas Harley.

ED. HARLEY to his father.

Sir—I trust the same mercy which conducted me safely hither hath comfortably preserved you. If that confidence did not refresh me, this journey would be very sad; but I dare not doubt the tender compassions of our heavenly Father to you, because I have alwaies experienced your tenderness to me. Thus, I beseech you, give me leave according to our Lord and Saviors precious logick to make some return for your fatherly love to me, with an assurance of an infinite Fatherly love to you. Sir, if our Lord God see it good to permitt Satan to discover his malice, be pleased to consider that your age and weakness, which encourage Satan to assault you: they doe much more assure you of victory, because all the retrenchments from your own ability to resist, doe place you more closely and imediately under the secure protection of the Lord of Hosts, who I doubt not will graciously avenge you of your spirituall adversary; will make His candle shine upon your head, and having sanctified all His dispensatins towards you, will fully assure you, that having given you His son, how shall He not with Him also freely give you all things. Thus humbly prayes he, who begs your blessing for, Sir,

 Your most obedient son,   EDW. HARLEY.

Birmichem, Feb. 2, 1653-4.
 To his most honored father,
Sir Robert Harley, Knt. of the Bath,
 at Ludlow, present these.

EDW. HARLEY to his father.

Sir—I bless God for your letter and for the testimony of His goodness to you, which I trust will be graceously continued and enlarged. I am not yet at a certainty whether I shall procure the money by the security of an assignation of your statute to the Earle of Lincolne, or by a new statute, but I doubt not a speedy dispatch, through Gods goodness. Wednesday last, the lord Protector rode in great state from Temple-bar to Grocers Hall. The lord Mayor rode bare, with the sword before him, and was knighted by him after the banquet, and the sword the Protector did then weare, he bestowed upon the Mayor. The Recorder his speech I present to you, enclosed. I beseeche the Lord in mercy confirme your health, according to His abundant mercy, which is the prayer of him, that humbly begs your blessinge, and is,

Sir,
Your most obedient Son,
EDW. HARLEY.

London, Old Bayley, 11 *Feb.* 1653-4.
For the Right Worshipfull
Sir Robert Harley, Kt. of the Bathe,
    at Ludlow, Shropshyre.

EDWARD HARLEY, on the day of his marriage, to his Father.

Sir—Although I have not heard since I parted from Ludlow concerning your health, I trust our gracious God continues your health towards a further degree of confirmation and strength. This day according to your leave, and by Gods mercy to me, I have consumated this great affaire heere, and my dear heart and I joyn in humbly begging your blessing. The most part of the 3000*l.* will be in a fewe daies at London. 1500*l.* of it is for Mr. Sherwyn. I desire to know whether Mr. Lacy shall have his money out of the remainder. My Lady Button is very desirous to have the joynture immediately settled, which I doubt cannot be wel-done before you speak with Mr. Powys, who is now on the circuit; therefore if please you, I think you may give my lady satisfaction for the present, if you acknowledg a statut of 8000*l.* to my Lady Button, with a defesance that you will settle a joynture within three or six months of 500*l.* per an. This may be done at Ludlow; and if you aprov it, I beseech you that it may be speedily dispatched hither. I think Mr. Davies of Wigmore can draw the defesance wel. My Lady Button is very desirus of a letter from you. She presents her service to you. When you think fit to writ of any privat business, I think, Sir, it may be better, if you pleas, to mak use of my sister Stanleys penn. Sir, I beseech the Lord in mercy continue your health and enlarge all spiritual comforts to you. So prayes, Sir,

Your most obedient son,

EDWARD HARLEY.

Tavistock, June 26, 1654.

Sir—I beseech you y^t our maryag may be kept privat.

To his most honored father,
Sir Robert Harley, Kt. of the Bathe,
At Ludlow, present these.

MARY HARLEY to her husband, Col. ED. HARLEY.

Deare Heart—I was very ill on Saturday last, and not abrode till to day. The duty as you desierid of the fast was this day performed, and the other of prayer every second Thursday shall be, if God pleas—it being your fathers command as well as yours. Mr. Shilton tells me Hurse cannot have either of the livings. I was forced to borrow money to paye Rutley 15*l.* 12*s.*; and I must borrow sume and the rest in my gold must pay Mr. Shiltons bill to Mr. Cloggie. The steward tells me none will be had. I know not what to doe for the house. I believe I must be forced to leve it, tho I should gladly do any service I am able. I have given your directions concerning the church to Mr. Davis, and to the steward for to bring hay, which he thinks, as he tells me, very difficult alredy, and it will be impossible, by that time he hath done plowing: so he would have too of the coach horses sent to be kept at Brompton. My brother came well home last Satturday, but the coach brook at Eacham, and came not till yesterday. Sir Robert and all are well, but your sad (and in your absence, deare heart,)

Unhappie, MARY HARLEY.

Sep. 16.

Pray write to my mother—my service to my brother, with my prayers for his health. We prayed for his recovery, which we hop will be sudaine. My brother presents his love to you. If you write to my mother, and send the inclosed you'll doe a great favour. My mother is grieved she heard not from me.

Sir EDWARD HARLEY to his Brother, announcing the birth of his son Robert, afterwards created Earl of Oxford.

Deare Brother—I thanke God I can give you the notice of the great mercy God hath pleased to vouchsafe us. Thursday, 5 Dec. between 7 and 8 in the evening my wife was very well delivered of a lusty boy, who was next day baptized and bears my fathers name, and through mercy my brother was recovered to so much strength as to be present. I desire you to joyn with us in thankfulness for this great mercy.

I desire to be comended to Mr. Hawes. Sir H. Lingen came not to town before this night. Monday morning, God willing, I shall speak with him, and I hope secure both Mr. Hawes and some others from further troubles. I hope you have received before this time some letters I wrote since W. Reynolds coming up, who brought all things safe.

I pray God bless the children, who I hope will be glad of theyr new brother, for they shall be loved still . . . . peice . . . . . leg and thigh. My sister is much better in health than when she came up. I pray God be with you.

  I am your most affectinat brother,   EDW. HARLEY.

Bow: Street, Dec: 7, 1661.

Directed—To the Worspl. Thomas Harley, Esq. at Bucknel.
Leave this with Mr. Edward Robinson, bookseller, at Ludlow.

No. II.

(1.)

The Protestation alluded to in Letter CVI. was no doubt that taken by the House of Commons 3rd May, 1641, to which is prefixed, in the Journals of that House, the following:—

"A Preamble, with the Protestation, made by the whole House of Commons, the 3 of May 1641, and assented unto, by the Lords of the Upper House, 4th of May.

"We, the Knights, Citizens, and Burgesses of the Commons House in Parliament, finding, to the Grief of our Hearts, that the designs of the priests and Jesuits, and other Adherents to the See of Rome, have of late more boldly and frequently put in Practice then formerly, to the Undermining and Danger of the Ruin of the true reformed Religion in his Majesty's Dominions established: and finding also, that there hath been, and having Cause to suspect there still are, even during the Sitting of Parliament, Endeavours to subvert the fundamental Laws of *England* and *Ireland*, and to introduce the Exercise of an arbitrary and tyrannical Government, by most pernicious and wicked Counsels, Plots, and Conspiracies: and that the long Intermission and unhappier Breach of Parliaments hath occasioned many illegal Taxations, whereupon the Subjects have been prosecuted and grieved: and that divers Innovations and Superstitions have been brought into the Church; Multitudes driven out of his Majesty's Dominions: Jealousies raised and fomented between the King and People; a Popish Army levied in *Ireland*, and Two Armies brought into the Bowels of this Kingdom, to the Hazard of his Majesty's Royal Person, the Consumption of the Revenue of the Crown, and the Treasure of this Realm: and lastly, finding the great Causes of Jealousy, Endeavours have been and are used, to bring the *English* Army into Misunderstanding of this Parliament, thereby to incline that Army by Force to bring to pass those wicked Counsels; have therefore thought good to join ourselves in a Declaration of our united Affections and Resolutions; and to make this ensuing Protestation:—

"I, A. B., do, in the Presence of Almighty God, promise, vow, and protest, to maintain and defend, as far as lawfully I may, with my Life, Power, and Estate, the true, reformed, Protestant Religion, expressed in the Doctrine of the Church of *England*, against all Popery and Popish Innovations, and according to the Duty of my Allegiance to his Majesty's Royal Person, Honour, and Estate; as also the Power and Privilege of Parliament, the lawful Rights and Liberties of the Subjects, and every Person that maketh this Protestation, in whatsoever he shall do, in the lawful Pursuance of the same: And to my Power, as far as lawfully I may, I will oppose and by good Ways and Means endeavour to bring to condign Punishment all such as shall, by Force, Practice, Counsel, Plots, Conspiracies, or otherwise, do any thing to the contrary in this present Protestation contained.

"And further, I shall, in all just and honourable Ways, endeavour to preserve the Union and Peace betwixt the Three Kingdoms of *England*, *Scotland*, and *Ireland*; and neither for Hope, Fear, nor other Respect, shall relinquish this Promise, Vow, and Protestation."

This protestation was immediately taken by the majority of the House then assembled, and directions were sent into the country for its being taken by sheriffs, magistrates, and others. It was not until 20th January, 1641-2, that Mr. Serjeant Wilde presented from his committee sitting at Grocers' Hall, the copy of a letter to be signed by the Speaker and sent to the several sheriffs of counties respectively, requiring "them and the justices of the peace of the counties to meet together in one place, as soon as possible they may, and then to take the protestation themselves; and then, dispersing themselves into their several divisions, to call together the minister, the constables, churchwardens, and overseers of the poor of every parish, and tender unto them the protestation, to be taken in their presence, and to desire them speedily to call together the inhabitants of their several parishes, both householders and others, being eighteen years of age and upwards, and to tender unto them the same protestation, and to take the names both of those who took it and of those who refuse, and to return them to the knights and burgesses, &c."

In consequence of this requirement, which was highly offensive to the gentry of Herefordshire, a declaration was got up and printed under the title of "The Declaration or Resolution of the County of Hereford:" on which occur the following notices in the Journal of the House of Commons:—

(2.)

"*Die Veneris,* 8° *Julii,* 1642. *Post meridiem.*
PROCEEDINGS OF THE HOUSE ON THE RESOLUTION OR DECLARATION OF THE COUNTY OF HEREFORD.

"*Resolved, &c.*—That the printed Paper intituled, 'The Declaration or Resolution of the County of Hereforde,' shall be referred to the Committee for Printing: Who are to sit To-morrow at Two o'clock, in the Exchequer Chamber.

"*Resolved, &c*—That   Hammon the Printer shall be forthwith summoned to attend this House, and be brought up in safe Custody.

"Mr. Maddison was called in, and did aver that he, being at a Stationer's Shop, and reading a Pamphlet intituled, "The Declaration or Resolution of the County of Hereford," and saying, that this was a foul Scandal upon the Parliament, and that the Author of it deserved to be whipt; one Sir Will. Boteler told him, that he deserved to be whipt for saying so; and that he would justify every Word in it: and that, by God he would slash him; and while he was talking with him, one Mr. Dutton, a Minister, came to him, and likewise said, that he deserved to be whipt; and he asked, Wherefore? And he replied, For speaking Nonsense, and for saying it was a Libel.

"*Resolved,*—That Mr. Dutton, the minister, shall be forthwith committed a Prisoner to the Gatehouse, there to remain during the Pleasure of the House, for carrying himself in a scornful Manner in the House, and for as much as in him lay, justifying the foulest and most scandalous Pamphlet that ever was raised or published against the Parliament.

"Mr. Dutton was again called in; and Mr. Speaker told him, that, by his carriage here towards the House, one might well judge of his Behaviour towards the Parliament out of the House: and that, as much as in him lay, he had justified one of the foulest and most scandalous libels that ever was raised or published against the Parliament: and then the Speaker pronounced the sentence against him aforesaid.

"*Ordered,*—That Sir William Boteler's bail shall be required to bring him in to-morrow morning.

"Same day.—Message from the Lords, by Judge Foster and Judge Mallet:—

"That the Lords do desire a present Conference by Committee of both Houses, concerning a Printed Paper intituled, 'A Declaration or Resolution of the County of Hereford.'

"Answer returned by the same messengers:—

"That this House will give a present meeting, as is desired.

"Sir William Lewis, Sir Rob. Harley, Sir John Evelyn are appointed managers of this conference.

"Two constables were called in, Who informed the House, that they were sent by the Justices of the Sessions at Newgate with Two Persons that were taken divulging the Printed Resolution of the County of Hereforde.

"The Men were called in, and confessed the same; and that they bought them of one Hamond.

"Sir Rob. Harley reports, from the Conference had with the Lords, That the Lords had brought unto them a printed Paper, which is a scandalous and infamous Libel in the name of the county of Hereforde, and do desire that this House will join with their Lordships in desiring the Knights that serve for that County to send down to know who in that County will avow the same: And, if any do, that they shall be prosecuted to the utmost, for setting forth such an infamous Libel.

"*Resolved*,—That this is a most scandalous and infamous Paper.

"*Resolved*,—That Jo. Hubbard and Evan Lewis shall be sent back to the Justices of Peace at the Sessions at Newgate, to be there proceeded against according to Law, for publishing an infamous and scandalous Libel.

"*Ordered*,—That Sir Rob. Harley do bring into the House To-Morrow Morning Two Letters he received from some of the Gentry of the County of Hereforde.

"*Resolved*,—That Hamon the printer shall be sent for as a Delinquent.

"11 July. *Ordered*,—That Mr. Venables be sent for forthwith to attend the House, and that he be examined at the Committee appointed for the Defence of the Kingdom concerning the printed Paper of the Resolution of Hereford; and that Sir Rob. Harley do attend that Committee with those letters he hath received from some Gentlemen of the county of Hereforde.

"20 July. *Resolved*,—That upon the humble petition of Evan Lewis and Rich. Hubbard, Prisoners in Newgate, by Order of this House, for selling about the Streets, a printed Paper, called '*the Resolution of the County of Hereford*,' they be forthwith released from any further Restraint."

The editor has been unable to find any copy of this declaration; but among Lady Frances Vernon Harcourt's collection, is the following paper, which embodies the views of Sir Wilm. Croft and others, who now more openly joined the King, and were shortly in arms against the Parliament.

(3.)

MS. endorsed, " Herefford Protestation."

THE PROTESTATION.

I—— beinge herevnto required doe willingly and in the presence of Almighty God solemnely vow and protest as followeth :—

1. That I beleeve noe power of pope or parliament can depose the soveraigne Lo. K. Charles, or absolve mee from my naturall allegiance and obedience vnto his royall person and successors.

2. That the two Howses of Parliament without the King's consent hath noe authority to make lawes, or to bind and oblige the subject by their ordinances.

3. Wherefore I beleeve that the Earls of Essex and Manchester, Sir Tho. Fairfax, Sir Will. Waller, Coll. Massie, together with all such as already have or hereafter shall take vp armes by authority and commission of the members of parliament of Westminster, pretendinge to fight for Kinge and parliament, doe thereby become actuall rebells, and all such ought with their adherents and partakers to be prosecuted and brought to condigne punishment.

4. That myselfe will never beare armes in their quarrell; but if I shal be thereunto called, will assist my soveraigne and his armyes in the defence of his royall person, crowne, and dignity, against all contrary fforces, vnto the vttermost of my skill and power, and with the hazard of my life and ffortunes.

5. That I will not discover the secretts of his Majestyes armyes to the rebells, nor hold any correspondence or intelligence with them. And all designes of theirs against our soveraignes armyes, or for surprizeinge or deliveringe vppe the cittyes of Worcester or Hereford, or of any other his Majestyes forts, I shall truly discover to whom it shall concerne, so soon as ever it comes unto my knowledge.

6. That his Majesties takeinge up of armes for the causes by himselfe so oft declared in print is just and necessary.

7. That I will endeavour all I may to hinder all popular tumults, riseings, randevous, meetings, confederancies, and associations of the people, townes, hundreds, and countyes which are not warranted to assemble by his Majesties express commission, or by power derived from him or by vertue of his comissions, and in the sense he meanes it.

8. I detest from my heart that seditious and trayterous late invented nationall covenant, and I promise never to take it.

All these particular articles I vow and promise sincerely to observe without equivocation or mentall reservation.

So helpe me God.

I doe strictly enjoyne, without exception, all commanders and souldyers, gentry, cittizens, ffree-holders and others within the county and cittye of Herefford to take this protestation, which is to be tendered vnto them by the High Sheriffe and Comissioners of the county, assisted with such a divine as they shall make choice of to that purpose; and that a scedule of their names who shall refuse to take the same is to be delivered vnto Sir William Bellendene, Comissary-Generall.

C. R.

(4.)

The Hereford Petition.

Die Mercurii, 4° May, 1642. *Journals of the House of Commons.*

The House being informed that divers Gentlemen of the County of Hereford were at the Door, who desired to present a Petition to this House:

They were called in; and did present the same, and then they withdrew; and their petition was read,—

The which being done, they were again called in; and Mr. Speaker, by the Command of the House, told them, that this House finds their Petition full of great Expressions of Duty to his Majesty, and of Love and Respects to this House and the Commonwealth, (for which they give you Thanks,) and full of great Concernment to the Commonwealth; which they command me to tell you, they will take into serious Consideration, so soon as may stand with * * *

The petition was as follows, here printed from a printed paper, endorsed in Sir Robert Harley's handwriting

"HEREFORDSHIRE PETITION, 1642."

"To the honorable, the Knights, Cittizens, and Bvrgesses of the Commons Hovse assembled in Parliament.

"The humble Petition of the High Sheriffe and divers of the Gentrey, Ministers, Freeholders, and Inhabitants of the county of *Hereford*.

"*Most humbly sheweth,*

"That with all thankfulnesse we acknowledge those many and great Blessings we have already received through God's mercy, the favour of our Gratious Soveraigne, the Wisdome, Councell, Sollicitation, and unwearied Paines and Patience of this Honorable Assembly, for the preservation of the Priviledges of Parliament, and liberties of the Subject, the removing of many of these Obstructions which hindred your good endevours; your zealous furthering of bleeding *Ireland's* Reliefe, earnest desire of disarming Papists, and securing of their persons; your prudent care in disposing the *Militia, Navie,* and places of Importance of this Kingdome to such persons of Trust as may (by God's blessing) give assurance of safetie to the King's Royall person, and good subjects of all his Majesties Dominions: your Pious Care to settle a Government in the Church according to the Word of God, your godly desires to prevent the Prophaning of the Lord's day; To take awny pluralities and *Non Residents,* and your zeale to provide Preaching Ministerie throughout the Kingdome, whereof this County stands in great neede, it now abounding with insufficient, Idle, and Scandalous Ministers, whereby the people generally are continued in Ignorance, Superstition, and prophanenesse, and are ready to become a prey to popish suducers, which Idolatrous profession hath of late yeares with much boldnesse appeared in this County: And wheras one of our cheife Commodities is the Native Wooll of this County, the price whereof is much fallen through the excessive importation of Spanish woolls, to our great impoverishing.

May it therefore please this Honorable House to continue your Prudence and Pious intentions and indeavours in all the Premisses not yett Accomplished, to hasten the speedy releife of Distressed and Gasping Ireland, *To remove evill Councellors, To take away the Votes of Popish Lords, Speedily to disarme the Papists, To settle a Godly and Learned Ministery, and to restraine the excessive Importation of Spanish Wooll.*

And wee shall be ready with chearefulnesse to contribute all possible Assistance our Prayers, lives, and livelyhoods may afford for the defence of his Maiesties Royall person, this Honorable House, and the preservation of the priviledges of Parliament.

London, Printed for *John Francke.* 1642.

No. III.

(1.)

LETTER FROM DR. NATHANIEL WRIGHT TO SIR ROBERT HARLEY.

To his much honoured friend SIR ROBERT HARLEY, Knight of the Most Noble Order of the Bathe, present these in Westminster.

Sr—If you can conveniently spare it, I desire that favour from you as to furnish me with the remainder of that mony which I disbursed for our Brompton soldiers in distresse. The account I left with you, and if you please to satisfye my request herein, this bearer (my brother-in-law) will convey it to me at his returne into these parts, which will be speedy. Were not my condition such as to enforse me to call upon you, I had much rather be silent, then sollicite you in this nature. I shall not need relate my wants, nor yet tell you of my sufferings: the last you in some measure know, and the former I sufficiently feele. I beseeche you pardon this freedome of expression, and accept of the humble tender of mine and my wifes love and service to yourself and yours, from him who is in all conditions, Sr,

Your most affectionate and most humble servant,

NATH: WRIGHT.

Salop, 9bris 10, '45.

(2.)

MEMORANDUM OF RENTS PAID BY SIR ROBERT HARLEY. 1639.

(In Sir Robert Harley's handwriting.)

1639. Rents yearly payd by mee.

	£	s.	d.
1. To ye kg for Kgsland	85	16	00
2. To ye kg for Wigmore parke	02	02	00
3. To ye kg for Bucton, &c.	00	14	04
4. To my Lo. Craven for Leintwarde	36	00	00
5. To my Lo. Craven for Mocktree	84	15	00
6. To ye kg for Burrington	21	10	11¼
7. To Sr Ro. Howard for Bucknill	00	00	00
8. To hym for the forrest, &c.	00	00	00
9. To Sr Wm Croft for my chiefe rent for Eyton	05	14	00
10. To ye bishop for Wigmore teithe	03	06	08
11. To hym for Leynthall Starks	04	04	00
12. To hym for Bucton	03	06	00
	247	08	11¼
13. To my Lady Wake	200	00	00
	447	08	11¼

(3.)

Particulars of Losses sustained by Sir Robert Harley since the Wars.

A particular of what loss my master, Sir Robert Harley, hath sustained by the enemy in the county of Hereford since these wars.

	£	s.	d.
Imp.—The stock of cattle of all sorts at	940	0	0
The loss of £1500 per annum for 3 years	4500	0	0
The castle itself being utterly ruined	3000	0	0
All the rich furniture and household goods belonging to the castle	2500	0	0
Two mills, with brew-houses and stalls and other out-houses, together with corn and hay, valued at	950	0	0
A study of books, valued at	200	0	0
Two parks wholly laid open and destroyed	500	0	0
Timber and other wood cut down and destroyed, valued at	300	0	0
Destroyed at least 500 deer.			
Destroyed more in corn at least	100	0	0
	12,990	0	0

This was brought to Westminster by the 23rd July, 1646.

SAML. SHELTON.
WM. BAYLEY.

(4.)

Rents paid to the King by Sir Robert Harley.

Endorsed—" Rents paid to the King by Sr Robert Harley."

Sr Robert Harleys estate in Herefordshire was from anno 1642 till May 1646, vnder the power of the Kings souldiers.

Aprill 16th, 1642.—The halfe years rent for Kingsland, Burrington, and Wigmore Parke was paid to Mr. William Geears, then receiver.

Aprill 11th, 1643?—The whole years rent was paid to Mr. Gervase Blackwall, receiver.

Octob. 16, 1643, was paid the halfe years rent to the said Mr. Blackwall.

No. IV.

(1.)

Letter 12 Aug. 1647, Signed, Denzell Holles, Walter Long, Will. Lewis, Jo. Clotworthy, William Waller, Ph. Stapilton, Anth. Nicoll, to Edwd. Harley.

Noble Sr—The place where you lodge and the necessity of our priuacy have denied vs of the opportunity of visitinge you, which wee have very much desired. Wee haue now gotten our passes to trauell, and beinge as carefull of you as of our selves, haue procured yours also, which wee send you heere inclosed. Wee intend to goe away speedily, and the most of vs into the Low Countryes, from whence wee shall (God willinge) giue you notice in what place wee shall stay. Sr, wee hartily pray for your health, and much desire the happinesse of your company, as a person of soe much honnor and worth, that wee have a very greate obligation vpon vs to be for euer, Sr,

Your very affectionate freinds and humble seruants,
 (Signed)
William Waller.	Will. Lewis.	Denzell Holles.
Ph. Stapilton.	Jo. Clotworthy.	Walter Long.
Anth: Nicoll.		

12th of Aug. 1647.

Endorsed—"From the 11."

(2.)

A Pass from the Speaker Lenthall, (11 Aug. 1647) for Col. Edward Harley to go beyond the sea.

Endorsed—" My pass to travel for six months."

By vertue of an order off the Howse of Commons, These are to will and require you to suffer the bearer hearoff, Collonell Edward Harley, a member of the Howse of Commons, wth his servants and twoe horses, to ship himselfe in any port wthin this kingdom to goe beyond the sea; heroff you may not fayle, as y^u will answer the contrary at your utmost perills. Dated ye 11th of August, 1647. This pass to continue for the space off six monthes, to be accounted from ye date of ye s^d order.

  (Signed)   Wm. Lenthall,
                   Speaker.

To all comaunders, officers and soldiers, both
 by sea and land, and to all others whom
  these may conserne.

No. V.

The Protestation at the King's Head, 12 Dec. 1648.

Endorsed—" Protestation at the King's Head, &c."

Wee whose names are hereunto subscribed, being members of the House of Comons and free men of England, doe hereby declare before God, and angells, and men, that the general and officers of the armye, being raysed by authority of Plt, and for defence and mayntenance of the priviledges therof, have not, nor ought to have, any powr or jurisdiction to apprehend, secure, detaine, imprison, or remove or psons fro place to place, by any color or authority whatsoever, nor yet to question or trye us or any of us by martiall lawe or otherwise, for any offence or crime whatsoever which can or shall be objected or apprehended against vs. And that the present imprisonment and removall of or psons is a high violation of the rights and priviledges of Plt, and of the fundamental lawes of ye land, and a higher vsurpation and exercise of an arbitrary and unlawful power than hath been heretofore appended to, or attempted by, this or any King [or] other Power whatsoever within these realmes. Notstanding w^h we and every of us doe declare our readynes to submit o^rselves to ye legall tryall of a free Plt for any cryme or misdemeanour that can or shall be objected agst us. In wittness whereof we have hereunto subscribed o^r names ye 12th of 10^{bris}, 1648.

(Signed)

   Edw. Massie.   William Waller.
   Lio. Copley.   John Clotworthy.

Att the King's Head in the Strand.

No. VI.

(1.)

Letter from Major Winthrop to Colonel Harley and Major Harley, 3 Aug. 1650.

To my honoured ffriends Col. HARLOWE and Major HARLOWE these present.

Gentlemen—I have received some commands from the Commissioners for the militia of this countye concerning yourselves, grounded (as I believe) upon some information of your disaffection to this present government, and therefore that I should send for you to my quarters at Leominster; but I shall only at present lett you know that they expect you should appear before them at Hereford, on Tuesday next, and so I remain,

       Gentlemen,
        Your friend and servant,
   (Signed)   S. Winthrop.

Leominster, 3 *August*, 1650.

(2.)

Letter from Colonel Harley to Major Winthrop.

Colonel HARLEY to Major WINTHROP.

Sir—I received by this bearer a letter from you dated this day, and directed to myself and my brother Major Harley (who hath been gone out of this country now four days), in which you express that you have received some commands, grounded as you believe upon information of our disaffection to the present government, from the commissioners of the militia, to send for us to your quarters at Leominster, where for the present you are, and let us know that the commissioners expect our appearance before them at Hereford, on Tuesday next.

Sir—After giving you thanks for your civility, I must take liberty something to wonder, that the commissioners for the militia should in such manner summon myself and brother, who are members of Parliament, who have from the beginning of the late unhappy troubles constantly and faithfully served the Parliament, and I am sure cannot be justly taxed with the least disaffection to it. If our coming into this country, our birthplace, and where God hath disposed the means of our livelyhood, be ill interpreted, it is without reason; for, I assure you, no design brought me hither, but the dispatch of some necessary occasions, concerning my father's estate, which being once dispatched, I shall, God willing, returne to London. This being all my business in these parts, I hope that liberty which is not denied to those who have been in armes against the Parliament, shall not be grudged to us who have lost our blood and suffered so much for the Parliament. But if this, which is nothing but the truth, do not satisfy you, I will, if please God, visit you on Monday next at Leominster.

(3.)

Colonel Harley's Promise to be in London.

Endorsed—" Promise when I was a prisoner at Hereford, August 10, 1650."

"For ten years space after this, I was not permitted any residence in Herefordshire. E. H."

I will, by the help of God, if my life and health permit, be at my father's house in Westminster, Saturday August 18, 1650, and continue there until the 1st day of September next following.

In witness whereunto I have put my hand this tenth day of August, 1650.

EDW. HARLEY.

(4.)

PASS FROM WROTH ROGERS TO COLONEL HARLEY TO TRAVEL FROM HEREFORD TO LONDON. 10 AUG. 1650.

Endorsed—" Pass from Wroth Rogers when I was disarmed and imprisoned. August 10, 1650. E. H."

These are to desire all officers and soldiers, and all others whom it may concern, to permit and suffer the bearer hereof, Collonell Edward Harley, with his three servants and fower horses, quietly to pass from the cittee of Hereford unto the cittee of London, wthout any trouble or molestation, hee acting nothing prejudiciall to the commonwealth.

Given under my hand this 10th day of August, 1650.

(Signed) WROTH ROGERS.

(5.)

SIR ROBERT HARLEY TO SIR HENRY VANE, WITH SIR HENRY VANE'S REPLY, AND A LETTER FROM SIR ROBERT TO EDWARD HARLEY, ON ONE SHEET. 20 AUG. 1650.

Sir ROBERT HARLEY to Sir HENRY VANE.

S^r—This waits on you to receave the further manifestation of y^r good favour towards, S^r,

Your affectionat friend and humble servant,

RO. HARLEY.

Westminster, Aug. 20th, 1650.

Directed—To his honorable friend,
    Sr Henry Vane, Kt.
        at Whitehall.

Below which is returned, on the same paper:—

S^r—I have enquired into your busines, and finde that your sons are under greete suspecion and not like to be removed suddenly from thence, unlesse there be some more urgent occasion for it then yet appeares, and I do perceave that the matter depending now as it does before the counsell, they will expect addresses to be made to themselves in this affair ; so rests,

S^r,

Your affectionate freend and humble servant,

H. VANE.

On the same sheet :—

Ned Harley—The enclosed will tell you what I haue done upon the news of both your brothers being confined in Bristol. I pray you quitt Herefordshire as soone as you can, and the Lord blesse you and return you with safety to your most loving father.

Ro. HARLEY.

Westminster, Aug. 20, 1650.

(6.)

MR. ROBERT HARLEY TO HIS BROTHER, FROM BRISTOL CASTLE.
9 Nov. 1650.

Major ROBERT HARLEY to his Brother THOMAS.

Deare Brother—I have receaved yours by my footman with Mr. Watts receipt and counsell of states letter, for doing the . . . the . . . I am not . . . but to gett suretys is the difficulty, I being not as yett prepared.

My love to my brother and sisters, and humble duty to my father : by the next you will heare of my continuance here or remoue, that, if please God, wee may see one another.

Your most affectionat,

Ro. HARLEY.

Bristoll Castell, 9 *Novr.* 1650.
For Mr. Thos. Harley,
at Sir Robert Harleys house,
Tuttle Street, Westminster.

No. VII.

(1.)

LETTER FROM EDWARD HARLEY TO THE MASTER AND FELLOWS OF CAIUS COLL. 14 DEC. 1658.

EDWARD HARLEY to the Reverend and Worthy the Master and Fellowes of Gonvil and Caius Colledg in Cambridg—present these.

Reverend and Worthy—The leas of the rectory of Folden in Norfolk, granted by your society to my wifes mother, the Lady Button, and by her death accrewing to us, wee desire in Gods fear, so far as lies in us, to restore that portion of the Lords to the seruice of the Lord. We would choos silently to discharge this duty; but we hope God will inclin the hearts of so worthy a school of the prophets, both to place a godly and lerned pastor at Folden, now voyd, and to perpetuat that mayntenance which I can only perform for a few years. In order to which we are willing to resign our leas upon these terms,—viz. That you wil promis under your hands to joyn your best endevors with ours, that assoon as may be, by act of Parlement, the profits of the rectory of Folden surmounting your rent reserued upon our leas, may be vnited to the vicarag, and settled for ever upon the incumbent minister at Folden; that until this vnion be effected, according to law, you will renew the leas for twenty-and one years future, either to myself or some other person of responsible estat and integrity, only in trust and for the use and benefit of the minister of Folden for the time being, which leassee shal also giv bond of 500 lb. penalty not to conuert the profits aforsaid to any other use then is expressed.

Concerning the next incumbent, I beseech you accept my thanks for your curteous offer by Mr. Naylor, of the nomination, of which favor I shall only desire this, that before you confer your presentation, the person may be aproved by my reverend friend Dr. Tuckney. I understand the benefit of my leas will augment the mayntenance to 100 lb. yearly, which wil be a comfortable subsistence for an able divine. To such an one I beseech God direct your choice, and bles your society, to send forth many faithful laborers into the vineyard of the Lord, who from thence may be transplanted to shine as the stars for ever. Thus prays

Your most assured friend to serve you,

EDW. HARLEY.

Decemb. 14, 1658.

(2.)

LETTER TO DR. TUCKNEY, MASTER OF ST. JOHN'S COLLEGE CAMBRIDGE.

EDWARD HARLEY to the Reverend Dr. TUCKNEY, Master of St. John's Colledg, and Regius Professor of Divinity in Cambridg, present these.

Reverend S^r—Whereas the Master and Fellowes of Caius Colledg have pleased in contemplation of some interest I hau in the impropriat rectory of Folden in Norfolk, to offer me the nomination of the next incumbent, now voyd, and in the colledges gift, of which favor I have only thus far accepted, to desire that the person the college intend to present may be first aproved by yourself, whom I beseech to be wel assured, that the person you shall approv, be orthodox in doctrin and disciplin, and of a godly conversation. Your acquaintance with my dear father, who is with God, encorages me in this boldness to trouble you, as your known worth gives me confidence to entrust you. I shal be most glad of any occasion to present you a thankful return from, S^r,

Your very faithful friend and servant, E. H.

Tawstok in Devon, Decemb: 14, 1658.

(3.)

MEMORANDUM SIGNED BY THE MASTER AND FELLOWS OF CAIUS COLLEGE, RELATIVE TO THE LIVING OF FOLDEN IN NORFOLK.

Endorsed—" Caius Colledge, concerning Ffolden."

July 2, 1662.

Whereas the vicarage of Ffoulden in the county of Norfolk is of so small value, that it is not a competent maintenance for a minister, We, the master and ffellows of Gonvil and Caius College (the undoubted patrons of the said vicarage), being desirous to add all possible encouragement to the future incumbent of the said vicarage, have jointly and vnanimously ordered and decreed the day and yere above written, that for the future the rectorie impropriate in Ffoulden aforesaid, belonging to the said college, shall be perpetually annexed to the said vicarage, and that the vicars thereof successively shall enjoy the same during their residence there, without payment of any ffiue or income. . . . . paying to the said college the ancient usually reserved rents. In witnesse whereof, we, the said master and ffellowes have subscribed our names, this 3rd day of July, in the year of our Lord 1662.

WILL. ADAMSON.   ROB. BRADY, Mr. or Keeper.
JO. FELTON.   WILLIAM BLANKE, y° Prd:
JO. ROBINSON.   JOHN GOSTLIN.
JO. ELLYS.   HENRY JENKES.
  WILLIAM LYNG.
  ED. GELSTHORP.
  WIL. NAILOR.
  . THRUSTON

No. VIII.

ORDER IN COUNCIL FOR THE APPREHENSION OF MAJOR ROBERT HARLEY. SIGNED HE. LAURENCE. 28 DEC. 1658.

Endorsed—" Copy of an Order of the Council of State for the apprehending Major Robert Harley. December 28°, 1658.

" By Richard Cromwel, (called) Protector.

" He was apprehended at Kynsham Court, at Mr. Thomas Blayneys. January, 1658-9."

In pursuance of an order of his Highnes and the Councell of the date hereof, These are to will and require you, immediately upon sight hereof, to

repaire unto the lodgings of Major Robert Harlowe, or unto any other pla[ce]
or places where you shall understand the said Major Robert Harlow to b[e]
and him the said Major Harlow to apprehend, and in safe custody to brin[g]
before the Councell to answer such matters as shall be objected against hi[m].
And all mayors, sheriffes, justices of the peace, constables, and other office[rs]
are required to be aiding and assisting in the due execution of the pr[e]
mises; and for so doing this shal be your sufficient warrant. Given [at]
Whitehall this 28th of December, 1658.

Signed in the name and by order of his Highnes and the Councell.

(Signed)   HE. LAWRENCE,
Presdt.

To Edward Dendy, Esq. S^{rt}
    at Armes, or to his deputy
       or deputies.

No. IX.

(1.)

LETTER FROM SIR EDWARD HARLEY TO THE LORD CHANCELLOR
CLARENDON. 12 DEC. 1665.

May it please your Lordship—I humbly address this to wipe o[ff]
that breath would intercept the clearness of your Lordship's favo[ur]
wherein (in that degree became me) I thought myself happy. My Lor[d]
Bishop of Hereford since his return from Parliament told me that yo[ur]
Lordship had acquainted him you had received some late informatio[n]
concerning me, as if I were not well affected, neither to the church n[or]
state, and that I countenanced factious persons. Particular instances [or]
proofs of this general accusation my Lord Bishop did not mention to m[e]

and if such were given to your Lordship, I doubt not most clearly to disprove or refute them.

I shall therefore (after most humble thanks for the notice your Lordship hath pleased thus to give me, wherein I hope I mistake not your favors towards me) beg leave to rectifye myself before your Lordship.

As for my religion, I thank God I can truly say I have no opinion but what is consonant to the Catholic faith and the doctrines of the Church of England, but what I have learned out of the Scriptures and the writings of the ancient fathers; accordingly, through God's help, I endeavour to lead my life, which, to clear me from all suspicion of schism, hath not only the present and sufficient evidences of a constant and reverend attendance upon divine service, but in times of danger had the testimony of many hazards, and expences in behalf of reverend persons of the church. I could say more, but I forbear, least I speak like a fool. My Lord, I wonder not that I am now reported to be a countenancer of factious persons, for I well remember when I served his Majesty in Dunkirk, it was commonly said, that the chaplains I brought into garrison were factious persons. But the truth was, I discarded the factious, and introduced learned and pious persons, who are now, one of them a prelate, the others, reverend divines in the church. I can now also truly averr, that I have not countenanced any factious persons, nor have such persons resorted to me, nor hath there been in my family any factious or unlawful meeting.

As for my affection to his Majesty's service, it is now twenty years since, upon that account I have constantly lost, done, and suffered: and in order to his Majesty's happy restoration I did, without the vanity of comparison, employ all the poor ability of my estate and person. My Lord, what I did then, I did out of duty—I had not any other design. My Lord General knew how unwillingly I undertook the command of Dunkirk. In that employment, I thank God, I served his Majesty with all fidelity and affection, and with as much devotion as ever my life is always at his Majesty's service.

In the beginning of July, I was visited extreamly with the gout in both my legs, from which affliction I have not been wholly free for ten days space, that kept me from attending my duty in Parliament. But in this part of the country, where I reside, I can truly affirm the King's service, in all respects, hath been diligently and faithfully managed.

My Lord Bishop* told me that the like information was brought to your Lordship, concerning my brother Thomas as concerning myself. As for him, though I had not sooner opportunity to signifye, I had a must grateful sense of your Lordship's favor in making him a Master in Chancery. He doth most humbly profess the like, and what I have alleadged for myself, I can do the same for him; that both his religion and loyalty are most affectionately orthodox and sincere. Having said thus much, I beseech I may add the tender of most humble service to your Lordship from my brother Robert, who still remains with me in a very weak condition. I hope your Lordship will vouchsafe credit to these lines of truth, in behalf of a poor family, which hath not deserved ill, I am confident, of those who have misrepresented us. I heartily forgive all the injury, except the necessity of so long a trouble to your Lordship, from, my Lord,

Your Lordship's most obedient, most humble servant,

E. HARLEY.

Brompton Brian, Dec. 12, 1665.

(2.)

LETTER FROM THE LORD CHANCELLOR TO SIR EDWARD HARLEY.
18 DEC. 1665.

Sir—Though I am very glad always to hear from you, yet I am very sorry that you had such an occasion to give yourself the trouble of writing to me the 12th of this month, when it seems you thought my friendship was lessened towards you. I make no doubt but I might say any thing to my Lord Bishop, which his Lordship sayth I did say to him; and that he meant no ill, either to you or me in the representation; but I do as well know that I have received no late informations concerning you which made the least impression on me to your prejudice. I know too well the humours of this age, and how frankly they speak of things and persons, according as they like or dislike, and I do in some degree know the temper of Herefordshire; and, if any information had about that time been given to me, to your prejudice, it is very probable I might communicate it to my Lord

* Dr. Herbert Croft.

Bishop, to receive his good testimony of you, without the least doubt of your sincerity either to church or state, which in truth I never had, since I was acquainted with you, and upon my conscience the king is well satisfied in both. Truely, I cannot remember that ever any body spoke to me to the disadvantage of your brother Thomas, and therefore I must confess to you, I was in some amazement when I read your letter. You will give better reason to be ill thought of, than you have yet done, if you are much troubled with the licence men take of talking, of whom they please, and what they please. It is an even lay that they who are bold with you one day, will be as bold with the king himself another day. I pray be confident, when I have any thing that makes your affections worthy to be questioned, I will let you know it, and receive your answer. I am heartily sorry poor Robin continues still weak. I pray commend me to him, and believe, that you shall always find me to be,

   Good Sir Edward,
    Your affectionat, humble servant,
       CLARENDON, Chancellor.

For Sr Edward Harley, Knight of
 the Bath, at Brompton Brian, in
 Herefordshire.   [Per Ludlow post.]

St. John's Colledge, 18° *December*, 1665.

(3.)

LETTER FROM SIR EDWARD HARLEY TO THE LORD CHANCELLOR.
28 JAN. 1665-6.

I presume too much, to offer to your Lordship the trouble of reading so many lines of no better subject than myself. I see, it is too true, that it is very difficult to undertake one's own cause, without committing great faults. Of one I am extremely sensible—that I have occasioned your Lordship the pains of answering my humble paper. I beg your pardon in all sincerity, yet I cannot but reckon it a happy fault, by which I am possessed of so many noble expressions of your Lordship's goodness and kindness, as your lines bestow upon me.

I have many reasons to believe my Lord Bishop's friendship to me, and specially because he hath several times related to me your Lordship's favourable discourse to him of me; but when I shall have the honor to wait on your Lordship, I shall, with your leave, make appear what I said on my own behalf was not altogether without cause. Though your Lordship be allways above the endeavour, be pleased to accept the affection that devotes me, my Lord,

Your Lordship's most obedient, most humble servant,

E. HARLEY.

Brompton Brian, January 28, 1665-6.

To my Lord Chancellor Clarendon, &c.

No. X.

(1.)

EXTRACT FROM A LETTER OF ROBERT HARLEY, ESQ. TO HIS FATHER, 14 MARCH, 1699-1700, RELATIVE TO DUNKIRK.

Lord Clarendon's memoirs are coming out. There are some letters, &c. confirmed by Sir Stephen Fox, that General Monk agreed to and pressed the selling Dunkirk, because Sir Edward Harley was turned out. An account of that and E. Macclesfield's proposal would be very acceptable.

(2.)

Sir EDWARD HARLEY'S Answer, dated 19 March, $\frac{1688}{9}$, wrote in my aunt Harley's hand.

I shall be very glad to see the memoirs you mention; but, as concerning your friend, once at Dunkirk, the sum of what he can say concerning himself is summed up in the 90th Psalm:—" We spend our years like a tale that is told." If the Lord please to spare his poor worm, an account shall be endeavoured for you, concerning that affair. What you mention concerning the Earl of Macclesfield's offer of 10,000*l.*; it is what many witnesses in several places, and upon several occasions, have heard his Lordship fully express, with undeserved regard and kindness, to the then governor of Dunkirk. What is said to be spoke by the Lord General Monk in relation to Colonel Harley and Dunkirk, hath many attestations, but it is hoped that, without mistake, it may be averred that the Earl of Montague was told by King Charles that he would not have parted with Dunkirk, if he could have been permitted to retain Colonel Harley in that post, which *he* would have preserved for his Majesty without extraordinary charge; but, said the king, " I am continually disturbed because he is represented to be a notorious Presbyterian." I shall not at this time add more upon that subject. I would be glad, if the Lord sees good, to represent to you that full scene.

No. XI.

Sir WILLIAM GREGORY to Sir EDWARD HARLEY.

Sir—Being sensible of the greate love that was betwene my Lord Scudamore and yourselfe, it makes me thinke it a necessary duty in me, to acquaint you of the time intended for his Lordship's interment, that soe, if your health and occasions will permitt, you may, if you please, performe your last civility to his Lordship's body, by accompanying it to the grave, wherein, I opine, it will be layed upon Thursday, the 8th of June, at Home Lacy church. We shall come that morning from Gloucester, and therefore I believe the funerall will not be, till about two of the clock. Sir, I begg your pardon for this trouble, and for my haste in it, but I have time only to subscribe my selfe,

Your most faithfull and humble servant,   W. GREGORY.

Grays Inn, ult: Maij, 1671.

No. XII.

(1.)

SIR EDWARD HARLEY'S RETROSPECT OF HIS LIFE ON ENTERING HIS FIFTIETH YEAR. 21 OCT. 1673.

I was born at Brompton Castle, 21st Oct. 1624.

I am now, through divine long suffering, at Brompton Brian, 49 years old.

O Lord! in thy hand is the breath of all mankind, and it is only God who holdeth our soul in life. But in most special manner I ought to praise my God, who preserved me from abortion at Burton-under-the-Hill. In this place, this day gave the light of life to poor clay, and for forty-nine years thou hast granted me life and favour, and thy visitation hath preserved my spirit. Lord, thou hast granted me life in the deliverances of life: when a child, from the chin-cough, measles, small-pox twice, and danger of drowning in the moat; when a man, from many perils in the wars, particularly when my horse was shot, when my arm was hurt, when a muskett-bullett, levelled at my heart, was bent flat against my armour, not reckoned of such proof, without any harm to myself. Many dangerous falls on horseback I have had, specially when I was wonderfully preserved, my horse stumbling and falling into a ditch near Orleton, in frosty weather, but was never by any fall much hurt. I have often been preserved in journeys and voyages from thieves; from waters, specially in a dangerous passage once at Newnham. Many times I crossed the sea between England and Flanders, allways safely; though once, in a great storm, constrained to lye at anchor 36 hours over against Graveling, 1661. I was delivered from the malitious accusation of the army, 1647, and my God made my speech in my defence in Parliament acceptable. That year I was preserved from the plague, of which my servant died, and at the same time recovered from a dangerous pestilential fever. In 1649 I had a long lingering distemper, which ended in a violent sickness with vomiting and purging at Wigmore; but, though the chastening was sore and deserved, I was not given over to death, but God restored me to health. Afterward I was preserved from the cruelty of that power which put to death holy Mr. Love. In 1654 I was recovered from a grievous ague, which had seized me in Devonshire. Some years I was visited with the gout, but through mercy the fits have been short, and my limbs restored to me; and now for above two years I have not been disabled with that disease. In 1640 God was pleased, with a fatherly wisdom and goodness, to visit me with a rupture, by which I was for many years kept humble and from many temptations. I used often many medicines and remedies prescribed by physitians and chirurgions, but without effect, yet after it had been upon me more than twenty years, it pleased God to heal that breach upon me, without the use of any remedy whatsoever, so that I have been perfectly well for several years. This is a most bountiful favour. O Lord! heal my soul of all vain desires, and accept my strength to serve the God of my life. O! let me never forget this signall blessing. Teach me, oh my God! to love thee with all my strength, and never to doubt the love of God Almighty, all sufficient, in whatever condition I shall be exercised, for my God is my life and the length of my days.

In all distress during the warrs, when my father lost all his estate, his houses burnt, and for three years had not any thing of his own for his family, we had allways meat to eat and raiment to put on. Praised be my God, that hath granted me the comforts of life, healthy constitution, usefull senses, money to pay my debts, power to build a convenient habitatio[n] blessing to repair many ruins in the estate of my father, and to enjoy [it] peaceably. Gracious was my God in giving me my first wife, now I trus[t] a blessed saint, who was a most affectionate, prudent, pious person, by who[m] God gave me, besides a very considerable portion, the mercy of four daug[h]ters. Two sleep, I trust, in Jesus, and live with God. Two now surviv[e] I hope, to glorifie God.

Gracious was my God, in giving to me my present wife, who hath bee[n] made the dear comfort of my life now above twelve years, and the moth[er] of four sons and a daughter, of which God was pleased to take my younge[st] son, in infancy, to His mercy.

Blessed be God! that hath granted me favour in the affection of m[y] father and my mother, who tenderly loved me, and wisely and carefully i[n]structed and corrected me. What am I, a poor worm, to have any estee[m] in the world, or to be accepted by thy saints? O Lord! by thy favour [I] was chosen of several parliaments; chosen, unknown to myself, Governor [of] Dunkirk, and there honoured to be serviceable to thy servants, and to ass[ist] the sanctification of thy holy sabbath.

How pretious are all thy thoughts of love unto me, O God! How gre[at] is the sum of them! The visitation of thy Spirit, O Lord! hath taug[ht] me the precious wonders of thy laws. From my birth, the lines have fall[en] unto me in pleasant places, for I have always heard the joyful sound of t[he] divine jubilee. Nay, Lord! this place, which was greatly waste, and f[or] divers years in the region of the shadow of death, for the sins and iniquiti[es] of my forefathers, who were idolators and sinners, and of me an unhol[y] vile wretch, now is made to me a goodly heritage; for we have a place [of] worship and a faithful dispenser of the Word of God.

Who is a God like unto our God, that pardons iniquity, transgressio[n] and sin? O Lord! for thy name's sake, heal my backslidings, love [me] freely, subdue all my iniquities, and cast all my sins into the depths of t[he] sea. My life is but a vapour. Oh! in Jesus Christ beget me, by the inco[r]ruptible seed of thy word, which liveth and abideth for ever, that I may [do] the will of God and abide for ever. Oh, Lord! I am the clay, be thou m[y] potter. Fashion this house of clay to be thy temple. Make me a vessel [of] praise and service to thy Majesty. Be not ashamed to be my God! ther[e] fore make me holy, as my God is holy, in all manner of conversation and godliness. Forsake not the work of thy hands, but keep me by thy power through faith into salvation, for the sake of Jesus Christ, in whom make me accepted, and partaker of the riches of thy grace, which hath abounded towards me, in all wisdom and prudence. Amen.

(2)

Sir Edward Harley's Retrospect on the Completion of his Fiftieth Year.

At Brompton Brian, 21 Oct. 1674.

I am this day, through divine patience, 50 years old. O Lord! I am not worthy the least of thy mercies. I have recorded some of the manifold loving kindnesses of the Almighty in the memorial of my last anniversary.

This year is now concluded to me in health, though it hath in every month of it been full of sorrow. Many dear friends taken away. After the death of Sir Robert Moray and my cousin Froysell, it pleased God to put an end to the pilgrimage of my brother Sir Robert Harley, Nov. 1673. In January at Westminster I was visited sharply with the griping of the gutts, but when I was under sentence of death it pleased God to cheer and raise me up. I returned from the Parlement in March. The weather being very bitter, I had no harm in that journey, but immediately after return, I was visited with the gout in both feet and hands. This fit was most painful and of longest continuance, yet now I am, blessed be God! comfortably free from that distemper. In November dyed my good friend Mr. Thomas Doughtie. In April, Sir Edward Massie; and, in a sad manner my cosin, Bartholomew Beal. In August, my dear neice Frances FitzJames, of the small-pox. Since that, my worthy friend Mr. Thomas Treherne, and my cosin Reads wife, both dead in the same day! and now my sister Palmer; while I, a poor unprofitable worm, am still spared. O, my God! the fiftieth year was in Canaan the year of Jubilee. Oh! that this may be to me the acceptable year of the Lord! wherein I may be released from the miserable chains of sloth and carelessness, which render me so vile in the eyes of the glory of my God. Lord! work in me for this same thing, by thy

Spirit, that I may be fervent in spirit, serving the Lord. I do not beg length of days, but with humble submission and resignation I beg to be spared to bring up my children, which in mercy are given me, to serve their generation according to the will of God, and that I may see the goodness of God to the Church in the land of my nativity, and be someway serviceable thereunto; that having seen the salvation of the Lord, I may depart in peace, my spirit being received by God who gave it, and my body sleeping in Jesus, until the last day, when both body and soul shall be glorified and be ever with the Lord, who loved and washed me from my sins in His blood. Even so, come Lord Jesus! come quickly. Amen.

NOTES TO THE LETTERS.

P. 1. *Lord Brooke.*—Fulke Grevile, Lord Brooke, was great-uncle to the lady Brilliana, her grandfather, Sir John Conway, having married his sister Eleanor. Collins, Peerage, vol. v. p. 225. Lond. ed. 1768.

Beaetham's Court.—Beauchamp Court, co. Warwick, the seat of Lord Brooke.

Tuddington.—Toddington, co. Gloucester, the seat of her grandfather, Sir John Tracy.

P. 2. *I hope the Parlament has spent as much time as will satisfy them in dooing nothing.*—Sir Robert Harley sat in the second Parliament of that year for the county of Hereford, from 6 Feb. 1625-6, to 15 June, 1626. (Willis, Notitia Parliamentaria.)

The payling of the nwe parke is made an end of.—The park adjoining Wigmore Castle was in a very decayed and neglected state, when it was granted to Sir Robert Harley.

P. 3. *I hope your clocke did you saruis betwne Glostre and my brother Brays.*—Sir Giles Bray, of Barrington, in the county of Gloucester, son of Edmund Bray, Esq. by Dorothy, daughter of Sir John Tracy, who married, secondly, Sir Edward Conway.

P. 4. *Mr. Pirson.*—The Rector of Brampton Bryan.

P. 5. *Present my beest love to my sister Wacke.*—A contraction, probably, of Helegenwagh, the third daughter of Lord Conway, wife of Sir W. Smith, of Hill Hall, co. Essex.

P. 6. *Ragley.*—The seat of Lord Viscount Conway, in Warwickshire.

Lady Veere.—She was the third daughter of Sir John Tracy, of Toddington, and aunt to the Lady Brilliana. Collins, Life of Vere, p. 342.

P. 7. *Ned Smith.*—Son of Sir Wm. Smith, by Helegenwagh, sister of Lady Brilliana.

P. 8. *Mrs. Willkinson.*—Wife of Dr. Willkinson, Principal of Magdalen Hall, Oxford. See Notes to the Introduction, p. xlix.

NOTES TO THE LETTERS.

P. 10. *I had not hard of Duke Roberts and my Lord Cravens being taken.*—Robert third son of the Elector Palatine and Elizabeth, daughter of King James, better known as Prince Rupert. In the battle of Lingen, in Westphalia, between the Emperor and Palatine, the forces of the latter were overpowered, and Duke Robert and Lord Craven made prisoners.

William Craven, eldest son of Sir William Craven, Lord Mayor of London (1611), having distinguished himself in foreign service, was knighted 4 March, 1626, and, eight days afterwards, created Baron Craven.

P. 12. *A booke printed by authority from the King, in which he has forbid the Booke of Common Prayer, and granted them a public fast.*—In Sept. 1638, the Marquis of Hamilton published a royal Proclamation in Scotland, which is " the Book " here alluded to.

P. 13. *Mrs. Pirson.*—Widow of the Rev. Thomas Pierson, the Rector of Brampton Bryan.

I thanke you for the Man in the Monne.—The Man in the Moon, by Domingo Gonzales, was the title of a posthumous work by Francis Godwin, Bishop of Hereford 1617—1633.

P. 14. *At Loudlow wheare the caus was hard.*—In the Court of the Council of the Marches of Wales.

P. 18. *I hope theare will no such things be imposed upon your lowes.*—That is, innovations in religious matters on Magdalen Hall.

P. 19. *By order of the Lords.*—The Lords of Privy Council, or the Lords Lieutenants of counties, issued orders to the magistrates and deputy lieutenants to take measures for keeping the peace and calling out and regulating the militia, in which Sir Robert Harley had a company : they were about this time usually trained by Low Country officers and soldiers. "Sargent Weare was one of these; he had been in Germany under Sir Thomas Conway."

Cousin Scriven.—Thomas Scriven of Frodesley, in co. Salop, colonel of a regiment of foot of the trained bands in that county: married Elizabeth daughter of Vincent Corbet or Moreton Corbet, and widow of Thomas Corbet. He was distinguished for his loyalty, and knighted, probably at Shrewsbury, soon after the battle of Edge Hill; and was buried in Condover Church, Salop.

For Forane newes, I beleeve you have hard that Briscake is taken.—Old Brisach or Brisac, a town of the Grand Duchy of Baden, once included in the Brisgau: it formerly stood on the west side of the Rhine, but since the river changed its course it is near the east bank of it, between Basle and Strasburg. It was regarded as a strong place, and sustained several seiges; the most remarkable was that here alluded to, when it was taken by Duke Bernard of Saxe Weimar. (Encyc. Metrop.)

The Curantes are liened againe.—Books of foreign news again licensed.

P. 21. *Mr. Penell: his mother was Sir Edwards Grevell's daughter, and so she was my cosen.*—Sir Edward Grevill being brother-in-law to Sir John Conway, his daughter was first cousin to Edward Viscount Conway, the father of the Lady Brilliana.

Mr. Scidamore that dwells hard by Heariford.—Mr. afterwards Sir John Scudamore, knight, eldest son of William Scudamore of Ballingham, co. Hereford, married Penelope sister of John, first Lord Scudamore. He was a distinguished traveller in Italy and other parts, a royalist, and took up arms in the King's cause, and was killed in a duel with Colonel David Hyde at Bristol, 12 May, 1645, and was there buried in the church of St. Werburgh.

P. 22. *Duke Robard and Lord Crauen prisoners.*—Prince Rupert was under restraint for upwards of three years: at length reluctantly liberated by the Emperor, through the mediation of Sir Thomas Roe, the English ambassador, upon solemn promise never again to bear arms against that prince.

P. 24. *Mr. Pirkins.*—Mr. Edward Perkins, under whose tutorage Edward Harley now was, at Magdalen Hall.

P. 25. *Lady Cope.*—Lady Elizabeth Cope, second daughter of Francis first Earl of Westmorland. She was wife of Sir John Cope, of Hanwell, Bart., and married secondly William Cope of Icomb, co. Gloucester. (Collins's Peerage, iii. p. 183.)

P. 27. *The holy Court.*—An English translation of "La Cour Sainte"—a devotional work of Nicholas Coussin, a learned jesuit, confessor to Louis XIII. This is perhaps the work alluded to in p. 13, where Lady B. says, " I would willingly have the French booke you write me word of . . . . for I had rather reade any thinge in that tounge then in Inglisch."

P. 31. *Theare is a booke which is rwitten by a papis that is conuerted; it discouers much.*—Probably "The Religion of Protestants a Safe Way to Salvation, by Will. Chillingworth, M.A." which was published in 1637 or 1638.

P. 32. *My Lord of Woster's sonne shall be generall of the hors.*—Edward Somerset, Lord Herbert of Ragland, afterwards known as Earl of Glamorgan, and second Marquis of Worcester, the author of " A Century of Inventions."

P. 37. *Good Mr. Stevenson.*—Vicar of Wigmore. The register of that parish records the baptism of one of his daughters by the name of Brilliana, in compliment to Lady Brilliana Harley.

P. 39. *The Act.*—Scholastic exercises at Oxford: again p. 45.

P. 46. *I haue sent some bessor stone, which you may take at a night when you goo to bede.*—Bezoars: concretions met with in the bodies of ruminant animals. They were celebrated for their supposed medicinal virtues, and considered as highly alexipharmic; so much so, that other medicines supposed to possess the same virtues obtained the name of bezoardics. So efficacious were they once thought, that they were eagerly bought for ten times their weight in gold. Besides being exhibited internally, they were worn round the neck, as preservatives against contagion. For this purpose, it is said, in Portugal it was customary to hire them at about ten shillings per day. It is needless to add, that the accounts of their extrordinary virtues must be now considered imaginary. See a further account in the Encyclopædia Metropolitana.

Orampotabely.—Aurum potabile. Another medicine rejected from the Materia Medica, but formerly much vaunted by empirics as a most powerful tonic. (Encyclopædia Metropolitana.)

P. 49. *Mr. Simons, a worthy minister, and three or fower more are gone into the Low Contreyes to shift for themselves.*—Escaping from the contributions required from ministers towards supplying the army: before alluded to in p. 37.

P. 51. *I thanke you for the King's booke.*—The large declaration concerning the tumults of Scotland, by the King, 1639, written by Dr. Balcanquall, Dean of Durham.

P. 63. *Letter* XLVIII.—Terminating the first series of Letters addressed to Edward Harley at Oxford.

P. 64. *Letter* XLIX.—Edward Harley returns again to Oxford.

P. 66. *I thanke you for the relation of the seae fight.*—A relation of the engagement between the Dutch and Spanish fleets in the Downs, which took place early in September.

P. 68. *Sir Richard Newpo,t.*—Created Lord Newport 1642. Brother of Sir Robert Harley's second wife.

P. 69. *If the venter of the Corrantes be in prison.*—Vendor of foreign news.

P. 72. *There is a Duch imbasodr, Mounsire Arttson, come over to excuse the fighting of the Duch ships upon the Inglisch cost.*—Van Aersen, Lord Somnelsdyke. Another object of this embassy was the marriage of the Prince of Orange with the Princess Mary. (Baillie's Letters, 29 Jan. 1640-1, vol. i. p. 294.)

P. 81. *Sir William Pelham hath refused to be knight of the shire.*—For Lincolnshire, in the first parliament of 1640, which met on the 17th April, and was dissolved on the 5th May following,

P. 84. *Mr. Blineman is goon into New Ingland.*—One of the Puritan ministers.

NOTES TO THE LETTERS. 255

P. 87. *On Tuesday next, if pleas God, your father will keep a day.*—In this parliament Sir Robert Harley and Sir Walter Pye represented the county of Hereford. He now sets apart a day for solemn prayer, in preparation for his duties in parliament.

P. 95. *On Sunday morning I receved a letter from your father, by which I found the news of the disolueing of the parlament to be true.*—On Sunday, the 10th May, Lady Brilliana hears from Sir Robert a confirmation of the rumour of the dissolution of parliament which took place on Tuesday (Die Martis) the 5th of May.

P. 100. *Letter* LXXXIII.—Ends another series of letters to Edward Harley at Oxford.

P. 101. *Letter* LXXXIV.—Finds Edward Harley with his father in London.

P. 103. *I heare that parlament is ajourned for ten days, but I defer my beleefe.*—A mere rumour. Parliament sat all December.

P. 105. *Mrs. Wallcots was with me this weake.*—The wife of Humphrey Walcot, of Walcot, Esq., whose funeral sermon, under the title of "The Gale of Opportunity," was published with that preached at the funeral of Sir Robert Harley, by Thos. Froysell, minister of Clun, in Shropshire.

Dr. Toby Mathue was with Mr. Plooden, wheare theare was great resort of papis, which makes some feare they haue some plots.—At Plowden Hall, near Walcot, the seat of a Catholic family who have enjoyed the estate, from which they derive their name, as far back as our records extend. Sir Toby Mathew was a Jesuit of the order of Politicians.

P. 106. *Mr. Tommes was at Brompton and helpt us in my family.*—In the religious exercises of the previous Wednesday. This was most probably John Tombes, B.D., a most eminent divine of his sect, settled at this time at Leominster, whom Calamy says, in his abridgment of Baxter's History of his Life and Times, "all the world must own to have been a very considerable man and excellent scholar, howsoever disinclined they may be to his particular opinions." See a list of his works in Calamy, and further particulars in Neal's History of the Puritans, and also in Wood's Athenæ, vol. iii. p. 1063.

P. 112. *I thought the Jesuet had bine acuesed of treson. I hope the King will yeald to the request of the parlament in that particular.*—The person alluded to was John Goodman, a priest and Jesuit, whose history is well known.

P. 117. *I hope my brother is not for Lord Straford: I hard my Lord Straford layed some of his actions to his charge.*—Lord Conway gave adverse evidence on Strafford's trial.

P. 118. *If you have bine to hear the Scots ministers, send me word how you like them.* —"The people throngs to our sermon, as ever yow saw any to Irwin communion: their crowd daylie increases. Six of us, Mr. Blair, Mr. Henderson, Mr. Borthick, Mr. Gillespie, Mr. Smith, and I preaches our tour about on Sunday and Thursday. In my last tour on the 3d verse of the 126th Psalm, 'The Lord hath done great things for us,' I spent much of an hour in ane historick narration, the best I could penn, of all that God had done for us fra the maid's commotion in the Cathedroll of Edinburgh to that present day: monie teares of compassion and joy did fall from the eyes of the English." Baillie's Letters, vol. i. p. 295.

I thanke you for the paper the Scots put into the Lords.—Many papers were put in for money on account of the 300,000l. granted in February to supply the wants of the army before it was disbanded. In the end of the following May 120,000l. of arrears were due. On the 19th June it was concluded that 100,000l. should be paid Midsummer 1642, and 200,000l. at Midsummer two years after. (May's Hist. of the Long Parliament.)

P. 121. *Letter* CVI. *misdated in the year.*—Letter CVI. 25 March, 1641, appears to be misdated and misplaced in the collection: it would naturally follow Letter CXLIII (19 March, 1641), in which it is said, " I hear the justices have sent up their answer why they would not take the Protestation—Sir Will. Croft governs all of them," and should be dated 1642. The protestation mentioned in it was, no doubt, that taken by the House of Commons 3 May, 1641, which was considered by the parliament " a true test of every good subject," " a shibboleth to distinguish the Ephramites from the Gileadites, that whosoever was well affected in religion and to the good of the commonwealth would take, and on the other side who would not take it was not well affected" (Denzel Holles' Speech to the House of Lords): and which was designed to be taken by all well-wishers to the Parliamentary cause. It appears from Letter CXVII., 21 May, 1641, to have been taken with great willingness at Brampton, Wigmore, and Lentwardine, where Sir Robert Harley's influence predominated, but it was not well received in the country; and, on the 20 Jan. 1641-2, a few days after the King's attempt to seize the *five* members, Serjeant Wilde brought up from his committee, for the signature of the Speaker, a copy of a letter to the sheriffs, requiring the justices of the peace and others, of 18 years of age and upwards, to take it. (See Appendix, p. 222.) The petition alluded to in this letter was probably the Hereford Petition, afterwards presented to the House, and well received by it in May, 1642. This letter acquaints us also with the views of Sir William Croft towards the Parliament, and soon after the raising of the standard at Nottingham in August, although he had been for some time under the displeasure of the King, he joined his majesty's army, and was with the King, to his great admiration, at Edge Hill.

P. 124. *Sir William Croft.*—Sir William Croft, of Croft Castle, in the county of Hereford, was son of Sir Herbert Croft, and born 1593: he represented Malmesbury in Parliament in 1625-1627. He was a gentleman of the Privy Chamber to King Charles; but, having evinced his dislike to the Duke of Buckingham, he was suspended from his office for three years, and on his murder banished from the court and dismissed. This treatment did not destroy his attachment to his royal master, in whose army he held the rank of colonel, and particularly distinguished himself at the battle of Edge Hill. He was taken prisoner at the surrender of Hereford on April 25th, 1643, but soon afterwards recovered his liberty, and was killed gallantly fighting in the royal cause, in a skirmish near Hopton Castle, or, as others say, near Stokesay Castle in Shropshire, July, 1645, and was buried in the chancel at Croft, where there is a slab to his memory. See Memoir of Sir James Croft in Southern and Nicolas' Retrospective Review and Historical Magazine, vol. i. p. 496. London.

P. 129. *I am glad my Lord Saye is Master of the Wards.*—"17 May, 1641. The Lord Cottington gave up his place of Master of the Wards, which the Lord Say had conferred on him." Whitelocke's Memorials, p. 44.

P. 130. *The Protestation was taken on Sabath day last at Brompton, Wigmore, and Lainterdine, with much willingness. I desire to know whether you took it.*—This protestation must have been that taken by the House of Commons on the 4th of May. The readiness with which it was taken marks the great influence of Sir Robert Harley in these places. It was much objected to and resisted in the country.

I have sent you a peuce of angelica rooat, you may carry it in your pocket, and bite sometimes of it.—" A pious and learned schoolmaster, that ventured to stay in London in the Great Plague of 1665, and was much employed, as some friends of mine that knew him and commended him assured me, to visit the sick, and distribute alms and relief to them, went indiscriminately to all sorts of infected, and even dying persons, to the number, as he told me, of nine hundred or a thousand. . . . . . I enquired what antidote he used: he replied, that next the protection of God, which so many sad objects made him the more fervently implore, and a constant fearlessness, the only preservative he used, besides good diet, were, half a spoonful or a spoonful of brandy five or six times a-day, especially when he went into infected places, and the bigness of a small nut, or less, of a root of Spanish angelica, of which he held in his mouth the quantity of a pepper-corn, or somewhat less, as often as he thought there was need." Relation iii. of Strange Reports, Robert Boyle's Works, vol. v. p. 102.

P. 131. *I am glad that justice is exicuted on my Lord Straford, whoo I thinke dyed like a Seneca, but not like one that had tasted of the mistery of godlyness.*—Wednesday, 12 May. "The Earl of Strafford beheaded on Tower hill. Some doubted whether his death had more of the Roman or the Christian, it was so full of both." Laud's Diary.

P. 135. *Rwit me word how the pasage was of Mr. Harberde Pris his carage in the parlament, becaus theare is such various reports of it.*—Mr. Herbert Price was burgess for Brecon in both parliaments of 1640. He is noted in Cobbett's Parliamentary History as one who left the Parliament and joined the King at Oxford, and was among the forty-six members who, on the call of the House, 16 June, 1642, were absent, when it was resolved "that those absent members whose names were now read shall not sit in the House till they have made their excuse to the Committee, and their excuse reported to the House, and that the House hath allowed it." Journ. H. Com. 16 June, 1642.

P. 136. *I am glad Corenell Goreing did so well cleere himself. We heare of many plots, &c.*—Lord Strafford's escape, it is said, had been planned. Master Goreing, eldest son of the Lord Goreing, was implicated in the charge, but, upon examination, dealt so clearly with the charge, and so far purged himself from evil intentions, that he was not at all committed by the Parliament. May's Hist. of the Long Parliament.

P. 140. *I thanke you for the acts of Parlament, and for Docter Downing booke.*—This was probably a book of the notorious Colybute Downing, of whom an account will be found in Wood's Athenæ, vol. iii. p. 106, too long to abstract, and too curious and edifying not to claim the reading of all who have access to it.

P. 142. *I thanke you for the King's manifest.*—Journ. H. Commons, 5 July, 1641. "The King's manifesto touching the Prince Elector read, and *Ordered*, That the House be resolved into a Committee on Wednesday next, at nine o'clock, to take into consideration *the manifesto* now received concerning the Prince Elector Palatine." Sir Robert Harley was of this Committee. The manifesto will be found in Nalson's Collections, vol. ii. p. 383.

P. 144. Letter cxxxiii. 9 *Aug.* 1641.—This letter terminates another series of letters addressed to Edward Harley, who now returns home from London.

Letter cxxxiv. *undated and misplaced.*—Letter cxxxiv. undated, contains allusions to Dr. Wright's exertions in the Hereford city election subsequent to the death of Mr. Weaver, Member for that place, which, it will be seen, took place in May, 1642: and also to a Proclamation in Shobdon church, which was most probably made after the receipt of the Speaker's letter to the sheriff; for Mr. Wigmore exercised at Shobdon a contrary influence to Sir Robert at Brampton. It would follow Letter clxxix., dated 2 July, 1642, which announces Sir W. Croft and Mr. Wigmore's intention of going to the King, or rather the previous letter, clxxviii. The original of Letter clxxix. is in a very decayed state, and the date in part obliterated: it was certainly written in the week of the 23rd, as it speaks of Wigmore fair to be held on the Monday following, which, according to the old style, took place on the 25th of July, which was on Monday, but before clxxviii. as it says Mr. Elton had not arrived to supper at 10 o'clock, whereas that letter says he came at four o'clock, no doubt of the following day. It would, there placed, terminate another series of letters addressed to Edward Harley before his return home; this it does as now printed.

P. 146. Letter cxxxv. 5 *Feb.* 1641-2.—Commences a new series addressed to Edw. Harley in London.

P. 147. *I doe much recoige in the King's answer to the pticion of both Houses, and that my brother was one of the sixe and threetie lords that voted against the bishopes.*—See Journ. H. Com. 7 Feb. 1641-2.

Answers to two petitions of the Lords and Commons, delivered 2 Feb. 1641, will be seen in the Appendix to May's Hist. of the Long Parliament. Oxford edition, 1854.

"Feb. 1641-2. The Lords pass the Bill for disabling persons in holy orders to have any place or vote in Parliament.

"Lord Conway was well affected to the Parliament and the Presbyterian discipline, and was one of the lords selected to be of the Assembly of Divines." (See the list in Neal's Hist. of the Puritans.)

"Sir Rob. Harley carried up this Bill with its amendments to the Lords." Journ. H. Com. 7 Feb. 1641-2.

P. 148. *In Hareford they have turned the tabell in the cathedroll, and taken away the cops and bastons and all such things. I hope they begine to see that the Lord is about to pury the Church of all such invencions of men.*—See the Order of the House of Commons on divers innovations in and about the worship of God. Journ. H. Com. 1 Sept. 1641.

P. 149. *I am glad to hear that Sir Jhon Conyars is leftenant of the Tower.*—On the removal of Sir John Byron, Sir John Conyars was made Lieutenant of the Tower, Jan. 1641-2. Whitelock, p. 53.

They are now about a peticion to the Parliament, which I hope will be ready to send up next weake.—A petition was on the 4th May, 1642, presented for Herefordshire, and well received by the House of Commons. See the petition in Appendix, p. 226.

We heare of letters that weare intersepted from my Lord Digbe.—Letters intercepted from Lord Digby to the Queen and Secretary Nicholas, on which the Parliament moved the King, " that he would desire the Queen not to correspond with Digby, nor any other persons whom his great council had proclaimed traytors. Jan. 1642." Whitelocke, p. 52.

P. 150. *Many feares did aris in the cuntry because the Kinge gave such a refusall to the requeste of both Howes.*—To the petition of both Houses concerning the militia, presented to his Majesty at Theobalds, 1 March, 1641.

It was a most remarqabell thinge that shipe was cast away in which thos fopperis weare.—See Journ. H. Commons, 2nd and 4th March, 1641-2.

P. 151. *Piner sends up 20l. to venture in the Irisch wars.*—24 Feb. 1641-2. The King assents to the votes of the Lords and Commons upon the propositions made for the speedy and effectual reducing of the Kingdom of Ireland. This was a scheme of adventure for raising money on the confiscated lands of the rebels in Ireland. See the scheme in Appendix to May's History, and in the Journals of the House of Commons.

260 NOTES TO THE LETTERS.

P. 152. *I did much long to receave the declaration to the King.*—"A new declaration of both Houses of Parliament sent to the King's most excellent Majesty, 16 March, upon his removall from Huntingdon to York." See May's Hist. Appendix, p. 493.

I heare the justices have sent up theare answer why they would not take the Protestation.— The Protestation of the 4th May, 1641, now demanded of all of eighteen years of age and upwards. See Appendix, p. 221, and note, page 121.

I hope shortly you will have the peticion from this conuty, but Sir Will. Croft disswaded it, as a thing unlawful to peticion.—See the petition in Appendix, p. 226. It was presented 4th May, 1642, and is again alluded to in pages 158—159.

P. 155. *Mr Gower is very well pleased that he is chosen on of the ministers.*—Journ. H. Com. 23 April, 1642. "Mr. John Green of Pencomb, and Mr. Stanley Gower of Brampton, were approved as divines for Herefordshire, fit to be consulted in the matters of the Church. The Bill for calling the Assembly of Godly and Learned Divines was read the third time 19 May, 1642." A list of them will be found in Rushworth Abridged, and Neal's History of the Puritans.

P. 158. *We hard the Kentiche peticion was brought by 3000 men, and that 3000 Loundoners meete them upon Blackeheath, and theare fought, and many weare killed.*—This was the celebrated Kentish Petition. Its reception is thus entered on the Journ. H. Com. 30 April, 1642: "The House being informed that divers gentlemen of the co. of Kent were at the door that desired to present a petition to the House, they were called in, presented their petition, and then withdrew. And their petition was read, and appeared to be the same that was formerly burnt, by order of both Houses, by the hands of the common hangman."

P. 159. *I hope something will be done to Docter Rogers.*—Dr. Henry Rogers, Canon Residentiary of Hereford Cathedral, and Rector of Stoke Edith, in Herefordshire. He was of Jesus College, Oxford, and became a famous preacher and schoolmaster. He was a member of the Convocation assembled with the Parliament of Nov. 1640, a decided Royalist, and, on the surrender of Hereford in April, 1643, was made prisoner. His preferments were sequestered, and his prebendal house, furniture, &c. bestowed on Dr. Timothy Woodroffe, a gifted chaplain, mentioned in the Introduction as having been promoted by Sir Robert Harley to the rectory of Kingsland, and a Parliamentary Preacher in Hereford cathedral. Wood informs us that Rogers had been acquainted with John Perse, alias Fisher, the Jesuit, with whom he had many disputes, and who, without authority, published an account of what had passed between them, which brought from Rogers an answer by way of Dialogue between Mr. Rogers and Mr. Fisher, 1633, to which Fisher published a reply, which was followed by Rogers in "The Protestant Church existent, and their Faith professed in all ages, and by whom. Lond. 1638." Wood's Athenæ, vol. iii, p. 31. Walker's Sufferings of the Clergy, part 2, p. 35.

P. 160. *I desire to heare how Sir Jhon Conyars comes off for Onell's escape.*—O'Neile escaped from the Tower, 5 May, 1642. "On May 13th, it was ordered that Sir Walter Erle do report the business of Mr. Daniel O'Neile's escape to-morrow morning. 17 May, Sir Walt. Erle reports the business of the escape; that the greatest matter of suspicion fell on Mrs. Sanders, who confessed she had once attempted it, but, being told of the danger of it, gave it over: notwithstanding that, many circumstances still stuck on her, for being at least knowing of his escape; and that therefore he had given order that she should put in good security for her appearance at such time as she should be required." See the Nicholas Correspondence, published with Diary and Correspondence of John Evelyn, vol. iv. p. 128.

Your father rwiteing to me by the post, and letting me knowe you weare to see the souldiers on Tuesday last, I toke it that that hindered you.—Journ. H. Com. Monday, 9 May, 1642. "*Ordered*, That the House shall meet to-morrow at eight, and adjourn at ten, to the end that such as please may see the militia of the city of London exercised."

They were assembled in Finsbury fields under the command of Philip Skippon, Major-General of all the city forces under the Parliament.

I thinke if Mr Schirbers be reproufed it would be very well.—William Sherbourn, D.D. Prebendary of Morton Parva, in the county of Hereford, suffered much for the King's cause, and lost all his preferments, to which he was re-admitted at the Restoration. He was Rector of Pembridge, where he died in 1679, aged ninety-two years. Walker says, "He had, at the persuasion of his old friend, the Earl of Essex, taken the Covenant, for which he was much disturbed in his last sickness." Walker's Sufferings of the Clergy, part 2, p. 36.

P. 161. *Sir Wm. Pelham rwites me word he has given up his liftenatcy, and his gooing to Yorks to the King.*—Early in May the Commons issued their ordinance for raising the militia, which the King commanded his subjects not to obey. On this, the Commons published a declaration, forbidding all persons to obey the King's proclamation. Orders were then sent into all the counties to muster the militia, and the King summoned the gentry of Yorkshire as a defence of his person.

P. 162. *The ocation of this letter is to let you knowe that Mr. Weafer is dead.*—Richard Weaver and Richard Seabourne, Esqs. were burgesses for the city of Hereford.

There had been previous rumours of Mr. Weaver's death, which had excited in the mind of the Lady Brilliana, a desire that her son Edward should succeed him. Dr. Wright had been actively engaged on that occasion, and is again now; but James Scudamore, Esq. appears to have been elected. Seabourne and Scudamore were Royalists, and, having joined the King at Oxford, were disabled by the House, when Edmund Weaver and Bennet Hoskins, Esqs. were elected in 1646. Willis's Notitia Parliamentaria, and Cobbett's Parl. History.

Sir Robert Harley's colleague was Fitzwilliam Coningsby, Esq. who was disabled 30 Oct. 1641 (Journ. H. Com.) as a monopolist, and was succeeded by Humphrey

Coningsby, Esq. who, having joined the King at Oxford, was also disabled, and made way for the election of Edward Harley in 1646.

P. 166. *I thinke we must all acknowledeg God's greate mercy that the plot for the takeing of Hull was discouered.*—Journ. H. Com. 27 May, 1642. "A letter from Sir John Hotham, concerning a treasonable attempt upon Hull, was this day read, and a letter from Beckwith, who was the great agent in that matter.

" *Ordered*, That this letter from Sir John Hotham of the 25 May, and the letter of Beckwith, and the other papers inclosed, shall be forthwith printed. *Resolved*, upon the question, That Thomas Beckwith, of Beverley, shall be forthwith sent for as a delinquent by the serjeant-at-arms attending this House." For particulars of the design upon Hull, see Rushworth Abridged, vol. iv. p. 351.

P. 167. *At Loudlow they seet up a May-pole and a thinge like a head vpon it, and so they did at Croft, and gathered a greate many about it, and shot at it in derision of Roundheads.*—Roundheads, the name imposed on the Parliamentarians. " The origin of this name is not certainly known : some say it was because the Puritans then commonly wore short hair, and the King's party long flowing hair. Some say it was because the Queen, at Strafford's trial, asked, who that round-headed man was (meaning Pym), because he spake so strongly." Baxter's Narrative of his Life and Times, quoted in Trench, on the Study of Words, p. 137.

In the Bishops' riot, Westminster, 1641, "Some cavaliers and discarded officers retained in the King's service who were walking near, indignant at the rudeness of the crowd, still more foolishly attacked the Roundheads with drawn swords." Buchanan's Hist. of Scotland, vol. iv. p. 66.

Journ. H. Com. 1 Feb. 1641. "*Ordered*, That the pamphlet entitled, The Resolution of the Roundheads, be referred to the Committee for Printing. Steph. Buckle, St. Martin's Lane, London, ordered to attend the Committee."

P. 169. *In my opinion it weare better to borrow money, if your father will give any, then to give his plate.*—Journ. H. Com. 10 June, 1642. An order for the bringing in of money, horses, and plate, to be repaid at 8 per cent. with full value of the plate, and consideration for the fashion, not exceeding 1*s*. per oz. Sir Robert responds to this order, and on 19th Sept. 1642 (Journ. H. Com.) saith, " he hath brought in three hundred and fifty pounds in plate, and will bring in one hundred and fifty pounds more, and provide two horses." Other notices, occur in the Journals, of moneys advanced by Sir Robert Harley. How zealously Lady Brilliana concurred with her husband appears from her readiness to send up the plate, and from this letter, in which she says, " This I doo not say, that I am unwilling to part with the plate, or any thing ells in this case : if your father cannot borrow money, I thinke I might finde out some in the cuntry to lend him some."

P. 173. *When Sir Will. Croft came to me, he came from my Lord Harbert.* 25 June 1642.—Lord Herbert was now busy in making levies in the King's cause under the Commission of Array.

I heare that Sir W. Croft has commanded the beacion now furnished and new piche put into it.—Into the beacon which formerly stood near the Beacon-gate, on Croft Ambry. Under authority of the Commission of Array, beacons were to be provided and other necessaries for better exercising the people and discovering sudden invasions and commotions.

P. 176. *The Kinge has sent a commistion to 12 of the justices to settle the milica.*—The Commission of Array for Leicestershire was issued 11 June, 1642. Rushworth Abridged, vol. iv. p. 401. On the 18th June, Serjeant Wilde reported that the Committee of Lords and Commons appointed to consider of the Commission of Array in Leicestershire were all of opinion, that it was against the law and against the liberty and property of the subject.

The Editor has not met with any copy of the Commission of Array for Herefordshire. Journal of the House of Commons, 21 Sept. 1642, "A warrant was read under the hands of Wallop Brabazon, Esq. Sir Will. Croft, Fitzwilliam Conningsbye, Thos. Price, Henry Lingen, Will. Rudhall, Esqs. Commissioners of Array for the co. of Hereford, directed to the high sheriff of the said county, requiring him thereby to raise such forces as he shall think fitting for the apprehending of Priamus Davies, who had been summoned by divers warrants from them, and had refused to appear, and for conveying him to his Majesty's gaol. On which, Mr. Davies having been called in and avowing it was a true copy of the warrant, it was *Resolved*, That Wallop Brabazon, Esq., Sir Wm. Croft, Knt., Fitzw. Conningsbye, Esq., Mr. Thos. Price, Mr. Henry Lingen, and Will. Rudhall, Esq. be forthwith sent for as delinquents."

The name of Priamus Davies occurs in the Register of Brampton Bryan.

The militia summoned to meet at Hereford on the 15th July was, no doubt, under the authority of the Commission of Array.

P. 180. *The captaine of the voluntiers is one Barell.*—James Barroll was Mayor of Hereford, 1639. Price's Hist. of Hereford, 1796.

P. 182. *My cosen Tomkins is as violent as ever, and many thinke that her very words is in the Heariford resolutions. I beleeve it was Mr. Mason's penning.*—Mary, the daughter of Sir Herbert Croft, and sister to Sir William Croft, was baptized at Croft, 21 Dec. 1598, and married Richard Tomkyns, of Monnington, in the county of Hereford.

Sir Herbert Croft having joined the Roman Catholic church, and taken up his residence at Douay, addressed "letters persuasive to his wife and children in England to take upon them the Catholic religion. These letters appear to have been answered, if not by his daughter Mary, in her name, as he afterwards printed a reply to the answer of his daughter M. C., which she made to a paper sent to her concerning the Roman church." Wood's Athenæ, vol. ii. 318.

By referring to the Appendix, p. 223, it will be seen that the declaration or resolution of the county of Hereford was regarded by the House of Commons as a most libell[ous] paper. The copies of it most probably shared the fate of Lord Digby's speech, Kentish petition, and other offensive papers, which were burnt by the common hangma[n]. The researches of James Edward Davis, of the Middle Temple, Esq. have brought to li[ght] a copy of it, "imprinted at London by a printed copie, 1642." It is found in vol. i[i of] the folio collection of Civil War Tracts, presented by King George III. to the Bri[tish] Museum.

P. 182. *Letter* CLXXIX. *misplaced.*—See p. 258, for a note on this transposition.

P. 186. *I would have rwite to him, but I durst not rwite upon papaper. Dear [M] rwite to me, though you rwite upon a peace of clothe, as this is.*—Letter CLXXXII. co[m]mences the last series of letters addressed to Edward Harley. It is written upon cloth [for] facility of concealment about the person.

Theare a 1000 dragoneare came into Barford 5 owers affther my Lord Harford[.] William Marquis of Hertford, under the Commission of Array, was appointed Lord Li[eu]tenant-General of Devon, Cornwall, Somerset, Dorset, Wilts, Southampton, Glouces[ter,] Bucks, Oxford, Hereford, and seven counties within the principality of Wales. Ma[y's] Hist. of the Long Parliament, p. 223.

P. 189. *The souldiers are goon before Gloster: theaire randevous is Sir Ro. Coo[k]howes. 25 Feb.* 1642-3.—"In Feb. the troops, 1500 foot and 500 horse, collected [by] Lord Herbert, advanced towards Gloster, and were intrenched at Highnam, within 2 m[iles] of the city, where, on the 22nd and 23rd March, they were completely routed by Sir W[m.] Waller and Genl. Massey." Introduction to Bibliotheca Gloucesteriensis, pp. xxx[v,] xxxvi.

P. 196. *I know not wheather this cessation of armes will stay them.*—In the propositi[ons] for peace presented from the Parliament to the King at Oxford, in 31 Jan. 1642-3, a[nd] in those sent back by the Commissioners to the Parliament, one was, that there be a ces[sa]tion of arms during the treaty. The treaty was still in debate. After many messag[es] between London and Oxford, the Commissioners were recalled, and returned to Londo[n] 17th April, 1643. May's Hist. of Long Parliament, 277-278.

P. 198. *I heare some say you have an imployment.*—Edward Harley was, about th[is] time, made Captain of a troop of horse in the Parliamentary army.

The report in the cuntry is that my Lord Capell comes very shortly to be Governor [of] Shrewsbury.—Sir Francis Ottley was at this time Governor of Shrewsbury, but the Prin[ce] of Wales was commander-in-chief, assisted by a council, and Arthur Lord Capell was co[n]stituted Lieut.-General under His Royal Highness, and took up his abode at that plac[e.] Owen and Blakeway's Hist. of Shrewsbury, vol. i. p. 433.

Honnest Petter taken. 6 *May,* 1643.—After the surrender of Hereford, 24 April, S[ir] W. Waller made a visit to Leominster, where there was some skirmishing. Petter pr[o]bably had been sent to pick up what information he could of events in that neighbou[r-] hood, and, in returning home, fell in with some of Sir W. Croft's friends about Mortimer's Cross, and was there made prisoner.

God has mightily been seen in Heareforshheere.—In the success attending Sir William Waller's attack upon Hereford, which surrendered to him on quarter, 24 April, 1643. Lord Scudamore, James Scudamore, Esq. M.P. for Hereford, Col. Herbert Price, M.P. for Brecon, Sir Rich. Cave, M.P. for Lichfield, Lieut.-Col. Coningsby, and his son, Humphrey Coningsby, M.P. for Herefordshire (five revolted members of the House of Commons), Sir Will. Croft, Sir Walter Pye, Sir Saml. Amby, and Drs. Rogers, Goodwin, and Evans of the cathedral, and many others, were made prisoners, and all carried to Gloucester. May's Hist. of the Long Parliament, p. 315.

Within three days, Sir W. Waller surprised Leominster, where he took good prize, and disarmed many of the royal party, and placing a garrison there, scoured the country to the gates of Worcester, where meeting with an unexpected repulse, he withdrew to Reading. Webb's Introduction to Bibliotheca Gloucesteriensis, p. xxxix.

P. 199. *I have sent you on to be of your troope, and have furnished him with a hors. The hors coost me 8l.*—Journ. H. Com. 22 March, 1642-3. "*Ordered*, That the four horses of the Lady Petre, three of Mr. White's of Bacons, three of Barnard's of Westland, one of Robert Goodyere, be all sent to my Lord General, to be employed for the publick service, but one, which is to be given to Edm. Brasier, who seized them; and that it be recommended unto my Lord General, that Capt. Harley may have the horses for the furnishing of his troop, and that Mr. Pym write a letter to my Lord General to this purpose."

P. 202. *We are still threatened, some souldiers are billeted at Pursla.*—5 or 6 miles north of Brampton Bryan.

Lef.-Councell Massey is commanded to be Gouernor of Gloster.—Soon after the surrender of Hereford. See Corbet's historical relation of the military government of Gloucester; also, notice of Col. Massie in Notes to Webb's Introduction to the Bibliotheca Gloucesteriensis, pp. clxxxix.—cciii. It will be seen by Edward Harley's retrospect on the completion of his fiftieth year, in the Appendix, p. 249, that Sir Edward Massie died in April, 1674.

In Lady Frances V. Harcourt's collections is the following letter, which, it is supposed, was written by Col. Massie's wife; the circumstance of his flight into Holland in the spring, 1648, makes it probable that she was left, like others in these sad times, in distress:—

"Noble Sir,—I lately receaved a letter from Capt. Blayney, in wch hee writes mee that hee hath given unto you, for my use, the sume of ffive pounds, wch ffive pounds I entreate you will bee pleased to sende unto mee by this bearer, my brother's servant, whereby you will oblige, Your friend and servant,

"CHRISTIAN MASSIE.

"To my honnord ffriend, Collonel Edward Harley, these, at Sr Robert Harley's house, in Tuttle Street, near the New Church, these present."

Endorsed, "Mrs. Massie's recept of 5*lb.* 25 Sep. '48."

CAMD. SOC. 2 M

NOTES TO THE LETTERS.

P. 203. *I hard from Loundoun that you, with Sir Arter Hasellrike, left Loundoun*
Friday was senight, and that your intentions weare to hast to Sir William Waller.—E
ward Harley now enters upon his military services. Lady Brilliana hears of his safe a
rival with Sir William Waller, where, says she, " the Lord of heaven and earth bless y
and presarue you. My hart is with you, and I know you beleeue it, for my life is boun
up with yours."

P. 204. *I am very sorry that my brother has doun what he has.*—" 10 June, 1643. T
Earl of Portland and Lord Viscount Conway, being accused by the Commons of bei
concerned in Edmund Waller's plot, were sequestered from the Lords, and committed, t
one to the custody of the Lord Mayor and the other to one of the sheriffs, but their lan
and goods not to be seized on till upon trial it appeared they were guilty. Not bei
proved, they were soon discharged." Cobbett's Parl. Hist. vol. iii. p. 131.

P. 205. *All Lancashere is cleared, only Latham howes. My Lord of Darby has l*
that county, which they take ill.—Lord Derby about this time was ordered off to the defen
of the Isle of Man, leaving Lady Derby in the possession of Latham House, now threaten
by the Parliament army. The siege of Latham House commenced in February, 1643
The Journal of this memorable siege has been several times printed from a MS. in t
Ashmolean Museum, Oxford.

P. 206. *I acknowledge the greate mercy of my God that He presarued you in so sharp*
fight when your hors was killed. 11 *July*, 1643.—This was probably in Edward Harle
first conflict, which must have been that which took place at Lansdown on the 5th Ju
1643, between Sir William Waller and Prince Maurice and Sir Ralph Hopton.

P. 207. *Sir William Vavasor has left Mr. Lingen with the souldiers.* 25 *Aug.* 1643
" Friday, August 11th. The Welsh forces, under Sir William Vavasor, advanced to t
Wineyard, where after two houres solemnity they with great valour tooke it, nobody bei
there to make a shot against them." Dorney's briefe and exact relation of the most m
teriall and remarkeable passages that hapned in the late well-formed (and as valien
defended) seige laid before the city of Gloucester. Bib. Gloucesteriensis, p. 212.

209. *There are some souldiers come to Lemster and three troopes of hors to Heariford w*
Sir William Vavasor, and they say they meane to visit Brompton againe.—Lady Brillian
troubles at Brampton began in the spring of 1642. In the absence of Sir Robert Harl
then engaged busily in Parliament, she had the anxiety of the management of his coun
affairs upon her mind. The payment of certain rents and charges upon his estate,
stated in page 229, due to the King, had been enforced in April of this year. The calli
out of the militia by the Parliament, and issuing of the commission of array by the Kin
brought matters to their ripeness, and made it necessary that every man should now se
his ground. Herefordshire stood well affected to the King ; Sir William Croft and oth

of chief influence immediately joined the royal standard, and in the autumn a strong muster in that cause was made in Herefordshire, and many outrages committed on each side. Communications took place, between the Marquis of Hertford, when at Hereford in December, and Lady Brilliana, who had already been kept under much annoyance and daily expectation of a siege. A council of war was held at Hereford in February, when it was decided to bring some Welsh soldiers against her, and blow up the place. Matters of more importance were going on at Gloucester, in the neighbourhood of which there was a rendezvous of Lord Herbert's forces, to which those from the country about Brampton were now ordered; but, notwithstanding their removal, a summons and threat of 600 men were sent to her. At this juncture (22 and 23 March, 1642-3) Sir William Waller, with Colonel Massey, attacked and completely defeated Lord Herbert's forces at Highnam, and, following up his success, shortly afterwards laid siege to the city of Hereford, which surrendered on 24th April, from which place he scoured the country, by way of Leominster, to Worcester. These events dismayed the royalists, and gave a little quiet to Brampton; but in June, Sir William Croft, Sir Walter Pye, and others, taken at Hereford, and recently prisoners at Bristol, were liberated, and soldiers again collecting in the neighbourhood, demanding free quarter and an assessment on the county of 1,200l. a-month, she was again under alarm. In the end of June, Lord Herbert and Colonel Vavasor went into Montgomeryshire to muster new levies, and on their return the siege of Brampton Bryan was commenced by Colonel Vavasor. By the letter of the 25th August it appears that, having done much injury to the place, he had then left it, and the soldiers there under the charge of Mr. Lingen (Colonel Lyngen), who must himself have quitted it within a fortnight, as this first siege commenced on the 26th July, and continued but six weeks.

The last letter, of the 9th October, shews that she was again threatened by Sir William Vavasor; within a few days of which, having " taken a greate coold," she departed this life.

Under the danger which threatened the church at Brampton, and which was very much injured in the siege, the Register had been most probably put away in safety, as it does not contain any record of Lady Brilliana's death or burial. Sir Robert was at this time much engaged in Parliament. The Journals of the House of Commons record his presence on the 7th, 9th, 17th, 19th, and 26th of October. On the 27th of this month it is ordered, That the Committee for the Western parts do meet this afternoon, at 3 o'clock, at Sir Robert Harley's house; and again on the 30th there is a similar order. No doubt the tidings of her death had then reached him.

INDEX.

Acton, Mr. 64
Adams (Lady Brilliana's cousin), 56, 64, 180.
Adamson, William, 239.
Aersen, Van, 72, 254.
Alldern, Mr. 164.
Ancram, Lord, 25.
Angelica root, 130, 257.
Arundel, Earl of, 25, 39, 74.
Ash, ———, 58.
Ashby de la Zouch, 37.
Ashley, Sir Jacob, 39.
Aurum potabile, 46, 254.

Bagly, ———, 146.
Balham, Mr. 78, 79, 84, 88, 108, 117, 118, 119, 125, 128, 130, 132, 133, 135, 137, 138, 141, 143, 144.
Ball, Mr. 84.
Banbury, 54.
Bardlam, 186.
Barker, Dr. 1, 5. 6, 27, 94.
Barrington, 17.
Barroll, James, 180, 263.
Barthy, Mr. 67.
Barton, Mary, 35.
Bath, 64.
Burgess, Mr. 167.
Baughly, Mr. 195.
Bayley, Mr. 190.
——— William, 230.
Beal, Bartholomew, 249.
——— Dr. 96.
——— Mr. 193.
Beauchamp's Court, 1.
Beeb, Roger, 94, 132.
Bellenden, Sir William, 226.
Berwick, 45, 48, 52, 57, 83.

Beverley, 215.
Bezoar stone, 46, 253.
Bishops, proceedings against the, 119, 135, 140, 143, 146, 147, 148.
Bishop's Castle, 6; election of members for, 87.
Blackfriars (London), 1.
Blackheath, 158.
Blackwall, Gervase, 231.
Blanke, William, 239.
Blayney (Lady Brilliana's cousin), 105.
——— Thomas, 239.
Bletchly, ———, 68, 72, 83, 94, 119.
Blineman, Mr. 37, 76, 84, 254.
Bond, ———, 189.
Borough, ———, 32, 45, 49, 61.
Boteler, sir William, 223.
Bower, Dr. 119.
Brabazon, Mr. 205.
Brady, Robert, 239.
Bramley, Mrs. 64.
Brandsheave, Capt. 51.
Bray, Sir Giles (Lady Brilliana's brother), 3, 8, 11, 17, 23, 24, 25, 36, 41, 44, 59, 65, 105, 128, 251.
——— Lady, 17, 41, 85.
Brereton, Sir William, 205, 207.
Brisack, 19, 27, 252.
Bristol, 4, 236.
Brompton (now Brampton) Bryan, co. Hereford; most of Lady Brilliana's letters are dated from this seat of Sir Robert Harley, and there are many references to news of Brompton and its neighbourhood; siege of Brompton Castle, xix. 207—209; protestation taken at, 130.
Brocklesby, 107, 130.
Brooke, Lord, 1, 49, 170, 251.

INDEX.

Broughton, Mr. 47, 49, 57, 63, 67, 69, 70, 71, 109, 116, 152, 153, 159, 161, 168, 212.
Buckle, 84.
———— ————, 6.
Bucknell, 67, 84, 135, 171, 229.
Buckton, 190, 229.
Burrington, 229, 231.
Bursell, Mrs. 141.
Burton, Mr. 104.
Button, Capt. 94.
———— Lady, 218, 219, 237.
Bytheway, Richard, 186.

Caius College, 237—239.
Calvin, 20, 52, 69.
Capel, Lord, 198, 200, 201, 205.
Carlisle, 45.
Casimir, Prince, 75.
Charles I. his expedition against the Scots in 1639, 30, 32, 35, 37, 45.
Chester, 207.
Child, Anthony, 41, 164.
Chillingworth's Safe Way, 31, 253.
Chokes *(sic)*, Lady, 48.
Clanver, 74, 78, 140, 141, 142, 144.
Clare, Lord, 172, 177.
Clarendon, Lord Chancellor, letter to Edward Harley, 242; publication of his memoirs, 244.
Cloggie, Mr. 219.
Clogie, Rev. Alexander, l—li.
Clotworthy, Sir John, 231, 233.
Colborne, ————, 45, 50, 96, 205.
———— John, 89, 146.
Collins, Capt. Increse, 215, 216.
Coningsby, Mr. 186, 187, 189, 191, 198, 205, 261.
Convocation, proceedings of, 96.
Conway (Edward Harley's cousin), 151.
———— Lady, 32, 33, 43, 128.
———— Ralph, 6.
———— Sir Thomas, 19.
———— 1st Viscount, 2, 3, 4.
———— 2nd Viscount, 12, 24, 117, 139, 147, 204, 255, 266; letter of to Edw. Harley, 213.
Conyers, Sir John, 146, 149, 160, 259, 261.
———— Lady, 150.
Cooke, Sir Robert, 189, 264.
———— Secretary, 73.
Cope, Lady, 25, 253.
Copley, Lionel, 233.

Corbet (Edward Harley's cousin), 35, 55.
———— Andrew, 86.
———— Sir Andrew, 34.
———— Sir Jhon, 86.
———— Lady, 34.
Cornwall (Lady Brilliana's cousin), 89, 105, 108, 148, 168.
———— (Edward Harley's cousin), 146.
———— Sir Gilbert, 14, 21.
———— Lady, 21.
Courants, the Weekly, 19, 32, 69, 252, 254.
Coxall, 178.
Cradock, Mr. 26, 31, 74, 78.
Craven, Lord, 10, 22, 229, 252.
Croft, 167.
———— Capt. 199.
———— (Edward Harley's cousin), 38, 43.
———— Sir James, xlii.
———— Robert, 182.
———— Sir William, 121, 122, 124, 133, 152, 156, 162, 163, 164, 173, 183, 192, 198, 225, 229, 256.
Cromwell, Richard, 239.
———— Oliver, riding in state through the city of London, 218.

Dale of Leintwardine, 193.
Dally, Edward, 139, 184.
Daniel (Lady Brilliana's cousin), 115.
Davies, Thomas, 213.
Davis (Lady Brilliana's cousin), 65, 68, 80, 97, 110, 116, 117, 127, 135, 136, 150, 171, 181, 206.
———— Mr. 2, 162, 163, 164, 170, 173, 178, 193, 219.
———— of Coxall, 178.
———— of Wigmore, 124, 178.
Dean, forest of, 188.
Deodate, Dr. 26, 32, 37, 38, 40, 41, 42, 78, 80, 97, 98, 134.
Derby, Lord, 205, 266.
Devereux, Sir Francis, 82.
Dewe, Mr. 145.
De Wort, John, 75.
Digby, Lord, 149, 259.
Doughty, Mr. 136.
———— Thomas, 249.
Dover, 215, 216.
Downing, Rev. Colybute, 140, 258.
Dunkirk, sale of, 241, 244, 245.
Dutton, Mr. 223.

Eatcham, 219.

INDEX.

Eaton, Mr. 205.
Edinburgh, 40.
Edwards, Mr. 84, 117, 135, 171.
Elector, Prince, 72, 75.
Ellis, John, 239.
Elton (Lady Brilliana's cousin), 163, 164.
—— Mr. 162, 164, 165, 182, 183.
Erasmus, 52, 53.
Essex, Earl of, 39, 45, 48, 179, 225.
Eure, Mr. 43.
Evelyn, Sir John, 224.
Eyton, 229.

Fairfax (Lady Brilliana's cousin), 114.
—— Lord, 215.
—— Sir Thomas, 225.
Felton, John, 239.
Fiennes, Mr. 125.
Finch, Lord Chief Justice, 32.
Fisher, Mr. 208.
FitzJames, Frances, 249.
Floyd, Mr. 168.
Folden, 237, 238.
Foster, Judge, 224.
Fox, Mr. 156.
—— Somerset, 32.
—— Sir Stephen, 244.
Foxe (Lady Brilliana's cousin), 39.
Froysell, Thomas, xlvi.
—— Rev. Thomas, xii. xxxi. 249.
Fumdwen, J. 185.

Gardnas (sic), ——, 205.
Gears, William, 231.
Gelsthorp, Edward, 239.
Gloucester, 3, 189, 198, 202, 246, 264.
—— Bishop of, 96.
Goodwin (Lady Brilliana's cousin), 93.
—— Mr. 86, 202.
Goodman, the Jesuit, 112, 255.
Goring, Colonel, 136.
Gostlin, John, 239.
Gower, Mrs. 47.
—— Rev. Stanley, Rector of Brampton Bryan, xvii.—xviii. xlviii. 18, 26, 35, 37, 53, 62, 86, 97, 98, 99, 100, 103, 106, 108, 109, 110, 111, 112, 113, 115, 118, 121, 126, 128, 141, 155, 158, 160, 189, 193, 260.
Graveling, 247.
Gray's Inn, 130.
Green, Mr. 208.
Gregory, Sir William, 245.

Greville, Sir Edward, 21, 253.
Griffiths, George, 15, 21, 35, 86, 88, 114, 185, 187.
—— Jack, 206.
—— Mr. 67, 105, 114, 134, 137, 142.
—— William, 178, 190.
Grocers' Hall, 218, 222.
Gwyn, Mr. 113, 118, 130, 139, 140, 141.

Hackluyt (Lady Brilliana's cousin), 41, 42, 61, 84, 118, 154, 155, 167, 189.
—— Richard, xlvii.
Hall, ——, 11, 14, 27, 73, 93, 151, 152.
Hamilton, Marquess, 51.
Hammon (the printer), 229.
Hanmer, 205.
Harley family, descent of, xli.
—— Brilliana, Lady, her parentage and connection, xii.; marriage, 24, 25; character, xiii.; her letters to Sir Robert Harley, 1—7; to her son Edward, 7—183, 185—209; to Mrs. Wallcot, 183—185; besieged in Brompton Bryan, xviii.—xix.; her children, xlix.; her death, xx. 267.
—— Brilliana, daughter of Lady Brilliana, 5, 18, 29, 42, 111, 126; journey to London, 153—158; enters the household of Lady Vere, 160, 161, 168, 172, 190, 192, 195, 201.
—— Dorothy, 60, 82, 161, 165, 167, 168, 169, 173.
—— Edward (afterwards Sir Edward), biographical notice of, xx.—xxix.; letters to at Oxford, 7—104; in London, 105—183, 185—209; services under the parliament, xxi. l. li.; letter inclosing his pass to travel, in 1647, 231; copy of pass, 232; further pass in 1650, 235; letters to Caius College, 237; to Lord Clarendon, 240, 243; to his brother Thomas, 216, 220; to his father, Sir Robert, 217, 218; answer to his son Robert about the sale of Dunkirk, 245; his retrospects of his life, 246, 249.
—— John, xlii.
—— Margaret, 57, 110.
—— Mary, letter to Edward Harley, 219.
—— the first Sir Robert, his parentage, vi.; education, ib.; knight of the Bath, ib.; returned to various Parliaments, vii. xliii. 251; his character, vii.; public

employments, vii. xliii. xliv.; letters to whilst in London, 1628, letters i. to viii. and xxvii.; references to in 1638, 14—36; in 1639, 38—82; his return to the Short Parliament, 1640, 84—87; references to whilst in London on that occasion, 88—95; other references in 1640, 96—101; attends the meeting of the Long Parliament, 100; references to his occupations therein and its proceedings, 100—206; a letter, from to his son Edward, xlix.; letter to, from his son Edward, 218; proceedings as to Herefordshire Declaration, 224—230; letter from Dr. Wright, 228; rents paid by, 229, 230; letter to Sir Henry Vane, and his reply, 235; losses in the civil war, x. 230; death, 11; funeral sermon, xii. xxxi.—xxxix.; marriages, xii.

—— the second Sir Robert, allusions to in Lady Brilliana's letters *passim*, 233; letter to his brother Edward, 236; order for his apprehension, 1658, 239; his death, 249.

—— Robert (afterwards first Earl of Oxford), 244.

—— Thomas, father of the first Sir Robert, xliii.

—— Thomas, son of Lady Brilliana, 5, 15, 18, 37, 115, 117, 119, 120, 122, 125, 126, 127, 128, 129, 172, 173.

Harvey, Mr. 95,
Haselrig, Sir Arthur, 203.
Haughton Castle, 207.
Havor, Mr. 145.
Hawes, Mr. 220.
Heath, Mr. 99.
Henrietta Maria, Queen, 40, 143, 198.
Herbert, Lord, 32, 173, 188, 196, 205, 253.

—— Mr. 86, 90, 100.

Hereford, City of, allusions to in Lady Brilliana's Letters, *passim*; musters and conduct of soldiery there, 3, 44; puritanical alterations in the cathedral, 148, 259; unpopularity of the parliament party there, 170, 179; surrender to Waller, 198, 265.

—— Bishop Coke of, 27, 36, 43, 44, 67.

—— Bishop Croft of, li. 240.

Herefordshire, anti-parliamentarian declaration of, 148, 158, 159; proceedings in parliament respecting, 223—225; reference to copy of this declaration, 264.

Hertford, Marquess of, 186, 264.
Hibbons, Mr. 79.
Hill, Mr. 176, 189, 192, 199, 204, 206.
Holland, Earl of, 57, 73.
Hollingworth, ——, 54, 83.
Hollis, Denzell, 231.
Holy Court (The), 27, 253.
Home Lacy, 246.
Hopkis, ——, 187, 193; (of Downend), 193.
Hopton, Sir Richard, 182.
Hoskins, Mr. 164.
Howard, Sir Robert, 87, 229.
Hubbard, John, 224.
—— Richard, 225.
Hubbins, Mrs. 141.
Hull, 166, 215, 262.
Hulley, ——, 59.
Hunks (Lady Brilliana's cousin), 6.
Hurse, ——, 219.
Husband, Mr. 141.
Hyde Park, 138.

Ireland, 58.

James, Mr. 104, 106, 170, 174, 188, 193.
Jeffreys, Capt. 195.
Jenkes, Henry, 239.
Jones, ——, 47, 50.

Kentish Petition, presentation of, 158, 260.
Kettleby, Nehemiah, 185.
Keynsham Court, 239.
King, Mr. 209.
King's Book, the, 51, 254.
Kingsland, 139, 148, 205, 229, 231.
Knight, ——, 196.
—— Mr. 137.
Knightly, Mr. 76.
Knighton, 203.
Kyrle (Lady Brilliana's cousin), 111.
—— Sir John, 64, 182.
—— Mr. 121.

Lacy, Mr. 2, 218.
Lane, Mr. 171.
Laneford, Mr. 122.
Lathom House, 205, 266.
Laud, Archbishop, 91, 129.
Lawes, Mr. 97.
Ledbury, 164, 179.
Lee, Sir Richard, 86.
Legg, ——, 190.

INDEX.

Legg, Mr. 196, 200.
Leintwardine, 43, 130, 213, 229.
Lenthall, William, 232.
Leominster, 6, 18, 98, 178, 209, 233, 234.
Lewis, Evan, 224, 225.
—— Sir William, 224, 231.
Lewson (sic), Lord, 1.
Leynthall Starks, 229.
Lincoln, Earl of, 218.
Lincoln's Inn, 127, 130, 155.
Ling, William, 239.
Lingen, Sir H. 220.
—— Mr. 205, 207.
Liquorice, 16.
Little, Mr. 7.
Littleton, Mrs. 172.
—— William, ib.
Long, Walter, 231.
Longford, ——, 56.
Longly, Mr. 12, 177.
Looker, ——, 11, 12, 85, 90, 129, 199.
Love, Mr. 247.
Lowe, Mr. 190, 193.
Luddington, 77.
Ludlow, 64, 86, 88, 123, 125, 137, 138, 167, 172, 174, 198, 201, 202, 218, 252.
Luke, Philip, 206.
Luther, Life of, 52.

Macclesfield, Earl of, 244, 245.
Macklin, ——, 189.
Mackworth, Mr. 114.
Maddison, Mr. 223.
Maidstone, 216.
Mainwaring, Lady, 6.
Mallet, Judge, 123, 224.
Man in the Moon, 13, 252.
Manchester, Earl of, 225.
Marrow, Lieut.-Col. 202.
Martin, ——, 17, 23, 102, 169, 175, 181.
Martyrs, Book of, 52.
Mason, Mr. 170, 182.
Massey, Col. 202, 205, 225, 265.
Massie, Edward, 233.
—— Sir Edward, 249.
Mathew, Dr. Toby, 105, 255.
Meyrick, Mr. 43.
Middlesex, Lord, 12.
Militia, musters of, 2, 18, 35, 36, 37, 48; King's commission for the, 176, 178.
Miller, Sir Nicholas, 215.
—— Thomas, 58, 61, 62, 76, 77, 81, 82, 107.
Mint, the, 216.
—— Mastership of, x. xlv.

Mocktree, 229.
Moene (sic), 60.
Monk, General, 244, 245.
Montague, Earl of, 245.
Montgomeryshire, election of knights for, 86.
Moore, Mr. 87, 108, 116, 123, 142, 143, 151, 153, 174, 200, 201, 204, 208.
—— Robert, 26.
—— Thomas, 147.
Moray, Sir Robert, 249.
Morgan, —— 104, 117.
—— Mr. 67, 200.
Mortimer's Cross, 198.
Morton, Lord, 25.

Nailor, William, 239.
Napier, Sir Robert, 86.
Naylor, Mr. 237.
Nelham, Mr. 86.
Newcastle, Lord, 215.
Newgate, 224, 225.
Newnham, 247.
Newport, Francis, 86.
—— Lady, 155.
—— Lord, 39.
—— Mr. 155.
—— Sir Richard, 68, 69, 254.
Nichol, Anthony, 231.
Northampton, Earl of, 102.
Northumberland, Earl of, 64.

Old, Mr. 155.
Old Bailey, 178.
Orleton, 247.
Osberson, Mrs. 138.
Oxenstiern, 109.
Oxford, Magdalen Hall, a Puritanical College, xx.; letters to Edward Harley whilst there, 7—104; few noblemen's sons there, 8; books cheaper there than at Worcester, 20; fire there, 22; people there inveigh against the Puritans, 40; Oxford apples, 65; plague there, 113; act at, 34, 39, 45, 61, 62, 63, 99, 253.

Paget, Lord, 170.
Palmer (Sir Edward Harley's sister), 249.
Parliament, meeting of the Long, 100.
Peacock, Rev. Thomas, Rector of Brampton Bryan, xv.
Pelham (Lady Brilliana's cousin), 59, 60, 111.
—— (Lady Brilliana's nephew), 38, 96, 104, 106, 201.

INDEX.

Pelham, Harry, 101, 114, 130.
—— Lady (Lady Brilliana's sister), 9, 27, 30, 32, 68, 81, 87.
—— Ned, 102.
—— Sir William (Lady Brilliana's brother-in-law), 32, 81, 102, 107, 130, 161, 254, 261.
Pennell, Mr. 21, 253.
Perkins, Edward, tutor to Edward Harley at Oxford, 9, 14, 24, 26, 31, 32, 33, 37, 38, 40, 41, 43, 49, 54, 56, 60, 63, 83, 95, 99, 253.
Petter, honest, 198, 200, 201, 202, 203, 208, 264.
Phillips, Mr. 179, 186, 189, 195, 200, 203, 208.
Piedmont, Collection for, xl. xlvi.
Pierpoint, Mr. 86.
Pierson, Mrs. 13, 22, 26, 29, 158, 252.
—— Rev. Thomas, Rector of Brampton Bryan, xv.—xvii. xlviii. 4.
Pinner, ——, 6, 43, 44, 139, 150, 151, 154, 155, 159, 190, 213.
—— Edward, 90, 91, 92, 93, 94, 190, 194.
—— Samuel, 83, 118, 128, 190.
Pitts, Mrs. 48.
Plowden, Mr. 105, 255.
Potter, ——, 154.
Powell, ——, 190, 197.
Powis, Mr. 218.
Presteign, 95, 188.
Price (Lady Brilliana's cousin), 6, 14, 18, 32, 37, 39, 40.
—— Herbert, 135, 257.
—— Mr. 164.
Pritchard, ——, 98, 155.
Prosser, ——, 186, 197, 208.
—— Thomas, 185.
Protestation of 3rd May, 1641, 130, 221, 257.
Prynne, William, 104.
Pursla, 201, 265.
Pye, Robert, 95.
—— Sir Walter, 84, 87, 198, 205.

Queen Mother's arrival, 9, 10.

Ragley, 1, 6, 251.
Ratesford (*sic*), Lord, 56.
Read (Sir Edward Harley's cousin), 249.
"Return of Prayer," 65.
Reynolds, W. 220.

Rice, ——, 107, 110, 143.
Richards, ——, 196.
Robert (Lady Brilliana's brother), 105.
Robinson, John, 239.
Rogers, Rev. Dr. 159, 171, 174, 260.
—— Mr. 87.
—— W. 235.
Roundheads, derision of, at Hereford, 170; at Ludlow, 167, 172, 262.
Rous, Mr. 211.
Rudall (cousin of Lady Brilliana), 48, 176.
Rupert, Prince, 10, 22, 252, 253.
Rutley, ——, 219.

St. John (Lady Brilliana's cousin), 117, 119. .
Salisbury, Lord, 172.
Sallwells, Mr. 99, 103.
Sankey, ——, 143, 165, 178, 206.
—— Capt. Lieut. 205.
Sanky, Richard, 94, 106, 118, 182.
Savile, Lord, 170.
Saxe Weimar, Duke of, 72.
Say, Lord, 49, 90, 129, 257.
Scotland, troubles in, 10, 12, 40, 45, 51, 57, 58, 72, 75, 99, 117, 118.
Scriven, Colonel, 19, 252.
Scudamore, John Lord, li.
—— Sir John, 2.
—— Lord, 124, 165, 166, 245.
—— Mr. 21, 48, 64, 124, 253.
Scurvygrass, 53.
Seaborne, Mr. 162, 164.
Shelton, Samuel, 230.
Sherborn, Rev. William, 160, 179, 261.
Sherwin, Mr. 218.
Shilton, Mr. 219.
Shobdon, 145, 176.
Shrewsbury, 15, 90, 123, 155, 171, 198, 203.
Simmons, Mr. reports of his health, 26—53; other references to, 49, 65, 69, 74, 76, 77, 84, 135, 254.
Smallman, ——, 14, 197.
—— Mr. 205.
Smith, *vide* Smyth.
Smith, Mr. 88, 153, 159, 178.
—— Edward, 7, 18, 22, 28, 31, 251.
Smyth (Lady Brilliana's cousin), 39, 40, 45, 101, 107, 110, 251.
—— (Edward Harley's cousin) 28, 35, 53, 55, 76, 86, 91, 121, 122, 128, 134, 137, 140, 151, 152, 154, 155, 158, 212, 213.

Smyth, Helengewagh Lady (sister to Lady Brilliana and referred to under the name of Wacke), 5, 48, 102, 105, 110, 128, 139.
Soldiers, misconduct of those of Shropshire, 97; of Hereford, 98.
Spain, King of, death of, 115.
Stanly, ——, 219.
Stanton, Elizabeth, 83.
Stapleton, Philip, 231.
Stevenson, Mr. 37, 108, 253.
—— Mrs. 14, 29, 37.
Stiche of Walford, 62.
Stiles, Mr. 205.
Storton, Dr. 49.
Strafford, Earl of, 104, 105, 114, 117, 125, 126, 127, 131, 257.

Taylor, Mr. 71, 72, 189, 195.
Temple, the, 127, 130.
Temple Bar, 218.
Tewkesbury, 53.
Thruston, ——, 239.
Toddington, 1, 251.
Tolson, John, xliii.
Tombes, Rev. John, 106, 255.
Tomkins (Lady Brilliana's cousin), 3, 30, 121, 182, 263.
—— Mr. 109.
Tracy, Sir John, 251.
—— Sir Robert, 8.
Trafford, Mrs. 26, 29, 32.
Traherne, Thomas, 249.
Tuckney, Dr. 237.
—— Dr. Anthony, li.

Vaughan (Lady Brilliana's cousin), 26, 45, 97, 99, 111, 113, 124, 164.
—— Mr. 2, 24, 64, 164.
Vavasour, Colonel, 205.
—— Sir William, 207, 209, 266.
Venables, Mr. 224.
Vere, Lady, 6, 76, 105, 114, 119, 126, 132, 157, 158, 160, 168, 172, 251; letter of, to Edward Harley, 213.
Voile, Mr. 107, 108, 137, 159.

Wacke, *see* Smyth, Helengewagh Lady.
Wake, Lady, 229.
Walcot, 76, 140.
—— Ann, 184.
—— Humphrey, 184.
—— John, 184, 185.
—— Mary, 184.

Walcot, Mr. 26, 31, 184, 185.
—— Mrs. 6, 26, 38, 91, 105, 144, 255; letters to, 183, 184.
Walker, Mr. 15.
Waller, Sir William, 202, 203, 204, 225, 231, 233.
Walls, John, 5, 83, 117.
Weare, ——, 19.
Weaver, Mr. M.P. for Hereford, 122, 154, 156, 162, 163, 165, 267.
Weobly, 109.
Westmoreland, Earl of, letters of to Ed. Harley, 214, 215.
—— Countess of, letter of, to Edward Harley, 215; other references to, 76, 105.
Whateley, 49, 54.
Whitchurch, 44.
Whitney, Lady, 79.
Wigmore, 36, 105, 122, 124, 130, 178, 209, 219, 229, 231.
—— Mr. 176, 182, 183, 186, 187, 205, 209, 213, 258.
—— (Lady Brilliana's cousin), 136, 138.
Wilde, Mr. Serj. 222.
Wilkinson, Rev. Dr. xlix. 31, 38.
—— Mrs. 8, 15, 27, 29, 36, 37, 66, 67, 72, 251.
Windebank, Secretary, 105.
Winthrop, S. 233.
Wistanstone, 164.
Witney, Mr. 124.
Wood, Mary, 6.
Woodhouse, ——, 42, 98, 117.
Worcester, 56, 64, 82, 178, 181, 182, 226.
—— Lord, 32.
Wortley, Sir Francis, 158.
Wright, Dr. Nathaniel, xlix. 80, 91, 92, 97, 98, 104, 105, 117, 119, 120, 121, 122, 124, 125, 127, 140, 144, 145, 151, 154, 155, 161, 162, 163, 164, 165, 170, 172, 174, 189, 192, 195, 196, 198, 201, 202, 206, 208; letter to Sir Robert Harley, 228.
—— Mrs. 192, 196, 198, 201.
Wycombe, High, 155, 156, 158.

Yates, Mr. 108, 112, 131, 153, 154, 155, 171, 172, 190, 193.
—— Mrs. 43, 104, 105, 108, 112.
York, 161, 170, 182.

LONDON:
J. B. NICHOLS AND SONS, PRINTERS,
PARLIAMENT-STREET.

Lightning Source UK Ltd.
Milton Keynes UK
30 August 2009

143189UK00002BA/1/A

NIHILISM

Nihilism
21st Century Revelations from a Devastating Mind

By Freydis

Published by Freydis

© Freydis 1998-2011CE, Nihilism Year 14

ISBN 978-1-4357-5480-5

Printed on Planet Earth

Cover Design by Freydis

Edited by Christian Lee

Seventh Edition – January 2011

Also written by Freydis:

The End of Zionism

- CONTENTS -

THE NIHILIST MANIFESTO - 12

WHAT IS NIHILISM?
Nihilism Defined - 17
The Historical Development of Nihilism - 19
The Russian Nihilists - 20
Anarchism - 21
Beyond Good and Evil - 23
A Little Perspective - 24
Nihilism as Philosophy - 26
280 Million Years of Nihilism - 28
What's Left? - 30

NIHILISM IN ACTION!
Objective Reality & Freewill - 34
The Pitfalls of Artificial Law - 35
War or Revolution? - 37
Systemic Self-Destruction - 40
Nihilism: Through the Eyes and Into the Minds - 45
A Brief History of Power - 46
Power, Sex, Revolution - 47

ANOMIE (DEATH TO THIS)
Death to Government - 51
Death to God - 53
Death to Ideology - 54
Death to Purpose - 55
Death to Culture - 57
Death to the Ego - 59
Death to the Money Morality - 60
Death to the Love Delusion - 62
Death to Philosophy - 64
Death to Liberty - 65
Death to the Y-Chromosome - 66
Death to Morality - 67

THE NIHILISTIC VISION - 70

HOW TO BE A NIHILIST
'Call Back Later, God's on Vacation' - 74
What is a Nihilist? - 75
Nihilism as Identity - 78
Becoming the Nihilist - 80
Activating the Nihilism - 82
Ever Deeper - Cynicism & Misanthropy - 83
Nihilism, Hedonism, and 'Using the System' - 85

THE HOLY FOOL
Beliefs and Rituals - 87
Mental Illness or Mental Religion? - 98
Why Do People Go to Church? - 99
Why Do People Believe? - 100
Belief and Purpose: The Challenge of Absurdity - 101
Defeating Religion, Superstition and the Culture of Stupidity - 106
Coping with Believers and Religious Zealots - 108
Overcoming Fear - 109

HISTORICAL NIHILISM
The Russian Revolutionaries - 110
Historical Context - 111
Severe Times Call for Severe Measures - 114

NIHILISM COMES TO AMERICA
National Myth Building - 117
What is America? - 118
A Few Great American Myths - 120
What Happened to America? - 132
America's Commercial Democracy becomes a Kleptocracy - 135

THE DOLLAR DISEASE
The Power of Money - 144
What is Money? - 147
Your Money is the Government's Debt - 148
The Almighty Dollar - 150
How the Great American Money Scam Works - 150

The Problem of Inflation - 153
Measuring Inflation in the Money Supply - 154
The Official Statistics are Bogus - 155
The 'Free-Market' is a Myth (and the Casino is Rigged) - 157
Welcome to the Debt Trap - 160
Widespread Institutional Failure - 162
The Beginning of the End - 166
Public Pain for Private Gain - 167
The Problem of Capitalism - 169
Solution - 171

THE MADNESS OF A MERETRICIOUS MILITARY
Useless Defense - 175
A Record of Failure - 179
America is Addicted to War - 182
Military Rife with Corruption, Fraud, Waste - 183
War Crimes and Atrocities - 185
Crime Time - 188
A Coup for Jesus? - 190
Deactivate the Standing Military and Unplug the War-Machine - 191

FAMILY AND NIHILISM
History of the Family Network - 193
Why Family? - 193
From Family to Society - 195
Imparting Values - 196
Childhood Development – Problem and Solution - 198
Plato and the Folly of Fear-Driven Authority - 200
Future of the Family - 202

REVOLUTION INTO EVOLUTION
Living Nihilism in the 21st Century - 204
Ethics - 204
Values - 206
Morality - 207
Context or Absurdity - 211
Meaning - 214
Environment - 216
Culture - 217

Life - 218
Fire: Not even the healthy are safe in a forest of disease - 221
Rage Beyond Right or Wrong - 224
21st Century Existence - 225

PROFILES IN NIHILISM
Mikhail Bakunin (1814-1876) - 228
Marcel Duchamp (1887-1968) - 229
Vera Figner (1852-1943) - 231
Gorgias (~485-378 BCE) - 232
Niccolo Machiavelli (1469-1527) - 233
Sergei Nechayev (1847-1882) - 234
Friedrich Nietzsche (1844-1900) - 235
The Red Army Faction [Baader Meinhof Gang] (1968-1998) - 235
Diogenes of Sinope (~404-323 BCE) - 236
Max Stirner (1806-1856) - 237

NIHILISM IN ART - 239

NIHILISM AND BEYOND
Food or Faith? - 246
Should I Vote? - 247
Where's the Truth? - 249
Consumerism and the Money Morality - 251
Total Extremes – A Thought Experiment in Nihilism - 253
Pitfalls of Philosophical Nihilism - 259
UFO – Alien Salvation - 260
Kafka & the Delusion of Freedom - 268
The Folly of Nationalism - 270
Math and Nihilism: Reduction to Common Elements - 274
Nihilism and Race - 275
Order & Chaos - Patterns, Science and Nihilism - 277

Appendix – NECHAYEV'S CATECHISM
'Catechism of a Revolutionist' By Sergei Nechayev - 280

QUESTIONS AND ANSWERS - 287

DEFINITIONS - 293

INDEX - 294

REFERENCES - 299

ABOUT THE AUTHOR - 310

Freydis

An Introductory Note

It's uncommon for a website to become a book, but then *Nihilism: The CounterOrder* is not your average Internet site. Since *The CounterOrder* has been online the responses from readers have been truly remarkable. In 1998 I really didn't think anyone else had the same nihilistic thoughts that I had. I built and published this website from handwritten notes so I could find out if I was really alone, to initiate a dialogue and perhaps even a mild controversy. I expected a torrent of rejection with only a few that would agree but what I actually received was the complete reverse! Today a common response is that 'I used to think I was the only one that thought the same way, and I didn't even have the word to describe my thoughts and feelings until I read about Nihilism'. And that's precisely how I felt when I first encountered nihilism. Remarkable indeed.

This printed book you are reading now is the product of great effort and careful consideration, offering a new and easier to read alternative that will enhance awareness of Nihilism. I'd like to thank the many Internet participants whose active involvement has encouraged the production of this book, and to acknowledge both the supportive fans and the harsh critics whose informative comments and challenging questions have greatly aided in the progressive development of Nihilism through a process of continuous improvement and clarification. And finally, a special thanks to everyone spreading the word – keep it up!

Freydis, January 2010

THE NIHILIST MANIFESTO

Why Nihilism?

Nihilism is considered evil, extreme, something so bad that many refuse to use the word to describe themselves even when the label would be apt. Others use the term to try and silence enemies.

Yet I consider myself a Nihilist and I'm not crazy or attention seeking, I'm just trying to label my feelings and ideas as accurately as possible. I look around and I don't see any belief set or political stripe that I can believe in, not even one I could feign allegiance to. This world offers me nothing to hope in, a society where cowards and failures are called heroes and made into role models, where war is called peace and death is called life. I hate what I see and despise those responsible for it all. Immigrants to America have been told the streets are paved in gold but all I see are potholes and weeds growing in the ever-expanding cracks. We're given garbage and told we can build skyscrapers with it. I'm sick of the lies, the foolish fantasies, and all the reeking fumes that support our pseudo-pop-culture built on vapid values. How does it make *you* feel?

So many problems and issues have become so complicated and convoluted yet we're socially compelled to keep trying the same things, to keep banging our heads against brick walls and each other to find a happy and acceptable solution; why? Who says I have to buy into this? Who says I have to buy into religion, traditional beliefs, and standard ideologies? Why am I being compelled to die for my country right or wrong? Why is our society placing so much effort into stopping drug abuse and suicide even as the rates of both continue to climb?

Maybe instead of treating the symptoms we should target the source – the utter lack of substance behind contemporary values. People kill themselves because they are driven by lies, people drug themselves to escape a living hell and find a dying peace. *Why not just blow it all to hell and at least create a chance of starting over?*

The typical answer within democracy is to just increase inclusiveness. By this reasoning the more people participate the more they will be happy with the outcome. Ha! What does it really generate? More talk, less action, more conflict and fewer useful results. Solutions never come from endless dialogue they come from movement and change. It's delusional to think that every situation has a solution achievable through construction, that every wound can be healed with a bandage. It's that stereotypical cockeyed optimism which deems every problem rectifiable through a smile and a nod. Destruction is often desirable, even the optimal solution, yet in our ambient culture it is always addressed as the last option, why?

Nietzsche once wrote, "All good things were formerly bad things." Maybe we should rethink guns, drugs and disease. I think I like every force humanity can't conquer, every force that destroys to live and forces the living to fight or die while creating a reason for life.

Now is the time to break what can be broken, to revaluate everything, and discover a totally new way of living. *Now is the time for Nihilism.*

Nihilism Defined

Nihilism is a view composed of skepticism coupled with reduction. 'Political' Nihilism is active, not passive, and dictionary-defined as the realization "that conditions in the social organization are so bad as to make destruction desirable for its own sake independent of any constructive program or possibility." In his 1861 novel <u>Fathers And Sons</u>, author Ivan Turgenev accurately defined this worldview, "A nihilist is a person who does not bow down to any authority, who does not accept any principle on faith, however much that principle may be revered."

A common but inaccurate description of nihilism is a "belief in nothing", a misleading phrase that defines the nihilist as one merely trading one belief for another. Instead we should substitute faith for belief where 'faith' is defined as the firm belief in something for which there is no proof, and therefore the nihilist is actually characterized by the *absence of faith*. A universal definition of nihilism could then well be the rejection of that which requires faith for salvation or actualization and would span to include anything from theology to secular ideology.

Within nihilism faith and similar values are discarded because they've no verifiable objective substance, they are invalid serving only as yet another exploitable lie never producing any strategically beneficial outcome. Faith is an imperative hazard to group and individual because it compels suspension of reason, critical analysis and common sense. Nietzsche once said that faith means not wanting to know. Faith is 'don't let those pesky facts get in the way of our political plan or our mystically ordained path to heaven'; faith is "do what I tell you because I said so". All things that can't be disproved need faith, utopia needs faith, idealism needs faith, spiritual salvation needs faith; *reject faith*.

The second element nihilism rejects is the belief in final purpose, that the universe is built upon non-random events and that everything is structured towards an eventual conclusive revelation. This is called teleology and it's the fatal flaw plaguing the whole rainbow of false solutions from Marxism to Buddhism and everything in between. Teleology compels obedience towards the fulfillment of "destiny" or "progress" or similar such grandiose goals. Teleology is used by despots and utopian dreamers alike as a coercive motivation leading only to yet another apocryphal apocalypse; the real way to lead humanity by the nose – tell them it's all part of the big plan so play along or else! It may even seem reasonable but there is not now and never has been any evidence the universe operates in a teleological way – there is no final purpose. *The universe does not operate according to human values!* This is the beautiful simplicity of nihilism that no other idea-set has. By breaking free from the tethers of teleology one is empowered in outlook and outcome because for the first time it's possible to find answers without proceeding from pre-existing perceptions. We're finally free to find out what's really out there and not just the partial evidence to support original pretext and faulty notions only making a hell on earth in the process; *reject teleology*.

Freydis

Active or Passive?

The randomness of nature is a powerful asset because it negates the credibility of teleology, that purposeful predestination that undermines self-determination. So you have the option to passively accept the socio-historically established concoction of false absolutes, 'truth' and moral laws that can be nothing but myth, or you can accept real for what it is and assume the healthier role of active participant constantly defining existence through perception and intelligence. In this way defining existence is predicated upon life, and a conscious awareness of sensory input combined with a critical interpretation of what that input means. And the more highly developed the consciousness, the greater the intelligence and the more effective and functional existence becomes.

Passivity is a myth. We are all intricately enmeshed within a dynamic system that doesn't just demand but compels active decision-making.

Direction

Often what appears to be the extreme message is actually just tomorrow's story today. One can ignore it and panic when it eventually arrives, or learn from it and be ahead of your time prescient, prepared, and devoid of fear and panic. We live in a dynamic era where traditional values have been warped by authorities to serve unjust ends contrary to public well-being. It's an era of contradiction that often necessitates counterintuitive conduct, where sanity is nihilism and patriotism is sedition. The recourse for survival within this context of the erosion of traditional meaning is nihilism.

Nihilism is the organic, reasoned response to artificial chaos, the intentional chaos manufactured by government, religion, and mass-media.

Nihilism

A plan is secondary to the ideas because the artificial structures around us, the outcome, is a product of the collective vision and once concepts are implemented details sort themselves out afterwards. The new will grow on the ash heaps of the old. Remember: today you have the luxury of making a decision no one else can make for you; choose carefully which side to be on.

"The beginning of a revolution is in reality the end of a belief."
– Gustave Le Bon

Death to God

Death to Government

Death to Philosophy

Death to Ideology

Death to Debt

Death to Morality

Beyond right and left, beyond right and wrong...

WHAT IS NIHILISM?

"The more the universe seems comprehensible, the more it also seems pointless." – Steven Weinberg, physicist

Nihilism Defined

Nihilism is primarily skepticism coupled with reduction, but in practical reality it takes on more than one facet which often leads to a confusion of definitions. In the most general sense nihilism has two primary classifications, the first is passive and usually goes by the term existential or 'social' nihilism and the second is active and is termed 'political' nihilism.

Existential nihilism is a passive world view which revolves around such topics as suffering and futility, and even has connections to Eastern mysticism like Buddhism. In a more direct sense existential 'social' nihilism is manifest within the sense of isolation, futility, angst, and the hopelessness of existence increasingly prevalent within the modern digital world, an effect referred to as the 'downward spiral'. A direct way to describe it might be 'detachment from everything'.

Words used to describe political nihilism include active, revolutionary, destructive, and even creative. Political nihilism is dictionary defined as the realization "that conditions in the social organization are so bad as to make destruction desirable for its own sake independent of any constructive program or possibility." It deals with authority and social structures rather than simply the introspective, personal emotions of existential nihilism.

Political nihilism especially is a worldview that's rational, logical, empirical, scientific and devoid of pointless, extraneous emotion. It's the logical psyche that distills everything down into what is known, what can be known and what can't be known. It's the realization that all values are ultimately relativistic and in some ways the simplicity of nihilism is its own complexity.

Nihilism

Nihilism: When conditions in the social organization are so unhealthy as to make destruction desirable for its own sake independent of any constructive program or possibility.

An estimable and succinct definition of a political nihilist comes from Ivan Turgenev's 1861 novel Fathers And Sons, "A nihilist is a person who does not bow down to any authority, who does not accept any principle on faith, however much that principle may be revered."

So the two classes of nihilism overlap but this book is mostly about the second stage, 'political' nihilism, for reasons of brevity because the existential angle when not stillborn generally leads to political nihilism anyway. Nihilism isn't something to just *talk* about it's something to *live*, and finally because political nihilism has real world history and experience as you'll read in this book concerning the Russian revolutionaries in *Historical Nihilism*. Ultimately however, the nihilistic direction one travels depends on what the individual wishes to make out of life.

To negate and circumvent the paradoxes and internal contradictions inherent within existential nihilism is the course of the 'political' nihilism you're reading. I don't want to use the philosophy lexicon any more than necessary nor the confusing verbosity of academia (just a few colorful adjectives where necessary); nihilism is the destruction of idle philosophy, the negation of idealism, the negation of mythology, and the destruction of perplexity along with the disingenuous despots that profit from it as the monopolist interpreters of artificial confusion. Therefore, 'political' Nihilism's definitions are:

1) When conditions in the social organization are so unhealthy as to make destruction desirable for its own sake independent of any constructive program or possibility. 2) A doctrine of skepticism coupled with reduction that refutes faith, teleology, arbitrary morality, sacred values and principles, heresy, blasphemy, and similar beliefs while maintaining that existing political, social, and economic institutions based on these beliefs must be destroyed. 3) A methodology for a biologically-based existence that rejects arbitrary

morality in favor of cause and effect and inviolate forces, predicated upon that which is objectively self-evident and without need of belief, within a sustainable mental and physical environment that promotes independent thinking and critical expression.

The Historical Development of Nihilism

The first nihilists were likely the Greek Sophists who lived about 2,500 years ago. They used oratorical skills and argumentative discourse to challenge the values upon which everyday beliefs rested. The Greek sophists, such as Gorgias, represented the beginning of philosophy and the first conflict between the traditional mystical belief system and a rational, skeptical view of the natural world. It was as basic as the difference between a worldview based on emotion and one on thought. Because the sophists challenged established beliefs they were often condemned by public authorities and critics as moral corrupters or worse.

One of the earliest nihilistic writers of the modern era was the Dane Soren Aabye Kierkegaard who lived from 1813 to 1855. Kierkegaard was a truly unique but also enigmatic philosopher who established the foundation of the philosophy later termed existentialism. Kierkegaard's existentialism was in many ways a negation of the ruling Hegelian philosophy, views deeply rooted in Kierkegaard's Lutheran Protestantism that reflected the ideals of the subjectivity of truth and the nature of life as a uniquely individual pursuit. To be brutally succinct existentialism posits that existence is based on experience and this experience is a uniquely individualized sensation, in other words 'my reality is not your reality'. Modern quantum physical 'philosophy' returned to this theme of solipsism during the late 20th century using empirical mathematics.

The philosopher-critic Max Stirner, who lived from 1806-1856, was similar to Kierkegaard in his existential viewpoint that placed rational self-interest over the herd-mentality, and most everything else as well. However, Stirner's harsh criticism of establishment institutions and contemporary values placed him closer to anarchism, and yet as he even criticized the values of anarchism he progressed into the realm of nihilism.

Travelling from the foundations of theory into revolutionary practice, the Russian Mikhail Bakunin, who lived from 1814-1876, took up action and revolution, and the destruction of idols and foolish beliefs, as a way of life. He circled the globe with a surfeit of revolutionary zeal and a limitless capacity for delivering motivating speeches, laying the foundation for anarchism and nihilism in the process.

The fiery Russian Sergei Nechayev (1847-1882), along with other revolutionaries of the era, carried the ideas of nihilism even further out of theory and into practice.

The Russian Nihilists

Political nihilism goes back at least to Russia during the last half of the 1800s as a revolutionary movement with the stated goal of overthrowing the despotic authority of the Czar.

> In Russia, nihilism became identified with a loosely organized revolutionary movement (c.1860-1917) that rejected the authority of the state, church, and family. ... The movement advocated a social arrangement based on rationalism and materialism as the sole source of knowledge and individual freedom as the highest goal. By rejecting man's spiritual essence in favor of a solely materialistic one, nihilists denounced God and religious authority as antithetical to freedom.[5]

By modern standards the Nihilists attempts at revolution were inconsistent and mostly ineffective – lobbing low quality munitions at the Czar and his family and even getting themselves blown up in the process. But what they lacked in equipment and tactics they made up for with vision, ideas, and an unparalleled intensity.

Freydis

The nihilists enjoyed shocking their parents by calling for an end to the old moral system, advocating, for instance, the extermination of everybody in Russia over the age of 25. In the 1860's many of these young intellectuals went to Switzerland, where the proper Swiss bourgeoisie were scandalized at the men with their hair cut long and the girls with their hair cut short, at their loud voices and insolent behaviour.[1]

The mark left by the Russian Nihilists was not in ephemeral political change but rather a revolution of ideas and attitudes, one that still resonates today. "The earnest young men and women [Nihilists] of the 1860's wanted to cut through every polite veneer, to get rid of all conventional sham, to get to the bottom of things."[4]

Anarchism

Nihilists and anarchists can both trace their roots to the intense personality of Mikhail Bakunin in the 19th century who succinctly reflected the nihilist sentiment with his famous statement: "Let us put our trust in the eternal spirit which destroys and annihilates only because it is the unsearchable and eternally creative source of all." Anarchism and nihilism are often confused, but looking deeper we can see that they view events from a different perspective. For example the anarchist says that 'no one has the authority to tell another what to do'. But the nihilist replies that if the one giving orders has a gun and the other not, then what do rights or authority matter? Indeed, what benefit is constitution at the moment of any criminal event?

The abuse and exploitation of power by illegitimate authority is as old as history because human behavior is primarily selfish and will usually take advantage of the situation as much as allowed. Right or wrong, authority and power remain. Nevertheless it's also true that the demand for fair treatment and equal opportunity are just as timeless. Human social development is a story of the constant struggle between the two forces. In this struggle the only healthy and functional structure remains one of robust checks and balances.

Nihilism

Anarchists are idealists that believe in subjective concepts such as peace, legal justice, and especially the universal noble nature of all individuals (at least under the proper social conditions). These myths can serve a constructive function, but all too often dogmatic attachment only serves to lead us astray. It's critical that we criticize and reconsider *even what we value most.*

The Nihilist realizes that history is abused and misconstrued through the formation of artificial lines and erroneous connections between disparate events, only to substantiate preconceived interpretations of reality, the classic teleological myth.

> We draw an imaginary thread through the ages to chart the course we judge to be the 'correct' one. All wrong views are ignored. This approach was dubbed the 'Whig' theory of history by Herbert Butterfield. The name derived from those past historians who treated history as a record of events that culminated in the political system dear to their own hearts: the liberal democracy.[2]

It's an understandable product of human evolution to not only detect patterns but also get carried away and concoct them as well.

> "[T]he human mind has evolved an ability to recognize geometrical patterns where none exist. What else might it be recognizing that does not exist?"[2]

Human nature sees things that aren't really there, just think of optical illusions or Rorschach ink-blot tests. Much of life is nothing interpreted as something. This is because dealing with the yawning absence necessitates the concoction of a something to grasp the nothing, thereby ignoring the perilous obvious by manufacturing a more malleable artificial myth. Yet the attitude of a Nihilist is contradictory to this because they seek to discern a more accurate understanding of reality at the moment, not as they *wish* to see which is the tragically typical way divorced from evidence and reasoned hypothesis. This includes the desire to view human character as it actually is and understand purpose within context.

Freydis

Beyond Good and Evil

Religious believers and philosophers alike frequently ask the question, 'does evil exist?', as if they need to be continually reassured that it does and we agree with them. Many are completely convinced that evil is everywhere, yet the same people are equally sure of luck, fate, and mysterious malevolent powers out to defeat all their noble efforts. But all these imaginary influences are simply projections of a selfish ego. In fact, *there is no natural evil, and no malicious intent exists within any forces of the universe.*

An old Russian proverb states, "There is no evil, but that it brings some good," revealing that even in standard Manichean theology every god has a devil and every good requires an evil to shadow it. Even to define evil as wholly immoral acts we still have to specify which set of moral of standards we're using as rule book. Is it the Bible? The Talmud? The I Ching?! Obviously, evil is a variable, yet nonetheless consistent elements of *healthy* and *unhealthy* can still be discerned within the boundaries of a species due to the shared genetic material. Actions and events that benefit the growth and well-being of the species, and the individuals within it, are colloquially, but consistently, termed good and the opposite as evil. For instance the chicken, as well as the human owner, considers the fox evil because he sneaks in to commit murder, yet the fox doesn't consider his species' carnivorous actions to be evil but rather entirely good because they mean food and survival. This analogy also reminds us that we can go much farther with symbiosis and cooperation than with warfare.

For intelligent creatures good and evil are unnecessary categories, they're loaded terms that intentionally obscure actual forces and events while impeding our ability to accurately comprehend both. We shouldn't view life and existence as a conflict between good and evil; to do so is both foolish and self-defeating because it requires us to declare war on ourselves, our instincts, and even unavoidable natural laws!

Nihilism

A Little Perspective

Everybody has an answer, but not just any answer, *the* answer. If you think about it it's truly amazing the sheer number of people that have the officially authorized monopoly on truth. This fact alone highlights the dissonance of absolute values and the misguided nature of idealism. What quantitative value would you place on your life? A life insurance corporation could concoct an exact dollar amount. But even that figure may be inflated; the chemical compounds that make up your body are only worth a few cents. But isn't life more valuable than gold, oil or other commodities? Think again; people *are* a renewable resource.

Which is cheaper to create human life or an ounce of gold? Gold can actually be synthesized in a cyclotron but the cost is astronomical, however human life, or any life, can be created virtually for free. Planet Earth is infested with perpetual self-replicators but the amount of platinum, for example, is finite. This self-righteous confidence manifests itself as an unlimited capacity for egoistic narcissism and self-magnification. Human arrogance conveniently assumes itself the apex of evolution yet in reality the corporal being is merely a disposable vehicle for the reproduction of genetic material, not the other way around! Perhaps the most profound realization of the 20th century remains mostly unknown for it is the genes that are the master and not the individual human created by them. This helps explain why many human cravings are harmful to the self but profitable to the genes, and the prevalence of certain self-destructive behaviors. And remarkably this is the true solution to the classic existential dilemma, why *life* is just *death* or as John Lennon once put it, "Why in the world are we here? Surely not to live in pain and fear," yet apparently we are! The human body isn't programmed for pain-free longevity, just long enough to reproduce physically and to perpetuate learned skills, which is why doctors will never run out of business. The biological boss may be too small to see but it's far too powerful to ignore.

If human value could be measured outside the skewed perspective of the collective ego it might look something like this; if only one individual existed on planet Earth they would be the most important human. If two people existed their individual significance would be divided in half (1/2). If six billion people existed on Earth what would the individual significance of each one be? A simple equation shows the value as the fractional percentage of the whole population plus any incidental, conjectural additives from education, training, intelligence etc. Presupposing this Marxian values system of universal equality the formula for individual human value is:

$1/p + (E/p)$ = individual human value

p = current world population
E = years of education, training, work experience.

So, in a world of six billion people your uneducated mass is 1/6000000000 or 1.67×10^{-10} of that whole. Your significance is 0.0000000167%. With a 12 year education your significance rockets upward to a factor of 2.167×10^{-9} or 0.0000002167%.

It's clear that overpopulation dramatically diminishes the value of human life. So, is it any wonder religion is so popular and why human nature so desperately seeks meaning and purpose even in the most ridiculous places? Why do so many people hide behind money fooling only themselves into thinking that wealth gives them significance? Isn't it painfully obvious why society invents artificial concepts of justice, morality, and ethics? The brutality and utter irrationality of the animal world is just outside the rusty gates of our  crumbling civilization. But isn't it comforting to know that as long as we're inside we have the warming illusion of fairness, equality and justice for all (that can afford it anyway)?

Nihilism

Self-delusion seems to be a defining quality of human behavior. Lies maintain our flimsy order, we find consolation in myths like 'what we do has significance' and 'God punishes the wicked'. The constant avalanche of empirical evidence to the contrary simply gets relegated to the third class bureau of irrational philosophers.

"Hypocrisy can flourish when goodness is defined not only as kind and altruistic behavior, but as sticking to the rules and obligations of the faith."[3] — Susan Blackmore

Our 'leaders' wage war in the name of peace and establish democracy with an iron fist. Our traditional values are warped; they reflect fantasy not reality. Our values are so removed from actual substance that fantasy becomes reality and truth becomes error. This is the primary difficulty in conveying the meaning of nihilism because all morally loaded concepts are biased against a lucid description of the nihilistic viewpoint. Nietzsche was addressing this issue when he wrote the title and the book <u>Beyond Good and Evil</u>. But it's not just a series of lies, it's a debasing and wholly aberrant structure. The problem is so deep that even the words to define it must be replaced with a new lexicon.

Nihilism as Philosophy

Nihilism is a rejection of philosophy and the metaphysical nebulae such reasoning inevitably descends into. Yet if one wants this out of nihilism they can construct it, even more so than other idea sets, but to do so only leads to paradox and contradiction like finding value in no-values or a literal belief in nothing; try the disbelief in gravity for instance. Nihilism is not absolutist voiding of values to create an imaginary milieu neutered of positive and negative forces, up or down because those are absurd situations, indeed i*dealistic* situations that are both impossible to achieve and dangerously delusional as goals. Unfortunately some nihilists get caught in this dim labyrinth of ethics and morality. Others jump head first into the maw as a demonstration of supposed mental prowess which explains existential nihilism's effervescent popularity among certain academics and similar insulated atoms of fantasy. Nihilism is the destruction of philosophy not the magnification of it! Reference Nietzsche's philosophy with a sledgehammer.

This existentialism is superfluous since such constructs are wholly elastic anyhow; they can and do mean whatever the proponent claims, generating the same foggy haze of intellectual opacity Nihilism disperses. In other words it's myth creation, although that doesn't render them insignificant or impotent in the mind of the public, myths have value for those that believe in them. The nihilists can't simply ignore the myth believers or the myths; instead the wise path is to seek understanding. Nihilism dissolves myth with the acid of reason and logic to illuminate their assumptions and underpinning structures to better understand and better act.

Nihilism challenges the assumptions supporting common values such as 'equality'; 'pity' and 'justice', but also terms of conclusion about human existence. Existential values, terms such as 'meaningless', 'pointless' and 'futile', are flawed because their definitions stem from the moral values that have hitherto been rejected. We have to criticize justice when events demonstrate that in court it's not whether one is guilty or not, but how persuasive their lawyer is, or how thoroughly the judge and jury have been rhetorically manipulated! 'Justice' is the confusing legalese that your high-priced barrister can spew in the courtroom like an oil slick in front of a pursuing vehicle. The rich go free while the poor go to prison. Why? Justice has been perverted beyond recognition, ironically through a dogmatic belief in its sanctity and immutability. It's clearly time to question the root assumptions.

Nihilism is a consequence of the personal realization that values and morals previously assumed indisputable are actually false, misguided or unworkable, and the ultimate esteem with which these morals have been uplifted leads to a catastrophic withdrawal to the opposite extreme when the deception is recognized. And while an acceptance of nihilism immediately returns a perspective of utter futility for life and universal existence, this perspective is not the final resolution. As Nietzsche once wrote in <u>The Will to Power</u>, "Nihilism represents a pathological transition phase..." Existence is not futile simply because the edifice of modern morality is inherently dysfunctional. Actually existence has even more purpose now because a proper perspective has been attained and a reason is [finally] clear – the complete destruction of the debasing, theologically derived moral order. Thus the nihilist is at base a creator of the highest magnitude and a survivor of the most intense metaphysical struggle of all time. The nihilist undergoes a personal evolution and has proven themselves the mental superiors to the herd and mob, they have proven their will and 'license' for continued existence and have successfully escaped from the circus of values. Once the transvaluation of values is complete an entirely new and sane perspective can be achieved.

280 Million Years of Nihilism

It's a characteristic of the human mind to turn simplicity into subjective complexity and to construe difficulty from life where none exists. Today the archetypal question for philosophers is "why are we here?" Ask a human and serious response will probably involve complex reasoning involving mystical deities or introspective analysis. But before we leave the final answer with humanity I think we need a second opinion.

Some 280 million years ago the first amphibians began life outside water. These Labryinthodonts named for their infolded tooth enamel typically had large triangular heads and wide, flat bodies that made them look like giant road-kill without the tread marks. Tetrapods like these crawled around on land eating worms, maybe a few bugs but basically whatever they could catch and digest. Not much to look at or admire yet they gave rise to all other land vertebrates, reptiles, birds, and yes eventually even literate humans.

If we could ask the same of a Permian tetrapod what mysterious, and enlightening answers would they provide? Perhaps something like "I don't understand the question; I just want to avoid death."

Freydis

Odd isn't it that they never had any goal or god, no soul or hope of an afterlife indeed they lacked *any* purpose beyond the brief struggle for life and yet millions of years later here we are reading this because of it, because they existed and evolved? We as humans exist in the same physical universe subject to the same rules of physics and biology, the same need for sea-water salinity body fluid, the same protein and amino acids ... *Decades of scientific inquiry and careful research all to reach the inescapable conclusion that the point is there is no point.* The joke is on us because we turned the absurdly simple into the dangerously complex.

The answer to "why are we here?" is no different for human, Labryinthodont, or jellyfish, because we live in the same world subject to the same physical limitations and end up in the same place after death. Well, some leave better fossils than others. Now we see why fear of death is such a natural instinct and why religion exerts so much concerted effort to contradict that instinct.

The human mind creates ethics, moral codes, rules to die by, excuses and justifications for the deepest epiphany and the most trivial event alike. Some even go so far as to hijack random events and misinterpret them as self-created, the psychological principle known as 'illusion of control'. Unfortunately the complexities of the human mind merely make it easier to believe in fantasy and entertain delusion. Such an effort to find greater significance where there really is none only leads to wayward guidance and specious justifications. Those concocted reasons are then used to justify what need not be justified like our continued existence except based upon lies, setting up everyone for the fall when the myth erodes. Everything would move onward quite smoothly without any human minds around to believe in God, Satan or any other fictions, it did before us and it will after. Instead the Nihilist is concerned with the things that matter *whether anyone believes in them or not*, and all the forces and factors that influence even the things that don't think.

Although evolution has no goal and our purpose may be just as elusive that doesn't void significance, it doesn't make action and consequence irrelevant, an important distinction too often confused within nihilism. Nihilism doesn't preclude significance or a naive refusal to extract lessons from history just as a lack of the traditional mystical goal does not necessitate futility. Extinction events, for example, are significant – after all, we wouldn't be here without them. The only cosmic justification supported by any tangible evidence is the impetus for continued existence, the self-justifying purpose of tautology. And truthfully demanding any further justification from most simply foments confusion and foolish behavior. Furthermore it's likely that anything beyond that basal maxim is just an artificial construction. So, nihilism is not an issue of existence so much as a series of questions regarding the value, if any, that those artificially constructed meanings have. Where do they take us and do we really want to end up there? And can we really outsmart natural selection, for instance?

What's Left?

Nihilism can appear very complicated because in the present moral milieu it's necessary to describe it in the terms of negatives and being against this or that. It's about accepting what is, and working within that framework to generate a lifestyle of efficacy and natural perspective. Too often our modern high-technology planet makes us think that if it looks confusing and it takes a Germanic scholar to analyze it then it must be complicated. What I'm saying is that you don't need any of that garbage. You don't need to believe in God or Beelzebub or anything else that can't be verified or tested in any way. You don't need to believe that human nature is intrinsically evil or in original sin. It takes so much vain effort to struggle with good and bad. Normal people literally torture themselves with ethical and moral quandaries in self-created dungeons that ultimately never matter. For this reason the nihilistic philosophy takes a beating in the arena of ideas because it's just a nothing ideology. That's why I like to call it an anti-ideology. It simply doesn't play by those rules because those rules are arbitrary; they exist only in the social-mindset. And if other people want to live within that self-torturing,

NIHILISM: FAITH NOT REQUIRED

intellect numbing fantasy world then I'm not going to stop them; have fun ... hating life.

It's important to realize too that Nihilism isn't like every other ideology that places a vague future goal in primacy and forces everything in the present to fit that fantasy. Nihilism is a counter-order, it is the opposite of every other ideology and theology that seeks to impose an absolute conception of the way everything should be because that's simply not how things really work. Life can't be controlled by an artificially concocted single universal answer or by building a perfect order that will last forever. Nihilism operates with the expectation that the future and its needs are always unknown and all we can really do is prepare ourselves to fit the present and try to meet whatever challenges arise in the ongoing process of existence; thus Nihilism isn't concerned so much with the aftermath as it is with the *here* and *now*, hence its very definition.

Many people spend great effort trying to determine what nihilism is, and it often seems perplexing because it is such a radically different viewpoint and mindset. Belief systems and ideologies are defined by what they are and what they value but nihilism is more defined by what isn't, it's about an absence rather than a presence. Nihilism is absence of faith, absence of teleology, lack of God, and so on. That's why I've always said, nihilism is where you go when you can't find anything to believe in. All that's left are the inescapable natural forces and that which is self-evident or verifiable.

It often seems more complex than it really is and indeed the more philosophers struggle to force it into the traditional ideological mold the less it's really nihilism. Is it hedonism? Is it immorality? Does it support capitalism, or socialism? Anything beyond the primary aspects are derivative and potentially arbitrary considerations, perhaps simply personal interpretations.

Change and acceptance of heterodoxy does not come without introspection. Human nature is so conditioned to social living that even the silliest social faux pas achieves monumental proportions; *people live for the trivial at the cost of living for the critical.* "Did I buy

Nihilism

the right brand of shoes? Am I using the right brand of toothpaste?" Who really has the twisted perspective?

And what *is* the point? The point is that even if you reject nihilism your relationship has not been severed because the entire social and political structure that we have to live within is programmed for self-destruction because it's all based on disingenuous ideas and promulgated through hollow rhetoric and plastic faces for near-term goals. And what do lies breed except vengeance and anger?

You may blame the violence, blame the anger, blame the nihilism, blame the effect not the cause, but nevertheless that dangerous dénouement will remain not far off and no one alive will avoid it.

As humbling as it is the scale and perhaps significance of humanity shrinks in accordance with the magnitude of our knowledge. A basic understanding of cosmology leads to the ultimate nihilism. Springing from a cosmic accident, life (apparently) has no purpose or value. We're just small beings crawling upon a tiny world at the edge of one of countless galaxies in an uncaring, unconcerned universe. The product of a series of astounding improbabilities destined to die after lifetime of meaningless suffering alone and afraid ... and if you think God made it all, isn't that even more degrading?!

Without a higher moral judge, nothing beyond life goes punished or rewarded. The fundamental moral quandary is that in order for moral rules to have validity they must have an ultimate arbiter, otherwise right and wrong dive into confusing waters of relativism. That ultimate arbiter has always been God, the final judge, where the buck stops, where even Earth's most evil and wicked run amok with free will get their comeuppance. The Bible says the Earth is the Devils domain (Isaiah 13:11 & Revelation 12:9, even though the Bible also says God created the Earth, Genesis 1:1). If that's what everyone expects, then that's all it will ever be. As a Nihilist I say it's *our* domain and we can make it a hell or a heaven. But as long as we prejudge the decision absolving ourselves of responsibility then it probably *will* be a realm for the Devil.

Freydis

When we conclude that we each only get one life, the goal becomes painfully obvious, as unpleasant as the sight of the predator messily devouring the prey in a wildlife documentary. I think humans are the gods, but the corporal package is a powerful dichotomy. Worm and god side by side. We need no higher power for justification or success, only the desire and willpower. Each human life has the potential, but unless one strives to be something higher they are only a worm. We *can* do anything the question is *will we*? Will we struggle in vain with the futile labels of olde, senselessly slaughtering each other over self-imposed polarities while disingenuous despots reap the profits from our collective bloodletting? Or will we choose the exit, and in this very dark room known as life not too many exit signs are visible. *The one I used is called nihilism.*

The only viable antidote to the terror of despotism is the arming of the individual mind with *fact* instead of fantasy and *firearms* instead of faith. – Freydis

NIHILISM IN ACTION!

Nihilism is sanity in an insane society

Objective Reality & Freewill

It's remarkable how even a modicum of logic and scientific philosophy demonstrates the difficulty of defining what is real and the rules to describe it. Like a sandpit the more you struggle in it the tougher it gets. So an important value to question is *objective reality*. The closest match might be scientific laws which are merely consistent principles and the most powerful ones are just statistical constructs.

This struggle to define objective reality implies a lack of objective truth, but really this philosophical assumption leads to neither clarity nor accurate interpretations. Even a state of total chaos has statistical uniformities. Consensus can be found and in fact it's remarkably prevalent. Commonality can be found and built upon at many levels but absolutes are less meaningful here than consistency; ultimate reality is fuzzy because it's a product of probabilities. The key is to utilize the solid and avoid the ambiguous, bet on the likely and not the unlikely.

Existence is largely defined by perception because reality is contextual.[1] If you perceive yourself as weak and without willpower then you'll find life is such. Conversely, if you perceive that you have the power to change things in your life, so it will be. In the same way we tend to find what we expect just as physicists contemplate how a photon can be both a wave and a particle. This essence doesn't mean that practical reality is an illusion, rather it is *multi-dimensional*.

The random and statistical qualities of nature are critical forces because they negate the credibility of teleology, that purposeful predestination that undermines freewill. So one actually has the option to passively accept the socio-historically established concoction of absolutes, truth and moral laws, the objective reality which can be nothing but myth. Or you can accept real for what it is and assume the healthier role of active participant constantly defining existence through perception and intelligence. In this way defining existence is predicated upon life, conscious awareness of sensory input combined with critical interpretation of what that input means. And the more highly developed the consciousness, or the greater the intelligence, the more effective and meaningful is existence.

Passivity is a myth. We are all intricately enmeshed within a dynamic system that doesn't just demand but compels active decision-making.

Hence the difference between passive 'social' and active 'political' nihilism is that one accepts whatever happens within futility and pointlessness while the other destroys/creates meaning and value. Which path a person takes is a personal decision within the limits of ability, and that means one does have choice; existence is not predetermined or fatally ordained. However, default answers and the compulsion of conformity shouldn't be overlooked. Reality is contextual.

The Pitfalls of Artificial Law

It may seem peculiar how terms like 'moral', 'liberal' and 'conservative' are used in conversation. People will tell you they're moral individuals but they don't say moral according to who or what even though every culture and religious order has different standards. They'll tell you they're liberal and one is supposed to assume they mean it politically instead of liberal users of peyote or stamps on heavy envelopes. 'Progress' is another favorite; progress is good but as in the spread of cancer? Or maybe they mean the spread of Wal-Mart's to every town in the world with at least 5,000 people?

But the consistent message people are trying to convey in conversation is their own subtle deviation from the political and social norm and from the ambient morality, which is to say from the

Nihilism

definitions and standards processed, packaged, and pumped into them by media, government, and church authorities. Since all these concepts are unable to be empirically codified they assume elastic values that are easily warped to serve despots and unhealthy outcome, which is why Nietzsche wisely stated:

"Morality is the best of all devices for leading mankind by the nose."

But moral laws aren't the only kind that can be warped to serve disingenuous ends. The greater the personal wealth and property one possesses the more laws are needed to protect that wealth. Conversely the less one owns the fewer laws are needed for protecting it. At a point of total poverty where one has nothing but the self they would only feel the need for laws against killing i.e. 'thou shalt not murder'. In other words the degree of law desired is directly proportional to the wealth in possession. Laws protect that vested power and the people owning it by providing consistent codified support for the control and distribution of that wealth. But even though the stated desire for legality is universal the interpretation of that legality is not, clearly varying between haves and have-nots, a schism fervently exploited by Marxists. Enter the lawyers who are mercenaries paid to reinterpret the law to favor the client. Since the rich have the money to buy the most powerful lawyers and since the establishment of precedent is defined through epic court battles, common law is gradually skewed in favor of those rich patrons; hence the emergence of a class-bifurcated, sanctimonious justice system and the erosion of legal fairness. Scientific research shows that in a police lineup witnesses' who choose an incorrect person are just as confident as those that choose the correct one because human memory fills in the blanks with assumptions. Furthermore juries are just as credulous of false

or inaccurate testimony as legitimate *because all that really matters is strength of conviction*. The criminal justice system warps science and the witness to its own ends because the only thing that matters in this setting is which side you're on – prosecution or defense.

Laws are typically employed to shield the incompetent and mitigate the influence of the capable. For example, a cop with a gun can be a greater danger than a 'criminal' because they have an official sanction to kill; their murder is backed by the concept of law. The government and legal institutions have no higher morality than the 'criminal' does; they are prone to heinous conduct just as, if not worse than the criminal is, without impartial oversight. One party can act with impunity; the other will be executed. So what of "rights"? Nihilism views rights as irrelevant because it's the underlying structures of morality and the roots of truth, myth and collective delusions that dictate significance. Morality and ethics are artificial byproducts of culture and through hypocrisy and abuse are warped into becoming illusory forces.

Some argue that money is a proxy for achievement, but this is false. Money is aggregated amongst the already wealthy. Nor does our capitalist society promote achievement through the educational establishment, the mythical system of western mandarinism perpetuated by certain intelligentsia members. The true nature of the system is based more on connections and wealth than merit. The number of slots to get on this escalator to social achievement is limited, and those already powerful get to choose who gets those slots. It has never been truer than today, the rich get richer while the poor get poorer.

War or Revolution?

Before I continue it is imperative that I clearly define the differences between war and revolution and their significance to Nihilism. All too often the two words are used interchangeably because they both convey a sense of violent action and social upheaval but they have very different meanings. Part of the problem involves the nature of modern warfare, which is increasingly an urban phenomenon that affects civilians even more than soldiers. Guerrilla warfare and counterinsurgency efforts all blur the distinction between revolution and warfare. But this doesn't mean the two concepts are synonymous; in fact warfare and revolution are opposites. A war is started by an established government and fought against an organized enemy. Revolution is an effort to overthrow and replace an established government or authority structure.

"It is better to deal with a government in difficulties than with one that has luck on its side," said Mayer Amschel Rothschild. "The best bargains can be found when the streets flow red with blood," is widely attributed to the Rothschilds as well. Cyclical, traditional European wars of the type funded by the Rothschilds culminated in World War One, once referred to as 'the war to end all wars'. Many bankers and rapacious industrialists gained fabulous wealth from the death and mutilation of millions. Just think of Sir Hiram Maxim who amassed a fortune from the invention of the machine gun, then consider that at Passchendaele in Belgium, on just one battlefield, 310,000 Allied soldiers were slaughtered so that side could gain just five miles of territory. *War serves only the monetary profit of kings and plutocrats.*

Revolution is an anti-war, ideally it's the effort to destabilize the machines of the industrialists and overthrow the kings. Still it would be naïve to think that many revolutions aren't manipulated by the same people they purport to overthrow.

Political leaders realized long ago that in order to achieve their goals and maintain the legitimacy of authority it was necessary to have the support of public opinion. Unfortunately the masses are conservative by nature and rarely desire to be dragged into the bloody machinations of their governments. The solution is to create the proper national event or circumstances with which to manipulate popular sentiment into supporting your campaign. This is called social engineering and like all tools it can be used to help or hurt. One infamous example involved F.D. Roosevelt who lured the Japanese into Pearl Harbor, neatly creating the proper domestic outrage required for entry into another suicidal escapade known as war.

It's ridiculous to assume these people will protect us from anything. The Russians, Germans, Japanese, even the British believed their governments would achieve greatness and keep them safe. I guess WW II was a rude awakening? How many used to think employment was guaranteed in a large corporation, or that housing values would never drop significantly? Apparently theft isn't a crime when it's sanctioned by authority. Support of this Empire is futile; the only choice is to destroy it for safety and sanity.

Too many idealistic crusaders fall for the trick of turning their revolutions into wars at the behest of established authority, in other words be sure to rub-out the right people and hit the correct target. The wise realize that the visible is a product of the invisible in the sense that ideas define outcome, values define product and the moral topology defines the superstructure; and if we think it's impossible it'll never happen but if we think it can it will. This is the true nature of the system we're dealing with.

It's an unfortunate fault of simplistic human nature to first target the visible elements. But to merely attack the visible superstructure of capitalism, church and politicians is doomed – the mistake of anarchism. The real enemies are the "demons" in the public consciousness, the myths and the lies, the foolish ideas and the self-destructive notions and secondly the people that preach it. The relativistic moral codes of "good" is this and "bad" is that, they're cynically reinvented by self-righteous leaderships to achieve misguided, mystical goals. And the intangible, non-verifiable goals make the sweetest bait because no one can claim otherwise! If you want to change a belief you must first change an environment because what the masses believe is formed by what they hear and see around them.

> "The great revolutions are those of manners and thought. Changing the name of a government does not transform the mentality of a people." – Gustave Le Bon

Nihilism

The strategic success of revolution is predicated upon reaching these roots. How? Employ the acidic dissolution of delusion. Ridicule the ridiculous; highlight absurdity, contradiction and irony. Make fun of the foolish and faithful alike but more importantly the notions they use; discredit delusion by every means available.

Second, propagate the replacement and fill the vacuum left by the discredited myths. Fill it with facts built from the boundaries of the known and the unknown in order to deal with the present and not some fictional afterlife. Counteract religious modes – convince the public that natural behavior and instinct are normal again. Work to build havens from mass-media and pop-cultural influences allowing anyone the freedom of independent thought and introspection unfettered by the corporate-sponsored, brand-positioned homogenized opinions doled out like drug-laced candy. Communicate the message, and the inveterate popularity of entertainment shouldn't be underestimated as a tool for changing opinion, it's the best way to connect with mass audiences. On a more localized level never begin with a frontal assault, but instead aim to first disarm your opponent by using humor or unexpected actions. And never forget the effect of reinforced statements, *one* voice is nonsense but *two* is the sound of authority – use it.

So when does the revolution start? It already has! Act accordingly in what you do and what you say. There's no half measure and no fence to sit on, everyone is a participant in this omnipresent psychological war because it has no front-line or boundaries. Every mind is a battlefield and every person with above room temperature body warmth and IQ is a combatant. Now's the time to decide which side to be on.

Systemic Self-Destruction

Nihilism is an awareness that *de*struction is at least as important as *con*struction, even more so when institutions have outlived their usefulness to become corrupt and unhealthy. Idealist crusades fail because they never remove the vestiges of the past order. Think of it biologically, would Homo sapiens have evolved out of the Mesozoic era, or would they have just been dino-snacks? We're here because of a previous *mass extinction!* The old order didn't mutate, it was catastrophically destroyed because that's the only way radical, meaningful change can occur. Revolutions often fail because the willpower to enact the necessary severity of change is lacking. Actually it's not just willpower it's the total vision that's usually lacking. Some call Karl Marx a revolutionary but Marxism isn't genuine revolution it's just rearranging the artificial order. Every ideology on the books is merely a convenient way to re-order the present situation; they just shuffle the same old cards and the people end up worse off than before. Nihilism plays a completely new game, but the old game of lies and myths always self-destructs eventually. These are the cycles of history, the recycling of flawed ideologies and our era is a prime example.

Every political ideology has been discredited as an affront to freedom and well-being. From capitalism to communism the blindly faithful never test and verify theory before implementation, so the fatal flaw is always the same – actualization; it's the predictable literalization of faith and myth. Besides producing voluminous hypocrisy and tyranny the byproduct of sham ideologies and fractional logic includes extensive pollution of both the human mind and the Earth's ecosystem. Think of the billions of dollars spent to produce nuclear, biological, and chemical weapons all to have them rust and leak in storage bunkers from Tooele to Tomsk-7. Millions toiling to produce ultra-deadly nerve gas and radioactive waste with a four and a half billion year half-life. Nihilists know who to 'thank'- and who to stop from doing it again.

Religion

Independent theologies and decentralized organizations have replaced the Church/State monopoly. With the loss of government support (money) the Church has revealed its true nature as the giant profit motivated, predatory scam that it is. The theological monopoly has been broken and now any faith is just as valid as any other. History will rate the separation of Church and State as one of the most critical pivots of the modern era. The secondary effect of this is that the national population doesn't know which faith to choose, and although religion can't be eliminated it can be easily replaced. Now all the addicts to God will have to make do with a pluralistic methadone.

Education

Every election season has its battle over education in some form or another. These conflicts only become more heated as relative values polarize amidst social disintegration and the concomitant increase of media attention on school violence. But this incessant emphasis on 'education' has little to do with training skills in socialization or adaptability and everything to do with myth indoctrination! This is why religious groups fight like hell for separate private or home schooling. Instead of learning critical reasoning skills useful for all applications, education has been turned into a process for molding and warping young when they're most impressionable in order to serve corporate demands, and not the needs of society and the intellectual development of the individual. Given the stunning uselessness of most school material within practical life, it seems difficult to explain the education scam otherwise, except perhaps as hollow tradition or keeping the kids off the streets for a few hours each day. Employers and authority powers all look for those stamped and notarized pieces of paper to effortlessly determine the gullibility and exploitability of a person, how quickly they'll latch on to authorized opinions and follow orders without questions, or at least that's how a cynic would posit degrees and diplomas are really being used.

Monarchy

Those inveterate despots and prostitutes for the Church, one of mankind's long lasting afflictions, the monarchy has finally been eliminated and relegated to a proper place in the dusty archives of history. Unfortunately the new master, the mass media, has simply replaced much of monarchic authority.

Nationalism

The nation no longer has any real meaning except as a vestigial tool to drag the public into fratricidal conflicts or generate enthusiastic rivalry for sporting events. The citizenry get the pain without the benefits of nationalism anymore because leaders fail to protect their citizens from external threats. Money, immigrants, religion, drugs and disease all cross political boundaries with impunity, ironically usually unmolested by nationalist politicians. The facile irony only masks the hypocrisy of the domestic leadership that parrots nationalist rhetoric yet acts in favor of international moneyed interests; *they talk local but act global*. The super-rich aren't restricted by nationalism, they and their money can move anywhere they want – and play one country against another for greater profits. Nationalism is just like religion, it's a trick used to exploit the poor and ignorant using faith, emotion and blind obedience.

Patriotism follows the same pattern of obsolescence because anymore it has been hijacked to mean obedience to the suicidal dictates of corrupt authority. As long as the domestic death-toll can be kept to a minimum war is good and noble because it generates employment and corporate profits.

> "Patriotism is the last refuge of a scoundrel."
> – Samuel Johnson, 1775

Traditional faith in the military establishment has become equally foolish. The creation of the professional military composed of volunteers drastically alters the equation, elevating imperialism and executive authority over the needs of the greater public. The worlds of the military and the civilian used to be intricately related. Now the two are rapidly spinning in opposite directions. Mistrust, ignorance, and incompetence have created a re-evaluation of the mission of the military and even its very necessity.

Nihilism

Mass Media

The character of the mass media is finally being viewed as the imperative threat to collective health that it really is. Democracy is a sham when the primary media filters and manipulates the vast majority of information voters need to accurately judge candidates and issues, while making a fortune broadcasting specious and vitriolic campaign advertisements. Not only do the same companies own the networks they're owned by the same people and the trend towards consolidation and mergers continues unabated.

Laws

Governments are drowning in a self-created morass of hyper-legislation. Criminality is not always a self-evident concept; laws create criminals. The beauty of legislative suffocation is that more laws mean more criminals and the more criminals on the streets the greater the need for more protective legislation. Lawmaking is the ultimate sinful addiction of corrupt regimes. Global economic and political aggregation is building a new tower of Babel.

This highlights a few elements of the decaying superstructure but to stop at that would be a fatal flaw — Marx's mistake. This decaying process has only begun and it's crucial it not end before being burnt to the ground and dead to the root. The nihilist plays an important role in this process but not as part of the dying system. The nihilist is *apart* from that system, the suicide orgy of everything attached to the crumbling edifice of dying gods. There's no reason to play games which can't be won or fight for lost causes.

Freydis

Nihilism: Through the Eyes and Into the Minds

The natural world and its inviolate rules consist largely of violence and dominance with a tenuous overlaid veneer of artificial order at certain moments; it's those news stories of conflict and suffering so distant and easy to disbelieve. If you keep glued to your TV and immersed in that fantasy world and if you go to church and get down on your knees in prayer every night just maybe that dark angel of reality will skip your house and take the next one ... or maybe you and your friends will be the one's in tomorrow's headlines. Too many are blinded by subjective morality, they fail to see the purpose Pol Pot and friends serve. It's that glimpse of the dark below, an animal realm foreign to our insulated world of fictional film and suburbia, that transient and mythical zone inhabited for a moment most believe is forever. Regardless of good or evil Pol Pot, whose despotic rule wiped-out one-fifth of the Cambodian population, brought that potential for brutality into the homes and media of not just a tormented South East Asia but an entire planet. He generates fear, we know how far and how fast the halo graced angel of man can fall from heaven and the wise who watch now have an impetus to keep from falling further.

So you see I'm trying to stretch that deadened range of sensation to include a fraction of the evil as well as the good, and if you don't like it you can't just change the channel or move to the suburbs. Escape is an illusion, peace is an illusion, deal with the war that we are all a part of and be prepared mentally and physically to defend and attack, otherwise you're just dead meat.

In any war you can't win without knowing the participants, who they are and what motivates them. Humanity consists of two simplified groups: the ones that think and the one's that only react. One group reasons with logic and the mind, the second from fear and intimidation. Don't hate the stupid, hate the ones that act stupid yet are capable of knowing better. The real target of immediacy isn't the crooked despots or the petty authoritarians, they're predictable and linear. The enemy is the middle class fence-sitters who grant support and mandate through jaded acquiescence and tacit

Nihilism

approval. The 9 to 5 taxpayer, cop's salary-paying drones suckling the teat of the myth machine, *the ones that just want to cooperate with this system and make a buck after taxes*, these are the ones that keep the Empires well oiled oppression machine grinding away day after day. Don't take the fight to the capitols or the cities where it's already at, take it to the suburbs. Attack the havens and safe-zones, the false insulation certain people enjoy at the expense of the rest of the planet while glibly sure everything is cute and fun because nothing bad happens here and TV says everything is perfect.

To attack directly, physically, may offer more of a thrill but it's dangerous and offers inferior benefit for the risk involved. Think like a social engineer, ideas are more powerful anyway. Take nihilism into the living room through the eyes and into the fearful minds of the public. Scare them with the facts, force the cognitive dissonance on the sheeple. Magnify conflict and inconsistencies, play the contradictory aspect of popular values against another. This will either make them Nihilists too or cause them to react with fear and hatred giving the Nihilists the upper hand of rationality and the authority of consistency. Remember, there's no need to be violent when the anti-Nihilists so easily assume that role which just establishes your opponent as a negative, impulsive force discredited by their own foolishness.

We tend to think of revolution to mean violent armed conflict such as in a civil war but a revolution can be entirely peaceful and non-violent, for a revolution is really just a radical, fundamental shift in individual and collective viewpoint.

A Brief History of Power

Within crude authority structures power is transmitted via violence, or at least the threat of violence. In less primitive authority systems power is primarily transmitted through mechanisms of money: bribes, kickbacks, and the various forms of financial corruption. Within more advanced authority structures power is mostly wielded through mechanisms of belief: faith, popular assumptions, and myths. This is why within the modern system of coercion through belief media control is so critical to authority because that's the means of manipulating the range of acceptable thoughts within the public mind.

So, just as power through violence and fear has become obsolete and strategically ineffective, coercion through belief is now becoming an obsolescent method of control. This development is largely due to advanced communications technology spreading practical ideas and information, along with the universal application of standardized and scientifically-based education. Eventually, with struggle, we will supplant the use of force and coercion with structures of social organization that are not based on whim or belief but built from impartial testing and verification, in other words, methods and ideas that actually function as intended in practice. When statement, intent and effect are matched then political and social hypocrisy are eliminated; the importance of this can't be exaggerated.

Despite the remarkable progression of human development we can still find examples of the various structures of power in different locations throughout our contemporary world. And when establishment authority loses legitimacy, through ineptitude and corruption or other reasons, they frequently resort to more crude forms of coercion in order to cement their hold on power. In this regard it's wise to remember that even within a political system based purely on power and force, the subjugated have every natural and inalienable right to resist and overthrow those in power over them. Of course whether they're able to or not is another matter, but the point is that an authority system based on power, whether stated as such or covered behind layers of hypocrisy and rhetoric, is one that's inherently unstable and where violence begets greater violence in cyclical fashion. At best this can be described as asymmetrical development.

Power, Sex, Revolution

Every monolithic establishment seems impossible to change when we're trapped within it, yet the revolution always seems inevitable in retrospect. Contrary to the view of the irrational pessimists human society *does* grow and develop, and even human nature evolves too. We're not doomed to repeat the past unless we fail to learn from it.

Vertical authority structures have been frequent features of the past 12,000 years of male-dominated human history. However, to believe that power and force are the only ways to structure a society is both profoundly foolish and historically myopic, even as such beliefs serve as convenient justification for contemporary abuses. The Paleolithic to the Neolithic era, around 6,000 to 60,000 years-ago and beyond, was the reverse – featuring successful civilizations structured around women.

The Cucuteni people, who inhabited southeastern Europe roughly 5,000 to 7,000 years ago, seem to have had a mindset of nihilistic renewal. Called Europe's first civilization, the Cucuteni would sacrifice whole cities every 60-80 years by intentionally burning thousands of their houses. They would then move and create another new settlement.[2]

In fact, the symbols and images of early human civilizations were almost exclusively of women, sometimes abstract and highly stylized. More recently these symbols were replaced by men while at the same time slavery and violence suddenly became commonplace.

In the 21st century, with the development of increasingly advanced reproductive technology like bio-engineered sperm, the human species has moved into a completely unprecedented and astonishing realm: a third sexual age that has effectively rendered the male sex biologically redundant.

Structured authority predicated upon force leaves much to be desired, most notably the stifling of human potential amid the upheaval of violence and brutality, both physical and psychological. Over millennia of accumulated experience, through wars and revolutions, and stepping-stone criticism by enlightened thinkers, the human species has devised means of structuring social authority, resources and power that strives towards more equitable formations that are therefore more stable and flexible, empowering greater numbers. This system in modern form revolves around concepts of equally distributed freedoms, rights of varying definition, and widespread expectations of fair treatment and open opportunity; *symmetrical development.* The concept of rules being equally applied to everyone, the ruler and ruled, and the realization that neither is inherently superior to the other, is a development as remarkable as it is revolutionary in human history.

The Russian Nihilists were a part of this process of human development, fighting to overthrow abusive and despotic authority and to build a society based on scientifically rational treatment for everyone. This kind of struggle doesn't come easy, it requires persistence and stamina, and especially a sober awareness of potential and pitfall, separating myth from facts. We don't have to exist under fear, torture and abuse. Freedom, peace, and cooperation are just as valid physical dimension within the virtually limitless realm of our universe, even superior because they confer unambiguous benefits to the vast majority involved within society; but we'll never arrive there using faith and hope, guided by belief and fictional saviors. *Together we have the potential to achieve anything with a vision and persistence.* The question is: will we try?

> "We must act, act perpetually in order to be human, in order to possess real awareness of ourselves." – Mikhail Bakunin

Many people blame nihilism for the evils of the world; some might even (erroneously) blame me as a proponent. Much of this antagonism is due to the nature of nihilism as an acidic affront to the everyday fantasy world most glibly inhabit. If all you want out of 'life' is a stupefying and delusional sense of false-security, then stay passive and ignorant, but you'll never see it coming to step out of the way when critical reality hits you like a ton of bricks.

Nihilism

Complacency may be cheap but its compound interest is deadly. Nevertheless even the most horrendous injustice is a lesson learned because it destroys the unhealthy delusion that ultimate responsibility for actions and consequences resides with ambiguous entities in mystical realms. The disabused realize, even if they choose not to accept, that ultimate responsibility resides within oneself. Life isn't fair because what's defined as 'fair' is self-centered and the universe simply does not revolve around any single person.

In a way that's all it is. That's all that's needed to revolutionize the planet because once a person finally realizes the totality of the lies that comprise everyday modern life they will become the greatest nihilist and radical imaginable.

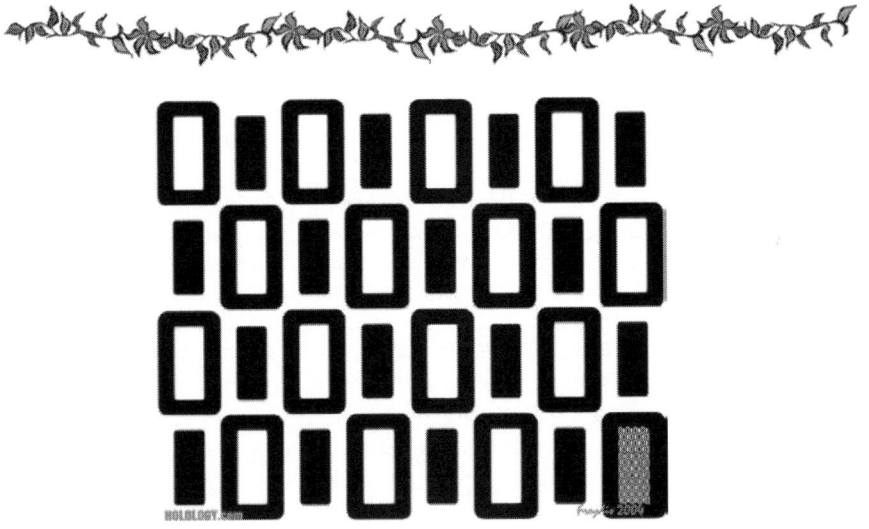

Something from Nothing (1/1=0+1), by Freydis, 2004

ANOMIE (DEATH TO THIS)

ANOMIE (n) social instability resulting from a breakdown of standards and values / alienation and uncertainty that comes from a lack of purpose or ideals.

Death to Government

Mass murder is not a natural state of affairs but rather one that must be organized and engineered by a central authority. From Stalin to Pol Pot only government powered by wayward ideology can compel its citizens to obey such destructive dictates.

It takes a government to create mass starvation; look at Zimbabwe today under the guidance of the racist Marxist Robert Mugabe. Why do North Koreans eat grass and sell human flesh for food? It's not because they don't know how to farm, it's because food production is controlled by the central authority.

But of course *our* government is safe and trustworthy so don't worry about it, right? Many forget that Hitler was democratically elected by a significant margin in a legitimate election. And who kicked all of the Japanese, legal citizens by the way, out of their homes and locked

Nihilism

them up in internment camps during World War II? That same U.S. government (and the Soviets too) tested atomic bombs on their very own soldiers, the same ones that fought to defend their country!

American soldiers soaking up the gamma rays on the beach at Enewetak atoll, 1956. Those nuclear blasts sure light up the nighttime darkness, eh?

The first atom bomb used in war was dropped on Hiroshima and targeted a Japanese military headquarters. However it's a little known fact that the American military knew they would vaporize not only 20,000 Japanese soldiers in their barracks but also American troops being held captive in a prison there! And what did the 'peacemaker' president Harry Truman have to say about that very event? "This is the greatest thing in history!" I rest my case.

"The US and the Soviet Union each spent the equivalent of 10 trillion dollars on the arms race." – Mikhail Gorbachev, July 2002

Even a cursory study of recent history provides a damning portrayal of the hazards of centralized authority, and the bigger and more distant it is from the people the worse it gets. *Never, ever, ever concede power to persons that can avoid the consequences resulting from their actions.*

Death to God

The stupidest, most mind stifling, self-destructive notions can always find an open opportunity to perpetuate in the skepticism-free safe haven of religion. Here are a few cursory examples:

⇨ Orthodox Jews won't touch a light switch on the Sabbath, many refuse to touch a phone to call an ambulance either and definitely not if the unfortunate victim happens to be a gentile.

⇨ Christianity still thinks evolution is a fiction, these are the same people that caged the great mind of Galileo under permanent house arrest for supporting the appalling heresy of *gasp* the Earth revolving around the sun and not the other way around! And if Galileo had been less famous he would have been tortured and executed like the Church wanted. The Christian Church used to put animals on trial for crimes against God and accepted cash payments for the forgiveness of sins – even for dead relatives!

⇨ Today, even though many Amish buildings are destroyed by lightning-induced fires they refuse to add lightning rods to their buildings because they believe such things are contrary to God's will.

⇨ And what of Islam that doesn't even want women to drive cars, and forces them to wear head-to-toe black robes in the broiling desert heat. Islam's hatred for women is only matched by Judaism's. In fact, misogyny is so much a general trait of all the dominant religions it may as well be a defining characteristic.

Nihilism

Confusing? Doesn't make sense? Of course – it's religion! The less logic it contains the more it can only be understood by faith, and faith means obedience to the interpreters of the manufactured confusion. This is the power of the priesthood class, they profit from ignorance and blind belief. As Bakunin stated, "Well, religion is a collective insanity, the more powerful because it is traditional folly, and because its origin is lost in the most remote antiquity."

Death to Ideology

Highlighted in a recent book review – the conveniently forgotten war crimes perpetrated by the Communist liberators of Germany. Those heroes of the Motherland somehow found the time between shaking hands with allied American soldiers and building 'Iron Curtains' to gang rape literally every woman they could get their hands on throughout eastern Europe. The author wryly states, "If anything, the events of 1945 reveal how thin the veneer of civilization can be when there is little fear of retribution. It also suggests a much darker side to male sexuality than we might care to admit."[1]

Yeah, no shit Sherlock, it doesn't take Andrea Dworkin to figure that one out. All animal species operate under the same sexual principle of reproduction by every means possible and (news flash) most of those bipeds so generously referred to as Homo sapiens have very little inner desire to actually act like human beings when they can act like animals instead. The sad truth is that most people will do about anything if they think they can get away with it.

> "The Red Army had managed to convince itself that because it had assumed the moral mission to liberate Europe from fascism it could behave entirely as it liked, both personally and politically."[1]

Death to communism, death to fascism, and death to everything in between. What did either side gain besides some 30 million dead?! Damn their wars.

Freydis

I've seen videos of World War II German news films; you should too if you get the chance. Germanic robots eagerly dying in pools of blood and mud just inches from that unreachable goal promised them by their benevolent leaders so their wives, sisters and daughters could be mass raped, tortured and murdered back home. Meanwhile those precious few with enough smarts to refuse to participate in the orgy get a slave manufactured, government stamped bullet implanted into their brain at mach two.

And just like clockwork, once again our benevolent leaders concoct another world war against evil, this time it's terrorism replete with all the typical propaganda – 'axis' of evil' and 'them against us' the Godly saints versus the filthy demons all perfectly packaged propaganda properly priced for all the citizens to gladly pay for in blood and taxes.

It's long overdue but Nihilism will steal their ammunition literally and figuratively once and for all. Communists will die for communism, fascists will die for fascism and the religious will die for religion, and with them all gone the nihilistic remainder will joyfully inherit the planet.

Death to Purpose

Here's a good way to start a conversation, just ask someone, "is there any rational purpose to cosmic existence?" Can they give a serious answer? And could this dearth of logical purpose explain rampant consumerism, drug abuse, entertainment escapism, and suicide?

So then, what *are* we here for? The intellectuals take a stab and walk away bloody. The misfiring synapses in Nietzsche's syphilis corroded brain spoke in mystical tones on the expression of power embodied in the Zarathustrian superman. Carl Sagan took a few hits off his joint and told us, it's all about fathoming the infinities of the cosmos, man. North American pioneer Freydis (the first) simply fought her way through the mess and took what she wanted. Freydis II implies that there is no reason, so don't waste the effort. Now true, taking advice from any of those persons should probably be accompanied by one of those lengthy legal warnings that come with computer software, but nevertheless the real problem is that everyone tries to find a reason regardless of the dangers. It's human nature. Although we may know why things are, none of it seems to serve any goal. Yet we're programmed to believe, or more accurately predisposed to believe, that everything has a goal and purpose. So we revert to mystical notions to avoid dealing with it. The result is religion, the manic faith in unassailable fiction as an intentional avoidance of the rational lack of logical purpose for existence beyond tautology.

Some are more predisposed than others to need convenient lies. Culture is really the vehicle with which all these irrational beliefs and practices are conveyed. Some people are so defined by their body of beliefs that they commit suicide when those cultural values and ideas are discredited. But what would *you* do if everything you'd been taught and all that you thought was true and your entire way of life was turned upside down overnight? Mass suicide is so common anymore it's practically a fashion statement. If cult leader Jim Jones had been alive during the 80s MTV would have been all over him like stink on a monkey.

'First-Nation' archaic cultures are the most obvious victims of anomie occurring from the head on collision between modern high-tech culture and stone-age subsistence living. But even within the modern western world the effects of science and technology are taking their toll – continually changing, revolutionizing, and discrediting tradition. School shooting anyone? Another kernel pops, the news crews package the carnage into a 60 second evening spot and everyone not dead takes an aspirin for the sense of mild unease and tries to get some sleep for the early work day tomorrow.

Rewind to the opposite extreme, now we see why intentionally irrational movements exerted such a significant influence during the tumultuous 20th century. From the pure emotional incitement of Dada art to the expression of raw animal power in Fascism, trying to not make sense actually takes a lot of effort and produces some strange results. Humanity slams into yet another cinder block wall. The people were just as exploitable as religious believers were because once again they had no objective references; they castrated their minds and robbed themselves of their only defense – skepticism and critical thought. So there you have it, within the modern milieu faith leads to suicide as the flawed notions are continually discredited, reason leads to nihilism, and irrationality leads to mass destruction. Decided yet?

The bottom line is that an awareness of continuity is necessary for sanity and contentment; if you study nothing else in life study history. In practice this means a comprehension of past coupled with a reasonable expectation of the self continuing into the future, in some form or another. This is the root psychology of human purpose. Basically all of human endeavor is wrapped up within the inveterate quest for immortality.

But even if everlasting life in a literal, physical sense is impossible it can nonetheless be achieved in a vicarious but very significant way. This practical immortality can take multiple forms from genetically similar offspring to more vague concepts like heroic altruism, fame, and glory. Indeed the most successful here have themselves interjected into the very fabric of culture, an estimable means of perpetuating legend to be sure. The secondary benefit to achieving these coveted statuses is that it enhances every other element of social success; celebrities never have any problems finding money or mates.

Death to Culture

Although culture is as palpable as it is immeasurable it's really just a collection of common beliefs, values, and ideas that slowly change with the winds of fashion and perception. Culture also functions as a means of conveying collective knowledge from one generation to the next; and indeed many animals have culture too, so it's not even unique to humans. As participants, willing or otherwise, culture serves as a dimension with which to perpetuate the concept of self.

Nihilism

Culture is proxy immortality for the participants, a selfish gift to the next generation.

The information being conveyed within culture doesn't even have to be useful, indeed most of culture is purely arbitrary and of no functional utility. Garbage and poison spread just as quickly as health and optimism. Much of cultural knowledge was useful in the past but isn't any longer, and may even be harmful to development, but it gets pushed forward by inertia and habit. And individual identities get wrapped up in culture when that's what one is born into and all one knows. However, if that culture is dying then the individual's identity bound to it is doomed as well. The outmoded or future-less culture is now effectively marooned along with the individuals encased inside it. Life becomes absurd and the values of death become more desirable than those of life (they get to the inevitable conclusion quicker). Collective suicide ensues, for without a cultural vehicle to perpetuate the self, life for the individual becomes meaningless as it lacks any future. Native tribes and similar archaic cultures are much more susceptible to this than modern cultures because they've been isolated and insulated from change for thousands of years.

Skyscraper, by Freydis

Freydis

A culture that isn't questioned or revaluated, destroyed and reinvented, is a hopeless loop of history repeating itself where subsequent generations must repeatedly toil against the same pain and wrestle the same fictional demons. Don't cling to culture or hide behind it − it's not a solid rock or an absolute value that must be, or even can be, perpetuated forever. To believe otherwise is to become a slave to your ancestors and the past, unable to adapt to the present, and doomed to a miserable future.

Death to the Ego

One of the recurring themes in nihilism is that individual worth is vastly inflated by the subjective self, or what's popularly referred to as the ego − that selfish urge inherent within human nature. For example, the belief in life after death didn't arise by accident. Just think of the alternate and how it limits actions. Eternal life is an illusion but a potent one. As the Romans discovered battling the barbarians of northern Europe, "All the Galatae, the Triballi, and many other barbarians believe in the soul's immortality, so they have no fear of death and go out to embrace danger."[2] A more contemporary example could include Jihad warriors and suicide bombers blasting body parts all over the street with unswerving faith in the fiction of a heavenly afterlife.

The misguided belief that the self is of utmost importance is an understandable survival tactic because it covers up existential doubts, but it can also lead to a skewed perception that nothing else matters, so when those feelings are at an emotional nadir suicide is the only way out. Much of self-destruction is commensurate with the degree of ambient social anomie, that being the realization of eroding values, disillusionment and failed beliefs − but only if one is so wrapped up in those illusions that you have no inner worth outside of them. Self-destruction is an egotistical expression. It's like saying 'I can't get the gratification my ego says I deserve so nothing matters anymore because it's only me that is of any importance'. Shortening perception down to the nearsighted limits of the Id and reflexive impulse is a bumpy ride indeed. It's like trying to steer a speeding car staring at the road directly beneath the front bumper.

Nihilism

Physics doesn't care, genetics is pitiless, and the whole universe doesn't give a damn because it's all operating on a time scale significantly longer than any single human life. For instance, if you were the only one on Earth, your value is 100 percent. Add another and it drops to 50 percent, four equals? And 6 billion equals? This is not negating individual value and input; it's just trying to put it in a more accurate context. Trade unions highlight this with the concept of worker solidarity and general strikes; meaning that although any single worker or individual can be easily replaced by another to work for the system, collectively the public has a significant power.

Ego value must be placed in proper perspective because inflated self-worth without the evidence to support it is not a pretty picture. It's time to tone the hyperbole down a bit and find something valid to substantiate your ego instead of just making it up.

Death to the Money Morality

Pol Pot was the only communist ever to have gone so far as to put his money where his mouth is, revolutionarily speaking, and ban currency entirely. It's also the only thing he ever regretted doing. Few Americans would ever dream of trying what Pol Pot did because they love money. But the love of money is also viewed as a negative thing so it's carried under the proxy banner of the 'free economy' of unfettered capitalist trade which sounds more acceptable because it implies that even people without any money can potentially acquire copious amounts of it too, someday, perhaps ... not.

However, anymore this disingenuousness is the source of significant criticism from both ends of the political spectrum. It may be called a 'free market' but that phrase could not be more misleading. If it's a free market why is everything regulated? And why do the rules keep changing? And why do the same people keep winning?

The true power of a government is money – the ability to print it, spend it and tax it. Rob authority of that power and you have an impotent regime, laws are useless and the military will quit if you don't pay them. *Pol Pot's lament!* Ultimately it's impossible to have any kind of equitable system and certainly not any element of social harmony within a true free market without vitiating the cultural values of the money morality.

Few know this but before World War II only a very few rich Americans had to pay any income taxes. It was not until Roosevelt's war and the trillions spent maintaining the ruse of the Cold War that average Americans had to pay anything to the federal government in income taxes! But as a side benefit to government, high taxes make subsidies that much more effective, meaning it enhances their ability to enact value goals. After all, a tax break doesn't work if you're not paying anything to begin with.

But first let's back up a bit, what is money or an economy anyway? Money is like water, it always flows downhill but what it does in between can be manipulated and the economy is like the topology, the surface land. Within a fluid and open economy the most powerful influence enacting desired values is the tax code. Taxes and money laws are like the dams and canals for waterways. It's a universal rule that a person will work harder if they think it benefits them personally, this is the 'secret' to capitalist success. An open economy plus regulated tax and financial codes create the incentive, and the entrepreneurs and industrialists go for the bait and construct the valued items and goals in the process.

Remember, money is a symbol, the cash you spend on beer, pizza, rent or anything else is called fiat currency because it's not backed by gold or anything of value except the reputation of the printing agency, in the case of America this is the Federal Reserve for bills and the Treasury for coins. Governments love this kind because the money supply can be inflated (printed up) at any time in any (reasonable) amount as deemed necessary for political or economic reasons. The consequence for this is a decline in value; for instance the British Pound has lost 100% of its value over 100 years, meaning what could be bought with a penny then, now takes an entire Pound note. America has a loophole called 'Dollar hegemony' but that's another story.

But the point is that money is a symbol, the tax policy is a tool, and both are value neutral in and of themselves. It would be self-destructive to eliminate them because it's not the money, it's not even the economy, it's the values, stupid (a bumper sticker slogan for nihilists)! The values and the people pushing those values are the problem; they use those tools to generate the product. Economics is riddled with value judgments, for example should we take the expensive option and recycle everything thereby increasing present living conditions? Or just throw it away decreasing living conditions but giving us more money to spend to perhaps fix the problem? Here's another fairly neutral example, the tax structure, coupled with values such as home ownership, privacy, and national defense created the interstate highway system, the suburbs, the private real estate market, and the axis of American money purchases: the house. Suburbia was crafted through favoritism in tax laws driven by a desire for neat, private, single family dwellings away from the city. A goal that simple probably generated the largest movement of people and construction endeavors in world history. Values drive the vision, and in an open economy the vision is built using money tools.

The industrialists and the entrepreneurs will always follow the money, they always follow the simplest and most consistent of rules: personal profit. Collective success comes not from vitiating these dupes but from manipulating them.

Death to the Love Delusion

Even the most enigmatic and bathetic of topics for poets and philosophers, love, is just simple chemicals in the brain. Sexual and maternal bonding is just oxytocin from the pituitary gland. Love is the triumph of group over individual, of gene over carrier; it's a temporary insanity of sorts that shuts down parts of the brain that might start asking inconvenient questions at the wrong time. At best, love is merely a synchronous delusion, or as H.L. Mencken put it, "love is the triumph of imagination over intelligence."

Love is primarily an irrational expression and this contention is supported by the stunningly typical expression of regret all relationships encounter when the chemicals wear off. Think of how many marriages end in divorce. Besides that, the modern divorce rate is more an expression of the freedom western society allows within relationships and the egregious allowances of love that have not been enjoyed on a comparable scale anywhere in recorded history. Instead of having a mate chosen by parents, clan, or lack of alternatives within cloistered societies, the decision rests solely upon the individual's personal discretion, or lack of it. So this decision is now determined by the fleeting whims of emotion with minimal social pressure for long-term success or even a fundamental compatibility between individuals! Thus cohabitation is increasingly popular because it's a superficial way of circumventing the issue of legal partnership entirely.

> And I feel like a beetle on its back
> And there's no way for me to get up
> Love'll get you like a case of anthrax,
> And that's something I don't want to catch
> - *Anthrax* by Gang of Four

The vast majority have no idea what they really want out of life or a relationship – it's all fantasies and imagination destined for a rude realization when it's too late anyway. The victims of this widespread stupidity, ignorance and social-incompetence are the children of such relationships. We'd all be better off if they'd just grasp the fact that *if you can't get it right don't do it at all*. Unfortunately for the rest of us, and social harmony in general, our present errant culture prides itself on perpetuating the triumph of love over reason as well as over mental and physical health.

Nihilism

Knowing this doesn't make the effect of love any less powerful but the awareness of being manipulated coupled with the powerlessness to rise above creates a maddening feeling, a negative stimulus in stark contrast to the positive of acquiescence. This demonstrates how much of human behavior has no thought involved at all but is just predictable reactions. Freedom? Liberty? One wonders!

"Marriage is the only adventure open to the cowardly." – Voltaire

The only inalienable rights are those derived from the genetic imperative, all else is fiction. And yet to defy that nature is not only counterproductive but essentially impossible. Nonetheless, genes can't plan ahead; they can only spread or go extinct based on circumstance. As sentient beings struggling to survive in an overpopulated world of diminishing resources we have the burden of making strategic decisions, and we must never ignore, through delusion or intent, our own fundamental biological elements.

Death to Philosophy

Albert Einstein once stated that, "The most incomprehensible thing about the universe is that it is comprehensible." Philosophy fixates on the apparent complexity of nature and classical thinkers ponder the grandeur and mystery of the universe. Yet one who constructs a conclusion using the building blocks of scientific knowledge eventually reaches a stunning, inescapable, and diametrically opposed conclusion. Existence is so absurdly simple it's utterly disheartening.

Yet simultaneously the source of life's excitement is the unknown, the chance and risk residing within all new encounters. Take it away, make everything predictable and knowable, the result is stasis, boredom, hatred for life and eventual suicide. Making things predictable has the unintended effect of eroding grandeur and destroying drama. Just think of the simple fact that the laws of the universe and biology are all even capable of being comprehended with a modicum of human effort. *The fact that things are both consistent and quite understandable is utterly devastating to philosophical thought.*

Popular perceptions are really just profound misunderstandings of simplicity. Welcome to reality – *mystery is dead, philosophy is dead, faith is dead, love is dead, and hedonism is boring.*

Death to Liberty

Like so many other ideals the populace desires, although they may wish for freedom from control they don't wish to live with the consequences. Wars are declared, invasions launched and authority enforced all in the name of freedom. Nearly every political or social movement and economic reform is based on precepts of freedom, liberty and so on. Free economics only enriches the already rich. Adam Smith's 18th century treatise <u>The Wealth of Nations</u> on unfettered market capitalism was the philosophical groundwork for Laissez Faire economics, or as he called it "a system of perfect liberty". Over 200 years later we've found that pure freedom does not and never has existed. What does exist, and always has, is a system of power and authority and each side continually attempting to maximize its own benefit, often at the expense of the other side. The ironic truth is that the most desirable system of government is one that *doesn't* function efficiently!

People don't really want freedom and liberty because that means other people will have freedom and liberty too. What most really want are safety and regulation with a double standard. People really want equal opportunity but no responsibility for their own failures within a system based on merit, but at the same time one that blocks new entrants in order to keep out the competition and hold what they've earned (or stolen). The only remotely effective system yet found of controlled power and the maintenance of freedom is one that pits one side against another in a standoff. For instance, the Mutual Assured Destruction (MAD) policy with the Cold War's nuclear weapons was 50 years of pseudo-peace.

In actuality, personal freedom and liberty is a lofty and hazy ideal that's continually being used by despots and democrats alike to sugarcoat their policy actions just long enough to get the public to swallow a poison pill. The French Revolution, one of the bloodiest and most fratricidal civil wars in history, was founded on the three ideals of liberty, equality, and fraternity. Despite the fervency of the participant's beliefs in those three values the outcome had little if anything connected to them, just the twisting torment of a hopelessly distorted society attempting to reconcile archaic values with modern realities. Not until a military dictator took power did any group begin to get the things they wanted, and it didn't take long for Napoleon to piss away France's military conquests after that! Hell of a long way to go just to get the metric system!

Real freedom and liberty is barely recognizable when compared to the nebulous ideal. Complete liberty is a myth and real freedom is a compromise because every human individual exists within, and because of, a complex network of social connections and inter-relationships. In practice nobody can just do anything they want because the freedom of one will invariably impinge upon the freedom of another.

Death to the Y-Chromosome

Many things are confusing because we're unable to see them in proper perspective due to bias or ignorance. Contrary to popular perception reality is not constructed in human dimensions. The real biological driving force is not the human body but the genes that build it, a concept first formulated by William Hamilton. Evolution works through the genes, not through the individual. "Our genes are not serving us at all. It is the other way round. We are serving them — faceless, thoughtless, and ruthless."[3] This is why sex is such a source of endless discord, contention and social trouble because the two opposing forms, XX and XY, are in direct competition with each other, with different needs and, very often, dissimilar goals.

Look around you and think for a moment. You'll eventually discover that essentially all our artificially induced problems can be traced back to man's reckless abuse of wealth, property, and power and woman's machinations to exploit male cravings for her own benefit. The Y-chromosome that creates men and sex has no conception of future or consequences; it only seeks to reproduce as rapidly and widely as possible without regard to anything else. In the process it has created a synthetic, toxic world that is killing and poisoning itself and everything else along with it. Clearly, this is an issue of profound proportion that takes us to the very roots of the established sociobiological order. Recognizing the true dimensions of a problem is the first step towards rectifying the situation.

Death to Morality

The time to take out the trash and clean up the human detritus is way past due, the stink of rot gets worse every day. The issue of waste product sterilization is no longer a *when* but a *how*. This is the contemporary world in the urban sewer of drug abuse, sexually transmitted diseases, violence and mental as well as environmental damage.

The primary source of our present pains of collective angst necessitating drastic actions is not in debate. It has had a death-grip on western civilization for centuries, culminating in the present lunge at world domination while yielding generation after generation of compounded mistakes. The death of all religious, mystical, theological, dogmatic and faith-based morality is the top task of true concern. These false morality systems are public enemy number 1, 2, 3 and 4000. Anything and everything 'good', 'evil' or ambivalent that works towards the total vitiation of them from the public conscience is more than preferable, it's necessary because it has put us in this chthonic wasteland we're collectively in today.

Nihilism

Religion and blind-faith contradict human nature and teaches everyone to hate their humanity, to hate and detest everything that they naturally are, to utterly despise the very reason for their existence and replace it entirely without question or criticism with a groveling belief in slavery to a mystical master. Instead of balance and order in life it only brings imbalance and disorder, a chronic sense of unease and an artificial chaos that can only be alleviated through deeper subservience to the all-mighty holy answer-man and his earthly representatives. Instead of normal human nature to love friends and hate enemies it teaches the fantasy of total (spiritual) love. Instead of criticism and independent thought it teaches obedience and repetitive oaths of faith.

In contrast to the do-what-God-and-his-holy-book-says morality, nihilistic morality is beautifully simple for it's to be what you are. A true freedom to be sure and yet no freedom is free. The catch is you must take responsibility for everything that you do. You can't deflect it to the Devil or to God but only to yourself. Nor has causality been repealed. If you look you'll notice that the universe has its own way of punishing intransigence because there's no 'free lunch' and every benefit has a cost, every reward comes with a price tag.

> "Indeed, against these [natural] laws revolt is not only forbidden - it is even impossible. We may misunderstand them or not know them at all, but we cannot disobey them; because they constitute the basis and fundamental conditions of our existence." – Mikhail Bakunin

Artificial law is primarily an exercise in futility because forcing someone to be something they aren't inevitably leads to repression, perversion, and anguish. Nihilism attacks judicial justice because it is based upon the whims of fashion and culture, meaning morality. It is not based upon fact or what actually happens; indeed most every historical example of morality is one of a square peg being forced through a round hole.

The destruction of all this sick system in its entirety is inevitable because it is wholly unsustainable, the only factor in question is how long will it take and how prolonged will the suffering be? Yet, even that inevitability will not stop the politicos, industrialists and media bosses, with their bevy of leeches and whores feeding off of it, from doing everything they can to keep it alive indefinitely.

No one really wants to swim in shit, but it's going to take a little more than chlorine to clean out this pool. *Try drain and refill*.

All for One, by Freydis, 2001 & 2008

THE NIHILISTIC VISION

The CounterOrder credo: To invert consensus, extract the reciprocal of orthodoxy, turn the world upside down, shake it and see what falls and what remains.

Many ask, what are the benefits of nihilism? In order to see the benefits you must first begin to visualize the nihilistic alternative. Although these images and ideas may seem anachronistic their power and significance should not be underestimated. *If you cannot imagine a new situation or event then you cannot achieve it.*

People build and perpetuate what they already know, not what they cannot visualize, this is why revolutions always seem impossible in the present yet inevitable in hindsight. Indeed, history has demonstrated over and over that outcome is defined by boundaries; redefine the boundaries and you will redefine the outcome.

The nihilistic vision is a positive result extracted from a negative event. This vision is very much an apocalypse but only for those that have had their chance and ruined it for everyone, the failing, ruling-class. Yet for everyone else interested in health and renewal it is a brilliant new dawn. This momentous change is of the near future, looming and portentous, angry and promising like a storm on the horizon. People fear the consequences but the shrewd revel in the bountiful opportunities bestowed by the aftermath, for the best time to rebuild is after the storm. For those who heed – prepare for the beginning, it's closer than you think.

The beginning is the end of sin. All transgressions both individual and collective are forgiven and national crimes annulled. There is no redemption ... but there is no guilt; there is flawed human conduct ... but no false justifications.

Freydis

Reformat the cities, those sprawling and putrid piles of poison. Dense population concentrations characteristic of the metropolis only serve to provide ideal incubators for virulent and ever more pernicious sicknesses. Deforestation and urban sprawl scatter and disturb natural wildlife allowing disease and vectors to thrive and spread when they would otherwise be kept in check by the natural balance of life. Once these cancers are razed localism will finally triumph over globalism; instead of blanket edicts from on high, rules and solutions will start and address where they're needed - locally. The power-pyramids will be crushed that fascists, elitists, and tyrants erect to insulate and perpetuate disproportionate authority while evading responsibility. In place of elitist force we'll have a naturally self-balancing and self-adjusting system characterized by mutual relations and a wide distribution of power. We will have respect and admiration for life and its infinite potential, rather than ruining it or paving over it!

Time will no longer accrue into infinity but rather will count down to the next beginning. The calendar will no longer start at 1 but end there. 100-1? 500-1? Details, details... At the top of time, all chains broken, all previous debts public and private will be annulled, all currency voided, all laws deleted.

All paper and electronic money will be zeroed out, and records will be purged to reset ownership and eliminate the tyranny of fictional wealth and the institutions that perpetuate it. Faceless bureaucrats can't manage your care in old age, or any age, without theft or mismanagement, because they have no inherent concern for your well being as only the self does. All buildup, all waste legislation, paperwork, and currency emptied and distributed for recycling and fuel for warming homes.

Nihilism

Reciprocally beneficial sexual intercourse is the worship of life and natural human behavior. Through the management of impulse and an awareness of instinctual purpose, rather than the futile attempt to ignore or misdirect, we will do away with associated perversion, repression, and mental illness. By breaking the binders that unnecessarily restrict our society we will create a realm of freedom to say what we feel and expound what we think, for a life to be used but not abused while seeking sensations and smarts amid the unclouded clarity of cogent comprehension. Your greatest gift is your mind and body; don't waste it – utilize it.

Everyone can have a new name. Finally, every individual will have the opportunity to describe themselves not as someone else decides but as *they* decide. What will matter is not what *role* you play in the dramatic farce of contemporary society but *who* you really are and what you can *contribute*. This will finally divide the parasites and the producers. Only those that participate to rebuild will receive any reward or status. The parasites receive nothing but ostracism and death.

Safe havens for solitude and sanity will exist in a physical and non-literal sense, allowing for introspection imagination and reasoning unfettered or oppressed by the intrusive presence of malevolent authority. *This freedom of the mind is as important to human life as air and water.*

Destruction to the false protectors of harmony and society: all police and military dissolved with their weapons distributed to the participatory social contributors because the only person that can really defend you is yourself. Through a network of individual militias collective and individual defense assumes its proper role. Thus we each gain freedom, self-sufficiency, purpose, and safety thereby creating healthier minds and bodies.

Freydis

A plan is secondary to the ideas because the artificial structures around us, the outcome, is a product of the collective vision and once concepts are implemented details sort themselves out afterwards. New and superior product will grow on the ash heap of the old.

The events of the 21st century will not be written by the powers of the 20th. These forces, though appearing unstoppable today, are nevertheless doomed by their very own endogenous flaws; their day in the sun is about to be done. Many will try to revive and reuse but they will all fail, merely replaying the same destructive inevitable. *The weaknesses of authorities are the strengths of freedom.*

World history is punctuated by deluded masters of conflict, Alexander the Great, Genghis Khan, Napoleon, and even Hitler. What are they known for? Conquering everything and unifying nothing. *The nihilistic vision will conquer nothing and unify everything.* Today you have the luxury of making the decision your descendants can't, choose carefully which side of the bulldozer to be on.

Towards the biologically-based civilization; from revolution into evolution, the new human species arrives.

"We are all atheists about most of the gods that humanity has ever believed in. Some of us just go one god further."
– Richard Dawkins

HOW TO BE A NIHILIST

'Call Back Later, God's on Vacation'

Oh, what a challenge rectifying the enormous evil in the world! Genocide, mass murder, serial killers, random shootings, rape, torture, mutilation in our next door neighbors house and on the other side of the planet in the dark of the jungle. Christ has answers, but most of them just lead to more questions and an ensuing maze of circular reasoning. They say hope and justice exists in God, lack of it is lack of God. Satan never one to be upstaged has answers too; evil's just part of the process man. But science doesn't have an answer. It leaves everyone wanting, 'please explain what we see and what we hear everyday'? Where is justice? Why can't we rectify our artificial notions of order with the worldwide reality we encounter every day?

We so need the lie drug.

The collective desperation for myth is palpable... send us a savior to correct our behavior!

Anyone who can live without the lie drug is a true nihilist. A nihilist can interface reality with all its beauty and unpleasant consequences with their personal sense of the tangible because the two are the same.

It is the nature of a broken man to seek answers. Likewise as anomie ensues, civilization disintegrates, and society fragments the spreading discontent and angst seeks a resolution. From the prophet to the savior neither stays in business long during times of wellness. Much like vultures they prosper during periods of decay. And unto them Jesus said: "They that be whole need not a physician, but they that are sick..." Matthew 9:12; always subversion before conversion.

Subversion may be inevitable but what you convert to is not. Anyone alive exposed to the post-modern pop pseudo-culture is diseased; we're all victims of this pernicious corrosion. Your reality is based on monstrous lies and disingenuous parables. Laws are capricious and their enforcement more so. Such pseudo-justice is merely a convenient performance intended to dupe the public into believing that law and order protect them. Realize more than anything else, power and its corollary of abuse make this diseased world go 'round. The nihilist knows this; they have progressed beyond this myth, beyond right and wrong. Justice is just power, present moral-legal framework is a myth and if you expect fairness you'll be burned.

You may already realize this but others don't yet. Soon they will though because valid ideas don't need advertising. The world seeks wisdom not the other way around. The desperate need for publicity is merely a sign of weakness, of hollow answers and non sequitur content posing as enlightenment. Legitimate ideas and solutions generate self-confidence and that confidence needs no saturating advertising campaign to persevere and permeate. Only trash and poison, products of unnatural consumption need to be hawked endlessly and pounded like nails into the brains of the delirious masses.

What is a Nihilist?

Often simply defining a nihilist is a challenge in itself because of the overall complexity of the topic and the disparity of conceptions. Sergius Stepniak a 19th century Russian Nihilist expressed the common view of Nihilists as "deniers of everything, striving after destruction for destruction's sake." But what does this mean in practice? Is it self-destruction and violence like some kind of stoned, self-immolating entertainer on a stage? (Hedonist) Or is it a calculating power-seeker who breaks rules to get what they want? (Machiavellian) Or could it even be an introspective, sober philosopher that has progressed beyond the need for petty attachments and has enough sense not to tamper with things that shouldn't be messed with? (Buddhist) All three stereotypes can be argued to fit as definitions of a nihilist.

But in addition one could also ask, could a nihilist simply be one that can't or doesn't care what anyone else thinks and thus acts in an anti-social manner? Is a nihilist just an egoist continually striving to magnify the self? Perhaps not believing anything then means the nihilist is just an opportunist – one thing today and something else tomorrow? Maybe it's just so completely subjective that a nihilist is just self-description and thus becomes whatever the individual is?

Common elements of the nihilist description:

- Lack of principles
- Lack of belief
- Lack of attachment (i.e. to the pre-existing social order)
- Self-description ("I'm a nihilist")
- Above heroes (perhaps because as a type-former they become one)
- Regards everything from the critical point of view

In practice this leads to conduct described as:

- Subversive
- Unorthodox
- Destructive
- Creative

Given that no one can deprive anyone else the ability to describe themselves as they see fit (whether the description is accurate or not is another matter), and also that everyone has different capacities and abilities, this labeling process yields different results for different people. Individual capacities vary widely within the human species, far more so than any other, and this makes social and biological categorizations difficult. We've got individuals that can design the most complex integrated circuits and mathematically comprehend the origins of the universe living next to imbeciles and hopelessly dysfunctional animals. I would label this effect an evolutionary divergence, but now I digress.

In other words, through the application of simplistic labels we can see one nihilist creating great works of art and another nihilist dying of a drug overdose in a dank alley. Actually, we are all driven by forces we cannot control and are presented with different opportunities in life. This doesn't violate the label nihilist; it just indicates an intrinsic randomness in life. Nihilism can be seen as the individual being what they naturally are, about taking the inner force and through practice and ambition destroying/creating the self and surroundings, either literally or figuratively.

Each of us is the unique accumulation of our thoughts and experiences, relationships, mistakes, and achievements. Don't try to be what you really aren't, be what you really are; you don't have to submit to the tyranny of imposed culture.

Nobody can be reborn, but you can make the most of what you are right now.

Since the human mind has a special ability to recall historical events and persons, we've expanded our function beyond simply survival and reproduction into a new category: that of being remembered. The ultimate Nihilist is one who recreates the world as a reflection of themselves, but from a very different perspective than tradition dictates because they operate with strength and confidence in their own capabilities, without adherence to current superstitions and traditions, or ambient beliefs and values.

The Nihilist is unorthodox, a tradition-violator, driven by the inner-force, and not attached or tied down by contemporary superstitions or beliefs.

Stepniak wasn't really bothered with disparate views and definitions because his conception of a Nihilist was limited to the range of his contemporary actors. Nonetheless, his conclusive definition remains as succinct today as any. Stepniak's true Nihilists of the 19th century emerged as:

Nihilism

The individual, tired of oppression, rose in all his pride and power, breaking the chains of ancient tradition, and recognizing no other guidance but his individual mind. Such were the true nihilists, the destroyers, who did not trouble themselves about what was to be built after them. They did not exactly deny everything, for they believed firmly, fanatically, in science and in the power of the individual mind. But they thought nothing else worth the slightest respect, and they attacked and sneered at family, religion, art, and social institutions, with all the more vehemence the higher they were held in the opinion of their countrymen.

Ultimately a Nihilist is only as capable and efficacious as they strive to be, while of course limited by circumstance and capacity, for just as Stepniak stated, a Nihilist recognizes no other guidance but his or her individual mind. In this dangerous and often hostile world intelligence and ingenuity are your only true allies.

Most people live in fear of their own death, yet we all know it will happen eventually. So, why not take control of the situation instead of simply becoming a victim of circumstance? Turn it around and say, "I want to die someday!" Revaluating the obvious grants us a new and portentous command because it presents the critical questions here as 'when' and 'how'?

Nihilism as Identity

An awareness of nihilism as a word to match an idea is more than superficial convenience, it forms the basis of *self*-identity. Furthermore, an awareness of this historically established concept grants meaning through the formation of a *collective* identity. Nihilism may never be a popular movement, it's caustic nature is feared and reviled, but it's a stage in personal evolution that unequivocally typifies a free-thinker, the exact archetype that is needed to direct and mold the remainder by being open to all ideas, even the unpopular and unorthodox, and by being intelligent and willing to experiment with new solutions; a new era needs new answers.

Nihilism is the antidote to the present moral-authority edifice. Nihilists deconstruct false values, highlight social absurdities, criticize fractional logic and challenge faith. They can speak like the Greek sophists and act like the Russian Nihilists to put the word 'nihilism' on the tip of every tongue. Nihilists negate lies and false reasoning and therefore the people behind them. And those people are the opposition, the anti-nihilists, the teleologists; they're obvious by their attachment to faith and false idols despite reason and evidence to the contrary. They form values and build models of reality based upon opinion and myth. But when confronted with anti-nihilist acrimony don't respond in kind, understand the psychological mechanics involved because they can't damage the underpinning logic so they attack the messenger. Indeed any emotional response to a rational argument is a sign of this. Their eventual introspection leads to difficult questions and the concomitant anger at being confronted with a new and uncomfortable situation. This forces the anti-nihilists to inflate their false-justifications or else drop all pretexts entirely. Practice, keep your mind sharp and your arguments cogent; challenge enough times and Nihilism wins – that's how the game is played.

> And whoever wants to be a creator in good and evil must first be an annihilator and break values. Thus the highest evil belongs to the greatest goodness: but this is – being creative. – Friedrich Nietzsche

All you have to do is critically examine the rules and resist control, especially mind control; don't let the 'experts' tell you what to do. Discredit through reason, rhetoric and evidence. What makes this wrong and that right? Why is this issue taboo and why is it wrong to ask that question? Question the fear and challenge the righteousness. Force them to substantiate opinion with fact and if they can't, analyze the implications.

Nihilism

The remainder of turned-off and burned-out people that hate everyone and the world are important even if they don't know it because the best place to begin a holistic evaluation is after losing faith in everything. And I'm saying there's a reason for this, why you hate everything and everyone. Certain people are directly responsible for your disenfranchisement, for giving you a world that doesn't give a *damn* about you, and are the source of your hate. Nihilism isn't about killing yourself because you've been burned. If that's all you want, go pretend to be a Satanist or smash windows and call yourself an anarchist. Instead it should be about defeating disingenuous leaders, pastors and politicians who've turned the world into hell from their lies. Incoherent hate only leads to violence and futile self-destruction. Coherent anger leads to positive change and vanquished enemies. Without coherence you only destroy yourself.

Becoming the Nihilist

To be a confident and effective Nihilist one needs to especially gain an awareness of 1) world events, and 2) personal culture and history. One must gain a sense of what is myth and what has validity, what is vapor and what is tangible because the only ones that can last in chaos are the ones that can see past it, able to comprehend time beyond the present and before your own. Most critically one must *know* the myths in order to understand them and rise above them. Once you understand these things you will realize where you come from and where you need to go, life will start to make sense and have purpose. You don't need to be rich, you don't even need the most friends and you certainly don't need popularity to be whole. Being a Nihilist is not about futility, self-destruction and giving up, although those feelings are inevitable they are absolutely not

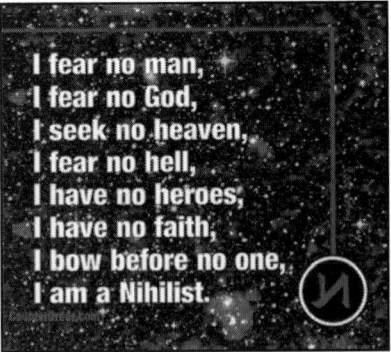

I fear no man,
I fear no God,
I seek no heaven,
I fear no hell,
I have no heroes,
I have no faith,
I bow before no one,
I am a Nihilist.

the final product, merely a critical stage. Remember that as long as you're alive you're changing the world if by no other means than your sheer existence. That's the baseline, but everyone can do better, change things in the proper direction rather than random futility. Turn off the TV and radio and instead read and search the Internet or go to the library. You can visit my *News: The Daily Irritant* web page at Holology where I try to deliver a few tidbits of edifying info every day. Look at what's evil and figure out why it's considered evil, look at good and figure out why it's good. Challenge popular beliefs and see what has factual support and evidence supporting it, and what's merely opinion. Compare and contrast different cultures and the values they employ. Find the similarities and study the differences; explore the various ways groups use to reach similar goals.

Next, write about what you've read, what you feel and what you think, because you'll remember it and you'll understand it better. This is what really builds intelligence in the sense of what the state education system supposedly wants but never achieves. Move on to new material and new ideas. You can get a start with my own essays covering nearly every issue under the sun at Holology.

Nihilism

It's usually better to listen first and speak later, if at all. Listen to what average people say about themselves and the world, they're rarely hesitant. Their ideas are defined by their environment, what they hear and see is what they believe. Thus what they espouse is a reflection of what the present order wants you to be also. Analyze it and mentally disentangle it. When you get a viewpoint absorb it then attempt to find the opposite viewpoint and absorb that too, often the truth lies between the poles. New and extreme 'avant-garde' ideas are great because they stretch the limits of the complacency and possibility and even if they're irrational and inaccurate they still get me thinking, wondering why they're in error and analyzing what validity they do have.

Activating the Nihilism

When people seek meaning they usually seek it through the promise of salvation delivered from an external source. Yet this path inevitably leaves them hurt and disillusioned because existence is built upon survival, and survival requires self-interest and an internal motivation. Warning: the self-interest of the savior may well contradict your own!

Some would argue that life is more than just survival, perhaps so but if this is the case only *you* can create a sustainable, valid reason for living beyond the inviolate basics. Even just sticking around to burn it all is a far more sustainable reason that will put more in your clenched fist than the hazy fog that most people grasp at for self-justification. Further, identity, a sense of self-worth, and a general reason for living all are enhanced when you're with others of the same interest because self-interest is not always mutually exclusive between individuals but often overlaps quite nicely. The challenge is to know who to work with and who to work against, who has the same self-interest as you and who has opposing ones.

> Remember: even on your own you can make a difference with Nihilism in action, because the revolution starts with you!

Freydis

Shatter complacency!
Defeat isolation!
Contradict habit!
Defy tradition!
Reorder routine!
Upset convention!
Rebel against convenience!
Create a superior alternative

Ever Deeper - Cynicism & Misanthropy

Famous filmmaker Francis Ford Coppola once said, "Cynicism is a very comforting thing to hide inside at a time of uncertainty." Nihilists are often viewed as complete cynics but cynicism is only useful when not simply a shield from critical analysis. A common error of nihilists is to simply eject most everything at once and remain at the bottom, but this is ultimately just as erroneous as believing in the original fantasies, it's just switching one blindness for another. Substantiate your negations and continually analyze without pretext because you may just find a certainty; so it's imperative to understand the reason, otherwise its purely unguided irrational emotion.

Misanthropy, the universal hatred for humanity, is a similar pitfall. Unfocused and baseless hate benefits no one and remains a serious disservice to nihilism often blocking earnest acceptance. Reasonable analysis and sound judgment, rather than the laziness of universal cynicism and uncritical rejection, will change the proponent from repellent to magnetic. The instant-gratification culture promotes impatient and impulsive behavior, but only through the enduring experience of patience will the gift of wisdom be granted. Patience is the opposite of the behavior

inculcated into the public, and wisdom is what our pop-cultural authorities fear most within the people.

You don't need to do anything illegal, immoral or unethical to be a nihilist, especially not for its own sake since that's pretty senseless. We only get one life, one shot because there's no heaven or afterlife. Accordingly it's wiser to accede to activism than acquiesce to passivism. Seek focus, answer the unknown using the known and avoid extraneous entanglements in all your efforts. Oppose the ambient culture of impulse and foolishness that defines what's popular and demands conformity just to herd the sheep. It's banking on maintaining your ignorance, gullibility and mental mediocrity to prevent scaring the faithful or making waves with destabilizing notions.

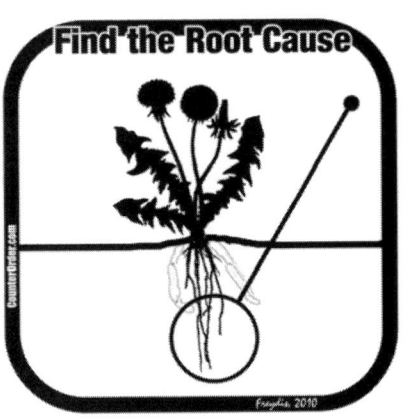

Regardless of who you are or what background you come from as soon as you are confronted by any belief or idea-set that opposes debate, refuses questioning and criticism - that indicates a faith, a religion and it should set off every warning alarm and red flashing klaxon in your head. Because religion isn't just repetitive rituals and praying to some spirit in the sky, religions are fundamentally defined as any idea-set that disallows a public challenge to its validity, and that definition extends to include even secular ideologies. To varying degrees of dogmatic fervor other religions enjoy privileged status and are presently shielded from criticism. And despite a contemporary era that prides itself on a postured attitude of jaded pragmatism, rejecting taboos and unenlightened views, a multitude of idols and sacred values that necessitate a closed mind and emotional attack-response still remain. Consider duopoly democracy, 'free-trade' and the 'free-market' economy, the six million Jewish holocaust (never mind the Armenian holocaust, or the millions of Chinese and Ukrainians starved to death by despots), the false choice between liberty or safety, human-caused global warming through carbon dioxide, state justice, national security as a justification for oppression and war, and if you think about it I'm sure you can come up with even more barriers of belief. The enemies of free minds and free-thought don't stop at the Church's door.

Any authority that mandates a belief and punishes public challenge of that belief is an enemy, and as a nihilist and a free-thinking human being any authority demanding allegiance to a faith or mandated ideology is enough to get me not just a trifle indignant. Of course that doesn't mean that discussion and communication can't, or shouldn't, be compartmentalized and organized appropriately, just as within the private and personal arena everyone should be free to say, listen to, and see what they want and exclude what they don't.

Nihilism, Hedonism, and 'Using the System'

People confuse this issue a lot so I'll restate it: what appears to be in one's own best interest is very often not. But before attacking the messenger blame your genetic makeup and millions of years of evolution! And this is the flaw in hedonism as well as some existential nihilists. Think of the fact that 60% of adult Americans are obese. These people wouldn't even consider themselves hedonists but they act in much the same way, impulsive, no self-discipline, most every action is for immediate gratification. But where does it take them? Do you get richer by spending on credit or careful savings and investment? Do you get stronger by slurping down fast food and over-salted high fat snack treats or moderated intake and exercise? Which would you rather be: weak, sick, poor and reactionary or healthy, rich and resolute? A common hedonist, or a nihilist? I'm not saying don't use the system and its resources to your advantage, but I am saying don't be disingenuous about it and there's a huge difference in practice. Be consistent and organized, because those profiteer types aren't nihilists, they're not anything except hypocrites, hopelessly chasing the winds of fashion. Lenin said it best, "The only thing that penetrates the opportunist's mind is what he sees around him."

The arena of metaphysics and especially politics is a pitiless battlefield, one of unparalleled tenacity and aggression. Nihilism is not for the faint of heart, but for those that understand it and know how to use it they possess an unsurpassed advantage. Nihilism is unique in that it has progressed beyond the hurdles of not just theology but ideology as well. Instead of faith and dogma defining action and range of imagination, chaining mind and body to the bottom in the process, nihilists are in a new frontier. No other group outside of research science actually promotes skepticism to such a profound extent that it's strong enough to question its own positions! And you're damn right people fear it, Christians and Communists hate it and Anarchists distrust it so you know it's on to something big; hostile reactions are typical because Nihilism is like a hydrogen bomb hovering over the heads of all the faith-driven believers.

So I hope it's crystal clear what this is about. It's not to be a contrarian or a rebel although I won't deny that has its moments; it's because faith and mandated ideologies are an imminent danger to freedom and free-minds everywhere. The inherently disingenuous fear opposing evidence and open public debate, those who know they're wrong and will do everything in their power to stop the questioning 'heretic' and prevent the nullification of their myths. The only reason to fear free expression of facts is to protect an edifice of lies anyway.

But this I say unto you, nihilism will be a fire under their feet, the more they attempt to stomp it out the more scorched will be their soles. They will dance the dance of death as they are consumed alive by the flames of the blaze they began.

"Life unquestioned is life lived in a religious state." – Godfrey Reggio

THE HOLY FOOL

"There's a sucker born every minute."

Few things are more embarrassing to witness than a flagrant display of belief in the ridiculous, especially when it occurs in people that are clearly smart enough to know better – if they would just try. Religious people are not all fools, although the vast majority excel at foolish thought and behavior, they just suffer from a weakness that predisposes them to slavishly adopt the facile beliefs surrounding them, especially when it comes with the imprimatur of authority. People that always want to do what is 'right' don't ask questions and will follow the rules regardless of the logic, or lack of it, underlying those rules.

Think of the most idiotic, asinine, foolish rituals and practices imaginable and some religion or cult somewhere has turned it into a sacred tenet of their belief system. The list of examples is nearly endless but a few are listed below. And remember that these religions and cults maintain that they alone are the one true faith and all the others are just heretics.

Beliefs and Rituals

> In many places in Africa it is quite polite when visiting friends or relatives to express one's sympathy with them for having such "ugly" or "unpleasant" children. The idea is that witches, always on the lookout for nice children to "eat" will be fooled by this naive stratagem. It is also common in such places to give children names that suggest disgrace or misfortune, for the same reason.[1]

Lightning burns down many Amish buildings but they refuse to use a simple metal lightning rod because it would contradict God's will. Many Amish won't even use buttons on their clothing.

Nihilism

Japanese doomsday cult Aum Shinrikyo ('supreme truth') was founded by Shoko Asahara who fancies himself the reincarnation of Jesus, among other things. Blind in one eye and nearly so in the other as a result of congenital syphilis, Shoko Asahara naturally gravitated towards a career in acupuncture. Aum Shinrikyo's beliefs consisted of hastening the arrival of an imminent apocalypse. Recruitment consisted of kidnapping, drugging and brainwashing. After their botched nerve gas attack on a Tokyo subway most of the key members were arrested and the remaining cast of flotsam changed their name to Aleph, generally repackaging the cult. Despite the façade change that was pre-planned anyway Aleph remains wildly unpopular amongst the Japanese public - go figure. Aum Shinrikyo had some highly educated scientists working on their arsenal of weapons of mass-destruction demonstrating that in a country where education consists of rote memorization rather than independent learning even educated people can fall prey to their own gullibility.

The Aztecs, considered "deeply religious people" by historians, performed human sacrifices in the most brutal and painful ways possible because they believed that if they stopped appeasing the god of death the world would end. This 'powerful' religion (and empire) proved to be no match for a few dirty Spaniards on horseback.

Buddhism doesn't technically have a god-deity but in practice the once human Buddha, often in the form of obese and gaudy statues, comes remarkably close. Buddhism fulfills the standard religious mold because it's based on escaping life, Earth and reality in general rather than in simply addressing it head-on as the Nihilist does. Buddhism like all beliefs forsakes the issue of the here and now for a fraudulent and impossible goal i.e. higher spiritual planes, nirvana, etc. Careless diet finished off Buddha Siddhartha who was sickened by tainted pork. The great Buddha died as he lived: carelessly ignoring the immediate significance of reality for escape in fantasy.

Tantric Buddhism of Bhutan:

> And the kernels of corn? They are the calculus of devotion. Each time the gray-haired woman named Tum Tum prostrates herself, she slides one of the 108 kernels (a sacred number) across the floor. In three months she has moved the kernels 95,000 times—1,000 prostrations a day—and will continue until she reaches 100,000. "Sometimes I get so tired I fall over," says Tum Tum, whose knees have left grooves in the floorboards. "But I won't stop. This is our tradition."[4]

Cargo cults sprang up as a result of the culture shock invasion and infection created by the American military bases built throughout the previously isolated south Pacific during World War II. The astounded natives didn't know what to make of these new people and their mysterious machines but they began to believe that all of it really belonged to them and not the thieving white man – they just had to lure it back. The cargo cult worshippers began to mimic the devices they had seen, making wooden copies of rifles, radios out of pots and rope, and idolizing dollar bills and photographs.  All they had to do was parade around acting like American soldiers and soon the giant metal ship would land and bring heaven along with it! Needless to say the believers are still waiting.

Cargo cults are an intriguing example of seemingly foolish rituals because they demonstrate the fundamental nature of belief: the human mind unsystematically grasping at explanations for unusual events using a forced context consisting of the limited range of everyday experiences. As the cargo cults show, the anthropocentric and teleological views of reality are fundamental flaws characterizing all belief systems.

The Catholic Church excommunicated many animals even as recently as the 20th century including eels, dogs, horses, and rats, to name a few. Ecclesiastical (religious) courts even put animals on trial. France in 1522 put all rats on trial for damaging barley crops but the case was eventually adjourned without verdict because the rats never showed up in the courtroom! And when court orders failed to alter the behavior of the offending animals or insects it was blamed on Satan. These numerous and lengthy legal trials against animals were funded through tithes paid to the Church by the public, i.e. taxes.[6]

Mexican priest Marcial Maciel, a serial pedophile, built a religious empire called the *Legion of Christ* with assets in excess of $20 billion. Yet, although his predatory sexual activities were known to Catholic authorities, it wasn't until 2010 that the Vatican officially stated that, after decades of refusing to punish Maciel, his behavior "constituted real crimes ... devoid of scruples and authentic religious sentiment." Maciel, called a "disgrace to humankind" by one of his victims, operated with impunity inside the patriarchal Church, using his unchecked authority to force obedience and silence upon his victims.[13]

The Church of Christ, Scientist (CCS), otherwise known as Christian Science, was founded by Mary Baker Glover Patterson Eddy who wrote the book <u>Science and Health with Key to the Scriptures</u>. CCS preaches that evil and sickness are jut illusions but with faith they can be overcome, spiritual powers are stronger than physical, and even denies the existence of all matter including the human body. Christian Scientists are notorious for refusing to receive medical treatment for themselves and their children with predictable consequences for everyone except the believers.

A Jewish sect known as the Essenes took observation of the Sabbath to a new level by refusing to use the toilet at all on that day. They considered using the bathroom an unclean act in the sight of God and as a consequence their latrines had to be located out of sight of the village, and not a minor distance either, scrolls from about 2,000 years ago indicate a distance of over a kilometer. This distance didn't even offer any health benefits because of the particular waste disposal methods the Essenes used, spreading disease and parasites.[2]

In Haiti, land of voodoo, a major worry is that witches will steal the body of a recently deceased relative. In order to prevent this from happening they will bury thread and a needle without an eye in with the body because this will keep the witches occupied for centuries as they attempt, in vain, to thread the needle and then forget about stealing the dead body.[1]

Hindus believe that certain animals are so sacred they can only be worshipped and never harmed. Consequently, cows wandering through a town will cause traffic jams and leave steaming piles of waste everywhere even as the humans live in disease and on the verge of starvation. Because Hanuman the monkey God is highly revered, aggressive monkeys are a common plague on rural Indian villages. Using their attentive monkey senses they are quick to detect weakness in the humans and often take over entire villages, carefully targeting the soft throat and genital regions of any puny human foolish enough to threaten their new domain. All efforts to convert the monkeys to the peaceful ways of the Buddhist and Hindu have met with failure; hopes remain high.

Lacking an abundance of ATM cash machines, and displaying a concern for women typical of nearly all religions, Hindu men that need a quick buck can, and do, burn their wives alive to collect the dowry.

Islam requires its followers to pray five times a day facing the direction of Mecca, preferably with the knees and forehead on the ground and the ass in the air. Islam strictly forbids pork and alcohol as well as any depiction of the human form, so for instance cross-walk signs in Middle Eastern countries will feature black silhouettes with the heads rubbed out! Despite the fact that Islam is one of the simplest religions around followers find no lack of details to interpret in different ways and then kill each other over the disagreement, as evinced by the bloody religious civil war in Iraq brought to you courtesy of the faith-based leadership of one George W. Bush.

In July 2008 Saudi Arabia's religious police that enforce Wahabist Islam announced a ban on the sale of cats and dogs, resurrecting an old rule in order to prevent men from using the animals as a means of meeting women, i.e. walking a dog in the park.[7]

Christianity isn't the only religion that has a problem with the human body in its natural form, conservative Islam even forbids unclothed bathing.

Genital mutilation is either highly suggested or outright mandatory for Islam, Judaism, Christianity, and many primitive tribal cultures as well. Various forms of self-inflicted mutilation can also be found in many religions and cults. Mutilation ceremonies are often conducted as a means of indicating the believer's faith, suffering and devotion for God.

Followers of the Jain sect often wear scarves or surgical masks to prevent breathing in an insect and snuffing out the life of a reincarnated soul.

Jehovah's Witnesses, notorious for endlessly pushing their 'Watchtower' tract onto anyone who can fog a mirror, refuse to serve in the military, salute a flag, or celebrate any holiday or birthday – apparently because their religion forbids them from forming an allegiance to an earthly power. JWs also believe that only 144,000 people will go to heaven and that they will remain behind to take over the Earth after everyone else is killed when the world ends ... soon, really, it will happen any day now!

Jews and Muslims believe that their animals must be slaughtered in particular ways otherwise the meat is 'unclean'. Unfortunately for the animals, scientific evidence, and modern sensibilities these religious slaughtering methods are torture killings.

> They bleed to death in what government advisers say is "very significant pain". ... Religious slaughter is exempt from the provisions of the Welfare of Animals (Slaughter or Killing) Regulations 1995, which insist that creatures such as cows, goats and chicken be stunned first. Under the Jewish shechita system, kosher cows, lambs and poultry have their throats slit and then bleed to death. Halal animals also bleed to death, but some of them are stunned after the incision is made, depending on the interpretation of the Koran.[5]

Even the non-religious end up supporting these practices when they buy meat because the extra cuts are sold in the regular market without any markings indicating how the animal was killed. And the scale of this activity is enormous. In Britain alone over 100 million animals a year are killed by kosher (Jewish law) and halal (Islamic law) methods.

Lunatic cult leader Jim Jones, infamous for forcing his flock to drink poisoned punch in the jungles of South America killing over 900 in mass suicide, came from the mainstream Christian denomination Disciples of Christ. But what pushed *him* over the edge?

For decades missionaries have been flying into Sub-Saharan Africa and spreading the Christian faith like a wildfire. The natives come from far and wide eager to get a free meal as much as they are to hear the gospel message delivered by enthusiastic and convincing white people, so strange they may as well have beamed down from a different galaxy. While the missionaries claim millions of saved souls by promising an unverifiable posthumous salvation, the unstated price is the present turned into a living hell. After the missionaries fly away on a silver bird the new foreign beliefs mix with ancient tribal superstitions, then add endemic over-population to the cocktail of mental poison and consider this little black nightmare coming at you straight out of Uganda. Praise the Lord and pass the machete it's the Lord's Resistance Army led by former Catholic altar boy turned professional psychotic Joseph Kony. The official mission of the LRA is to turn Uganda into a theocracy based on the Biblical Ten Commandments. The LRA spreads fear and gains recruits by capturing and mutilating children and forcing them to kill their parents – and that's on a good day. Christian missionaries, Joseph Kony and the LRA are powerful testament to the words of Voltaire who once stated, "Those who can make you believe absurdities can make you commit atrocities."

Ancestor worship is a resilient tradition in Chinese culture, never fully extinguished by secular Maoist Communism. The tradition called minghun (afterlife marriage) involves burying a dead woman along with a dead unmarried man, after a posthumous marriage ceremony, in order to ensure his happiness in the afterlife. Although illegal it is not uncommon for profit-seekers to kill women and sell them as 'ghost brides'! Minghun is just one particularly egregious belief-practice characterizing a culture that places a higher value on women dead than alive.[3]

The Holy Book of Mormon originated from metal plates buried in a forest in New York that were discovered by Joseph Smith, Jr. after supposedly being guided to the secret location by God, Jesus and an angel named Moroni. Smith hid behind a sheet and translated the mysterious symbols to his followers using special glasses found with the plates. The origin of the Mormon religion reads like a joke without a punch-line yet over 10,000,000 members of the Church of Jesus Christ of Latter-day Saints (LDS) really believe what's written in their holy book. The Mormons didn't get to be so numerous on the basis of an appealing set of beliefs; they got there the good ol' fashioned way: *brainwashed from birth*. They're ordered to marry and have children if they want to attain the 'highest levels of divinity'. Brigham Young had between 28 and 49 wives (but who's counting, right?), and although polygamy is no longer *officially* sanctioned by the Church of LDS, it is nonetheless still practiced. Polygamist Mormons have turned their religious beliefs into a financial scam because the second (third and fourth, etc.) wives are viewed by the state as unmarried single women with children (where present) and no assets, so they qualify for taxpayer-funded welfare benefits.

Orthodox Jews take adherence to rules and rituals to an extreme, refusing to use mechanical and electrical devices or do any kind of work, including cooking, driving, or cutting hair on the Sabbath. Public transportation is shut-down on the Sabbath, and rabbis control all Jewish marriage and divorce in Israel.[8] Influential Rabbi Yosef Shalom Elyashiv proclaimed that Jews can't wear Crocs shoes on Yom Kippur because they're too comfortable. Halacha (Jewish law) forbids the use of any electrical devices on the Sabbath, so Orthodox Jews have specially built (Shabbat) elevators that operate without the need to touch any buttons or switches. But even that's not safe enough because some Jews argue that simply the weight of the rider still increases the electricity used and therefore violates Halacha![11]

Adding insult to injury, upon marriage Orthodox Jewish women have their heads shaved and the hair turned into a wig for them to wear![10] Yes, the G-d of Orthodox Judaism is a *very* active deity obsessed with minutia, and not surprisingly just about everything that happens is caused by God. Otherwise, like all forms of Judaism, it's based on a severe form of exclusivity where all gentiles are the lowest form of life and all Jews are the highest; multiple, and often imaginative, forms of duplicitous behavior stem from this warped belief.

Judaism, known worldwide for its wealth of 'wisdom' and 'wholesome traditions', has its own version of the Taliban who exert enormous influence within Israel. Jewish fundamentalists enforce G-d's rules vigilante style by assaulting women who dress or act inappropriately, like wearing red clothing because the bright color attracts attention. They also demand and receive gender-segregated public busses (women sit in the back – *waaaay* in the back), vandalize clothing stores they don't like, and torch music and electronics stores for ruining souls. "Three years ago, a son of Israel's Sephardi chief rabbi, Shlomo Amar, was accused of kidnapping a 17-year-old boy, beating him at knifepoint and terrorizing him with snarling dogs because he had sought the attentions of the accused's unchaperoned sister."[9] And that's just in their free-time when Zionists aren't shooting Palestinians in the guts and building settlements with oversized Israeli flags on stolen land.

> Religious vigilantes operate in a society that has granted their community influence well beyond its numbers — partly out of a commitment to revive the great centers of Jewish scholarship destroyed in the Holocaust, but also because the Orthodox are perennial king-makers in Israeli coalition politics.[9]

Traditional Jewish religious laws exert enormous influence upon society in Israel, even trumping secular laws. Jews in Israel can only get married under Halacha rules, and these rules have no minimum age limit for marriage. Throughout the world the slaughter of animals through torture killing, and every other aspect of diet, are regulated by kosher rules that are so arcane and bizarre that not even the Rabbis can agree on them, but they make a small fortune putting their kosher stamp on as many food, and even non-food, products as possible. Kosher marks can even be found on *laundry detergent*, revealing that it's all just a scam anyway – and you get to pay for it through the added price!

In Roman Catholicism, Catholics are forbidden to eat meat on Friday as decreed in the law of abstinence. In a marriage between a Catholic and a non-Catholic, the Catholic is required to convert the non-believer; and of course the kids will be raised Catholic. It's now well known that many priests have been found guilty of child abuse and pedophilia. Despite what Church officials have stated, shocking incidents of pedophilia were not rare or isolated but were in fact *systemic*, and occurred over a period of decades in Catholic schools, reformatories, orphanages, and other institutions around the world. Even more appalling, Church authorities knew what was going on but chose to cover-up the acts and shield the perpetrators, rather than stop the sexual-abuse of children under their control. And it's not just sexual abuse either, the Catholic Church, and associated enterprises, has always been a bastion of physical violence and psychological abuse targeted at the young and vulnerable. The Church's perversity is pervasive, persistent and it extends all the way to the top. The Pope's brother, Georg Ratzinger, was in charge of a boys choir that a former student described as being run on "a sophisticated system of sadistic punishments in connection with sexual lust".[12] The Catholic Church has unequivocally demonstrated the terrible hazard of unaccountable authority while totally undermining the supposed moral righteousness of their religion.

Saint Nicholas was a bishop in Turkey, martyred in the year 305. St. Nicholas is better known today as Santa Claus and once did double duty as the patron saint of pawnbrokers and beer drinkers. Sadly you may need to find another deity to pray to as you binge drink since Nicholas was un-sainted by the Catholic Church in 1969.

The Seventh-day Adventist church is based upon the hallucinatory visions experienced by Ellen Gould White after sustaining a serious head injury. The SDA church is fanatical about vegetarianism, the imminence of Jesus' second coming AKA the end of the world, and the fact that the seventh day of rest is on *Saturday* not *Sunday!* The infamous Branch Davidian cult leader David Koresh split off from the SDA church.

Nihilism

The Church of Scientology originated in 1952 with science fiction writer L. Ron Hubbard and his <u>Dianetics</u> book. Scientology believes in past and present lives as well as the strong financial and mental control of its flock.

People that follow animistic religion in Siberia are careful to watch what they say and how they express it because malicious spirits eavesdrop on conversations and will attempt to sabotage human efforts. Yet by simply using metaphorical language when discussing important topics they are protected against the machination of evil spirits because the spirits, despite superhuman powers, cannot understand language expressed in metaphors.[1]

Apologies to any religion, cult or belief system not maligned or listed. *Gullibility is divine, thus sayeth the Lord.*

Can I get an 'Amen'?!

Mental Illness or Mental Religion?

When some people fervently believe in ghosts or when they follow commanding 'voices in their head' they're treated as delusional, crazy or even psychopathic. These people are given medical treatment and brain-chemical balancing drugs in order to manage their mental illness. Yet when people profess the most intense beliefs in certain other things no one has ever really seen, such as demons, Allah, God, angels, heaven, hell, and so on, these people are treated with the greatest of reverence and social respect and even made into leaders and wise gurus who become rich from the donations of their faithful followers!

What's the difference here? The fantasies and delusions are equally foolish whether it's the belief and obedience to a psychotic voice in the head or an imaginary deity residing in some magical place no one can see. Religious beliefs should be placed in the same class as mental sickness or any other serious psychological disorder that degrades the quality of life and the individual's ability to deal with reality.

One of the fundamental (but understandable) flaws with modern psychology is its assumption that sanity is defined using the mental character of the majority as a benchmark. But this standard isn't really objective, it's subjective and merely based on a relational comparison that's used incorrectly to define an aberrant standard for mental health. *Just because many people believe in something that doesn't make it valid, and just because a lie is repeated a billion times that doesn't make it any more truthful than it was to begin with.*

Why Do People Go to Church?

For many people church attendance is just about gaining a level of acceptance and trying to find solace with others. Church is about the comfort that comes from fitting into a crowd where the shared belief is just a common delusion. Another unstated benefit of church attendance is the intellectual equalization effect, which is especially appealing for lukewarm minds. It can be quite comforting to be with a friendly crowd that all hold the same childish beliefs because it puts all the members on the same (low) intellectual plane.

Many people say that religion doesn't really hurt anyone because at least it gives people something to believe in and a reason to work together but those benefits can be gained from any idea-set as long as it's consistent. All people are really gaining from religion is the comfort that comes from a life of staid habit and the illusory elimination of ambiguity from knowledge. By pretending to hold an absolute truth life becomes much easier because sides and boundaries are clearly defined and everything becomes black and white. This is just like saying life is easier as a slave because you don't have to think for yourself and someone else makes all the tough decisions for you. It may be true but it is hardly a desirable status!

Why Do People Believe?

Beliefs are difficult to explain using standard terminology precisely because they seem to defy common sense. Human beliefs are so often detrimental to the individual, forced to maintain them with considerable effort against all evidence to the contrary, that the model of the *meme* was introduced to try and explain the phenomenon. Memes are used to explain how beliefs can take hold of a mind and spread even though they are so often surprisingly useless to the believer. Memes are the equivalent of genes except instead of being part of physical reproduction they function to reproduce ideas. However, just like a virus memes need an external host with which to replicate, hence the human mind works quite well as a vehicle to convey and magnify ideas and beliefs without regard to the benefit of the host but merely for the benefit of the meme and its increased propagation.

Despite the convincing appeal of the meme model, other explanations can suffice to explain the spread and tenacity of beliefs such as simple human social dynamics – the need for acceptance, the protection that comes from cooperation, and the stability that comes from consistency and habit made even more stable through artificial, reality-immune constructions.

Individuals that lack a sufficient sense of personal efficacy in life, be it of thought or action, will default towards authoritarian modes of living where everything is divided between the powerful that dominate and the weak that submit. But in reality personal power is all in the mind and outside of obvious physical limitations everyone is only as constrained as they think they are. And this is another reason why the stranglehold of religion on the mind is such an insidious threat, it intentionally constrains the efficacy of the individual and it engenders the belief in a fundamentally false authoritarian view of reality based upon the exploitation of one group over another, just as God dominates his creations and the priests deliver orders for their flock to obey, and so on down the line. Further, in this warped world of faith, salvation can only arrive from an external, and by definition, more powerful source. The only real 'salvation' that can ever be achieved has to be self-motivated, but this is why people that have a weak sense of personal efficacy also lack any sense of personal responsibility – *I have no power to control my life therefore nothing I do is my fault.* Welcome to the hell that religion and belief creates.

> "No matter what the Church authorities tell you to do – do it. If it's right, it's right. If it's wrong, they'll be accountable, not you."
> – Chauncey G. Webb (Mormon) 1903

How this strong versus weak power distribution forms is never fully explained except through tautology and the excuse of divine intervention. But in practice the 'strong' get to the top because they create their own free will, they seize opportunities and lead an active and engaged existence. While the 'weak' achieve their status because they accept the authoritarian order and agree to live a passive and unengaged life disconnected from responsibility and any sense of real efficacy.

Always remember: belief is a choice

The lesson of Nihilism, contrary to religious belief, is to *not* run from life, 'evil', and the world in general but instead to meet it head-on with aggression and aplomb.

Belief and Purpose: The Challenge of Absurdity

I've stated before that a reduction to the level of survival is a convenient basis for a common cause, but what exactly does a person really need for survival? Food, shelter, and clothing are tangible, standard issue necessities sufficient for a non-sentient being. But humans have complex minds attached to their physical

Nihilism

bodies and they've evolved as social creatures that exist within, and because of, collective interdependence.

Consequently, a sense of community is another element necessary to human survival. Because humans have a conscious awareness of reality they also have another need, which is a sense of identity, or to put it another way, a social context with which to place themselves in relation to other persons and objects in time and space. Finally, every person needs a sense of self-worth and a purpose within that context of community and identity otherwise they are faced with a very potent absurdity that must be mentally rectified one way or another to maintain sanity.

When community and the necessary sense of social bonding to others breaks down individuals become isolated and alienated from their social and physical environment. Individuals cut-off without any social context lose their sense of purpose in life because the individual either cannot deliver any value to society or what they can do or produce is not needed by society, consequently they lose a sense of purpose in life. If this situation carries on long enough then existence becomes an absurdity for without any purpose or point to anything the individual lacks any reason to continue the struggle of life. Thus the thinking goes that 'if I'm worthless, then so is everything around me, and life is pointless'. At this stage the individual becomes like a computer on a classic episode of *Star Trek* that self-destructs when faced with a reflective non sequitur as the ego returns conflicting and erratic output from the irrational input.

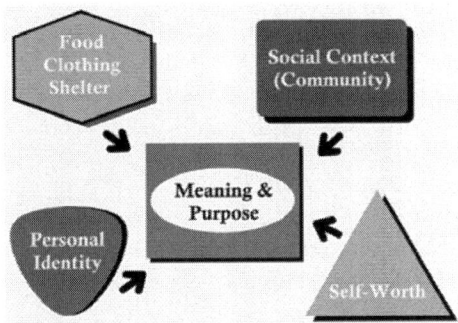

This is the unstable and anti-social state of mind that the school shooters find themselves trapped within. Full of anger from an ego cheated of its sustenance these kids ask themselves: 'if no one wants me and I have no purpose, then why am I here?' The resulting spree of violence and self-destruction from this chain of thought is sometimes referred to as an expression of nihilism. But nihilism is a *result* not a *cause* of anomie! A society that makes vast segments of its own feel worthless and redundant is a society on the road to ruin anyway.

It may well be that school shooters are acting rationally but basing their actions upon irrational input; however this alone is not enough to produce the outburst of deadly violence. Psychotropic drugs have been used by nearly all of the school shooters. Anti-depressant medication, such as Prozac and Luvox, can lower inhibitions and in extreme cases the individual begins to live in a dream where the counter-balancing force of intellect is no longer sufficient to prevent the emotional response from taking over. When this is combined with a conditioning to violence through an immersion and obsession with shooting and killing, such as through movies and games, this individual may eventually act out in a deadly school shooting.

The religious and superstitious take another track to the absurdity of existence, they argue: "... since I *am* here, then I *must* have a purpose!" However, this is merely employing an absurdity they like to counteract an absurdity they don't like. Superstition and religious beliefs are just a means of psychological self-preservation in a situation that is full of apparent absurdities; they protect the ego by mitigating the influence of the simplified logic of self-destruction. Like a duckling that will follow the first thing it sees after hatching from its egg people also imprint by adopting whatever belief system they discover upon self-awareness, usually the beliefs of their parents, and so the cycle continues.

But what is religion and spiritual belief really about, what is it trying to find? Religion is really just the attempt to find some sort of cosmic meaning that comports with subjective values and generates a divine purpose behind everything, but since such a thing doesn't exist it must be concocted! These convoluted efforts to circumvent absurdity indicate the importance of purpose and self-worth to the

Nihilism

health and survival of the human psyche. Widespread feelings of inadequacy compound the problem as they are propagated throughout cultures influenced by the incestuous echo chamber of corporate driven mass-media, promoting unrealistically high expectations and standards in wealth, beauty, and social esteem (fame). Today many people work longer hours not because they actually have to but because they think they have to; they need the extra cash to compete for the status symbols of living based on mass-consumption. Instead of one car, now they need three. Instead of one television sufficing now they need three – one for the bedroom, one for the living room, one for the den. Instead of a 1200 square foot ranch house being enough for a family of five, now a family of three needs at least a 2800 square foot home. The issue is: given that competition is instinctive, what do we compete for when we already have everything we need?! So, this is not really an issue of competition, which is woven into human nature, but rather the character of the competition itself and the metric people are using to rate their self-worth.

In an environment of foolish competition it becomes imperative that we reassess the values that are driving us to collective self-destruction one individual at a time. Today we live in a cultural environment that is largely antithetic to human mental and psychological health and one that even promotes anti-social behavior through TV, music, films, and a broad assortment of media, while many physical structures fracture community and direct human interaction. A surfeit of primary desires such as food, clothing, personal time, and entertainment, far beyond the survival level is such a recent phenomenon in history that human nature has not yet evolved an adequate response to deal with it. Consequently, self-destructive behaviors emerge such as eating to sickness and obesity or promiscuous sex until death by virulent disease.

> "Our brains misfire when presented with a situation to which we have not evolved a response."
> – Evolutionary biologist Robert Trivers, 2005

Although teenage school shooters are probably the most visible product of the absurdity of existence without meaning they are by no means the only expression. Indeed modern existence has become a veritable carnival of self-destruction. The hedonistic lifestyles of many gay men are another example, for once one assumes a completely homosexual lifestyle their purpose as a biological being is entirely negated for they cannot reproduce and their sense of chronological context is lost. Without a biological purpose or context homosexual men have a redundant existence, and for many in this state all they have left is to seek short-term pleasure even at the cost of a painful death by horrible diseases in the longer-term.

The existential dilemma is largely a problem of social redundancy. An individual that has no sense of purpose becomes introspective and depressed. Thus as social and economic redundancy has increased in modern society so has depression, suicide, and similar deleterious mental and physical conditions.

There's no such thing as meaning without context, for such a situation is an absurdity. Meaning is a subjective creation that emerges from the confluence of four primary elements: food-shelter-clothing, self-worth, identity, and the social context of community. Individual purpose is meaning directed into action; the solution is action in a social context because purpose, just like life itself, is a tautology – *you create it by doing it*.

Nihilism

Defeating Religion, Superstition and the Culture of Stupidity

The gap between the world of the believers and the faithless is so deep and profound that it really marks a rift in the species, a biological differentiation between the thinkers and the drones. Everything in our modern world from space travel to electronics to modern medical care is a result of the rational thinkers, the people who have ceased to believe in and use God as their guidance at least long enough to function productively according to rational thought. The sky won't come crashing down upon us all when we challenge the authenticity of religion and beliefs. The public once believed that when a train topped 50 miles an hour it would crash into a wall of air and that human powered flight was impossible because God didn't give people wings. Faith never built a train or an airplane – careful objective research, engineering and construction did!

The essence of belief is *escape*; it is about inventing a comfortable lie to avoid an uncomfortable reality, a reality that many believers are completely incapable of processing. A surprising number of humans are simply unable to exist in a universe that doesn't revolve around an anthropocentric, self-centered perception of events that provides them with answers to every question in monochrome simplicity. Believers are incapable of interfacing with reality because reality requires independent thought and responsibility.

Our biological evolution operates on a scale far in excess of our own lives. In the meantime we have to operate with the material already present, such as it is. We can't directly change the religious faithful because their beliefs are carefully constructed to be immune to

common sense while the believers are programmed to be resistant to all reason and logical counter-arguments. But we can do it indirectly by changing the environment, by altering the cultural landscape. The majority of religious followers are not really beyond hope; they merely follow the course of least resistance along the cultural topography, like a river down a valley. The path to collective health and sanity requires a revision of the constraints of culture, ambient values and the standards of acceptability. We have to begin to make the cultural environment less friendly and tolerant of superstition, foolish belief and other forms of willful stupidity.

Mock the Christians and every ridiculous notion they hold so dear but can never prove or substantiate in any way; make them *embarrassed and ashamed* to continue believing in their childish fantasies. The religious should feel embarrassed not because they can never be anything but hopeless losers but because they don't really *have* to be hopeless losers! Since believing is a choice, religion is a case of optional maladaption to the environment. *Where is the excuse?!*

Mock all the religious be they Mormon or Baptist, Sunni or Shiite, Orthodox or Hassidic, or anything else. Our world is too small and dangerous to allow collectively suicidal beliefs to perpetuate and inflict suffering upon everyone regardless of whether they've earned it or not. No more excuses for gullibility; no more special exceptions for foolish behavior, and especially not for the fools that promote it. Instead, promote intelligence, criticism, healthy skepticism, and a challenging intellectual environment that doesn't roll over and die just to make people feel good about their self-inflicted disabilities.

Nihilism

Coping with Believers and Religious Zealots

For those that have progressed beyond faith and belief for moral and intellectual guidance in life it can be a frequent challenge dealing with coworkers, neighbors, and strangers who are outgoing moral conservatives, religious fundamentalists, self-righteous Christians, and the like. So, what can you say or do to convince them otherwise – or at least get them to tone-down the threats that you're going to hell as a nihilist, atheist, or anarchist?

There's probably no single thing you or anyone else can say that will instantly alter habitual mindsets. But over time people really *do* change their views on important matters, yet it only occurs after deep consideration and frequently only after years of internal debate and personal turmoil. Besides words and debate the best demonstration is to lead by example; show that you don't need religious guidance and authority to have a productive life with healthy social interactions.

In order to effectively address the situation you need to get an idea of the religious mindset that you're up against. The previous writing here, such as *Why Do People Go to Church*? explains much of the psychology and social factors involved. For many believers God and faith offer *certainty*; with faith they finally 'know' something that can't be rescinded or made obsolete through progress and development – 'the God I follow is in charge and as long as I follow orders I have nothing to worry about'. This (imaginary) certainty gives the believer an anchor in the stormy sea of life. The believer looks out into a big world and sees that technology is constantly rebuilding everything around us; secular culture is continually growing and changing, and that science (being a process of hypothesis and verification) is constantly being revised. But for the believer, 'God and my Holy Book are always the same!'

Some despair that after working on enlightening a believer they realize, after another week of church and Bible study, the believer is right back at the beginning! The social network that the religious have is the major force holding them in tight orbit around their stellar black hole of faith. Unless you can convince them to stop going, the best thing to do is start (or join with) another social network to counteract the onslaught of superstition. This can be done a variety of ways, a word-of-mouth meeting at a friend's house, an online forum, or a scheduled event.

Overcoming Fear

Much of the resistance to dumping belief is simply a fear of the unknown and the ever-present threat of damnation and hell for disbelief. But which hell are you afraid of? If you're a Christian then you're going to Muslim Hell, and vice versa. You can't believe in every God, so what makes you sure the one you chose isn't the wrong one? There's a multitude of ways the absurdity can be thrown back in the face of the believer. Humor and satire are very effective ways of revealing foolishness masked by routine and tradition.

Ultimately it's not enough to highlight foolishness, we have to offer something that's appealing and reassuring without the need for faith and religion. Planet Earth is filled with unique experiences, interesting places, different people and ideas. The universe is filled with mind-bending oddities and peculiar forces that are waiting to be discovered and explained. There's no real reason to fear it or to concoct myths in order to hide it from an open mind. Existence is much brighter and rewarding without specious rules and imaginary barriers.

In an insecure society many people strive to be what they are not.
– Freydis

HISTORICAL NIHILISM

The Russian Revolutionaries

Although nihilism is often thought of as a vague concept relegated to the arena of philosophy, or perhaps as the unavoidable conclusion to post-modernist thought, nihilism does have a strong historical background that deserves greater recognition. The most significant manifestation of nihilism in recent history also coincides with its most active and organized expression, that of the Russian nihilist revolutionaries who rose to prominence in the 1860s.

The Russian nihilists (the Russian word for nihilist is nigilist) tend to be associated with violence, revolution, and terrorist acts such as the assassination of Czar Alexander II by the 'Will of the People' group. But although violent acts get recorded in the history books often the lasting impact is carried through non-violent ideas and identities. The Russian Nihilists were intriguing in this regard for their history is like that of an iceberg – only a small portion of their total character is readily visible. Indeed, much of the violent acts associated with the attempted overthrow of the monarchy occurred under the auspices of other groups such as anarchists, Marxists and narodnichestvo populists in the 1870s, rather than those directly associated with the Nihilists themselves who were much more complex than the over-simplified 'terrorist' label attached to them by autocratic authorities.

> Nihilism was not so much a corpus of formal beliefs and programs (like populism, liberalism, Marxism) as it was a cluster of attitudes and social values and a set of behavioral affects—manners, dress, friendship patterns. In short, it was an ethos.[2]

Freydis

Historical Context

In order to understand who the Russian Nihilists were we first have to understand what they fought against and why. Europe in the 19th century was a time of dramatic changes — political, economic, and social. Industrialization created fantastic wealth disparities and entirely new classes of people as the old aristocratic power system transformed into a plutocratic one. Cities grew rapidly and traditional agrarian lifestyles were decimated in favor of the cramped urban life of wage slavery. Imperial Russia experienced many of these difficult changes but events often took on a more extreme character than that of Western Europe and social development for Russia has always been both painful and slow.

All of the wiser Russian monarchs realized that their system of serfdom, with a social structure of the very few existing on the backs of the very many, was not sustainable and would end in bloody rebellion sooner or later. The problem was implementing reforms that were both effective and politically realistic. By the middle of the 19th century the forces of state repression coupled with the longevity of the problem had already created such an intolerable situation that fixing the system through reform was essentially impossible. The only reasonable answer to this kind of situation is nihilism; the only way to live is to destroy. Russia had become a stifling, backwards country run by a ruling elite grown fabulously wealthy through rampant natural resource extraction. The Russian government had become completely disconnected from its subjects and new information and new ideas were impossible to prevent from seeping into the country from the heated and bubbling social scene in Western Europe. Even a brutal and violent police-state could not stop the Nihilists, other dedicated revolutionaries, or the inevitable outcome of the conflict.

The heart of Russian Nihilism was about breaking with the failures of the past and about crafting a new identity. This was the meaning of the 'Fathers and Sons' phrase used at the time and remembered today in Turgenev's novel of the same name.

Nihilism

Whereas the "fathers" grew up on German idealistic philosophy and romanticism in general, with its emphasis on the metaphysical, religious, aesthetic, and historical approaches to reality, the "sons," led by such young radicals as Nicholas Chernyshevsky, Nicholas Dobroliubov, and Dmitrii Pisarev, hoisted the banner of utilitarianism, positivism, materialism, and especially "realism." "Nihilism" — and also in large part "realism," particularly "critical realism" — meant above all else a fundamental rebellion against accepted values and standards: against abstract thought and family control, against lyric poetry and school discipline, against religion and rhetoric. The earnest young men and women of the 1860's wanted to cut through every polite veneer, to get rid of all conventional sham, to get to the bottom of things. What they usually considered real and worthwhile included the natural and physical sciences — for that was the age when science came to be greatly admired in the Western world — simple and sincere human relations, and a society based on knowledge and reason rather than ignorance, prejudice, exploitation, and oppression.[1]

This was about the destruction of idols, about burning the dead wood of society. And the Russian Nihilists were quite revolutionary, especially given the context of the time and location they existed in, for they include sections of the population that had little if any representation before. Women for example played a key role and included some of the most motivated and charismatic characters of the time period, like Vera Figner and Sophia Perovskaia. The Russian word for a female nihilist is *nigilistka*.

> "If the feminists wanted to change pieces of the world, the nihilists wanted to change the world itself, though not necessarily through political action."[3]

It's important to point out that the nihilist ethos of the time was primarily individualistic and not always politically revolutionary; some radical nihilist attitudes precluded ideological or political orientation.

"While nihilism emancipated the young Russian radicals from any allegiance to the established order, it was, to repeat a point, individual rather than social by its very nature and lacked a positive program — both Pisarev and Turgenev's hero Bazarov died young."[7] Clothing, attitude, communications style, all were portions of the new nihilist outlook. The clothing style sought functionality and usefulness over frivolous fashion. The 'revolt in the dress' of the nigilistka went something like this:

> One of the most interesting and widely remarked features of the *nigilistka* was her personal appearance. Discarding the "muslin, ribbons, feathers, parasols, and flowers" of the Russian lady, the archetypical girl of the nihilist persuasion in the 1860's wore a plain dark woolen dress, which fell straight and loose from the waist with white cuffs and collar as the only embellishments. The hair was cut short and worn straight, and the wearer frequently assumed dark glasses.[4]

Nigilistka fashion was about more than just juvenile rebellion against bourgeoisie fashion because instead of simply contradicting established forms it went on to create its own identity. Self-empowerment was the reason behind much of this. "The machinery of sexual attraction through outward appearance that led into slavery was discarded by the new woman whose nihilist creed taught her that she must make her way with knowledge and action rather than feminine wiles."[4] Even deeper than changes in superficial appearance existed a new and quite profound realization, for the *nigilistka* understood that life had to be defined internally and not solely by external authorities or values. "To establish her identity, she needed a cause or a "path," rather than just a man."[4] An interesting departure also occurred in communications style. "The typical *nigilistka,* like her male comrade, rejected the conventional hypocrisy of interpersonal relations and tended to be direct to the point of rudeness..."[4]

Nihilism

Severe Times Call for Severe Measures

Seeing their efforts at social change only being met with police brutality and increasing repression by despotic authority the revolutionaries reassessed their tactics. Peter Tkachev and Sergei Nechayev were two that felt severe times call for severe measures – the revolution was only getting started.

> Several years of revolutionary conspiracy, terrorism, and assassination ensued. The first instances of violence occurred more or less spontaneously, sometimes as countermeasures against brutal police officials. Thus, early in 1878 Vera Zasulich shot and wounded the military governor of St. Petersburg, General Theodore Trepov, who had ordered a political prisoner to be flogged; a jury failed to convict her, with the result that political cases were withdrawn from regular judicial procedure. But before long an organization emerged which consciously put terrorism at the center of its activity. The conspiratorial revolutionary society "Land and Freedom," founded in 1876, split in 1879 into two groups: the "Black Partition," or "Total Land Repartition," which emphasized gradualism and propaganda, and the "Will of the People" which mounted an all-out terroristic offensive against the government. Members of the "Will of the People" believed that, because of the highly centralized nature of the Russian state, a few assassinations could do tremendous damage to the regime, as well as provide the requisite political instruction for the educated society and the masses. They selected the emperor, Alexander II, as their chief target and condemned him to death. What followed has been described as an "emperor hunt" and in certain ways it defies imagination. The Executive Committee of the "Will of the People" included only about thirty men and women, led by such persons as Andrew Zheliabov who came from the serfs and Sophia Perovskaia who

came from Russia's highest administrative class, but it fought the Russian Empire.[6]

After the assassination of the tsar some began to question the strategic usefulness of the spiraling violence, but few alternatives existed in the oppressive milieu of Imperial Russia. Subsequent monarchs Alexander III and Nicholas II only became more reactionary and narrow-minded while simultaneously voiding even minimal public freedoms.

> Murder and the gibbet captivated the imagination of our young people; and the weaker their nerves and the more oppressive their surroundings, the greater was their sense of exaltation at the thought of revolutionary terror.[5]
> – Vera Figner

The Russian Nihilists were smart, dedicated, and possessed a tenacity that was unparalleled. These were revolutionaries that were well aware of the nature of the political system they were in conflict with but nonetheless they still failed to acquire two critical elements. Without a clear and cohesive social program the Nihilists lacked strategic sustainability for their revolutionary movement. Although they achieved their tactical goal of assassinating the top-level authority figures their wider objective of gaining greater freedom of movement and ideas still remained elusive. It seems that the necessary time-scale of their struggle was longer than anticipated and the entrenched nature of the system and the culture of fear and subservience to autocratic rulers that it rested upon was much deeper than realized; 1,000 years of tradition simply can't be thrown out in a decade. But since the social program is secondary to immediate plans in a larger sense I think the primary problem affecting the 19th century Russian revolutionaries had more

Nihilism

to do with communications limitations than anything else because they had most everything going for them except numbers. Lacking the ability to reach the Russian public, except on the smallest scale, made widespread and coordinated revolt practically impossible. Publishing technology was easy for despotic regimes to control while radio and cheap printing didn't arrive in widespread use until the early 20th century.

Although the political violence may have had questionable strategic value the cultural shift in views, attitudes, and ideas made significant contributions that lasted long after the Russian Nihilists themselves had left the scene.

> Such were the true nihilists, the destroyers, who did not trouble themselves about what was to be built after them. They did not exactly deny everything, for they believed firmly, fanatically, in science and in the power of the individual mind. But they thought nothing else worth the slightest respect, and they attacked and sneered at family, religion, art, and social institutions, with all the more vehemence the higher they were held in the opinion of their countrymen. – Sergius Stepniak

"Nobody realizes that some people expend tremendous energy merely to be normal." – Albert Camus

Freydis

NIHILISM COMES TO AMERICA

"We hate this system that we're trapped in but we don't know who has trapped us or how. We don't even know what our cage looks like because we have never seen it from the outside." – Gore Vidal

National Myth Building

The United States exerts an enormous influence upon world events, that much is obvious, but what is less clear are the reasons for why America does the things it does, and even more so, why Americans act, think and vote the way they do. The myths, shared beliefs, and unquestioned assumptions that collectively define the American entity are the keys to deciphering this puzzle.

For many the decline of the United States' institutional integrity began with the Watergate scandal and the revelation of widespread criminal conduct on the part of the Nixon administration in the early 70s. Although these events were an eye-opener for the American public they were nonetheless too easy to discount as just a singular event with a singular source. In this regard the 90s were a formative decade because we could see so many other things falling apart, often for the first time.

It's important to realize that we didn't get where we are today by accident, sudden event or happenstance. It's a long process of very poor collective judgment and multiple mistakes. Much of the process that has led to the large scale social, political, and economic problems featured today have to do with the collection of beliefs and myths that drive American decision-making.

Kids growing up in America are fed a steady diet of stories, fabrications, and outright lies about their national history. This myth building is not uncommon throughout the world but what makes America more unique is the fact that the vast majority *actually believe* the stories!

Nihilism

Russian and Chinese intellectuals of my acquaintance who came to America in the 1990s after living in this atmosphere of private cynicism toward public ideology often reacted with utter astonishment, and some fear, to the way in which ordinary Americans glorify their country's beliefs, institutions, laws and economic practices in private conversations, not just as a matter of defensive patriotism, but with a sincere belief in their validity for all mankind: "They actually believe all this! No-one is forcing them to say it!"[4]

This startling lack of skepticism and eagerness to believe is one of the main reasons why America is characterized by rampant jingoistic adventurism, mindless patriotism and slavish devotion to executive authority in times of national distress. As a result of these military adventures (always launched with the most noble of intentions) the United States is seen around the world as a serious threat to global safety and well-being.

While manic conservatism and paranoia wax and wane over time what remains tragically consistent is the fact that so much of the country as a whole has demonstrated a notable inability to mature or to learn from past mistakes. Witness the obvious folly of repeating the Vietnam fiasco in Iraq just three decades later. As long as the majority of Americans continue to live in a fantasy world of flawed beliefs and phony historical myths about their country they will continue to elect disingenuous and incompetent leaders who intentionally exploit the American public's naiveté and ignorance to advance foolish, even disastrous agendas for the USA, and the world as well.

What is America?

The easiest way to explain America is to describe the basic dichotomy that divides it into two parts. One segment of America is urban, the other is rural. One is typified by the 'blue' states courted by the Democratic Party and the other the 'red' states by the Republicans. Sometimes they cooperate but more often they conflict. To put it bluntly, the rural segment is characterized by a fear of change because they perceive that everything was better in the past, while the urban segment seeks it out because they see that everything could be better in the future. This struggle between progress and regression is hardly a new development, and considering the rapid social and technological change in the USA it's not surprising that the country is a cultural battleground in the 21st century.

Although this cultural conflict always seems monumental at any given moment it's quite evident from the historical record that it all eventually leads in one direction. The people willing to embrace new ideas and innovations are the ones that gain the most, while those who shun change and innovation are outpaced and superseded by the ones that do. This seems simple enough, but America's mythology is very deeply rooted in visions of the purity and desirability of the rural mindset and philosophy. While low-population density lifestyles are desirable to many people, and with valid reason, they are increasingly anachronistic or just plain impossible given the size of America's current population as opposed to what it was just 100 years ago. The mythology of the rural American lifestyle lives on even as it becomes increasingly impractical to implement and unrealistic in its applicability to the problems and issues of modern life.

Many politicians play upon these myths and anachronistic beliefs to aggrandize their own narrow agendas. This is what creates the irony of rural Americans voting for the Republican Party that promises them cultural conservatism but delivers real financial gains to the wealthy urban class at the very expense of the increasingly impoverished rural voters! This is just more evidence that religion is a disease of the mind that weakens and eventually kills the victim. Clearly, corrupt and cynical political and religious authorities have found this cultural dichotomy a very profitable conflict to exploit for personal gain. They pit one side against the other to get elected and use fear to raise funding and pass punitive legislation.

Nihilism

A Few Great American Myths

Myth: The 'America Dream' can make anyone rich if they just work hard enough

Republicans, in economic and political collusion with religious leaders, have conned the American voter by exploiting their beliefs and myths of America's past to enact an economic agenda that the working class would never support otherwise because it is destructive towards their own well being. The Democrats, because they're beholden to the same wealthy influence, have aided this process by not offering any alternative economic model! Clearly there is desperation for honest representation in the United States, so much so that many American's are willing to suspend disbelief to vote out of faith. Many voters, mostly rural, white and religious, have opted to vote for the Republicans in order to preserve their conceptions of tradition and cultural conservatism. They will gain neither for multiple reasons, perhaps the most obvious being that the policies of neo-liberal capitalism they are supporting with their votes are antithetic to the very values they're trying to preserve.

In order to increase profits for the wealthy ownership class at the expense of labor the ruling rich must do many things that are both unpopular and socially destabilizing. This is because placing capital in primacy over labor means putting workers and wages last on the priorities list behind making more in financial profit for the capitalists. Economic globalization featuring 'outsourcing' and 'offshoring' of employment, engineered economic disruptions for private gain, such as the Thai Bhat collapse that triggered the 1997 Asian financial crisis, and the long-standing abuse of the US Dollar in a scheme known as 'Dollar Hegemony' to fulfill imperial political objectives around the world through pseudo-benevolent instruments like the World Bank and the IMF, are all prime examples.

Placing capital first also creates another serious consequence - it forces labor to follow the money, rather than the other way around, and in a globalized marketplace that means millions of people uproot and migrate to where they think the jobs are. Simultaneously, capital is constantly seeking to find the lowest priced labor to setup a factory, creating a global economy that looks like a dog chasing his tail on top of an increasingly unstable one-legged table. In the process, large scale immigration creates massive social and economic turmoil. The United States is ground-zero for this problem with millions from Mexico alone having entered the country illegally, bringing with them cheap unskilled labor but also enormous needs like special language education, medical care and a litany of other social and police service requirements. Practically all of the costs associated with meeting these needs are offloaded by business and industry onto the public, i.e. the taxpayers. The taxpayers predictably rebel at rising tax rates, government looks for the easiest place to cut spending in social services, assistance for the working class evaporates and wealth becomes increasingly unequally spread around, while the competition at the bottom just gets fiercer.

The truth is that *capital only looks out for capital* and without factoring in the needs of labor, or anything else, we are left with a very distorted and unstable socio-economic system that generates widespread suffering and injustice – the birthplace of revolution. Remember that.

So, having been collectively conditioned to reject the social and economic concepts and solutions that can actually help them, it's not surprising that the American public's views on work, wealth, and the mechanisms behind them are so completely distorted by national myths and flawed beliefs that they're easy prey for scams and the phony promises of disingenuous politicians and con-artist alike. It's especially sad to see how the myth of the 'American Dream', where anyone can get a job and become middle class through concerted labor, continues to influence American values and decisions long after the 'Dream' has ceased to exist.

Myth: America is the greatest country in the world and a beacon of hope, freedom and democracy to the rest

Nihilism

Statements like this are so full of hubris and national arrogance they can only portend a country ready to take a hard fall when they stumble over reality. Most people are proud of their country even if for no other reason than habit and enculturation, but that doesn't give them license to force that perceived greatness upon everyone else. This is especially valid advice considering recent events. The intensity and appeal of America's 'beacon of hope' has been massively diminished during the Clinton and Bush administrations, mostly through fantastic foreign policy follies. For instance: lobbing cruise missiles into an aspirin factory in Sudan and then lying to the world to convince them it was making chemical weapons (Clinton). Or lying to the world to convince them Saddam Hussein was responsible for the 9/11 attacks on the US (Bush).

The grotesque abuse that occurred in the Abu Ghraib prison and the continuing injustices on display in the Guantánamo Bay concentration camp have had a major impact on world opinion, even as influential American authorities do everything they can to convince their domestic audience of the necessity and nobility of these efforts. Perhaps the most egregious foreign policy folly (in the last six months) was on display during the recent war between Lebanon and Israel where the Bush administration literally reversed policy 180 degrees against (formerly) pro-western Lebanon so as to grant Israel free reign to demolish the country with their air and ground assault. All that just to try and set an example by punishing the minor resistance group Hezbollah, which enjoys vast regional support. The attack on Lebanon was a foolish and completely counter-productive effort that put both Israel and the United States clearly in the loser category. Bush called it a success against terrorism.

- 122 -

Egregious examples of state terrorism and mass-murder through war are acceptable largely because of the allowance granted to the national leadership from the common belief in the American psyche that the United States fights noble and heroic wars against tyranny and in support of freedom, democracy, and so on. Obviously, the impact of this myth has significantly declined since the fiasco in Vietnam and amidst the ever widening gap between official policy and actual events, but it still has the power to sway many American minds largely because *intentions* are used to gauge the morality of actions.

The most important way in which World War II shaped the moral and technological tenor of mass destruction was the erosion in the course of war of the stigma associated with the systematic targeting of civilian populations from the air, and elimination of the constraints, which for some years had restrained certain air powers from area bombing. What was new was both the scale of killing made possible by the new technologies and the routinization of mass killing or state terrorism. ...

Every US president from Roosevelt to George W. Bush has endorsed *in practice* an approach to warfare that targets entire populations for annihilation, one that eliminates all vestiges of distinction between combatant and noncombatant, with deadly consequences. The awesome power of the atomic bomb has obscured the fact that this strategy came of age in the firebombing of Tokyo and became the centerpiece of US war making from that time forward. ...

Nihilism

American self-conceptions of benevolence and justice have remained fixed not on the reality of the killing of noncombatants but on the combination of American intentions in combat and generosity in charting postwar recovery in all wars since 1945.[7]

Now when the world hears that America promises to bring them democracy they laugh and reach for their rifles. So many successive Presidential administrations have abused the terms freedom and democracy to justify the exact opposite – economic exploitation and trans-national plunder, that the world equates a democracy crusade to mean threats and even military occupation.

The violence and civic disorder on display in Iraq, Afghanistan, Pakistan, and elsewhere, are exactly what America's 'democracy and freedom' mean to everyone that isn't isolated and brainwashed by the Washington echo-chamber. The world's reaction to this is hardly surprising. Russia, China, Venezuela, and just about everyone else in one form or another, has moved to build alternate political, cultural and economic alliances outside of the influence of the United States. So while America's dominant leadership is busy trying to establish their 20th century empire of exclusionary benefit to take it all at everyone else's expense, most of the rest of the world is struggling to build a multi-polar order for tentative co-existence built around international institutions. An example of this is the Shanghai Cooperation Organization (SCO), a new economic and political bond between China, Russia, several Central Asian nations, and more eager to join. Despite the geo-political significance of the SCO it's nearly impossible to find any reference to this new alliance in America's domestic mainstream media.

The three largest massacres of innocent people in a single-day have all been performed by the United States' war-machine:

1. The firebombing of Tokyo, March 9, 1945. As many as 120,000 civilians were burned alive or suffocated in the inferno.

2. The atomic-bombing of Hiroshima Japan on August 6, 1945 instantly incinerated 70,000, and eventually killed up to 200,000.

3. The atomic-bombing of Nagasaki Japan on August 9, 1945 instantly killed 40,000.

Myth: America is the richest country in the world with the highest standard of living

America is not the richest country in the world when national income is divided by population, that distinction belongs to Luxembourg. Although the rankings vary slightly by year, the World Bank in 2005 ranks the top as Luxembourg, Norway, Switzerland, Bermuda, Denmark, Iceland, and then the United States. This statistic is misleading because it averages everyone together and does not reveal how the wealth is distributed. America has most of the world's billionaires and enormous capital resources but the wealth is very unevenly distributed. The United States contains the fabulous wealth of Manhattan but also the abject poverty of the Native American reservations of the Dakotas. The distribution of wealth is measured by the gini coefficient where 0 is total equality and 1 is total inequality i.e. only one person gets all the income. Using this measure the U$A is sandwiched between Senegal and Ghana with a score of 40.8! For further comparison, Mexico has 54.6 and Canada has 33.1.

It is true that the USA has a very fluid economic system that will employ almost anyone, at least temporarily, but the benefits, and sometimes the wages too, that are paid are typically below the standards of other modern developed countries. For example, many unemployed or poorly paid Mexicans illegally cross the border and risk arrest and deportation in order to find jobs to the north. The work is there on the other side but it's dangerous, the pay is minimal and the health care benefits non-existent. When these people get injured their employer typically fires them and then all the healthcare costs of these disposable illegal workers are transferred to the state that then has to move the costs onto the taxpayers. The United States is one of the few countries where this public rip-off is legal. This also explains why America has so many millionaires and why so many of the wealthy are in love with the 'neo-liberal' trickle-up politico-economic philosophy of the Bush administration. The businessmen at the top make a fortune off of this scam, the pain is spread out amongst millions of mostly oblivious taxpayers and the disposable workers are used up and thrown away. Immigrants were once told that the streets are paved with gold in America. In reality the streets have many potholes and the economic machine chews up workers and spits them out while the social services needed by everyone that isn't rich gradually dwindle away.

The national wealth is a fascinating parable as well. The United States is a debtor country that spends far more than it earns. The USA requires over $2 billion every day in foreign investment just to maintain the current economic level. That is not a misprint, $2,000,000,000 every day! Most of the money needed to keep America solvent comes from Japan, China, and Saudi Arabia. Money buys influence, so who really owns America in the 21st century? Indeed, Americans are surprisingly oblivious to the economic developments occurring around the world. China, India and Russia are just three examples of countries that are experiencing rapid economic growth. Around the world the US is being surpassed in everything from wireless and high-speed Internet to steel production.

> The irony is that many Americans think we're rich and China is poor. Exactly the opposite is true. This is because the removal of gold's backing from paper money has

created a virtual explosion in credit and liquidity. The sheer amount of liquidity around the globe is incalculable.

While some people do become richer in this system, funny money actually punishes working people who save money. It devalues the value of your work and your savings, even though you may feel wealthier.[6]

Only labor can create capital. Capital cannot create labor nor can it create capital – it can only attract more capital like a magnet attracts iron filings. This is why labor rich countries, such as China and India, have a bright economic future for growth once they become organized for production, as China has done. Capital rich countries spend most of their effort shuffling around phony money to create the illusion of wealth; it's called the 'service' economy.

Myth: America is a noble Christian nation run by honest Christian leaders

Christianity was the dominant religion of America's early settlers but they *did not* share the same interpretations of their Holy Book, a fact that has lead to much conflict then, just as it does today. It's also conveniently forgotten that the major founders of the United States, such as George Washington and Thomas Jefferson, were Freemasons too, so does that make it a Freemason nation? Religious and political leaders that use the Christian nation ploy are just cynically manipulating public sentiment because the Constitution has always been unambiguous in the need to keep Church and State separate for the very reason that, even within Christianity, much disagreement exists. In reality America has always been a multi-religious country and has spawned multiple conflicting new sects since its political inception, such as Mormonism, Jehovah's Witnesses, and the Seventh Day Adventists.

Nihilism

Billionaire Mormon presidential candidate Mitt Romney's December 2007 campaign statements form a perfect example of the warped views on religion and politics infecting contemporary American culture:

> Espousing one of the main distortions of the religious right, Romney claimed that "in recent years, the notion of the separation of church and state has been taken by some well beyond its original meaning." He castigated the defenders of the constitutional principle of separation of church and state for seeking "to remove from the public domain any acknowledgment of God." He continued, "Religion is seen as merely a private affair with no place in public life. It is as if they are intent on establishing a new religion in America—the religion of secularism."
>
> For all Romney's vilification, secularism is not a religion. The separation of church and state leaves individuals free to worship or not, as they see fit, without any government prohibition or encouragement. One of the epoch-making and entirely progressive features of the American Revolution was that it dealt a major blow against the use of state coercion to enforce the subordination of mankind to various forms of religious dogma. ...
>
> Turning history on its head, Romney claimed in his speech that the US Constitution, the first in the world to mandate the separation of church and state, was somehow founded on religious principles. "The founders proscribed the establishment of a state religion," he said, "but they did not countenance the elimination of religion from the public square. We are a nation 'Under God,' and in God we do indeed trust."
>
> In fact, the pledge of allegiance, whose daily recitation is required of most US school children, was devised only in the 1890s. It made no mention of religion, with the words "under God" added only during the early 1950s, at the

height of McCarthy witch-hunt, to distinguish patriotic Americanism from "godless communism."

The Constitution makes no mention of such religious conceptions as the basis of the political organization of the country. It explicitly bans any religious test to hold any public office: the president may adhere to any religion, or none at all.[8]

One of the most troubling aspects within American culture is the marriage of religious conservatism and American myth perpetuation. Religious groups, particularly the fundamentalists and evangelical Protestants, invest an extraordinary amount of money and effort into inflating and perpetuating select stories and myths about America's history and position in the world, for example that the United States is, and must be, a wholly Christian nation and that it's a model the rest of the world must embrace. The USA is, after all, the new Israel for a special people destined to lead the world out of darkness and sin with its inherently superior morality and culture, or so that's how the new evangelists for this version of America see it! The Reagan years saw the ascendancy of the American myth as a god-fearing nation of believers standing up, and eventually defeating, the 'evil', atheist, communist Soviet Empire. The Bush administration has continued and magnified  this trend to exploit fear and paranoia, consistently using images of a world in black and white where every conflict is a battle between good and evil in order to stifle debate and deactivate critical thought on the part of the public.

This kind of religious nationalism is fueled both by religious moralism and by a paranoia fed in turn by a feeling of cultural embattlement. In the words of Richard Hofstadter: "Since what is at stake is always a conflict between good and evil, the quality needed is not a willingness to compromise but the will to fight things out to the finish.

Nihilism

Nothing but total victory will do. Since the enemy is thought of as being totally evil and utterly unappeasable, he must be totally eliminated.... This demand for unqualified victories leads to the formulation of hopelessly demanding and unrealistic goals, and since these goals are not even remotely attainable, failure constantly heightens the paranoid's frustration.[5]

Conservative religious groups and their political allies have been intentionally mixing state and religion for decades but with increasing emphasis and resources since the 1980s. This is an especially threatening force in a country that owes its continued existence to a strict separation between secular government and private belief.

Recent history has repeatedly demonstrated that the official institution of the Church, regardless of the denomination, is hardly a model of moral purity and noble guidance. Infamous televangelists Jim and Tammy Faye Bakker were icons of the 1980s with their PTL and 700 Club TV shows, operating under the auspices of Pat Robertson's media-empire. Millions of Americans were shocked to learn about their Cadillacs, mansions and air-conditioned dog houses, even though they sent the Bakker's check after check to do 'God's work' without asking any questions. More recently the Catholic Church was involved in a massive legal case involving multiple Priests all over the world who have been convicted of pedophilic child abuse that spanned decades. The unholy marriage of politics and religion has already burned many of those foolish enough to get involved in it, the paragon of Christian morality Ralph Reed and the Christian Coalition for instance, and his relationship with super(corrupt)-lobbyist Jack Abramoff; more on that below.

Despite the steady flow of scandals leaking out most Americans have difficulty internalizing the significance of these isolated events and connecting them into a cohesive whole, consequently they vastly underestimate the corruption that occurs in business, politics, and the religious establishment. The purity and sanctity of America and her leaders is a very tenacious belief on the public mind. People outside the American bubble don't have this problem. Japanese business and political travelers have been known to make the statement, Jakarta or Washington D.C., what's the difference? Indonesia (Jakarta) is notorious for its corrupt political system and in reality Washington D.C. is not far off. In many ways it is a sophisticated corruption that has to hide in order to shield itself from the public outrage that comes from exposure. But behind the scenes the scale of America's institutional crime is staggering.

Myth: The United States is the freest country in the world.

Freedom is a value that lacks a universal definition since it is in fact more of a luxury than a necessity, thus making this statement difficult to prove. Nonetheless, history has shown that a large degree of freedom is a requirement for creating the kind of society that is most successful and desirable by the vast majority. So it's true that the US has a great allowance for public freedom as written into the Constitution, however the actual implementation of that allowance, which is what really counts, is under constant attack from special interests, politicians, and many short-sighted others. This has been the situation ever since the US Constitution was ratified, yet these Constitutional rights have held up remarkably well in practice for over 200 years. This is a testament to both a well written document and a collective desire to interpret those codified freedoms as broadly as possible.

Freedom of speech and public expression are easily the greatest things the United States still has going for it, and indeed that is why it's placed as the *first* amendment in the Bill of Rights. And an especially important element of free speech is the ability of the public to criticize their leaders without fear of retribution. This is a freedom that is rarely allowed anywhere else and one of the main reasons dictatorships, in one form or another, are so widespread even in the 21st century.

To its national credit criticism is open and vigorous in America, but unfortunately it's mostly channeled at innocuous targets and subjects that are very unlikely to actually create substantive social, political, or economic change. *Dissent is not dead in the United States, it just lacks diversity and impact.*

As long as the American public remains vigilant against the forces that want freedom stifled and eliminated, and maintains constant pressure on their leadership class to do the same, they will continue to enjoy the benefits of one of the most free societies in the world. This desirable outcome doesn't just happen automatically, it requires continuous civic engagement in ideas and events, be they local or global, as well as a constant effort to push the boundaries and expand the range of ideas and discussion, for otherwise those boundaries will shrink to the point that we will be reduced to a voting choice of only one candidate while accepting only one ideology and one view of things approved by authorities.

Backwards Focused Vision

It's ironic that even though America has most everything it needs to succeed and flourish in the future, widespread intolerance and a lack of legitimate, open, diverse and inclusive debate on issues of crucial national significance are leading the country into a regressive and reactionary mode that is as foolish as it is self-defeating. National ideals and myths shape the future and as it is now America is trying to create an impractical, and indeed impossible, future based on a mostly erroneous perception of its past and present national condition. People with open minds and open eyes to witness the rapid decay of institutional integrity can grasp the significance of the anomie around them. It should be no surprise that nihilism is spreading in America; what else is left?

What Happened to America?

One beneficial aspect that has emerged from the raw deceit and brutality of America's national rulers is the way it has motivated many people to speak out, produce documentaries, write books, and basically just *do something* to counteract everything harmful that's being forced down from the top. With major scandals breaking at a frenetic pace, just keeping track of what's going on has become an industry in itself. The scale and numerical volume of scandal and turmoil are like zebra stripes to the American public, a confusing maelstrom where individual events can't be discerned in order to form a coherent pattern and trend, much to their collective loss.

Amidst the avalanche of information and events what does it really signify? What happened to America and its institutions, and where is the country headed? Well, let's start with the money. America has a Congress that is completely out of control, writing $100 billion dollar blank checks practically every six months for the worldwide war against all the President's enemies. The President and Congress love these emergency spending bills because Congress get to throw in every kickback and pork project they can think of while the President gets a blank check to wage war on the world, enrich his cronies, and look like a patriotic tough-guy in the process. The latest cost of the war in Iraq and Afghanistan, both of which are being lost at a rate that makes Vietnam look like a raging success story, is now up to $10 billion per month with no end in sight.

Now this brings us to the Pentagon, another American institution run amok under the wayward guidance of Zionist neo-conservatives and civilian war hawks like Donald Rumsfeld. The official budget for the Defense Department is running near half a trillion dollars per year, more than every other country combined! But the real budget of this military juggernaut is closer to $750 billion, as revealed by the astute Chalmers Johnson, former military man and now anti-imperialist, *What happened to the US Congress?*

> The government isn't working right. There's no proper supervision. The founders, the authors of the constitution, regarded the supreme organ to be Congress. The mystery to me - more than the huge expansion of executive branch powers we've seen since the neo-conservatives and

George Bush came to power - is: Why has Congress failed us so completely? ...

This is the beast we're trying to analyze, to understand, and it seems to me today unstoppable. Put it this way: James Madison, the author of our constitution, said the right that controls all other rights is the right to get information. If you don't have this, the others don't matter. The Bill of Rights doesn't work if you can't find out what's going on. Secrecy has been going crazy in this country for a long time, but it's become worse by orders of magnitude under the present administration. When John Ashcroft became attorney general, he issued orders that access to the Freedom of Information Act should be made as difficult as possible.

Just paying for the war on Iraq this year alone will consume almost as much as the departments of Education, Justice and Homeland Security put together![1] So with a virtually unlimited budget and a vengeful leadership eager  to seek out and persecute new enemies, the Pentagon has joined forces with spy agencies, like NSA and the new and deceptively innocuous sounding Department of Homeland Security (DHS), to monitor and interdict public dissent, be it a peace march or a private discussion group, all in contravention of the spirit of the Constitution as well as decades of legal precedent against such invasive actions. The TALON program and elaborate data mining efforts are just small pieces that managed to leak out from a much larger, concerted spy effort.[2] The Pentagon and DHS can't distinguish between a harmless peace rally and violent saboteur because they're all the same threat to the nascent American police state. Everyone is a potential terrorist waiting to happen.

The institutionalized torture, intimidation, and humiliation perpetrated on Iraqi captives by American soldiers that leaked out from the Abu Ghraib prison did more to damage American esteem throughout the world than anything in recent memory, even the My Lai massacre in Vietnam only comes close. But always remember that what happened there was just 'follow the leader' and when the punishment has to be handed out in a corrupt and hypocritical society it's always the followers that take the blame. Once national credibility is lost, like it was at Abu Ghraib, the only tool an empire has left to get what it demands is fear and intimidation and then the world really sees what's behind the mask of benevolence!

America's Commercial Democracy becomes a Kleptocracy

Government corruption has reached record proportions with top level politicians falling from grace like so many angels being kicked out of heaven. The escapades of 'super-lobbyist' Jack Abramoff have managed to tarnish or take down multiple politicians from both parties, but most notably the saintly House Majority leader Tom Delay, once described as "a very religious guy".[11] This one scandal alone is so convoluted and extensive as to be far beyond what I can relay within the limitations of one written article. The Republican congressman from San Diego, Randy 'Duke' Cunningham, is serving eight years and four months in prison for taking $2.4 million in bribes from defense contractors. In April 2006 the former governor of Illinois, George Ryan, was found guilty of all charges leveled against him including fraud, racketeering, and tax evasion.[3] Incompetence and corruption within the U.S. federal government has reached astounding levels under the Bush/Cheney regime. And let's not forget the Enron scandal that saw President W. Bush in league with Enron CEO Kenneth Lay to cynically deregulate

Nihilism

and rig the energy industry to favor private corporations. These are just the guys getting caught, so think about what else is going on that hasn't even been revealed yet!

Given this kind of environment, the massive banking crisis of 2007-2008, and the political response, shouldn't come as too much of a surprise. Having failed to rectify the situation, America's national leaders have in fact succeeded in making the situation far worse by delivering billions, if not trillions, of dollars directly to the larcenous mega-banks and swindling billionaires who caused the collapse in the first place. Yet at the same time national leaders claim they have no money to provide jobs, rebuild a crumbling country, or provide necessary social services!

As the opening act of the *second* financial bubble-collapse, the 'robo-signing' scandal of 2010 has revealed America's mega-banks having systematically and illegally falsified documents in order to take the homes of millions of Americans through foreclosures. This fiasco implicates every major institutional player in criminal corruption. Goldman Sachs, Bank of America, GMAC, Citigroup, Wells Fargo, JP Morgan Chase, and PNC Financial all continue to steal and receive federal bailouts while the corporate executives take home millions of dollars in pay and bonuses.

> The rampant falsification of loan documents has now raised doubts over the solvency of the entire mortgage security industry. The "robo-signers" basic task was to supply affidavits to courts in lieu of the actual documents related to ownership.[9]

Freydis

The corporate mass-media misdirect the blame towards the homeowners, and the federal government, under the Obama regime, has put all their effort into shielding the mega-banks and billionaires while refusing to even put a pause on home foreclosures! Lenders falsified signatures, shredded documents, and even faked notary stamps. Agencies tasked with monitoring the mortgage industry, such as the Federal Reserve, the Office of the Comptroller of the Currency, and the Office of Thrift Supervision, have done nothing to stop the scam. The courts and legal system have consistently favored the richest of the rich, tossing out families from their homes just so banks can seize a house they can't even find a buyer for!

They may wear suits and ties, but only to hide the obvious: these aren't the actions of respectable people; these are the actions of thieves, rapists and plunderers. This is an environment that only breeds deceit and brutal exploitation. Even greedy  and short-sighted cynics have to think twice before climbing on board this short ride because the rest of the sleazy gang will only take you down with them. As the saying goes, *when you lie down with dogs you'll get up with fleas.*

The Lobby

Money is not the only disease infecting America's body politic. As if financial fraud and kickbacks weren't trouble enough, now we have to add dual loyalty and outright treachery to the mix because of a five-ton elephant stinking up the room known as the Israel lobby. This interest group has become so powerful, due to decades of shielding from public scrutiny and debate, that most people are too afraid or too crooked to even talk about it in public. It takes two tenured professors to carefully document a critical report on the subject just to get the issue into the mainstream for a brief moment;

Nihilism

an effort that earns them the predictable slew of irrational abuse from the raving media mouthpieces.

> Moreover, the Lobby's campaign to squelch debate about Israel is unhealthy for democracy. Silencing skeptics by organizing blacklists and boycotts—or by suggesting that critics are anti-Semites—violates the principle of open debate upon which democracy depends. The inability of the U.S. Congress to conduct a genuine debate on these vital issues paralyzes the entire process of democratic deliberation. Israel's backers should be free to make their case and to challenge those who disagree with them. But efforts to stifle debate by intimidation must be roundly condemned by those who believe in free speech and open discussion of important public issues.[10]

The harm caused by the Israel Lobby is incalculable, as decades of special protection from criticism and scrutiny have directly generated the current political environment of fraud and rampant corruption that plagues the federal government. The Israel Lobby's political immunity means that every other lobby and special interest group, from weapons to pharmaceuticals to prisons and everything in between, can spread and thrive while merrily manipulating government policy too. Special interest lobbying cannot be stopped because to do so would require punishing the Israel Lobby as well, or adding a very obvious special exception that would only make the scam even more blatant, so the problem just expands out of control. And for a country thoroughly dependent on imported oil, choosing sides in the Middle East and blindly supporting the Zionist state of Israel at every opportunity is nothing short of *national suicide*.

After all this we've still got people who think everything is just fine because America looks pretty much the same as it used to. But under the influence of passive entertainment, television and commercial broadcast news, the public can barely

- 138 -

remember what happened yesterday; and of course they can't really recall what went on a few years ago. Danny Schechter, a former mass media employee and now professional media analyst, created an informative and revealing documentary titled *Weapons of Mass Deception* where he shows the power of mass media television news to influence and manipulate public opinion, in this case to support the war on Iraq. Schechter details multiple aspects of the modern mass media machine and how it has become little more than a propaganda outlet for the established powers.

This crumbling and wholly corrupt establishment has not self-corrected, it's still not being regulated or supervised by oversight bodies, and instead it continues to impoverish the people at an accelerating pace, robbing millions of families of homes, jobs, and indeed any stake in the system at all! Even if you want to believe that the political leadership is democratically elected, it's apparent they're not responding to democratic input or democratic needs.

You can run from America but you can't hide from it

These corporate and political scandals aren't just business as usual if for no other reason than the unprecedented volume and scale of them in totality, but also because we are witnessing the unraveling of the very fabric of representative democracy as the process of voting and elections are distorted and corrupted beyond recognition. The end result is a public that protests without being heard and votes without anything changing and is ultimately robbed of any legal recourse for making their voices and needs heard and understood by the political leadership. President Kennedy's speech writer said it best, "Those who make peaceful revolution impossible only make violent revolution inevitable."

Investigative reporter and filmmaker Greg Palast made *Bush family fortunes – The Best Democracy Money Can Buy* (2004) DVD, an insightful and provocative documentary that shows how the Bush dynasty has used its influence in office for decades to build up their personal fortunes through special connections, such as with the Saudi monarchy and the infamous Carlyle Group, and then plowed the profits back into their own reelection campaigns. Palast explains that the contested Florida election in 2000 was lost due to intentional disenfranchisement of Black voters using a doctored roster of out of state convicted felons.

Vote rigging is a tactic that both sides, Republican and Democrat, want to see continue because it favors the incumbent and they both believe that by perpetuating it they can win at this charade. Palast goes so far as to suggest that the Supreme Court was a party to the corruption in the Florida election as well. If this is the case then America as a Republic and as a democracy is completely lost because no institution remains that is free of massive corruption. Not the Presidency, not Congress, and now not even the Supreme Court. No matter how much effort the public puts into it through agitation and protest, the system cannot fix itself anymore because all legitimate institutions have been corrupted to become part of the problem implacably opposed to the solution! The cynical saying, *if voting changed anything it would be illegal*, has never been more true. Read between the lines: *Bush's Family Fortunes* is a call to revolution in the United States because it is increasingly apparent that nothing else can rectify the situation.

The Illusion of Reform

The United States, and much of the western world, doesn't have anything approaching democracy. When the only way to win an election is through fraud or by out-spending your opponents on advertising, it's not a democracy. Establishment authorities repeatedly call the political machine a democracy to deflect legitimate criticism of what the system really is – a plutocratic and kleptocratic oligarchy. This is marketing 101; if you want to sell crap you don't tell the customer it's crap, you tell them it's solid gold and they're fools to want anything else!

The present situation is especially pathetic because we actually know most of the answers and we have legitimate solutions, but in practice it's impossible to enact any of them because the system is intentionally structured to resist progressive and socially-beneficial reform. This is why we can't elect a leader that will save us, and even though it's fairly simple to make laws and regulations to fix the obvious problems, genuine legislative solutions remain nothing more than another mirage on the horizon. For instance, it would be a simple matter in theory to make all elections funded through a pool of taxpayer money. Public funding of elections would mean everyone gets the same amount and then the contest is based on real issues and the candidate's merit, rather than purchased advertising. But we won't see this happen. Even the most noble and well-meaning President can't get anything changed of great significance. The President is kept in a bubble to prevent him hearing the cries of the people and to stop him from actually making valid popular decisions that favor the electorate. And the apparent ease of reform is part of the deception; it's what keeps so many people voting in the false hope of changing the system.

The Fuse Burns Shorter

The founding figures of the United States, who fought a bloody revolution against a tyrant and carefully crafted the Constitution, knew full well that swindlers in black hats like Abramoff would come along and link up with greedy, smiling scumbags like Delay and then proceed to merrily sell out their country and electorate. They knew that corruption was inevitable but they did the best they could to prevent it by writing down a Constitution and creating a system of checks and balances, two political parties and three separate branches of government, to watch over each other. But they also knew that it was up to the people in the end to keep things from getting completely fouled up and out of hand. Yet if through apathy and ignorance they still drop the ball, it's the responsibility of the citizenry to initiate a revolution.

So when Thomas Jefferson wrote, "The tree of liberty must be refreshed from time to time with the blood of patriots and tyrants," he wasn't being philosophical or metaphoric, he meant it in a literal sense because violent revolution is exactly what Jefferson and others had to do themselves.

Nihilism

Waiting for it all to collapse may feel nice, but unfortunately the aftermath won't work out the way you want it to unless you've planned ahead and prepared before it's too late. This edifice of hypocrisy and corruption that surrounds all of us is much more likely to descend into something more oppressive and stifling than to implode all neat and simple. No, this is a monster that will kill *you* if you don't kill it first. Maybe the death won't be a physical one, or maybe it will, but nonetheless the established machinery will continue to grind away at your economic well being, reducing you to the wage slavery of a modern day peasant. The machinery will usurp your mind, stealing your intellectual freedom and turning you into a mental slave through fear and the manipulated forces of social conformity.

Too many Americans are still part of the problem, living in denial while deluding themselves into believing they can get rich even if everything and everyone else gets the shaft.

We can't afford to wait for the perfect solution to be concocted before we get started because if we wait it will never arrive. Problems get solved by addressing them head-on, by doing them and not by just debating them. Americans need to be able to *visualize* revolution if they are to ever actualize it. They need the imagery, the symbols and the words to conceptualize it and to express it because it can't get started until the people can imagine it really happening here and with their participation. We need to make a concerted effort to attack and discredit the fear, superstition, apathy and ignorance that allows the machine of Empire to perpetuate and accelerate, to start wars in the name of peace and to spy and repress in the name of freedom.

Revolution is like an investment – you don't spend all the money you earn every day on savings, you take a small part and build it up piece by piece, and then eventually you have enough to achieve your goal. Through a multitude of small efforts we eventually accumulate enough power to achieve our vision.

Freydis

Every successful insurgency follows a similar pattern; we have to build up a new system that functions independently from the corrupt establishment, while at the same time actively tearing down and discrediting the existing institutions that oppress, lie, and rob us on a daily basis.

Be the Revolution

Amidst epic financial exploitation, brutal state violence, and the appalling economic *and intellectual* impoverishment of the vast majority, the only practical and functional response is massive widespread protest – any way and every way possible. Consider every tactic that will disorder daily events and disrupt business as usual. As the fuse burns in America, millions of people in France have taken to the streets to protest, while shutting down refineries and fuel delivery in order to force authorities to take notice, all within yet another supposedly democratic country where the rulers refuse to respond to democratic statements.

Push until authorities respond as democratic rulers or topple as tyrants, because conditions in the social organization have reached the point where destruction is desirable for its own sake, independent of any constructive program or possibility. *This* is the place to start and *now* is the time for Nihilism.

You can't control your own life until you start to think for yourself.
– Freydis

Nihilism

THE DOLLAR DISEASE

The Power of Money

No other artificial force affects us on daily basis the way money does. From institutions and individuals, governments and churches, to the wage earner and the illegal immigrant, money is the primary concern and motivating factor for much of human action within society, even if it isn't always admitted as such in public discussion. In this regard we are all economic entities enmeshed within an artificially constructed economic grid that regulates our choices, influences our thoughts, affects our identity, and remains practically impossible to evade.

In a world where billions of people struggle every day just to find enough food to eat it's peculiar that nuclear weapons are so often considered the greatest threat to human life; money is far more dangerous. Millions of people literally live or die based on the economic policies established in New York and Washington DC. Money is ubiquitous and possesses a deadly corruptibility on large scales; perhaps only disease can rival it in capacity for widespread harm.

This artificial grid that distributes wealth and resources in our society is called an economy. An economy is a system for allocating resources, but where the resources go and who gets them is ultimately determined by some form of values. Yet established economic systems are based mostly on assumptions and ideology. Verifiable research is thin but theory is great. And although allocation of resources within the framework of an economy is initially justified based upon ideological or theological guidelines, in practice wealth and resources accumulate in the greatest degree with those that already have the most of both. In other words the rich get richer. At this point the economic order becomes an exercise in power and authority justifying its own excess through ideology and religion. This makes the rich inherently conservative in political and social outlook because they need stability in order to preserve their wealth and status. It's interesting that all U.S. currency is marked with the statement "In God we trust" intermixing, money, government, and divine authority into one piece. This official statement must refer to the royal 'we' because I'm not putting any trust in this economic system and after you finish reading this chapter you won't either!

As important as it is economics remains a confusing topic with actual events difficult to predict using established theories because cause and effect are often unclear and billions of individuals are all making different decisions based upon a constantly changing series of events.

Economics has long been a watering hole for cranks and charlatans. Convincing theory is easy to concoct and just as easy to foist on the gullible and the greedy. Economics remains a warren of fraud because it's impossible to predict how millions of individuals are going to act or react to any given economic situation. About all we can be certain of are the basic elements of supply and demand and after that economics is in many ways just a mislabeled branch of psychology. Nevertheless demand for predictive economic theories is as insatiable as capitalism's demand for increasing profits. Economists along with their unverifiable crystal-ball theories are the modern equivalent of the sawbones doctors of medicine 150 years ago. Regardless of whether they kill the patient or accidentally save a life the public is often compelled to seek their services for lack of a superior alternative.

With wealth and power intricately linked the few that posses it have the greatest influence upon choosing and propagating contemporary economic theory, and so established economic theory is, not coincidentally, conservative in outlook and structured to support those already in power and those that are already wealthy. The validity and actual efficiency of the economic theories and guidelines that emerge from this money morality are rarely, if ever, questioned by establishment society. Indeed, the fact that these economic theories and beliefs are socially dysfunctional, strategically counter-productive, and often antithetic to social development and cohesion is either ignored or attacked. For example Milton Friedman, treated

Nihilism

as something between a genius and *the* god of modern economic theory by establishment authorities, encapsulated his attitude with the statement, "So the question is, do corporate executives, provided they stay within the law, have responsibilities in their business activities other than to make as much money for their stockholders as possible? And my answer to that is, no, they do not." Ayn Rand (born Alissa Rosenbaum) developed a flimsy ideology now used to justify greed, personal excess, and obscene wealth-disparity that is increasingly popular amongst CEOs and other overpaid corporate executives[1]. Ayn Rand was a personal mentor to Alan Greenspan the former U.S. Federal Reserve Chairman and maestro of massive monetary inflation. The current Federal Reserve Chairman, Ben Shalom Bernanke, has quickly picked up where Greenspan left off despite initial rhetoric to the contrary.

Although most of the economic pain in the U.S. has manifest during the W. Bush administration both political parties participated in hollowing out the US economy. Most notable was the Clinton administration's economic 'miracle' performed by Robert Rubin, another god of the money morality and sage of modern economics, in the form of 'Rubinomics'. Rubin's strategy was to work with Greenspan at the Federal Reserve to inflate the money supply and use creative accounting techniques to make a bleeding federal budget deficit look like a surplus while slashing government regulation of the financial sector to generate a frenzy of foolish speculation, boosting the stock market and creating the superficial appearance of a robust and healthy economy.

> *The infamous North American Free Trade Agreement (NAFTA) was intensely promoted by both Rubin and Greenspan. NAFTA hasn't created more jobs as promised, but it has depressed wages and exaggerated wealth disparity.*

Rubin used the enormous volume of Dollars in circulation as a foreign policy weapon, offloading inflation overseas on to manufacturing countries and compelling everyone to adopt the U.S.

Dollar for trade or as their primary currency. This system of Dollar hegemony robs smaller nations of the ability to manage or regulate their own economies and generates widespread suffering and social turmoil as manufacturing countries compete against each other in a race to cut wages and lower costs for exporting products to the U.S. market.

Most developing nations now realize after painful experience that by using currencies other than the U.S. dollar and shunning loans from U.S. controlled pseudo-economic assistance agencies, such as the IMF and World Bank, they can actually raise wages and grow a healthy domestic economy in reality and not just in meaningless rhetoric. But due to the wizards of monetary fraud like Friedman, Greenspan, and Rubin, America's financial capital and international credibility have vanished like a malevolent magic act, while concocting the greatest wealth disparity in world history between the ultra-rich and everyone else.

What is Money?

Money has historically been a physical object, usually of uncommon substance – it could be seashells, it could be feathers, it could be shiny metal. Form is not particularly important, although one has to wonder about the giant stone money of Yap Island, how practical was that? But at least theft was unlikely!

> The stone money of Yap, though not legal tender in the international currency market, is still used as legal tender on the island. The value of these limestone, donut-shaped coins varies, though not according to size. Today the money is still owned but not moved, even though ownership may change.[2]

The important aspect of traditional money is that it's of a finite quantity because when the supply of objects used as money increases so do the prices of everything being traded. This is because the seller wants to get as much in trade as they can, and with more money floating around in everyone's pockets it's easier to charge more for products. This effect of rising prices stemming from a growing supply of money is called inflation, but more on that in a moment.

Your Money is the Government's Debt

In 1971 President Richard Nixon removed the U.S. Dollar from the gold standard creating a currency that can be produced in unlimited amounts and cannot be redeemed for anything but more debt, employing the bogus economic notions of Milton Friedman as theoretical justification for unlimited expansion of the national money supply. The disastrous and expensive war on Southeast Asia made it abundantly clear to Nixon and the military-industrial complex that they needed cash – and lots of it, and having already burned through the national gold supply and generated a financial crisis of confidence the switch to a fiat currency was a welcome, if extremely short-sighted maneuver. Since 1971 the US Dollar has depreciated at an annual rate of 10% relative to gold.

> Before 1971, the introduction of $1 new debt used to increase the GDP by as much as $3 or more. Since 1971, this ratio started its precipitous decline that has continued to this day without interruption. It went negative in 2006, forecasting the financial crisis that broke a year later. The reason for the decline is that irredeemable debt causes capital destruction. It adds nothing to the per capita quota of capital invested in aid of production. Indeed, it may take away from it. As it displaces real capital, which represents the deployment of more and better tools, productivity declines. The laws of physics, unlike human beings, cannot be conned. Irredeemable debt may only create make-belief capital.
>
> By confusing capital and credit, Friedmanite economics obliterates truth. It makes the cost of running the merry-go-round of debt-breeding disappear. It makes capital destruction invisible. The stock of accumulated capital supporting world production, large as it may be, is not

inexhaustible. When it is exhausted, the music stops and the merry-go-round comes to a screechy halt. It does not happen everywhere all at the same time, but it will happen everywhere sooner or later.[3]

Modern money has lost the connection to finite physical substance becoming a fiat currency that can be produced without limit. Since governments control the supply of official currency through a legal monopoly, and since the currency has no backing by gold or silver or any other finite substance, the temptation to create more money for the government to spend is enormous and *always* abused. Fiat currency creates speculative bubbles that are inevitably followed by crashes or economic recessions. The unlimited money supply is its own problem and its own solution, because adding more money to the economy in the right places and at the right time can give the economy a boost and potentially lessen the impact of a recession. In this process the economy rises and falls like a roller-coaster over the decades but one trend increases consistently and that's inflation, because the loans used to fund new money are not repaid. Indeed they cannot be repaid because our money is debt, and the debt is money.

This system of fiat currency that we are all forced to interact with is also one of irredeemable debt. The money supply is the debt, and the more debt issued the more money can be injected into the economy. Not only that but since interest is being paid on all of this debt it means that the money supply must keep expanding in order to meet the need for more and more funding to pay for it all. And since none of this money is backed by anything of value, not gold, not silver, not even copper, nothing but pure perception, this monetary system is inherently inflationary. Inflation will inevitably ruin the value of our artificial absurdity called fiat currency. The U.S. Dollar and all other fiat currencies are simply *fictional* capital.

> And since almost every dollar in existence was created out of thin air at the instant someone borrowed from a bank

Nihilism

(as that is the bizarre kind of economy that we have in the United States), every one of these borrowers was then obligated to pay back more than was borrowed, and all that interest compounds and compounds, which means that the money supply must keep growing in a geometric fashion forever, too, compounding and compounding.[4]

The Almighty Dollar

In the post-World War II era the United States with its almighty Dollar has dominated the world economy and acted as the currency of choice for savings and investment. This system is known as Dollar hegemony and it has conferred significant benefits to the United States both economically and politically, but turmoil and uneven gains to the rest of the world. Succinctly, the producing countries sell their products to the largest market in the world, the U.S.A., and in return they have to take Dollars as payment, yet the U.S. government can produce as many Dollars as they desire thereby keeping prices low and sending inflation back overseas. However, in order to keep the Dollar hegemony scheme in operation the United States has to continually create new capital or otherwise entice back home the Dollars sent overseas. Creating new money is relatively easy but it comes with a steep price, bringing the Dollars back to the U.S. is less painful but it requires interest bearing loans called Treasury bills.

How the Great American Money Scam Works

The simplest way to manufacture more money is to print it and distribute it throughout the economy. This method is easy but also the most inflationary. The typical method is to sell bonds i.e. loans to the government in the form of Treasury bills. The cash from these sales is then distributed in various ways throughout the economy, deposited in banks, spent on building roads, spent on war, etc. By using bonds to create money the overall supply is closer to a balance and thus less prone to inflation. However the word 'bond' in this case is very misleading because federal debt is not like a car or home loan that is steadily being repaid interest and principle. Only the interest on the debt is ever paid back and the more debt the more interest. And since the interest has to be paid no matter what, new money has to be created. Thus this system is not only inherently inflationary but also inflationary at a rapidly escalating pace! So, more loans are issued in order to generate more capital and this new money is then used to pay the interest on the existing loans. This is the definition of a check kiting scheme and it is of course illegal, except when government does it.

As long as someone is willing to trade his or her cash for another loan paying a small amount of interest then the scheme continues, at least until hyperinflation sets in and everyone has to use a wheelbarrow full of 1,000,000 notes to buy a loaf of bread.

> Treasury bonds, contrary to appearances, are no more redeemable than Federal Reserve notes. It's all very neat: the notes are backed by the bonds, and the bonds are redeemable by the notes. Therefore each is valued in terms of itself, rather than by an independent outside asset. Each is an irredeemable liability of the US government. The whole scheme boils down to a farce. It is check-kiting at the highest level.
>
> At maturity the bonds are replaced by another with a more distant maturity date, or they are ostensibly paid in the form of irredeemable currency. The issuer of either type of debt is usurping a privilege without accepting the countervailing duty. They issue obligations without taking any further responsibility for their fate or for the effect they have on the economy. Moreover, a double standard of justice is involved. Check-kiting is a crime under the Criminal Code. That is, provided that it is perpetrated by private individuals. Practiced at the highest level, check-kiting is the corner-stone of the monetary system.[3]

In the United States the Federal Reserve is specifically charged with maintaining the stability and integrity of the national money supply. In practice this requires keeping inflation low and interest rates high enough to promote savings but not so high as to stifle growth by making loans for new development too expensive. The Chairman of the Federal Reserve is supposed to be an independent and objective force for carefully managing the financial integrity of the national money supply. Yet from 1987-2006 the powerful and (once) highly revered Fed Chairman Alan Greenspan didn't do any of these things. Instead Greenspan worked hand in glove with the political establishment to fulfill patently political objectives, abusing the monetary system like it was a giant campaign donation fund while printing money to bail out the super-rich who made terrible investment decisions. His policy of monetary inflation has made the rich richer, the poor poorer and the economic order far less stable. Following Greenspan's disastrous lead, central Banks across the world, fearing the collapse of their own fiat currency scams, are in the process of selling massive hordes of their gold to buy up paper currency! If ever there was an insane investment that would qualify. But they need to keep the price of gold low in relation to their money otherwise gold will become an attractive alternative and they will lose the central bank luxury of printing new cash at will. So now our national currencies are competing in a race to reach the bottom in value.

> Fed policy is creating widespread economic distortions. By re-inflating the economy to rescue banks and housing markets, the Fed is making the public liable for mistakes it did not make and pay for the gains reaped by speculators and debt holders. Private gains from speculative booms remain private, while the Fed passes on private losses to the public. The homeless, eating much less, are paying for bolstering the value of homeowners' asset.

> Indeed, inflation is known to impose a heavy tax on cash balances and incomes in favor of debt holders be they government or private. The higher is inflation, the higher the tax burden imposed by the Fed. As inflation accelerates and the dollar depreciates, real incomes fall; consequently, vulnerable people in many countries can afford less food and the basic amenities of life.[5]

Freydis

The Problem of Inflation

Massive inflation of the money supply coupled with deregulation of markets has turned the world economy into a casino where the rich and the ultra-rich spend billions of dollars in a frenzy of speculative investment searching for a profit in the latest economic bubble and buying controlling stakes in national assets formerly considered to be public goods protected from speculation and private ownership, like housing, water, power, and transportation infrastructure.

Inflation doesn't harm the rich, they don't worry about having enough money to buy food, they're concerned about the hedge fund going bust that they have $500 million parked in, so they do all they can to prop up the stock market and give the middle finger to middle America (and the rest of the world too). Indeed the wealthy actually enjoy inflation, at least in moderation, especially when it's channeled into the price of assets like property, stocks, and commodities. The rich benefit from inflation because it makes them even richer but everyone middle class, or with even less money suffers, particulary when inflation moves into commodity prices and consumer products as this makes buying the daily necessities, like food and fuel, increasingly difficult. Business and industry owners also enjoy inflation just as long as it doesn't translate into higher wages for employees.

After inflating assets for decades the rapidly growing surplus of money has finally begun to affect the prices of consumer products. Inflation reaching average consumers has hit extraordinary levels as I write this in May 2008, in one year oil prices have doubled, gasoline prices have increased nearly 40 percent, heating oil 90 percent, egg prices have jumped 40 percent, corn 72 percent and flour has risen 50 percent just since January! Fertilizer prices have soared with phosphate up 200% in 2007 and potash 100%, the important industrial chemical sulfur has increased in price *1000%* in just a year, and primary and precious metals have all jumped in cost; basically every major commodity has risen in price feeding into even greater cost increases in every finished product. And this is only the beginning.

Nihilism

Measuring Inflation in the Money Supply

Measuring the total money supply in order to gauge the scale and pace of inflation has been fairly simple using the measure called M3, however since 2006 the Federal Reserve discontinued tracking of M3 (surprised?) making this task more difficult. Another measurement called MZM (Money of Zero Maturity) tracks growth in the money supply as a close proxy for M3 and can be viewed at the St. Louis Federal Reserve website. Recent expansion of the total money supply is stunning; the 5 year MZM chart is nearly vertical during the first four months of 2008 and has increased by an incredible 1.3 *trillion* dollars between May 2007 and May 2008!

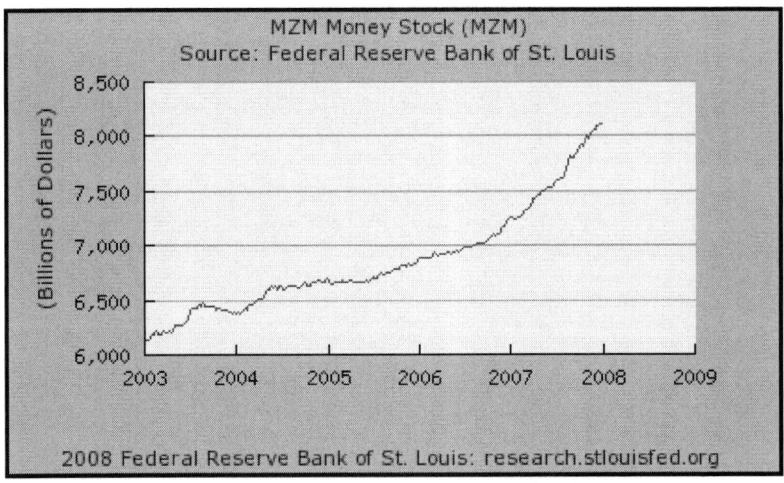

Another measurement tool of more practical application to the consumer for tracking inflation, and thus the continual devaluation of the Dollar currency, is available at the Minneapolis Fed's website, it calculates the value of the Dollar for any given year based on CPI. But, as you'll learn in a moment, CPI understates the actual scale of inflation eating away at the value of the Dollar.

As a side note, for about a decade the U.S. government has been redesigning the Dollar for the official purposes of making the paper currency more difficult to counterfeit. Yet no private counterfeiter in the world can compete with the federal government expanding its own money supply by billions of dollars every day! The threat from counterfeiting pales in comparison to the inflationary damage the government is inflicting on its money. It seems to me that the currency redesigns have much less to do with defeating counterfeiters than acting as a covert method of pumping more cash into the economy. After all, they never recall the old money, both the new and the old are legal tender and where's the need to redesign the $10 and $5 bill? Who's going to counterfeit a $5 bill, I mean really?!

> "Charles Ponzi was deemed an unprincipled conman to insulate unregulated capitalism itself from being revealed as a systemic Ponzi scheme." – Henry C K Liu

Mismanage an economy badly enough and you get not just creeping inflation but *hyperinflation*. The African country of Zimbabwe is experiencing hyperinflation thanks to the foolish economic guidance of tyrant Robert Mugabe. The official inflation rate is over 1,000,000%, and a loaf of bread costs 200 million Zimbabwe dollars, enough to buy 12 new cars ten years ago.

The Official Statistics are Bogus

The Federal government intentionally hides the true scale of inflation for several reasons, obviously because they're the cause of it, second because it raises prices and that's highly unpopular, and third because higher inflation means that the federal government has to pay more for all inflation indexed outlays such as Social Security for retirees.

Official government statistics are manipulated in order to put the spin on the numbers that the political establishment wants the public to receive. Some statistics are conveniently left out, many key statistics are just buried in the data dump and ignored by the financial mass-media, and some are corrupted through outright fraud. For example the official rate of economic growth in the U.S. is positive, currently a very anemic amount of less than one percent. But to get the real rate of growth you have to subtract inflation, so in reality the national economy is actually shrinking in size! Similarly the official Federal Reserve determined interest rate is positive, a few percent, but the real interest rate is actually negative because inflation has to be factored in. So the government is actually paying banks to take loans and the national economy is still declining! The Consumer Price Index (CPI) is supposed to measure inflation affecting consumers by tracking price changes for household products. But CPI is notoriously bogus because it removes the most inflationary elements as officials claim the numbers are too 'volatile' or 'cyclical'.

> In other words, when prices of basic food commodities, including bread and butter so necessary for children, triple or quadruple, this causes no concern to the Fed, because they are not part of core inflation. However, when toys prices go up by 10%, they may become of some concern to the Fed, signaling that core inflation is rising! But with workers struggling to put food on table, they are less concerned with buying toys. Hence, toy prices may never increase, core inflation may not rise, and the Fed may never respond to racing energy and food prices.[8]

Unemployment numbers are highly questionable as well. The official US unemployment rate is about 5% but honest assessments place it closer to 12%. The demographic and regional unemployment rates vary greatly throughout the country, anyone that has been unemployed for awhile or has to take a part time job or take a pay cut doesn't get counted, the massive prison population is excluded from unemployment statistics, and the official numbers still don't characterize how many people actually earn a living wage.

Worker productivity statistics prop up another capitalist canard, that greater worker productivity (the amount of output per hour of work) creates higher living standards for workers. The cruel corollary implies that if your living standards don't increase then you have to work harder for longer hours in order to make it happen. Yet U.S. living standards have been falling for at least 30 years while at the same time worker productivity has been rapidly increasing. In fact the connection between effort and gain only holds if production actually benefits the people doing all the work! It's clear that what's really happening is that people are working harder for longer hours and still experiencing a very tangible decline in living standards just so that a tiny oligarchy can become even wealthier at an ever quickening pace. "According to the US Census Bureau, the median US Household income fell by $1,043 from 1999 through 2006, the last year for which figures are available. Labor Department statistics suggests that real wages have fallen a further 2.4 percent in the past year alone."[13] So why does anyone continue to support an establishment that, unless you are already fabulously wealthy, guarantees that you will be poorer a few years from now?! The simplest rule of macroeconomics is the first one ignored in a corporate-friendly political environment: wages are directly proportionally to genuine economic growth. Workers with less income spend less and economic decline invariably ensues, while greater wages deliver greater prosperity.

The view that official statistics present is the attitude of those with wealth and political power. Information like unemployment statistics need only affirm that most everyone has some kind of job that keeps them tired, occupied, and paying taxes so they aren't out protesting or otherwise causing trouble for authorities. Palpable problems that should be numerically represented, such as inadequate wages, a rapidly escalating cost of living, and socially destabilizing income disparities between executives and general employees, are simply irrelevant to the billionaires and their sycophantic policy-makers.

The 'Free-Market' is a Myth (and the Casino is Rigged)

Proponents of a laissez-faire economic system like to claim the 'free-market' is a natural evolutionary product, a result of the strong triumphing over the weak, but in reality it's merely a self-justifying morality as short-sighted as it is contrived. In the same mindset notorious Enron con-artist Jeffrey Skilling looked at Richard

Dawkins' book The Selfish Gene and conveniently misinterpreted it as a biological justification for greed and anti-social selfish behavior!

> Yet survival of the fittest among the animal kingdom is practiced only between species, while intra-specie cooperation is the general law. The symbiotic interdependence of different species is well recognized in all ecological systems. Moreover, the laissez-faire market system is far from a natural phenomenon, but a contrived mechanism with the purpose of reconciling individual pursuit of self interest with the welfare of society.[10]

The very existence of a central bank in the guise of the Federal Reserve blatantly contradicts the supposed existence of a free-market. No such thing as a free-market really exists and indeed economic regulation of at least minimal form are both necessary and unavoidable. The US Treasury and the Federal Reserve are continually intervening in the marketplace to prevent crashes, for instance through the covert Plunge Protection Team (PPT), to boost the appeal of the national currency (by suppressing the price of gold for instance), to support political agendas, and even to aid political campaigns through market manipulation! Not to mention extensive financial manipulation on an international scale aimed at achieving foreign policy objectives favorable to the New York and Washington DC establishment.

Very large banks and corporations operate on the assumption that they are Too Big To Fail (TBTF) and will receive a government bailout if they ever get into serious financial trouble because their collapse would simply be too devastating to the national economy. Not only does this secret insurance create an unfair business advantage it also injects a very dangerous hazard into the marketplace by tempting the TBTF into reckless behavior. On Friday March 14, 2008 the Federal Reserve made the unprecedented decision to directly fund JP Morgan Chase bank's purchase of the insolvent Bear Stearns investment company to keep them from collapsing after incurring billions of dollars in losses on bad investments. Founded in 1923 Bear Sterns was the fifth largest investment bank in the U.S. and the U.S. Securities and Exchange Commission (SEC), undoubtedly knowing otherwise, claimed the company was "well-capitalized" right up until the moment it (surprise) wasn't!

> Capital can cross national borders to where cost and wages are lowest, but workers cannot go where wages are highest because of immigration restrictions. The net effect is global wage stagnation in the midst of spectacular multinational corporate profits that results in global overcapacity. [...]
>
> [F]ree markets require sophisticated, complex and dynamic regulations to restrict the ability of market participants to manipulate prices through monopolistic practices, rendering highly problematic the literal meaning of an unregulated free market. Totally free markets tend to end in market failures. This is particularly true in money markets as finance is infinitely more pliant that physical goods. [...]
>
> [M]arket participants seldom act with equal information or full understanding of the effects of their actions. Market fundamentalism is a theory that suggests the right path to a watering hole can best be found by blind men pulling at different directions for uncoordinated reasons. The fundamental problem with market fundamentalism is the ability of market participants to maximize advantage by externalizing cost or penalties outside of the market onto the real economy. Free markets require regulation to remain free.[17]

Exploding the free-market myth has enormous consequences since it forms the foundation of modern economics. Maintaining the lie means that the people cannot adequately prepare or respond to events and the elite cabal of insiders can exploit the national treasury to manipulate the financial markets behind the curtain like malevolent magicians.

Nihilism

In addition to creating a privileged class, the manipulation also has little democratic legitimacy in the sense that the citizenry has not given its consent. This has tangible ramifications. By not informing the public, successive U.S. administrations have employed a dangerous policy response that is subject to the worst possible abuse. In this regard, the line between national necessity and political expediency has no doubt been perilously blurred.[6]

We need to drop this erroneous myth of a free market and start calling things as they really are, not what some wish them to be.

Welcome to the Debt Trap

Having established a fiat currency system based on irredeemable public debt the working class public have had little choice but to follow the lead of officials and structure their own finances upon debt and private loans, racking up more and more as the national currency inflates and the purchasing power diminishes.

> Households are simply not saving anything. Real average weekly earnings of production and non-supervisory workers - over 75% of all us payrolls - have been stagnant since the mid 1970s. If we use 2005 dollars and the CPI-U (consumer price index for urban consumers), average weekly earnings decreased by about $1 per week over the 30-year interval 1975-2005. The folks have thus stopped saving and have taken on massive amounts of housing and consumer debt.

> A look through the Federal Reserve's Flow of Funds Accounts of the United States, or Z1, released in September 19, is a traumatic experience. It reveals the contours of America's debt disaster in stark statistics that grow worse with each passing quarter. In 1999, total outstanding household debt was $6.4 trillion. As of the end of the second quarter of 2006 total outstanding household debt was $12.3 trillion.

Household debt has increased by almost as much since 1999 as the sum total of all debt accumulated by all households across the preceding 220-year history of the US. In 1999, household mortgage debt stood at $4.4 trillion. At the close of the second quarter of 2006 it had more than doubled to $9.33 trillion. In 1999, consumer credit outstanding was measured at $1.6 trillion.[7]

A commonly held and erroneous belief, particularly prevalent in the United States, is that 'if you're not rich yet then it's your own fault, so shut-up and work harder'. Yet the capricious cruelties of debt and finance within the capitalist structure  contradict this perception on a daily basis. This situation of rising personal debt and declining income eventually leads to a debt trap where obligations exceed assets and income, and the only recourse is bankruptcy. Until then delusions remain an ever popular alternative to facing a bleak but correctable reality. Widely held assumptions also aid in this process of passive oppression.

In the United States, despite productivity gains of 44.5 percent, no improvement in wages occurred for most workers between 1979 and 1998. Similarly, the median male wage in 2000 was below the level in 1979![18]

Capitalist authority's best defense against popular insurrection continues to be the lottery, successfully preying upon the average human mind's incapacity to comprehend large numbers, to generate an illusionary incentive to participate within an exploitative economic system with the vain hope that great wealth can easily be achieved by anyone! The lottery sates the greed need without any fundamental shift in wealth or progressive changes to society; it's a marvel of social-engineering through psychology. The multi-million dollar lottery is probably the ultimate tool for pacifying the public's materialistic desires - it is the state's insurance against revolution.

Never forget: debt is pure fiction. Monetary debt is an artificial value that can be abused by tyrants for brutal exploitation, just as it can be instantly deleted with the push of a button, or the stroke of a pen.

Widespread Institutional Failure

Accounting companies play an important role in maintaining the integrity of the economy by producing accurate and trustworthy financial records, yet since the Enron scandal all of the major U.S. public accounting firms such as Arthur Andersen, KPMG, and PricewaterhouseCoopers, have been involved in fraud and/or negligence by actively supporting, or failing to reveal, billions of dollars in falsified financial reports and bogus accounting practices on the part of their corporate clients. Even within the boundaries of the law, thoroughly skewed to favor private wealth, corporate accounting has become so rife with deception and fraud that U.S. companies can now, after a successful lobbying campaign, claim *losses* on debt as *gains* in revenue! Bear Sterns for instance legally claimed a $305 million profit using this accounting trick in February 2008 and then promptly melted down the next month.[11]

Arcane formulas for repackaging paper assets to yield quick profits proliferate as the money supply is inflated and regulations are cut, making the true value of debt and equity increasingly difficult to discern. In this situation reliable ratings become crucial for sustaining the international casino economy. Rating agencies are entrusted with making accurate and reliable determinations on the quality and integrity of corporations, stocks, bonds, and even governments. Yet trust placed in them has been ruined by the collapse of the repackaged debt market. Investments that the ratings agencies claimed to be rock-solid safe and low risk have turned out to be *worthless*, leading to billions and billions of dollars in losses for banks and investment companies around the world. In the US, and by extension the world economy, Standard & Poor's, Moody's, and Fimalac's Fitch Ratings together control 98 percent of the market. Besides having monopolistic control, largely due to the negligence of US government regulators, they also operate under an inherent conflict of interest by taking payment from the companies whose debt they analyze. All of them incorrectly rated subprime mortgage debt, generating more than $400 billion of market losses since the scam started disintegrating in 2007.[9] S&P gave Orange County California an AA-rating right before the county filed for the largest-ever municipal bankruptcy. Enron had investment-grade stamps of approval from S&P, Moody's and Fitch until four days before they filed for, what was then, the biggest US bankruptcy. S&P, Moody's, and Fitch graded Lehman debt A-1 the day it filed for bankruptcy,[16] a collapse ultimately calculated to be *$639 billion*. Far from being disbanded, or even officially reprimanded, corrupt ratings corporations continue to grade debt for the multitude of federal schemes designed to rescue private corporations using public wealth.

Official agencies tasked with oversight of the marketplace, such as the Securities and Exchange Commission (SEC) in the U.S., have facilitated systemic collapse through inaction and outright corruption. Called the largest Ponzi scheme in history, in December 2008 Bernard Madoff, former chairman of the NASDAQ stock exchange and treasurer of the American Jewish Congress, was arrested for perpetrating an estimated $65,000,000,000 swindle on investors. Besides neatly typifying the inane avarice of contemporary finance-capitalism, Madoff is just one of many egregious examples of the SEC completely failing to do its official job – protecting fairness and integrity in the national financial system.

> Madoff admitted that he did not know how to properly record a credit default swap. He said he called a number of major banks, and none of them knew either. They had just been keeping their transactions off their official records. Madoff said that "today, lots of trades are done off the books because people don't know what to do with them."[19]

Nihilism

Not only did the SEC fail to address specific allegations sent to them regarding Madoff's scheme going back to at least 1999, but a former SEC attorney named Eric Swanson is married to Madoff's niece and was part of a team tasked with investigating Madoff in 1999 and 2004; both instances resulted in no action. Not only that, but the U.S. attorney general Michael Mukasey had to remove himself from the criminal investigation due to a conflict of interest.[14] In an ironic twist, since Madoff is Jewish, just like Attorney General Mukasey and like the majority of hedge-fund money-magicians, his enterprise was granted millions of dollars from Jewish charities through personal connections. The spectacular collapse of Madoff's swindle not only further undermines a rickety economic system but will also impair worldwide Zionist machinations.[15]

"People lost money because they had faith in government." – Harry Markopolos,
speaking to the House Financial Services subcommittee about the SEC colluding with Madoff, February 2009.

These problems aren't limited to just the United States. In January 2009 we were treated to the scandal dubbed 'India's Enron'. The Indian company Satyam, a multi-national business empire built on job outsourcing to low-wage locations, was using fictional accounting and claiming at least a billion dollars in cash that did not exist, among other things. Adding irony to fraud the name *Satyam* is from *satya* meaning 'truth' in Sanskrit, and yet this was a mainstream and respected operation that even earned multiple awards. Byrraju Ramalinga Raju, the CEO, won the Ernst & Young 2007 entrepreneur of the year award, and in 2008 one for excellence in corporate governance from the London-based World Council for Corporate Governance. Even more pathetic, Satyam's accounting was being managed by PricewaterhouseCoopers – how did they miss a billion dollar discrepancy, *again?*

The rot and corruption pervading the world financial system goes all the way to the very top. The Bank for International Settlements (BIS) in Switzerland, the central bank for all the other central banks of the world, embraced the popular foolishness of irredeemable fiat currency in 2003, abandoning gold as a monetary basis and eliminating the final source capable of providing real capital to stop a global credit crash. This is capitalism without any capital!

> The banks no longer trust each other. Last August, as mortgage-backed securities unraveled, finances froze up worldwide. Why? Because the banks knew how much undisclosed junk they had on their own books. Who could say what the next fellow had? Overnight lending between banks—the process that ensures that every bank has funds when it needs them—fell apart. This is a very big deal.
>
> Since August [2007], America's big banks have been wards of the Fed, and those in Europe equally so of the Bank of England and the European Central Bank. The system survives because central banks keep the lending windows open, and the result is that—except for one instance in Britain— the public has not pulled out of the banks. Let's be clear. The private financial markets did actually fail. It's only the fact that the public trusts government that keeps the system from dissolving in panic.[12]

Our fraudulent monetary system indicts nearly every institution and pillar of society – the universities teaching bogus theory, the elected leaders making foolish and near-sighted decisions based on conveniently selective interpretations of economics, the legal system upholding the scam, and of course the commercial mass-media for failing to do any critical analysis or skeptical inquiry despite the obvious failings engulfing us all.

> The captains of the banking system in effect deny and defy that basic law. They are leading a blind crowd of mesmerized people to the brink where momentum may sweep most of them into the abyss to their financial destruction. Yet not one university in the world has issued a warning, and not one court of justice allowed indictments

Nihilism

to be heard from individuals and institutions charging that the issuance of irredeemable debt is a crude form of fraud, calling for the punishment of the swindlers issuing it, whether they are in the Treasury or in the central bank. The behavior of universities and courts in this regard could not be more reprehensible. Rather than acting to protect the weak, they act to cover up plundering by the mighty.[3]

Widespread institutional failure doesn't merely describe contemporary finance it aptly describes every other element of society as well. Economic turmoil is just one symptom of a much deeper and more severe illness. When large corporations are on the verge of bankruptcy they tell the world they're more financially sound than ever, and as major recession looms and consumer prices soar governments and establishment stooges proudly proclaim everything to be sunshine and rainbows. But now more than ever it's clear to objective and honest observers that we live in a hollow artificial world based on lies and manufactured from theft that can only be sustained though a concerted campaign of deception and subterfuge.

The Beginning of the End

By October 2008 prices and world markets are being wildly distorted as financial institutions make increasingly desperate speculative bets in the casino economy, trying to recover from enormous losses by 'doubling-down' on market gambles. Government intervention has expanded to include virtually every aspect of the economy including buying stocks to sustain the stock market and providing massive loans to banks and major corporations at low interest rates while trading the worthless paper collateral of financial institutions for taxpayer money in the 'trash for cash' scheme. Widespread reactionary government intervention is further distorting markets by removing the constraints of supply and demand and preventing broken companies and institutions from going bankrupt. Stock markets are rising while consumer confidence plunges to record lows. Home prices throughout the U.S. continue to fall – a situation previously considered impossible for any length of time. Precious metal prices on traded paper are falling but physical supplies are quickly vanishing in the face of massive demand! U.S. banks are racing to get cheap loans from the Federal Reserve so they can buy up rivals and eliminate competition.

Public Pain for Private Gain

Everything that political authorities and establishment economists have been preaching to us on how our economy is supposed to operate, on the importance of the free market and free-trade, it's all been completely inverted or discarded without a second thought or official explanation! Now this scam of epic proportions has nothing left to hide behind and all the values that sustained it have turned out to be lies and illusions. And yet authorities still try to perpetuate the same system as if it only needs a few minor repairs and it's back to business as usual! What kind of economic system crashes every ten years (1987, 1997, and 2007) and has to be bailed out by the government?

> "Is it the end of capitalism? It seems to say it's a loss of belief in the things we claimed to have believed in."
> – Robert Brusca, economist, Fall 2008.

Ever greater wealth is being concentrated into fewer and fewer hands. It's apparent that regardless of what establishment economists and similar pseudo-experts claim the only purpose of this system is to take money from the public and convert it into private profit with the direct result being increasing poverty, unemployment, and government funding cuts for everything that doesn't assist this process. Authorities behind this scam will do whatever it takes and say whatever they have to in order to perpetuate it. The bankers, the billionaires, the central banks, the presidents, and the prime ministers, they're all doing everything they can to keep the political and economic power structure exactly the same and they'll spend any amount of national treasure and change any laws in order to do it. They may disagree on the methods but the ultimate aspiration is the same.

Nihilism

Nonetheless it's clear to honest observers that the world economy is in a serious state of decline and genuine recovery is unlikely any time soon. Indeed the current situation is unusually grim with major banks and financial institutions failing and central banks in Europe and the USA pumping billions of dollars into the economy every day desperately trying to keep their world afloat and prevent a credit crash. We've entered a new Great Depression. With food and fuel prices skyrocketing riots over inflation and high prices are breaking out all over the globe. Governments are feeling the heat and millions are going hungry while wealthy speculators reap billions in profits from the turmoil.

Throughout North America and Europe banking and corporate rulers are using all of their financial, political, and media influence to compel their stooges in power to divert billions of public dollars into the sweaty hands of big business, using the pretext of budget deficits to force 'austerity measures' on the people. This is a familiar maneuver perpetrated for decades upon national victims throughout South and Central America by the notorious IMF and World Bank, leaving the wreckage of poverty and wage-slavery in their wake. As government goons, sold-out union bosses, and a disingenuous mass-media betray them, the people are rapidly realizing that these so-called austerity measures don't apply to actual causes of broken budgets, like massive bank bailouts and endless wars.

The ultra-rich aren't going to suffer in a national bankruptcy, they'll profit from it by buying public assets to turn a private profit. Then we'll be subservient not to a government that at least has to feign the trappings of democracy and at least make the attempt to receive public criticism, but to a new clique of tyrants unaccountable to anyone and who justify their authority simply by having more money than most everyone else! Yet, *it doesn't have to be this way.* Much of the trouble stem from the fact that those holding the greatest degree of economic power or influence are not held accountable for their actions and decisions. Social responsibility is not in proportion to the scale of personal wealth and the disproportionate influence that it confers upon the rich within capitalist society. We desperately need to call things what they really are, and we need political and economic transparency. Meanwhile, charlatan leaders in economics and supposed 'experts' are treated like gods or mystics that shouldn't be questioned or criticized.

When the people can no longer afford food and gasoline *then* they will start to care about these things even if they aren't able to understand what's happening or who's really responsible. And as the people of the West are increasingly impoverished and exploited through fraudulent austerity measures and the liquidation of public assets for private gain, the financial ruling class only hastens their own demise by triggering fires of rage that will coalesce into an uncontrollable inferno, consuming them in the flames of revolution.

In order to tactically rectify the current macroeconomic situation, where supply exceeds demand, political authorities can either allow asset prices to fall or they can raise wages so that the working public can afford to buy. However in this debt-based economy if asset prices decline it will lead to corporate bankruptcies, but if asset prices are boosted through market intervention it will inevitably lead to major economic distortion and hyperinflation. The political leadership has decided to use taxpayer wealth for reinflating the debt-based asset bubble when it should be used to raise wages, employment, and quality of life. The decision of the political leadership to support asset prices for near-term gain indicates the interests they truly serve, just as it will invariably lead to macroeconomic collapse and widespread social turmoil.

The Problem of Capitalism

The established capitalist economic order is collapsing around us, even as authorities do everything they can to prolong a hopelessly broken system and to prevent any alteration in the status quo or (heaven forbid) a redistribution of resources. But an economic collapse won't fix what is broken, nor will it resolve the root of the problem. Unless the root values, beliefs, and assumptions are revaluated and rectified another economic order will be reconstructed within the same diseased environment, perpetuating the same injustice and hypocrisy.

Nihilism

History has shown that money is just as inescapable as authority, so the issue is not the tools and technology but the values driving the minds using the tools. The trouble results from the meaning and the representation ascribed to the symbols – the moral interpretations. *The problem of capitalism is the belief in money as a social savior and as a valid solution to human problems.* Indeed, it's painfully clear amid widespread damage to the natural environment and similar socially unstable practices that establishment capitalism doesn't encompass the full consequences of cause and effect. Establishment capitalism narrowly proscribes the boundaries of causality to concoct a convenient ideological view of events that fails to factor in the future costs and consequences of actions and decisions.

The politico-economic order cannot be saved, but it can be replaced

We have to envision a radical departure leading to a superior alternative but the landscape of contemporary economic thought is being monopolized by outdated ideologies and dominated by the dead gods and false saviors of debt-based economics, such as John Maynard Keynes. Our economic order has failed because it was built on fictional wealth and flawed assumptions instead of factual evidence and real resources, because the unchallenged gods of economics sold us convenient fictions like the belief that people with the most money are more valuable than those that have less, and that in a free market money only goes to those that earn it or deserve it most. Today the chosen few that possess the most money define morality, *but their days are numbered and their time remaining is very short.*

The decay of establishment capitalism and widespread economic disorder provide us with an unparalleled opportunity, one not seen in nearly 100 years. Now we have a chance to separate money from political influence, to demolish the money morality where right and wrong are determined by the quantity and possession of cash, and to overthrow the gods and usurp the beliefs that support this fraudulent and failed order that denigrates everything that doesn't have a price tag on it. It's imperative that we *demolish* the power structure that sustains the ultra-rich and allows them to function with impunity regardless of the state of the economy. We have to *undermine* the American culture that admires and adulates the wealthy largely based upon the mistaken belief that they can become super-rich too.

Consider these things now and prepare to act because I can hear the sound of rioting getting louder and I can see the glow of fires in the street getting brighter.

Solution

Over a period of decades we've been socially debased and economically colonized without most even realizing it. Millions of families have been turned into serfs, tied to a little plot of land with their house on it that they bought from the bank, because property prices have fallen so far they can't even sell it to move and get a job somewhere else! Yet even as unemployment increases amidst the wreckage of widespread economic failure, we shouldn't miss the fact that in the developed world we already have everything we need to succeed, both collectively and individually. We have smart and educated people, a multitude of natural resources, powerful tools and technology, and plenty of capital. The underlying problem is not a lack of resources, rather it's simply that we aren't using what we have effectively, or at all, mostly because it's locked-up out of reach of the many for the benefit of the few.

Remember: when you become jobless and hungry, it's not the end of the world for the billionaires (who've never had it better); it's just the end of world for <u>you</u>. So, what are you going to do about it – go down alone, or get organized?

A few hundred years ago the people of North America were colonized too, then by monarchal England. The King had a choice: he could spend a sufficient amount of money to build up America in infrastructure and social capital so the citizens would support him and his country, or he could spend little to nothing and extract as much in treasure and resources as possible while risking the wrath of an exploited people. Given the greed and arrogance characteristic of royalty in general, the King, of course, chose the path of maximum short-term gain. As a result colonial Americans had to take care of themselves, and eventually they simply didn't need England, the King, or his taxes. And although the King didn't give up control without a fight, we all know which side won the war.

Working people around the world, from Buenos Aires Argentina and Guangzhou China to Los Angeles California, and everywhere in between, are colonized and exploited in the same way, but this time it's not by a king, it's by an elitist clique of international billionaires and the institutions they've established to serve their interests, like the World Trade Organization (WTO) and the International Monetary Fund (IMF), that exclude the needs of billions of people being directly affected. Now, unless we choose to be slaves to the capital of billionaires, we must learn to take care of ourselves and those around us – not because government can't, or shouldn't, take care of its people with social programs, education, health care, and employment, but because the ones in charge refuse. If the government won't support the people then the people won't support the government.

The first step to rectify this situation is to radically revaluate and revise the broken values that define the politico-economic structures distributing our resources. In this regard we have no shortage of alternative plans, yet no matter how noble the intentions of the proponents or how appealing the plans may seem we must test before implementation in order to accurately verify that the plan actually functions as promised! Indeed, it's crucial that we implement an open process of scientific verification as an established methodology throughout the economic and political realm. In this regard ideology and beliefs must be discarded because they only impede the necessary process of impartial testing and verification.
As the myths of money begin to fall away, such as the belief that you have to have dollars to be someone and that only the rich are important, a whole new realm of opportunities is opened for novel ideas and the participation of people previously excluded. Alternatives to hierarchical capitalism already exist and are increasingly popular. Community currencies are popping up all over, particularly in places that are Dollar poor but labor rich. Other capital alternatives are only

limited by human imagination and effort, take for example the community tool library in Portland Oregon – why buy a tool if you only need to use it a few times?

Indeed, solutions to our crisis of massively broken debt-based casino-capitalism already exists in nascent form. For the first time in history we have everything we need to seize control of capital from the bankers and billionaires and to finally place it under the control of the rightful owners – the people who work every day to produce it. We don't need Marx or Mussolini, financial 'experts' or ideology, all we basically need is an impartial network for sharing capital (Internet) built on a set of clear and simple, fairly-enforced rules that everyone can follow. A universal network of peer-peer direct lending will form the basis for the radically different financial architecture of the 21st century, flattening the authority-pyramid and forming a natural balance of power.

When the truth becomes unpatriotic national disaster soon follows.
– Freydis

Nihilism

THE MADNESS OF A MERETRICIOUS MILITARY

The historical justification for a military is that a nation needs a potent armed defense to counteract aggression from rival nations. Yet even within the boundaries of this outdated and generous conception recent events have aptly demonstrated that a national military out of proportion to valid potential threats becomes a very serious threat on its own. In his final speech as President the former General Dwight Eisenhower warned of America's military-industrial complex growing into an unstoppable and pernicious threat to the freedom and well-being of the country, yet if it was a looming problem in 1961 it's a raging catastrophe over 40 years and trillions of dollars later.

Today western countries have become military-police states that relentlessly monitor and spy on their own citizens, where the only reliable jobs anyone can find are working for the police or the military-industrial complex, where public and even private expression are censored and outlawed using bogus euphemisms like 'hate speech', and where the highest courts are divided on guaranteeing the most elementary of civil and political protections like habeas corpus! Under the Bush-Cheney regime the most outrageous and once unthinkable acts of state brutality and oppression have become commonplace. The highest officials admit to promoting the physical torture of government opponents and this is considered legally acceptable simply by referring to their tyrannical effort as a 'war' and labeling opponents 'terrorists'. Throughout this process America's military institution has been an integral participant.

The military has not worked to protect the Constitution and the well-being of Americans, or anyone else, but has instead violated the Constitution while decimating legal protections and the physical safety of the people. From the gratuitous brutality of Abu Ghraib prison in Iraq to the showcase concentration camp in Guantanamo Bay Cuba, the ongoing civilian slaughter in Iraq and Afghanistan, and yet more that remains hidden from the public eye, the military as an institution is the embodiment of hypocrisy and parasitism, it is a meretricious institution in desperate need of total revaluation.

Useless Defense

The military in contemporary American culture has practically become a holy institution, open criticism of which is taboo for fear of failing to 'support the troops'. Yet anyone that truly cared about the troops would not want them placed in danger of being killed, particularly for a foolish and counterproductive conflict. The truth is that no real problem exists in our modern world that can be solved by the military or military force. Even RAND, a famous think-tank that does research in support of the U.S. military-industrial complex, concludes that the war on terrorism is a failure and that the military cannot solve what is, at worst, an issue for law-enforcement. Military involvement only makes the problem worse.³ NATO cannot win in Afghanistan just as the U.S. can't win in Iraq, or anywhere else, by the use of military force for this very fact. The very act of self-preservation using deadly force inevitably kills innocent civilians, inflaming tensions and creating new enemies until the entire country is outraged against the occupying military and all hope of victory is lost. If the occupation goes on long enough, in defiance of public opinion, the entire region will become inflamed and then you've really got problems. This is exactly what's happening in Afghanistan that's now spreading like a wildfire into nuclear-armed Pakistan, pushing that country into civil war and economic collapse.

For a classic example of the ironic foolishness characteristic of the whole 'War on Terrorism' consider the September 2008 attempted assassination of a former CIA asset in Pakistan by US forces using a pilotless drone aircraft. Instead of killing Jalaluddin Haqqani, who was paid thousands of dollars to fight against the Soviet Union during the 1980s, the *five* missiles instead killed 23 people (including eight children), blatantly violated Pakistan's political sovereignty, and thoroughly inflamed already high regional tensions. This kind of event has CIA written all over it. Mission accomplished![11]

On the topic of blowback, the explosion of illegal immigration and gang-violence roiling the United States is largely a byproduct of disastrous U.S. military and CIA polices used in Central America during the 1980s as part of the Cold War Ideological fight between the U.S. and Soviet empires. Civil wars and insurgencies raged as Central America was flooded with weapons, just as paramilitary forces were trained by the U.S. military and the CIA in assassination and torture, justified as: 'why should we do all the killing and take the blame for it when we can fund proxies to do it for us?' This policy of manufacturing death-squads, now referred to as the 'Salvador Option', is credited to John Negroponte who started out with the CIA's Phoenix Program during the Vietnam War in which some 40,000 Vietnamese were assassinated. Negroponte later resurrected the death-squads as militias in Iraq, greatly enhancing the carnage of an ultra-violent religious civil war, all justified as a classic divide-and-conquer tactic.[12]

Although the actual threat from Soviet forces in Central America was manufactured the aftermath of these civil wars brought very real poverty, corruption, and social destabilization, while crime, drugs, and gangs filled the dual voids of political authority and economic necessity. Now U.S. policies in the region have arrived full-circle back in the United States through massive illegal immigration, gang-warfare, and illegal drugs, although not surprisingly the blame for this crisis is hardly ever apportioned properly. The gang Mara Salvatrucha 13 (MS-13), known for its brutality, is a typical example of this boomerang effect, having fled El Salvador and establishing themselves in Los Angeles California. Today MS-13 has grown so large that it is considered a trans-national threat to the stability of entire countries, with an estimated total size of 50,000 gang members and at least 10,000 in the United States.

Ideology rooted in nationalism and imperialism sponsored the wars, Catholic religious culture that shuns contraceptives and promotes violence-ridden male-dominated societies has generated the overpopulation crisis, decades of exploitative U.S. economic policies have economically and environmentally hollowed-out the region, while the hypocritical 'War on Drugs' has created the economic opportunity, yet America still tries in vain to only solve the symptoms while ignoring the root causes!

The very fact we have international bodies and forums means that for any given international problem we can use dialogue and negotiation instead of military force. These very bodies directly negate the necessity and the very purpose of an offensive military capacity. And for this reason the Bush-Cheney administration has put enormous effort into abrogating international arms treaties and undermining international forums for dialogue, such as the United Nations (UN), and co-opting and hijacking international institutions such as the International Atomic Energy Agency (IAEA) for nuclear non-proliferation.[8] As long as these outlets of dialogue and negotiation exist the military has no validity, and since the United States has overwhelming military superiority, it means that a venal national leadership can't use military force to intimidate and steal at will.

> There is a common starting point to any strategy of both insurgencies and contra-insurgencies. Who has the legitimacy? Now, with the International Court of Justice, the human rights treaties and the progress of liberal democracy, not to torture is not only a need, but an obligation. Winning depends on how you conduct yourself. Could an officer in an extreme case use some degree of physical violence to extract information from a prisoner? No, doing it could hurt the overall political strategy, as it has happened in Iraq. When you mistreat your detainees,

you stimulate their opposition, their hate. – Former Salvadorian guerrilla leader Joaquin Villalobos, May 2004.

Even allowing for the continuation of the outdated relic known as the state an offensive military is counter-productive, and in the USA it's even unconstitutional because only a citizen militia, not a standing army, was ever meant to exist! The United States was established as a Republic to be defended by a citizen militia – never by a permanently staffed career army. That was the idea behind the National Guard (the only military force in the United States that has any Constitutional legitimacy) a part-time citizen militia that is under the control of the State governors and only placed under the control of the President during a national crisis. The reasoning against a full-time military should be clear by now: a standing military is an open invitation for wars of imperial aggression and conflicts for profit and it will eventually lead to a dictatorial president and corrupt Congress. And that's exactly what the United States has today.

"A standing army is one of the greatest mischiefs that can possibly happen." – President James Madison

This all started because of World War II, specifically the fact that the soldiers were not completely demobilized at the end of the conflict as they had been after previous wars. This standing army obviously needed something to do to justify a continued existence hence the Korean War, then Vietnam, and so on. At least during these conflicts most of the soldiers were drafted into service and that put a brake on how far the Executive branch of government could drag the American people

along. Vietnam changed that. Widespread public resistance to a brutal and futile conflict forced a shattered Army with its prestige in tatters to rebuild as an all volunteer force. By only employing volunteers the U.S. military removed the last resistance factor to opportunistic warfare and today the military is just a mercenary corps that refers to the President as their Commander in Chief and will salute, and shoot at, whatever he tells them to kill as long as their paychecks keep coming. Anyone that doesn't agree with this situation will leave and be replaced by someone that won't think as much and is more willing to follow orders without asking questions.

A Record of Failure

The Vietnam fiasco killed an estimated 5,000,000 people, and resulted in an abysmal strategic failure for the United States, yet the same mistakes are repeated thirty years later in Iraq and Afghanistan. It's apparent that the U.S. national leadership is irresponsible, unaccountable, incapable of learning from the past, and granted far too much power. Basically, every instance of military force has failed in the last century and today if a superior force engages a weaker one and achieves a decisive victory the contest only reverts to a guerrilla war and insurgency that eventually defeats the superior military. And in the age of nuclear weapons for two powers of relatively equal capacity to engage militarily is mass-suicide!

> "The technology of war is out of control; I'm a warrior, but my conclusion is that war is obsolete." – Former U.S. Army Major Douglas Rokke

If you want a war then prepare for one because the greater the national military buildup the more other countries are forced to expand their own militaries in order to compensate for their own defense. This is why a large military ceases to become the defensive force it claims to be as justification and actually becomes a force that generates turmoil and the very problems it purports to solve. The military establishment sees enemies and threats everywhere yet all of America's enemies and villains over the past century have been concocted and self-created opponents. Indeed the Pentagon, and associated spy-agencies such as the CIA, are like a fire department staffed by arsonists. Imperial Japan would never have attacked the United States during WWII if not for America placing a chokehold on them by denying them oil in trade; it was an act of sheer desperation on the part of Japan. Hitler's Germany never had any desire to attack the United States or step foot anywhere in the western hemisphere, and Hitler even owned land in Colorado! The entire Cold War was concocted by the direct actions of the United States government first by building up the Soviet Union to fight the Wehrmacht through massive assistance in resources and military hardware, and then by devastating Nazi Germany so thoroughly that the Soviets could easily take over half of Europe!

They rig wars and intentionally trigger conflicts, then write the history books, turn the opponents into ridiculous fictional monsters, then make themselves the heroes who fought a valiant defense in a conflict that was foisted upon them by evil forces. Hypocrisy saturates the Department of Defense, right down to the name. Officially tasked with ensuring the safety and security of the nation it has instead enhanced and motivated a multitude of threats, while creating *new* hazards within the country and around the world. Throughout the world the military has, and continues to be, an absolute disaster upon the natural environment. The Pentagon is the largest single polluter in the U.S. and is responsible for 129 out of 1,255 'Superfund' waste sites. Numerous highly toxic chemicals regularly pollute the water supply near military and weapons production facilities, such as the carcinogenic degreaser TCE, and perchlorate – known to harm the thyroid, particularly in infants, leading to a decreased IQ and behavioral problems. Due to the potential for massive financial and legal liability the Pentagon goes to extraordinary lengths to avoid taking responsibility for their environmental damage, often using intimidation and threats against local government and manipulating EPA research to trivialize the hazards from chemical pollution.[14]

The massive mess from decades of reckless nuclear weapons development is staggering. Millions of gallons of radioactive and highly volatile transuranic liquid waste stew inside corroding tanks in the desert of central Washington State at the Hanford site. These tanks have to be continually monitored and stirred otherwise the contents will explode! And Russia's situation is even more appalling, one of their tanks even blew up. Thousands of tons of chemical weapons, stored in tanks, bombs, and everything else the war-planners could dream up, now corrode away and leak while waiting to be destroyed in Russia and the United States.

Over a period of decades the U.S. military secretly dumped millions of pounds of, now leaking, nerve and mustard chemical agents near Hawaii, Alaska, both the East and West coasts of the U.S., and elsewhere. The dump-sites weren't catalogued and the scale of the environmental mess has only recently come to light due to injuries from fishing activity.[13] Farmers in Western Europe still plow up poison-gas containing shells leftover from World War I, and unexploded bombs dropped from Allied aircraft during WWII stifle construction projects in Germany. Mines and cluster-bombs regularly maim and kill worldwide, long after the wars ended.

Millions of people have died because of the actions of the U.S. government and its military yet both are considered heroes! Perhaps as a testament to the effectiveness and pervasiveness of the propaganda, combined with a very short collective memory, many Americans believe that their military is the only institution left that still functions properly.

Even if a big military was a useful tool it's painfully obvious that it's bleeding America dry in money and international prestige. One of the reasons for high fuel prices, and oil-related wars, is the insatiable demand of the Pentagon's oil-

Nihilism

consuming war machinery. Indeed, the U.S. Department of Defense is the largest single user of fuel in the world, consuming more than the entire country of Sweden *every day!* For example, one B-52 bomber burns up 47,000 gallons (178,000 liters) on just one average mission, and American military bases in Iraq and Afghanistan consume 90 million gallons of fuel each month.[18] The U.S. government has spent an astonishing five trillion dollars for the 'War on Terrorism' between the attacks of September 11, 2001 and 2008.[15] Ironically, a bloated military-industrial complex is one of the major forces that pushed the Soviet Empire into collapse, and America is repeating the same stupid mistake; once again this demonstrates the total lack of any capacity for reflective national self-analysis. Intellectual bankruptcy precedes economic bankruptcy.

> They may want a lot of things associated with war - the comradeship, the thrill that comes from holding a weapon. I think this is what confuses people. Thrills, comradeship, all of that can come in many different ways; it comes from war, though, only when people are manipulated into it. To me the strongest argument against an inherent drive to war is the extent to which governments have to resort to get people to go to war, the huge amounts of propaganda and deception of which we had an example very recently. And don't forget coercion. So I discard that idea of a natural inclination to war. – Howard Zinn

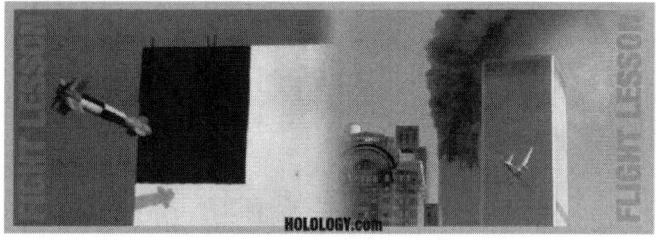

America is Addicted to War

Just since the second World War America has attacked and bombed China 1945-46 and 1950-53, Korea 1950-53, Guatemala 1954 and

1967-69, Indonesia 1958, Cuba 1959-60, the Belgian Congo 1964, Peru 1965, Laos 1964-73, Vietnam 1961-73, Cambodia 1969-70, Grenada 1983, Libya 1986, El Salvador 1980s, Nicaragua 1980s, Panama 1989, Iraq 1991 to present, Bosnia 1995, Sudan 1998, Serbia 1999, Afghanistan 2001 to present, as well as various 'dirty-wars' and clandestine operations too numerous (or not publicly known) to mention. The U.S. economy has become so lopsided and dependent upon warfare that it has undercut the structural sustainability of the nation and helped push it into recession. Only direct government spending from the wars are keeping the domestic economy temporarily afloat, barely, and sustaining enough jobs to keep it out of depression. In the process the military-industrial complex is now taking what is profitable external warfare for them and turning it inwards, selling it as security against threats largely created by the very offensive external wars the industry itself has fomented amidst an environment of rampant paranoia and fear. U.S. based Lockheed Martin is the world's largest defense contractor but is also a key contractor to Britain's Royal Mail, while rival Northrop Grumman also sells everything from billion-dollar war-toys to fingerprint ID system to the British police-state. Both corporations see a profitable future selling their expensive pseudo-security to the fearful.[3]

Military Rife with Corruption, Fraud, Waste

Add together huge amounts of money, weak or non-existent oversight, and insider deal-making and you have the perfect recipe for massive fraud and corruption – exactly the character of most military business deals. The war on Iraq has been one long parade of scam and scandal, billions of taxpayer dollars given away in 'cost-plus' contracts handed out to Bush administration favorites without any open bidding or competition. But even outside of war similar events occur; take for example the sad story of military base housing.

> The military's nationwide housing privatization program started small in the late 1990s after Congress authorized it, and accelerated under the Bush administration. Now

Nihilism

two dozen private companies control nearly every military home – about 178,000 – a quarter of them in Texas and California.[5]

This example is replete with the usual indicators: contracts given to suspicious companies, millions spent, little to show for it, and a whistle-blower unable to rectify the situation.

> When the Navy questioned American Eagle about Jack's claims, his boss ordered Jack to stop talking to Navy officials. Instead, he gave the Navy 20,000 pages of documents to prove his point. He was fired in March 2006.[5]

As is typically the case, the deal with the builder American Eagle was setup by a former military officer, General Merrill McPeak. Sen. Mark Pryor of Arkansas: "One of the great mysteries is how this company got the contract in the first place," Pryor said of American Eagle. "Wow. There should have been red flags going off all over the place."[5]

Pentagon spending detracts from everything else the nation needs, from medical care to education and infrastructure development. Don't forget that every dollar spent on bullets and fighter planes means a dollar that can't be spent on something else, like education, exploration and science, or national infrastructure. Nobody really knows the exact amount but a trillion dollars a year is a reasonable estimate of how much gets sucked into the black hole of the military-espionage-industrial complex every year.

Former top-level Pentagon official Thomas P. Christie:

> [W]e don't know where the hell all this money is! We can't track where our money is going. And we've known this for 20 or 30 years. We've had Pentagon comptroller after comptroller say, "Okay, we're gonna get it fixed," and then they throw their arms up in despair. [...]

You've got two things happening: First, everything we're developing and buying is costing an arm and a leg. And second, you're justifying it based on a questionable projected threat.

I really despair about getting a handle on this because it isn't just the Defense Department, it's also Congress. It's a military-industrial and congressional complex that is going full steam, and any attempt to draw back on that will be met with defeat, unfortunately. And I don't care which administration comes in. Once you've got all this stuff going down the pike, these big systems — they are jobs programs.[6]

Military and related spending is out of control in the U.S., politically it has become a welfare subsidy for big business and wasteful jobs to placate voters, it's economic socialism in a country that professes a hatred for socialism.

War Crimes and Atrocities

"The Americans brought electricity to my ass before they brought it to my house." – A former detainee in Iraq's notorious Abu Ghraib prison.

Through the self-inflicted blindness of nationalism and patriotism the public in western countries generally views their military as an idealized, clean, honest group of soldiers, but the reality is quite different. Even honest people forced into horrific situations will act in brutal and violent ways, committing war crimes and atrocities left and right.

A recent investigation of declassified documents from the Korean War has revealed that the U.S. military intentionally attacked, napalmed, and killed Korean refugees, then blamed the mass-killing on the North Koreans! The western public blindly accepted that the North Koreans as communists must have been responsible for the massacres. Hundreds of similar incidents have come to light, often against great resistance on the part of authorities. At No Gun Ri in 1950 an estimated 400 died at American hands, mostly women and children. At one point U.S. forces were ordered to attack anyone wearing white believing that the people in white were communist infiltrators. Only problem was that just about *everyone* in Korea was wearing white.

> Investigator Kang Eun-ji said high priority is being given to reviewing attacks earlier in 1950 on refugees gathered in fields west of the Naktong River, in North Korean-occupied areas of the far south, while U.S. forces were dug in east of the river. One U.S. air attack on 2,000 refugees assembled Aug. 20, 1950, at Haman, near Masan, killed almost 200, survivors reported. "There were many similar incidents — refugees gathered in certain places, and there were air strikes," she said.[4]

Since secret documents are usually declassified automatically after 50 years one can only imagine what kinds of atrocities and cover-ups we will discover about the U.S. war on Southeast Asia.

The first Gulf War, under the auspices of the first President Bush, was marketed to the domestic public as entertainment; remember the videos of laser-guided bombs falling through airshafts? It was presented as a painless and affordable war even though it really wasn't. Although the air-assault on Iraq actually continued between the two ground wars, the second announced war on Iraq, under the command of the second Bush President, was a tightly controlled presentation with western media directly controlled by the military leadership, while alternative media were openly intimidated and killed, such as in the attacks on Al Jazeera TV stations in Iraq and Afghanistan, and numerous other cases of independent journalists being imprisoned or killed.

With a timid, complicit, or just neutralized mass media it's easy for the government to cover up atrocities and paint a pretty picture of a clean war, or even an entertaining war. Censorship is rife in the current wars on Iraq and Afghanistan, even going so far as to try and block a medical book designed to assist combat surgeons simply because it shows images of wounded soldiers, thereby revealing the true nature of combat!

> Censors also tried to prevent the book from getting a copyright and the international standard book number letting it be sold commercially, Lounsbury said. ... Kevin Kiley, a retired lieutenant general who was the army's surgeon general when the book was being prepared, said some higher-ups in the military had been worried that the pictures "could be spun politically to show the horrors of war."[2]

As the professional and mercenary military replaces conscription censorship becomes necessary for masking the true costs of war both in blood and in treasure.

> I had always idealized the military, like we were going out to fight the Nazis, and had real moral high ground. When I got over [to Iraq], I was shocked by the brutality. My whole first tour, I can honestly say I never saw an Iraqi guy who deserved to die, who had weapons or was attacking us or anything. In many instances American soldiers took really bad decisions that killed innocent Iraqis. I had a hard time reconciling that with what I had thought I would be doing. By the time my second tour was over, I had morphed into a killer. A lot of people don't understand what war actually is. I don't know what's worse: being charged with felony or

Nihilism

having a head full of insanity. – US Army Specialist Michael St Clair, 2009.

Crime Time

Many that enlist in the military are already just one step away from prison in civilian life, but after basic training they can properly use firearms and they've learned how to kill other people. As long as soldiers are killing 'bad guys', enemies, and anyone the President labels a terrorist this is publicly accepted as perfectly wonderful. But after being trained to kill and then performing the task soldiers sometimes point the gun in a direction not officially sanctioned by God or government and continue their killing back home, terminating either themselves or someone else. Murders often reach the headlines, but small scale events are frequently missed. For example, the town of Killeen Texas, just outside the massive Fort Hood Army base, has seen a surge of violent crime (up 22%) and domestic abuse (up 75%) since the start of wars on Afghanistan and Iraq in 2001.[17]

Compounding the problem of troublesome troops, the U.S. military is struggling to fill the ranks depleted by combat casualties and has been forced to drastically lower entry standards in order to meet recruitment quotas. The physical and psychological trauma of combat, coupled with the ambient social and political hypocrisy of the conflict's grueling military occupation of foreign nations, enhances already statistically high levels of crime and deadly violence committed by the troops. But in a large country these violent events are easily ignored by the general public in favor of appealing myths about combat heroism and national victory. In 2008 the suicide statistics for active-duty soldiers reached a record level. The last time it was this high was the late 1960s during the war on Vietnam and as the U.S. military was falling apart from the inside.[9] The situation for female soldiers is even worse; women who've been in the military have a suicide risk triple that of non-veterans.[19] The pervasive presence of sexual violence throughout the military is undoubtedly a contributing factor. Incidents of rape and sexual trauma are increasing in the US military. According to the US

Department of Veterans Affairs, women are twice as likely to be sexually assaulted in the military as in the civilian population. But in fact, the numbers indicate that most victims are male and most incidents either go unreported or are ignored by military authorities. *The military is a great place to be a rapist*; in addition to the complicit environment, only eight percent of sex crimes that get investigated lead to prosecution, compared to a 40 percent arrest rate in the civilian realm.[20]

The Pacific nation of Fiji offers us a prime example of the detrimental blowback effect resulting from the militarization of society. Soldiers from the small nation of Fiji work for cash around the world on various military missions, such as 'peacekeepers' for the UN or for the U.S. and NATO wars on Iraq and Afghanistan.

> The Fijian military (RFMF) is larger than that of any other Pacific island nation and it is extremely well "connected" to international power brokers. It is also "independently wealthy" as a result of controlling several questionable mercenary schemes supportive of foreign interventions of both the United States and United Kingdom. More than 3000 Fijians serve in the British Army. Some of those mercenaries were once active members of the Fijian army. The government allows soldiers, particularly officers, to transit from military service to join private security firms, which in turn pay it a fee.[10]

Although Fiji likes the income, and doesn't mind the killing when it's thousands of miles away, when these mercenaries are out of a job they come home and all they know how to do is harass and intimidate civilians, set up roadblocks, censor the media, and stage coups. Fiji's corrupt and violent military institution is steadily eroding the social and economic fabric of the country and taking everyone with them on the road to ruin.

Fiji demonstrates that, although there may be no 'right' or 'wrong' in a cosmic sense, cause and effect remain alive and well and we will all eventually reap what we sow, as exemplified by the military madness of a nation believing it can kill with impunity overseas and not be internally affected.

A Coup for Jesus?

Most Americans probably think of a coup d'état as something that could only happen in a third-world banana republic, but anymore America is, sadly, not far from the mark with consecutive Presidential administrations staffing leadership positions in critical government agencies with progressively more and more incompetent and corrupt friends and cronies. And if that wasn't trouble enough the U.S. military has become a veritable bastion of conservative, if not outright fundamentalist, Christianity. This characteristic helps to explain the military institutions zeal for killing Muslims and fighting wars for Israel.

The rebuilding of the U.S. military into a volunteer corps after the disaster in Southeast Asia coincided with the popularity of Evangelical Christianity during the late 1970s and 1980s, typified by the public statements of President Carter as a "born again" Christian. With the approval of top authorities, believing it a means of improving fighting spirit, the military quickly became a haven for Christians. Within military culture public prayer and chapel attendance went from acceptable, to a suggestion, and into a mandatory event. Today militant evangelical Christianity has infected the United States military from top to bottom. According to James Carroll, a Christian apologist and former Catholic priest who grew up in the halls of military power in the Pentagon, "At the Air Force Academy, "Team Jesus" was one of the nicknames for the football team and one of the most vociferous evangelical Christian proselytizers was the football coach." And a screening of Mel Gibson's fundamentalist slasher flick *The Passion of the Christ* was even force-fed to cadets as an official Air Force event![16]

Generals and other top-level military leaders have enormous offensive capacities under their direct control, for instance ballistic missile submarine commanders can launch their nuclear-armed missiles to reach-out and annihilate almost any spot on the globe, and they can see the USA falling apart and her international prestige in tatters just like everyone else. A coup staged by religious conservatives under the pretense of restoring America to her former glory and establishing a Christian theocracy using a warped interpretation of the Constitution as legal cover is, unfortunately, not nearly as far-fetched as it may seem. And who's going to stand in the way of their 155mm howitzers and tell them otherwise if the Generals decide to order it?

Deactivate the Standing Military and Unplug the War-Machine

> It's very disturbing. I've seen good people in the Pentagon, good people in the military, all the way to the top, just throw their hands up in frustration: "No way we can turn this ship around and get it in the right direction." And that's unfortunate. You just gotta come in and scrap the whole process. ... What needs to be done can't be done bit by bit. It's got to be revolutionary.[6] – Thomas P. Christie

The military-industrial and espionage institutions cannot be repaired, many have tried over the decades and all have failed, the inertia is simply too great. The only viable solution is to dismantle and demolish the entire institutional system and in its place create an armed and trained citizen defense force. With the establishment of a well-armed citizenry you eliminate the need for a costly and parasitic military-espionage-industrial complex and you eliminate the possibility of tyrannical government and despotic rulers. Aggression from outside is useless because no one can hope to conquer millions of thoroughly armed people willing to defend their freedom, and other states no longer have any need to maintain large standing militaries of their own. If we fail to do this we will end up under the calloused thumb of a desperate military dictatorship on the path to national bankruptcy and worldwide catastrophe.

FAMILY AND NIHILISM

More than once I've been queried on the nature of nihilism as it relates to family and child-raising. Is nihilism compatible with family? What influence does it have? The question of family really hasn't been adequately answered for the modern age. The conservatives can easily push an opinion based on inapplicable historical examples, but trying to recreate the past is doomed without an adequate allowance for contemporary issues. Yet trying to redefine family is fraught with peril and controversy and really the only answer is one of expediency for the moment - think ahead and use what works. Be they politically conservative or liberal, when adopting concepts for the guidance and formation of a family you should be wary of advice from experts long on faith and short on fact.

I'm no substitute for a doctor and maybe not even a decent magazine on the topic but I'll try and cover what I know from experience and analysis. If you the reader really wants the answers on this issue just read Maria Montessori's incredible book The Montessori Method. Maria takes Nietzsche's philosophy and turns it into reality, but more on that later.

Anyway, it's clear that kids grow and go through stages. Early development is probably the most mechanical, yet also the most important in physical aspects for future health in mind and body which are dependent upon proper care here. As they get older and more mobile they start to interact with others of the same and older ages, they learn the forces of authority, power and the effects of feedback from interacting with others. We can see that really all development is based on trial and error and I would posit that we probably learn more from errors than immediate successes in life. So, attempting things, especially new things is important, in some cases it comes naturally in others it should be encouraged, at least in safe and reasonable ways.

Much of raising a child is mechanical, devoid of ideology, and is similar across cultures. All kids need food, shelter, clothing, exercise, education, and similar fundamentals. Because of the similarity and necessity these factors can be safely ignored for the sake of brevity in this assessment. Besides that, humans have very long childhood developments and much of this is due to the need to learn the vast amounts of information and skills necessary not just for survival but for success as well.

History of the Family Network

Conformity to family or near clan can be useful and served its purpose when society was small, homogenous and cohesive, but in today's faceless urban society of millions, conformity and group allegiance is often not just useless but self-defeating. Like many other concepts it conveyed a benefit at one time in the past for small societies but today it has been warped and twisted to hurt, not help, the average person. If one understands this they can properly act but if not they're doomed to powerlessness and confusion. Now more than ever it's imperative to carefully choose your allies when possible. Family may change its name, and even its form slightly, but the fundamental concepts are not going away anytime soon because they're hardwired into our being. The social need for family cannot be ignored without peril, only substitutions are allowed.

Why Family?

Family has loads of cultural baggage and mythology attached to it, making analysis superficially challenging and confusing, but it's fundamentally a very mechanical process. Having kids is a practical method of extending the self. Immortality is the goal of every perpetuating entity and humans do this through genes and/or memes and both paths involve sacrifice. Reproducing is striving for immortality and doing this genetically involves your standard biological reproduction. The sacrifice to yourself, from a genetic perspective, is that only a portion of your genetic material is perpetuated, but the idea is to offset this by finding a mate genetically similar but different enough to avoid too many deleterious recessive genes from popping out in the product (baby). This process occurs constantly around the world but the participants rarely have even an inkling of what's really going on behind the

Nihilism

scenes. The genes still win anyway, and in fact stupidity, to a limited extent, is to the genes advantage because those types are unable to comprehend much besides sex. Sex is the cheapest, most basal form of entertainment possible (violence is second).

Memetic (cultural) immortality is also known as fame; it's the perpetuation of the ideas and thoughts of the originator into the larger pool of collective minds. The sacrifice here is that one has limited control over the outcome – great ideas often get warped or misinterpreted, but the outcome is not diluted by the necessity of a partner.

Family is a support element to enhance the process of reproduction, primarily biological perpetuation, but memetic reproduction is predicated upon a healthy biological source anyway. So the fact is that a child cannot live and grow without some kind of social support network, a family in other words, and since human childhood is so long, nearly two decades, the family has to be able to provide for the child's mental and physical needs at least that long or the perpetuation process is stunted.

Adoption of a non-genetically related child is a compromise usually born out of necessity coupled with the manifestation of very powerful hormonal and psychological needs built into the human essence. But for the sake of brevity I'm going to just focus on the parents and the child and ignore these minor details and state that the child is a reflection of the parent to varying degrees. This reflection is intentional, as previously mentioned.

Gangs

Modern gangs are the product of a very primal need coupled with contemporary economic and social factors. Gangs represent an inherent human desire for authority structures along with the childhood need for guidance from mentors. So, gangs are primarily a symptom of large youth populations within a socially unstable and economically eroded environment that's often exacerbated by the decay of traditional values. Not surprisingly, places like Guatemala,

Afghanistan, and Los Angeles California are prime examples of this phenomenon. Broken social networks initiate and perpetuate gang societies – kids lack healthy and reliable adult role models, then grow up and act out accordingly. As the political power of government decays, gangs rise to fill the local need for social stability. Established authority structures are widely ineffective against this problem because they only *police* and *punish* rather than address and rectify the deeper social roots of the crisis, namely kids growing up without the guidance they really need. And the lack of close bonds with more wise and experienced adults and parents has many causes. Increasing incarceration rates have broken up many families, putting one or more parents behind bars for years. Wars and violent conflicts kill off parents and leave broken families behind; drugs and disease, like HIV in Africa, cause early deaths too.

From Family to Society

The needs of children, and therefore society, around the world are at root fairly simple, and ideological or theological values are secondary interchangeable accoutrements mostly serving to form bonds of group connectedness through ritual and routine. Unfortunately, these secondary values complicate the realization of valid solutions to serious family-based problems. Kids need wise and reliable adult role models. Very young parents lack both capacities. Parents that see little connection to their kids, perhaps because they aren't genetically related or simply due to unfit personality, will let down their kids and thus society at large as well. It's important to emphasize that childhood problems are eventually society's problems.

Broad generalizations for the social model can be difficult to make. What form should a family take? Does a family have to have two parents? Does a car have to have four wheels? No, but it works better that way. Ultimately the quality of the parent is a lot more important than the quantity. In some cultures kids have multiple parents, or they learn from the entire clan as a group, and this is usually more useful to the child than the isolated atoms

Nihilism

characterizing modern families. Healthy exposure is important, as is the socialization process itself. The children of larger families are usually psychologically healthier than those of very small ones because the children of larger families have learned how to properly interact with others and that their actions and words have direct consequences. Interacting with those of the opposite sex and people from different backgrounds is equally important for the same reason.

Imparting Values

This is the real nexus for our focus on nihilism. What's good and what's bad? Nothing. What does that mean? Nothing. All right, now that we've cleared that up ... the point is that we can think anything we want and no matter how much we believe in it that won't ever make fantasies real. No matter how much mind-altering drugs one consumes that won't change the consistent nature of that which exists outside our minds and bodies and continues long after we're gone and without regard for our own inflated egos – only the ability to perceive and respond to it.

Perfectly Dysfunctional, by Freydis, 2005

Since children are a reflection of the parent, equally the values of the parent will be impressed upon the offspring, whether intentional or not. This does not guarantee a mindless clone parroting the parent's ideas and rhetoric when they get older. Parents can only impart a substratum in the minds of the child, as far as values and ideology are concerned, and the more resistant to criticism are these values and ideas the greater the longevity in the mind and attitude of the child. And this resistance can be acquired through blind faith in religious dictums or solid logic of an objective argument. But ultimately imparting a solid framework for thinking and learning is much more important to the child than just isolated facts and orders. It's not just 'that's the way it is', but instead 'this is why' and 'this is how we reach the conclusion'.

Beliefs and values are a crutch, a mental shortcut to avoid the need for justification of an opinion. Parents employ this constantly for obvious reasons. Parents tell kids not to curse, for example, but kids demand a reason to back up the argument, especially when the parents curse anyway. This need for validity in the argument has increased especially as force becomes less culturally palatable in molding the child's mind and attitudes. Very often the arguments parents give out are either contradicted by their own actions or simply the standard 'do what I tell you and don't question' line. Neither one works in the long run because the kids see the contradiction and react accordingly. Blatant contradictions and double standards are probably the most serious flaw in parenting, and indeed form a major problem within society as well.

If parents would simply justify the reasons for demanded behaviors, and then apply and follow their own philosophy and moral demands in their own lives, this would solve the vast majority of parent-child conflicts, especially in the rebellious teen years. And yet the religiosity of the parents is likely the greatest obstacle in this path, for faith compels behavior blatantly out of synch with reality. Parents are leaders, they have to lead by example not by mere words; it's rare for a kid to end up better mentally and emotionally balanced than their parents – think about it.

Nihilism

Guidance and role models are very important to human child development. Everything they see, hear and sense is going into the formation of their attitude and world-view. Kids act based upon what they see, what they hear, and their overall surroundings, and since they're only around their parents a portion of the time their influences include peers and related culture such as television, magazines and music. This is why parents are often apoplectic over the content and character of mass media programs. For the most part the producers of these programs are only concerned with profits so they'll distribute almost anything if it can catch an audience long enough for the advertising sponsors to make a sale. In this culture the audience is a commodity to be exploited and their minds to be warped into the most profitable course of action for the ones who control the dominant media outlets. Once again, only substitutions are allowed. In order to win this battle the parent has to make a valid substitution to the child for the undesired content.

Childhood Development – Problem and Solution

Pick whichever philosopher you like, from Nietzsche to Buddha, they, like most everyone else attempting to rectify what's broken with society, remain trapped in a reactionary mode trying to undo the harm already burned into most everyone's brain from childhood. The sad truth is that warped authorities wreck us from the start and we quickly become psychologically damaged in one way or another before we even become adults. Most of this is due to the heavy imprint of rigid authority forcing children to meet adult goals and a failure to see the world from the perspective of a child. Realizing this, Maria Montessori wrote a book based on her research into early childhood learning and development. The Montessori Method was a revolutionary production in the early 20th century, and it remains today as a profoundly important guide to how children can learn to properly interact with other people, forces, and objects. Maria reached some of the most critical elements of the human experience, mind, power, authority and personal efficacy, and developed a functional path to a healthy adulthood in a way that Nietzsche tried but couldn't. Children want to grow and learn, but they need the tools and an environment that allows them to do so on their own terms.

Long-term research has found that the greatest factor in determining success in life is not intelligence, although that certainly helps, but rather it's *self-control* that matters most. Lack of self-control is manifest as impulsive aggression, hyperactivity, lack of persistence, inattention and impulsivity. Kids with lower levels of self-control are more likely to be overweight, have sexually transmitted diseases, get caught raising a child in a young single-parent household, and to suffer from poor financial planning among other things.

Learning how to control their impulses, starting as young as three, greatly improves the chances of healthy and successful life once they become adults.[1] And in order to develop self-control kids need to be presented with consistency between words and deeds by parents and role models, and to grasp the concept that they can't have everything they want immediately, or at all, without effort; learning cause and effect in realistic scenarios. Similarly, many speak of protecting the innocence of youth, but that's a misleading and ultimately foolish way to frame the issue. It's not about insulating kids inside a bubble; it's about giving them the appropriate tools and skills so that they can properly interact with their environment. And in order to learn how to properly interact they have to try things themselves within a safe situation.

It's difficult task to objectively study ourselves as a species. Researchers into animal intelligence and behavior are painfully careful to avoid making assumptions and injecting human bias into the experiments, yet researches studying human infants rarely make the same efforts. For instance, the boy reaches for the truck – but is he really attracted to the vehicle or simply the object with wheels on it that moves? The girl reaches for the doll, but what aspect of the object is really attracting her attention? Infant minds are not like adult minds and we shouldn't make assumptions in that regard or we risk making dangerously flawed behavior and values associations. Indeed, how much of our adult character is really natural development, and how much is forced socialization that perpetuates stale habit and tired tradition?

Most of our greater social problems can be solved before they even occur by creating a healthy and functional environment for childhood development. The reactionary need for ideology, theology, and complex social solutions to shape people into a coherent mass would largely be eliminated because a better world will automatically emerge from the use of a scientifically established, observational-based environment for childhood development.

Plato and the Folly of Fear-Driven Authority

Original communist authoritarian Plato in The Republic theorized that the family has to be abolished in order to create a regulated state where men and women's roles are interchangeable. Basically the government tells the little people 'hey, *we're* your family now!', and even goes so far as to pick who breeds with whom. In this case family no longer serves the individual but rather the state, and individual identity is transferred to that abstract, political supra-entity.

Family has been co-opted for the service of government more than once in history. Third Reich Germany and Communist Romania are two poignant examples which spring to mind. The belief behind this, and that which motivated Plato as well, is that every man and woman has an innate ability, basically a destiny, that they must follow in order that community is served and their own potential is maximized. In other words, some people are born good at making shoes and others at giving orders, some are naturally slaves and others are born to be masters. These roles are determined at birth but then the elite detect it at a young age and place them in training to maximize their given skills for the intended social position. It's a totally rigid, top-down, elitist system, the 'anthill' society.

The problem with this belief is that it's defeated by the true nature of reality, for some are good at many things, some aren't good at anything, and in the meantime the skills needed by society are constantly changing. Maybe that unemployable drifter in ancient

Greece would be a wealthy software engineer now. What would the Emperor of China do today if he stepped off a bus in downtown Saint Louis? Silly examples maybe, but the point is still made. As even a cursory study of biology in the natural environment indicates, a wide variety of strategies for personal and collective success exist, with success defined as making the most of the surrounding environment.

The individual freedom to choose your strategy, ideally with serious thought and consideration involved in the decision, is critically important because otherwise the trouble arrives when one despot or authority group tries to impose their own values and strategy upon others. This inevitably leads to dictatorship, authoritarian brutality, rebellion and eventual social collapse. A sustainable and beneficial social system necessitates a fluid and flexible society that maximizes personal opportunity within an environment that accepts innovation and novel or radical ideas. Anything less is simply trading short-term stability for long term failure.

Every member of the group has to have a solid sense of ownership or participation in *process*, *product*, and *outcome* or it will inevitably fail spectacularly no matter how glorious the start or lofty the founding ideals. Further, contrary to Plato you can't breed humans like cattle because we don't know our ultimate goal to breed towards! It's easy to control the biological characteristics of cattle because all they have to 'do' is taste good after you cook 'em. We can't know the future or the skills needed to meet future needs; the best we can possibly do is make educated guesses about the future and try to produce smart generalists capable of quickly adapting.

A root problem here is the blind faith in control – the belief that we *can* control things and that we *should*, and further, that the product will be *superior* to what would arrive on its own without some dictator ordering it to happen. People fear chaos and they fear disorder, especially when it is foreign to their rigid, heavily regulated lives. But disorder is the natural state of events, it is what created us through evolution and about the only thing we can really rely on strategically. This disorder and random course of events that we cannot, and

Nihilism

indeed should not control, will shape our collective and individual future regardless of the magnitude of our egos.

Some of the most dynamic and powerful countries in history are a testament to the power of minimal control and a maximum allowance of freedom. It's amazing what can happen if you just let people be free, let them do what they want to do without micro-managing their lives or forcing them to participate in some artificial authority monstrosity of 'The State' or 'The Church'. If people want to have families let them have families; if they don't, let them do without.

Future of the Family

With the advent of in vitro fertilization and other artificial reproduction techniques the classic process of sexual reproduction is segueing into obsolescence. The astounding implications of this radical step in human evolution are only now beginning to be recognized. Technology that enables biological reproduction for otherwise sterile individuals will eventually lead to an entire population unable to reproduce naturally, unless genetic repairs are made at some point. And in this regard biotechnology is a perfect complement, for that is exactly what it will do. In the relatively near future biotechnological tools and knowledge will progress to the level where the basic elements that build life are as easy for us to use as plastic toy building blocks. This is the awesome power of reduction set into action; nihilistic and ineluctable, it breaks the complex down into functional elements. Eventually we'll be able to build life and rearrange it as desired. The potential is practically unlimited, for we can become literally whatever we want to be and anything becomes possible – we can cut and paste, edit out diseases, edit in new attributes, and even create entirely new life forms. The potential for progression is awesome, and the potential peril equally so; the significance of biotechnology is roughly equivalent to splitting the atom. The strategic issue becomes – what do we create with these building blocks and what are the consequences?

Humans have already reached the stage where we can't survive at all without our advanced technology. So, whether this technology is 'good' or 'bad' is a specious question because the development is unavoidable and inevitable. To ban or to hide from technological development is self-defeating for, like all technology, as fast as one narrow-minded clique rejects it another less conservative group picks it up and gains a massive advantage over the rest. Instead, it's time for us to collectively acquire the maturity and intellectual development to use our tools appropriately and to properly deal with the consequences. We have to start interfacing with people and forces, what we traditionally call reality, based on what's consistent and verifiable, not based on belief and assumption. This way of thinking can't just be for adults, it has to start in childhood to become a reliable methodology for productive living.

We must overthrow the material and moral conditions of our present-day life. ... We must first purify our atmosphere and completely transform the milieu in which we live; for it corrupts our instinct and our will, and constricts our heart and our intelligence.
— Mikhail Bakunin

Nihilism

REVOLUTION INTO EVOLUTION

Living Nihilism in the 21st Century

Once the superficial and unnecessary pieces are stripped away we're left with the unavoidable, and the unavoidable is always of particular concern to the nihilist, and most any thinker, with death being the most obvious factor. But what about the much more important time before the end? How do we live as Nihilists? The following contains some conclusions.

Ethics

Reading an article about the cancerous corporate growth patterns of Starbucks Coffee Inc. made me think about a contradiction between words and action that seems quite common. Why are stated values and the subsequent actions of individuals so often contradictory? For instance, why do people rail against a company like Starbucks but then turn right around and buy their over-priced, over-roasted coffee anyway? Or another example, and I'm sure the reader can imagine many more, why do people so often complain about the quality of television programs but then spend hours watching them anyway? Why does the public patronize their own self-described 'evil' institutions purely out of choice and in blatant contradiction to their own expressed values? Clearly something is going on here that's deeper than appearances suggest.

It seems likely that either impulse continually overpowers reason or many people are simply making complaints and criticism not based on their own reasoning but rather on group-think – attempting to ascertain and adopt group values. But whatever the reason for it, hypocritical behavior as compared to self-expressed personal values cannot be psychologically healthy for it leads the individual into a chronic state of self-debasement.

The disconnect between words and action carried out over time leads to a perpetual state of hypocrisy and wears down the subconscious, rendering the individual a floating, baseless consumer that says whatever others want to hear while attempting to sound logical but acting purely on whim and impulse. It's not surprising that so many people turn to religion in this kind of environment, a veritable sandstorm of hypocritical values and rationalization of behavior.

Religious morality provides a sense of center and focus, an ethical context with which to reference throughout daily life. It doesn't matter that the beliefs are based on archaic fantasies and have little or no bearing on modern life, or that one believer is just as happily deluded in their faith as every other regardless of how and who they worship. The beliefs are not what matter, rather it is the framework and sense of context that creates a structure for the adherents to base their daily lives upon. This code of ethics leads to psychological health by eliminating the internal and external value-action hypocrisy.

Everyone needs a code and structure for living that they can aspire towards but also one that they can actually follow in practice, not just desire to follow, so that their words will match their deeds – a critical element of mental health. This is also why religious believers tend to be more honest in daily interactions and more likely to follow through on their promises. Success here means making a conscious effort to always match words to actions. Doing this empowers the individual as well because they gain the authority of coherence and the mental stability of consistency. This is all the belief-need really is; many people think it requires faith and attachment to arbitrary rules from mystical deities but in fact it's simply an intentional effort by the individual to act on what they speak and speak to what they do. This is also why it's so important to recognize the limitations placed upon action by human nature because ignoring or denying the limits leads to a perpetual state of defeat in mind and body.

To construct this necessary framework for daily life one must first have a solid awareness of what they can do, meaning one's own practical capacities for decision-making. In other words simply stating that Starbucks is a rip-off is not enough if one drives past one of their stores every day on the way to work and has a coffee addiction, because they'll soon find their best plans foiled by need and impulse! Something has to change, either the impulses are curbed, redirected, or one's words change to match the impulses. *Say what you do and do what you say.*

Values

Human machinations are often explained as the inveterate search for happiness, and while this explanation suffices to a minimal degree in casual philosophical discussion in fact the human mind is not so simple that it just seeks happiness in every action and decision. Many people seek things that don't make them happy, power for instance. Many people seek to become Presidents, Prime Ministers and dictators but look at how much trouble they get out of the bargain when and if they arrive? Or what about fame; the famous say 'don't be famous - it isn't worth it', but who listens? *Something deeper is going on here...*

In reality the human mind, and the body supporting it, is enmeshed within a complex system of relationships, connections, and interactions and we have to very carefully, continually and with great effort, map out a path and measure our actions against the consequences and impacts that our efforts will have upon the people, objects and connections in our environment. Unless they're a woefully dysfunctional psychopath, people aren't little atoms bouncing around trying to feel good all the time and the few fools that try this don't last very long! It seems surprising how few seem to recognize this fairly simple concept of interconnections and, perhaps because it's so difficult to quantify, this misunderstanding is especially common in the male mind.

Most important to recognize is that humans are not living beings that can exist independently; humans are not one-celled organisms, they are highly networked, social creatures. We all exist inside, and because of, a complex network of relations formed between objects, individuals, and an ever-changing array of groups composed of both. Our goals and values are a direct result of that system we are enmeshed within.

Hypothetically, the choice of which value system we adopt depends on what kind of goal we want to achieve but in practice we rarely know exactly what we want and even less often how to get it. So the entire argument that characterizes philosophy and metaphysics, as a dissection of the individual human mind and body, is a charade and it just ends in the same dead-end of argument because it doesn't aim towards or find the root of the issue.

The message emanating from the reduction-oriented methodology of nihilism concerning values is simply that because of our tenuous and constantly changing situation our values and goals are not absolutes but are in a continual flux. Consequently our values are not fixed but actually quite relative. For various reasons we typically use great effort to hide this value ambiguity by concocting false absolutes, such as through myths and religious beliefs held together by dogma, but in the end our actions reveal this for the delusional foolishness that it is.

The fully and properly developed human mind and body are seeking more than simple short-term self-interest, but also seeking to better fit into the vast and often complex surrounding environmental network. This entails a constant process of adaptation, questioning, solution seeking and struggle while continually creating and destroying the networks that characterize our social and physical environment. Because of this, in this struggle called life the Nihilist has a profound awareness to not hold anything sacred and never get too attached to anything.

Morality

To help explain the basics of morality consider this situation: someone stranded alone on an island cannot act immorally for there is no God and there is no posthumous judgment of deeds except by earthly survivors. Similarly as Ayn Rand once stated, no situation without a decision can have a moral component. So if you have no choice or context, or if an outside value system is imposed upon you, then you have no morality – you cannot be moral or immoral in action or thought.

Nihilism

Indeed morality itself is a product of society, of interconnections, of social bonds and the inevitable search for power equilibrium between individuals. Further, moral codes serve as tools of control but not necessarily always as a top-down imposed authority force but very often as a means of balancing power between individuals, of keeping 'them' from getting more than 'me'. Morality changes over time and indeed is itself largely relative and culturally derivative. But the social and psychological effects are nonetheless quite real even if inconsistent and plagued by chronic efforts to 'cheat' or for 'me' to get more than 'they' do.

I remember an old episode of the *Twilight Zone* where a crew of space explorers crash-lands on what they think is a distant, desert planet. They proceed to battle each other over diminishing water supplies, and thus personal survival, only to eventually discover that they actually crashed in the Mojave Desert and civilization was just over the hill. I think the implied, made-for-TV feel-good message was that one should always value human life and not be greedy. But on a practical level the true message is that regardless of the pre-existing cultural and moral overlay, ultimately human behavior, meaning 'right' and 'wrong', is contextually defined and founded upon the basal law of personal survival and propagation.

Using another fictional example, consider the classic novel by HG Wells, The island of Dr. Moreau, where the doctor tortures animals using the excuse of scientific progress – what moral position does this have? None? But the doctor could not do this without continual assistance from the outside world through supplies, food, and so on. So Doctor Moreau is not isolated, he is connected to a larger society and can be judged by its dominate moral codes. Regardless of the morality of his actions, the ethics of his research are easily criticized for the wayward results that were produced, not to mention the Doctors original motives that were based purely on faith in achieving a questionable goal. So now that he is connected to the outside, most would consider Dr. Moreau's actions to be morally wrong. Here is where nihilism enters for it argues that 'wrong' or 'right' are secondary not primary as most, especially religious views, would hold. Right or wrong are irrelevant if in this case Dr. Moreau can get away with what he's doing. This is why using morality as a social security system is one very dangerous way to live and why authority must jump in like an 800 pound gorilla and take over to hold a society together with an outcome that is more vast and convoluted than the original simple problem could have possibly ever produced on its own.

Human morality, as it's traditionally employed, is an artificial construction, and as such it can be changed to be almost anything.

While there's no right or wrong in a cosmic sense we nonetheless still exist within a universal framework of cause and effect. And within the boundaries of cause and effect it's clear from even a passing view that certain behaviors are more functional than others – for instance, cooperation is more universally beneficial than conflict, or even competition in most cases. These facts are obscured by common cultural myths, such as the belief in 'dog-eat-dog' struggles and a zero-sum world. This misreading of Darwin's theories only serves as a convenient excuse to justify otherwise unacceptable actions of abuse and exploitation, actions that are ultimately self-defeating anyway.

Further, because humans are social creatures we need guidelines and protocol in one form or another in order to function collectively on even a rudimentary level. Morality emerges as an inevitable byproduct of the social interactions of multiple participants. So, although much of morality is cultural variable, consistent underlying elements can be found. These consistent elements first emerge as a result of personal interactions, primarily acquired through the socialization process in childhood.

The reason we need to reconsider and reassess the values within our moral codes, along with our cultural concepts of right and what's considered wrong, is that by continually taking them on assumption we can easily be led astray or compelled to do things that are harmful to ourselves and others. Not all moral rules are equally valid, just as the rules must inevitably change as circumstances evolve, and that's why it's important to recognize where these rules that compel us to act in certain ways are coming from to begin with.

The really remarkable aspect of morality is that in many instances the rules can be mathematically described, using game theory for instance. Even more important, these quantifiable values are not restricted to humans, and in fact also serve to describe the behavior of other animal species as well. Because morality is a byproduct of social living other social and intelligent species, such as birds and apes, display the same moral behavior that humans must, emphasizing the universally applicable aspect of many moral guidelines and behavior patterns.[5] Intelligent social animals display the same needs for justice and fair-treatment that humans do, and will even react in similar fashion when injustice is manifest.

> It is part of a long evolutionary history in which cooperation and equity go hand in hand, even though it is undeniable that we have also a hierarchical streak. This is equally true for other primates, not to mention for canines, but no species accepts these vertical arrangements 100 per cent of the time.[8]

It's often believed that morality comes from religion, but scientific research into animal behavior, moral rules, and game theory analysis, clearly indicates that morality does not come from religion or religious beliefs. Actually, religion *hijacks* moral rules and associated behavior to serve ulterior motives. Basic morality is hard-wired into us as social beings.[6]

Unless mentally or psychologically damaged we intrinsically know, with the aid of the socialization process, how to behave because of consistent cause and effect and because the majority of interactions are reciprocal in nature. In other words, *you reap what you sow.*

The problem of morality and misbehavior boils down to at least two deficiencies residing in the individual, and at least one can be corrected. The first is a *lack of power*. The core problem is lack of personal efficacy and those who perceive themselves as powerless, selling freedom to authority for a sense of security, and an equilibrium at the bottom where if 'I' can't have it 'no one' can. Fear of loss, also fear of the other, fear that others will gain at my expense hence the desire to submit to social conformity and specious rules just to try and hold on to what little 'I' have now. Especially in a transitional society people are very insecure and they will cling desperately to whatever scraps they've already acquired in life.

The first deficiency is largely an issue of education and the things people learn as they grow and develop. For instance, if while growing up you're always told what to do, criticized for minor details and had parents or authority do things for you or to you, then a lack of efficacy, lack of self-worth, and a need to strike at something inside or outside can result later in life. In this case perspectives of power become perverted and appeals to authority forces may appear the only way to rectify internal deficiencies; if enough individuals are this way they form a society of concomitant character. The second deficiency is partially a cumulative issue stemming from the first and also external large scale factors such as environmental and economic instability.

Those who control the images rule the world. As such it's critical to manage your inputs, because our individual characters are deeply influenced by external factors, from physical substances to the intangibles of images thoughts and ideas — it all comes together to create who you are. So, if you want to control who you are you must control what you absorb — your surroundings in people, places and things.

Context or Absurdity

As we've learned already morality is relative and meaning is contextual. Our own meaning is encapsulated in personal identity, and identity is the interface of our own self-value or worth and the outside external composed of others. An individual isolated on an island can have no identity, or maximum identity which is effectively the same, zero or infinite. But they have no future as well so everything they do is ultimately meaningless, although not necessarily immediately meaningless since survival is an immediate need and everything which works towards fulfilling that need is meaningful, it has value. But since this poor lonesome being is doomed to die anyway and they have no social context to create meaning for everyday life then their sum is zero. Life for someone permanently stranded alone and destined to die alone is thus absurd, it's meaningless. *Everything is absurd without a society to contextualize action and value, as well as a future to perpetuate the self.* Similarly if reality is solipsistic then it's absurd since we (or just I) are all stranded alone on islands, metaphysically speaking.

But now we can see that meaning is a two part issue consisting of the immediate personal and the strategic non-personal. Long-term meaning can only come through perpetuation of the self in some form; it is an extension of tactical meaning. Although tactical meaning is more important it is not what one considers when philosophizing, it is not what obsesses philosophers and theologians. Strategic meaning is the age old question, why are we here? Does anything matter? And so on. Although one could logically argue these vague issues don't even matter, there seems to be a fundamental psychological need to be convinced they do. While it's possible to explain this desire as just an extension of the instinctive survival motive being projected through an intelligent mind attempting to find a means of lengthening existence, it probably has something to do with the human body being a vehicle for the genes to perpetuate on a time-scale far in excess of any single person and human nature evolving within societies.

Both strategic and tactical meaning is firmly rooted in the genetic core of every living being. This is not fanciful but quite real even though widely misunderstood and misinterpreted, and thus abused and perverted in practice. This genetic drive is clouded in euphemisms and mystique, the soul, the spirit, love, and so on. The simplicity of meaning, life, and everything is its own deception within the intelligent and introspective human mind, and further, people tend to manufacture complexity to mask responsibility. Maria Montessori, one of the most profound genius' of 20th century social science (because she operated based on *observation* not *assumption*), once wrote, "A great deal of time and intellectual force are lost in the world, because the false seems great and the truth so small and insignificant."

Meaning truly is 'all in the mind' because your own personal perspective and attitude literally determines whether you live or you commit suicide. *The will to live is biological; the will to die is psychological.* The physical universe doesn't care at all one way or the other and will continue humming away long after you are gone, just as it did long before you were around. Our very identity is defined by relative connections. *If you want to alter who you are you must control what surrounds you, what the inputs are.* Identity, just like meaning itself, is largely (but not completely discounting genetic origins) relative to surroundings.

Laughter is a necessary defense mechanism against absurdity.

Many people prefer denial, they choose to believe in fantasies and get high on the veritable buffet of pop-drugs from God to TV to heroin (it's all the same) in order to escape, but the price they pay for a temporary feeling of happiness is going through life wearing a thick blindfold and both arms tied behind their back, metaphorically speaking. In truth most of humanity is far, far too weak to accept anything but cultural narcotics and self-delusions. Yet for these sad specimens in a very dangerous world where intelligence and cunning are your one true ally, suffering, confusion, and anguish are their only rewards. As Nietzsche said through Zarathustra, "To many men life is a failure; a poison-worm gnaweth at their heart. Then let

Nihilism

them see to it that their dying is all the more a success." So, let the dying begin.

Fortunately as a species we can adapt and overcome, or else we wouldn't still be here on this planet, but nevertheless the ones that can't adapt will die. In a world of anomie and rapid change, nihilism often acts as a fitness test for survival; those that can only see meaninglessness and futility self-destruct through suicide, the survivors overcome, and the successful see opportunity, challenge, and new experiences.

Meaning

First of all meaning is relative, it is relational. Take anything out of context and it loses its meaning and becomes absurd. This is why meaning seems so transient and difficult to define, it is not a 'something' it is a 'because of' (derivative). Ultimately the reason we seek meaning is to establish our social position and context, and to find a sense of happiness, or at least a sense of momentary ease. The existentialist position delves into this and eventually concludes that happiness is impossible. This view satisfies no one and only highlights the flaws of the existentialist position, for although they are correct in realizing that conflict is inherent in all social interactions they are not correct in concluding that harmony cannot emerge from the fracas of life.

Obviously no one wants to be redundant and feel useless or that their place and potential are a waste. Marx was closer to the truth by realizing that human worth is connected to what we do, labor is key to happiness. Nietzsche was closer still by connecting values to the internal will-force.

If you look around you'll find that some of the happiest and most optimistic people are those that own their own business. They work hard but remain upbeat and I think there's more to this than just personality. Any healthy person will put enormous effort into an endeavor if it fulfills at least two qualifications:

1. It's something they are interested in and enjoy dealing with.
2. The rewards from the endeavor are unambiguously returned to them personally, preferably with a direct connection between the effort (input) and the reward (output).

The third qualification is the frosting on the cake so to speak,

3. Other people also gain from the endeavor.

If all three are met then that's generally a happy person.

Further, the happiness principle involved here has nothing to do with capitalism since profit in terms of money is a secondary issue. Profit is just a means of perpetuating the enterprise and quantifying the reward. After all, many people work in non-profit businesses that serve the community and take little or no pay for their often very significant personal efforts; they're rewarded through principle three. Indeed selfishness and the inveterate need for personal profit in life is a vastly misunderstood concept that muddles some critically important aspects of human nature. The real question here is: are we gaining from taking or gaining from giving?

An interesting example which demonstrates the importance of principle two is that of video games where the connection between action and reward could not be more clear – and that's the appeal! Even deeper than that is the action, the 'labor' part. Being productive (or at least active) does two very important things, it occupies the mind with concrete and substantive issues, and it connects the physical world with the mental being.

The easy and overly convenient life spawns a general lack of meaning and purpose. Instead, expand the known limits, explore, climb a mountain, learn new things, push your physical and mental boundaries, accomplish the 'impossible'. Rediscover purpose through resistance, friction, and challenge. The easy life kills us, but the difficult life invigorates us.

Nihilism

Environment

Over millions of years we as a species, like other life, have adapted to fit our environment because failure to do so inexorably leads to death and even extinction. This basic rule of existence hasn't changed; we still must fit our surroundings or suffer the pitiless consequences. Yet our technological development is so profound and potent that we have begun to create our *own* environment apart from the natural realm that interactively created us as biological beings. Our artificial technological environment is currently incompatible with the natural environment, as evident from the widespread ecological devastation that has been perpetrated upon the natural world's life forms, oceans, atmosphere, and land. Primary responsibility for the devastation of the natural world can be traced back to religious beliefs, particularly the Jewish and Christian holy book of Genesis, dictating that the Earth's life and elements are for man to use as his property, generating a pernicious mindset that views everything as a resource to be endlessly exploited for private profit.

Although humanity is being compelled to develop a wisdom beyond religiously-derived resource exploitation, the artificial changes to the natural world have become so pronounced that we have actually generated an entirely new geological era, transitioning from the Holocene that began at the end of the most recent ice-age, into the *anthropocene*, meaning that human activities are marking the Earth in ways that will be detectable millions of years in the future, and altering our surroundings on a significant scale in the process.

When you fit your environment it no longer seems 'chaotic' and 'evil'. Think of a swamp – to outsiders it appears to be a miserable and disorderly realm of darkness and decay, but to the native inhabitants it's a paradise to thrive in.

So, not only do *we* have to be compatible with our artificial environment, but *it* also has to be compatible with the natural world, or we'll run out of resources amidst ecological collapse. Fortunately we have the technology to adjust our artificial realm, and the power to alter ourselves to fit within it. Unfortunately our collective wisdom in decision-making is often lacking, and this is the crux of the matter, for just as religious mentalities got us into this mess, strategically-sound scientific methods can get us out.

In the meantime, it's critical to recognize that the main physical reason for widespread environmental degradation, disease, wars, and even uncivil behavior, is simply a result of crowded living and the *overpopulation* of our own species as rated against the limited space and material we have on this small planet.

> "The more crowded it gets, the cheaper life becomes, and the easier it becomes to exploit people." – Donna Locke, 2006

We have several choices and they aren't mutually exclusive. We can reduce our population numbers, drastically increase our resource efficiency, or leave Earth and expand our frontier.

Culture

Although culture is as palpable as it is immeasurable and complex it's really just a collection of common beliefs, values, and ideas that slowly change with the winds of fashion and perception. Culture functions as a means of conveying collective knowledge from one generation to the next; and indeed many animals have culture too, so it's not even unique to humans. As participants, willing or otherwise, culture also serves as a dimension with which to perpetuate the concept of self. Culture is proxy immortality for the participants, a selfish gift to the next generation.

> [T]he force of culture shapes both behaviour and biology across generations. Culture has been confused with genes because behavioural studies are short-term, while culture operates on the scale of generations with a kind of tyranny and force that has not been widely recognised. – Sue Savage-Rumbaugh, 2010

Nihilism

Much of cultural knowledge was useful in the past but isn't any longer, and may even be harmful to development, but it gets pushed forward by inertia and habit. So, a culture that isn't questioned or revaluated, destroyed and reinvented, is a hopeless loop of history repeating itself where subsequent generations must repeatedly toil against the same pain and wrestle the same fictional demons. Culture unquestioned is just habit – it's the comfort of routine within the context of perceived history.

It's entirely natural for youth to revolt against the culture of their parents and their ancestors in order to test the necessity and validity of established cultural notions, to rid the world of dead and obsolescent ideas and harmful beliefs, and at the same time to craft an identity for themselves that's built from the foundation of the past and combined with their assessment of the present in order to survive and prosper in the future.

Now we know what culture comes from and what purpose it serves, so the important issue is what values are our culture based upon and perpetuating? If it's based upon faith in fantasy it will inevitably crumble to dust and spin everyone attached into disorder and self-destruction. If it's based instead on facts, skepticism, and a verifiable methodology it will have greater longevity while generating peace and prosperity for the cultural participants.

Life

What's the meaning of life? Where did life come from? These have long been fundamental human questions motivating theologians, philosophers, and scientists searching for answers. From as far back as can be discerned the fundamental algorithm for everything around us is the ability to be copied and extenuated. Anything that can fulfill this role will spread and succeed to varying degrees based on multiple factors, such as copying fidelity or cleverness in avoiding hazards and outwitting opponents. This is the root *meaning* of life; a tautology in that life exists because it exists, and continues to do so because it can adapt and overcome.

As the scale of our awareness increases our often inflated sense of self-importance shrinks in significance. And things are not always what they seem because we so often distort actual events through the lens of our selfish impulses. We now realize that, contrary to ego-driven beliefs, a human being, like all life, is the vehicle for genetic continuity. The reproducing animal is actually just the form genes use to spread and perpetuate. The ego-cult of the individual has been overthrown, yet the critical concept here is the act of replication, for even ideas moving through a sea of culture can outlast genes.

Where life came from isn't certain, but the basic outline is already known. From spectrographs scientists can detect that life's primary chemicals form in clouds of interstellar gas, a chemical soup warmed by a steady stream of cosmic radiation. Comets and asteroids bombarded the early Earth and delivered the basic chemical ingredients needed for life, such as water and amino acids.

> Curiously, almost every living organism on Earth uses left-handed amino acids instead of their right-handed counterparts. In the 1990s, scientists found that meteorites contain up to 15% more of the left version too. That suggests space rocks bombarding the early Earth biased its chemistry so that life used left-handed amino acids instead of right.[3]

Convincing evidence indicates life could have originated in underwater alkaline vents, consisting of bubbly rocks riddled with labyrinthine pores, which existed before Earth had an oxygen atmosphere.

> The last common ancestor of all life was not a free-living cell at all, but a porous rock riddled with bubbly iron-sulphur membranes that catalysed primordial biochemical reactions. Powered by hydrogen and proton gradients, this natural flow reactor filled up with organic chemicals, giving rise to proto-life that eventually broke out as the first living cells - not once but twice, giving rise to the bacteria and the archaea.[7]

Nihilism

This ingenious idea solves the mystery of two key elements necessary for cellular life – an energy source and a discrete package to protect the special chemical reactions. If this is the case the necessary situation and ingredients for life to begin must be remarkably common throughout the universe.

But if life really did originate on Earth it did so suspiciously fast – as soon as possible, immediately after Earth's formation during tumultuous volcanic cataclysms and violent meteorite impacts. Since the necessary situation and ingredients for life to begin must be common throughout the universe, it's not a great leap to consider the possibility of a cosmic origin for life in a theory called panspermia or exogenesis. In two separate experiments India launched rockets to search for signs of life in the upper atmosphere, in what was thought to be an inhospitable region for living things considering the high-levels of radiation. Yet life they did find – three previously unknown species of bacteria.[4] Incredibly, these two experiments establish that life *can* survive in outer space.

Whether life started here on Earth, or somewhere in space and was delivered to Earth by a comet or asteroid, the point is that our very physical existence is the direct result of cosmic events. Jumping from inorganic chemicals to self-perpetuating cells, life eventually evolved into sentient beings capable of recognizing what's happened!

The logical conclusion is that life must be ubiquitous, even if it's isolated and hidden from our currently very limited capacities for detection. This realization contains enormous significance. As living beings we are not unique or alone in the universe. No longer is Earth an anomaly and we can establish a context for our existence as a part of the greater universe. Our effort and struggle doesn't have to die here, alone and forgotten.

For tens of thousands of years people have gazed into the night-sky at an amazing multitude of scattered fires. They invented stories and elaborate religious beliefs to explain the burning lights. The ancient Greeks developed philosophy as a way to explain events and forces through subjective rhetoric. The scientific method was developed and it competed with philosophy and religion, eventually superseding both by providing objective, verifiable, and predictive conclusions. Between religion and philosophy, and between philosophy and science, someone imagined a different state of affairs and others helped to create it. Philosophy was overthrown and the burning spots in the sky turned out to be stars, and the stars turned out to have planets of their own, and someday we'll even find out what's on those planets.

Meanwhile the natural forces on our small and dynamic planet are continually creating the new by destroying the old, and a balance emerges from this natural state of chaos. Yet human effort so often struggles to retain the status quo long after it transforms from a benefit into a burden. It was once a blasphemy to suggest that the Earth revolved around the Sun rather than being the center of everything. Even today natural selection and biological evolution are attacked as heretical. Similarly it was once only the family, and then it was only the tribe, then the nation, the empire, the state, the global institution, and now the network. Despite the force of cultural inertia and social conservatism, superior ideas and predictive methodologies inexorably supplant the useless and ineffective.

Fire: Not even the healthy are safe in a forest of disease

Nihilism is often best conveyed within the context of biological parallels because they're so concisely applicable to our own survival. A prime example resides in the vast stretches of forested wilderness within western North America. If you live near or visit the forests you will see the death toll, the sick and dying trees, grim monuments to a dilemma generated by a hundred years of human error and human 'solutions'. Thousands of square miles showcase natural systems driven to unnatural states and forming an imbalanced order that presently defies resolution except through complete devastation.

A hundred years ago the western North American forests consisted of about 70 percent ponderosa pine and 30 percent Douglas and grand firs. Today the order is reversed, and this is a major problem

Nihilism

because harmful budworms attack, eat, and kill firs, but they don't eat ponderosa pines. Errant conservation programs, often necessary as a result of human development encroaching ever further into the forests, have had unintended consequences because prevention of all forest fires has created a very unnatural state.

Ponderosa pines need regular fires and before fire suppression efforts took place a ground fire would burn through the forests about once every ten years. These ground fires cleared underbrush, giving young pines space to grow, and with naturally fire-resistant bark the mature pines thrived. But without regular clearing fires the small trees and undergrowth multiply and this benefits Douglas firs that tolerate more shade better than pines. The Douglas firs have spread across the American West at the expense of fire-resistant pines. When fire does occur in a forest filled with underbrush the fire easily leaps to the tops of trees, creating an uncontrollable crown fire. When a crown fire occurs it's so severe that firefighters can only back off and defend elsewhere.

As budworm infestations spread so do the pernicious effects, eventually creating a 'stand-replacement event', a fire that burns the entire forest to the bare ground. As one expert put it, "The forest is ripe for catastrophic change."

Every summer news crews cover the outbreaks of forest fires and each year the conflagrations become more widespread, tougher to control, and more deadly to homes and fire fighters. Fire, usually in the form of lightning strikes, is a natural part of the forest life-cycle serving to clear out forest-floor detritus and prevent tree overcrowding. These natural periodic burns prevent the large scale unnatural holocaust conflagrations we now witness every summer. This is the result of a dogmatic approach to forest 'conservation' guided by wayward environmental activism and coupled with

mistaken government and industrial attempts to alter equilibrium and exploit nature as a 'resource'. Consequently the only way the forest can be saved is to leave it alone, let it burn to the ground, and allow the trees to start all over and grow back from seed.

The same malevolent parties responsible for reducing the western forests to a state of lingering death have brought human life to an equally unhealthy nadir. Blame government for horrendously flawed and short sighted policy. Blame monomaniacal environmentalism and the legion of similar dogmatic ideologies. Blame mass-media for conveying erroneous and overly simplified filtered views of reality, Smokey Bear cartoon truth, manic fire prevention and 'build a house in the woods'; all the while failing to properly explain the science behind the fires or the danger of living in the wilderness. Blame industry for logging off the natural life to begin with and either clear cutting or replanting with the wrong trees as well as importing foreign species that take over and wreak havoc, all for improved pulp production, faster growth or whatever the reason.

Nihilism is not abstract philosophy, it's tangible and of imperative significance. Much as our forests have become unstable and doomed to destruction, warped to where sickness, disease and death are endemic, so has our own society. The forest of our society has become deadly to the human inhabitants, a natural system chronically corrupted, the equilibrium fractured and our environment driven to unnatural states. But it's a slow change, just slow enough that most can entertain the notion everything is fine while those perplexing problems will all be rectified without personal price or harmful collective consequence. But in parallel with the spread of subconscious unease comes knowledge of what few can admit even to themselves – the end is very near and there's only one way out.

To a Nihilist, destruction for survival is not counterintuitive it's just common sense, and all the technology, all the faith, all the prayer and all the effort to stop it will not tarry that eventual event.

Nihilism

Rage Beyond Right or Wrong

The early years of the 21st century have already featured increasingly widespread and violent outbursts of suburban youth-driven rage, growing from the ranks of the impoverished, into the working class, and now including even the middle class. The deliberate police shooting of 15-year-old Alexandros Grigoropoulos in Greece sparked riots and protests in December 2008, but this was only the catalyst that released simmering anger over much greater social and economic trouble. As a result thousands of Greeks staged street protests and violent riots, attacking police and property and creating the most severe civil unrest since the collapse of Greece's military dictatorship in 1974.[1] Yet unlike traditional public protests planned and organized to address one, or a few, key issues and then the demonstrators return home afterwards, the new rage is notable for spontaneity and a lack of clear aim on the part of those involved.

Actions in the Paris suburbs, and other cities in France in 2005 and 2007, and across Greece in December 2008, are potent examples of this new rage. Indeed, this is nihilism by dictionary definition: *When conditions in the social organization are so unhealthy as to make destruction desirable for its own sake independent of any constructive program or possibility.* After seeing peaceful demonstrations ignored by authorities, voting produce no substantive political change, and the gap between the rich and the poor and what those in power *do* and what everyone else *needs* grow ever wider, it's only natural that violent and unfocused anger emerges from chronic injustice and disenfranchisement.

The post-anarchists have no heroes, nothing to believe in, no progressive future to look forward to, and everything around them is FUBAR. This is pure nihilism; it's all wrong so tear it all down. This is a generation of nihilists without a label, living in an anomic world, many lacking even a name to call themselves or a symbol for recognition! It may be an unspoken nihilistic rage, but in the process we're reminded that the only way to be heard by those in power is through violent outbursts because peaceful protests are ignored. In order for your voice and concerns to be recognized by those in power you have to shake things up and force authorities to respond. And without a resolution and a solution the rage only grows.

> [T]he new generation of urban guerrillas has tried neither to garner popular support nor explain its actions. Instead, the Sect of Revolutionaries, believed by experts to be a branch of Revolutionary Struggle - a group that made its debut with a rocket attack on the US embassy in 2007, and also thought to be behind the attack on Citibank - has stood out for its cold cynicism and marked lack of ideology. "We don't do politics, we do guerrilla warfare," it declared [in Greece, February 2009].[2]

So, while authorities try to suppress the nihilism, and philosophers debate how bad it is, the sentiment remains and spreads regardless of official opinion. This amorphous revolt has to be carried through to the natural conclusion, otherwise it's just like government's attempted rescue of the broken economy – bailing out criminal billionaires and busted banks when if we just allowed natural failure we could purge the mistakes, punish the guilty, and move on.

Once you begin to visualize a world that is different, a system that we like and want to participate in as opposed to the current corrupt authority-establishment predicated upon mass-disenfranchisement, you've made the first step towards creating it.

21st Century Existence

Existence is predicated upon by relationships, just as meaning emerges from the interactions of those living relationships. So just as primitive human societies, and indeed most life, functions in a nominal state of equilibrium with surrounding environment, we must form a new state of nominal balance between our surroundings and ourselves expressed through an array of relationships. Technologically primitive humans had to do this through myths and beliefs that were gradually developed over hundreds, even thousands of years based on continuous and steady interactions with a relatively stable natural environment.

Yet today we live in an advanced, primarily artificial, environment crafted by our own enterprise and structured for our own short-term benefit – but at long-term costs that are rarely included in near term expenses. If we are to survive individually and collectively our new equilibrium must be one based upon the same consistent, verifiable, and predictable forces that we use to build our surroundings – primarily physics, math, and science in general. This requires a radically different approach to living than what we have experienced in our collective past, just as our own environment has already radically changed from traditional lifestyle patterns.

Although we can't go back to a stagnant past, we *can* go forward into a dynamic and fruitful future. But evolution doesn't occur without cost or sacrifice. Archaic and traditional beliefs still dominate social values and assumptions even though every structure we have built has been through a completely different viewpoint, that of reason and science. The values and beliefs that many still cling to now lead us collectively into self-defeating dead-ends while our words, abstracted ideas, and expressions are all too often contradicted by our real actions based on necessity or desire. As has become painfully obvious amidst a record-breaking economic crisis, epic ideological collapse, gory religious wars, and widespread anomie, much of what has been accepted as truth has turned out to be abominable lies, while holy gods have failed, and supposedly overwhelming authorities have crumbled to dust under scrutiny and public challenge.

As the social scientist Gustave Le Bon once stated, "The beginning of a revolution is in reality the end of a belief." Take a cue from Mikhail Bakunin and ignite the fires of revolution around the globe, one belief at a time.

Until our words match our deeds, and our deeds match our words, until our values are finally based upon consistent elements, we will only foolishly struggle against inviolate forces while wallowing in a morass of suffering, internal contradiction, and detrimental social hypocrisy. In order to overcome we must test to find weakness, while openly challenging assumptions and established beliefs so we can learn what remains valid and what is simply myth. In life it's not enough to just be told the answers and ordered what to do, because some answers may be correct for one but not for another, or invalid in a different time or place. This is why 'learning' by command is one of the most blatant and harmful flaws of the establishment education system. Ultimately you have to learn the answers on your own, but more importantly we all need a robust methodology to be able to find valid answers regardless of the time, place, or situation. Remember, *you can't control your own life until you start to think for yourself.*

Just as Maria Montessori did what Friedrich Nietzsche could not do as a philosopher – turn radical ideas into a practical methodology, so it is today in the 21st century we need a revolution to establish a methodology that allows us to evolve and develop on a social and environmental level in conjunction with our technology, so one force doesn't far exceed the other.

As Nihilists we are terminators of belief, enemies of social hypocrisy, and opponents of a society that forces aberrant and contradictory behavior creating schizophrenic values and mental anguish. In this way Nihilists are catalysts, they're lightning bolts setting fire to the diseased and dying forest and compelling a new paradigm to grow in the newfound absence, the nothingness of a healthy and invigorating apocalypse.

Those who can't imagine a different future are doomed to repeat the past. – Freydis

PROFILES IN NIHILISM

Nihilistic figures aren't as rare as many might assume, they're simply unrecognized or misunderstood. So, in an effort to rectify that issue, here are some famous nihilistic historical characters:

Mikhail Bakunin (1814-1876)

Mikhail Bakunin: "Founder of Nihilism and apostle of anarchy."
– Alexander Herzen

Mikhail Bakunin was born into a wealthy Russian family in 1814 and even from an early age his rebellious personal nature and outlook set him at odds against the ruling class he emerged from. Unsatisfied with life in a stagnant aristocracy he sacrificed it all to become a revolutionary.

Bakunin rejected philosophy, detested love and sought to destroy harmony because it meant stagnation and limitation of potential. Indeed his entire worldview was one of action and rebellion even if simply for its own sake regardless of aim or goal. A completed task, be it a revolution, a book, or even a sentence, was anathema to Bakunin because it meant one could go no further, it left nothing else to do! "We must act, act perpetually in order to be human ... in order to possess real awareness of ourselves." The purpose of life to Bakunin resided in the process not the goal!

Bakunin wanted action, he placed movement over passive thought and this was his charm because he meshed so well with the turbulent milieu of his era. Bakunin became an icon and a legend. Rumor and myth about his escapes from the secret police and his own talk of direct action created an aura of the superhuman revolutionary, fulfilling the eras need for a leader and hero even if his actual deeds often failed to fulfill the myths around him.

Bakunin refused to accept the limitation of the present and took nothing for granted. "The commonplace is the most terrible phantom binding us with vain but strong, invisible chains." Bakunin's view discarded the standard moral, aesthetic and even emotional elements and distilled everything down to just thought and revolt!

Even at the time Bakunin was often difficult to describe and even more difficult to categorize ideologically within the context of his 19th century contemporaries. Bakunin gained from process rather than accomplishment in life, whether the process had aim or not wasn't so much the issue as the act itself. And although his direct involvement in revolutionary activities was often limited Bakunin had a much greater impact on contemporary, and even future ideas. His primary surviving work is the book God and the State, a potent patchwork of ideas and musings on history, revolution, religion and authority.

Bakunin's destructive words influenced the Nihilists in the 1860s characterized by the clean-sweep revolution. "...the modern rebels believe, as Bazarov and Pisarev and Bakunin believed, that the first requirement is the clean sweep, the total destruction of the present system; the rest is not their business. The future must look after itself. Better anarchy than prison; there is nothing in between."[1]

Marcel Duchamp (1887-1968)

Marcel Duchamp was a dada artist whose approach was intentional, calculated, concise, and even reductionist. Instead of making art through randomness, as some other dada artists attempted to do, he took the opposite course and made art through calculation. Hans Richter, a contemporary of Duchamp, referred to him as "the nihilist of art".

Nihilism

> His purpose was to administer a strong purgative to an age riddled with lies – and to the society which had brought it into being – an age of shame for which he found an artistic counterpart in the shape of a Mona Lisa with a moustache. – Hans Richter, 1964

Duchamp is most famous for his 'ready-made' art where he would take a manufactured object, sign it, reposition it, and then present it as a finished work. But this wasn't a cynical endeavor to exploit a gullible public for cash, it was an effort to attack and challenge the values upholding art and establishment society around him. In 1917 Duchamp took a urinal and turned it over, signed it 'R. Mutt' and submitted it to an art show! His ready-mades weren't meant to be admired in an aesthetic sense and because of this he challenged the belief in art as something holy and placed on a high pedestal, art as something distant and divorced from life.

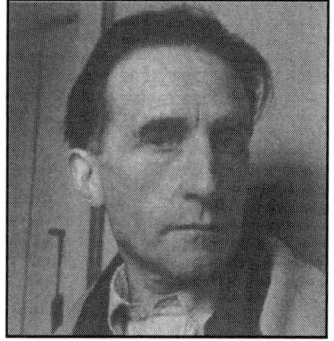

It's interesting to note that Duchamp didn't agree with the attitudes and direction taken by Pop Art and Neo-Dada that arrived several decades later. Although those newer art movements took many of the concepts from dada art (1916-1922), instead of being anti-establishment and anti-authority, as dada was, Pop Art only created a new entertainment commodity for the wealthy to consume. In a letter dated November 10, 1962 Marcel Duchamp wrote:

> This Neo-Dada, which they call New Realism, Pop Art, Assemblages, etc., is an easy way out, and lives on what Dada did. When I discovered ready-mades I thought to discourage aesthetics. In Neo-Dada they have taken my ready-mades and found aesthetic beauty in them. I threw the bottle-rack and the urinal into their faces as a challenge and now they admire them for their aesthetic beauty.[2]

Freydis

Vera Figner (1852-1943)

Vera Figner was born into a wealthy family in Kazan Russia. She wanted to become a doctor but Russian society wouldn't allow it because she was a woman, so she left and went to Switzerland to study. In Geneva she met many other Russians who were frustrated by the backwardness of Russian society and outraged by the repression and police-state terrorism inflicted upon anyone that openly questioned Tsarist authority. Vera rapidly acquired a revolutionary worldview, returned to Russia, and joined the Land and Liberty revolutionary group. She subsequently went with the radical People's Will faction when it split off in 1879. In two years she became the leader of the group, and then planned the successful assassination of Tsar Alexander II that occurred in 1881.

Vera Figner had the courage to challenge a political establishment where property, wealth, and power were all controlled by a small (male) portion of the population, elite that used their influence to perpetuate a dysfunctional society where most Russians lived in severe poverty as feudal slaves. Never one to waste time or mince words, she always took the direct approach: "Murder and the gibbet captivated the imagination of our young people; and the weaker their nerves and the more oppressive their surroundings, the greater was their sense of exaltation at the thought of revolutionary terror." It's simple cause and effect – you reap what you sow; when the forces of authority make an environment that disallows peaceful change, they make violent revolution inevitable.

Vera Figner was a very remarkable woman who survived a death-sentence, prison, exile to Siberia, the Bolshevik revolution, the Bolshevik's *themselves*, and she still lived to be over 90.

Nihilism

Gorgias (~485-378 BCE)

Gorgias, also known as 'The Nihilist', came from Sicily and went on to fame and fortune as one of the most successful sophists in Greece. He was so adept at rhetoric that he verbally negated 'truth' and elevated argumentative discourse into primacy. Indeed Gorgias claimed to be able to train others to sway opinion regardless of knowledge of the subject utilizing his methods of rhetoric alone. One reputed tactic was to demolish an opponent's seriousness with humor and their humor with seriousness.

> ...it must have had a beginning. Its being must have arisen either from being, or from not-being. If it arose from being, there is no beginning. If it arose from not-being, this is impossible, since something cannot arise out of nothing.
> – Gorgias, a master of logical maneuvering.

With the success of rhetoric Gorgias believed that words have relativistic meanings and since the definitions can change then the meaning becomes debatable. Rhetoric in this case is thus more important than any underlying meaning attached to the words; persuasion negates objective truth since truth is subjective, being defined by opinion which is variable.

Gorgias and other Greek sophists represented the beginning of philosophy and the first conflict between the traditional mystical belief system and a rational, skeptical view of the natural world. It was as basic as the difference between a worldview built on emotion and one on thought. Because the sophists challenged established beliefs they were often condemned by public authorities and critics as moral corrupters or worse.

By leading a frenetically transient lifestyle and talking his way out of trouble, Gorgias, evaded both the city-state taxman, made a comfortable sum on appearance fees long before it became fashionable by unemployed politicians and washed-up actors, and is reported to have lived to be over a hundred.

Freydis

Niccolo Machiavelli (1469-1527)

Irving Kristol is purported to have once called Machiavelli "the first nihilist". As you can tell after reading this book he's definitely not the first, but it's still an intriguing and provocative assessment of a notable character. Machiavelli was a Florentine statesman and a remarkably observant student of human nature. His book The Prince is an apt tool for gaining and maintaining political power as well as the policy making of expediency. Niccolo was a nihilist in the sense that he didn't allow morality in planning or ethics in his treatise to obstruct his judgment, although he was certainly aware of the implications of his endeavor. Consequently he constructed a product that despite complaints and condemnation remains useful and accessible to anyone.

Niccolo used his mastery of history, especially the Roman politicians, to form patterns and draw logical conclusions. He called 'em as he saw 'em, a pragmatism perhaps more accurately categorized within chronology as opportunism but that's just a sign of understandable ambition. Still the infamy ascribed to Machiavelli is remarkably inappropriate given the logical simplicity of his conclusions. *"Men in general judge rather by the eye than by the hand, for every one can see but few can touch. Every one sees what you seem, but few know what you are."* Machiavelli's message was not a justification of authoritarian excess but the political prudence of a perpetually placated public.

The bottom line is that it's much easier for the people to prevent abuses of power when they actually understand how authorities manipulate and misuse it against them, and this is what makes Machiavelli so important even today. "He [Machiavelli] professed to teach kings; but it was the people he really taught." – Jean-Jacques Rousseau.

Nihilism

Sergei Nechayev (1847-1882)

The Russian Revolutionary era of the second half of the 19th century was characterized by some very fiery personalities, like Michael Bakunin. But if the rest were intense, Sergei Nechayev was a thermobaric bomb!

For a while Sergei Nechayev operated in an ideological gray area between radical anarchism and political nihilism. But after publishing his 'Catechism of a Revolutionist' and promoting the most violent means to justify a destructive end, the anarchists expressed concern and trepidation over both Nechayev's methods and his highly focused and conspicuous lack of moral boundaries.

And when it came to revolutionary focus Nechayev was downright laser-like. His modus operandi was nihilistic in that he desired destruction of the polity regardless of any constructive future, or at

least it wasn't a concern for the present. But by placing all the emphasis upon eliminating the political and social system of oppression and censorship without offering a vision of superior alternative it not only limited popular appeal but this manic adherence to the 'Revolutionist' precepts essentially became one of a questionable faith anyway.

Still, given the brutal context of feudal Tsarist Russia there was logic to his methodology because whether you criticized the Tsars fashion sense or threatened to kill his entire family and the little dog too, you'd still end up doing the same 20 years of hard labor when caught by the secret police. Nechayev correctly surmised the lack of benefit to half-measure within the revolution.

Freydis

Friedrich Nietzsche (1844-1900)

Nietzsche was a philosopher and writer that still defies simplistic characterization. Although in most cases he did not consider himself a nihilist he did contribute greatly to the concept in its modern form. Having stated that for clarity, Nietzsche definitely did display nihilistic characteristics. Nietzsche was quite unafraid to venture into dangerous territory and to craft new powerful ideas while breaking from the burden of tradition and the past. He was a pioneer of the mind that was unlike any of his contemporaries and distant leaps away from any antecedents. In a religious era he broke with God and became an atheist. When most people embraced self-defeat by believing in a pre-determined, static world, Nietzsche embraced self-actualization and the burning ambition to alter human events on a cosmic scale. Nietzsche's appeal emerges from the combination of his intellect and literary talent to craft myth and imagery in an inspirational form.

The Red Army Faction [Baader Meinhof Gang] (1968-1998)

The Rote Armee Fraktion (RAF), more commonly known as the Baader Meinhof Gang, was a revolutionary group founded by Andreas "the whole system is shit" Baader and journalist Ulrike Meinhof in West Germany around 1968. Amidst an environment of student-led protest and government/corporate-created carnage in Southeast Asia, the RAF fought back against oppressive powers, leaving a trail of targeted violence and destruction while branching out to connect with other European and Middle Eastern revolutionary groups.

Nihilism

The intent of the RAF was to create an atmosphere of instability in West Germany in order to expose the Federal government as a tyrannical regime masked behind rhetoric of being a democracy. The RAF saw the German public as a reactionary mass that had been usurped by consumerism into serving the commercial capitalist enterprise. As a consequence they concluded that individual expressions of revolutionary action could ignite a new social consciousness.

In the process the West German government became even more authoritarian, nullifying legal rights to stomp out the 'Red menace' without a second thought.

Despite numerous brazen and high-profile actions the RAF succumbed to tactical and strategic mistakes, alienating some of their public support base and leading to the arrest of their main leaders, while struggling against an increasingly fearful, safety-seeking populace. But ultimately, it was the end of the Vietnam War and a general change in social and political climate that eroded their momentum. Nonetheless, the RAF had a remarkable cohesion and intensity that made them the most enduring urban revolutionary group in the western world, lasting around 30 years, while transcending social mores and trite political categories of left and right to move beyond into a realm of socio-political nihilism.

Diogenes of Sinope (~404-323 BCE)

Diogenes of Sinope was a remarkable thinker of classical Greece, one of the Cynics who were known for defying convention, deriding superstition, rejecting money and kings, being scornful of sophisms, and disdainful of Plato. Diogenes concluded that each individual must be guided by reason, otherwise, like an animal, she will need to be lead by a leash. Reasoned thought can plan ahead and prevent repeated mistakes.

In an encounter with the egotistical conqueror Alexander the Great, after being asked if he wanted anything, Diogenes replied, "Stand a little less between me and the sun."

Diogenes had a talent for undercutting social and religious conventions and subverting political power through rhetoric and humor, but his contentious character wasn't merely for the sake of rebellion. Diogenes aimed to promote reason over reaction, and consideration of action over blind animal instinct.

Max Stirner (1806-1856)

Max Stirner, born as Johann Kaspar Schmidt in Bayreuth Germany, was a unique but awkward nihilistic and existential critic who placed the individual in primacy as the defining value of existence. He wrote in The Ego and His Own about living from self-driven principles where values are based on personal preferences. In his writing Stirner expressed an intense nihilism, criticizing religions, ideologies, establishment institutions and modern values as hollow and antagonistic to the self-driven individual.

Despite over 150 years of sporadic circulation in intellectual circles Stirner has continually failed to gain any significant traction, with major thinkers and philosophers refusing to even admit an awareness of his ideas. Part of the trouble is Stirner severe viewpoint, the rest his nearly impenetrable writing that's exceptionally difficult to read. Stirner expressed anarchistic sentiment yet he attacked the values of anarchism. His extremely individualistic attitudes are usually seen as anti-social and dissociative if carried out in practice. Nonetheless, Stirner's nihilistic impact on western thought deserves reconsideration. Self-interest is basically how people act anyway but their behavior becomes perverted in outcome because it's masked by cultural myths and delusions concerning social order. Reduction to the universal need

Nihilism

for self-preservation can actually create a durable common element for collective efforts if clearly articulated and commonly recognized.

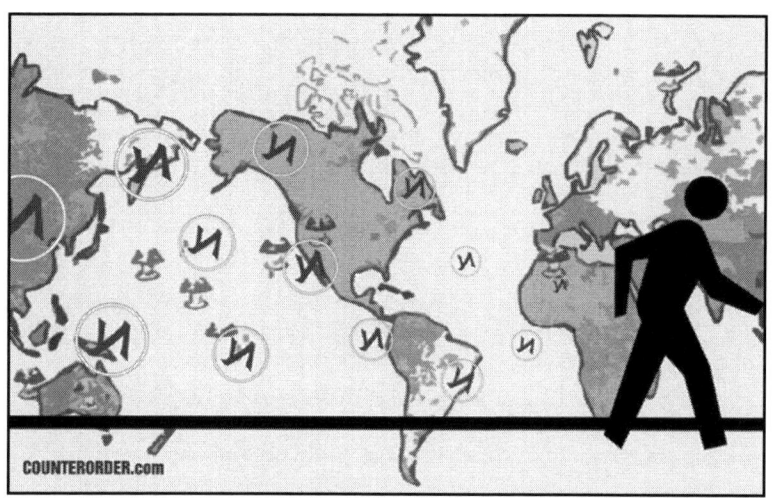

Worldwide Noman, by Freydis, 2005

"Don't accept the old order, get rid of it." – Johnny Rotten

Freydis

NIHILISM IN ART

Although Dada is probably the most closely associated art genre with nihilism, it's not the only one containing nihilistic elements. Nihilism can be found in the art of Surrealism, Futurism, even Pop-art.

Futurism sought to overcome the weight of the past while promoting technological elements of the future, intending to bludgeon the public with shock effects.

> We must break down the gates of life to test the bolts and the padlocks! Let us go! Here is the very first sunrise on earth! Nothing equals the splendor of its red sword which strikes for the first time in our millennial darkness." – F. T. Marinetti, 1909

Founded by Filippo Tommaso Emilio Marinetti with the publication of his Futurist Manifesto in 1909, Futurism was a response to the ossified, backwards-looking conservatism of early 20th century Europe, and Italy in particular. Intentionally provocative and inflammatory, Emilio Marinetti's Manifesto was a call to rebellion and grand action that sought to build a new and vibrant future, while rejecting establishment culture trapped in a mythical past.

> [T]he Futurist programme was based on the refusal of all closed and predetermined forms, on the exigency of a constant renewal of the arts, and the affirmation of the individual's creative mind above all social hierarchy.[1]

In their manifestos of 1909 to 1913 the Futurists celebrated the dynamism of great cities, the energy and destructive force of modern inventions. The hectic, deafening chaos of a mechanized world would destroy the old morality, the old society, the outmoded human product. They saw the cycle of death and rebirth repeated in men's entanglement with the machine, with electric power and kinetic force.[2]

While Futurism was an unstable mixture of anarchistic attitudes and militaristic passions, Dada on the other hand was thoroughly anti-establishment and opposed to military authority. Both Futurism and dada shared a disdain for tradition. Futurism became a classic example of justified rebellion discredited by misplaced idealism; Dada outlasted Futurism because it didn't have that same weakness; nevertheless it didn't take too long before even the dadaists themselves disliked dada because the art was always secondary to the emotion – rejection, alienation, and anger. Dada was largely a reaction to the bourgeoisie nationalist carnage and fratricide of the First World War. Dada is often referred to as 'nihilistic art', mostly because it was often devoid of rules and in direct conflict with many contemporary values.

> This dissolution was the ultimate in everything that Dada represented, philosophically and morally; everything must be pulled apart, not a screw left in it customary place, the screw-holes wrenched out of shape, the screw, like man himself, set on its way towards new functions which could only be known after the total negation of everything that had existed before. Until then: riot destruction, defiance, confusion. The role of chance, not as an extension of the scope of art, but as a principle of dissolution and anarchy. In art, anti-art.[3]

All of the above mentioned art genres are derivatives of reality, they're perceptions and subjective interpretations, and that's perhaps the primary appeal. Personally, I tend to see the most nihilistic art as being views and depictions of things and events as they naturally are, because these objects and forces aren't good or bad, they just are until subjectively interpreted. But then again that's mostly what art is about anyway – subjective and emotional interpretations of objective events. Enter 'New Realism':

Whereas the Impressionists believed that art should record visual impressions left by actual experience, and the Expressionists strove to reveal an inner, emotional reality, the New Realists strove to objectively catalog everyday life. Their focus was broad and unsparing, embracing all aspects of existence, no matter how sordid or mundane.[4]

Examples of this 'Neue Sachlichkeit,' (German for New Realism), also called Objectivism, can be seen in the work of Karl Blossfeldt as well as his contemporaries like George Grosz and Otto Dix. Indeed, 1930s Germany seems to have been a watershed for this, and other revolutionary forms.

Neue Sachlichkeit can be a truly remarkable art form with the capacity to convey ideas and concepts in seemingly unlikely ways. Just showing a thing as it is, and even calling it what it is, has significant impact within the context of our American(ized) culture where every product and idea must be obfuscated by the smokescreen of 'spin' and propaganda; this is the reality of unreality where unintended killing of civilians on the battlefield becomes 'collateral damage', where software flaws are called 'features' and where increased consumption is not considered waste but 'boosting the economy'.

Optical art has connections to futurism, neue sachlichkeit, and surrealism too, but it's most widely seen as an outgrowth of Pop-art because of the chronological overlap. Bridget Riley is one of the most well known artists in the genre of Op Art, and M.C. Escher also falls into this category.

> What all Op artists share in common is a relinquishment of any fixed vantage point on the part of the viewer, which, together with a multi-focal composite compells [sic] the eye to ever-fresh perception. This is under-scored by an elimination of the artist's personal touch, in an attempt to concentrate solely on the objective, optical event taking place on the surface. The visual unrest of Op Art reflects

an urge not only to keep the eye moving but to set the work of art itself in motion.[5]

The popular works of the Dutch artist MC Escher are usually referred to as Optical Art; they revealed the challenges of perspective and dimension by creating new views of common and imaginary objects or settings. Richard Estes, a Photorealist, painted everyday objects and urban locations from photographs.

Out of Order, by Freydis, 2002

Heironymous Bosch, Delvaux, Dali, and Magritte are generally classified as surrealistic artists in its various forms. Many other artists across genres created works that strongly conveyed nihilistic themes, intentionally or otherwise. Edward Kienholz is a personal favorite for his use of readily available materials from junkyards and thrift stores to construct reflective commentary on society and contemporary values. The rest are nihilistic at least in the sense the artists challenge convention to create new forms and aesthetic expressions. As their methods and products become accepted, admired and even institutionalized over time, it often illuminates the fungible nature of values, the influence of authorized approval, and the coercion of conformity.

> All is not as it appears to be, Magritte is saying; the picture thus presents a challenge to ordered society and an assault on the accepted way in which people see and think.[6]

With an ever-expanding array of genres, styles, code-words, good and bad, right ways and wrong ways, the official art world can seem thoroughly complicated. And yet most of the artificial complexity is simply bullshit.

The role of popular artist appeals to narcissistic personalities because it's something that can generate positive identity as well as an aura of special skills that therefore magnify the uniqueness and importance of the artist. This is a boat everybody wants to be on since people want to be congratulated and sought after. Yet it loses its value when *anyone* can be an artist, hence the creation of those widespread cliques and elitist clubs. Special interpretations and ways of being an artist are meant to exclude the majority in order to magnify the minority. This is the inveterate search for a monopoly through the power of definition. The clique that can define what art actually is to the masses gains enormous power and coveted prestige. Connect the dots: today's art movements are no better than others, the artists are no better either, they just hold a very transitory monopoly.

Nihilism

"It [conceptual art] is the product of over-indulged middle-class bloated egos who patronise real people with fake understanding." – Ivan Massow, chairman of the Institute of Contemporary Arts, January 2002.

Given that typically the only genuine 'concept' in conceptual art is the alliance of ego and money, this is not a surprising turn of events. Clearly the art world is in desperate need of a replacement genre and I suggest a more nihilistic alternative.

A Nihilist filters the sound out of the noise, they view these elements through the lens of critical reduction and conclude that all art, be it a 30,000-year-old cave painting in France or a crucifix in a jar of urine, has a crucial common element – the evocation of emotion, the conveyance of a message. Art is communication and superior art is superior communication. Everything else is icing on the cake. Beauty, colors, form, style, all just accessories designed to enhance spread and popularity of the ideas ensconced within the art. Everyone can be an artist, but the best artists have a superior ability to convey ideas and emotions.

I think beauty can only be generated by natural forces and mimicked by the human artist. True beauty resides within the wispy colors of a nebular cloud or the intricate veins of a green leaf, hence the art most widely deemed 'beautiful' consists of accurate depictions of nature, be it an Ingres portrait or a Church nature scene. Otherwise aesthetic values are primarily subjective and ancillary to the issue of art anyway, it just makes a good thing better.

Art is simply a means of communication, and whatever means that's effective is valid, and then some. It's not about style or training or name or prestige, it's about evoking emotion and ideas. Art is simply a vehicle, a means of conveying a message but it also contains significant subjective qualities.

Ultimately art should be more than just a source of passive bemusement; it should be a participatory activity. When art is a recipe rather than static monstrosities collecting dust in pretentious museums, art where the viewer is part of the process, they become artists as well. Not only does this dissolve the repulsive elitism staining modern art but it becomes entertaining and enlightening too because there's nothing holy or mystical about art or the qualities an artist must possess. This is the most nihilistic and democratized art movement I can think of because it has no set genre and no clique is defining what's acceptable. Every artist creates what they are best at creating and what's most appealing to them while anyone else that appreciates the same material can use the recipe, the instructions to create their own version, slightly changed to suit themselves. Paint the walls, post on the Internet, wear it on your shirts, it doesn't matter. The more you practice the better the product looks. Give it a try.

As long as war remains financially profitable, its application to every problem (both real and imagined) will only increase. – Freydis

NIHILISM AND BEYOND

This chapter includes various articles written between 1998 and 2008 that elaborate upon Nihilism and related issues.

Food or Faith?

Jesus said "It is written: 'Man does not live on bread alone, but on every word that comes from the mouth of God." (Matthew 4:4) in an attempt to justify religion as one of life's daily necessities. But despite the counterintuitive word of God through Jesus, man can and does live on bread alone. Meaning that no one has died from spiritual malnutrition or a dearth of philosophy, indeed no one has even gotten sick from lack of faith in God or any 'higher power'!

In actuality it's clear that we have food and then we have faith and since nihilism is beyond transient values, 'beyond good and evil', nihilism is with the *food* and not the *faith*. The faith is interchangeable; it's a fungible, extraneous desire, not a mandatory necessity. Food is a constant required by all living things but faith is a variable, and a very insidious variable to be certain because it means whatever authorities and officially sanctioned interpreters declare it to mean.

> "There is nothing so absurd that it has not been said by philosophers." – Cicero

The universe doesn't hide anything from us; there is no intentional mischievousness inherent within nature. A God is not out there trying to conceal the secrets of life and the universe from us all. I've written before that the interpreters ruin the world and indeed they do because it is they who invent the fictions, create the fantasies and beliefs. Everything is already out there, all the answers are staring back at us. But if one wants to see things that aren't there, they must be interpreted or concocted out of the existing universal order. Now at times there are certain tactical advantages to creating fantasy worlds and convincing others to play along, but these benefits are inevitably negated by strategic events.

A guess without a test is a waste. Unverifiable philosophizing and 'interpreting' the universe requires immense effort with no commensurate benefit for doing so and is ultimately indicative of a person with far too much free time.

For the wages of unreality is death

To think that an artificially manufactured belief or interpretation is a life necessity is a serious and ultimately mortal mistake; such thinking displays a serious cognitive dysfunction – *it is a disease.* A nihilist does not 'believe' in nihilism because nihilism offers nothing for anyone to believe in. Nihilism is a label and symbol for the realization of the order, chaos and continual processes that are already out there and always will be.

Should I Vote?

Is the glass half full or is it half empty? Deciding whether to vote or not is the same sort of question – the answer depends on your perspective and sentiment at the given moment, but the short answer is *yes*, so let me explain.

Politics is the shit in life you can't escape from, so even though the dominant political parties that almost always win the elections (Democrat & Republican, Labour & Tory, etc.) don't represent me or my interests, and probably don't represent you either, the decisions they make in office will still affect us nonetheless. That leaves us in a quandary. If we don't vote at all they will definitely win the election and can claim a mandate based on the sizeable majority of the votes

Nihilism

that put them in office. If we do vote and participate in an election system that is a sham we risk justifying it, but can at least exert a small influence upon the outcome while at the same time gaining a legitimate allowance for criticism by virtue of participation. I like to think of voting as renewing my license to criticize the democratic political system.

If you look at the low voter turnout in the average election in the United States, for example, the pseudo-democratic system doesn't need mass participation to justify itself. So I think to criticize voting as simply supporting a broken system is misleading and perhaps even over-simplified. Everyone is told that what we have now is representative democracy and it's the greatest thing invented since sliced bread so very few people are willing to take the risk of openly criticizing it. Consequently the most practical and rational option is to vote in a way that maximizes the message being conveyed to the elected officials. The two ways to do this are:

- Vote for the main opposition party to create maximum political turmoil and gridlock.
- Vote for a 'third' candidate / minor party that will actually represent your interests.

Many have rued the truism that *if voting changed anything it would be illegal*. But we have to put voting in perspective. Don't expect radical change to occur but don't completely discount the impact that your vote can have – it may not be much but it is there if you want to use it. This brings me to another major question: why are voters so afraid to vote for a minor party candidate even though the two party duopoly is so obviously corrupted, useless, and even outright malevolent towards the public?

I think part of the issue is related to a difference in viewpoints between generations. Voters that are middle aged and older are still convinced that they can elect Party Left or Party Right and solve everything. Conversely, skepticism and cynicism towards the two-party duopoly is widespread among youth today.

Another major impediment to seeing what's really going on is the *sports spectator effect* – the popular desire to be a part of the winning team through vicarious association, in this case by voting for the candidate that gets elected. People have to stop thinking about 'winning' in the election. Nobody is really *winning* anything in this system except the candidate that gets their meat-hooks into office and the lobbyists and special interest groups they're funneling the kickbacks too. Voting just to be a vicarious winner, instead of voting for the candidate that really represents you, is about as asinine as you can get, yet that is exactly how many voters behave!

Finally, the people that vote most often are the ones that feel they have something invested in the social and political order and as such they tend to not want it to change radically, or at all, because that could negatively impact their interests. This is why the richer the voter is the more likely they are to vote for a conservative, and vice versa. People that are disenfranchised and disaffected have much less invested in the status quo and thus they typically see no benefit to participating or supporting it and so they don't vote. Unfortunately this short term self-interest only serves to justify and perpetuate the status quo, creating a self-fulfilling prophecy.

Where's the Truth?

The primary process under the rubric of nihilism is skepticism, it is to take as little for granted as possible and that includes nihilism itself. Philosophical nihilism is inherently contradictory, for instance to state that 'no truth exists' is just as rigid and principled as the more common assertion that a singular truth does exist. Nevertheless some people still try to use one or the other. Both are absurd, although the one of philosophical nihilism is more obvious.

Absurdity can be entertaining and enlightening but only in the way that outdated fad becomes kitsch and is therefore 'cute' and collectible. A message is contained within it all but it's not a facile one. Absurdity really indicates a lack of complete information; *absurdity is an error message.*

The fact that some people attach so strongly to either one demonstrates that an irrational undercurrent runs through human nature. In the case of 'no truth' (anti-science) it's part rebellion, part ignorance and part fear: fear of order that might defeat their own beliefs in self-determination, or more specifically the belief in the right to 'do whatever I want to do'. In the case of the other pole, the 'one truth', it's a wish to have everything taken care of and the belief in a holy deity that controls everything and all blessing will follow from obedience.

Science originates from the 'one truth' view and not too surprisingly it generates some intense antagonism in the public because it doesn't make either group happy, it undercuts free-will and also God. But the ideas behind science are completely sound: to try and find some pattern in the disorder, to try and employ some kind of consistent algorithm to find consistent results. I think the scientific method is the best tool of its kind around, so far, but it has its limits. Mikhail Bakunin once stated, "Between thought and life there is a wide abyss." Science can generate completely accurate and truthful statements but upon application in human society they can fail miserably. Even more, technology often fails even after science succeeds.

Everyone wants to find 'truth' but it can't be found like a search for a singular entity, like some jungle explorer searching for a legendary gold idol. The search for 'truth' is the search for a definition. As humans we all start from a very distorted perspective because in order to exist we must value our life, yet the continuing order of the universe cares not a bit about us one way or the other and suicide changes nothing. But the universe is definitely not irrational; in fact if anything it is maddeningly predictable, at least on the size-scale that we exist at. Humans live by values but the universe does not – it offers possibilities but does not favor one over the other. Ultimately moral right and wrong are products of the ego, after all no one wants to be 'wrong' and everyone wants to be 'right'!

Even amongst the disparity a common element can be found and I think that the natural survival instinct will suffice. It creates an internal sense of true and false but one that is not necessarily transferable to others. Nihilism can state that the overall picture does not create any absolute right and wrong, true or false, but the concept is nonetheless quite significant to the individual. So it could be said that true and false are both absolute and relative at the same time. The interface between all of the viewpoints creates a deceptive complexity; our sense of reality is the interface between all of them perpetually interacting. Indeed, trying to find a truth here is an atrocious calculus problem. This is why scientific reduction often fails in deciphering human actions and living reality, but adding it all up also proves problematic because it's never accurate, only an estimate. Truth, at least on the social level and perhaps a universal level, is statistical.

Consumerism and the Money Morality

Consumerism as we think of it today has its origins in the post WWII era of industrial production surplus, the result of mass production techniques and the commodities made available by a worldwide transportation system coupled with the socio-political need to maintain minimal unemployment. In the 1950s America propaganda pushed on the public made it clear that the duty of every citizen in a 'free' capitalistic country was to buy as many products as they could. Not surprisingly a materialistic consumer-driven society emerged and has been refined over the decades since then. Consequently, the dominant value system is structured upon spending and acquiring money and increasingly the morality of good and bad are measured using dollars.

Nihilism

The beauty of this new morality is the quantifiable nature of it. This is a radical departure from all known previous moral orders that have been mostly arbitrary having been based on habit and tradition with the express, if often unstated, purpose of keeping things from changing.

This is a remarkable development in human history but it clearly leaves much to be desired since as we know capital is a sticky substance – it makes the rich richer and the poor poorer.

That this new morality is materialistic, quantifiable, and often merit-based and change friendly is not undesirable, and indeed these qualities are an inevitable consequence of rational development. Rather, the source of the problem is that the equation here is incomplete. The consumerist, capitalistic value system is circular and self-referential; it fails to include the negative externalities of industrial production, for example. Nor is it able to include intangible qualities such as beauty or friendship. Further, the moral foundation of this value system is based on a tautology in that rich is good and poor is bad, that winners win and the losers lose and the winners are perceived as being inherently better than the losers – a flawed interpretation of Darwinism twisted and perverted to substantiate a preordained conclusion.

The value of money is not being questioned or even being measured in a valid context. People structure their entire lives based on the search for monetary wealth (and the products it can buy), it is the desire for money just to have more money. The effort is pointless because it has no context just as consumers are divorced from meaning and a separate identity outside of the money loop. Consumers are strongly discouraged from finding or forming independent meaning and identity, and especially from questioning the established value system of consumer driven capitalism, just as under more traditional moral authority codes.

Taking a grand view of events I have to conclude that the moral values of contemporary consumer driven capitalism are an intermediate stage in the progression towards a system that adequately includes human needs and the needs of the natural environment around us.

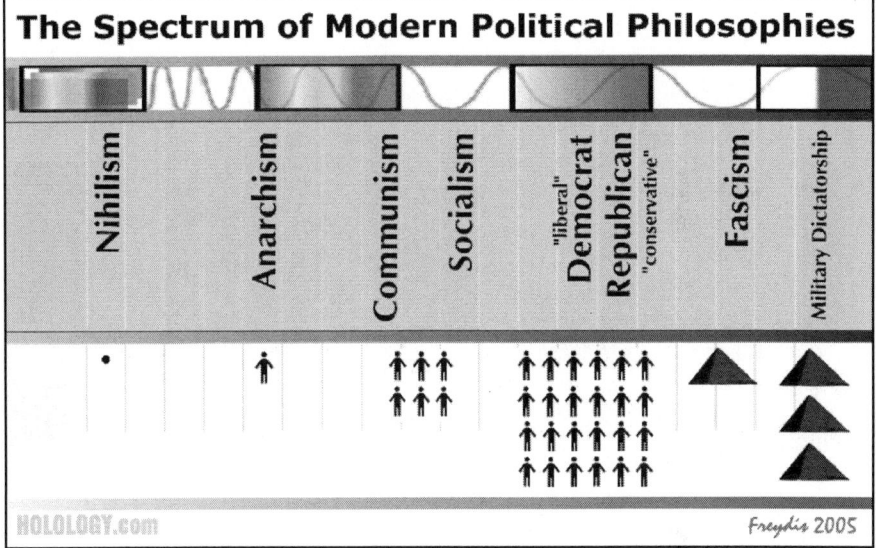

Total Extremes – A Thought Experiment in Nihilism

To understand the middle it helps to study the extremes. This being the case, just what do the extremes look like on a universal scale? It seems that the two extreme poles are difficult to describe because they bear no resemblance to anything we experience on a daily basis or indeed anything in the known universe, they are theoretical but extremely simple constructions.

Nihilism

The singular universe of 'One' is that of complete sameness in everything. Imagine looking at a metal plate painted white and perfectly smooth – try to distinguish anything from anything else – you can't. This universe is a one, no values can be formed here because everything is just one-thing and it's all the same so distance, time, all values used to describe it are completely inapplicable. In this realm of the singularity the individual is useless, or more accurately, just impossible.

Nihilism, in the philosophical sense, is applicable in the singularity universe because no values can be employed to describe anything inside it and no choices can even be made, indeed everything here is completely frozen, static, timeless.

Infinite. The opposite extreme is one where everything is different from everything else and no order or pattern can ever be discerned or extrapolated – it is pure chaos. In this universe forming values would be

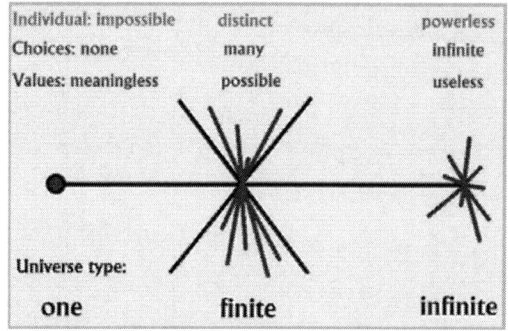

possible, indeed any action would be possible, but at the same time completely useless. In other words if you eat a sandwich today you might feel full, but tomorrow if you eat a sandwich it might make you feel hungry. Values are useless in a chaotic realm because consequence doesn't follow action on a consistent basis so any action taken now to serve a single purpose may or may not generate the same result later. The individual here can act but they are powerless nonetheless because they cannot predict or generate any consistent results. This is a bit of a cheat for purposes of visualization because in the chaotic universe no individual could exist since stable form requires a consistent pattern. It's interesting to consider that even this chaos can still be rationally described (because of the simple physical laws governing it).

Obviously we exist in a universe that is far removed from either extreme, convenient for us because we wouldn't be around otherwise. Our universe is somewhere on a scale between the two extreme poles, it is finite and thus a distinct and discrete range of options exists. Anytime a limited range of options exists so does the necessity of choosing, some options will be better than others, but here the trick is *determining* that value. This is the universe we live in, it is one of order and often murky but still discernable patterns. Our universe is consistent but large enough to still feature unknowns and limitations beyond which it is impossible to perceive, generating a small but still significant amount of randomness.

It's quite possible that both extremes are attached to the life cycle of our own universe. We can extrapolate the past by rewinding the detected expansion of the universe to a singularity (the sameness of one) and possibly predict the future as a progression to chaos, just random energy.

Although in this universe it is possible to have a functional value system it may not be a sound one! What matters is the criteria used, the perspective – this is a universe created from the product of multiple, complex interactions and relationships. *Our present universe is one of relative values overlaid on a substratum of inviolate physical rules.* From an objective and cosmological perspective no set of adopted values is any better than the other since none can change the ultimate confinement of time and space within the universe – the original existential dilemma.

Reduction to the simplest form generates clarity but one that is often misleading because of its distance from the everyday complexity we actually experience. Practical reality is subjective, it dictates a continual need to judge, act and react. Just as entropy is so often misunderstood to mean chaos cannot be avoided, so is everyday life an exercise in erroneous contradictions. The existential dilemma can be broken because human life is not infinite but highly proscribed – this is what creates order out of the disorder. The Second Law of Thermodynamics, which defines entropy, is not an absolute but merely a construct of averages, it merely states the most *likely*

Nihilism

outcome; allowances exist for localized and temporary contradictions of entropy. Not only that but the equations only pertain to closed systems, Earth for instance is an open system because it gains energy, mostly from the sun.

We actually live in a very dynamic setting where things really *do* change. Order can and does emerge from chaos, but it's an order that needs to be questioned for even the values behind it can be changed. Actually, if I had any point when I started writing this I can't remember it, but that one works as well as any.

Graphic: *Universe Types*, by Freydis, 2004.

Acting Out

As a kid in school I was so fantastically bored the only way I could survive was to escape into my own mind and imagination. In middle school, while on the interminable bus rides I was always stuck on, I would imagine blowing things up with my anti-matter gun. I'd build and perfect the gun in my mind and watch the destruction. Earlier, in elementary school I wrote and illustrated a short story based on the 'Mr. Men' book series; the character I created was called *Mr. Destruction*.

Not surprisingly my teachers were always on my case, and this was before the panic and fear today with the school shootings. If I were a kid in school today I'd probably have my own dedicated security camera. But it was quite unnecessary and actually had the opposite effect because it just heightened the sense of antagonism between authority and me. I get twitchy thinking about what a kid like me has to go through in public school today.

It seemed like anytime I expressed myself in a genuine way I ended up in a parent-teacher conference! I got the message real fast, act yourself and get punished. But in retrospect I don't think my case is really all that unusual. This learned disingenuousness is widespread. Psychologists call this *cognitive dissonance*, the act of holding two contradictory beliefs at once, and it's pervasive as it is insidious in modern culture. This is the root of schizophrenia because the mind literally develops a schism, it's split in half and reality assumes two forms: the part we know is true and the part we have to act like it is true. So as a child grows up they continually want to act in an instinctive and internally-motivated way but they can't because repressive morality and culture constrain them. When compelled to obey flawed beliefs and wayward ideologies, anger, resentment and even insanity will ensue. The social psychologist John Dewey was on to this and his conclusions actually got him called a nihilist.

People are suppressed and unnecessarily stifled all the time, they have to release but don't know how; they beat up their girlfriend or yell at family or just kill themselves slowly with a TV remote and a beer, or fast with a bullet and a gun. This is one of the main reasons behind recreational drug use – it's a pathetic way of stripping off that shell and being free to act as we really want to, and the drug effects are used as an excuse so it becomes socially tolerable behavior. Drug abuse increases, senseless violence increases, anger and hostility increase, all in conjunction with the rising levels of hypocrisy, double standards and forced behavior patterns within society. The coercion of conformity weighs down on everyone like a ton of bricks: you have to act this way, you have to look like this, you have to want these products, over and over and over until people crack, they blow up. Then the pundits wonder aloud 'how could this happen, we need tougher penalties!' Or 'why does everything seems so phony and shallow in society; we need more old time religion!'

Shakespeare once wrote (*As You Like It*, II, vii, 139-143), "All the world's a stage, and all the men and women merely players." A playwright *would* say something like that; still the sentiment has a significant amount of truth to it. Pretending you are something that you're really not is a human capacity, it allows for greater depth of character. But when it's forced rather than just play it assumes a very sinister role in human development. The fear of being controlled and losing your mind are two themes that recur throughout contemporary literature, movies and other forms of discussion. In fact the storyline of <u>Dr. Jekyll and Mr. Hyde</u> is one of the most used and repeated themes in all of cinema; the human mind is split and behavior follows suit. Eventually the schizophrenia gets so severe that a person loses any ability to distinguish between what they're pretending to be and what they really are (or were). So, much like an actor that does a single role so much that they become the character rather than themselves, the line is not just blurred but erased in the mind and one finds that they really have been taken over; they have lost themselves only to become a clone and a slave to something they don't even understand. They've lost all freedom and their freewill has been usurped. Life becomes worse than a living hell because once original identity is lost no viable way exists to regain it!

Sometimes the chokehold of oppression is so strong that the only outlet is a mass hysteria whereby individual suffering is projected into collective behavior. These epidemics of insanity are more common than might be thought; Nietzsche mentions some of them in <u>Genealogy of Morals</u>, III, #21. Any culture, even archaic ones, are potentially affected by mass insanity so long as they remain rigid and incapable of accommodating human behavior driven by innate desires or individual, independent expression.

The bottom line is that in order to be mentally healthy everyone must have two things. First they must have at least part of their identity set apart from everyone and everything else around them; the freedom of self-definition is crucial to human mental health. We all have to have at least a corner where we don't have to pretend, where we don't have to lie, where we don't have to always act in the 'appropriate' way because without it we're slaves. Second, a person must have some control over their physical surroundings, as Maria Montessori very wisely surmised. But this is just a derivative of the mental independence already described for the mind reaches outwards; human behavior crafts the outside to reflect the inside.

"All human victories, all human progress, stand upon the inner force." – Maria Montessori

Drawing: *Mr. Destruction*, by Freydis, age 9.

Pitfalls of Philosophical Nihilism

To take a position called 'nihilism' and proceed to make such bald statements as 'nothing is real' or 'nothing can be known' defeats the proponent as soon as they start. After all, how can one assert that 'nothing can be known' without some means of knowing that statement to be true?! This is stillborn philosophy.

In this nebula of philosophical nihilism, meaning becomes absurd through a willful ignorance, a manufactured monopole reality of idealistic constructs with no bearing on real life. False absolutes only mislead rather than edify. A steady diet of air or rhetoric they'll both starve you to death with the same rapidity. Reality and the meaning extracted from it are relatives not absolutes.

Pitfalls of Universality

Another flaw of this idealistic, philosophical nihilism is that of universality. If nothing is the same or capable of being compared then it leads to an inability to form any conclusions or predictions because everything is unique and totally different. Noted crackpot Charles Fort wrote on this view in his <u>Book of The Damned</u> (1919); but try proving it! Some have gone to the opposite extreme and concluded that everything is the same, a basically equivalent statement. Electrons for instance are the same no matter where we find them. Certainly given modern research the 'everything is the

Nihilism

same' conclusion has more weight to it. But ultimately neither one is adequate because both are misleading, unreal perspectives; not to mention the fact these distinctions are based upon artificial and usually arbitrary categorizations.

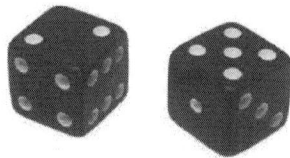

The 'universalist' position is easily demolished, just look at a pair of dice. All dice are (meant to be) exactly the same but take two and roll them; the part that concerns us is not that we have two of the same dice but that we have two numbers and a relation between the two. Differences can occur from a combination of similar elements.

The universalists have used nihilism to break it down but missed the message in the fragments. We have to shift perspectives, universality misses the point, for it's not what separate entities are in themselves, it's what's between them that matters. It's the *relationships* and the *interactions* that form meaning and the substance we deal with on a daily basis.

――――――――――――――――――――――

UFO – Alien Salvation

Nihilism is reduction as an action – and a powerful action it is. By breaking things down we can gain a sense of what works and what doesn't, what's faith-based and what's self-evident, and eventually even get a grasp on what exists independently of the human mind and what is merely an illusionary product of it. Today let's try the colorful issue of *Unidentified Flying Objects* (UFO's). UFO's *are* real but only in the sense that unexplained natural occurrences have been recorded and magnified by the forces of human imagination into becoming extraordinary events.

Limits of Human Perception

The range of our human senses is very proscribed, and generally within that range quite sensitive and accurate, but only within the limits of common occurrences. Any unusual event, especially brief ones, are inherently riddled with errors because the mind connected to the senses, such as vision and hearing, have to do two very difficult things – quickly detect a sensation and then make a judgment as to what it is. The most critical factor is determining just what we saw or heard. We always jump to conclusions in this sort of case even if they're wildly wrong because it's the safe thing to do. Nothing is more dangerous, at least from a psychological perspective, than a giant strange unknown that can't be categorized, it's just too scary. It's much simpler to put an unusual event into a context we are familiar with and then ignore or entertain alternative views afterwards.

Further, our determination of the event is always limited by what we're already aware of because, obviously, we cannot relate to something we've never encountered before or have no previous experience with. This is why observers always employ the lexicon they are familiar with in describing chance encounters. If they see a disc shaped object it becomes a flying saucer. If they see a bright glowing object it becomes an alien craft, rather than the very bright planet Venus for instance, because more people are familiar with UFO's as spaceships than they are with typical astronomical events. If an astronomer, someone who studies the above for a living, sees an unusual sky event they will probably label it a meteor or a satellite, but if the average person sees the same thing they 'know' it's something more fantastic. The general public is much more familiar with imaginary details of space aliens than with scientifically categorized phenomena, consequently the general consensus becomes one of associating an intelligent extraterrestrial with these events.

Nihilism

Too Fast to Figure Out?

The short duration of UFO sightings is another serious problem in making accurate determinations as to their origins. Any sudden event, even the most mundane, poses serious challenges to the human mind in comprehension. Police know this effect well because they interview witnesses to sudden crimes, like a purse-snatching, and the witnesses are notorious for imagining details that can be proven to never have been present even though they will swear they 'saw a gun' or 'the crook was Black', and so on. This is because the human mind only gets a portion of the whole picture through the limitations of the senses and is forced to compensate and fill in the blanks using pre-existing prejudices and judgments. Similarly, police lineups to identify the culprit are useless in court without corroborating evidence. Try any optical illusion, like in a puzzle book, and you'll realize how easy it is to be fooled by the limitations of human vision.

Issues of perspective also impose limitations upon what can be accurately detected with the naked eye. For instance, it's very difficult to gauge depth and thus relative size of an object placed against a background without any distinguishing features, such as the sky; a flying hubcap can appear to be a giant silvery craft. Similarly, judgments of an object's speed are equally misleading against indistinct backgrounds; a passing airplane in the blackness of night could appear to be a distant, speeding spaceship.

These perceptual limitations are a key factor in both debunking the supposed alien associations with extraordinary events and at the same time understanding why so many people are adamant in such assertions.

Any picture or view using only one sense cannot be relied on to be what it appears, indeed as any simple optical illusion will testify seeing may be believing but it's only believing in a self-created fiction! The substantive determination of any unusual event based solely on one sense or slice of the electromagnetic spectrum, such as that from visible wavelength light, is essentially meaningless.

This is why still photographs of UFO's, or indeed any controversial phenomenon, proves absolutely nothing even without the fact it can be easily manipulated electronically or photographically. And even less useful is personal testimony since, as we've already figured out by now, people are very easily fooled; this is especially true when they are influenced by large groups due to the power of suggestion and of course the standard limitations of the human senses and the human mind to interpret it all.

Multi-Spectral is Mandatory

Any unusual phenomenon has to be analyzed using data from multiple slices of the electromagnetic spectrum to even come close to making a solid determination as to just what it is. A tentative start in this direction can be achieved by combing radar reports with personal sightings. Air-traffic radars are all over the developed world, every major city has at least one. But again, these instruments have serious limitations; radar is easily fooled - ask the Air Force. Every radar operator knows, especially on older radars, that blips and spurious readings are a constant problem and always turn out to be caused by natural phenomenon when anyone takes the time to look, and they usually don't waste the effort. Technology attempts to compensate for things like flocks of birds, rain and dense clouds which can create mistaken identities, by limiting the radio frequency range or electronically filtering them out. Basically, we have to understand that air-traffic control radars are carefully designed to detect large aluminum objects of a certain size and shape (commercial aircraft!), and anything that falls outside that narrow description is either not detected or comes up as a blip, an unknown error reading - in other words it tells the radar operator virtually nothing. In cases of serious danger to either air-traffic safety or national defense the obvious reaction is to scramble a fighter and find out what this error reading really is, if anything. But once again we're back to the above mentioned problem because the pilot in the jet sent to inspect only has his own two eyes and perhaps radar in the aircraft nose cone.

Nihilism

People can tell you what they *saw* but that absolutely does not mean that's what was really *there* no matter what their social rank, personal credibility or how convinced they seem.

Ideally any unusual event needs to be corroborated by multiple pieces of spectral evidence, and not just visual wavelength light and a certain wavelength of microwaves from radar. Infrared, ultraviolet, all are helpful in figuring out what 'it' is and the more data the better determination one can make. Secondly, any unusual event has to be repeated otherwise it is just a fluke, a meaningless aberration. Trying to identify a singular extraordinary event is like trying to draw a chart with only one data point – it can't be done. We have to have at least two, and preferably more, similar occurrences in order to make any kind of accurate determination in the case of these fleeting, momentary encounters.

Unknown Events

When encountering and trying to understand the unknown always apply Occam's Razor. There are a lot of unknown things still out there, especially in environments that are remote or poorly studied, but none of them have ever proven to be supernatural or beyond the bounds of physical description. High atmospheric altitudes are a prime example of unexplored regions full of the unknown. Weird flashing lights in the high-sky? Just very recently over the ocean in East Asia a totally new form of lightning was discovered which traveled upwards from high cloud levels.

No matter how incredible some events may seem at first sight they always turn out to follow the same laws of physics as everything else, upon closer inspection. Anyone betting on the mystical answer or the wildly unlikely in life is making a losing wager of embarrassing proportions.

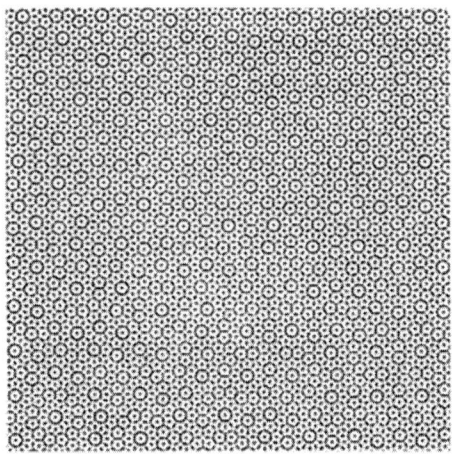

The human eye is easily tricked into detecting movement where there really is none. If you look at this picture for a few moments you can start to see patterns, motions and a 'bubbling' effect.

Spiritual aspects of the UFO

A few people have even taken their unwavering faith in intelligent extraterrestrials and turned it into a full blown cult - and remember, a religion is just a cult that survives cultural evolution long enough to become socially acceptable and traditional. But the belief in alien life visiting Earth in the form of space ships as a UFO is a fantasy, especially considering that alien beings probably wouldn't remotely care about our own welfare. The technological levels required to even attempt interstellar space travel are so immense that if such alien beings did arrive they would view humans as we view a busy colony of ants. This myth is a testament to the enormously inflated human ego and sense of elevated place in the universe, for such visiting aliens wouldn't even bother to stomp on our anthill because it wouldn't be worth the effort to get their feet dirty! Nonetheless this myth of alien visitors is an especially informative one concerning human nature and spiritual needs. There is a common human desire for a savior in life, someone or something to come down and deliver us from doom, protect us from our dangerous folly and generally make all problems go away and leave us feeling warm and fuzzy without struggle or criticism.

But some people have this need more than others do; they often feel like they have little power or control over their lives and feel buffeted by inexplicable external events. They believe that only an outside person or group can ever help them. This erroneous attitude is especially attractive because acceptance of the alternative of personal empowerment necessitates responsibility for personal actions and outcome.

But others who think for themselves and feel able to take control of their lives, manage events, and plan ahead to minimize externally oriented problems, they respond positively to a realization of personal 'salvation'.

The only savior possible (if any) has to come from inside, ultimately everyone is their own savior because only *you* can ever save *you*. The more someone refuses to accept personal responsibility in outcome the more powerless they become and the more desperate is the need for external rescue.

Change

Change is a reaction to discomfort and the discomfort of new ideas and challenges to pre-existing notions in mind or environment. Social-scale change is the art of finding ways to make as many people constructively uncomfortable as possible, it's turning it all upside-down from the inside-out. Yet to generate discomfort is classified by the dictatorship of public opinion as evil, therefore change is "evil". A very "black art" indeed. So fear the "evil" and be afraid, be very afraid, after all it might even help you.

Freydis

How many killed by the Church?

How many killed by nihilism?

Any questions?

Nihilism

Kafka & the Delusion of Freedom

Franz Kafka lived in Prague during the late 19th and early 20th centuries. Kafka was a unique and enigmatic author who enjoyed reading his stories to an informal audience but rejected having them published. In fact the only reason anyone outside his circle of friends ever got the chance to read most of his writings was because his best friend ignored Kafka's final wishes and kept, rather than burned, his collected works. This is even more ironic when considering the fact that Kafka is deemed by some to be one of the most important figures in modern literature, which is largely because his writing presaged and codified much of the angst and individual alienation pervading contemporary western society.

I think my personal favorite novel is The Trial because it so neatly typifies every element of Kafka's core themes and writing style. But in general the primary theme that reoccurs beneath the superficial phantasmagoria is that even though things often make no sense one still has to try anyway; *existence is struggle*. So one can either accept this fundamental ... or accept it - the only alternative is denial and the only potential difference resides within your personal attitude and perceptions of it all.

Kafka's most famous novel, The Metamorphosis (1912), typifies this situation where the main character wakes one morning to realize he has been transformed into a giant beetle:

> But when once again, heaving a sigh after similar efforts, he lay there just as before, and once again saw his little legs battling one another even more pitifully, if that were possible - when he could find no possibility of bringing calm and order into that arbitrary turmoil - he told himself again that he couldn't possibly stay in bed, and that the most sensible thing was to make every sacrifice if there existed even the smallest hope of thereby freeing himself from bed. But at the same time he didn't forget to remind himself occasionally that the calmest possible reflection is far preferable to desperate decisions.

Freydis

Not because he thinks he can necessarily defeat this bizarre turn of events but because Gregor realizes that dealing with the situation at hand always assumes primacy; a sort of pragmatic existentialism, a logic perhaps as superficially ridiculous as the situation itself. The most striking continuity is that all of Kafka's main characters address the ludicrous, random, crushing weight of the outside world upon themselves in a rational manner, just like in a dream where even the most outrageous and nonsensical events remain unquestioned but rather directly addressed just as they are. This is both the literary appeal of his novels and a source of the symbolism involved.

A more obscure but at least as enlightening novel of this primary theme comes from A Report to an Academy (1917) which is about a captured ape (or monkey) forced to become something he isn't. How much of this story is intentional or not is open for debate but the powerful symbolism is nonetheless inescapable:

> They told me later on that I made unusually little noise, from which they concluded that I would either go under, or else, if I managed to live through the first, critical period, I would be extremely trainable. I lived through that period. Muffled sobbing, painful searching for fleas, weary licking of a coconut, banging the side of the crate with my cranium, sticking out my tongue whenever someone approached - those were my first occupations in my new life. But, throughout it all, only that one feeling: no way out. Today, naturally, I can only sketch from hindsight, and in human words, what I then felt as an ape, and therefore I am sketching it incorrectly, but even if I can no longer attain the old apish truth, my description isn't basically off course, and no doubt about it.

> And yet, up to then, I had had so many ways out and now no longer one. I had boxed myself in. If I had been nailed down that couldn't have subtracted from my freedom of action. Why so? Scratch the skin between your toes till it bleeds, and you still won't find the reason. Press yourself backwards against the bars until they nearly cut you in

Nihilism

two, you won't find the reason. I had no way out, but had to create one for myself, because without it I couldn't live. Always up against the side of that crate - I would definitely have dropped dead. But, for Hagenbeck, apes belong at the side of the crate - so I stopped being an ape. A lucid, elegant train of thought, which I must have somehow hatched out with my belly, because apes think with their belly.

I'm afraid that it may not be clearly understood what I mean by "a way out." I am using the phrase in its most common and most comprehensive sense. I purposely do not say "freedom." I don't mean that expansive feeling of freedom on all sides. As an ape I might have known it, and I've met human beings who long for it. As for me, however, I didn't desire freedom then, and I don't now. Incidentally: human beings fool themselves all too often on the subject of freedom. And just as freedom counts among the loftiest feelings, so does the corresponding delusion count among the loftiest.

Living in the Past While Blind to the Present: The Folly of Nationalism

It's very easy to romanticize the distant past precisely because it *is* beyond our own memory and experience. Traditionalists and nationalists selectively recall an idealized history in order to convince themselves that everything was better way back when, and that if we all just revert to the 'simpler traditional lifestyle' everything will fit into place and be perfect again.

Actually, the overall well-being of everyone has improved drastically over the past century in direct proportion to technological development. In general even the poorest of the poor are better fed and healthier than they would have been just 100 years ago, and the vast group in the middle now have previously undreamt of capacities at their command. Indeed this fantastic increase in well-being has directly led to the trouble of over-population. So of course we still have significant problems to overcome but our ancestors had much greater problems plaguing their difficult and precarious lives, and with fewer tools at their disposal to solve them!

These changes have occurred so rapidly that we have not collectively had time to adapt to them, but that doesn't mean we cannot or should not adapt to them. Traditionalism is sacrificing the present trying to live in the past, and yearning for a way of life that can't be regained even if it was desirable. But even more to the point, the fundamental problem with nationalism is that there are more groups of people calling themselves a nation than there is physical space to create their nations. Israel and Palestine is a classic example of the problem of nationalism. Both groups require land to be called a nation yet their claims overlap, so the contest descends into a pitiless war between two implacably opposed sides that slaughter each other in bloody conflict. Europe fought violent and futile nationalist wars for centuries, millions died on the battlefield, and nothing changed – they would just start all over again a few years later! These wars weren't even successful as population growth control! Or look at the Balkans, the former Yugoslavia, for another prime example of the rotten results of nationalism. All fractured into tiny nations that aren't even viable independent entities, these people have been slaughtering each other over nationalism for hundreds of years and getting nowhere because of it. Nationalism is a recipe for stagnation and decay because you can't develop and progress when you spend your time killing your neighbors over differences, real or imagined.

Nationalism is a characteristic disease of delusional authoritarian egomaniacs.

Once you head down this path every trivial detail becomes a point of contention and a reason to exclude someone from the 'nation', splintering into even more opposing sects and generating an

Nihilism

endless series of wars for blood and soil. Nationalists are willing to play because they believe they can win the war and crush the other side once and for all through genocide. Yet victory is never guaranteed. National Socialist Germany was convinced they would win during WWII, yet the Germans ended up narrowly avoiding extinction. And one of the main reasons we have to achieve collective cooperation and not foolish competition is the state of modern weapons technology. In an age of nuclear weapons, and even more hazardous chemical and germ-weapons of mass destruction, warfare no longer threatens the well-being of an isolated nation; it literally threatens the survival of all life on our small planet.

Nationalism is toxic glue for holding a group together; it works for awhile but the disastrous consequences soon outweigh the short-term benefits.

Nationalist ideologues have always been reactionary counter-revolutionaries because they don't have anything of their own to bring to the table that's new or widely appealing. Instead they market unrealistic myths from the past while usurping and redirecting contemporary competitive ideologies. This is exactly what Hitler did so effectively against the communist revolution in pre-WWII Germany; he took the appealing elements of revolutionary communism while claiming national ownership over an international movement, added racialism, and then repackaged it all as 'National Socialism'. The mistake the German people made, and one that cost the lives of millions of them, was not in choosing National Socialism over Communism, it was in investing unchecked power in one individual! This is why, if we allow ourselves to have any kind of government at all, it must not only be under constant scrutiny within a robust system of checks and balances, but even more importantly it must be as impartial and value-neutral as possible.

GIGAPLEX CINEMA

NEVER AGAIN II	R	G	MARS NEEDS MOISTURE
NOT ON WEDNESDAY	PG	PG	ANGEL OF AMNESIA
MURDER ON THE FAIRWAY	PG13	R	THE NETWORK TERMINATOR
WARRANTY EXPIRED	R	G	KILLER PHYTOPLANKTON FROM PLUTO
VISION WORTH FIGHTING FOR - The Roger Corman Story	PG	PG13	A THIN WHITE LINE
DUNSTIN CHECKS OUT	PG	R	RETURN OF THE TELEVISION RERUNS
PAYBACK WITH INTEREST	R	PG	FREE WALLY
CODE NAME SPREAD EAGLE 1	PG13	R	CONVICTED FOR LAWBREAKING III
UNITED WE STOOD	PG	NC17	LOST IN MOOSEHORN
A BRIDGE TOO BROKEN	R	PG13	SPRING II: DANDELIONS REVENGE
YOU SUNK MY BATTLESHIP III	G	PG	WHERE THE FOODS AT
SimMOVIE	G	PG13	THE FISCAL FACTOR
BATMAN V. ROBIN	PG13	R	EXECUTIVE INDECISION
IT CAME FROM BOLLYWOOD	NC17	PG	MONKEY SAW, MONKEY DID
FRESH FROM NEW JERSEY	R	PG	LIVE ON STAGE! The Movie
FISTFIGHT OVER TOKYO	G	R	REQUIEM FOR A RAILING KILL
PINBALL PANIC II	PG	G	DISCONTINUE *THIS!*
DUDE, I CAN'T FEEL MY LEGS!	PG13	PG	NO REFUND IV
FAHRENHEIT 98.6	PG	G	THE MUPPETS TAKE MISSISSAUGA
CRY FOR HELP-The Adam Sandler Story	R	PG13	JUMP TO YOUR DEATH
THEY CAME TO LITIGATE	R	PG	THE THEATER HAD AIR CONDITIONING

freydis 2002

Nihilism

Math and Nihilism: Reduction to Common Elements

Nihilism is an extreme form of skepticism because it questions everything and takes nothing for granted. And yet this way of thinking can result in questioning the very value of symbols themselves; does math really describe the nature of the universe or is it an artificial construction of remarkable convenience? One of the dictionary definitions for nihilism is that "nothing can be known" so technically a nihilist could say, these symbols of language and math are all false and we can't communicate or truly know anything. Towering intellects have debated this issue and still walked away with inconclusive or nonexistent results. For the moment we have to accept that math is a very powerful descriptive tool and leave it at that. And besides, ultimately we can't really know that we don't know.

Mathematics and nihilism are worth comparing in the sense that both are self-evident truth conveyed through value neutral symbols. Neither should require belief in anything in order to achieve an agreed upon result. Like adding one apple with another apple gives you two apples. The issue is that math uses numbers but nihilism must use words; numbers are singular and objective while words have multiple shades of subjectivity. Nihilistic concepts are inherently difficult to convey using contemporary value-laden language. So, one answer is to create a new language, a common set of symbols, but of course that's easier said than done.

Reduction to common elements is akin to building useful symbolism and generating new language much as computers use the simplest language of all – just ones and zeros on/off binary language. Life itself is coded similarly in a language of only four letters but with incredible constructive powers. Why? Because it's so simple it can easily build repetitive complexity; it's the power of symmetry.

As we progress beyond the predictable bounds of theology and ideology we travel into uncharted waters which necessitate a new understanding of morality, values, and even a new language – meaning a new set of symbols necessary to convey nihilistic concepts. It will take everything at our disposal to create that language, that map to common understanding, because the unpleasant alternative is palpable – do or die, try or fail.

Nihilism and Race

Nihilism does not uphold race as a value any more than it tells us one culture is arbitrarily better than another. We're all biological entities built with genetic code and then defined and refined through our intellectual capacities and our remarkable ability to adapt, overcome and prosper. Much of this success is due to the fact that humans are mentally malleable beings whose rise to the top of the food-chain has been a direct result of adopting new ideas and developing new tools and technology.

Race is a subset of species, sometimes referred to as a sub-species, and a species is defined as a group that can reproduce together. Organisms within a species group, like races, can reproduce together. Human races are relatively new creations, formed under the intense pressures of natural selection in the harsh environment of the last ice-age. Because races can intermix they will, it can't be wrong in an evolutionary sense because it's biologically and physically possible. The only limitation is geography and the speed of travel, that's why human races have been preserved in many parts of the world. However, as everyone can tell these limitations of space and distance no longer hold true. Intermixing is what normally happens when separate populations come into contact; the only remarkable difference today is the scale of the event. Whereas in the past it was only a few individuals, for instance the European conquistadors that explored Central and South America centuries ago, now it's entire populations.[1]

Because many of the physically characteristic traits of specific races are recessive genes, blue eyes and blonde hair for example, they will no longer show up in the superficial attributes of the hybrid population except in rare cases. This doesn't necessarily mean that recessive genes no longer exist at all and go extinct; in fact since the goal of a gene is to spread as widely as possible they can actually gain from this. This demonstrates the very complex process of conflict and interaction occurring on the genetic level, far beyond what we are aware of at our own macroscopic scale.

We naturally grow and develop through continual interaction and synthesis

As even a cursory study of biology in the natural environment indicates there are a wide variety of strategies for personal and collective success, with success defined as adaptation to make the most of the surrounding environment. The individual freedom to choose your strategy, ideally with serious thought and consideration involved in the decision, is critically important because otherwise the real trouble arrives when one despot, or authority group, tries to impose their own values and strategy upon others. This inevitably leads to dictatorship, authoritarian brutality, and eventual social collapse.

Actual events and technological developments have already far outpaced the traditional conceptions of race and reproduction. The real story is far more fascinating anyway when we consider the revolution in biotechnology. At some point in the relatively near future the tools and knowledge of biotechnology will progress to the point where genes, DNA, and the basic elements that build life are as fungible as plastic building blocks. This elemental simplicity is nihilism because it is ineluctable. Eventually we'll be able to build life and rearrange it as desired. The potential is practically unlimited, for we can become literally whatever we want to be and anything becomes possible – we can cut and paste, edit out diseases, edit in new attributes, and even create entirely new life forms. The real issue is what do we create with these building blocks and what are the consequences?

To ask 'is this technology good or bad' is to ask a specious question because the technology is inevitable. We mustn't hide from it or try and ban what's physically possible because, like all technology, as fast as one narrow-minded clique rejects it another less conservative group picks it up and gains a massive advantage over the rest. Instead, it's time to collectively develop the maturity and intellectual development to properly deal with the forces and consequences of our tools and to develop a social culture that has an adequate allowance for the inevitable impact of change.

> "It is not the strongest of the species that survives, nor the most intelligent that survives. It is the one that is the most adaptable to change." – Charles Darwin

1. For a remarkable look at the genetic history of European explorers, and the story of the Y-chromosome's decay, read <u>Adam's Curse</u>, by Bryan Sykes, 2004.

Order & Chaos - Patterns, Science and Nihilism

From particles to planets we can find strikingly similar patterns across the spectrum of scales, times, and places. The Standard (atomic) Model has been used for a long time to illustrate how the electrons circle the atomic nucleus similar to the orbit of planets around the 'nucleus' of a sun in the solar system. Despite the fantastic difference in size both models have proved to have remarkably useful predictive powers. Similar evidence of unseen common structures can be found everywhere. The sphere is representational of everything from a particle to an atom to a planet, why? Because it's simple, it's the perfect geometry – one dimensional - it only has one side! And fractal geometry for instance can graphically depict complexity from simplicity using math.

So when we look at different scales, times, or places, these useful similarities can be found because fundamental algorithms, simple formulas and repetitive structures, are creating the complexity we exist within. This is the physical parallel to the social mechanisms of primary human concern. The Nihilist should always be asking, what are the roots? What is the simplest common element to explain the evidence? Remember the principle of Occam's razor, the simplest answer is usually correct.

This is the science in nihilism; it's an understanding that complexity is just the interaction of multiple simplicities. Roots lead to the superstructure. And when you divide nothing you get two entities, one positive and a matching negative – for instance an electron and an antiproton. *Everything, in a literal sense, is actually the fractured symmetry of nothing.*

One of the most powerful appeals of nihilism is its use as a tool for understanding life, reality, and your own place within it all. So think about it - one common element often overlooked is the fact all human life comes from the same source biologically speaking, or that an electron is the same anywhere and anytime in the universe; these elements have both consistency and universality.

Tune out the noise, eliminate the chaff, and seek the substance

Most look at the universe in bewilderment wondering how God created such depth and complexity. Yet "God" didn't build anything, with the parameters defined everything else built itself by filling in the blanks. It's all defined by very concise algorithms, geometric and dimensional boundaries. Similarly most gawk at society and world events only to quickly give up in exasperation – 'it's so complex and so confusing, how did it get this way?' Sociologically speaking, it's all just filling in open space between the artificial boundaries.

Freydis

The populace is trained by TV and pop-culture to remain unfocused and incapable of the coherent thought so threatening to authority, or figuring anything out besides which button changes the volume and which the channel. Those ones are lost, they're enjoying the rapids of the mainstream on the ship of establishment headed for the waterfall. But the ones reading this, the ones able to think and act, they will survive and prosper because they're not on the ship. So don't be blinded by the bright lights of muddled immediacy and the short-lived products of panic and desperation. Focus on the boundaries themselves, the errant parameters continually creating confusion and disorganization. Most everything that has been built up, packaged and marketed – the values and the limits are just fraud and sham. If you attach to that system either willingly or by default you'll inevitably sink with that ship of lies and plastic promises.

"The precise moment at which a great belief is doomed is easily recognizable; it is the moment when its value begins to be called into question." – Gustave Le Bon

Appendix – NECHAYEV'S CATECHISM

There are notable differences between the cultural and political situation of late 19th century Europe and our 21st century world. The weight of oppressive authority is nowhere near as crushing today as then, especially in comparison to Tsarist Russia. The situation for the masses was so bleak as to make death through violence more attractive than life in slavery; America is no Palestine and California is no Gaza Strip, if you know what I mean.

The severity of revolutionary action has to be matched to the lack of freedom to express dissenting ideas within the region of operations. Otherwise you'll just be blown out of the water by public rejection and police reaction. Fortunately, today we have many (peaceful) tools that they did not. Nonetheless it's still prudent to prepare for the worst.

Sergei Nechayev had the focus of a laser beam. His tenacity was admirable and his methodology scores points for attempting to address more than merely the physical infrastructure so typical of Marxism and other one dimensional "revolutions". And if nothing else, 'The Catechism' certainly stirred up debate and generated enthusiasm for the revolutionary effort.

'Catechism of a Revolutionist' By Sergei Nechayev, 1869

PRINCIPLES BY WHICH THE REVOLUTIONARY MUST BE GUIDED IN THE ATTITUDE OF THE REVOLUTIONARY TOWARDS HIMSELF

1. The revolutionary is a dedicated man. He has no interests of his own, no affairs, no feelings, no attachments, no belongings, not even a name. Everything in him is absorbed by a single exclusive interest, a single thought, a single passion - the revolution.

2. In the very depths of his being, not only in words but also in deeds, he has broken every tie with the civil order and the entire cultivated world, with all its laws, proprieties, social conventions and its ethical rules. He is an implacable enemy of this world, and if he continues to live in it, that is only to destroy it more effectively.

3. The revolutionary despises all doctrinarism and has rejected the mundane sciences, leaving them to future generations. He knows of only one science, the science of destruction. To this end, and this end alone, he will study mechanics, physics, chemistry, and perhaps medicine. To this end he will study day and night the living science: people, their characters and circumstances and all the features of the present social order at all possible levels. His sole and constant object is the immediate destruction of this vile order.

4. He despises public opinion. He despises and abhors the existing social ethic in all its manifestations and expressions. For him, everything is moral which assists the triumph of revolution. Immoral and criminal is everything which stands in its way.

5. The revolutionary is a dedicated man, merciless towards the state and towards the whole of educated and privileged society in general; and he must expect no mercy from them either. Between him and them there exists, declared or undeclared, an unceasing and irreconcilable war for life and death. He must discipline himself to endure torture.

6. Hard towards himself, he must be hard towards others also. All the tender and effeminate emotions of kinship, friendship, love, gratitude and even honor must be stifled in him by a cold and single-minded passion for the revolutionary cause. There exists for him only one delight, one consolation, one reward and one gratification - the success of the revolution. Night and day he must have but one thought, one aim - merciless destruction. In cold-blooded and tireless pursuit of this aim, he must be prepared both to die himself and to destroy with his own hands everything that stands in the way of its achievement.

Nihilism

7. The nature of the true revolutionary has no place for any romanticism, any sentimentality, rapture or enthusiasm. It has no place either for personal hatred or vengeance. The revolutionary passion, which in him becomes a habitual state of mind, must at every moment be combined with cold calculation. Always and everywhere he must be not what the promptings of his personal inclinations would have him be, but what the general interest of the revolution prescribes.

THE ATTITUDE OF THE REVOLUTIONARY TOWARDS HIS COMRADES IN REVOLUTION

8. The revolutionary considers his friend and holds dear only a person who has shown himself in practice to be as much a revolutionary as he himself. The extent of his friendship, devotion and other obligations towards his comrade is determined only by their degree of usefulness in the practical work of total revolutionary destruction.

9. The need for solidarity among revolutionaries is self-evident. In it lies the whole strength of revolutionary work. Revolutionary comrades who possess the same degree of revolutionary understanding and passion should, as far as possible, discuss all important matters together and come to unanimous decisions. But in implementing a plan decided upon in this manner, each man should as far as possible rely on himself. In performing a series of destructive actions each man must act for himself and have recourse to the advice and help of his comrades only if this is necessary for the success of the plan.

10. Each comrade should have under him several revolutionaries of the second or third category, that is, comrades who are not completely initiated. He should regard them as portions of a common fund of revolutionary capital, placed at his disposal. He should expend his portion of the capital economically, always attempting to derive the utmost possible benefit from it.

Himself he should regard as capital consecrated to the triumph of the revolutionary cause; but as capital which he may not dispose of independently without the consent of the entire company of the fully initiated comrades.

11. When a comrade gets into trouble, the revolutionary, in deciding whether he should be rescued or not, must think not in terms of his personal feelings but only of the good of the revolutionary cause.

Therefore he must balance, on the one hand, the usefulness of the comrade, and on the other, the amount of revolutionary energy that would necessarily be expended on his deliverance, and must settle for whichever is the weightier consideration.

THE ATTITUDE OF THE REVOLUTIONARY TOWARDS SOCIETY

12. The admission of a new member, who has proved himself not by words but by deeds, may be decided upon only by unanimous agreement.

13. The revolutionary enters into the world of the state, of class and of so-called culture, and lives in it only because he has faith in its speedy and total destruction.

He is not a revolutionary if he feels pity for anything in this world. If he is able to, he must face the annihilation of a situation, of a relationship or of any person who is part of this world - everything and everyone must be equally odious to him. All the worse for him if he has family, friends and loved ones in this world; he is no revolutionary if he can stay his hand.

14. Aiming at merciless destruction the revolutionary can and sometimes even must live within society while pretending to be quite other than what he is. The revolutionary must penetrate everywhere, among all the lowest and the middle classes, into the houses of commerce, the church, the mansions of the rich, the world of the

Nihilism

bureaucracy, the military and of literature, the Third Section [Secret Police] and even the Winter Palace.

15. All of this putrid society must be split up into several categories: the first category comprises those to be condemned immediately to death. The society should compose a list of these condemned persons in order of the relative harm they may do to the successful progress of the revolutionary cause, and thus in order of their removal.

16. In compiling these lists and deciding the order referred to above, the guiding principal must not be the individual acts of villainy committed by the person, nor even by the hatred he provokes among the society or the people. This villainy and hatred, however, may to a certain extent be useful, since they help to incite popular rebellion. The guiding principle must be the measure of service the person's death will necessarily render to the revolutionary cause.

Therefore, in the first instance all those must be annihilated who are especially harmful to the revolutionary organization, and whose sudden and violent deaths will also inspire the greatest fear in the government and, by depriving it of its cleverest and most energetic figures, will shatter its strength.

17. The second category must consist of those who are granted temporary respite to live, solely in order that their goofy behavior shall drive the people to inevitable revolt.

18. To the third category belong a multitude of high-ranking cattle, or personages distinguished neither for any particular intelligence no for energy, but who, because of their position, enjoy wealth, connections, influence and power. They must be exploited in every possible fashion and way; they must be enmeshed and confused, and, when we have found out as much as we can about their dirty secrets, we must make them our beasts of burden, as if they were but mere oxen of the field. Their power, connections, influence, gold and energy thus become an inexhaustible treasure-house and an effective aid to our various enterprises.

19. The fourth category consists of politically ambitious persons and liberals of various hues. With them we can conspire according to their own programs, pretending that we are blindly following them, while in fact we are taking control of them, rooting out all their secrets and compromising them to the utmost, so that they are irreversibly implicated and can be employed to create disorder in the state.

20. The fifth category is comprised of doctrinaires, conspirators, revolutionaries, all those who are given to drunken bullshitting, whether before audiences or on paper. They must be continually incited and forced into making violent declarations of practical intent, as a result of which the majority will vanish without trace and real revolutionary gain will accrue from a few.

21. The sixth, and an important category, is that of women. They should be divided into three main types: first, those frivolous, thoughtless, and fluff-headed women who we may use as we use the third and fourth categories of men; second, women who are ardent, gifted, and devoted, but do not belong to us because they have not yet achieved a real, passionless, and practical revolutionary understanding: these must be used like the men of the fifth category; and, finally there are the women who are with us completely, that is, who have been fully initiated and have accepted our program in its entirety. We should regard these women as the most valuable of our treasures, whose assistance we cannot do without.

THE ATTITUDE OF OUR SOCIETY TOWARDS THE PEOPLE

22. Our society has only one aim – the total emancipation and happiness of the people, that is, the common laborers. But, convinced that their emancipation and the achievement of this happiness can be realized only by means of an all-destroying popular revolution, our society will employ all its power and all its resources in order to promote an intensification and an increase I those calamities and horrors which must finally exhaust the patience of the people and drive it to a popular uprising.

Nihilism

23. By "popular revolution" our society does not mean a regulated movement on the classical French model - a movement which has always been restrained by the notion of property and the traditional social order of our so-called civilization and morality, which has until now always confined itself to the overthrow of one political structure merely to substitute another, and has striven thus to create the so-called revolutionary state. The only revolution that can save the people is one that eradicates the entire state system and exterminates all state traditions of the regime and classes on Earth.

24. Therefore our society does not intend to impose on the people any organization from above. Any future organization will undoubtedly take shape through the movement and life of our people, but that is a task for future generations. Our task is terrible, total, universal, merciless destruction.

25. Therefore, in drawing closer to the people, we must ally ourselves above all with those elements of the popular life which, ever since the very foundation of the state power of Moscow, have never ceased to protest, not only in words but in deeds, against everything directly or indirectly connected with the state: against the nobility, against the bureaucracy, against the priests, against the world of the merchant guilds, and against the tight-fisted hillbilly land pirate. But we shall ally ourselves with the intrepid world of brigands, who are the only true revolutionaries in Russia.

26. To knit this world into a single invincible and all-destroying force – that is the purpose of our entire organization, our conspiracy, and our task.

"It is impossible to modify the convictions of men without also modifying their existence." – Gustave Le Bon

QUESTIONS AND ANSWERS

Freydis answers a few frequently asked questions concerning nihilism:

Q: What is *Nihilism: The CounterOrder*?
A: *Nihilism: The CounterOrder* is a website and communications network for Nihilists that was started in 1998 by Freydis, and operates under the domain name of CounterOrder.com with the word 'counterorder' being a synonym for revolution. This revolution need not be violent just as it can be a radical change in physical surroundings or a radical alteration in perceptions and way of thinking within an individual mind. Indeed, you may already be a revolutionary!

Q: "What is nihilism?"
A: A purified definition of nihilism is reduction to that which is ineluctable, which is a short way of saying that nihilism is about dealing with those elements and facts that cannot be avoided, vitiated or abrogated, while accepting that all else is shades of illusion. Nihilism is an understanding of what morality is (a byproduct of social living that's warped through the abuse of power), where good and evil come from, and the influence of those forces. Morality defines everyone's actions; it defines the legal structure that punishes, the limitations on our thoughts and ideas, the range of response to any given situation. Think of why they have too many cattle in India and the concomitant range of disease and starvation.

Q: "Who are the Nihilists?"
A: Anyone who follows and comprehends the tenets of Nihilism. At present it's mostly limited to informal and often individualistic expression largely due to widespread misunderstanding, public misconceptions, or simply a lack of awareness. However that is rapidly changing, starting here.

Q: Where did the Nihilism symbol come from?
A: I sketched the rudimentary design for the Nihilism symbol when I was in High School. Later, when I developed the website, I

Nihilism

converted the sketch into a digital design using an obscure font for the reversed 'N'. There's no hidden meaning in the design, it's merely intended as a quick, simple, and appealing means of identifying Nihilism and Nihilists.

Q: "What's the difference between Nihilism and Anarchism?"
A: Anarchism is against authority, the idea being that all authority is repressive and should be abolished. To a Nihilist authority in some form is unavoidable and repressive government is just a symptom of a much deeper problem, secondary to what really matters. If all one is concerned with is tyrannical rule, if that's all you want to solve, go for it but you won't ever make any permanent change because you're pulling up the weeds and leaving the roots in the ground. Nihilism is fundamentally much more significant because it strikes at the roots, it strikes at perception and morality.

Q: "What's the difference between nihilism and atheism?"
A: Atheism says 'don't believe in God' while nihilism says 'don't believe in anything', so nihilists are atheists but atheists are not necessarily nihilists.

Q: "Does evil exist?"
A: Certainly harmful and unhealthy events occur all the time, but evil in the abstract or spiritual sense, as most people take the word 'evil' to mean, is purely fictional. According to a Gallup poll done in June of 2001, 41 percent of Americans not only believe in the existence of Satan but also that people can be possessed by him. The unshakable conviction controlling many in America, and the rest of the uneducated and mis-educated world, is that evil is not only very real but very tangible as well. Yet good and evil are really just self-justifications for destructive lies and otherwise unpalatable actions. For example, people like President George W. Bush and Vice President Dick Cheney, who made grandiose speeches about defeating "evildoers" in the wake of the September 11th attacks, ordered the establishment of secret prisons and the kidnapping and torture of thousands of people, most of whom were completely innocent anyway, all in the name of fighting evil. In the imperative battle against evil there can be no quarter, no room for objectivity and no second guessing of self-righteousness. It should be painfully

clear by now that the belief in evil, and the moral obedience that belief compels, is the real hazard.

Q: "Isn't Nihilism just an excuse for hedonism?"
A: No. Nihilism is rejection of guilt, the moral nose ring, because it fuels environmental theologies and an endless series of self-abasement ideologies. Nihilism is dropping guilt and becoming human; it's the acceptance of instinct that minimizes mental illness and repressed aggression. Ultimately the choice of hedonism is open but nature has an uncanny ability to punish the foolish, then neighbors will find a way to deliver comeuppance to the rest compelled to flaunt the limits of reasonable behavior. You may be able to do anything you want but that doesn't mean you necessarily should. Besides, hedonism is unhealthy because it's slavery to compulsion. Likewise it's acutely obvious as the population gets fatter and weaker that *imbalanced pleasure is just postponed pain*. So understanding cause and effect within our biological limitations and defining appropriate conduct is a reflection of self-respect and sanity. And pleasure is a biologically evolved response to certain behavior and stimuli, that genetic imperative which is the real owner of the human soul. News flash: your MTV rebel is just a deluded slave.

Q: "Is life pointless?"
A: No, the purpose of all life is to reproduce itself, and every other function is an extension of that necessity.

Q: "Why do we die?"
A: The succinct answer is so that new things can grow, to prevent stagnation and eventual extinction.

Q: "Since I'm going to die then what's the point of anything?"
A: If all you live for is to die then there's no other point to anything you do in between now and the end. The physical body is of limited endurance but we as intelligent human beings exist in other realms besides just the physical body, we have minds and a consciousness and we can think up new ideas, ruminate on existing ideas, invent, destroy, and pass on both our genetic material and our mental ideas as well. Don't sell your existence short, use every minute of it!

Nihilism

Q: "Is there life after death?"
A: The human life is a vehicle for genetic continuity and in this case life is very nearly immortal because the genetic material (is supposed to flow) on indefinitely, vacillating between the male or female container and perhaps ironically evolving and changing as little as possible. This is why civilization developed and why (barring extraneous influences) like mates with like.

Q: "What is the point (of anything / everything)?"
A: The universe may be pointless when measured using human values but this is because the universe didn't come into existence for human enjoyment. Rather, human life adapted to fit pre-existing conditions that the universe already contained. The universe exists independently of human life – the natural order is not anthropocentric. Many times we get the 'wrong' answer because we ask the 'wrong' question. We shouldn't ask "why is everything pointless" but instead "why do we believe it's pointless?"

Q: "How is it possible to know anything at all?"
A: You can't, but we can make guesses that usually suffice. These guesses are based upon experience stemming from the illusion of time creating a sense of past and knowledge of previous occurrences. Most everything else is a statistical construction; nonetheless most things around are so predictable and normative that this guessing is equivalent to knowing. "Our experience hitherto justifies us in believing that nature is the realization of the simplest conceivable mathematical ideas." - Albert Einstein

Q: "Is religion really that awful?"
A: One common question goes like this: If there's no 'meaning' to life then doesn't it make sense to do whatever makes you happy and not think about things that don't make you happy? In other words since ignorance is bliss why learn anything? Another version essentially replaces the word 'ignorance' with 'religion' – if there's no 'meaning' to life and religion makes people happy, why rain on their party trying to disabuse them of their beliefs? This question seems more rhetorical than serious to me, but nonetheless as often as it's asked it would seem to merit an answer. The explanation could go

on for pages but to be succinct it boils down to two points. First of all stupidity is not healthy for anybody. Seeing through superstition and illusion is a critical task because it prevents the individual from being exploited in life. Second, the religious, believing they hold a monopoly on truth, are compelled to force everyone else to believe the same things that they do, and that means a conflict is inevitable. Nihilism and religion cannot co-exist because the believers cannot allow it.

Q: What is the difference between existentialism and nihilism?
A: Existentialism is a category of philosophy that deals with the individual and their struggle to interact in life and define what is real; it concerns the difficulties of existence, hence the name. Famous existentialists include Sartre and Kierkegaard. Existentialism constructs elaborate philosophical structures trying to define some basic terms and it can all get quite murky, but basically existentialism concludes that everyone is isolated and life is just angst. Existentialism starts with many of the same issues as nihilism, such as defining real, the nature and purpose of existence, and the nature of individual goals too. Nihilism at root is significantly simpler than existentialism because it rejects those philosophical constructions and the intangibles that create endless debate. I suppose the primary difference is that existentialists maintain a set of beliefs that eventually build to state that unhappiness can be overcome but nihilism would maintain that unhappiness is either inevitable or irrelevant. Author Robert G. Olson, who wrote the informative book <u>An Introduction to Existentialism</u> (1962), refers to existentialism as nihilism in effect but not in intent. I think that sums it up pretty well. Existentialism is really just taking the very long and torturous route only to get to nihilism in the end.

Q: Does postmodernism relate to nihilism?
A: Postmodernism seems to have originated as an art movement and was at some point picked up in academia and turned into a form of theory or philosophy. The more I've studied postmodernism the less substance I can find in it, so I'm not sure the question can be answered directly. Any objective analysis of the whole postmodernism language and set of ideas has to conclude that it is

either a bad joke taken seriously or one of the greatest academic frauds ever perpetrated on an unsuspecting public.

Q: "How did *Nihilism: The CounterOrder* get started?"
A: I began studying nihilism in 1993 after I discovered the term by happenstance while browsing through an encyclopedia of Sociology. The realization of nihilism as a word and a concept was eye-opening to say the least; it matched my views and feelings on the world and the more I studied it the more fascinated I became. Reading, thinking, and writing at a frenetic pace by 1998 I had accumulated a substantial collection of handwritten notes. With the arrival of the Internet as a functional medium the progression to a website was a natural outcome. The rapidly expanding content of my *Social Engineering Notebook* split into *Holology* (Holology.com) and *Nihilism: The CounterOrder* website. Much of the core content and many of the symbols and aesthetic design elements originated from drawings created during extended periods of High School boredom. It's amazing how minor events and decisions can have such a significant impact over time.

Nihilism: The CounterOrder and related productions, on and offline, exist for several reasons but primarily so that other Nihilists realize that they are not alone in the way they think and feel. If you want things to change you've got to alter the perspective first, and in order to do that you've got to interject radical and potent ideas into the culture. So if any goal can be ascribed to this effort it would be that much of what I'm trying to do is build a methodology that allows people to be what they are naturally without the need for superstition and fantasy to provide a false sense of protection.

"True genius is creative and makes all from nothing."
– Jean-Jacques Rousseau

DEFINITIONS

Anomie: Instability that comes from the breakdown of standards and values within society. The alienation and uncertainty resulting from a lack of direction and broken ideals.

Apostasy: To reject or renounce a belief-set or religious faith, to revolt.

Existentialism: A philosophy concerning the difficulties of individual existence in a world where knowledge and morality are uncertain.

Faith: The firm belief in something for which there is no proof.

Heretic: One who dissents from religious dogma or breaks from accepted beliefs; nonconformist.

Heterodox: View or opinion that is different from, or in opposition to, an accepted standard or religion; unconventional, unorthodox.

Iconoclast: Image destroyer. Destruction of religious symbols and or one who opposes their worship. One who attacks established beliefs and associated institutions.

nihilism: A viewpoint that traditional beliefs and values are mortally flawed, unfounded. The imperative desire for the wholesale destruction of existing values, beliefs and associated institutions.

Nihilism: The ideas and concepts of nihilism put into action.

Revolution: Fundamental change in worldview, and/or a radical socio-political and economic transformation.

INDEX

—A—
Abramoff
  Jack, 130, 135, 141
Abu Ghraib, 122, 135, 174, 185
Al Jazeera, 187
Anarchism, 21
Anarchists, 86
atheists, 73
avant-garde, 82
Aztecs, 88

—B—
Bakker
  Jim and Tammy Faye, 130
Bakunin
  Michael, 21, 49, 54, 68, 228, 229, 250
Bear Sterns, 158, 162
Bible, 32
Blossfeldt
  Karl, 241, 310
Bosch
  Heironymous, 242
Buddha, 88, 198
Buddhism, 14, 17, 88, 89
Buddhist, 75, 91

—C—
Camus
  Albert, 116
capitalist, 37, 60, 61, 161, 169
Cargo cults, 89, 90
Carroll
  James, 190

Cheney
  Vice President Richard, 135, 174, 177, 288
China, 124, 126, 127, 201
Christian Coalition, 130
Christianity, 53, 92, 127, 190
Christians, 86, 107
Christie
  Thomas P., 184, 191
CIA, 176, 180
communism, 41, 54, 55, 129
Constitution, 127, 128, 129, 131, 134, 141
CPI
  Consumer Price Index, 154, 156, 160
cult, 56, 87, 88, 89, 93, 97, 98, 265
cynicism, 83, 118, 248
Czar, 20, 110

—D—
Dada, 56
Dawkins
  Richard, 73, 158
Democracy, 139
Democratic Party, 118
Dix
  Otto, 241
Dollar hegemony, 62, 147, 150
Duchamp
  Marcel, 229, 230
Dworkin
  Andrea, 54

—E—

Einstein
  Albert, 64
Eisenhower
  President Dwight, 174
entropy, 255
Escher
  MC, 241, 242
evolution, 22, 24, 29, 53, 73, 78, 85, 106, 201, 265
existentialism, 27, 269
Existentialism, 291, 293

—F—

family, 20, 62, 78, 104, 112, 116, 139, 192, 193, 194, 195, 200, 228, 257, 283
fascism, 54, 55
Federal Reserve, 61, 146, 151, 154, 156, 158, 160
fiat currency, 61, 148, 149, 152, 160, 165
Figner
  Vera, 112, 115, 231
Fiji, 189
food, 51, 85, 96, 105, 144, 152, 153, 156, 192, 246, 301
Fort
  Charles, 259
Friedman
  Milton, 145, 147, 148
Futurism, 239, 240

—G—

Galileo, 53
Gang of Four, 63
gangs, 194
genes, 24, 66, 100, 193, 212, 219
Genghis Khan, 73
Genital mutilation, 92
gini coefficient, 125
Gorbachev
  Mikhail, 52
Gorgias, 19, 232
Greece
  (protests), 201, 224, 225
Greenspan
  Alan, 146, 147, 152
Grosz
  George, 241
Guantanamo Bay, 122

—H—

Hamilton
  William, 66
Hedonist, 75
Hezbollah, 122
Hitler
  Adolf, 51, 73
HIV, 195
Holology, 81
Hubbard
  L. Ron, 98
hyperinflation, 151, 155

—I—

IAEA
  International Atomic Energy Agency, 177
illegal immigration, 176
imperialism, 177
Iraq, 92, 118, 124, 133, 134, 139
Islam, 92

—J—
Jefferson
  President Thomas, 127, 141
Jewish, 91, 93, 95, 96, 163,
  164, 216
Johnson
  Chalmers, 133
Judaism, 53, 92, 95, 96
justice, 25, 36, 68, 74, 75,
  124, 151, 165

—K—
Kafka
  Franz, 268, 269
Keynes
  John Maynard, 170
Kienholz
  Edward, 242
Kierkegaard
  Soren Aabye, 19, 291
Kony
  Joseph, 94
Koresh
  David, 97
kosher, 93, 96

—L—
Le Bon
  Gustave, 16, 39, 226, 279, 286
Lenin
  V.I., 85
Liu
  Henry C.K., 155
Lords Resistance Army
  (LRA), 94

—M—
Machiavelli
  Niccolo, 233
Machiavellian, 75
Maciel
  Marcial, 90
Madoff
  Bernard, 163, 164
Marx
  Karl, 41, 44
Marxism, 14, 41, 110, 280
Matthew
  Book of, 74, 246
Maxim
  Sir Hiram, 38
memes, 100, 193
Mencken
  H.L., 63
mental illness, 98
misogyny, 53
Montessori
  Maria, 192, 258, 259
Mormon, 94, 101, 107, 128
Mr. Destruction, 256, 259
MS-13
  Mara Salvatrucha 13, 176
Mugabe
  Robert, 51, 155
Mutual Assured Destruction
  (MAD), 66

—N—
Napoleon, 66, 73
nationalism, 43, 129, 177, 185
NATO, 175, 189
Nechayev
  Sergei, 20, 114, 234, 280
neo-conservatives, 133
Neolithic, 48

Neue Sachlichkeit
 (New Realism), 241
Nietzsche
 Friedrich, 13, 14, 26, 27, 28, 36, 55, 79, 192, 198, 213, 214, 227, 235, 258
Nigilistka, 113
Nixon
 President Richard, 117, 148
No Gun Ri, 186

—O—
Occam's Razor, 264
overpopulation, 177

—P—
Palast
 Greg, 139, 140
Paleolithic, 48
Passchendaele
 WWI Battlefield, 38
Pisarev
 Dmitrii, 112, 113, 229
Plato, 200, 201
Pol Pot, 45, 51, 60, 61
post-anarchists, 224
postmodernism, 291
PPT
 Plunge Protection Team, 158
psychology, 57, 99, 145, 162

—R—
RAF
 Red Army Faction, 235, 236
Rand
 Ayn, 146, 305
Republic, 140, 178, 200
Republican Party, 119

Republicans, 119, 120
Riley
 Bridget, 241
Rothschild, 38
Rubin
 Robert, 146, 147, 305
Rumsfeld
 Donald, 133
Russia, 20, 21, 111, 115, 124, 126, 181, 231, 234, 280, 286

—S—
Sagan
 Carl, 55
salvation, 14, 82, 101, 266
Sartre, 291
Satan, 29, 74, 90, 288
Schechter
 Danny, 139
schizophrenia, 257, 258
Scientology, 98
SEC
 Securities and Exchange Commission, 159
Shanghai Cooperation Organization, 124
skepticism, 13, 17, 18, 53, 57, 86, 107, 118, 248, 249, 274
Skilling
 Jeffrey, 157
Smith
 Adam, 65, 94, 95, 305
Stepniak
 Sergius, 75, 77, 78
Stirner
 Max, 19, 237

suicide, 12, 44, 55, 56, 57, 59,
   65, 94, 105, 138, 250

—T—
TBTF
   Too Big To Fail, 158
teleology, 14, 15, 18, 31
Truman
   President Harry, 52
Turgenev
   Ivan, 13, 18, 111, 113
TV, 45, 81, 104, 130, 198,
   257, 279

—U—
UFO
   Unidentified Flying Object,
      260, 261, 262, 263, 265
UN
   United Nations, 177
universe, 14, 17, 29, 32, 50,
   60, 64, 65, 68, 106, 246,
   247, 250, 253, 254, 255,
   265, 274, 278

—V—
Venezuela, 124
Vietnam, 118, 123, 133, 135,
   178, 179, 183
voodoo, 91
vote, 117, 120, 247, 248, 249

—W—
World War II, 52, 55, 61, 89,
   123, 150, 178
World War One, 38

—Y—
Yap Island
   stone money of, 147
Y-chromosome, 67, 277

—Z—
Zasulich
   Vera, 114
Zimbabwe, 51, 155
Zionist, 133, 138

REFERENCES

What is Nihilism?

1. A History of Civilization, Brinton, pages 300-301, Prentice Hall 1960.
2. The World Within The World by John D. Barrow, pages 334 & 332, Oxford University Press 1988.
3. The Meme Machine by Susan Blackmore, page 189, Oxford University Press 1999.
4. A History of Russia, sixth edition, by Nicholas V. Riasanovsky, Oxford University Press 2000, page 381.
5. The Internet Encyclopedia of Philosophy, *nihilism*,
   http://www.utm.edu/research/iep/n/nihilism.htm

Chapter images in sequence:

The Power of Faith, by Freydis, 2005
Nihilism, by Freydis
Nihilism: Faith Not Required, by Freydis

Nihilism in Action!

1. The World Within The World by John D. Barrow, page 137, Oxford University Press, 1988.
2. *7,000 years ago, Neolithic optical art flourished*, by Rossella Lorenzi, MSNBC, September 22, 2008,
   http://www.msnbc.msn.com/id/26839697/

Chapter images in sequence:

Tiger having eaten professor, painting by Frederick Stuart Church, 1905
Save the Earth: Recycle Your Beliefs, by Freydis, 2005
...and justice for all, by Freydis, 2005
The 'Venus of Willendorf' figurine from central Europe, approximately 25,000 years old.

Nihilism

A figurine from the Cucuteni people of southeast Europe, approximately 6,000 years ago.

Anomie (Death to This)

1. Berlin: The Downfall 1945, by Antony Beevor 2002.
2. Life of Pythagoras, by Lamblichus, Book XX, ~300CE
3. Adam's Curse by Bryan Sykes, 2004.

Chapter images in sequence:

The Dance of Death by Wolgemut, 1493
Photo of U.S. nuclear testing in the Pacific, 1956
Die for the Government, by Freydis, 2005
Photo of a church's double-entendre sign, undated
Conquer Ego (icon), by Freydis, 2010
Cosmic Tourist ('Original Sin' comic), by Freydis, 2008

The Nihilistic Vision

Chapter images in sequence:

Reduce, Reset, Reorder, by Freydis, 2005
Photo comparing skulls of a Neanderthal and a modern human, undated
Photo of a galaxy, undated

How to be a Nihilist

Chapter images in sequence:

I am a Nihilist, by Freydis, 2007
Patriotic Subversion, by Freydis, 2010
Find the Root Cause (icon), by Freydis, 2010

Freydis

The Holy Fool

1. Religion Explained – The Evolutionary Origins of Religious Thought, by Pascal Boyer, 2001, Basic Books.
2. *Toilet tied to tale of Dead Sea Scrolls*, by Alan Boyle, MSNBC, November 15, 2006, http://www.msnbc.msn.com/id/15689591/
3. *Ghost brides are murdered to give dead bachelors a wife in the afterlife*, by Jane Macartney, The Times (UK). January 26, 2007, http://www.timesonline.co.uk/article/0,,3-2566549,00.html
4. *Bhutan's Enlightened Experiment*, by Brook Larmer, National Geographic magazine, March 2008 vol.213 no.3, p. 132.
5. *Halal and kosher meat should not be slipped in to food chain, says minister*, by Martin Hickman, The Independent (UK), April 7, 2008, http://www.independent.co.uk/news/uk/home-news/halal-and-kosher-meat-should-not-be-slipped-in-to-food-chain-says-minister-805396.html
6. Weird History 101, by John Richard Stephens, 1997, Adams Media, p.126-131.
7. *Saudi religious police ban pet cats and dogs*, AFP, July 30, 2008, http://news.yahoo.com/s/afp/20080730/wl_mideast_afp/saudireligionanimaloffbeat;_ylt=A9G_R29T3ZBIO0oAOAxvaA8F
8. Like most any other religion, variations in interpretation lead to different behavior patterns. Some Orthodox Jews will break Sabbath rules in emergencies, nevertheless the point still remains that these kinds of harsh holy orders exist and are usually obeyed by followers of the faith.
9. *Jewish 'modesty patrols' sow fear in Israel*, by Amy Teibel, AP, October 4, 2008, http://news.yahoo.com/s/ap/20081004/ap_on_re_mi_ea/ml_israel_enforcing_modesty;_ylt=A9G_R20InOdljglAtBdvaA8F
10. The Thirteenth Tribe, by Arthur Koestler, 1976, Random House publishing, (first American edition), p.157.
11. *Rabbinical ruling causes havoc on elevators*, by Tia Goldenberg, AP, October 26, 2009, http://news.yahoo.com/s/ap/20091026/ap_on_re_mi_ea/ml_israel_elevator_debate
12. *Pope's brother linked to new claims of child abuse by clergy*, by Jerome Taylor, The Independent (UK), March 9, 2010, http://www.independent.co.uk/news/world/europe/popes-brother-linked-to-new-claims-of-child-abuse-by-clergy-1918357.html

Nihilism

13. *Mexico hit hard by Vatican's repudiation of Legion's founder*, by Tim Johnson, McClatchy, May 11, 2010,
http://www.mcclatchydc.com/2010/05/11/93925/mexican-priest-scorned-but-religious.html

Chapter images in sequence:

Aztec fun times in Mesoamerica - *gimme that old time religion!*
Keep the faith: cargo cult natives wait for salvation and prosperity
A Shiite Muslim beats his head with a sword and bleeds for Allah
A Jim Jones supporter with her homemade sign
Place All Refuse in Can, by Freydis, 2004
(Generating meaning and purpose), by Freydis, 2005
Winners are just the first losers in a foolish competition, by Freydis, 2004
JWPP ('Original Sin' comic), by Freydis, 2001
We're Not Buying God, by Freydis, 2004

Historical Nihilism

A. A History of Russia, sixth edition, by Nicholas V. Riasanovsky, Oxford University Press, 2000.
B. The Women's Liberation Movement in Russia – Feminism, Nihilism, and Bolshevism 1860-1930, by Richard Stites, Princeton University Press, 1978.

1. Reference A pg. 381
2. Reference B pg. 99-100
3. Reference B pg. 101
4. Reference B pg. 104
5. Reference B pg. 146
6. Reference A pg. 384
7. Reference A pg. 448

Top image: *Student Nihilist*, painted by Ilya Repin, 1883
Bottom image: *The Revolutionary Meeting*, painted by Ilya Repin, 1883

Freydis

Nihilism Comes to America

1. *Study says final tab may double*, Washington Post via Chicago Tribune, April 27, 2006,
http://www.chicagotribune.com/news/nationworld/chi-0604270180apr27,1,6705322.story?coll=chi-newsnationworld-hed
2. *Pentagon Steps Up Intelligence Efforts Inside U.S. Borders*, by Robert Block and Jay Solomon, Wall Street Journal, April 2006.
3. *Former Illinois governor guilty of corruption*, Reuters, April 17, 2006
http://today.reuters.com/news/articlenews.aspx?type=politicsNews&storyid=2006-04-17T202234Z_01_N17403948_RTRUKOC_0_US-CRIME-RYAN.xml
4. America Right or Wrong - An Anatomy of American Nationalism, by Anatol Lieven, 2004, page 50, Oxford Univ. Press.
5. ibid, page 149.
6. *The Last Days of the Dollar*, by Robert Kiyosaki, October 17, 2006, http://finance.yahoo.com/columnist/article/richricher/10932
7. *A Forgotten Holocaust: US Bombing Strategy, the Destruction of Japanese Cities and the American Way of War from the Pacific War to Iraq*, by Mark Selden, Japan Focus, May 2, 2007, http://www.japanfocus.org/products/details/2414
8. *US presidential campaign: Romney denounces secularism in bid for Christian fundamentalist backing*, by Patrick Martin, WSWS, December 7, 2007,
http://www.wsws.org/articles/2007/dec2007/romn-d07.shtml
9. *Wall Street, White House blame homeowners in foreclosure crisis*, by Tom Eley, WSWS, 16 October 2010,
http://www.wsws.org/articles/2010/oct2010/bank-o16.shtml
10. *The Israel Lobby and U.S. Foreign Policy*, by John J. Mearsheimer and Stephen M. Walt, page 41,
http://ksgnotes1.harvard.edu/Research/wpaper.nsf/rwp/RWP06-011
11. *Billions: The Politics of Influence in the United States, China and Israel*, by Peter Dale Scott and Connie Bruck, Japan Focus, July 25, 2008,
http://www.japanfocus.org/_P__D__Scott___C__Bruck-Billions__The_Politics_of_Influence_in_the_United_States__China_and_Israel

Nihilism

Chapter images in sequence:

Support our Terrorists, bumper sticker by Freydis
Justifying the War on Terrorism ('Original Sin' comic), by Freydis, 2001
(support the troops) ... until they all come home (in coffins), by Freydis
Kultur Terror II, by Freydis, 2005
Osama bin Laden Thanks Allah for George W. Bush, by Freydis 2007
God -less America, by Freydis
Photo of a grimacing Defense Secretary Donald Rumsfeld
Returned to Sender, by Freydis
Police photo of a grinning former House Majority leader Tom Delay
Too Big To Fail, Too Rich to Lose, by Freydis, 2008
They reap impoverishment from a promise of salvation, by Freydis 2010
Regime Change Starts at Home, bumper sticker by Freydis

The Dollar Disease

1. *CEOs Pushing Ayn Rand Studies Use Money to Overcome Resistance*, by Matthew Keenan, Bloomberg news, April 11, 2008,
   http://www.bloomberg.com/apps/news?pid=20601109&sid=as6BR0QV4KE8&refer=news
2. *Sights of Yap*, Federated States of Micronesia tourism office,
   http://www.visit-micronesia.fm/eng/yap/sights.html
3. *The twilight of irredeemable debt*, by Antal E Fekete, Asia Times Online, May 2, 2008,
   http://www.atimes.com/atimes/Global_Economy/JE02Dj05.html
4. *TFC goes down on the upside*, by The Mogambo Guru, Asia Times Online, February 29, 2008,
   http://www.atimes.com/atimes/Global_Economy/JB29Dj01.html
5. *The Fed's deformed maturity*, by Hossein Askari and Noureddine Krichene, Asia Times Online, May 8, 2008,
   http://www.atimes.com/atimes/Global_Economy/JE08Dj03.html
6. *Move Over, Adam Smith: The Visible Hand of Uncle Sam*, by John Embry and Andrew Hepburn Sprott Asset Management, August 2005; http://www.sprott.com/pdf/TheVisibleHand.pdf

7. *Hard US lessons, harder landings*, by Max Fraad Wolff, Asia Times Online, November 21, 2006,
   http://www.atimes.com/atimes/Global_Economy/HK21Dj02.html
8. *Fed pause promises financial disaster*, by Hossein Askari and Noureddine Krichene, Asia Times Online, May 20, 2008,
   http://www.atimes.com/atimes/Global_Economy/JE20Dj06.html
9. *Moody's stock suffers record plunge on rating error*, by Walden Siew, Reuters, May 21, 2008,
   http://biz.yahoo.com/rb/080521/moodys_shares_glitch.html
10. *Rubin's poisoned chalice*, by Henry C K Liu, Asia Times Online, May 21, 2008,
    http://www.atimes.com/atimes/Global_Economy/JE21Dj01.html
11. *Wall Street Says -2 + -2 = 4 as Liabilities Get New Bond Math*, by Bradley Keoun, Bloomberg, June 2, 2008,
    http://www.bloomberg.com/apps/news?pid=20601109&sid=a2ppBYA0ELaU&refer=news
12. *December Surprise*, by James K. Galbraith, Mother Jones Magazine, July/August 2008, p. 40.
13. *Banks sharply increased fees as US households fell deeper into debt*, by Andre Damon, WSWS, July 25, 2008,
    http://www.wsws.org/articles/2008/jul2008/debt-j25.shtml
14. *AG takes himself out of Madoff fraud probe*, by Pete Yost and Marcy Gordon, AP, December 17, 2008,
    http://biz.yahoo.com/ap/081217/madoff_scandal.html
15. *Madoff scheme hits Jewish charities hard*, by Jocelyn Noveck, AP via Business Week, December 16, 2008,
    http://www.businessweek.com/ap/financialnews/D9543FDO0.htm
16. *Flawed Credit Ratings Reap Profits as Regulators Fail (Update1)*, by David Evans and Caroline Salas, Bloomberg, April 29, 2009,
    http://www.bloomberg.com/apps/news?pid=20601109&sid=au4olx.judz4&refer=news
17. *Integrity deficit has its price*, by Henry CK Liu, Asia Times, August 20, 2009,
    http://www.atimes.com/atimes/Global_Economy/KH20Dj02.html
18. *Things are getting better?*, by Max Fraad Wolff, Asia Times Online, September 24, 2009,
    http://www.atimes.com/atimes/Global_Economy/KI24Dj04.html
19. *Documents reveal SEC complicity in Madoff Ponzi scheme*, by Andre Damon, WSWS, November 6, 2009,
    http://www.wsws.org/articles/2009/nov2009/mado-n06.shtml

Nihilism

Chapter images in sequence:

In God we Mistrust, by Freydis
MZM chart from Federal Reserve data, May 2008
"Worker productivity is the key factor in rising living standards" by Freydis, 2008

The Madness of a Meretricious Military

1. *Defence groups turn focus to security at* home, by Sylvia Pfeifer, Financial Times, August 4, 2008, http://www.ft.com/cms/s/0/cdd2deb6-61bb-11dd-af94-000077b07658.html
2. *A surgeon's guidebook to the horrors of battle*, by Donald G. Mcneil Jr. International Herald Tribune, August 5, 2008, http://www.iht.com/articles/2008/08/05/healthscience/05surg.php
3. *Strategy Against Al-Qaeda Faulted*, by Joby Warrick, Washington Post, July 30, 2008, http://www.washingtonpost.com/wp-dyn/content/article/2008/07/29/AR2008072902041.html
4. *Seoul probes civilian `massacres' by US*, by Charles J. Hanley and Jae-Soon Chang, AP, August 3, 2008, http://news.yahoo.com/s/ap/20080803/ap_on_re_as/korea_us_refugee_killings;_ylt=AsfkzqYZXFrN1oNVi0vWx2JvaA8F
5. *In military housing disaster, a whistle-blower awaits vindication*, by Eric Nalder, Seattle Post-Intelligencer, August 7, 2008, http://seattlepi.nwsource.com/local/373921_militaryhousing07.html?source=mypi
6. *All Guns, No Butter*, by George Kenney, In These Times magazine, August, 2008, http://www.inthesetimes.com/article/3808/all_guns_no_butter/
7. *The devastation of Iraq*, by Dahr Jamail, Asia Times Online, January 11, 2005, http://www.atimes.com/atimes/Middle_East/GA11Ak01.html
8. *Twilight of the NPT? The US, Syria, Iran, North Korea and the Control of Nuclear Weapons*, by China Hand, Japan Focus, May 9, 2008, http://www.japanfocus.org/products/details/2749
9. *Soldiers' Suicide Rate On Pace to Set Record*, by Ann Scott Tyson, Washington Post, September 5, 2008, http://www.washingtonpost.com/wp-dyn/content/article/2008/09/04/AR2008090403333.html

10. *Fiji's Mercenary Military, the US and the Politics of Coup D'état*, by Andre Vltchek, Japan Focus, August 30, 2008, http://www.japanfocus.org/_Andre_Vltchek-Fiji___s_Mercenary_Military__the_US_and_the_Politics_of_Coup_D___tat
11. *U.S. attack on Taliban kills 23 in Pakistan*, by Jane Perlez and Pir Zubair Shah, International Herald Tribune, September 9, 2008, http://www.iht.com/articles/2008/09/09/asia/09pstan.php
12. *Negroponte and the escalation of death*, by Dahr Jamail, Asia Times Online, January 11, 2007, http://www.atimes.com/atimes/Middle_East/IA11Ak03.html
13. *The Deadliness Below*, by John M.R. Bull, Newport News Daily Press, October 30, 2005, http://www.dailypress.com/news/local/dp-02761sy0oct30,0,3545637.story
14. *EPA Unlikely to Limit Perchlorate in Tap Water*, by Juliet Eilperin, Washington Post, September 22, 2008, http://www.washingtonpost.com/wp-dyn/content/article/2008/09/21/AR2008092102352.html?hpid=topnews
15. *Pentagon spending growth outpaces auditors*, by Jon Ward, Washington Times, October 20, 2008, http://washingtontimes.com/news/2008/oct/20/pentagon-spending-growth-outpaces-auditors/
16. *US exceptionalism meets Team Jesus*, an interview by Tom Engelhardt, Asia Times Online, September 21, 2007. http://www.atimes.com/atimes/Middle_East/II21Ak02.html
17. *At Army Base, Some Violence Is Too Familiar*, by Michael Moss & Ray Rivera, New York Times, November 9, 2009, http://www.nytimes.com/2009/11/10/us/10post.html
18. *Kick ass - or buy gas*, by Nick Turse, Asia Times Online, June 19, 2010, http://www.atimes.com/atimes/Global_Economy/LF19Dj02.html
19. *Women's suicide risk rises sharply after military service*, by Joe Rojas-Burke, December 02, 2010, The Oregonian, http://www.oregonlive.com/health/index.ssf/2010/12/womens_suicide_risk_rises_shar.html
20. *Rape rampant in US military*, by Dahr Jamail, Al Jazeera, December 21, 2010, http://english.aljazeera.net/indepth/features/2010/12/2010122182546344551.html

Chapter images in sequence:

It's Not Vietnam Again ('Original Sin' comic), by Freydis, 2008
Daddy's Greasin' Gooks ('Original Sin' comic), by Freydis, 2001

Nihilism

Partners in Freedom (Bush, Nixon, TV), by Freydis, 2004
Fight Lesson, by Freydis, 2006
The Empire's Visionary Leader, by Freydis, 2008

Family and Nihilism

1. *Children's Self-Control Predicts Health, Wealth*, by Jessica Marshall, Discovery News, January 24, 2011,
http://news.discovery.com/human/children-self-control-success-110124.html

Revolution into Evolution

1. *Policeman 'aimed in direction of' Greek schoolboy*, by Helena Smith, The Observer (UK), January 18, 2009,
http://www.guardian.co.uk/world/2009/jan/18/greece-riots-korkoneas
2. *Death threat to Greek media as terrorists plot bomb havoc*, by Helena Smith, The Guardian, February 22, 2009, (italics added for emphasis), http://www.guardian.co.uk/world/2009/feb/22/greek-terrorism-guerrilla-group
3. *Watery asteroids may explain why life is 'left-handed'*, by Hazel Muir, New Scientist, March 17, 2009,
http://www.newscientist.com/article/dn16779-watery-asteroids-may-explain-why-life-is-lefthanded.html
4. *Discovery of New Microorganisms in the Stratosphere*, ISRO, March 16, 2009, http://www.isro.org/pressrelease/Mar16_2009.htm
5. The documentary *Animal Minds* (1999) presents an incredible look into intelligent animal life that reveals the inner workings of moral behavior in social animals, and much more.
6. For an interesting explanation of how a basic moral sense is built into us and the way that religion hijacks it read Religion Explained – The Evolutionary Origins of Religious Thought, by Pascal Boyer, 2001, Basic Books.
7. *Was our oldest ancestor a proton-powered rock?*, by Nick Lane, New Scientist, October 19, 2009,
http://www.newscientist.com/article/mg20427306.200-was-our-oldest-ancestor-a-protonpowered-rock.html?full=true
8. *Fair play: Monkeys share our sense of injustice*, by Frans de Waal, New Scientist, November 11, 2009,
http://www.newscientist.com/article/mg20427341.100-fair-play-monkeys-share-our-sense-of-injustice.html

Freydis

Profiles in Nihilism

1. Russian Thinkers, by Isaiah Berlin, 1978, p. 301, Viking Press.
2. Dada art and anti-art, by Hans Richter, 1964, translated from the German by David Blitt, 2004, pages 207-208, Thames & Hudson world of art.

Nihilism in Art

1. *The Italian Sources of Futurism*, by Giovanni Lista; extracted from Futurism, 2009, page 51, Centre Pompidou, first edition.
2. World War I and the Weimar Artists, by Mathias Eberle, 1985, Yale University Press.
3. Dada - art and anti-art, by Hans Richter, pg. 48, 1964/1965/1997, Thames & Hudson Ltd.
4. Natural Art Forms, by Karl Blossfeldt (originally printed in 1932), Dover.
5. Art of the 20th Century Volume I, by Karl Ruhrberg, 2005, page 347, Taschen GmbH.
6. The Art book, 1994, Phaidon Press Ltd.

ABOUT THE AUTHOR

Freydis is the nom de guerre for an artist, author, thinker, revolutionary, and critical analyst of political and social issues within a strategic context. Freydis is best known for creating and maintaining the highly regarded and unique website *Nihilism: The CounterOrder*, and the even more extensive website *Holology: the Social Engineering Notebook* containing commentary and analysis on a wide variety of important topics. Freydis also operates the *Symposium for Nihilism* communications network connecting Nihilists around the world.

Freydis' prolonged university study covered numerous fields beginning with engineering and political science, progressing to geography and network engineering, and finally arriving at community development before eventually concluding that libraries offer a more rewarding educational experience at a drastically reduced price.

Originally from Portland Oregon, Freydis currently lives and works in St. Louis Missouri with his collection of carnivorous plants and half-finished art projects.

Freydis

Freydis in Oahu, Hawaii 2008

For More Nihilism visit *Nihilism: The CounterOrder* at

www.CounterOrder.com

Also visit,
www.Holology.com
http://twitter.com/Holology

Printed in Great Britain
by Amazon.co.uk, Ltd.,
Marston Gate.